1993

Love Matthew

GEORGIA PLACE-NAMES

By

Kenneth K. Krakow

Macon   WINSHIP PRESS   1975

GEORGIA PLACES NAMES
First Edition

Copyright © 1975 by Kenneth K. Krakow

Library of Congress Card Number: 75-5230
ISBN 0-915430-00-2 Hard Cover Edition
ISBN 0-915430-01-0 Soft Cover Edition

Published by

WINSHIP PRESS
Mercer University Station
Post Office Box 859
Macon, Georgia 31207

Designed and Printed in the United States by

OMNIPRESS INC.
Macon, Georgia

To my wife, Marian

Without whose help,
criticism, patience,
encouragement,
and understanding,
this book could never
have been produced.

I feel a sense of pride in the history and heroic deeds accomplished by my forebears, and shall endeavor to so live so that my State will be proud of me for doing my bit to make the State a better Commonwealth for future generations.

— from the Georgian's Creed

History is all explained by geography.

— Robert Penn Warren

INTRODUCTION

The origin of the name of a county, town, river, or any geographical feature prominent enough to have been given a name always excites the imagination of people who live in or around that community or place. But often it excites an outsider even more. Such is the case of Kenneth Kemler Krakow, a native of Iowa, who has been in Georgia for six years. During these years he has sought the origin of every place name in this state.

Krakow came to Georgia directly from North Carolina, where he had been assistant director of food services at the University in Chapel Hill. In 1967 he came to Mercer University in Macon, Georgia, to fill the position of director of food services. But this alumnus of Michigan State University had a continuing interest in education and an insatiable appetite for new knowledge. He was not satisfied to be merely a member of the administrative staff; he felt a desire to try the curriculum of this Southern institution. He registered for courses in History leading to the degree of Master of Education, and among these courses was my History 245, The History of Georgia.

When we agreed that he might do a term paper on place names in Georgia, little did I realize that I had a potential onomastic scholar on my hands, or in my hair! And from that time to the present he has been constantly "in my hair" as he has worked to expand his term paper into this book. But I have enjoyed every hour of it; and I find, now that I have read his manuscript through, that I am quite favorably impressed by the industry, the insight, and the patience of our Yankee friend who in less than six years has learned more about Georgia place names than his teacher has learned in a period eight times as long.

Krakow's interest in place names was not something that began in my Georgia History class. Actually, he had developed an interest in the general subject during a career in management of food services that enabled him to live in far away places such as Paris, France, for instance. As a first lieutenant in the United States Army, he managed a mess hall in what had previously been a large restaurant on the Champs Elysees. At war's end he resumed an interrupted education at Michigan State and there married a native, Marian June Tompkins. She shares with him his enthusiasm for place names and their derivations, and has worked with him in compiling this volume. On Krakow's graduation the couple moved to Chicago where the young husband found employment at the Hotel Morrison and their first son was born. In 1948 they moved to Rochester, Minnesota, where Krakow operated his own restaurant, managed a hotel dining room, and added three more children to the family. In 1955 the Krakows moved to Southern California where he worked as a sales representative for a national food concern, and later as food services director of a large hospital in San Bernadino. It was in California that he first began to be seriously interested in the derivation of place names, as he searched out the sources of the interesting town names he encountered there.

Krakow has made his book more useful and easier to use by following a simple alphabetical arrangement rather than a topical one. He has indicated in every instance possible, in the limited space he has had to devote to the research, the origin of thousands of place names. Some are derived from the names of persons; some from geographical features, some from places similarly named; some are taken from the Bible, other literary works, or mythology; some are alterations of existing or old names; some were inspired by anecdotes or special events; and some would not fit any of these categories. Particular attention is given to definitions of Indian names, which abound in Georgia.

The compiler, a self-confessed novice in terms of the length of time he has been in Georgia, has had the advantage of many before him spending years gathering such information. To those he acknowledges his indebtedness, and cites the ones he considers most reliable. Sometimes he cites more than one source when not able to determine which should be accepted as authentic. He, of course, recognizes the pioneering work in this area done by the late Professor John H. Goff of Emory University, whose publications and notes are deposited in the State Department of Archives and History.

An examination of the extensive bibliography shows the scope of Krakow's diligent research. Every possible source that seemed authentic was examined as soon as the compiler was aware of its existence. Local citizens and county historians have sometimes caused doubts by telling fantastic tales of the origins of certain names. Krakow has tried to protect himself in cases of doubt by indicating that such stories are merely heresay. Although critical of the veracity of some of the stories, he often leaves the reader the burden of separating fact from fancy.

Many will find this book useful, and even more will find it interesting. They will learn how "Puddleville" became Adel, and how a segment was extracted from the word "Philadelphia" by a pioneer citizen who wanted a more dignified name for his town. They will be able to trace the spelling of Ossabaw Island through its various forms, from Ossebah, Ussybaw, Hussaper, Hussaba, and Opispa, or the Chattahoochee River from Tchattauchi and Chatty Hoochee to its present form, with several variations in between. They will find legends surrounding the origins of such places as "Rising Fawn," "Talking Rock," "Po Biddy Cross Road," and "Fargo." They will choose what seems to them to be the most reasonable answer to the question of the origin of the name for Fulton County, and many others over which controversy stirs. Genealogists will find helpful suggestions from the many family names to which place names are associated. All this and . . . I can't say "Heaven too," because there is no "Heaven" nor is there a "Hell." That is, not in Georgia. But, yes Virginia, there is a "Santa Claus."

As Krakow readily admits, his compilation as it goes to press has reached no final point of perfection nor completeness. He expects readers to verify or challenge any questionable statement; it is a continuing process—open-ended, one might say. Many who use this book will undoubtedly suggest additional entries which can be incorporated later in a revised edition.

Spencer B. King, Jr.
Mercer University
Macon, Georgia

CONTENTS

PREFACE

The place-names of a state reflect various aspects of its nature and its culture, and phases of its history. Knowing the stories behind the names of places encountered in Georgia goes far to help one understand the state better.

The people of Georgia are proud of their state's rich historical heritage, and it is hoped that this volume will provide them a convenient source of background material in encyclopedic form. With the coming celebration of our nation's bicentennial, the American Name Society is actively encouraging all of the states to complete such place-name surveys by 1976.

Place-name research is relatively new in the United States, and until quite recently, very few states have been subject to any comprehensive treatment. However, in Europe, the investigation into the origin and meaning of names has been studied for a great many years as a branch of philology or etymology. The Germans have been the pioneers and teachers, although the English have completed some creditable work in this field.

Since this field of study is so new, there are no precise guide lines as to what categories of names are to be properly included in such reference books at this. Most compilers seem to make different arbitrary decisions as to what is included, aside from the obvious coverage of cities, towns, counties, and rivers. For example, R. M. Hanson in his 1969 book on *Virginia Place Names*, includes bridges, tunnels, railroad companies, peninsulas, streets and buildings. Robert L. Ramsay's *Introduction to a Survey of Missouri Names* (1934) lists names of such things as churches and schools. On the other hand, for example, a more specialized coverage is found in William D. Overman's 1959 place-name book, *Ohio Town Names*.

This volume includes information on the creation, naming, size, and derivation of all 159 of the present counties of Georgia, as well as some which no longer exist, such as Bourbon County, Campbell County, Frederica County, Milton County, Savannah County, and the original Walton County, which was located in what is now determined to be North Carolina. All of the counties of Georgia were created by acts of the state legislature (except the eight Constitutional Counties, q.v.) on the dates indicated at the entry for each county. As succeeding counties were formed from earlier ones, the original areas naturally decreased. The area indicated herein is the present size of each county.

Also included here are the cities and towns, plus all the county seats and some militia districts, as well as crossroads and rural communities. Dates of incorporation of cities and towns given are the earliest that were found in the official state records of when approved by acts of the legislature. Within the county entries are given dates when courthouses were destroyed by fires or acts of God, to indicate where official records may have been lost. Many of the dead towns of Georgia are listed here, as are a great many rural post offices, which in some cases existed only briefly, sometimes in the postmaster's home or place of business. Names of some of the principal Indian towns and villages are also included.

The major islands and rivers have been included, as well as lakes, dams, reservoirs, and a large number of the state's many streams. Herein also are the names of mountains, valleys, passes, bluffs, ferries, river bends, swamps, bridges and ridges. Nearly all of Georgia's state parks are here, as well as some former Indian trails, early military roads, etc. Also included are the military installations, as well as the great many forts, past and present, and information as to the founding and naming of colleges and universities.

The general intention is to include so many general categories that this compilation will interest and be of value to the greater number of persons.

The names on the map of Georgia record the peculiarities of her long and varied history. This region has been inhabited for at least 10,000 years, as has been established by evidence found at the Ocmulgee Mounds of Macon. John Goff has pointed out that the oldest recored place-names found in our state are Appalachee and Aucilla, both early Indian names.

Many of the streams, as well as some towns and a few counties, preserve Indian names to remind us of those who originally dwelt on this land. Names of Cherokee derivation are found mostly in the northern mountainous section of Georgia, where these Indians lived and established a constitutional government before this state systematically drove all of the natives from its borders in 1838. The Seminole Indians (who were originally Muscogees) lived in the far south, mostly near Florida and in the vicinity of the Okefenokee Swamp. Most of the remainder of the state was occupied by the Creek Indians, which were predominantly Muskogean. When these Indians were found living along Ochise Creek (the Ocmulgee River), the early white explorers referred to them as the Ochise Creek Indians, later shortened to "Creek Indians."

The first white men to set foot in what is now Georgia were Spanish explorers under the leadership of Hernando DeSoto, searching for gold here from 1539 to 1542. The spanish called the region Bimini and LaFlorida, and named their first island settlement Guale. They put their early missions on The Golden Isles of Georgia's coast, and these islands were then given Spanish names.

The permanent settlement of the state began with the establishment of Georgia by General James Edward Oglethorpe in 1733. Additional settlers came soon afterwards from England, as well as some Salzburgers from Germany, followed by others from the Carolinas and Virginia and from Kentucky and Tennessee.

Names of English places and people were among the first to be applied to Georgia places. Some of the original counties were named for Englishmen who were sympathetic to the colonies in their disputes with the mother country.

Yankees were also attracted to Georgia, such as Henry Harding Tift, Samuel Griswold, and Philander H. Fitzgerald. Their names were to be found on the Georgia map, as well as other northerners like Robert Fulton, DeWitt Clinton, and Zebulon Pike, and some Yankee cities like Albany, Duluth, Boston, and Philadelphia (Adel.).

As Greece supplied classical columns to "Georgian" architecture adopted in the new state, it also supplied names for some of its towns. Charles Lagondakis (in the *Georgia Historical Quarterly)*) has pointed out the Greek derivations of place-names such as, Athens, Climax, Eudora, Omega, Sparta, and Ypsilanti.

The American Revolution produced many of Georgia's place-names, such as Greene, Jasper, Lincoln, Newton, Paulding, Pulaski, Washington, and Wayne counties. The only county in the state to be named for a woman is Hart County, named for Nancy Hart. She was a colorful figure of the Revolution, who according to legend, singlehandedly captured a group of Tories who were afterwards executed. Clarke County, which is the smallest in area, was named for Revolutionary hero, General Elijah Clarke. After the war he attempted to establish his Trans-Oconee Republic in the vicinity of today's Milledgeville, much to the dismay of President George Washington.

Some of Georgia's place-names are reminiscent of the Civil War. We have a Jeff Davis County named for Jefferson Davis, who was president of the Confederacy, and Stephens County named for Alexander Stephens, who was the vice president. Confederate leader Robert Toombs was remembered by the naming of Toombs County and also the town of Toomsboro. Evans County, Turner County, and Wheeler County were also named for noted officers of the Confederacy.

Such place-names are easily enough found. But the authorities are not always in agreement as to others, and it is not always possible to establish with any certainty which derivation is the most reliable. Therefore, the compiler has included all suggested derivations found, often indicating the sources used. When it is indicated that the derivation of a place is unknown, this of course means that no authority has been found by the compiler to explain the origin of the particular place-name in question.

No attempt has been made towards strict uniformity of treatment for all the entries in this work, because of the wide variance in the present information available. However, a standard procedure for handling of the counties has been used here, wherein the date of creation is first given, followed by its size in square miles, and then an explanation of from whom or what the county in question was named. Much of this particular information was taken from the most recent edition of the *Georgia Official and Statistical Register,* which is published by the Georgia Department of Archives and History. Following the information regarding the derivation of the county name will be the designation of the county seat. Incidentally, where the name of each county seat is shown in the alphabetically listing, it will be so designated by the abbreviation "CS."

Every effort was made toward achieving the highest possible accuracy in the information presented here. It must be pointed out however, that by the nature of this field of study, there can be a very few absolutes, particularly in regard to the origins of the names of places. Even in those rare instances when it isrecorded at the time it is done that a particular name is to be given to a place, there is frequently an omission as to why it was given, or exactly to whom the name refers. Even in the naming of counties, there have been disagreements as to which of several persons with the same name were meant to be so honored, such as in the cases of Brantley County, Cobb County, Fulton County, and White County.

In many instances, legends have been invented to explain how some of Georgia's towns were named, which are often more fascinating than the true derivations. Some have related how Georgia's first city was named when a young maiden was drowning, and a call came out to "Save Anna!" thus the place was called SAVANNAH. Or it was often said that ALMA in Bacon County was named from the initial letters of Georgia's succesive state capitals: Augusta, Louisville, Milledgeville, and Atlanta. And a story came out that the old town of HAHIRA in Lowndes County was given this name because of a railroad engineer named Hira, whose friends, would call to him, "Hey Hira!"

The NACOOCHEE RIVER of White County and LAKE NACOOCHEE in Rabun County were supposedly named for an incident when an Indian maiden called Nacoochee jumped to her death after her father, the chieftan, prevented her marriage to a brave of an alien tribe, with whom she was in love. Another Indian legend relates to the naming of Dade County's town of RISING FAWN, in which the Cherokee chief there named his newborn daughter from the first thing he saw the morning the infant was born, a fawn rising from over the nearby hill. The Madison County community of POCATALIGO was so named according to a legend which tells of a method of urginga balky mule to move, and that is to, "Poke 'e tail 'e go." And one of the most ridiculous stories told of the naming of RESACA in Gordon County, wwhich which a young Indian brave commanded "Re-sacka!" after the sack was lifted to reveal the unattractive face of a prospective bride. These and other legends were created by some who were unaware of the actual derivations of these Georgia place-names.

The most obscure place-names of course are those of Indian origin. These dialects are seldom translatable word-for-word, hence there are often several interpretations of the meanings of a given Indian name. The Cherokee Indians of Georgia were the only native Americans to have created an alphabet and a written language, but this has not proven to be of particular help in translating their place-names into English. The guttural Indian rendering of their words have been written as they sounded to DeSoto, Bartram, Hawkins, Mooney, and others. Some of the more common spellings of Indian place-names have been included in this compilation: "Okefenokee" has been recorded with over 77 different spellings!

In the course of this research, every name listed was first located on one or more maps to verify its location, and to determine whether the place exists today. This was also done in order to be able to indicate as reliably as possible the present status of the place listed. Current road maps of Georgia as well as of the individual counties were examined, and also current atlases. The state Department of Archives and History provided the use of its vast collection of maps dating back to the founding of Georgia.

Individual histories have been written of only about two-thirds of Georgia's counties. Most of these furnish information on the founding and naming of their towns, and in some instances other place-names. Generally, these county histories were written and published in response to a resolution passed by the State Assembly, August 23, 1929, requesting that all counties in Georgia have their individual histories written and published before the State's bicentennial celebration on Georgia Day, February 12, 1933. Some of the counties compiled with this request, but there remained about 100 which did not. A number of these have since been published, and these too were consulted, as were some city histories, such as Athens, Columbus, Macon, Milledgeville, Rome, Savannah, etc. The most helpful of these has been Franklin M. Garrett's two-volume, *Atlanta and Environs,* published in 1954.

The first book to be written on Georgia place-names was the Reverend Adiel Sherwood's *Gazeteer of the State of Georgia,* which was publshed in several editions beginning in 1827. This contains alphabetically listed places, with descriptions and occasional derivations. In 1855, Reverend George White issued his *Historical Collections of Georgia,* which proved helpful for the earlier periods of settlement. A more comprehensive source was Lucien Lamar Knight's two-volume *Georgia Landmarks and Legends,* which was published in 1913. Another useful source was the three-volume, *Cyclopedia of Georgia,* published in 1906 by Govenor Allen D. Candler and General Clement A. Evans, which provides good descriptions of the counties, cities, and towns, as well as the leading personages of the state.

An excellent source book used was, *Georgia, A Guide to its Towns and Countryside,* compiled by WPA writers, and published by the Georgia Board of Education in 1940. Undoubtedly the most useful, thorough, and reliable source of information on Georgia place-names is the extensive work compiled by the late John H. Goff of Emory University. Much of this was published over a period of years in the *Georgia Mineral Newsletter,* in the series, "A Short Study in Georgia Place-Names." Additional information was also obtained from Goff's place-name files and unpublished papers in the custody of the state's Surveyor-General Department. One of the most recent compilations to appear is Hal E. Brinkley's handy little booklet, *How Georgia Got Her Names,* which was copyrighted in 1967.

Much of the information used here has come from historical markers which have been erected throughout the state by the Georgia Historical Commission. Those of us who are interested in our state's history are indebted to Carroll Proctor Scruggs, who compiled and published in 1973 the complete texts of these 1,752 *Georgia Historical Markers.*

Some of the data used was obtained by written inquirers and also by personally travelling throughout the state to question residents as to the name derivations of their own localities. Also, a great deal of information was found in the pages of the daily newspapers in the state, particularly anniversary editions, and in such periodicals as *Georgia Magazine* and *Georgia Historical Quarterly.*

It is with much pleasure that appreciation is expressed for the help and encouragement offered by Dr. Spencer Bidwell King, Jr. of Mercer University, who read the manuscript in the first draft, corrected historical inaccuracies, as well as making innumerable constructive suggestions. His student also thanks Dr. King for providing the delightful introduction for the volume. Valuable assistance has been provided by Mrs. Pat Bryant of the State of Georgia Surveyor-General Department, who made available the maps and records in her custody. The compiler is grateful for the efforts of Mrs. Bryant's associate, Mr. Marion R. Hemperley, who read the manuscript in its entirety, correcting factual errors therein. Mr. Dumont Bunn of the Mercer University Library was helpful in aiding the compiler as to the form of presentation, and helped procure place-name source material from other libraries. Whatever faults and inaccuracies that may remain are the responsibility of this writer alone.

The compiler is grateful for the help and cooperation received by those who supplied needed information, aided in the research, and helped in many other ways towards the completion of this effort. Some of those who contributed in these ways are: Jewell R. Alverson, Lora Burns, Leah Chanin, Kenneth Cherry, Ed Corson, Mrs. Joseph C. Coward, Helen W. Coxon, S. H. Croft, Mrs. Henry Dunham, J. E. Earnest, Hubert Hamilton, Ruth Harben, Hazel M. Harvey, Herman Huhn, Cindy Hinebaugh, Jimmy Jones, W. W. "Billy" Keith, Jr., Betty Kemp, Katherine E. Mann, Daniel Lamar Metz, Jr., Elizabeth Middlebrooks, Violet Moore, Mary Overby, W. S. Palmer, Joseph Parham, John R. Patterson, Milton L. Ready, C. P. A. C. "Chris" Reynolds, Nell W. Rogers, Perry U. Rozier, Anna E. Schnikel, Don L. Shadburn, Mary Singleton, Emory P. Smith, Jr., Marion Smith, J. Clayton Stephens, Jr., Claude G. Stevens, Mrs. Ray Tench, Tommy Toles, Solon W. Ware, Jr., John W. Watson, and Miriam L. Wheeler.

One of the frustrating aspects of this endeavor is the fact that a great deal of documentation is lacking, or at least very difficult to locate if it does exist. Therefore, the compiler would like to invite correspondence from individuals who are able to supply any additions to or corrections of the data recorded here, which would be useful for a possible revised edition of this work.

Kenneth K. Krakow
Macon, Georgia

MILITIA DISTRICTS

The state of Georgia is divided into 159 counties, and each county is subdivided into further political divisions known as militia districts. This is the only state to have such a designation, although other states do divide their counties into smaller units, usually called townships.

Georgia's militia dates back to colonial days and was authorized by the General Assembly April 16, 1751. The original intention was to provide protection against the Indians. All able-bodied male white citizens, between the ages of 18 and 45 (unless exempt) were at that time enrolled into the militia.

Each militia district was served by a company of approximately 100 men who elected one of their members to be the captain in charge. The districts were at first named for the captain, but confusion arose because of duplications of names and changes in command. It was then decided to use the present system, numbering the districts, beginning with the first organized. Besides using the numbers, some districts have retained the original names for the first captain, others have been named for prominent men, towns or communities, or from other origins.

The militia was under the direct command of the governor, and could not be sent out of the state, and could only be used to repel invasion and preserve order. After the Indians were finally driven from the state, the militia organization gradually took on a sort of social aspect.

During the Civil War, the Conscription Act of the Confederacy in effect wiped out the state militia by forcing its men into the regular Confederate Army. In the Twentieth Century, some of the militia companies became National Guard units for service in the Mexican conflict of 1916, and some went on coast guard duty against the Germans in World War I.

Today the militia district is the ultimate unit in Georgia's political division, and is no longer military in nature. Each district is entitled to one justice of the peace, elected by the people, and one notary public, recommended by the grand jury, and both commissioned by the governor; two baliffs, elected by the people, and commissioned by the ordinary, and one justice court each month, and a voting precinct.

A

AARON, Bulloch County. A rural community located 14 miles northwest of Statesboro. Named for the Biblical brother of Moses.

A B A C, Tift College. This railroad station name is an acronym formed from the initials of Abraham Baldwin Agricultural College located here.

ABBEVILLE, CS Wilcox County. Incorporated September 15, 1883. Sixty acres were given by David Fitzgerald for the county seat. It was said to have been either named for Abbie McNally or for Fitzgerald's wife. Brinkley says it was named for the famous Abbeville District of South Carolina, which was settled by French Huguenots, and was the home of Vice President John C. Calhoun.

ABERCORN, Chatham County. An early community which was located about fifteen miles above Savannah on ABERCORN CREEK, which stream was named for this settlement. The place was named by General Oglethorpe for the Duke of Abercorn, who encouraged Oglethorpe's philanthropies. Ten families comprised the original settlement which was established in 1733. The place was abandoned in 1737 as conditions in the area caused sickness and death from malarial fevers. ABERCORN STREET in Savannah was also named for the Duke of Abercorn.

ABERDEEN, Fayette County. Incorporated as a town August 18, 1911, and named for the city in Scotland. This former community has now become part of PEACHTREE CITY, and is a stop on the Atlantic Coast Line Railroad.

ABNER, Spalding County. This was the former name of DREWRYVILLE (q.v.).

ABRAHAM BALDWIN AGRICULTUR-AL COLLEGE, Tifton. Founded in 1908 as the SECOND DISTRICT AGRICULTURAL AND MECHANICAL SCHOOL. The present name is in honor of the founder of the University of Georgia (*see* Baldwin County). The college came under the State University System in 1933.

ACHENAHATCHEE CREEK. A Creek Indian name which means CEDAR CREEK (q.v.).

A-CON-HOLLO-WA TAL-LO-FA, Clay County. The Indians' name for a village at the site of the present FORT GAINES (q.v.).

ACORN CREEK, Carroll County. Rises at Whitesburg and flows southwesterly. Named for the former Creek town of ACORNTOWN, which was located at the junction of this stream and the Chattahoochee River.

ACTON, Harris County. A former post office in south Harris County which was named by Revolutionary veterans for the old colonial ACTON DISTRICT in Christ Church Parish. Acton was a former borough of London which was a center of English Puritanism.

ACWORTH, Cobb County. Incorporated as a town December 1, 1860. Earlier called NORTHCUTT STATION, it was named in 1843 by Joseph L. Gregg for the New Hampshire town which was named for the English nobleman, Lord Acworth. It was also thought to have been named for Paul Ackerly from Brooklyn, New York, who was an early president of Acworth Mills here.

ADAIRSVILLE, Bartow County. Settled in 1825 by a Scot, Walter S. Adair, who married into the Cherokee Nation. Incorporated as a town February 8, 1854. The Adairs lived five miles north of here at Oothcalooga (Calhoun).

ADAMS BRIDGE, E. CUYLER, Wilkinson County. Spans Turkey Creek three miles east of Allentown on Georgia highway 112. Named March 25, 1958 to honor civic leader E. C. Adams, who was a mail carrier for 33 years.

ADAMS PARK, Twiggs County. A railroad stop four miles south of Bullard station. Named for President John Adams, due to his popularity following the XYZ affair with France in 1797-98.

ADAMSVILLE, Fulton County. Now part of Atlanta, this former community was believed named for an early settler called Adams. It was recorded that G. W. Adams was a farmer here in 1882. This place was previously called LICK SKILLET(q.v.). *See also* Howell's Ferry Road.

ADEL, CS Cook County. Pronounced "Aydell'" or "Uh-dell'." Incorporated October 3, 1889. A pioneer settler, Joel J. "Uncle Jack" Parish was the first postmaster here, and wished to change the name of the town from PUDDLEVILLE. To create the new name, he struck out the first and last four letters from the name Philadelphia which he saw on a crocus sack. The name was changed July 22, 1873.

ADKINS, Crisp County. An early settlement which was located in the Western section of the county. Named for a William Adkins who came here from Washington County before 1842.

ADRIAN, Johnson and Emanuel counties. The post office was established in 1891, and the town was chartered December 19, 1899. The county line forms a large "Z" through Adrian, which came about because of a local feud. Derivation of the name is not known.

ADSBORO (Militia) DISTRICT, Morgan County. This is a coined name which arose from an incident in which a man shaping a timber with an adz, hit himself in the knee.

AERIAL, Habersham County. A community located eight miles west of Clarkesville on Georgia 17. Brinkley said it was named for its location among the lofty and aerial mountains.

AFRICA (Militia) DISTRICT, Heard County. Bonner wrote that this name was inspired by the wilderness of the region, and not by the ancestry of its inhabitants.

AGNES SCOTT COLLEGE, Decatur. Founded in 1889 as DECATUR FEMALE SEMINARY by Dr. Frank H. Gaines. In 1890 the name was changed to AGNES SCOTT INSTITUTE in honor of the mother of its generous benefactor, Colonel George Washington Scott (1829-1903), Cavalry CSA (*see also* Scottdale). It was given its present name in 1906.

AH-YEH-LI A-LO-HEE, Hart County. Also spelled A-YEH-LI A-LO-HE (q.v.).

ALABAHA CREEK (or RIVER), Pierce County. This is another form of the Creek Indian word *Alapaha* (q.v.). It is a north-bank tributary of the Great Satilla River.

ALACOOCHEE RIVER, Irwin County. This name appears on an 1823 map and is believed to have been meant to apply to Willacoochee Creek (q.v.). But if authentic, the name probably means "Little Potato," from the Creek Indian *ahalak,* "potato," and *"uchi,* "little."

ALAMO, CS Wheeler County. Incorporated August 16, 1909. The name first suggested for this town was McCrae to honor a prominent landowner here, Judge John McCrae, who later became a state senator. Since the name was already in use, his daughter Christian McCrae suggested the name Alamo after the famous mission at San Antonio, Texas, the scene of a brutal massacre in 1836. *Alamo* is a Spanish word meaning "cottonwood" or "poplar."

ALAPAHA, Barrien County. Incorporated September 29, 1881. This town bears the name of the nearby ALAPAHA RIVER which flows southward from Dooly County to enter the Suwannee River in Florida. It is called the cleanest river in Georgia. Old timers pronounce it "Loppy-haw." The LITTLE ALAPAHA RIVER was earlier known as FLORIDA CREEK, a name of Spanish derivation meaning "flowered" or "flowery." Variations of spelling have included LOPAHA, ALOPAHA, LOPPAHAW, and LOW HAW. It is said by some to be from the Creek Indian word *apala,* signifying "on the other side," but it is more likely from the Timicua Indian word *Arapaha: ara,* "bear," and *paha,* "house." It has also been thought to mean "alligator." This was the site of an early Seminole Indian town also named Alapaha. Lakeland (q.v.) in Lanier County was formerly called ALAPAHA. *See also* Alabaha Creek.

ALAPAHOOCHEE RIVER, Lowndes County. The name means "Little Alapaha." This stream is formed about ten miles southeast of Valdosta where Mud Swamp and Grand Bay unite. It runs into the Alapaha River (q.v.) at the Georgia-Florida line.

ALBANY, CS Dougherty County. Called "City of Opportunity." Locally pronounced "All ben' ny" or "Al bain' ny." Named for the capital city of New York State, which was named for the Duke of York's Scottish title, Duke of Albany. The name was adopted because both cities are located on rivers at the head of navigation. The site was selected and purchased in 1836 by Alexander Shotwell, a Quaker from New Jersey. The town was settled by Nelson Tift, October 1836, and he secured a charter for the city December 27, 1838. TIFT PARK was named for Colonel Tift, founder of the town (*see* Tift County), and MILLS MUNICIPAL STADIUM was named in honor of Hugh M. Mills (1885-1952), school teacher and athletic coach. ALBANY STATE COLLEGE was established here in 1903 as the ALBANY BIBLE AND MANUAL TRAINING INSTITUTE. It became GEORGIA NORMAL AND AGRICULTURAL COLLEGE in 1917, and the present name was adopted in 1943.

ALBANY JUNIOR COLLEGE was established here in 1966.

ALBANY, Jones County. This was the early
name of CLINTON (q.v.).

ALCOVY, Newton County. This stop on the
Georgia Railroad is located northeast of
Covington. Is named after the ALCOVY
RIVER which flows southward from
Gwinnett County through Newton County
into Jackson Lake. The Muskogean Indian
name of the river was ULCOFAUHATCHIE,
which William Read translates to mean, "A
river among pawpaw trees," from *ulcofau,*
"pawpaws-among," and *-hatchie,* "creek."
The name has also been spelled ALCOVA
and ALCOVEE.

ALECKS CREEK, Wayne County. Has also
been spelled ALEX and ELLIS Creek. It was
named for a lower Creek Indian chief called
Alleck or Captain Alleck, who once lived near
its mouth on the Altamaha River. His name is
derived from the Muskogean Indian word,
aleckcha or *alikcha,* meaning "doctor." *See
also* Doctortown.

ALEXANDER, Burke County. Incorporated
December 16, 1851. A community located nine
miles southeast of Waynesboro on Georgia 24.
First established as Alexander Village and
Academy Company, it was settled in 1849 and
named for early settler, Hugh Alexander.

ALEXANDER H. STEPHENS STATE
PARK, Crawfordville. Named in honor of the
vice president of the Confederate States, Alexander H. Stephens. His home Liberty Hall, a
museum, Lake Liberty, and a monument to
his honor are included in the 1,161 acre park.
See also Stephens County.

ALEXANDERVILLE, Madison County.
The previous name of MADISON SPRINGS
(q.v.). Named for James Alexander, who with
William Dearing purchased the site in 1816 to
develop a resort.

ALEXANDRIA, Elbert County. Founded
about 1797; its location was believed to have
been near the Savannah River, a few miles
below where Ruckersville was settled.
Believed to have been named after Alexandria, Virginia.

ALLATOONA, Bartow County. This community is located on ALLATOONA CREEK,
and was established as a gold mining village
of the 1840's and 1850's. It is probably a

Cherokee Indian name of unknown meaning;
resembles "toonigh," once a common name
for Cherokee men. Brinkley states it was
named after the city of Altoona,
Pennsylvania. An important engagement of
the Civil War was fought here October 5, 1864.
The settlement is about six miles southeast of
Cartersville, and is a stop on the Louisville
and Nashville Railroad, near the 19,200-acre
ALLATOONA LAKE (or RESERVOIR).

ALLEN GAP, Gilmer County. Named for an
early settler here, Billy Allen.

ALLEN('S) MILL, Carroll County. A community located near Villa Rica. When first
settled, a Mr. E. M. Allen had a general store
and mill here.

ALLENSVILLE, Forsyth County. This was
the fifth post office in the county when it was
established, September 30, 1837. It was
located in the lower section of the county near
Shiloh. The first postmaster was Beverly
Allen. The name of the post office was
changed January 13, 1846 to VICKERY'S
CREEK (q.v.). *See also* Beverly.

ALLENTOWN, Located at the junction of
four counties: Wilkinson, Twiggs, Laurens,
and Bleckley. Named for the early
postmaster, John Allen. The town was incorporated December 7, 1901, when the first
aldermen included J. W. Allen and W.M.
Allen.

ALLIGATOR. This name is derived from the
Spanish *el lagarto,* "the lizard." Before
thousands were killed for their hides,
alligators were seen more commonly in the
coastal plains of Georgia. This has been
reflected in many of the state's place-names,
such as the community of ALLIGATOR in
Telfair County. ALLIGATOR BAY is in
southwest Bryan County, and ALLIGATOR
HOLE in eastern Early County was recorded
on an 1820 map. A map of 1764 shows an
ALLIGATOR POND in Jenkins County. The
name of streams called ALLIGATOR
CREEK has been noted in the following counties: Baker, Clinch, Dodge-Laurens-Wheeler,
Mitchell, Telfair, Toombs, and Ware.

ALLONAHACHEE CREEK, Stewart
County. This name is derived from the Muscogean Indian words, *alunaha,* "wild potato,"
and *hachi,* "creek."

ALMA, CS Bacon County. Called "The
Queen City." Incorporated August 21, 1906. A

group of residents were trying to decide on a name for their community, when their friend, a Mr. Sheridan arrived on the scene. He was a "drummer" (salesman) from Macon who offered the name of his wife Alma. Bernice McCullar has pointed out that this town name is made up of the first letters of the four Georgia capitals: Augusta, Louisville, Milledgeville, and Atlanta.

ALMON, Newton County. This town had a post office from 1886 to 1931. The first postmaster here was Thomas J. Almond.

ALPHARETTA, Fulton County. Incorporated December 11, 1858. Was the county seat of the former Milton County (q.v.). Prior to 1858 the town was called NEW PROSPECT CAMPGROUND. The name is a variant of Alfarata, the fictional Indian girl of the 19th century song, *The Blue Juniata.* Alpharetta has also been thought to have been coined from the first letter of the Greek alphabet.

ALPINE, Chattooga County. A former village three miles south of Menlo on ALPINE CREEK. Because of its location in the mountainous region of Georgia, this community took its name from the Swiss Alps. Settled by the Force family of Augusta, this was the home of George Guess (1770-1843), the Indian called Sequoyah (q.v.).

ALSTON, Montgomery County. Incorporated as a town August 3, 1910. Named for the early settler family of Alex Alston.

ALTAMA, Glynn County. This was the name given to a 2,000-acre plantation which was established in 1815 and purchased by the Shakers in 1898. The former ALTAMAHA PARK was later located at this site. For derivation, *see* Altamaha.

ALTAMAHA. Prounounced "All'-ta-ma-haw'." This was the name of an early community in Tattnall County, ten miles southwest of Reidsville, near the river from which it took its name. It was possibly situated at about the same location as an earlier Indian settlement of Tama (q.v.). In the days of Spanish possession, the islands and coastal lands of present Georgia were referred to as Guale (q.v.), and the inland region of mythical riches as Tama. The ALTAMAHA RIVER flowing through the middle of this region was apparently called by the Spaniards, AL TAMA (*al* in Spanish, "to

the"), and later extended by the Indians to Altamaha. In his poem *The Desserted Village* (1770), the English author, Oliver Goldsmith, referred to the river as the "Altama." This name was mentioned by Hernando DeSoto's chroniclers in 1540 as the name of a province, and is claimed to be a Creek Indian adaption of a Timicua Indian name. The river has also been called A-LOT-AMAHA. Some have claimed a derivation from the Spanish *alta-mia,* signifying "deep earthen plate (or dish)." It has also been suggested that the name is from the Timicua Indian, *holahta,* "chief," and *paha,* "lodge," to mean "chief's lodge." Another interpretation has been that it means "treacherous waters." Altamaha was also the name of a Yamassee Indian chief. A map of Georgia during the Spanish era shows this river labeled RIO DE TALAJE (*see* Talaje). The only town which has endured on this great river is Darien.

ALTO, Habersham County. Incorporated December 16, 1895. Previous names were LONGVIEW STATION, LULAH and ROUL. The name of this town is from the Italian, *alto,* meaning "high," in reference to its elevation, 1,395 feet above sea level. The Georgia Industrial Institute here is on the site of the former state tuberculosis sanitarium. The rural community of ALTO in Madison County is located five miles north of Comer.

AMBOY, Turner County. Community located seven miles northeast of Ashburn. Named from the city in New Jersey, an Algonquin Indian word referring to a valley.

AMERICUS, CS Sumter County. Founded in 1832, the post office was established January 15, 1833. The town was incorporated and made county seat December 22, 1832. Named for the Western Continents, which in turn were named for Amerigo Vespucci (1451-1512). Americus, the masculine of America, was suggested by a Mr. Cobb, who placed it in a hat with other proposed names. Charles A. Lindbergh made his first solo flight at Souther Field (q.v.) here in 1923.

AMICALOLA, Dawson County. Pronounced "Ahm-a-ku-lo-la." A former community in the western section of the county, named for AMICALOLA CREEK, on which it was located. The stream rises in the AMICALOLA MOUNTAINS in the northern section of the county, and flows southwesterly until it reaches the Etowah River. The name means "tumbling waters," from the Cherokee

Indian words, *ama*, "water," and *kalola*, "tumbling." This refers to the series of seven waterfalls of this stream called AMICALOLA FALLS, which have a total fall of 929 feet. These are the highest waterfalls in the state and are located within 263-acre AMICALOLA FALLS STATE PARK. AM(M)ACALOLA CAMP GROUND was established in this vicinity December 18, 1860 by the Methodist Episcopal Church. Past variations in spelling have included AMAKALOLA, ARMICALOLA and UM-MAH CALOLOKE.

AMITY, Lincoln County. This community's name means harmony and friendliness. The AMITY SCHOOL DISTRICT here was incorporated August 17, 1903.

AMSTERDAM, Decatur County. This community is located 16 miles southeast of Bainbridge, and was named for the city in Holland.

ANDERSONVILLE, Cobb County. This community was located on U. S. Highway 41 between Big Shanty and Acworth, but ceased to exist after the railroad by-passed the area. The derivation of the name is not known.

ANDERSONVILLE, Sumter County. Incorporated January 18, 1881. First known as ANDERSON or ANDERSON STATION, after a Mr. Anderson the original settler. During the Civil War the Confederate States Military Prison, CAMP SUMTER, was established here (1863), and was generally referred to and later formally named ANDERSONVILLE PRISON. This consisted of twenty-eight acres of stockaded area which was used to confine about 40,000 captured Union soldiers, of whom 12,462 died in a thirteen month period, and lie buried in ANDERSONVILLE PRISON CEMETERY adjoining the prison camp. The stockade has been designated a National Historic Site under the National Park Service, and is now called ANDERSONVILLE PRISON PARK. A monument stands in the "square" of Andersonville village to honor the prison commandant, Captain Henry Wirz (1822-1865), and as a protest against his execution. He was condemned to death after a trial at which he was charged with excessive cruelty to the prisoners here. ANDERSONVILLE TRAIL was the official designation given an 80-mile tourist loop off of Interstate Highway 75, which includes the towns of Cordele, De

Soto, Americus, Andersonville, Oglethorpe, Montezuma, Marshallville, and Perry.

ANDREW COLLEGE, Cuthbert. Claims to have the second oldest charter (1854) in the United States for an educational institution conferring degrees upon women. It is now coeducational. Originally named ANDREW FEMALE COLLEGE in honor of Methodist Bishop, James Osgood Andrew (1794-1871).

ANGELICA CREEK, Sumter County. Located in the northern part of the county just above Americus. Was at one time labeled MUCKALOOCHEE, and was probably first called NOTOSAHATCHIE, after the Angelica plant that the Creek Indians found growing here, which they used for medicine.

ANGUILLA, Glynn County. A community located eight miles northwest of Brunswick on Georgia 32. Named for the Caribbean island of Angilla, from where Sea Island Cotton was introduced into Georgia.

ANNA RUBY FALLS, White County. Located five miles northeast of Helen, they are also known as RUBY FALLS (q.v.).

ANNEEWAKEE CREEK, Douglas County. Flows southeastward from near Douglasville to join the Chattahoochee River. First called ANNAWAKA CREEK (1827), the name is thought to have been derived from a Cherokee family named, Anakwan-ki. The possible meaning is "Cow (Cattle) People," from *ani*, "clan," and *waca*, "cow."

ANNIEDELL, Floyd County. A community located 12 miles west of South Rome. Named for the Cherokee woman, Sadayi, known to white traders as Annie Ax.

ANTIOCH, Stewart County. Incorporated as a town December 30, 1851, it was named for the Antioch Baptist Church, established here in 1839. Derivation is from Antioch, the ancient capital of Syria, which is now Antakya, Turkey. This Georgia community was also known as HANNAHATCHEE (q.v.), and is now called LOUVALE (q.v.). *See also* STEPHENS.

APALACHEE. This is the oldest recorded Indian name in Georgia, according to Goff. It is a name that was given to a former community in Oconee County, and was named for the APALACHEE RIVER on which it was located. This was formerly called the South Branch of the Oconee River, and before that named CHULAPOCCA (q.v.). There is at present a community called APALACHEE in upper Morgan County. It was settled before 1820 and incorporated August 22, 1907. The railroad station here was first named FLORENCE, for Florence Few, a daughter of Joe C. Few. The name was already in use, so about 1896 the name Apalachee was adopted. The name is derived from the Apalachee (or Apalachi) Indian tribe of the Creek Confederation. The meaning may be from the Hitchiti Indian word *apalahchi,* "those on the other side" (as opposed to allies), "those who lived beyond the mountains," or possibly from the Choctaw, *apelachi,* "helpers" or "allies." Derivation can also be traced from the former Indian town of Apalachee (or Apalachen), which was in the vicinity of today's Tallahassee, Florida. This place was mentioned by Alvar Nunez de Vaca.(1490?-1557) in the account of the Narvaez expedition of 1528. The Spaniards under Hernando De Soto (1500?-1557) first applied the name to the APPLACHIAN MOUNTAINS in 1539. This range includes all of the eastern United States mountains from Alabama and Georgia to northern Maine. Through this range runs the APPALACHIAN TRAIL, the longest trail in the world, which extends 2,065 miles from Springer Mountain in Georgia to Mount Katahdin in Maine.

APALACHICOLA. A former Indian village located south of Caveta (q.v.) on the west side of the Chattahoochee River. The exact location is not known. APALACHICOLA FORT (or *Presidio)* was built at this site in 1689 by Captain Primo de Rivera for protection against the English. In the summer of 1691, the garrison was withdrawn and the fort was completely destroyed to prevent the English from occupying it. The name comes either from the tribal name Apalachicolas, an Indian confederacy called Lower Creeks by the English, or from the Choctaw Indian word *Apelach-okla,* "The helping people" or "Allies." The name was shaped by the early Spaniards to the appearance of a Spanish name for RIO APALACHICOLA. This is the APALACHICOLA RIVER, which is formed by the meeting of the Chattahoochee and Flint Rivers, and flows through Florida to the Gulf of Mexico.

APOLLO, Putnam County. This former community was named for Apollo, the Greek god of light, music, poetry, and pastoral pursuits.

APPLE VALLEY, Jackson County. This rural community was founded by Judge W. J. Colquitt of Athens, who planted apple orchards in this valley. The post office served here from June 29, 1877 to August 31, 1903.

APPLING, CS Columbia County. Settled in 1772 by William Appling who conveyed the land on which the court house was established December 10, 1807. The previous county seat was Cobbham (q.v.), now a dead town.

APPLING COUNTY. Created December 14, 1818 with 514 square miles acquired by Creek Indian cessions of August 9, 1814 and January 22, 1818. Named for Colonel Daniel Appling (1787-1818), a native Georgian and noted soldier of the War of 1812. The county seat is Baxley (q.v.).

ARABI, Crisp County. Incorporated as a town September 14, 1891. In 1888 the original settlers met to name their railroad stop, and "agreed on this name after a great deal of discussion." It is said to have been derived from a family name.

ARAGON, Polk County. Incorporated as a city July 23, 1914. Was named after the mineral, aragonite, which has been mined in this area for use as a bleaching compound.

ARCADE, Jackson County, Incorporated August 17, 1909 to enable the establishment of a school here, which was to be housed in an arcade type building. This is now called "The Beer Capital of Georgia," because it sells about 500,000 cases of beer a year at a low tax rate in an otherwise dry county.

ARCADIA, Liberty County. An early community named for the land of idyllic joys in Peloponnesus, Greece, which was inhabited by a pastoral people. This community is now known as MIDWAY (q.v.).

ARCH, Forsyth County. A former community which was located in the northeast section of the county. Named for the Cherokee scribe, John Arch, whose tribal name was A'tsi.

ARCHIBOOKTA CREEK, Webster County. This Creek Indian name found on an 1826 map means "Corn Cob Creek." The present name of the stream is HARRELL MILL CREEK (q.v.).

ARGYLE, Clinch County. Incorporated as a town November 18, 1901. Established in 1885 when it was first known as SAUSSY to honor a Mr. Clement Saussy. The present name was used beginning in 1899 to commemorate Fort Argyle (q.v.) in Bryan County.

ARGYLE ISLAND, Chatham County. Located in the lower Savannah River, it was probably named for Archibald Campbell, 3rd duke of Argyle (1682-1761).

ARKAQUIA CREEK, Union County. Also spelled ARKAQUA, it flows southwesterly into the Nottely River three miles below Blairsville. Named for a Cherokee Indian man who lived nearby.

ARKWRIGHT, Bibb County. Formerly called HOLTON (q.v.), this community on the Ocmulgee River is the site of the Arkwright Power Plant which was named for Preston S. Arkwright, founder and early president of the Georgia Power Company.

ARLINGTON, Calhoun and Early counties. "Garden Spot of the World and Southwestern Georgia" Established in May 1873 and incorporated as a town September 13, 1881. Was the county seat of Calhoun County until August 6, 1929 when the seat was moved to Morgan (q.v.). Named for the estate of General Robert E. Lee in Virginia near Washington, D. C., which is now a national cemetery.

ARMSTRONG STATE COLLEGE, Savannah. Founded in 1935 as ARMSTRONG JUNIOR COLLEGE. Was first housed in the Armstrong Building, a gift to the city from the family of George F. Armstrong. The college entered the State University System in 1959 when the present name was adopted.

ARMUCHEE, Floyd County. This town is located on ARMUCHEE CREEK, which arises in Chattooga County, and flows into the Oostanaula River. The name is a

Cherokee word that is thought to mean "hominy," or may be from the Choctaw, *alumushi,* "hiding place." Sartain stated that it means "land of the flowers." Brinkley says it was named for Am ma choo, an old Cherokee warrior who was protected by a land grant in the 1817 treaty.

ARNCO (MILLS), Coweta County. A community located about five miles northwest of Newnan. This is a coined name for the cotton mill established here by a Mr. Arnold and a Mr. Cole.

ARNOLD (MILL), Fulton County. A community in the upper section of the county which was named for Givens White Arnold, a settler of old Milton County.

ARNOLD ROAD, Barrow County. Located eight miles east of Winder. When this road was in Jackson County, a village of ARNOLDSVILLE or ARNOLD'S STORE was established here. Mr. T. B. Arnold had a general store here. The place was also called BARBERS CREEK (q.v.), named from the nearby stream.

ARNOLDSVILLE, Oglethorpe County. Incorporated as a city April 23, 1969. Settled about 1881 on the site of the former CHEROKEE CORNER community (q.v.). In 1896 the name of the post office was changed to Arnoldsville, named for Mr. Nat D. Arnold, who was one of the largest farmers in the county.

ARP (or BILL ARP), Banks County. A community located about five miles northeast of Homer. For derivation, *see* Bill Arp, Douglas County.

ASBESTOS, White County. A former community in the eastern part of the county, named for the fire resistant mineral, asbestos, mined here.

ASBURY, Troup County. A community located nine miles north of La Grange, named for Bishop Francis Asbury (1745-1816), first American consecrated bishop of the Methodist Episcopal Church. It is now called HARRISONVILLE.

ASCALON, Walker County. An early post office which was located in the northern section of the county, 18 miles above LaFayette. Named for the Biblical city of Ashkelon in Israel, which is today spelled Ashqelon.

ASHANTILLY PLANTATION, McIntosh County. Located just east of Darien, and was the home (1818) of Thomas Spalding (*see* Spalding County). Named for the Barony of Ashantilly, Perthshire, Scotland.

ASHBURN, CS Turner County. Incorporated December 26, 1890. Named for W.W. Ashburn, early settler who came here from Eastman. Was previously named MARION by Mr. Ashburn and J. S. Betts when they purchased land here about 1888. The place had first been called TROUP-VILLE CROSSROADS.

ASKA, Fannin County. A community located eight miles southeast of Blue Ridge. A form of the Cherokee word, *asi,* "a winter house."

ATCO, Bartow County. An acronym for American Textile Company, which established a plant here. This community is now a part of Cartersville.

ATHENS, CS Clarke County. Called "The Classical City." Incorporated December 8, 1806 when the county seat was moved here from Watkinsville. Of over forty Athenses in the U. S., Athens, Georgia is the largest and best known. The name was reportedly selected by the Trustees of the University of Georgia (q.v.) upon its establishment here. Some have believed that the name was suggested by Milledge or Meigs, but more recently, University of Georgia professor, E. Merton Coulter, surmised that the local postmaster selected the name. It was named for the capital of Greece, which name is believed to have been derived from the name of the Olympian goddess Athena, and as John Milton, the English poet once said, "Athens is the mother of arts and eloquence." The original settlement here was called CEDAR SHOALS (q.v.). The street names of Athens reflect the men in its history: BALDWIN STREET was named for Abraham Baldwin (1754-1897), who introduced the bill in the state legislature to authorize the new university, MILLEDGE AVENUE for John Milledge (1757-1818), who donated the land for the university. MEIGS, CHURCH, and WADDELL streets were named for Josiah Meigs, Alonzo Church, and Moses Waddell who were early university presidents. FINDLAY STREET honors James Findlay, the founder of the university Library, and LUMPKIN STREET commemorates Governor Wilson Lumpkin (1783-1870), who lived in Athens. FRANKLIN STREET was named for noted resident

Leonidas Franklin, and GRADY AVENUE for William S. Grady, businessman of Athens who died in the Civil War. Old MARKET STREET was later changed to WASHINGTON STREET to honor our country's first president.

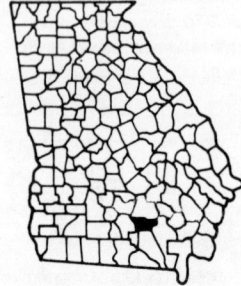

ATKINSON COUNTY. Created August 15, 1917 with 318 square miles taken from parts of Clinch and Coffee counties. It was named in honor of state representative, William Yates Atkinson (1854-1899), who became speaker of the State house, and later governor in 1894. He was born in Meriwether County. The county seat is Pearson (q.v.).

ATLANTA, capital of the State and CS of Fulton County. The Indians first had a settlement at STANDING PEACHTREE (q.v.) where Atlanta now stands. However the first permanent white settlers were James Montgomery (*see* Montgomery Ferry Road), and Hardy Ivy (c. 1780-1844) who came from South Carolina in 1833, and built a log cabin near the present Five Points (q.v.). He is remembered in Atlanta today by IVY STREET (q.v.). His arrival was twelve years after the territory was opened by treaty with the Creek Indians. As other settlers arrived the settlement was sometimes called CANE-BRAKE, but the first official name was the post office called WHITE HALL (q.v.) which was established June 9, 1835. This name is today preserved as WHITE HALL STREET. Colonel Abbott Hall Brisbane surveyed the area for the railroad, and placed a bench mark in early September 1837 between the present Forsyth Street and the old Gas Works. This was referred to as the railroad terminus, and the first cluster of shacks was called TERMINUS. This name was used by early settlers here between 1845 and 1850, although it was never official. In 1839 it was suggested by some that the early settlement be called "Deanville" for early resident Lemuel Dean.

Another suggestion was to call it "Thrasherville" (q.v.) for John J. Thrasher (1818-1899), who with a partner operated the first store here. About 1842, former governor Wilson Lumpkin declined the suggestion that the new town be named "Lumpkin" in his honor, and suggested it be called "Mitchell," for Samuel Mitchell who gave the land for the railroad terminus. However Mitchell and chief engineer of the Western and Atlantic Railroad, Charles Fenton Mercer Garnett (for whom GARNETT STREET is named) decided to name the town for Lumpkin's youngest daughter, Martha. It was incorporated under the name MARTHASVILLE on December 23, 1842. The United States Post Office also recognized the place as Marthasville at that time. The present name was chosen by J. Edgar Thomson, chief engineer of the Georgia Railroad, who was asked by his boss in 1845 to suggest a new name for the depot. He mailed his reply, "Eureka! — ATLANTA, the terminus of the Western & Atlantic Railroad — Atlantic, Masculine; Atlanta, feminine— a coined word, and if you think it will suit, adopt it." The town was still officially called Marthasville, but the freight all began coming in marked "Atlanta," and the town was thereafter called by this name. Atlanta was incorporated as a city December 29, 1845, at which time its population had grown to 2,000 inhabitants. It became the county seat November 7, 1853 when Fulton County was formed. Atlanta became the capital of the state April 20, 1868, when it was transferred from Milledgeville. Many nicknames have been applied to Atlanta, including: "Black Ankle" (1820's), "Mud City" (1872), "Empire City of the Empire State," "The Chicago of the South (1873), "The Cracker City" (1885), "Capital City," "The Magic City" (1892), "The Windy City," "Gate City" (q.v.), "Gait City" (1911), "The Dogwood City," "Gone With the Wind City," "Scarlett's Town," and "Sin City" (1954). *See also* Zero Mile Post.

ATLANTA UNIVERSITY, Atlanta. A private coeducational institution which was chartered in 1867 to provide higher education for freed slaves. It became a graduate school for students from Spelman and Morehouse colleges in 1929, Morris Brown College in 1932 and Clark College in 1941.

ATLANTA GENERAL DEPOT, Forest Park. Deactivated in 1974 to become FORT GILLEM (q.v.).

ATLANTIC COASTAL HIGHWAY, U. S. Highway 17. Descriptively named after the Atlantic Ocean, which name is thought to have been derived from that of the lost continent of Atlantis in Greek legend. It was also said to be named for Atlas the legendary giant who carried the world on his shoulders. The highway extends from Maine to Florida, and was paved through Savannah in 1924. The stretch between Darien and Savannah was first built by General Oglethorpe's engineers, Augustine and Tolme, following the route of an old Indian trail.

ATLANTIC INTRACOASTAL WATERWAY. This descriptively named busy passageway for small craft stretches from Maine to Miami, and runs along the inland side of Georgia's Golden Isles (q.v.).

ATTAPULGUS, Decatur County. Incorporated August 7, 1914. The name of this town is pronounced "Atteepulgus" by old timers. Was previously known as BOROUGH OF PLEASANT GROVE, and before that was called HACK. Many variations of spelling have been found such as, TAPHULGEE, ATLAPALGAS (1817), ALLAPULGES (1818). and ATEAPULGUS (1891). Some say it is from the Indian, itu-pulga, "boring holes in wood to make a fire," while others believe it is from the Creek Indian word, *attap' halgi,* "dogwood grove." In this locale is also found BIG ATTAPULGUS CREEK and LITTLE ATTAPULGUS CREEK (q.v.). The clay found in this region is a fuller's earth containing a mineral which has been labeled attapulgite, known chemically as hydrous aluminum magnesium silicate.

ATTICA, Jackson County. The name of this community is a Greek word pertaining to the Athenians.

AUBURN, Barrow County. Incorporated September 13, 1881. This town is thought to have been named for the imaginary community in British author, Oliver Goldsmith's poem, "The Deserted Village" (1770).

AU CHE HA CHEE. This was the Indian name of the LITTLE OCMULGEE RIVER (q.v.), and probably means "Little River," from *ochee,* "small (or little," and *hachi,* "creek."

AUCHUMPKEE CREEK, Crawford County. A tributary of the Flint River called OAK CHUNK locally. The Muscogean Indian word means "hickory-all-about." This name has also been interpreted as being a garbled version of *otialgi*, the Muskogean word for "islands."

AUCILLA RIVER, Thomas County. The second oldest recorded Indian name in Georgia (after Apalachee q.v.), as it was mentioned in 1539 by the chroniclers of Hernando DeSoto (c. 1500-1542). Various spellings have included ASSILLI, AUSSILLE, OSSILLA, and OCILLA. The name is derived from a Timicua Indian settlement in Florida, written variously as Agile, Axille, Aguile, and Ochile. There was at one time a post office of AUCILLA in Thomas County, located eighteen miles northeast of Thomasville. AUCILLA SWAMP is located in southeast Thomas and southwest Brooks counties.

AUDUBON, Gordon County. A community located ten miles northeast of Calhoun. Believed named for American ornithologist, John James Audubon.

AUGUSTA, CS Richmond County. Called "Garden City of the South" and "Golf Capital of the U.S." Established in 1735, this is the second oldest settlement in the state after Savannah. It was incorporated as a town in 1789, and as a city in January 1798. General James Edward Oglethorpe, founder of the colony of Georgia gave it the name of the Princess of Wales, Augusta, the mother of King George III. FORT AUGUSTA (q.v.), which was sometimes called KING'S FORT, was built here in 1736 by order of the Colonial Trustees, and its site is presently identified by a Celtic cross located between St. Paul's Church and the river. Augusta was the state capital from 1786 to 1796. AUGUSTA CANAL was built here in 1845-46 by Colonel Henry H. Cumming to produce water power for a cotton mill. AUGUSTA COLLEGE was established here as JUNIOR COLLEGE OF AUGUSTA in 1925, utilizing the RICHMOND ACADEMY (q.v.) building on Bay Street. Its present name was adopted in 1958 when it became part of the University System of Georgia. OLIVER GENERAL HOSPITAL of Augusta was named for Colonel Robert T. Oliver (1868-1937), dental surgeon of the AEF in 1918, and later head of the American Dental Association. MEDICAL COLLEGE OF GEORGIA was founded in Augusta in 1828, and is part of the University System of Georgia.

AUGUSTINE CREEK, Chatham County. Flows into the Savannah River at Port Wentworth. Erroneously labeled on maps as ST. AUGUSTINE CREEK. It was named for Walter Augustine, who had a sawmill on this stream.

AURARIA, Lumpkin County. An old gold-mining town south of Dahlonega, which was the first gold-mining town in American history. It was the provisional county seat when the county was first organized in 1832. The following year Dahlonega was designated the county seat. The village was first called DEAN(S) after William Dean who had built a cabin here in 1832, and then NUCK-OLLSVILLE for Nathaniel Nuckolls who set up a small tavern here. It was called "Scuffle-Town" by some. John C. Calhoun (1782-1850), South Carolina statesman and vice president of the United States (1825-1832), owned a mine near here and wished to establish a new name for the community. Doctor Croft, a friend from South Carolina, suggested to him the name *Aureola,* meaning "gold" or "Shining like gold." The settlers however, preferred to call their place Auraria, the meaning of which is approximately the same, "gold mine" or "gold region." The name was actually selected by Major John Powell, a prominent citizen here and professional gold miner.

AUSMAC, Decatur County. This is a station on the Seaboard Airline Railroad, six miles northwest of Bainbridge. It is a coined name created from the surnames of two men called Ausley and McCaskill, who were in the turpentine trade here.

AUSTELL, Cobb County. Incorporated September 4, 1885. Was established near Sweetwater Creek at the site of a former Indian town. It was first named CAUSEY'S CHAPEL for an early settler family, and afterwards called IRVINE, after A. H. Irvine who was postmaster and owned a general store here. In 1882 the village was called CIN-CINNATI JUNCTION. The present name is for General Alfred Austell (1814-1881), a leading financier in the early development of Georgia, and founder of the Atlanta National Bank. He was at one time owner of AUSTELL'S FERRY, originally known as Gorman's Ferry (q.v.), which crossed the Chattahoochee between south Fulton and Douglas counties from about 1870 to 1937. *See also* Factory Shoals.

AVALON, Stephens County. Incorporated August 9, 1909. The name for this town is a Celtic word meaning "Island of Apples," and refers to an earthly paradise which was the legendary home of King Arthur.

AVIRETT, Decatur County. This former village was located about eight miles southwest of Bainbridge. Abner Avirett was the postmaster here in 1882.

AVONDALE, Bibb County. Located south of Macon. AVONDALE, McDuffie County. This was a former post office located near Dearing. AVONDALE ESTATES, DeKalb County. Incorporated January 1, 1927. This Atlanta suburb was created on land purchased by G. F. Willis in 1924. This is a coined name derived from the Upper Avon River in England which flows past Stratford, William Shakespear's birthplace. The post office of INGLESIDE (q.v.) was here originally. AVON (or AVON HALL) was the name of the William Neyle Habersham summer home on the Vernon River near Savannah, which was destroyed by fire in early 1971.

AXSON, Atkinson County. This community was first called MACDONALD'S MILL, for James MacDonald who built a sawmill here. Georgia State representative Charlie Stewart had political differences with the mill owner,

and therefore had the name changed. The present name was then chosen by President Woodrow Wilson (1856-1924), who named the place in honor of his wife, Ellen Louise Axson (1860-1914). *See also* Woodrow Wilson College of Law.

A-YEH-LI A-LO-HEE, Hart County. This site, originally a Cherokee Indian assembly ground, is located three miles southwest of Hartwell, where the Indians' paths to trading posts crossed. This Cherokee Indian name is purported to mean "Center of the World." On October 25, 1923, a granite marker was unveiled here in commemoration of the Cherokees. Vigorous efforts were made by some to establish the Hart County seat here.

AYERS(VILLE), Stephens County. Located five miles west of Toccoa. This community was settled about 1810 by Nathaniel and Jeremiah Ayers.

AZALIA, Screven County. This community was located six miles below Sylvania. Was probably named for the large flowering shrub of the genus *rhododendron*.

AZILIA. A proposed name for an English colony where Georgia was later founded, generally referred to by the full name, MARGRAVATE OF AZILIA (q.v.).

B

BACK RIVER, Savannah. Descriptive name for the channel of the Savannah River, flowing in back of Hutchinson's Island, on the South Carolina side. Early records show that this designation was used about the time of General James Edward Oglethorpe's arrival. *See also* Front River.

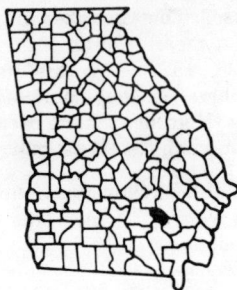

BACON COUNTY. Created July 27, 1914 with 293 square miles taken from Appling, Pierce, and Ware counties. The county seat is Alma (q.v.). The county was named for Augustus Octavius Bacon (1839-1914), who was born in Bryan County, but made Macon his home. He was speaker in the Georgia House of Representatives, later became U. S. Senator from Georgia, and served as president pro tempore of the Senate after the death of Vice-President James S. Sherman. He bequeathed a 117-acre tract to the city of Macon named BACONSFIELD PARK in honor of his two sons. The park was returned to the heirs in January 1970 as the result of a U. S. Supreme Court decision concerned with the stipulation in the will of Senator Bacon that the park was for white people only.

BACONTON, Mitchell County. Incorporated August 6, 1903. This town was founded by and named for Major Robert J. Bacon (1830-1907), lawyer and planter who came here from LaGrange, Troup County in 1858, and purchased land to take up farming. He was a graduate of the University of Georgia, Athens at its 50th anniversary commencement in 1851. His home was known as "Liberty Hall."

BAD CREEK, Rabun County. The name is quite descriptive of this stream flowing in a rugged area in the lower part of the county. Nearby is Worse Creek which runs parallel to it, and both flow into the Chattooga River.

BAGGS CREEK, Lumpkin County. An extreme upper tributary of the Chestatee River, in the northeast section of the county. Supposedly named for a Cherokee Indian family called Bagg who lived along the stream until 1819.

BAHIA DE GUALQUINI, Glynn County. The Spanish name of SAINT SIMONS SOUND (q.v.), which translates, "Bay of Gualquini" (*see* Gualquini).

BAILEY'S MILL, Camden County. An early settlement which was located on the Satilla River two miles southeast of Burntfort. John S. Bailey owned a general store and a sawmill here.

BAINBRIDGE, CS Decatur County. Incorporated as a town December 22, 1829. In 1765, John Burgess operated an Indian trading post in this vicinity. Brinkley said it was originally called FORT HUGHES (q.v.). The present city was founded December 19, 1823, and was named for William Bainbridge (1774-1833), who once commanded the celebrated frigate *U. S. Constitution*, nicknamed "Old Ironsides" (*see also* Gascoigne's Bluff).

BAIRDSTOWN, Oglethorpe County. A community located on the Greene County line which was settled in 1825. It was originally called HURRICANE BRANCH, and later changed to honor a Mr. Baird who lived here.

BAKER COUNTY. Created December 12, 1825 with 355 square miles taken from Early County. Named for Colonel John Baker (? - 1792), affluent farmer, soldier of the American Revolution, and Indian fighter. He represented Liberty County in the Georgia House of Representatives. The county seat is

Newton (q.v.). The court house was destroyed by floods in 1925 and 1929.

BAKER'S FERRY, Elbert County. This ferry crossed the Broad River southwest of Elberton, and was named for L. H. Baker, its owner and operator.

BALD MOUNTAIN, Murray County. Elevation is 4,010 feet, and located 12 miles northeast of Chatsworth. The name "Bald" is used to designate a peak without trees at its summit.

BALD MOUNTAIN PARK, Towns County. Located two miles south of Hiawassee near LITTLE BALD MOUNTAIN (4,450 feet elevation), and almost one mile north of BRASSTOWN BALD (q.v.). The site of the park was previously called FODDER CREEK (q.v.).

BALDWIN, Habersham County. Incorporated December 17, 1896, the town now extends into Banks County. Named for Joseph A. Baldwin, an official of the Atlanta-Charlotte Airline Railroad.

BALDWIN COUNTY. An original county, created May 11, 1803 and June 26, 1806 following Creek cessions of June 16, 1802 and November 14, 1805. It now comprises an area of 257 square miles, and was named in honor of Abraham Baldwin (1754-1807) a native of Connecticut who moved to Savannah in 1784 and there began to practice law. He was a signer from Georgia of the Federal Constitution in 1787, and was a state legislator, and one of the founders of the University at Athens. The county seat is Milledgeville (q.v.). The court house was destroyed by fire in 1861.

BALDWIN STATE PARK, Baldwin Coun-

ty. A 700-acre park located west of Milledgeville, opened in 1975.

BALL GROUND, Cherokee County. This name is a survival of Indian days, when the site of the present town was used by the Cherokee Indians for their national pastime, the ball-play. The name BALL GROUND was also applied to a crossroads in south Murray County, which is included in Georgia Militia District No. 1807, known as the BALL GROUND DISTRICT.

BALL PLAY CREEK, Lumpkin County. This stream enters the Chestatee River three miles east of Dahlonega, and is named after the Cherokee Indians' once popular game, the ball-play. A recent state map of Lumpkin County erroneously shows this stream labeled PECKS MILL CREEK, after a mill located thereupon.

BANKHEAD HIGHWAY. U. S. Highway 78 between Atlanta, Georgia, and Birmingham, Alabama. Believed named for William Brockman Bankhead (1874-1940) of Alabama, who served in the U. S. Congress (1917-1940).

BANKS BRIDGE, O.H., Jasper County. Spans Murder Creek on Georgia 83. Named March 4, 1964 for Mr. Banks, bank president and mayor of Shady Dale.

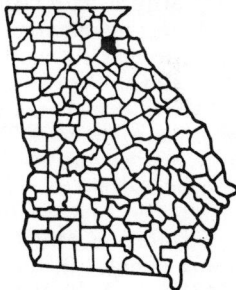

BANKS COUNTY. Created December 11, 1858 with 231 square miles taken from Franklin and Habersham counties. It was named for a noted surgeon, Dr. Richard E. Banks (1784-1850), who took up practice in Ruckersville, Elbert County, then moved to Gainesville, Hall County in 1832. The county seat is Homer (q.v.).

BANKSVILLE, Jackson County. This rural community was located about nine miles southeast of Homer when the site was in Banks County. Named for Dr. Richard Banks (*see* Banks County).

BANNING, Carroll County. An early post office. *See* BOWENVILLE.

BARBER, Colquitt County. A former community located five miles northeast of Moultrie. Named for Moultrie banker and industrialist, William H. Barber.

BARBER'S CREEK, Barrow and Oconee counties. Rises just east of Russell and flows southeasterly to McNutt Creek just before that stream enters the Middle Oconee River above Watkinsville. Named for the early settler family of Robert Barber.

BARBOUR ISLAND, McIntosh County. Lies across the Wahoo River from South Newport. It is thought to have been named for John Barber, who first settled here in 1740 with General Oglethorpe's permission. Records of 1757 list the place as BARBER'S ISLAND. BARBOUR ISLAND RIVER drains into Sapelo Sound and forms the west boundary of Barbour Island.

BAREFOOT (or BEARFOOT), Towns County. A little spot located where the old Hiawassee Trail crossed the present U. S. 16 in the eastern section of the county. The name either signifies "bear track" or a place where residents had to go without shoes.

BARKCAMP (Militia) DISTRICT, Burke County. This district contains one of the early communities of Georgia. Its main settlement at BARKCAMP CROSSROADS is located six miles above Midville, and was one of the earliest post offices in the state. The original community of BARKCAMP is believed to have been three miles southeast of the present crossroads, on the east side of BARKCAMP CREEK (a tributary of Mill Creek). This earlier site was recorded in the 1760's and 1770's as CASE'S OLD PLACE (q.v.). The name is derived from a "barkcamp" which was a crude shelter, similar to a lean-to, with a roof and siding of bark. These were frequently erected by early cattlemen and hunters. Another BARKCAMP (Militia) DISTRICT is located in northwest Hall County. It took its name from a former site known as BARKCAMP, located to the northwest of today's community of Price, where it is said that early travellers going to and from the mountains stopped to camp.

BARNESVILLE, CS Lamar County. Set-

tled in 1826 and incorporated February 20, 1854. This town was named for an early settler, Gideon Barnes, who ran a tavern here and operated a stage line between Macon and Columbus. Located here is Gordon Junior College (q.v.).

BARNEY, Brooks County. Incorporated as a town August 6, 1903. Community was settled in the 1830's by William Folsom. The South Georgia Railroad was built through here in 1897 when the present name was adopted, which is for one of the owners of the Barney-Smith Car Company of Ohio (railroad equipment suppliers). The post office was transferred here from Foster (q.v.) in 1897.

BARNSLEY GARDENS, Bartow County. Located midway between Cartersville and Rome, six miles from Kingston. It was built just prior to the Civil War on 10,000 acres purchased by Sir Godfrey Barnsley (1805?-1873), scion of British nobility, who was the wealthiest man of Savannah. These once beautiful gardens have recently fallen into neglect.

BARRETTSVILLE, Dawson County. This community was located seven miles south of Dawsonville on the Etowah River. It is believed to have been named for the first postmaster, J. M. Barrett.

BARRIMACKE, Camden County. Located at the northeast tip of Cumberland Island. This early community of about twenty-four families was settled in 1740, but they deserted the place shortly afterward. The derivation of the name is unknown.

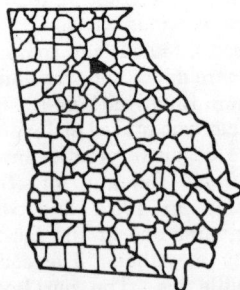

BARROW COUNTY. Created July 7, 1914, comprising 171 square miles taken from

Gwinnett, Jackson, and Walton counties. It was named for the chancellor of the University of Georgia, David Crenshaw "Uncle Dave" Barrow (1852-1929). The county seat is Winder (q.v.).

BARTLETT'S FERRY DAM, Harris County. This dam was built 1923-26 at the site of the former BARTLETT'S FERRY, which crossed the Chattahoochee River here. The name is a misspelling of Dr. Simpson W. Bartley's name. This early ferry operator was a minister who owned lands here. The dam created Lake Harding (q.v.).

BARTOW, Jefferson County. Incorporated September 20, 1887. This town was originally called SPIER'S TURNOUT (q.v.), but the name was later changed to honor General Francis S. Bartow (*see* Bartow County).

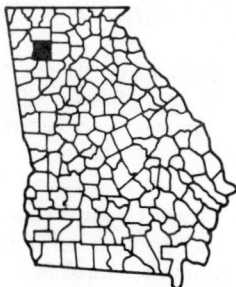

BARTOW COUNTY. Created December 3, 1832 with 463 square miles taken from Cherokee County. It was originally named CASS COUNTY (q.v.), but was changed December 6, 1861 after General Lewis Cass alienated his southern friends with his views on slavery. The present name was selected to honor Brigadier General Francis Stebbins Bartow (1816-1861), who was a state senator from Chatham County. He died in the first battle of Manassas Plains to become the first Confederate general to be killed in the Civil War. He was elected a member of the First Confederate Congress from the Savannah District, and was responsible for the selection of the Confederate gray uniforms. Cartersville (q.v.) is the county seat.

BARWICK, Brooks and Thomas counties. Incorporated August 17, 1903. This border town originated as a Georgia Northern Railroad stop in 1891-92, and was built on lands that were owned by T. M. and John Massey. The post office opened in 1894 with

John Massey the first postmaster. The name is of unknown origin.

BASTONVILLE, Glascock County. This was the fourth post office in the county, and the first postmaster was Nathan T. Baston. Located ten miles southeast of Warrenton, it served this area from January 31, 1890 to April 30, 1902.

BATH, Richmond County. Located six miles west of Hephzibah, this locale was originally called RICHMOND BATHS after the therapeutic springs here.

BATTEY GENERAL HOSPITAL, Floyd County. *See* Rome.

BATTLE CREEK, Lumpkin County. This stream was given its name after a bloody fight in gold rush days when some Georgians ran off some Tennessee "gold diggers."

BATTLE HILL, Fulton County. Incorporated as a town December 16, 1895, and was so named because its entire town limits were the site of the July 28, 1864 Battle of Ezra Church. This community, in the Vicinity of the present Mozley Park, was absorbed in the 1910 expansion of Greater Atlanta.

BAXLEY, CS Appling County. Incorporated February 23, 1875, the town was named for William Baxley, an early settler who came from North Carolina. The county seat was moved here from Holmesville (q.v.) in 1874. Georgia's first nuclear power plant is on a 2,200-acre site north of here on the Altamaha River. Completed in 1974, the $330 million EDWIN I. HATCH PLANT produces 800,000 kw of power daily.

BAY CREEK (Militia) DISTRICT, Gwinnett County. Located just above Loganville. There was formerly a community of BAY CREEK, seven miles southeast of Lawrenceville on the stream from which it took its name.

BEACON CREEK, McIntosh County. Located on Wolf Island at the mouth of the Altamaha River, and named after a marker located near its mouth. This stream has been mislabeled BEAVER CREEK on some maps.

BEALL SPRINGS, Warren County. Located seven miles southwest of Warrenton on S1097. Ceded to the state in 1773 after which the Beall family acquired the property.

BEAR CREEK, Terrell County. *See* LOCHOCHEE CREEK.

BEAR CREEK STATION, Henry County. Established in 1848 as a stop on the Macon and Western Railroad. Named after the stream which rises near Hampton and flows through a corner of Spalding County where it enters the Flint River. The town of BEAR CREEK was incorporated here August 23, 1872, and the name was changed to HAMPTON (q.v.) in 1873.

BEARDS BLUFF, Long County. Located along the northeast bank of the Altamaha River just below the entrance of BEARDS CREEK, from which its name is derived. Beards Creek forms the boundary between Long and Tattnall counties. Derivation is uncertain, but is apparently for one of three pioneers here, Edmund, George, or Matthew Beard. *See also* Fort Telfair.

BEARFOOT, Towns County. *See* BAREFOOT.

BEAULIEU, Chatham County. Pronounced "Bewley." Located at the mouth of the Vernon River, south of Savannah, this community was settled in 1739 by William Stephens (1671-1753), the first "president" of Georgia (1743-50). It was reportedly named after a manor of the Duke of Montgomery. However, Charles C. Jones records it as BEWLIE, taken from the name of a manor of the Duke of Montague.

BEAVER. In Georgia there are many places with "beaver" in the name to denote where beavers had been active in earlier days. BEAVER CREEK in Jackson County was called JARATHOGGIN by the Indians. Other streams named BEAVER CREEK are in Bibb, Candler, Macon, Putnam, and Stewart Counties (*see also* HOG CRAWL CREEK). Streams called BEAVERDAM CREEK are found in Burke, Lamar, Screven, and Upson counties (*see also* PHILEMA CREEK). BEAVERDAM BRANCH is a stream name found in Richmond, Washington, and Wilkinson counties. The name BEAVER RUN has been noted in Douglas and Schley counties by John Goff, as well as BEAVER POND in Muscogee (1797) and Wilkes counties. A BEAVER RUIN CREEK is located in Clarke County. Goff says this name refers to an extensive area which a colony of beavers had flooded and devastated with a network of dams. Another

BEAVER RUIN CREEK is in Gwinnett County. Brinkley says this stream was named for a Cherokee, Beaver Toter, whose house and ferry were washed away during a flash flood. A BEAVER MOUNTAIN is found in Murray County, and a community of BEAVERDALE is located in northeast Whitfield County. *See also* INTACHCOOCHEE, INTACKCULGUA, and TURKEY CREEK.

BEAVER SLIDE, Atlanta. This was the name used in referring to a row of shacks on the east side of Ivy Street in the block just north of Decatur Street, in the early days. It was once a respectable community, but after the Civil War it fell from its former state. The Negroes gave the section this name after it became a dive and hangout for criminals.

BEECH CREEK, Jackson County. Named for the beech trees of the vicinity. The early name for this stream was TAURALABOOLE or TAURULABOOLE, meaning "Screaming Panther Creek."

BEL AIR, Richmond County. This rural community is located two miles west of Augusta city limits on U. S. Highway 78-278. The name is a French phrase meaning "good air."

BELFAST, Bryan County. This rural community, located about seven miles south of Richmond Hill, was named from the city in Northern Ireland. The BELFAST RIVER is located in lower Bryan County.

BELLE VISTA, Glynn County. The name of this community is from the French, and means "beautiful view."

BELL, ERNEST A., BRIDGE, Charlton County. Crosses St. Marys River east of St. George. Named to honor Charlton County Commissioner Bell.

BELL HIGHWAY. *See* Vereen Bell Highway.

BELL(E)VILLE, Evans County. A community located seven miles west of Claxton. Incorporated March 10, 1959. Established in 1890 with the coming of the railroad, and was named for James Bell Smith's mother, who was Miss Fannie Bell before her marriage. The railroaders claimed Belleville was named in honor of the lovely ladies of the town. The town of BELLVILLE in Richmond County was incorporated December 6, 1861.

BELOIT, Lee County. A rural community in

the southeast section of the county, it was incorporated August 4, 1903. The name is believed transferred from the city in Wisconsin.

BEMBRY'S (OLD) MILL, Pulaski County. Was located about four miles southeast of Hawkinsville. It stood on the property for which the first deed in the county was recorded, November 7, 1807. Named for early owner, Miles Bembry, who was sheriff of the county, and one of its largest landowners.

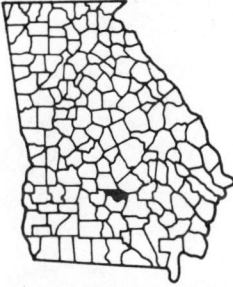

BEN HILL COUNTY. Created July 31, 1906 with 255 square miles taken from Irwin and Wilcox counties. It was named for U. S. Senator Benjamin Harvey Hill (1823-1882), Whig leader who strongly opposed the Reconstruction measures. Born in Hillsboro, Jasper County, he was a state representative and senator from Troup County. The county seat is Fitzgerald (q.v.).

BEN HILL, Fulton County.. This was a hamlet located nine miles southwest of Atlanta. Its name prior to 1880 was MOUNT GILEAD CROSS ROADS. It then took the name of Senator Benjamin Hill (*see* Ben Hill County).

BENJAMIN HAWKINS, CAMP, Peach County. Boy Scout camp located north of Byron, named for Colonel Benjamin Hawkin (1754-1816), the famous Indian agent. *See also* Hawkinsville.

BEREA, Jackson County. This former post office was established five miles southeast of Commerce in 1897. The name is derived from the ancient city of Berea in Macedonia, which is today called Veroia.

BERKLEY, Madison County. Name of the railroad station of CARLTON (q.v.). *See also* TRIP.

BERLIN, Colquitt County. This town was named for the capital city of Germany. The name was changed to LENS (q.v.) during World War I, and afterwards reverted to Berlin.

BERNER, Monroe County. When the Macon and Brunswick Railroad brought tracks through here about 1822, the station was called FRANKVILLE, until the turn of the century. The community was named for Colonel Bob Berner of Forsyth.

BERRIEN, Dooly County. Located at the site of the present VIENNA (q.v.), it is believed to have been originally called BROWNVILLE. The name was changed to Berrien November 25, 1824 when the town became Dooly's first county seat. Afterwards the seat was moved to Drayton and then returned to Berrien in 1839. The name was changed to CENTERVILLE in 1840, and to the present name of Vienna, February 8, 1841.

BERRIEN COUNTY. Created February 25, 1856 with 466 square miles taken from Coffee, Irwin, and Lowndes counties. Named for U. S. Senator and Attorney General, Judge John MacPherson Berrien (1781-1856) of Savannah, but originally from Princeton N. J. The county seat is Nashville (q.v.).

BERRY COLLEGE, Mount Berry. Located in Floyd County on the northwest outskirts of Rome (q.v.). This institution, with BERRY ACADEMY, occupies the nation's largest campus, on 30,000 acres. It was opened in 1902 and named for its founder, Martha Berry (1866-1942). The chapel-like HENRY FORD DINING HALL was named in honor of its donor (*see also* Ford Island).

BERRYTON, Chattooga County. This village is located on Raccoon Creek, and was probably named for John Berry of Rome who developed a textile mill here.

BETHANY, Jefferson County. This old community was an active ante-bellum trade center. It was named when orphans from Bethesda (q.v.) Orphanage in Savannah were refugees here during the Civil War. The town is now called WADLEY (q.v.). An earlier BETHANY was settled in 1751 by John Gerar William DeBrahm and the German Salzburgers in what is now Effingham County. It was north of their other settlement of Ebenezer (q.v.).

BETHESDA, Chatham County. An orphanage located about ten miles southwest of Savannah. The name means "house of mercy." The Reverend George Whitefield gave it this name when he established one of the first orphanages in the United States here in March, 1740. *See also* Bethany and Whitfield County. BETHESDA is also the name of a community located four miles east of Union Point in Greene County.

BETHLEHEM, Barrow County. Called "The Christmas Town of Georgia." Incorporated in 1902, the name is derived from that of the Bethlehem Methodist Church and campground here, which were incorporated December 20, 1860. Some of the street names here are MARY, JOSEPH, JUDEA, AND STAR. Found also here are ANGEL, CHRISTMAS, AND MANGER avenues. A live Nativity scene is staged annually in Bethlehem during the yule season.

BETTY(S) CREEK, Rabun County. Arises in the North Carolina mountains and flows into Georgia, across Rabun County, to join the Little Tennessee River at Dillard. It was previously called LITTLE BETTY'S CREEK, after a Cherokee Indian widow known as Little Betty who lived at Eastertoy (q.v.). An earlier name of this stream was VALLEY CREEK.

BETWEEN, Walton County. Settled in the 1850's and incorporated August 17, 1908. Mr. George Schaeffer, who was the husband of the postmaster of Monroe, chose this name for the community because of its location equidistant between Monroe and Loganville.

BEVERLY, Elbert County. Incorporated as a town from August 22, 1907 to 1919. This community is located on Beaverdam Creek, about two miles east of Middleton. It was named for wealthy Virginian, Mr. Beverly Allen, who kept a tavern here. Allen was charged, found guilty, and imprisoned for the June 1794 killing of U.S. Marshall, Robert

Forsyth, father of John Forsyth (1780-1841), who later became governor of Georgia. Later released, he moved to Kentucky where he lived to be 90. This community has also been known as PEARL (q.v.).

BEWLIE, Chatham County. *See* BEAULIEU.

BIBB CITY, Muscogee County. A long established community located on the northeast edge of Columbus. Named for Dr. Bibb (*see* Bibb County).

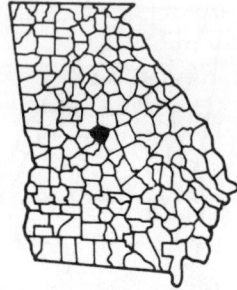

BIBB COUNTY. Created December 9, 1822 with 254 square miles taken from Houston, Jones, Monroe, and Twiggs counties. It was named in honor of William Wyatt Bibb, M. D. (1780-1820), a native Virginian who studied medicine in Pennsylvania. He moved to Elbert County, Georgia and served in the U. S. House of Representatives and later in the U.S. Senate. Bibb was appointed governor of the Territory of Alabama in 1816 and was subsequently elected the first governor of that state. There was at one time a sentiment in the Georgia General Assembly to change the name of Bibb County to Mercer County. The county seat is Macon (q.v.).

BIEWLY, Chatham County. An alternate spelling of BEAULIEU (q.v.).

BIG ATTAPULGUS CREEK, Decatur County. This stream heads near Climax and flows southerly into Florida. For derivation, *see* Attapulgus.

BIG BALD MOUNTAIN, Gilmer County. A 4,081-foot peak located in the northeast section of the county. The descriptive name indicates that there are no trees at its summit.

BIG BEND, Charlton County. This name refers to the region of the lower section of the county, bordered on three sides by Florida, and formed by the "big bend" of the St. Marys River.

BIG COTTON INDIAN CREEK, Henry County. *See* COTTON RIVER.

BIG CREEK, Forsyth County. A community located six miles south of Cumming on Georgia highway 141. Named from the nearby stream called BIG CREEK.

BIG CREEK. Streams with this descriptive name are found in Early, Forsyth, Jefferson, Lanier, Laurens, and Thomas counties. It is generally translated from the Muskogean Indian name HATCHEETHLUCCO. *See also* UPATOI CREEK.

BIG HOUSE CREEK, Wilcox County. *See* HOUSE CREEK.

BIG INDIAN CREEK. Rises at Fort Valley, flows southerly to form the boundary of Peach and Macon counties, crosses southeasterly through Houston County to the Ocmulgee River. Has also been called BIG WARRIOR CREEK. Named for the Creek Indian chief, Tustinugee, who was noted for his physical size.

BIG OAK, Twiggs County. A former settlement in the northern part of the county, named for the trees of the area. The post office existed here from December 28, 1895 to January 14, 1904.

BIG SANDY, Twiggs County. Also called MYRICK'S MILL (q.v.), this rural community was located four miles northeast oi Fitzpatrick. It was so named because of its being near BIG SANDY CREEK, which rises in Twiggs County and flows through Wilkinson County to join the Oconee River in Laurens County. The post office was established here from June 2, 1879 to May 15, 1903.

BIG SAVANNAH, Dawson County. This section of the county is now referred to as SAVANNAH, and it comprises the SAVANNAH (Militia) DISTRICT. The post office of Big Savannah was established about 1874 at the site of the present DOUGHERTY (q.v.). A Cherokee Indian settlement called TENSAWATTEE (q.v.) had been here previously. This section boasts fine bottom lands along the Etowah River, and was named Big Savannah because of the open, moist, meadow-like area where grass or reed cane grew in abundance.

BIG SHANTY, Cobb County. The early settlement on the site of the present KENNESAW (q.v.). At one time the dwellings of railroad construction workers were on a hill here. The steep grade of the railroad at this point was called "that big grade to the shanties," and afterwards shortened to Big Shanty. It has also been said that the place was given this early name because of a particularly large and well-built shanty which once dominated the scene. There exists today the BIG SHANTY ELEMENTARY SCHOOL in Kennesaw, and BIG SHANTY (Militia) DISTRICT, in which Kennesaw is located. *See also* MORROW.

BILL ARP, Douglas County. This community was named for Southern humorist, Charles Henry Smith (1826-1903), who was for a short time editor of the *Rome Commercial,* and who wrote under the name "Bill Arp." *See also* Arp.

BILLY'S ISLAND and BILLY'S LAKE, Charlton County. This 60-acre lake is the largest in the Okefenokee Swamp, in which the island is also located. They were named for the famed Seminole Indian chief, Billy Bowlegs, who lived in the swamp as late as 1840. His Indian name was *Olac-to-mico,* and he is said to have been born in Wiregrass, Georgia about 1804. A town of 600 population grew up on the island after 1909 near Hebard Lumber Company plant.

BIMINI. This was the early name of what is the present day coastal Georgia, before it was called GUALE (q.v.). This is probably of Spanish origin.

BIRDSONG BRIDGE, FRANK G., Troup County. Spans the Chattahoochee River on State Route 109 between LaGrange, Georgia, and Roanoke, Alabama. Mr. Birdsong was a member of the Board of Commissioners of Roads and Revenue of Troup County. The bridge was named March 17, 1958.

BIRDSVILLE, Jenkins County. This post office was established in 1813 in what was then Burke County. It was named for the first postmaster, Captain Samuel Bird of the County militia, and was located on the Jones plantation, which had been established in 1764 by Francis Jones. The post office was later closed, and afterwards reopened as HERNDON (q.v.) in 1854. BIRDSVILLE AIRPORT is located nine miles northwest of Millen.

BIRDWOOD JUNIOR COLLEGE, Thomasville, Thomas County. Opened in 1954 by the Primitive Baptist Church on the former Birdwood Plantation.

BIRMINGHAM, Bartow County. Named after the city in England. This was the former name of CARTERSVILLE (q.v.).

BISHOP, Oconee County. Incorporated December 26, 1890 with W. H. Bishop, one of the original councilmen.

BLACKANKLE. As applied to a section or locale, this name is found in Chatham, Upson, and Fannin counties and denotes an area of deep, fertile, black soil. BLACK ANKLE CREEK is located in lower Fannin County, and flows into Toccoa River.

BLACKBEARD ISLAND, McIntosh County. Lies northeast of Sapelo Island. It was so named because of its early use by pirates, including Edward Teach (? - 1718), known as "Blackbeard," who established his headquarters here in 1716. It is now federally controlled, and is called BLACKBEARD ISLAND NATIONAL WILDLIFE REFUGE.

BLACKBURN STATE PARK, Auraria. This 193-acre park is located seven miles southwest of Dahlonega, in the richest section of the gold belt. Named in honor of its donor, Wayne W. Blackburn, who now resides in Clearwater, Florida.

BLACK CREEK. This stream in Bulloch and Bryan counties was translated from the Creek Indian word *Weelustee,* meaning "black water." The two major branches of the stream are now called UPPER BLACK CREEK and LOWER BLACK CREEK. In post-Revolutionary years these branches were called FIRST BLACK CREEK and SECOND BLACK CREEK respectively. BLACK CREEK in Ware County was a translation from the original WILASTIHACHI, or "Water Black Stream." A community of BLACK CREEK was once located twelve miles southeast of Sylvania on the stream of that name in Screven County.

BLACK HALL, Fulton County. *See* White Hall.

BLACK JACK ISLAND, Ware County. This island is five miles long, and is located in the south central section of Okefenokee Swamp. It got its name on account of the abundance of "black-jack" oak growing on the island.

BLACKJACK MOUNTAIN, Carroll County. With an elevation of 1,550 feet, it is located about eight miles south of Bowdon. It is so named because of all the blackjack oak growing on this mountain.

BLACKSHEAR, CS Pierce County. Named in honor of General David Blackshear (1764-1837), who commanded the troops who constructed BLACKSHEAR ROAD (or BLACKSHEAR TRAIL) in 1814 between Hartford and the Flint River. Fort Early (q.v.) was then built at this latter terminal of the road, and many years later a dam was constructed here on the Flint River to create the 8,000-acre LAKE BLACKSHEAR of Lee and Sumter counties. BLACKSHEAR'S FERRY in Laurens County was located four and one-half miles north of Dublin on the Oconee River. It was previously called TRAMBLE AND BATEY FERRY for the prior owners. The name was changed after General David Blackshear took over the ferry while he was assigned to drive out the Indians and to survey the lands. General Blackshear later built his home, "Springfield Plantation," one-half mile eastward from the site of the ferry. BLACKSHEAR'S MILL was the name of the post office near here from July 5, 1878 to December 17, 1879.

BLAINE, Gilmer County. This dead town was named for James Gillespie Blaine (1830-1893), who was a U. S. Senator from Maine, Secretary of State, and presidential nominee in 1884. This town was originally called TALKING ROCK (q.v.) and was named Blaine after the name Talking Rock was transferred to the community of Loves (q.v.). *See also* CORNELIA.

BLAIR LINE. Surveyed in the early 1800's by James Blair as the boundary between Georgia and the Cherokee Nation. It is described by a marker in Habersham County at the junction of Georgia highways 115 and 105.

BLAIRSVILLE, CS Union County. Incorporated December 26, 1835. Named for Francis Preston Blair, Sr. (1791-1876) from Kentucky, editor of the newspaper, *Washington Globe,* which was established to promote Andrew Jackson's re-election. His Washington D. C. home, Blair House, is now government property. The county seat was established in Blairsville in 1835.

BLAKELY, CS Early County. Incorporated October 24, 1870. This town is called the "Peanut Capital of the World." It was named in honor of Captain Johnston Blakely, who was lost at sea aboard the sloop *U. S. S. Wasp* in the War of 1812.

BLANTON, Lowndes County. A rural community in the southeast corner of the county. Established in 1896, and named for local landowner, J.N. Blanton.

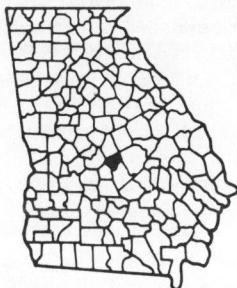

BLECKELY COUNTY. Created July 30, 1912 with 219 square miles taken from Pulaski County. It was named in honor of Logan Edward Bleckley (1827-1907), a philosopher and poet, who became Chief Justice of the Supreme Court of Georgia. The county seat is Cochran (q.v.). Also named in his honor is the LOGAN E. BLECKLEY HIGHWAY, that portion of U.S. Highway 23-441 (formerly Georgia Highway 15) which extends from the North Carolina State line in Rabun County to the Habersham County line.

BLECKLEY MOUNTAIN, Rabun County. *See* OLD SCREAMER MOUNTAIN.

BLITCH, Bullock County. This early community was believed named for its postmaster, W. H. Blitch, who owned a general store here. It is at a "five points" intersection, nine miles north of Statesboro.

BLOOD MOUNTAIN, Union County. A legend relates that before the white men came, a savage Indian war was fought at Slaughter Gap (q.v.) near here between the Cherokee and Creek nations. It is said that blood ran down the mountain sides and colored the waters, which is the reason for the name. The top of the 4,458-foot mountain is within Vogel State Park (q.v.).

BLOODY BRANCH, Charlton County. Arises northwest of Burntfort, and was named to commemorate an Indian massacre of 1794. At that time, a settler named James Keene and one of his four children were killed when a group of twenty Indians attacked him and his family by this stream.

BLOODY MARSH, St. Simons Island. Located between the lighthouse at St. Simons and the old citadel of Frederica (q.v.). So named for the historic and fierce battle fought here July 7, 1742 against the Spanish invaders.

BLOUNT, Monroe County. A community ten miles north of Forsyth. Named in honor of Congressman James H. Blount (*see* Blountsville), who served in the U. S. House of Representatives from 1872 to 1892.

BLOUNT(S)VILLE, Jones County. Located about eight miles north of Gray on Georgia Highway 129. Named for the James Blount family of Plymouth, North Carolina and Jones County, Georgia. Before the Civil War this was a busy community, with a wagon factory, state coach station and post office. The town was founded before 1817 and disappeared following the severe destruction it suffered during the war. *See also* Blount, Monroe County.

BLUE BLUFF, Burke County. Located two miles below Hancock Landing. Named for the native clay here, a bluish-grey glauconitic marl.

BLUE JOHN CREEK, Troup County. Rises in LaGrange and flows south to join Long Cane Creek which then enters the Chattahoochee River near West Point. Some think that the name refers to its color, like "blue john," a frontier expression that means skim milk.

BLUE RIDGE, CS Fannin County. Incorporated October 24, 1887, and named for the Blue Ridge Mountains, as was nearby BLUE RIDGE LAKE. The BLUE RIDGE MOUNTAINS are the easternmost of the Appalachians, and extend from north Georgia to western Virginia. They were first given this name by the early settlers who observed that from a distance they were "like ranges of blue clouds." The county seat was transferred here from Morganton (q.v.), August 13, 1895.

BLUE SHIN (Militia) DISTRICT, Dougherty County. So named because the configuration of the district on the map resembles a swollen foreleg. There is also a region in northwest Heard County which has long been called BLUE SHIN.

BLUE SPRINGS, Brooks County. This resort community was active in the 1870's, and was named from a spring east of Quitman on the Withlacoochee River. A community known as BOSTON (q.v.) existed here previously. Another BLUE SPRINGS is found in Harris County, located six miles west of Hamilton at the base of Pine Mountain. It has a capacity of one million gallons a day, and was named for the color of the clear blue spring water. BLUE SPRINGS was the original name of RADIUM SPRINGS (q.v.) located in Dougherty County, and was also the early name of SWORDS (q.v.) in Morgan County.

BLUFF SPRINGS, Pike County. Incorporated in 1853, this former community was located two miles southeast of Zebulon, and took its name from the Bluff Springs Camp Ground here.

BLUFF TRAIL. This old road had previously been known as UPPER UCHEE PATH (q.v.). In 1807, surveyor William Dowsing Sr. gave it the name of Bluff Trail, after the bluff opposite the mouth of Crooked Creek where this stream enters the Ocmulgee River in Twiggs County.

BOARDTOWN CREEK, Gilmer County. This stream in the northeast section of the county flows southward to join the Ellijay River. It was named for BOARDTOWN, a former Indian community in this region.

BOBBY BROWN STATE PARK, Elbert County. This 664-acre park, situated between the Broad and Savannah rivers, is located eighteen miles southeast of Elberton at the site of old Dartmouth (q.v.). Was named in honor of Lieutenant Robert T. Brown, U. S. Navy, who died in World War II. Lieutenant Brown was the son of U. S. Congressman Paul Brown of Elberton.

BOBBY JONES EXPRESSWAY, Richmond County. Georgia Highway 232, west of Augusta, Named in honor of Robert Tyre (Bobby) Jones, Jr. of Atlanta, five times winner of the National Amateur golf championship.

BOGGY GUT CREEK, Burke County. Flows into the Savannah River near Shell Bluff Landing (q.v.). Was descriptively named, the word "Gut" meaning channel or stream.

BOLD SPRING(S), Walton County. This rural community was settled in the northwest section of the county about 1899, and was named for the big bubbling springs at the original site of the settlement, which was later moved several miles to another location. It was incorporated as a village August 17, 1908 under the name WILLIAMSVILLE, and then reverted to its original name August 9, 1909.

BOLINGBROKE, Monroe County. Incorporated as a town July 30, 1912. This old community is near the southeast border of the county on U. S. Highway 23-41. The post office was established here March 16, 1824, and first called STALLINGS STORE for John Stallings, the original postmaster. The name of the post office was changed to PRATTVILLE (q.v.) August 8, 1844, at which time it was said to have been located about one and one-half miles west of the present Bolingbroke. The post office name was next changed to COLAPARCHEE (q.v.) September 10, 1850. Finally, it was named Bolingbroke, August 28, 1866, for "Lord" Bolingbroke, Henry St. John, Viscount Bolingbroke (1678-1751), English statesman and author. When the Central of Georgia Railroad was built, this stop was called CRAWFORDS CROSSING (or STATION). The president of the railroad, William Wadley, purchased a 1,360-acre plantation here, where he moved to live in 1873, and named it Great Hill Place. The house was built in the 1820's and still stands on this property, which was sold by the Wadley estate in 1974. It was Mr. Wadley who selected the name Bolingbroke. *See also* Wadley.

BOLIVAR, Bartow County. Pronounced "Bol' i ver." This little station on the Louisville and Nashville Railroad was named in honor of General Simon Bolivar (1783-1830) who overthrew Spanish rule in South America.

BOLTON, Fulton County. Incorporated December 29, 1893, and named for Charles L. Bolton, who was a state railroad commissioner. It had also been called BOLTON-VILLE, FULTON, and ICEVILLE (for the ice plant of the Atlanta Brewery Company). The town was located on the Chattahoochee River near the present BOLTON BRIDGE and BOLTON ROAD in Atlanta, and is now a section of Atlanta.

BONAIRE, Houston County. Incorporated as a town August 7, 1912. This community is named from the French phrase, *bon aire,* meaning "good air."

BONAVENTURE, Savannah. This cemetery takes the name of the former plantation here, which was named by its owner, Colonel John Mulryne, who came here from Charleston about 1760. San Buenaventure was the name of an old Spanish mission on St. Simons Island.

BOND'S MILL, Twiggs County. This early post office was located fifteen miles southwest of Jeffersonville. Postmaster John T. Bond owned a steam-operated grist mill here in the 1880's.

BOND'S TRAIL. This name was sometimes applied to JACKSON'S TRAIL (q.v.), and was named for a thrifty Indian trader called Bond.

BONNY CLABBER BLUFF, Laurens County. Located on the west bank of the Oconee River in the lower section of the county. It is thought to be a "poverty name" for the bluff, and is probably an Anglicized Irish expression for sour buttermilk. *See also* Buttermilk.

BONY BLUFF, Echols County. Located nine miles southeast of Fargo. So named because the sand here contains large fragments of blackened bones, sharks' teeth, and other fossils.

BOOGER BOTTOM, Hall County. This site was of archeological interest because of an ancient mound located here. However it is now beneath the waters of Lake Lanier. "Booger" is an old American slang term for hobgoblin. The name was apparently descriptive of this low area where spirits were reputedly found.

BOOTH, Jackson County. This was a post office from 1890 to 1895, and was named for the postmaster, James M. Booth.

BOOTH'S FERRY, Jones County. Named for Zachariah Booth who ran a ferry which crossed the Ocmulgee River below today's Juliette. BOOTH'S FERRY ROAD, Jones County, is named for this former ferry.

BOSTON, Brooks County. This former village of the 1840's and 1850's was located on the Withlacoochee River east of Quitman. It was named in honor of Thomas M. Boston of Lowndes County. He discovered a mineral spring here, after which the community was later given the name BLUE SPRINGS (q.v.).

BOSTON, Thomas County. This town was chartered October 24, 1870, and was named for its first settler, Captain Thomas Boston, who came in 1831.

BOSTWICK, Morgan County. Incorporated as a town in 1902. Named after John Bostwick, the man who did the most to bring about development and growth of this town.

BOURBON COUNTY. This former county was created February 7, 1785, at which time the western boundary of the State of Georgia was at the Mississippi River (as directed by the Treaty of Paris in 1763). It was believed named for the famed ruling family of France. Thomas Green attempted to organize this county, but it embraced largely the western part of the region which Spain was claiming, and the Spanish authorities resisted his efforts to occupy the territory. It was located in what is now the State of Mississippi, and was bounded by the Mississippi River on the west, the Yazoo River on the north, the unrelinquished Indian lands on the east, and the 31 degree parallel of latitude to the south. On February 1, 1788, the General Assembly of Georgia repealed the act creating Bourbon County in an effort to reduce the diplomatic strife with Spain.

BOWDEN, Douglas County. Early name of LITHIA SPRINGS. *See* Salt Springs.

BOWDON, Carroll County. Pronounced to rhyme with "how-done." Incorporated as the town of BOWDEN (sic) December 13, 1859, and had originally been called CERRO GORDO (q.v.). It was named to honor U. S. Representative from Alabama, Franklin Welch Bowdon (1817-1857), who was instrumental in getting a post office for the early community. Incorporated as the city of Bowdon on March 7, 1957. Located here was BOWDON STATE NORMAL AND INDUSTRIAL COLLEGE, which was established here in 1855 by Charles A. McDaniel as BOWDON COLLEGIATE INSTITUTE.

BOWEN'S MILL, Ben Hill County. This was a post office of the 1880's which was also called BOWENSVILLE. Postmaster R. V. Bowen operated a grist mill here. The 100-acre BOWEN'S MILL LAKE was created by a dam on House Creek, constructed here in 1870. The lake drained away after the dam collapsed in 1949.

BOWENVILLE, Carroll County. A rural community located nine miles southeast of Carrollton; named for the first postmaster, William Bowen. The name of the post office was later changed to BANNING.

BOWERSVILLE, Hart County. Incorporated as a town September 4, 1883. Was an early settlement of old Franklin County, named for William F. Bowers who owned the land on which the settlement began.

BOWLING GREEN (Militia) DISTRICT, Oglethorpe County. Located south of Lexington. Named from a race track once owned by Ferdinand Phinizy.

BOWMAN, Elbert County. Incorporated August 22, 1907. This town was named in honor of Thomas J. Bowman of Elberton who helped finance the Elberton Airline Railroad.

BOXANKLE, Monroe County. A former community which was located six miles north of Forsyth, where Boxankle Road (q.v.) meets Johnstonville Road. It is said that some men were here watching a cockfight, and two men began fighting. One knocked the other over a wooden box and broke his ankle. This is said to be how the community got its name. *See also* Richland, Stewart County.

BOXANKLE ROAD, Monroe County. Extends northwest from U. S. 23 about three miles north of Forsyth. Named from the early community of Boxankle (q.v.).

BOX SPRINGS, Talbot County. Incorporated as a town from August 4, 1913 to August 13, 1931. This community is located in the southwest corner of the county. In June 1853, railroad workers boxed a spring near the tracks to provide water for the locomotives, which gave the place its name. It was first called BOX SPRING, but the Post Office Department adopted the present name in 1958 after people had added the "s" over the years. In this same section of the county is located the BOX SPRINGS (Militia) DISTRICT.

BOYKEN, Miller County. A community located five miles southeast of Colquitt. Incorporated as a town August 4, 1903.

BOYNTON, Catoosa County. Located four miles west of Ringgold on Georgia highway 2. Settled as PEAVINE in 1850. Renamed to honor General H. V. Boynton, the first commissioner of the Chicamauga-Chattanooga Battlefield Park (q.v.). Incorporated as a town August 22, 1907.

BOY'S ESTATE, McIntosh County. *See* SANTO DOMINGO BOYS ESTATE.

BRADLEY, Jones County. A community located three miles northwest of Gray. Named for the pioneer family of John W. Bradley, Jr.

BRAINERD ROAD, Chattooga and Walker

counties. Name is derived from the Brainerd Mission, which was located near the present site of Chattanooga, Tennessee. It was a school for Indians, established by Reverend Cyrus Kingsbury, and it existed from 1817 to 1838.

BRANCHVILLE, Mitchell County. This rural community is located ten miles west of PELHAM. Named for Colonel W. Branch, (son of Governor John Branch of North Carolina), who came here from Decatur to settle in 1864. The place was later called FAIRCLOTH (q.v.) temporarily, because at that time there existed another post office in Georgia named Branchville.

BRANDON, McDuffie County. Located in the northern section of the county near Little River. This was one of the earliest settlements of upper Georgia, and was established about 1752-1754 by Edmund Grey, a pretended Quaker and his frontiersmen. They abandoned this settlement to move to New Hanover (q.v.) in April 1755. The derivation of the name is unknown. Later a group of Quakers, led by a Joseph Mattock, settled here and named the settlement WRIGHTSBOROUGH (q.v.).

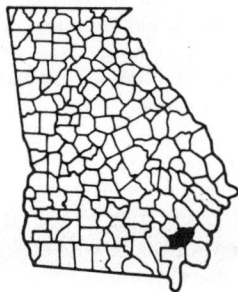

BRANTLEY COUNTY. Created August 14, 1920 with 447 square miles taken from Charlton, Pierce, and Wayne counties. Named for State Senator William Gordon Brantley (1860-1934) of Brunswick. Some earlier sources claimed that the county was named for Benjamin D. Brantley (1832-1891). The county seat is Nahunta (q.v.).

BRASELTON, Jackson County. Pronounced "Bra-zel-ton." First settled in 1884 when John O. Braselton opened a store here. The post office was established in 1916 and the town was incorporated August 21, 1916.

BRASSTOWN, Towns County. This settlement located eight miles southwest of Hiawassee was formerly called TRACK ROCK (q.v.). The name Brasstown is a misinterpretation of a Cherokee Indian word *Itse' yi,* which actually means "town of the green valley" or "a place made green with vegetation." It was confused with a similar Cherokee Indian word, *Untsai' yi,* which translates "brass." BRASSTOWN BALD, Union County. This is the highest point in Georgia with an elevation of 4,784 feet. This mountain peak was formerly called the SUMMIT OF MOUNT ENOTAH. The present name was taken from the nearby settlement of Brasstown. BRASSTOWN CREEK of Union and Towns counties, and BRASSTOWN MOUNTAIN of Union County were also named for the community of Brasstown.

BREAD TOWN, Dawson County. This former Cherokee Indian settlement was located on the lower end of Amicalola Creek, on the present site of the Lockheed nuclear facility. The name was apparently translated from the Cherokee, *Gatu-yi.*

BREASTWORKS BRANCH, Early County. This stream near Blakely was named for an old stockade found near its banks.

BREMEN, Haralson County. "Clothing Center of the South". Pronounced "Breemen." Incorporated as a town September 1883. This city was previously called REPOSE (q.v.). Its present name came from the famous seaport city of Germany.

BRENAU COLLEGE, Gainesville. Chartered in 1878 as the GEORGIA BAPTIST SEMINARY, although it was never owned or supported by the church. It is a nonsecterian, liberal arts college for women. The present name is a coined word from the German, *brennen,* "to refine," and the Latin word, *aurum,* meaning "gold." WILKES HALL (Food Service) was the first building erected on the campus, and it is named for the school's first president, Dr. W. C. Wilkes.

BRENT, Monroe County. A community located five miles southwest of Forsyth. The name originated with the Thomas Y. Brent family, who came here from Louisville, Kentucky.

BREWTON, Laurens County. Incorporated as the town of BRUTON August 20, 1889. The Wrightsville and Tennille Railroad established a station here in 1884, and named it BRUTON after the nearby Bruton Creek. The name was changed December 16, 1895 to Brewton.

BREWTON-PARKER COLLEGE, Mt. Vernon. Established in 1904 as a Baptist high school. In 1927 it became BREWTON-PARKER JUNIOR COLLEGE, and in 1948 control was transferred to the Georgia Baptist Convention. The present name was adopted in 1958. It is named in honor of Dr. John Carter Brewton (1854-1939), the founder, and Mr. C. B. Parker, a generous benefactor.

BRICK STORE, Newton County. When first settled in 1818, it was proposed that a town named "Winton" would be established here. This was considered the original county seat when the first superior court of Newton County convened here April 15, 1822. The present name was adopted after Solomon Graves built the first brick building in the county here, which was constructed of brick which were made in England and hauled by oxen-pulled wagons from the Savannah wharf. The structure still stands, and is located one-fifth of a mile east of Hub Junction (q.v.). A post office existed here from 1851 to 1866.

BRICKYARD HILL, Lumpkin County. This hill near Dahlonega extends from Last Chance Creek to Cane Creek. At the foot of this hill was a brickyard which made bricks used in the construction of North Georgia College, the local court house, and the former United States mint here.

BRIDGEBORO, Worth County. Incorporated as a town August 1, 1912. A community located 14 miles southwest of Sylvester. Derivation of the name is unknown.

BRIER CREEK. Spelled BRYAR CREEK on a 1780 map. Flows southeasterly through Screven County and enters the Savannah River east of Sylvania. The Indian name of the stream was KANUGU 'LA or "Scratchers," referring to the rich growth of briers along the banks. BRIER CREEK was the name of a former settlement and shipping point on the Savannah River.

BRIGHTON, Tift County. A former community which was located four miles northeast of Tifton in what was then Irwin County. Was believed settled by a Mr. Jim Walker, who had but one arm. The post office was established here about 1900. Ida Belle Williams said it was named by Captain

Henry Harding Tift for a town near his home in Mystic, Connecticut. BRIGHTON (Militia) DISTRICT is located in the northeast section of Tift County.

BRINSON, Decatur County. Incorporated as a town August 22, 1907. Was first known as MOUNT ZION community, after the Methodist Church here. The post office was called SPRING CREEK, and the first postmaster was Simeon Brinson, who was also the town's first mayor.

BRINSONVILLE, Jenkins County. A former community, recorded in 1883 as being in what was then Burke County, and was located on the Ogeechee River four miles from Millen. It is believed to have been named for the Brinson family who were early settlers here.

BRISTOL, Macon County. This former community was incorporated as a town December 31, 1838, presumably named from the city in England. It was originally called TRAVELERS REST (q.v.).

BRISTOL, Pierce County. Located ten miles north of Blackshear. Originally called Lightsey after Jack Lightsey. It was said that Lem Lightsey named it after the city of Bristol, England.

BROAD RIVER, Elbert County. This descriptively named river runs along the south border of the county, and was formerly called DART RIVER (q.v.). Earlier names were SALIVAGE RIVER (1733 map) and SALIVEGEE RIVER (1789 map).

BROCKTON, Jackson County. This community is located about five miles east of Jefferson. The first postmaster, Charles O. Brock, established the post office here June 11, 1895. The office closed January 31, 1902.

BROKEN ARROW (Militia) DISTRICT, Walton County. To the Indians, a broken arrow ordinarily signified "peace." It has also been supposed by some that in this instance the name was derived because of the abundance of discarded arrowheads found in the area. A little hamlet known as BROKEN ARROW existed in this section of Walton County's early days, and may have had some remote kinship with the well known Indian town of the same name that once existed on the Chattahoochee River.

BRONCO, Walker County. Located five miles southwest of LaFayette. Because of the wild, rustic location in this woodsy region, the name proposed for the first post office of this community was Sylvan Bower. After postal authorities rejected this name, the Spanish word *Bronco* was selected as a name descriptive of a wild, bucking horse.

BRONWOOD, Terrell County. Previously BROWN'S STATION, incorporated September 24, 1883.

BROOKFIELD, Tift County. This town was founded in the Fall of 1870 with the opening of a store and lumber mill. The name is descriptive of its location by a small stream which is a tributary of the Withlacoochee River.

BROOKLET, Bulloch County. Incorporated as a town August 21, 1906.

BROOKLYN, Stewart County. This community in the northeast section of the county may have been named for the borough of New York City. However, the name was most likely chosen to suggest an area of pleasant surroundings. BROOKLYN was once the designation of a section of Atlanta at the intersection of Marietta and Walton streets. BROOKLYN is also the name that is applied to a southwest section of Athens in Clarke County.

BROOKS, Fayette County. Incorporated as a town from August 3, 1910 to August 16, 1913. Located twelve miles south of Fayetteville, it was named in 1850 for Hilary Brooks who moved here from Henry County in 1840. The first name of this community was SHARON GROVE (1835). It was changed to HAISTENTOWN in 1840 for "Aunt Peggy" Haisten and her husband, who were the first white settlers, having arrived here in 1819.

BROOKS COUNTY. Created December 11, 1858 with 492 square miles taken from Lowndes and Thomas counties. Named in honor of Preston Smith Brooks (1819-1857) of South Carolina. U. S. Congressman Brooks, a captain in the Mexican War, gained notoriety when he caned Senator Charles Sumner of Massachusetts in the Capitol at Washington, because of a speech by Sumner which was offensive to the South.

BROOKTON, Hall County. A community located ten miles north of Gainesville. Named for the John Prescott Brooke family who settled the area in 1825.

BROOMTOWN VALLEY, Walker County. Located near Summerville, it is named for an Indian chief known as "The Broom" or "Old Broom." Also in Walker County is a small stream in the west central section called BROOM BRANCH, which is an affluent of Boggy Gut Creek. There was also at one time a community of BROOMTOWN, located five miles west of Summerville in Chattooga County. BROOMTOWN ROAD is the name given to Georgia Highway 337, which runs southwest from LaFayette in Walker County, down through Broomtown Valley.

BROTHERSVILLE, Richmond County. Named in honor of the Anderson brothers, James, Augustus, and Elisha Jr., who built the first homes here. The place is now called HEPHZIBAH (q.v.), and has also been referred to as LOST ARCADIA (q.v.).

BROWN'S CROSSING, Baldwin County. This was once a stop on the Georgia Railroad, sometimes called BROWN'S STATION. In the 1880's, C. E. Brown was the postmaster, and D. W. Brown was the railroad agent who also operated a gin and a grist mill here. This dead town is located where Pancras Road crosses Camp Creek, and is the site of an annual crafts fair held in October, having begun in 1970.

BROWN'S MOUNT, Bibb County. Named for George A. Brown who first owned the property. This ancient prehistoric Indian mound is located near the Ocmulgee River about seven miles below Macon, and still has traces of an old fortification.

BROWNSVILLE, Paulding County. This rural community is located about eleven miles south of Dallas, and was possibly named for an early Methodist minister here, Reverend John Brown.

BROWNWOOD, Morgan County. This rural community is located five miles southwest of Madison, and was named for James Neville Brown, a prominent landowner of the vicinity.

BROXTON, Coffee County. Incorporated as a city July 27, 1904. This town was first called GULLY BRANCH, then later took its name from nearby BROXTON CREEK. This stream was thought to have been named for Henry Broxton, early settler here from South Carolina.

BRUNSWICK, CS Glynn County. Called "Port City." This is Georgia's second busiest seaport and is a shrimp processing center. Originally a plantation settlement was here prior to 1770 known as CARR'S FIELD, for settler Mark Carr. Founded in 1771 and chartered December 3, 1813, it was named in honor of England's King George III who was of the house of Hanover, or Brunswick. This has the lowest elevation of any city in Georgia, 14 feet above sea level. GEORGE STREET here was named for King George III. BRUNSWICK JUNIOR COLLEGE, a unit of the University System of Georgia, was founded here in 1961.

BRYAN COUNTY. Created December 19, 1793 with 439 square miles taken from Chatham County. Named in honor of Jonathan Bryan (1708-1788), who came from South Carolina with General James Edward Oglethorpe, to help establish the Georgia Colony at Savannah. A patriot of the Revolution, Bryan was later a judge and state representative from Chatham County. The county seat is Pembroke (q.v.).

BRYAN, Bryan County. This was the original county seat, sometimes called BRYAN COURT HOUSE, and also known as EDEN (q.v.). Was recorded as the county seat in 1883; the seat was later moved to Clyde (q.v.) nearby.

BRYAN('S) NECK, Bryan County. This descriptive name is given to the narrow, lower part of the county between the Great Ogeechee and Medway rivers.

BUCHANAN, CS Haralson County. Incorporated December 22, 1857. Named for the fifteenth president of the United States, James Buchanan (1791-1868) of Pennsylvania, who served immediately prior to Abraham Lincoln. He strongly favored the maintenance of slavery.

BUCK CREEK. Arises in Marion County, flows through Schley County into Macon County where it enters the Flint River. It is presumed that the original surveyor shot or saw a male "buck" deer in the vicinity of the stream he so named. The Indians called the stream OPILTHLUCCO, "Big Swamp." Another BUCK CREEK is located in Screven County.

BUCKHEAD, Fulton County. Incorporated as a town August 17, 1908. Now a part of Atlanta, this community was settled in 1838 by Henry Irby (1807-1879), for whom the post office of Irbyville (q.v.) was named. It was said that a man killed a buck deer and nailed its head to a tree near the store here, and it remained there for some time. The place was therefore called Buckhead. It might have been Irby himself who shot the deer.

BUCKHEAD, Morgan County. This village is located eight miles east of Madison. Benjamin Fitzpatrick first settled here with other families from Greene County. When hunting here they killed a huge buck deer and hung its head on the branch of a tree, which gave rise to the community's name.

BUCK HORN, Haralson County. This rural community west of Villa Rica was one of the earliest settlements of Carroll County. First to arrive about 1833 was G. H. West. Isaac E. Cobb who came next, once killed a buck and nailed its horns in front of his house to give the place its name.

BUCKTOWN (Militia) DISTRICT, Gilmer County. Located in the eastern section of the county, it was once a part of Tickanetley District, but was organized as a separate district in 1892. It was named at the suggestion of T. H. Tabor who had long kept the antlers from a buck which had been killed in the area and exhibited in Ellijay.

BUDAPEST, Haralson County. This community was named by Hungarian winemakers from Budapest, Hungary who settled here.

BUENA VISTA, CS Marion County. Became the county seat in 1849 after the original county seat at Tazewell (q.v.) was destroyed by fire. It was incorporated January 26, 1850. The original community here was called PEA RIDGE (q.v.), and it was established about a mile and a half from the site of Kings Town, home of the Uchee Indian chiefs. It was named in honor of General Zachary Taylor's noted victory over Santa Ana at Buena Vista, Mexico, February 22-23, 1847. The name is Spanish and literally translated it means "good view."

BUFFALO CREEK, Brantley County. Was presumably given this name when the original surveyor either shot or saw a buffalo in the vicinity.

BUFFALO LICK, Greene County. An early settlement was started here in 1773. Located about one and a half miles east of Union Point. Named for a rock with a salty taste which attracted buffaloes.

BUFFINGTON (or FORT BUFFINGTON), Cherokee County. Established in the 1830's as a stockade or fort for use in rounding up Cherokee Indians for removal to the west in 1838. This community is thought to have been named for a mixed blood Cherokee, Joshua Buffington.

BUFORD, Gwinnett County. Pronounced "Bew' ferd," to rhyme with "You' ferd." Incorporated as a town August 24, 1872. Called "The Leather City." Established in 1868 as a stop on the railroad that ran from Atlanta to Charlotte, N.C. Named for the president of the road, Colonel A. S. Buford, by Thomas S. Garner and Larkin Smith, stockholders of the railroad, who first developed this area.

BUFORD DAM, Forsyth County. Built by the U.S. Corps of Engineers, and completed in 1957 to create Lake Lanier (q.v.). The dam took its name from the nearby town of Buford (q.v.).

BUGABOO ISLAND, Ware County. Located near Chase Prairie in Okefenokee Swamp. The name refers to an incident when an early deer hunter became frightened of a fearful noise which turned out to be from two trees rubbing together in the wind.

BULLARD, Twiggs County. This name was first given to a railroad station located about a mile east of the Ocmulgee River. It was named for the Daniel Bullard family. Mr. Bullard was a wealthy plantation owner and business man who owned land on the east bank of the Ocmulgee River. The present settlement is about a mile and-a-half east of the station. The post office of Bullard existed from May 10, 1870 to January 31, 1923.

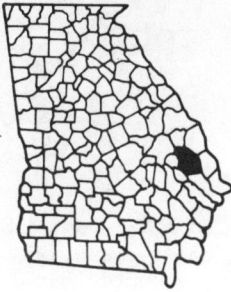

BULLOCH COUNTY. Created February 8, 1796 with 684 square miles taken from Bryan and Screven counties. Named for Archibald Bulloch (1729-1777), one of the most distinguished of Georgia's Revolutionary patriots. He was also congressman, speaker of the House of Representatives, and acting governor of Georgia (1775-1777). The county seat is Statesboro (q.v.).

BULLOCHVILLE, Meriwether County. Was incorporated December 20, 1893. Believed to have been named for Benjamin F. Bulloch who settled here in 1891. The name of the town was changed to WARM SPRINGS (q.v.) August 6, 1924.

BULLSBORO, Coweta County. An early trading station and settlement. This was the first county seat, and was located about two and one-half miles northeast of what is now Newnan. Derivation of the name is unknown.

BULL SLUICE, Fulton County. Located about six miles below Roswell on the Chattahoochee River; This shoal was given its name by the Cherokee Indians. A suggestion to change the name to MORGAN FALLS (q.v.) was at first refused by the public, but the change was made nevertheless.

BUNCOMBE (Militia) DISTRICT, Haralson County. This name was taken from Buncombe County in North Carolina, which was there named for Colonel Edward Buncombe (1742-1778), a soldier of the Revolution. There are also militia districts named BUNCOMBE in Oconee, Polk, and Walton counties, which name was probably brought in by newcomers from North Carolina. *See also* LOGANVILLE.

BURDEN (Militia) DISTRICT, Jones County. Named for early settler Thomas Liles

Burden (born 1809) who came to Jones County from South Carolina.

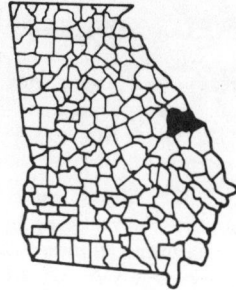

BURKE COUNTY. Created February 5, 1777 with 832 square miles acquired by the Creek cession of May 20, 1733. This is an original county, previously organized as the PARISH OF ST. GEORGE (q.v.). It is the state's second largest county in area. It was named for English political writer, Edmund Burke (1729-1797), who advanced theories of liberty and human rights, and who favored conciliation with the colonies. The county seat is Waynesboro (q.v.). The court house was destroyed by fires in 1825 and 1856.

BURNSIDE, Chatham County. A former community named for an early settler, James Burnside. It is now a part of the settlement of MONTGOMERY, located south of Savannah. Located here also is BURNSIDE ISLAND and the BURNSIDE RIVER.

BURNTFORT, Charlton County. A community located on the Satilla River, twelve miles from Folkston. It acquired its name from the traditional story that there once existed a fort here which was built by South Carolina between 1715 and 1725, and was destroyed by fire.

BURNT VILLAGE, Troup County. Was located on the west bank of the Chattahoochee River at the mouth of Wehadka Creek, due west of LaGrange. Prior to 1793 this was the great central point of the Muskogee tribe of the Creek Nation. In that year, a Major Adams led an attack of white men who killed the Indians and burned their town as revenge after Indian attacks on frontier settlements.

BURTON LAKE, Rabun County. *See* LAKE BURTON.

BURTSBORO, Lumpkin County. A rural community seven miles southwest of

Dahlonega. Named for Ray and W. J. Burt who operated a general store here.

BUSH CREEK, Heard County. *See* LOO-CHAU PO-GAU.

BUSHNELL, Coffee County. A former community which was located six miles northwest of Douglas on the Seaboard Railroad. Incorporated as a town from August 22, 1907 to August 17, 1908. A Mr. G. L. Bush was one of the town councilmen.

BUTLER, CS Taylor County. The town was incorporated February 8, 1854. Named for General William Orlando Butler (1791-1880), who was commander of the United States Army in Mexico. He was candidate for vice-president on the ticket with General Lewis Cass of Michigan in 1848.

BUTLER ISLAND, McIntosh County. This island is located at the mouth of the Altamaha River just below Darien. It was owned by Major Pierce Butler (1745?-1822), an Irish-born British army officer who came to America in 1776. He was elected from South Carolina to sit in the first meeting of the U. S. Senate, which convened in New York City. His grandson, Pierce Mease, who at his grandfather's wish had taken the surname of Butler, married the noted British actress, Frances Anne "Fanny" Kemble (1809-1893), who was the author of, *Journal of a Georgian Plantation in 1838-1839.* This devastating book which was critical of slavery, was written during a four-month stay here and at BUTLER(S) POINT on St. Simons Island. This famous estate, location of Major Butler's widely known Hampton Plantation, was also named for Major Butler, who provided sanctuary here for Vice-President Aaron Burr after the latter had killed Alexander Hamilton in the famous duel in 1804.

BUTTERMILK. Some of the following may be "poor mouthing" names, referring to persons, who because of their poverty status, had to survive on buttermilk. Others may refer to bodies of water with a whitish buttermilk - like appearance. Some of these are: BUTTERMILK BLUFF, located where I-95 crosses the Camden County line at the St. Marys River. BUTTERMILK BOTTOMS, which was the name of an old section of Atlanta; BUTTERMILK CREEK, Cobb County; and BUTTERMILK SHOALS on the Ocmulgee River near Hawkinsville. BUTTERMILK SOUND, McIntosh County, is located at the mouth of the Altamaha River.

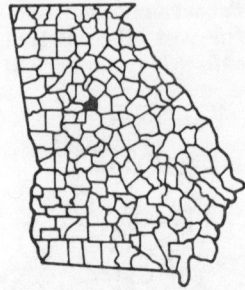

BUTTS COUNTY. Created December 24, 1825 with 185 square miles taken from Henry and Monroe counties. Named for Captain Samuel Butts (1777-1814), who lost his life January 27, 1814 in the battle of Challibbee against the Upper Creek Indians. The county seat is Jackson (q.v.).

BUZZARD FLOPPER CREEK, Cherokee County. This stream arises near the upper edge of Lathamtown and flows northward to join Smithwick Creek, which flows into the Etowah River south of Ball Ground. Believed to have been named for a Cherokee Indian called Buzzard Flopper (or (Flapper) who lived on the Etowah River.

BUZZARD ROOST, Taylor County. This was a former Indian settlement on the west bank of the Flint River, and was an out-settlement of the Cusetta Indians, whose main center was where the present Fort Benning Army reservation now stands. The name is translated from the Muskogee Indian word, *sulenojuh,* which means, "having buzzards." A post office named BUZZARD ROOST, in the southwest corner of Twiggs County existed from May 20, 1872 until January 6, 1891. One legend claims that the name was gradually acquired because Indians then frequently lay on the ground here to sleep off intoxication. Another account relates that when the Macon and Brunswick Railway was being built, right of way was solicited from the landowner at this point, Robert R. Slappy. He granted the request with the provision that he be allowed to name the station. Being a practical joker, Mr. Slappy named the station Buzzard Roost to infuriate his friends and kinsmen. In 1885 the name was changed to WESTLAKE (q.v.). BUZZARD ROOST in Fulton County was the early name of SANDTOWN (q.v.), and was probably named for BUZZARD ROOST ISLAND in Cobb County. This island is located at the south corner of the county in the Chattahoochee

River, and was named for the Buzzard Roost tribe of Indians from Alabama. BUZZARD ROOST LAKE in Charlton County is located in the Okefenokee Swamp. It was so named because of its being a favorite roosting or gathering place for buzzards. *See also* MILL CREEK GAP.

BYROMVILLE, Dooly County. Incorporated August 19, 1905. Named for early settler, William H. Byrom who purchased 800 acres of land here in 1852, where he built his home in 1859. The community that developed here was first named FRIENDSHIP for the Friendship Methodist Church. The town was first settled in 1829 by N. Thomas Swearington; his home built that year still stands. The post office opened July 1, 1853.

BYRON, Dougherty County. A former community located five miles northwest of Albany. Also recorded as BRYAN, it was named for Lord Byron, *(see* Byron, Peach County). This was the original county seat of Baker County, and was so designated December 16, 1828. The seat was moved to Newton in 1832.

BYRON, Peach County. Incorporated as a town March 3, 1874. Settled about 1820, and named for English writer, George Noel Gordon, Lord Byron (1788-1824), by the founder of the town, a Mr. Richardson, who was an admirer of Lord Byron. The previous name of the community was JACKSON, for the many Jackson families settled here. The name changed when it was found that another place called Jackson already existed in Georgia. This was the site of the South's largest "pop festival" which was held during the weekend of July 4, 1970 *(see also* Echeconnee Creek).

C

CABANISS, Monroe County. A community located eight miles northeast of Forsyth. Named for Judge E. G. Cabaniss of Forsyth. It was previously called GULLETTSVILLE (q.v.). *See also* Oglethorpe, Macon County.

CADWELL, Laurens County. Incorporated as a town August 22, 1907. Land for the town was donated by Mrs. Rebecca L. Cadwell, and it was named for her first husband, Matthew Cadwell. One of the first four councilmen appointed here was C. C. Cadwell. The place is 17 miles southwest of Dublin.

CAHELEE CREEK, Early County. Located in the western part of the county. The name was altered from the previous COHELEE (q.v.).

CAINS, Gwinnett County. Also called HOG MOUNTAIN (q.v.). Named for the John Cain store and post office.

CAIRO, CS Grady County. Pronounced "Kayro." Incorporated as a town October 28, 1870, and designated the county seat when Grady County was formed in 1905. It was believed named for the city in Egypt, but Brinkley says it was named for Cairo, Ill. This has become the center of the syrup trade in Georgia.

CALAMIT, Barrow County. An old settlement on the Okoloco Trail (q.v.), 3½ miles southeast of Winder. It means "place of rest," and was so named because of a huge chestnut tree here providing shade and shelter.

CALHOUN, CS Gordon County. "Cherokee Indian Capital." Named for Senator John Calhoun (*see* Calhoun County) in 1850 and incorporated as a town January 12, 1852. It was previously named DAWSONVILLE for a Mr. Dawson who owned a general store here in early times. Before this the Indians called their town here, OOTHCALOGA (*see* Oothcalooga), USTANALI (q.v.), and NEW ECHOTA (q.v.).

CALHOUN COUNTY. Created February 20, 1854 with 289 square miles taken from Baker and Early counties. Named for the famous statesman from South Carolina, Senator John Caldwell Calhoun (1782-1850), noted orator and leader in the Southern fight for slavery and states' rights (*see also* Calhoun Mine). The county seat is Morgan (q.v.). The court house was destroyed by fires in 1888 and 1920.

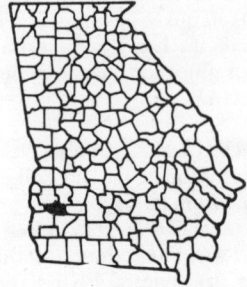

CALHOUN DAM, Lumpkin County. Also named for Senator Calhoun (*see* Calhoun County), it was located about two miles south of Dahlonega on the Chestatee River.

CALHOUN MINE, Lumpkin County. Located south of Dahlonega, it was named after Senator John Calhoun (*see* Calhoun County) after he had purchased this mine, which is where deer-hunter Benjamin Parks first discovered gold in 1828. The senator took almost $1,000 worth of gold from the mine daily. *See also* Auraria.

CALHOUN'S FERRY. Crawford County. Named for Samuel Calhoun, who was authorized to, at one time, operate a ferry across the Flint River.

CALLAWAY GARDENS, Pine Mountain. This park comprises 2,500 acres on the northern slopes of Pine Mountain in Harris County, and was opened to the public in 1952. Was developed by Cason J. Callaway of LaGrange, and named in honor of his mother Ida Cason Callaway. He was the son of Fuller E. Callaway, founder of Callaway Mills of LaGrange, and the father of Howard Hollis "Bo" Callaway, U. S. Congressman (1965-1967), now president of Callaway Gardens Corporation, and appointed Secretary of the Army in 1973.

CALLICO CORNER(S), Coweta County. Settled before 1840. The name was believed to be attributed to the early residents here named Colley. On June 1, 1852 this community became GRANTVILLE (q.v.).

CAMAC'S ROCK, Dade County. Located near Nickojack Creek on the summit of Rackoon Mountain, it indicated what at one time was determined to be the northwest corner of the state. Named after James Camac, mathematician, who helped locate this exact site in 1818. *See also* Ellicott Rock.

CAMAK, Warren County. Incorporated as a town December 22, 1898. Named for James Camak of Athens, newspaper editor and first president of the Georgia Railroad.

CAMDEN COUNTY. Created February 5, 1777 with 656 square miles acquired by Creek cessions of November 10, 1763 and November 12, 1785. An original county previously organized in 1765 as the parishes of Saint Thomas and Saint Mary. Named for Sir Charles Pratt, Earl of Camden (1714-1794), English jurist who opposed the English ministry's attitude towards the colonies. He was chief justice and lord chancellor of England. The county seat is Woodbine (q.v.).

CAMELOT, Clayton County. A suburban area near Jonesboro. In British fable, Camelot was the legendary place where King Arthur held his court.

CAMERON MILLS, Telfair County. In 1882, records show that postmaster J. W. Cameron owned a grist mill here. The community here is now called COBBVILLE (q.v.).

CAMILLA, CS Mitchell County. "The Hub City" Incorporated as a town December 14, 1858. Named for Camilla Mitchell, the daughter of Governor David B. Mitchell (*see* Mitchell County), when she was 19. She later married a Mr. Groves and lived in Marietta.

CAMPBELL COUNTY. Created December 20, 1828 from Carroll, Coweta, DeKalb, and Fayette Counties. The county seat was Campbellton (q.v.) and then Fairburn (q.v.). Campbell County was merged into Fulton County January 1, 1932. It was named in honor of Colonel Duncan G. Campbell (1787-1828), a noted Georgia lawyer, who was a member of the legislature, a commissioner to the Indians, and a strong advocate of the higher education of women.

CAMPBELLTON, Fulton County. Settled in 1829 and incorporated December 3, 1829. This was the original county seat of Campbell County (q.v.), located nine miles northwest of Fairburn. It was named for Georgia statesman Colonel Duncan G. Campbell by Frank Irwin, who owned the land on a hill overlooking the Chattahoochee River where the town was established. After the railroads bypassed the town, the court house was moved to Fairburn (by 1870), and eventually this became a ghost town.

CAMP BRANCH. This stream rises in Ware County and flows southward to enter the Suwannee River in Charlton County. Thought to have been named by the survey party who made camp near the stream.

CAMP CORNELIA, Charlton County. A site at the eastern entrance of the Okefenokee Swamp. Named by Captain Henry Jackson for his daughter Cornelia. *See also* Jackson's Folly.

CAMP CRAWFORD, Decatur County. *See* FORT SCOTT.

CAMP CREEK, Union County. This old community derived its name from the fact that it was located on Camp and Dooley Creeks, twelve miles northwest of Blairsville.

CAMP EATON, Forsyth County. Earlier name of CAMP GILMER (q.v.). Senator John Henry Eaton (1790-1856) was Secretary of War (1829-31).

CAMP GILMER, Forsyth County. Named for George Gilmer (*see* Gilmer County). The original name was CAMP EATON when first constructed by U. S. troops in 1829. Was located at the present community of Hightower.

CAMP GORDON, Augusta. Named for John Brown Gordon (1832-1904), who was a lieutenant general in the Civil War, and governor of Georgia from 1887 to 1890. The name of the post was changed to FORT GORDON in 1956 when this became a permanent army post. *See also* Camp John B. Gordon.

CAMP HARRIS, Macon. Established opposite Crumps Park in 1917 as a tent camp for troop mobilization for the Mexican border conflict. Was commanded by Macon's

General Walter A. Harris, and named by Adjutant J. Van Holt Nash in honor of Georgia's governor at that time, Nathaniel Edwin Harris (1846-1929).

CAMP JOHN B. GORDON, Chamblee. Established July 18, 1917 as a World War I cantonment, and was named in honor of General John B. Gordon (*see* Camp Gordon). The camp was abandoned December 13, 1919 after which this section was for years known locally as CAMP GORDON. During World War II the site was used for the establishment of a Naval Air Base and Lawson General Hospital (q.v.).

CAMP LAWTON, Jenkins County. Was located at Magnolia Springs, five miles north of Millen. The camp served as a Confederate prison in 1864, where thousands of Union prisoners were confined during the closing months of the Civil War. Named for Brigadier General Alexander Robert Lawton (1818-1896), a graduate of West Point and Harvard University. He was quartermaster general of the Confederate Army. He later served in both houses of the state legislature, and was appointed U. S. minister to Russia in 1887.

CAMP McDONALD, Cobb County. Established by Governor Joseph E. Brown as a training camp for Confederate soldiers. Named for Governor Charles James McDonald (1793-1860) of Cobb County.

CAMP MILNER, Griffin. A Confederate cavalry camp, named for Ben Milner, who was a prominent Spalding County man. The name was changed to CAMP NORTHEN (q.v.) in 1898.

CAMP NORTHEN Griffin. Established as CAMP MILNER (q.v.) during the Civil War. Named in 1898 for Georgia governor, William Jonathan Northen (1835-1913), and used for a training camp and mobilization center during the Spanish-American War. Here now is the Municipal Park of Griffin.

CAMP OGLETHORPE, Macon. Named April 30, 1844 for the founder of Georgia, James Edward Oglethorpe (*see* Oglethorpe County). Was located at Seventh and Hawthorne streets, and used for a parade and camp ground. Macon's OGLETHORPE STREET was named from the camp.

CAMP PINCKNEY, Charlton County. This former community and boat landing was located on the St. Marys River below Folkston. It was said that a Captain Pinckney camped here with troops during the Indian Wars. It was possibly Thomas Pinckney, son of Governor Charles Pinckney of South Carolina.

CAMP STEPHENS, Spalding County. Was located north of Griffin on McIntosh Road. This was a Confederate Infantry camp, named for Alexander Stephens (*see* Stephens County).

CAMP STEWART, Bryan, Evans, Liberty, and Long counties. Now called FORT STEWART, it was named for General Daniel Stewart (1761-1820), an ancestor of President Theodore Roosevelt, who fought in the Revolution and the War of 1812. General Stewart's home was Tranquil Plantation near Riceboro.

CAMPTON, Walton County. Incorporated as a town August 23, 1905 at the site of William F. Camp's storehouse. This rural community is located about five miles north of Monroe. The post office was opened in 1888, and was originally called CAMP'S STATION after railroad agent Joseph Ray Camp.

CAMP WHEELER, Bibb County. Was located east of Macon at Holly Bluff, and was established in July 1917. It was used for training about 300,000 soldiers during both world wars. After World War I, Camp Wheeler was ordered abandoned December 9, 1918, and was then rebuilt on the same site in 1940-41, after which it became the nation's largest replacement center. It was named for Major General Joseph Wheeler (1835-1906) of Augusta, a noted general for the Confederacy in the Civil War who also served the U. S. Army in the Spanish American War. General Wheeler was also a U. S. congressman and an author. A nearby residential area of Macon is now called WHEELER HEIGHTS. There is also a WHEELER ROAD that runs past the site of the former camp from Macon southeastward into Twiggs County. *See also* Wheeler County and Emery Highway.

CAMP WRIGHT, Bibb County. Established near Macon in early 1864 by, and named for, General Marcus Joseph Wright (1831-1922), CSA.

CAMP WILL-A-WAY, Barrow County. *See* WILL-A-WAY RECREATION AREA.

CANDLER COUNTY. Created July 14, 1914 with 251 square miles taken from Bulloch, Emanuel, and Tattnall counties. Named in honor of Governor Allen Daniel Candler (1834-1910), who served in the state legislature, was Secretary of State, and governor of Georgia from 1898 to 1902. In the Civil War, he lost an eye at Jonesboro. He afterwards became known as the "one-eyed plow-boy from Pigeon Roost" (his being born near Pigeon Roost gold mine in Lumpkin County). He edited the Colonial, Revolutionary, and Confederate records of the state. The county seat is Metter (q.v.). The community of CANDLER, Hall County was incorporated as a town August 15, 1910. It is located five and one-half miles southeast of Gainesville on Georgia highway 60. It was also named for Governor Candler, as was the CANDLER (Militia) DISTRICT of Hall County.

CANOOCHEE, Emanuel County. Incorporated August 19, 1912, this town was named from that of an ancient Indian country or province, recorded as Canosi, of uncertain meaning.

CANOOCHEE RIVER (or CREEK). Rises in Emanuel County and flows southeastward to the Ogeechee River in Bryan County. It may be of the same derivation as the town by this name in Emanuel County, although it has also been thought to be from the Creek, *Ikanodshi,* "Graves are There." A more likely derivation is from *Kanooche,* meaning "Little Ground." Former variations of spelling have been CANOUCHIE, CANOCHE, and CONOOCHEE.

CANOY, Lee County. This is an old spot northeast of Leesburg which was the site of Jack Kennard's settlement. The Indians couldn't pronounce Jack's last name, and the Kennards later called themselves "Canards." The name Canoy evolved as a further variation from the same source.

CANTON, CS Cherokee County. "The Broiler City" Pronounced "Can'-tun." The place was first called CHEROKEE COURT HOUSE when the post office was established in 1832. It was incorporated under the name of ETOWAH (q.v.) in 1833, and then changed to Canton December 18, 1834 for China's great silk center. Judge Joseph Donaldson brought in 100,000 silk worms and put out many mulberry trees, hoping to develop a thriving silk industry here. It has been said by some that the name was chosen as the village was thought to be antipodal to Canton, China.

CANTON CREEK, Cherokee County. Flows westerly to join the Etowah River at Canton, from which it was named.

CAPRON, Dooly County. This former community was located on the Flint River twelve miles northwest of Vienna. Said to have been named for a Confederate war hero by the name of Capron.

CARBONDALE, Whitfield County. A community located eight miles south of Dalton on the Southern Railway. First called COVE CITY for its location at the mouth of a cove. Later named for the railroad coal (carbon) stop.

CAREY, Greene County. This is the station where the Georgia Railroad crosses the Oconee River, and it was named for James Carey, for many years an employee of the railroad. The post office formerly here was named LITCH, after a Mr. Litchfield who had a store here, and no doubt was also the postmaster.

CARLIER SPRINGS, Floyd County. Named after Louis Henry Carlier, who helped General L. J. B. LeHardy establish a Belgian colony here in 1848, which existed thirty years. It was located three miles east of Rome, and was sometimes referred to as LeHARDY SPRINGS.

CARLTON, Madison County. Incorporated December 20, 1892. This town is known by two names. After being established, it was found that freight shipments were frequently routed to Carrollton by mistake. To avoid this confusion, the railroad name of BERKLEY was adopted for the station here.

CARNESVILLE, CS Franklin County. Designated county seat November 29, 1806 and incorporated as a village December 7, 1807. Named for noted judge and congressman, Thomas Peter Carnes (1762-1822) of Clarke County. CARNES ROAD of Augusta was also named for Judge Carnes.

CARMEL MISSION, Gilmer County. This was the name of the second mission to the Indians in the State of Georgia since the time of the Spaniards, and was named for the Carmelites (an order of the Roman Catholic Church). It was located near Talona (q.v.), where it was established from 1819 to 1839, and its main building stood for ninety-seven years, until 1918.

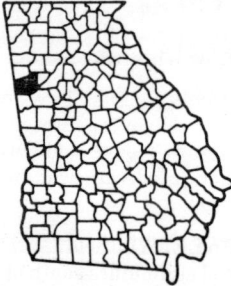

CARROLL COUNTY. Created June 9, 1825 and December 11, 1826 with 495 square miles acquired by Creek cessions of January 24, 1826, March 31, 1826, and November 15, 1827. This was an original county, named for Charles Carroll (1737-1832), a Maryland patriot, U. S. congressman and senator, who was a signer of the Declaration of Independence. In its early history it was often called "Free State of Carroll" because of its large size and independent character. The county seat is Carollton (q.v.).

CARROLLTON, CS Carroll County. "The Friendly City." The original county seat was so designated May 31, 1827, and was located at a site eight miles northwest of the present county seat. Now referred to as OLD CARROLLTON, it was first called simply CARROLL COURT HOUSE. The new county seat was authorized November 14, 1829, and at first named TROUPSVILLE (q.v.). The state legislature met December 22, 1829 and incorporated the town under the name of Carrollton, after the name of Charles Carroll's old colonial home on Chesapeake Bay. LAKE CARROLL is located in the northeast section of Carrollton.

CARRS (STATION), Hancock County. This railroad stop is located about ten miles southwest of Sparta. Believed named for J. D. Carr, who owned a general store here and was a railroad and express agent.

CARRY'S SOCK ISLAND, Okefenokee Swamp. Was so named becuase it is in the shape of a stocking.

CARTECAY, Gilmer County. This was an old Indian settlement, and is now a rural community about six miles southeast of Ellijay. The name is from a Cherokee Indian word meaning "bread valley." Spelling variations and previous names have been CARTECAY, CORTIKEYEH, KANTIKA, CARTIKEE, and CROSS ROAD. CARTECAY (Militia) DISTRICT in the southeast section of the county was named from the town. CARTECAY RIVER (or CREEK) of Gilmer County is located in the CARTECAY VALLEY, all with the same variation. The river is a tributary of the Coosawattee River.

CARTER ISLAND, Baldwin County. Located in the Oconee River just below Lake Sinclair Dam. Named for Farish Carter (*see* Carters).

CARTERS, Murray County. This once active settlement was the living and industrial center of Farish Carter's vast plantation. He purchased this 15,000 - acre plantation about 1832 from Judge John Martin, treasurer of the Cherokee Nation. It was originally called COOSAWATTEE, after the prominent river flowing throgh the plantation. He gave it the name CARTER'S QUARTERS, and it was also known as ROCK SPRING plantation. *See also* Cartersville.

CARTERS DAM, Murray County. This dam was built on the Coosawatee River by the U.S. Army Corps of Engineers at the vicinity of Carters (q.v.). It is the largest earth-rock dam east of the Mississippi River, constructed from 1963 to 1975 at a cost of $106 million.

CARTERS LAKE, Gilmer and Murray County. This 3,200 - acre lake is the reservoir on the Coosawattee River created by Carters Dam (q.v.).

CARTERSVILLE, CS Bartow County. Incorporated as a town February 8, 1854, and again in 1872, after its destruction in the Civil War. Was originally called BIRMINGHAM by some Englishmen who settled here in 1832. It was later changed to Cartersville in honor of Colonel Farish Carter (1780-1861) of

Milledgeville (*see also* Scottsboro), who was one of the wealthiest of Georgia's ante-bellum landowners, and one of the largest slave-owners in the state. *See also* Carters, and FAIRBURN.

CASE'S OLD PLACE, Burke County. An early settlement which was also known as WILLIAM CASE'S OLD SETTLEMENT and CASE'S CAMP. It is belived that William Case was a trespasser on Indian lands where he grazed his cattle. The settlement was later called BARKCAMP (q.v.).

CASEY'S (Militia) DISTRICT, Fulton County. Named for Hiram Casey, one of the earliest settlers of the county, and for many years justice of peace.

CASEY'S HILL, Atlanta. Located between Peachtree and Proctors creeks, near the Chattahoochee River. Named for John A. Casey (1820-1907) who lived on this hill.

CASSANDRA, Walker County. A rural community located nine miles northwest of LaFayette on Georgia highway 193. Was first known as HINIARD'S CROSSROAD. The name is from Greek mythology, in which Cassandra was a Trojan princess who learned the art of prophesy from Apollo, but was never believed. A Dr. Thornbury, who was a Methodist preacher and physician, settled here after having crossed the Atlantic on a ship called *Cassandra,* and suggested the town be given this name.

CASS COUNTY. Created December 3, 1832 with 463 square miles taken from part of Cherokee County. The name was changed to BARTOW COUNTY December 6, 1861, when it was no longer desired to retain the name of a Yankee from Michigan. General Lewis Cass (1782-1866) was Secretary of War under President Jackson, later minister to France, and the Secretary of State under President Buchanan.

CASSVILLE, Bartow County. Was designated the county seat in 1832, laid out in 1833, and incorporated as a town December 27, 1843. It was named for the county, but changed to MANASSAS (q.v.) in 1861 when the county became Bartow. The new name for the county seat was recognized by the Confederate authorities, but not by the U. S. postal officials. The name change was said to be the cause of the town's utter destruction by Union forces in 1864.

CASUPPY CREEK, Wilkes County. Labeled on maps of 1784 and 1785 as CASUPPY FORK and COSUPPY FORK. This is evidently a branch of Kettle Creek in the southwest section of the county. The name is derived from Kosalu, an early name of the Savannah River.

CATATOGA. This name was given to an old Cherokee town of uncertain location, and means "New-settlement-place."

CATAULA, Harris County. Settled about 1829, the post office was opened in 1836. Located in the lower part of the county on the stream for which it was named. Besides the town, there is also a CATAULA (Militia) DISTRICT here.

CATAULA CREEK. Rises in Talbot County and joins Mulberry Creek in Harris County. The name is from the Muskogee word *kitali,* which means "dead (or withered) mulberry." Hawkins called the stream KETALEE.

CAT CREEK, Lowndes County. This former community was established about 1858 by Mitchell Griffin, and it was named for the stream on which it was located. It was about twelve miles northeast of Valdosta. The stream rises in Berrien County and is a tributary of the Withlacoochee River.

CATOOSA COUNTY. Created December 5, 1853 with 167 square miles taken from Walker and Whitfield counties. The name is derived from the Cherokee word *catoosa.* The meaning is not certain, but is is said to have been from an Indian chief who lived at CATOOSA SPRINGS, four miles east of Ringgold. It also may be from the Cherokee word *gatusi,* signifying "hill," "small mountain," or "high place." Another theory is that is is from the Cherokee *gatu' gitse,* meaning "new settlement place." The county seat is Ringgold (q.v.).

CAUSTON(S) BLUFF, Chatham County. Named for Thomas Causton, General Oglethorpe's bailiff and storekeeper. Fort Bartow (q.v.) was established here.

CAVE SPRING, Floyd County. Incorporated as a village January 22, 1852. Henry W. Grady called this town, "One of the most beautiful spots in all the land." It was so named becuase of the bountiful spring that eminates from a cave, providing water for the community and for Little Cedar Creek. Cave Spring was the home of Chief David Vann (see Vann's Creek).

CAVETA (FORT). Built in 1702 and named after a former town of the Coweta Indians. This early settlement on the Chattahoochee River was burned to the ground by the English in 1685. The exact location is unknown. See also Coweta County.

CAWTHON, Greene County. This rural community is located eleven miles south of Greensboro. The postmaster in 1882 was J. W. Cawthon, who had a general store here, as well as a gin and grist and saw mills.

CEDAR, Jackson County. This former community was located midway between Braselton and Pendergrass on Georgia highway 60. The post office was established here from March 30, 1901 to June 30, 1902. This is one of the many placenames in the state that are derived from the large number of cedar trees in the region. Another rural community named CEDAR is located three miles northwest of Winder in Barrow County. Nearby is the community of CEDAR HILL, which is at the site of a formerly active Indian town that was called POGANIP, which means "cold weather." In the vicinity of these places in Barrow County is a stream named CEDAR CREEK which flows into a pond on the northwest edge of Winder. CEDAR CREEK in Clarke County is southeast of Athens, and flows into the Oconee River, while the CEDAR CREEK in Crisp County goes into the Flint River. Another CEDAR CREEK rises in northeast Marion County, then runs through the south section of Taylor County, and enters Whitewater Creek at Ideal in Macon County. The CEDAR CREEK which flows into the Coosa River in Floyd County originates in Polk County, flowing by its county seat, CEDARTOWN. This town was incorporated and made county seat February 8, 1854 and named for the numerous red cedar trees growing here. There was once

a Creek town of this name in the area. Then there is a CEDAR CREEK which rises in northern Tattnall County and flows through western Evans County to enter the Canoochee River above Claxton. And a rural community called CEDAR GROVE is near the south border of Laurens County. Incorporated as a town August 17, 1908 to August 19, 1918. It was settled about 1890, and named by Cornelius Clark, as he selected this name for a church built near some cedar trees growing in a graveyard. Another community called CEDAR GROVE is located seven miles west of LaFayette in Walker County. Just east of Dalton in Whitfield County is a rise called CEDAR RIDGE, and in eastern Union County is CEDAR MOUNTAIN, with an elevation of 4,041 feet. CEDAR SHOALS are in the Yellow River at Porterdale in Newton County, and another CEDAR SHOALS in Clarke County on the Oconee River gave its name to the original community that later became Athens. The community of CEDAR SPRINGS in Early County is located fifteen miles southwest of Blakely. Its name is derived from a group of springs which are east of the village. See also Hannahatchie.

CELEOTCHEE CREEK, Talbot County. Also spelled CELEOTH. This stream rises near Manchester and flows easterly to join Lazer Creek before that stream enters the Flint River. May be from the Muskogee, okcotuh, "muskrat," and oochee, "small," i.e. "Small Muskrat."

CEMENT, Bartow County. Incorporated October 9, 1891. Located one and one-half miles north of Kingston. Early postmaster George H. Waring manufactured hudraulic cement here, and so named the post office. The population has dwindled from about 200 to zero.

CEMOCHECHOBEE CREEK. Rises in Randolph County and flows westward through Clay County to enter the Chattahoochee River north of Ft. Gaines. Derivation is from the Hitchiti, samochi, "sand," and chobi, "big," or "Big Sandy Creek." See also Wakafudsky.

CENCHAT, Walker County. This rural community is located four miles northwest of Chickamauga on Georgia highway 193. This is a coined word to describe where the Central of Georgia crosses the Chattanooga Southern Railroad.

CENTER, Jackson County. Incorporated as a town August 21, 1906. The first post office was established here in 1826 and called BASCOBEL. In 1899 the village was named for a railroad man from Athens, a Mr. Center of the firm Center and Reeves.

CENTERPOINT, Carroll County. Located about four miles south of Temple. Named for its approximately equal distance from Carrollton and Villa Rica.

CENTER POST, Walker County. This community is located seven miles southwest of LaFayette on Georgia highway 337. The name came about as the place was the midway point between Bronco and Trion on the old mail route.

CENTER · VILLAGE, Charlton County. This now extinct community was also called CENTERVILLE. Was located two miles northeast of the center of present Folkston, near Camp Pinckney (q.v.). It was settled about 1800 after which it became an active trading center, but declined after the Civil War with the coming of the railroad.

CENTERVILLE, Early County. This rural community is halfway between Hilton and Damascus, as well as halfway between Blakely and Mayhaw (Miller County).

CENTERVILLE, Houston County. Incorporated as a city March 25, 1958. Mitchell F. Ethridge settled here and opened a store about 1885. The name derived from the fact that it was located halfway between Macon and Perry, as well as halfway between Byron and Wellston (Warner Robins). Since there was already a Centerville in Georgia, the name was changed for a while to HATTIE after the oldest Ethridge daughter, until the post office was moved to Perry.

CENTERVILLE, Talbot County. This community is located in the center of the county, and was laid out as the county seat about 1827, before Talbotton was selected for this designation.

CENTERVILLE, Walton County. This was the original name of JERSEY (q.v.).

CENTERVILLE, Wilkes County. Originally spelled CENTREVILLE, it was so named due to its being at the mid-point between Washington and Lexington. This community is located twelve miles west of Washington on U. S. highway 78.

CENTRALHATCHEE, Heard County. Incorporated as a town August 15, 1903, this community was named for the stream on which it is located.

CENTRALHATCHEE CREEK, Heard County. Rises at Ephesus and flows southwesterly to enter the Chattahoochee River at Franklin. This name is derived by folk-etymology from the Muskogean, *Sandalakwahachi,* "Perch (fish) - Stream." An earlier recorded form of the name was SUNDALHATCHEE.

CERES, Crawford County. This former community was located near the Flint River, five miles north of Knoxville. Was named for the ancient Roman goddess of agriculture, and the word stands for "growth." The community was also known as HOPEWELL.

CERRO GORDO, Carroll County. This post office was authorized in September 1847. The derivation of the name is Spanish, meaning "fat (or round) hill." The name was changed to BOWDON (q.v.) July 1848.

CEYLON, Camden County. Now merely a triangulation station, it is located about four miles east of Woodbine. Named for the island south of India.

CHALYBEATE SPRINGS, Meriwether County. Pronounced "Ka-lib-e-at." Located one mile east of Manchester. This was once a popular resort named for the springs here. Chalybeate means "containing iron salts or minerals" as mineral spring water.

CHAMBLEE, DeKalb County. Pronounced "Cham-blee'." Incorporated as a town August 17, 1908. The original name of the place was ROSWELL JUNCTION, but when this name was submitted to the U. S. Post Office department in 1881, it was found that the name was already in use. So the officials in Washington instead arbitrarily took the name of one of the petitioners for the post office name. There was once a village of CHAMBLEE on Chenubee Creek in Terrell County.

CHAPEL HILL, Twiggs County. This former post office opened April 14, 1837, and was named for the first postmaster, Thomas Chapel. There is at present a rural community of CHAPEL HILL located in Douglas County, with its name apparently derived from the university town in North Carolina.

CHAPPELL, Lamar County. Was settled in 1821 when it was named UNIONVILLE, which name it retained until Lamar County was formed in 1920. This community was given its present name for businessman H. A. Chappell. CHAPPELL (Militia) DISTRICT located in this section was also named for Mr. Chappell.

CHARING, Taylor County. A community located 12 miles southwest of Butler. Incorporated as a town from August 19, 1912 to August 13, 1915.

CHARLIE(S) CREEK, Towns County. Rises in North Carolina and flows southeasterly to the Tallulah River. Named for the principal Cherokee chief, Charlie Hicks. Named also for him is CHARLIE MOUNTAIN in Rabun County. With an elevation of 2,990 feet, it is located east of Lake Burton.

CHARLTON COUNTY. Created February 11, 1854 with 799 square miles taken from part of Camden County. Named in honor of one of Georgia's foremost jurists, Robert Milledge Charlton (1807-1854), once mayor of Savannah, and later elected to the U. S. Senate in 1852. The county seat is Folkston (q.v.). Its courthouse was destroyed by fire at Traders Hill in 1877 and at Folkston in 1928. CHARLTON STREET in Savannah was also named in honor of Senator Charlton.

CHASTAIN, Thomas County. A rural community located near the northern border of the county. Early residents here were J. A. Chastain, a teacher, and B. E. Chastain, a farmer.

CHATHAM COUNTY. Pronounced "Chattum." Created February 5, 1777 with 441 square miles acquired by Creek cession of May 20, 1733. This was an original county, previously organized in 1758 as the parishes of SAINT PHILIP and CHRIST CHURCH. Named for the same individual as Pittsburgh,

Pennsylvania, William Lord Pitt, the Earl of Chatham (1708-1778), noted prime minister of England, who vigorously opposed the harsh measures taken with regard to the American colonies in 1774-75. The county seat is Savannah (q.v.). *See also* Savannah County.

CHATSWORTH, CS Murray County. Incorporated as a town August 18, 1906. Judge W. W. "Billy" Keith said that the name came about after the railroad came through, and a board or sign fell off of a freight car on which was printed the name "Chatsworth." It was placed on a pole by the tracks, and the place was thereafter known by this name. Chatsworth in England was the seat of the Duke of Devonshire in the county of Derby. Brinkley on the other hand said that the town was named for a railroad official.

CHATTAHOOCHEE, Fulton County. This former community was located on the Southern Railway where the present U. S. highway 78-278 crosses the river for which it was named. Before 1899, the place was called OAKDALE.

CHATTAHOOCHEE COUNTY. Created February 13, 1854 with 253 square miles taken from parts of Marion and Muscogee counties. Named for the river which forms its western border. The county seat is Cusseta (q.v.).

CHATTAHOOCHEE, LAKE, Clay, Quitman, and Stewart counties. Said to have been named by the state assembly of Georgia. Was formed by the Walter F. George Dam on the Chattahoochee River at Ft. Gaines. It is also called LAKE GEORGE, LAKE EUFALA, and WALTER F. GEORGE RESERVOIR (q.v.).

CHATTAHOOCHEE NATIONAL FOREST. Consists of nearly two million acres in twenty Georgia counties of the northern mountainous regions of the state. It was established in 1936 by proclamation of President Franklin D. Roosevelt, and took its name from the principle river of the area.

CHATTAHOOCHEE OLD TOWN, Heard County. This was an old Indian village which was located near the present town of Franklin, on the west bank of the river for which it was named, or possibly vice versa. John Goff found a 1738 map where it was spelled CHATAHUCHEE.

CHATTAHOOCHEE PALISADES STATE PARK, Cobb and Fulton counties. Comprises 377 acres along the Chattahoochee River north of Atlanta. Established with a $1.89 million grant from the U. S. Department of the Interior, September 26, 1972. Lieutenant General William T. Sherman crossed here with his Union troups in the Civil War.

CHATTAHOOCHEE PARK, Hall County. This former park was located on the former Lake Warner (q.v.).

CHATTAHOOCHEE RIVER. Pronounced locally, "Chatty-hoochee." This great river is about 560 miles in length, and originates in tributaries of Habersham, Towns, and Union counties. It was believed named for an early Indian town of CHAT-TO-HO-CHE which was located on the Chattahoochee River near today's town of Franklin. The name probably meant "Corn Rock," "Pounded Rock," "Meal Rock," or "Flour Rock," from *Uchee*, "corn" and *Hochee*, "pounded (or beaten)." It has also been said to be derived from the Indian words *Chatta*, "Sparkling," "Flowered," or "Marked," and *Ochee*, "Rocks." Benjamin Hawkins spelled it CHATTA HO CHEE. The French wrote it SCHATTAOUCHI and CHACTAS-OU-GUY. Other variations from old maps included: CATAHOOCHE, CHATTAHUCES, CHATAHOUCHY, CHATTA UCHEE, and CHATTY HOOCHIE. The Yuchi Indians called this river the TIAH.

CHATTANOOGA CREEK, Walker County. Flows northerly, on the east of Lookout Mountain, into Tennessee. Derived from the Muskogean, meaning "Rock-coming-to-a-point," probably referring to Lookout Mountain. CHATTANOOGA MOUNTAIN in Dade County and CHATTANOOGA VALLEY (Militia) DISTRICT in northwest Walker County were from the same derivation.

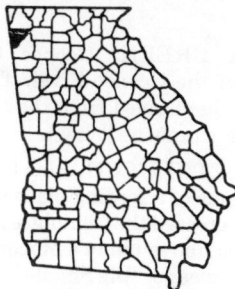

CHATTOOGA COUNTY. Created December 28, 1838 with 317 square miles taken from parts of Floyd and Walker counties. Named for the Chattooga River which flows through the middle of the county. The county seat is Summerville (q.v.).

CHATTOOGA LAKES STATE PARK, Chattoga County. Descriptively named, this new state park is located three miles southeast of Summerville on Marble Springs Road.

CHATTOOGA RIVER. Rises in Walker County and flows through Chattooga County, then continues southwesterly to join the Coosa River in Alabama. The name is from that of an early Cherokee Indian town of *Cha tu' gi,* which was located east of Clayton in South Carolina. The meaning is not known for sure, but some think it is derived from the Cherokee word, *Tsatu' gi,* which may mean "He drank by sips" or "He has crossed the stream and come out on the other side." John Mooney said it means, "Throw it out (away)." Others think it is a variation of the Cherokee word *Chatauga*, which means "chicken." Some variations of spelling have included CHATOOGA, CHATUGA, and CHATTUGIE. Another CHATTOOGA RIVER runs along the east border of Rabun County, and is an upper extension of the Savannah River; and its tributary, the WEST CHATTOOGA RIVER in eastern Rabun County. Was formerly called GUINEKELOKEE, an old Cherokee name of unknown meaning. CHATTOOGA was also the former name of LaFAYETTE (q.v.) in Walker County. Was incorporated as Chattooga and made county seat January 22, 1835.

CHATTOOGAVILLE, Chattooga County. A community in the southern part of the county, named for the Chattooga River (q.v.).

CHATUGE LAKE, Towns County. Extends from Hiawassee northwestward into North Carolina. For derivation, *see* Chattooga River.

CHAUGA CREEK, Oconee County. A tributary of the Oconee River. The name is thought to be derived from the Creek word, *chahki,* which means "shoal."

CHAUKEETHLUCCO, Bibb County. This was the name of a fording place where Toms Path (q.v.) crossed the Ocmulgee River about seven miles above today's Macon. The Muskogee word means, "Big Shoals," from, *chaki,* "shoals" and *thlako,* "big."

CHAU, KE THLUCCO. A former Indian town located upriver from Philpots old ferry in the big bend of the Chattahoochee River on the Heard-Troup county line. For derivation, *see* Chaukeethlucco.

CHAUNCEY, Dodge County. This town was incorporated September 11, 1883. Named in honor of Mr. Chauncey of New Hampshire, who promised to erect a church here, but died before it was accomplished.

CHEAP, Banks County. Another name for the former community of WILMOTS (q.v.).

CHEATHAM HILL, Cobb County. An elevation west of Marietta. Named for Confederate general, Benjamin Franklin Cheatham (1820-1886), whose division defended this site June 27, 1864.

CHECHERO (Militia) DISTRICT, Rabun County. Located in the southern part of the county. Named for a Cherokee settlement, CHEROCHEE (or CHICHEROHE), which was destroyed in the American Revolution.

CHEHA(W), Lee County. A former Indian village near the present town of Leesburg. It was also called CHE-RAW and AU-MUC-CUL-LA, and was the home of the Chehaw Indian tribe, for which it was named. Also named for these Indians was CHEHAW CREEK in southeastern Putnam County. This stream is now called JENKINS BRANCH. CHEHAW PATH was the name of an old trail that extended to northeast Putnam County from Toms Path in southwest Jones County. CHEHAW STATE PARK in

Lee County is located two miles northeast of Albany. This 586-acre park was named for the Chehaw Indians. *See also* Chiaha.

CHELOCCONENEAUHASSE. A Creek Indian name which means, "old horse path," and was commonly referred to as the LOWER CREEK TRADING PATH. It extended between Augusta to the Creek towns below today's Columbus.

CHENOCETAH MOUNTAIN. Habersham County. With an elevation of 1,829 feet, it is located just south of Mount Airy. A Cherokee Indian name of unknown meaning, which name was lost for several years when this was called GRIFFIN MOUNTAIN and TOWER MOUNTAIN.

CHEPUCKY. This former community was located on CHEPUCKY ISLAND in the southwest section of Okefenokee Swamp. This was the site of an old Indian town called CHEPUCKY-TO-LO-FA, which means "Chepucky's Town."

CHERAW, Lee County. A variation of CHEHAW (q.v.).

CHEROKEE COUNTY. Created December 21, 1830 and December 24 and 26, 1831 with a present area of 414 square miles. This was an original county which was acquired by Cherokee cession of December 29, 1835. When formed the county contained 6,900 square miles which was then occupied by the Cherokee Indians, and was therefore given this name. James Mooney said that the derivation of the Indian word *Cherokee* has no meaning in the Cherokee language, and its origin is uncertain, but various theories have been suggested. Some say it may mean "upland field," in reference to the topography of this tribe's vast homeland, extending through the southern states. Another theory is that it is from the Muskogee Indian word *tcikoli,* meaning "people of a different speech," or from the word *cheera,* meaning "fire," or *a-che- la,* "he takes fire." It has also been said it is from the Indian word *Tsalagi* or *Tsaragi,* to mean "Ancient Tobacco People." "Red Fire Men," "Children of the sun," or "Brave Men." Also it may have come from *Chiluk-ki,ki,* the name applied to the Cherokee Indians by the Choctaws, which means "Cave People." The English had spelled the name CHERAKAE (1674), or CHARAKEYS (1715), and the French wrote CHIAQUIS. TSA-LA-GI is the form used at present. The county seat is Canton (q.v.). The court house was destroyed by fire in 1865 and 1928. The community of CHEROKEE in Cherokee County was originally an Indian settlement, named SWEET WATER TOWN. This name has also been applied to a stream, CHEROKEE BRANCH in the CHEROKEE VALLEY located in Catoosa County, between White Oak Mountain on the west and CHEROKEE RIDGE on the east. In this same county is also found CHEROKEE SPRINGS, which was once a summer resort. CHEROKEE CORNER was located in Oglethorpe County, eight miles west of Lexington on Athens Road. It was established in the 1770's by colonial governors to regulate Indian trade. CHEROKEE MILLS is a community in Cherokee County, located eight miles southeast of Canton. CHEROKEE TRAIL is a mountain road in the southeast section of Dade County.

CHERRY LOG, Gilmer County. This is the name the Cherokee Indians gave to their old settlement here, nine miles northeast of Ellijay. CHERRY LOG (Militia) DISTRICT in the northeast section of the county was named after this early community.

CHESSER(S) ISLAND, Charlton County. Located about two miles southwest of Camp Cornelia (q.v.). Named after an early settler on this island in the Okefenokee Swamp, W. T. Chesser, who moved here from Tattnall County in 1858.

CHESTATEE, Forsyth County. This community located in the northeast section of the county was called ATSUNSTA TI YI by the Indians. The CHESTATEE RIVER is an upper tributary of the Chattahoochee River, which rises in Lumpkin County, runs between White and Habersham counties, and enters Lake Sidney Lanier in Hall County. The upper part of Lake Lanier is named CHESTATEE BAY. The Cherokee word *chestatee* means "pine torch place" or "place of the

lights," so named because the deer hunters used torches when hunting by the river at night.

CHESTER, Dodge County. Incorporated December 17, 1902. This town was founded about 1890 by Mr. June Williams and H. M. Hancock, and named for the town of Chester, New York.

CHESTNUT FLAT, Walker County. This rural community was so named because of the abundance of chestnut trees here when the early settlers arrived. There is also a community of CHESTNUT GAP, located five miles northeast of Blue Ridge in Fannin County.

CHESTNUT MOUNTAIN, Hall County. First known as PRICE MOUNTAIN, renamed for the early settler family of J. T. Chestnut.

CHIAHA, Floyd County. Also spelled ICHIAHA, TCHIAHA, and CHEHAW (q.v.). This was a Lower Creek town on the west bank of the Chattahoochee River. The Chiaha Indians had other villages on the Flint River. A town called CHIAHA, "where otters live," existed among the Cherokee Indians; this is the name that they had called their town at the site where ROME (q.v.) now stands.

CHICKAMAUGA, Walker County. This town is located on the west fork of the Chickamauga River. It was first called CRAWFISH SPRING after an Indian Chief Crawfish who lived here. Incorporated September 11, 1891, when the name of the place was changed to Chickamauga after the river of that name. It is located in CHICKAMAUGA (Militia) DISTRICT of upper Walker County.

CHICKAMAUGA RIVER. Flows through Catoosa, Walker, and Whitfield counties. It is pronounced "Chick-a-mog'a," or by old timers, "Chicky-mawgee." Early settlers were told by the Cherokee Indians that it means "River of Death," because of so much sickness and death from malaria and other fevers when they dwelt along its banks. It has been claimed by some that the name is from the Cherokee, *chacama,* "good," and *kah,* "place." Another interpretation is that it means "The dwelling place of the chief." The name is actually from the Muskogean *Tchiskamaga,* which means "To become filled with snags or roots," "Sluggish or dead water." A branch of the Cherokee Indians, known as the

Chickamaugas, inhabited five villages on the Tennessee River.

CHICKMAUGA AND CHATTANOOGA NATIONAL MILITARY PARK, Catoosa and Walker counties. Established August 19, 1890, it consists of 8,127 acres, part of which is in Tennessee. This is the oldest and largest national military park administered by the Federal government. In the Fall of 1863, more American lives were lost here than in any other battle in our history, when the casualties totaled about 18,000 killed, wounded, and mising out of 66,000 engaged.

CHICKASAWHATCHEE, Terrell County. Earlier known as Hortonville (1847). This community was named for the stream on which is is located. Incorporated as a village March 3, 1856 (Lee County).

CHICKASAWHATCHEE CREEK. Flows from Terrell County into Baker County where it enters the Flint River. Was formerly written CHICKASYHATCHY, which is a Hichiti Indian word meaning "Council House Creek," with reference to a council house, attracted by American folk-etymology to the name of the well-known Chickasaw Indian tribe (*See also* Chicken Road). CHICKASAWHATCHEE SWAMP in Baker County has also been written CHICKASAWHACHEE.

CHICKEN ROAD. Has also been called CHICKASAW INDIAN TRAIL. It extended from the Oconee River near Dublin, to Hartford on the Ocmulgee River in Pulaski County, and was orignally part of the Uchee Path (q.v.). It is thought to have been named after the Chickasaw Indians who had used this trail. They lived mostly in Mississippi and neighboring states, and were called "Chicazo" by DeSoto, and "Tchikasa" by the Creek Indians. *Chickasaw* may mean "rebellion," and refer to a separation of the Chickasaw Indians from the Creeks and Choctaws.

CHICOPEE, Hall County. Pronounced "Chick'-a-pee." This is a mill town below Gainesville. The Chicopee Manufacturing Company of Chicopee, Massachusetts established a mill on a 3,500-acre site here which was previously occupied by the Hall County Home and Farm. Chicopee was said to be the name of an Indian chief of a tribe from Canada that settled in the mountains of western Massachusetts. This is an Algonquian Indian word which may mean "swift water," or possibly "birch-bark place."

CHIEF McINTOSH LAKE, Indian Springs State Park (q.v.). Named after General William McIntosh, a half-breed Creek Indian chief, who was murdered by fellow Indians after he had signed away their remaining land to the white men in the Treaty of February 12, 1825. *See also* Coweta County.

THE CHIEFTAINS, Rome. Located in the Riverside community, on the banks of the Oostanaula River. This was an old Indian trading post, and the home of John Ridge, chief of the Cherokees. It was here that the U. S. - Cherokee Treaty was signed which removed the Cherokees to Oklahoma.

CHILDERS CREEK, McDuffie County. Was named for an early settler who lived near the stream.

CHILD TO(A)TERS CREEK, Dawson County. Named for a prominent full blood Cherokee who lived at the Big Savannah (q.v.) settlement. It is now called RUSSELLS CREEK (q.v.).

CHINA HILL, Telfair County. Located about six miles west of Jacksonville. The name of this community is derived from the numerous china trees which adorn the crest and brow of the nearby hill.

CHIPLEY, Harris County. Established about 1879-80, and named for railroad promoter, Colonel W. D. Chipley. It was incorporated in 1883. The original community here was named HOOD (q.v.). In 1958 the name of the town was changed from Chipley to PINE MOUNTAIN, which was thought to be a more attractive name to attract tourists.

CHISHOLM, Stewart County. Pronounced "Chizzum." Probably derived from a family name. This was the early name of RICHLAND (q.v.).

CHISSEHULCAH CREEK, Muscogee County. Enters the Chattahoochee River north of Columbus. This stream was mentioned by Benjamin Hawkins as CHUSETHLOCCO and CHISSE HULKUHA. It is thought to mean "Crawling Rat(s) Creek," or "Place of Bluebirds." The present name is ROARING CREEK.

CHOCTAHATCHEE CREEK. Rises in northwestern Sumter County and flows southwesterly to enter Kinchafoonee Creek in Webster County. Was probably first named from the Chatot tribe of Muskogee Indians with a later substitution from the name of the better known tribe, Choctaw.

CHOESTOE, Union County. This community is located seven miles southeast of Blairsville. The name is probably the same as "Choestea," from the Cherokee, *tsistu-yi,* "rabbit place."

CHOICE'S STORE, Gwinnett County. Was located 11 miles southwest of Lawrenceville. Settled in 1824 and named for postmaster John Choice.

CHOKEE, Lee County. This is a rural community in the northeast section of the county. The name is shortened from the Creek Indian word *Chokeefichickee,* with obscure derivation. It may mean "Rotunda raised on a mound." CHOKEE CREEK rises at Leslie in Sumter County and flows southward through Lee County to enter the Flint River below Lake Balckshear Dam.

CHOKEELIGA CREEK, Lee County. Located in the northwest section of the county. The name has also been spelled CHOKEELIGEE, and is of Muskogean origin, meaning "House there," with reference to a council house, or "Council House-stands-there."

CHOPPED OAK, Habersham County. An early Indian rendezvous where many Indian trails crossed, which was on a hill between Cornelia and Baldwin. This was where the Indians recorded trophies of battle by taking a gash in a great oak tree here, for every scalp taken. The Cherokee name of the site was DIGALU YATUNYI, "Where it is chopped (or gashed)." CHOPPED OAK CHURCH is about three miles east of Hollywood, Habersham County.

CHRIST CHURCH PARISH. Created January 11, 1758 when the colony was divided into eight parishes. This was the most populous, and included all of the present Chatham County and the adjacent islands. It was named for Christ Episcopal Church, the "mother church" of the colony, which was founded in 1733.

CHRISTMAS BRANCH, Stewart County. An upper tributary of Hannahatchee Creek which commences at the northwest edge of Richland. This name was first applied by surveyor John G. Scruggs when he recorded this stream on December 25, 1825. CHRISTMAS CREEK of Cumberland Island is a channel which enters the Atlantic Ocean at the upper end of the island.

CHRISTOPHER, Chattahoochee County.

A stop on the Central of Georgia Railway, three miles notheast of Cusseta. Named to complement a "sister city," Columbus.

CHULA, Tift County. The first post office of this community was named RUBY, and soon after changed to Chula, thought to be the Muskogean Indian name meaning "flowers." It has also been suggested by Stewart that this is a Muskogean word meaning "fox." Brinkley says the place was named for Chula Vista, California. Was incorporated as a town August 15, 1904 to August 1, 1906.

CHULAPOCCA. This is an obsolete name of the APALACHEE RIVER (q.v.), and may mean "Pine trunk (or stem)" or may mean "Fox Ball."

CHULIA, Floyd County. A former community southeast of Rome. Named for an old Cherokee warrior, Chulioa.

CHUPEE CREEK. This was an early name given to the present TOBESOFKEE CREEK (q.v.). The derivation is from the Creek Indian word *chapa,* "halfway."

CHURCH HILL, Marion County. A settlement 12 miles south of Buena Vista on Georgia 41. Was so named because of the many churches here.

CISCO, Murray County. A community located 14 miles north of Chatsworth. Named for the old Etowah Indian province of CHISCA, which name is from *Siskowit,* a Cherokee Indian word for a kind of a trout of an oily nature.

CLARK COLLEGE, Atlanta. Founded in 1869 by the Freedman's Aid Society of the Methodist Episcopal Church. Named in honor of Augusta Clark Cole, who contributed a large portion of the funds for its founding.

CLARKDALE, Cobb County. The Clark Thread Co. erected a mill here in 1932 and named the village in honor of the Clark family. This community is located within CLARKDALE (Militia) DISTRICT, northwest of Austell.

CLARKE COUNTY. Created December 5, 1801 from a portion of Jackson County. This is the smallest county in the state, comprising 125 square miles. It was named for Elijah Clarke (1733-1799) of North Carolina, a distinguished soldier of the Revolution, and the "Hero of Hornets Nest." He later served in the U.S. House of Representatives from Wilkes

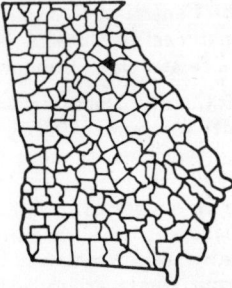

County. *See also* Elijah Clark (sic) State Park and Trans-Oconee Republic. The county seat is Athens (q.v.).

CLARKSBORO(UGH), Jackson County. This post office was established from 1813 to 1903, and was located seven miles southeast of Jefferson. It was the county seat of Jackson County from 1796 to 1802, and was named for Elijah Clarke (*see* Clarke County).

CLARKESVILLE, CS Habersham County. Incorporated as a village and made county seat November 26, 1823. Named for General John C. Clark (1776-1832) of North Carolina, son of the Revolutionary hero, Elijah Clarke. John Clark was governor of Georgia (1819-1823). *See also* Jack's Creek.

CLARK HILL DAM. Constructed by the U.S. Corps of Engineers beginning in 1946, on the Savannah River, 21 miles above Augusta. It is over one mile long, the concrete section being 2,282 feet in length. This dam created CLARK HILL RESERVOIR, including a lake 39 miles long on the Savannah River, 25 miles long on Georgia's Little River, and 17 miles long on South Carolina's Little River. The shore line extends 1,200 miles. The dam and reservoir were named for Elijah Clarke (*see* Clarke County). The town of Clarks Hill is on the South Carolina side of the dam.

CLARK'S MILL, Crawford County. A grist mill on Spring Creek five miles southeast of Knoxville. Was operated by E.S., J.B. and J.J. Clark in the 1880's, serving a community of reportedly 200 souls.

CLARKSTON, DeKalb County. This community northeast of Decatur opened a post office October 9, 1876, and was incorporated December 12, 1882. Named for Colonel W. W. Clark, prominent lawyer from Covington and director of The Georgia Railroad.

CLAXTON, Evans County. "Fruit Cake Capital" Incorporated as a city July 28, 1911.

It was first proposed to call the town Hendricks to honor the founding family here. Georgia at that time already had a post office by this name, so it was named for a popular actress of the time, Kate Claxton (1878-1924).

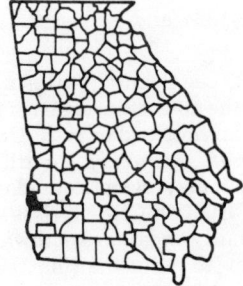

CLAY COUNTY. Created February 16, 1854 with 224 square miles taken from portions of Early and Randolph counties. Named for Henry Clay (1777-1852), Secretary of State, Speaker of the House of Representatives, and U. S. Senator from Kentucky. The county seat is Fort Gaines (q.v.).

CLAYTON, CS Rabun County. This site was selected as the county seat in 1821, with the name to be CLAYTONSVILLE in honor of Judge Augustin S. Clayton, who held the first sessions of the superior court of the county. December 13, 1823 the town was incorporated and made the county seat. At this time the name was shortened to Clayton. The land was acquired in 1824 from Solomon Beck to erect a court house. *See also* Clayton County.

CLAYTON COUNTY. Created November 30, 1858 with 149 square miles taken from parts of Fayette and Henry counties. Named after Augustin Smith Clayton (1783-1839), originally from Virginia, and a noted judge, who served in the House of Representatives from Clarke County, and was also elected to the State Senate. *See also* Clayton. The county seat is Jonesboro (q.v.).

CLAYTON JUNIOR COLLEGE, Morrow. Named for and established in 1968 by the Clayton County Board of Education. Opened in 1969.

CLEAR CREEK, DeKalb County. The post office of this name was in operation from 1831 to 1839, and was the third post office to be established in the county. It was located in the approximate area of Sherwood Forest subdivision, and was named for the stream which flows through Piedmont Park, and continues northward to enter Peachtree Creek. *See also* Mud Creek.

CLEOLA, Harris County. This community was established as a station on the Southern Railroad about 1887. Named by Mr. Jess Milner in honor of a girl friend.

CLERMONT, Hall County. Incorporated as a town August 11, 1913. Was settled in the late 1800's and first called DIP (q.v.). The present name of the town means "clear mountain" and was suggested by high school principal, "Professor" Will Johnson.

CLEVELAND, CS White County. Established in 1857 and incorporated as a town August 18, 1870. The early name of the community here was MT. YONAH after the prominent mountain nearby (*see* Brasstown Bald). The derivation of the present name is uncertain, but is thought to have been named in honor of Colonel Benjamin Cleveland (1738-1806), hero of King's Mountain.

CLIFTON MILLS, Miller County. A community, also called TWILIGHT, which was located six miles south of Colquitt. In the 1880's, J. S. Clifton ran a general store, gin, grist, and saw mills here. Only the Twilight Church remains.

CLIMAX, Decatur County. Originally called BAINBRIDGE JUNCTION, and changed to Climax in 1833 when the town was laid out. The post office was established January 31, 1902, and the town was incorporated August 11, 1905. The name is from the Greek word *klimax,* to describe the order of plants and animals in the natural environment.

CLINCH COUNTY. Created February 14, 1850 with 796 square miles taken from parts of Lowndes and Ware counties. Named in honor of General Duncan Lamont Clinch (1784-1849) of North Carolina, veteran of the

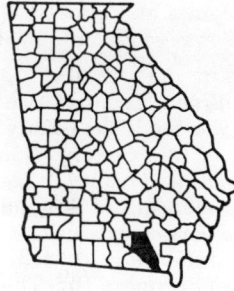

War of 1812 and the Indian wars in Florida during 1836-1838, and was elected to U. S. Congress in 1844. The county seat is Homerville (q.v.). The court house was destroyed by fires in 1846 and 1857.

CLINTON, Jones County. Incorporated as a town December 4, 1816. This community is located two miles south of Gray, and was originally called ALBANY (in 1808). Was designated the county seat in 1809 at which time the name was changed to Clinton in honor of Governor DeWitt Clinton (1768-1828) of New York. It was given this name by Revolutionary War veterans who first settled here, and were Masons wishing to honor Clinton, who was a Grandmaster. The county seat was moved to Gray in 1905. This was the site of the old CLINTON FEMALE ACADEMY, incorporated by the state December 15, 1821 and CLINTON FEMALE SEMINARY, founded in 1828 by Thomas B. Slade. Samuel Griswold came from Burlington, Connecticut about 1818 and established Georgia's first iron foundry here in 1820. This factory made more cotton gins than any place in the world. He moved to the site of Griswoldville (q.v.) in 1849 to be near the railroad. The town of Clinton died, partly from destruction by General Sherman's men, but mostly because the residents rejected having the railroad pass through the community.

CLOUDLAND, Chattooga County. A community located about two miles northwest of Menlo, named for a Savannah investor, A. C. Cloud.

CLOUDLAND CANYON STATE PARK, Dade County. Located twenty miles northwest of LaFayette in old Cherokee Indian territory. This 1,699-acre park takes its name from the descriptively named canyon here, also referred to as the "Grand Canyon of North Georgia." *See also* Sitton's Gulch.

CLYATT(E)VILLE, Lowndes County. This town was named for one of the first settlers here, Mr. James M. Clyatt. CLYATT MILL CREEK flows south into Withlacoochee Creek here.

CLYDE, Bryan County. Also known as EDEN, it was made the county seat at the beginning of this century. Named for Sir Colin Campbell (1792-1863) Lord Clyde, a noted field marshall of Scotland. The community no longer exists, although Clyde cemetery remains, located six miles northwest of Richmond Hill. The county seat is now Pembroke (q.v.). CLYDE CREEK of Bryan County flows into the Canoochee River just above Richmond Hill.

CLYO, Effingham County. The name of this community is a variant of Clio.

COAHULLA CREEK, Whitfield County. Rises at the north boundary of the county and flows southerly to enter the Conasauga River southeast of Dalton. The name is an Anglecized form of Ka' lahu, an old Cherokee chief known as All Bones, or may be a corruption of Cohutta (q.v.).

COAL MOUNTAIN, Forsyth County. This post office existed from March 8, 1834 to February 21, 1907. It is believed to have been named for some of the Cole family (sometimes spelled in early records as "Coal"), early settlers here.

COAT CREEK, Jefferson County. *See* GREAT COAT CREEK.

COBB COUNTY. Created December 3, 1832 with 346 square miles from part of Cherokee County. Most authorities state that it was named for Judge Thomas Willis Cobb (1784-1835) from Virginia, who served as colonel in the Revolutionary War, and later as a state congressman. Other sources have claimed the county was named for Colonel John Cobb, brother of Thomas Cobb, who followed him to

Georgia. The county seat is Marietta (q.v.). The court house was destroyed by fire in 1864.

COBBHAM, McDuffie County. This town was located about ten miles north of Thomson, and was the county seat of Columbia County when it was first cut off from Richmond County in 1790. The post office was established in the 1830's. It was named after Captain Thomas Cobb, officer of the Revolution who owned lands here.

COBBTOWN, Tattnall County. Incorporated as a town August 23, 1905. The post office of CORSICA (q.v.) was established here previously. It is not known for which Cobb family this town was named.

COBBVILLE, Telfair County. A community on Horse Creek, eleven miles southwest of McRae. It was formerly called CAMERON MILLS (q.v.).

COCHECALECHEE RIVER. This was shown as a tributary of the Chattahoochee River on early maps, but the exact location is not determined. The Creek Indian name means "broken arrow."

COCHRAN, CS Bleckley County. Incorporated March 19, 1869. Settled in the 1850's, it was originally named DYKESBORO (q.v.). When the railroad came through, the name was changed to honor the president of the Macon and Brunswick Railroad, Judge Arthur E. Cochran.

COCHRAN FIELD, Bibb County. This airport serving Macon and vicinity was built in 1941 and used as a basic flying training school in World War II. It was originally named for Lt. Robert James Cochran (1895-1918), who was killed while engaged in aerial combat with German planes near Toul, France. The present name is LEWIS B. WILSON AIRPORT (*see* Macon).

COCHRAN'S MILL, Mitchell County. A former station on the Seaboard Coast Line Railroad, six miles north of Camilla. Mr. G. C. Cochran operated a general store here as well as grist and saw mills. *See also* FLINT.

COCKSPUR FORT, Chatham County. A drawing of 1764 shows this fort at the entrance of the Savannah River on Cockspur Island (q.v.).

COCKSPUR ISLAND, Chatham County. Originally called PEEPER ISLAND (q.v.), it is also called LONG ISLAND (q.v.). Located near the mouth of the Savannah River, it is the island on which Fort Pulaski (q.v.) is located. It is called "Cockspur" because of the shape of the reef which points toward the sound.

COE, Tattnall County. A post office (c.1900) which was located 13 miles southeast of Reidsville. The name is from the Choctaw, *coi,* "panther."

COFACHIQUI, Richmond County. Sometimes spelled COFITACHEQUI (q.v.). This was an old Creek Indian town on Silver Bluff (q.v.), about 25 miles down the Savannah River from Augusta. Was the name of an Indian chief or possibly an Indian princess, or may mean "Dogwood Town." The name was shown on the Sanson map of 1656, which plotted DeSoto's explorations.

COFAQUI, Baldwin County. This was the Indian town where DeSoto and his men were so royally entertained. It is believed to have been at the site of the later Oconee Town (q.v.). The village is thought to have been located on the east bank of the Oconee River about six miles south of Milledgeville near Rock Landing (q.v.). Derivation of the name is unknown.

COFFEE BLUFFS, Chatham County. Located on the Little Ogeechee River near Vernonburg. Was believed named for the Coffee family here.

COFFEE COUNTY. Created February 9, 1854 with 613 square miles taken from Clinch, Irwin, Telfair, and Ware Counties. Named for General John E. Coffee (1782-1836), soldier of the War of 1812 and the Creek War, and later elected to both houses of the state legislature. This part of the state is known as the Wiregrass Region (q.v.). The county seat is Douglas (q.v.). The court house was destroyed by fires in 1898 and 1938. Also named for

General Coffee is the community of COFFEE in southeast Bacon County.

COFFEE ROAD. Authorized in 1822, and named for General John Coffee of Telfair County, who supervised its construction. This was a major stage coach and mail route which began at Jacksonville in Telfair County and wound southwestward toward the Florida line.

COFITACHEQUI, Richmond County. Also spelled COFACHIQUI (q.v.). This was said to be the fabled Indian city of gold for which DeSoto was searching in the 1540's.

COHELEE CREEK, Early County. It is now spelled CAHALEE CREEK. The Creek Indian name may possibly mean "Standing Cane," but more likely it means "Good Cane Creek," or possibly "Good Cane Place." Brinkley says it is a short form of COCHECALECHEE, which became known as "broken arrow."

COHUTTA, Whitfield County. This community near the Tennessee line was incorporated for ten years, beginning December 3, 1895. The Cherokee Indian name *cohutta* means "frog," or may mean "a shed roof supported on poles," from *gahuta yi.* The same name is applied to the COHUTTA MOUNTAINS in Gilmer County, sometimes called THE GREAT SMOKIES. COHUTTA MOUNTAIN in Murray County is located in the southwest section of Fort Mountain State Park, and its peak is 2,716 feet above sea level. MOUNT COHUTTA in Fannin County is 5,155 feet in elevation. There was once an active community of COHUTTA SPRINGS in northern Murray County, located on the Conasauga River.

COLAPARCHEE CREEK. Rises at Bolingbroke in Monroe County and flows into northwest Bibb County, after which it enters Rocky Creek. The name is derived from the Creek root word *kalapi,* to produce the translation, "White oak tree Creek." However another source interprets the name to mean "Seven Creek," the number of streams to be crossed to reach a principal Indian town. COLAPARCHEE has been said to be an early name of the community of BOLINGBROKE (q.v.) as well as that of a plantation near there, and also the name of a road in northwest Bibb County. The name has also been spelled COLOPARCHEE.

COLBERT, Madison County. This town was incorporated under the name FIVE FORKS December 8, 1899 and changed to Colbert August 11, 1909. Derivation of this name is unknown.

COLDWATER, Elbert County. This rural community is located north of Elberton, and has been settled for over 200 years. It was named after the old Coldwater Methodist Church here. The church was named for nearby COLDWATER CREEK, which rises in Hart County and flows south into Elbert County, then goes into the Savannah River east of Ruckersville.

COLE CITY, Dade County. This town was incorporated in 1873. The name is a corruption of the word "coal" in reference to the Dade County Coal Co. here.

COLEMAN, Randolph County. Incorporated as a town October 23, 1889. Derivation is unknown.

COLEMAN POND, Irwin County. Located in the northwest corner of the county, in the Third District. It was named for a Mr. Coleman who owned the pond in the early days.

COLEMAN'S LAKE, Emanuel County. Incorporated as a city March 4, 1953. The community was named for the lake of the same name which is backwater from the Ogeechee River. This is now a campground owned by brothers Heyward and O. T. Fulghum.

COLEOTCHEE CREEK, Talbot County. A tributary of Big Lazar Creek, it rises southeast of Manchester, and flows easterly. The name is from the creek, *kala,* "white oak," and *hachi,* "creek."

COLERAIN(E), Camden County. Located seven miles west of the present town of Kingsland, it was established December 1, 1786 by traders James Armstrong and James Seagrove. This was an important early settlement of Camden County, and was the site of Fort Pickering (q.v.). It was previously a Spanish settlement, and before that an Indian town, having been named for the Indian chief Coleraine. However, Brinkley says the name comes from Ireland. This former trading town was supplanted by Center Village (q.v.) about six miles north of here, but it too no longer exists.

COLLEGEBORO, Bulloch County. This former post office was named after Georgia Southern College, located on the south side of Statesboro.

COLLEGE PARK, Fulton County. Established in 1890 as the suburban town of MANCHESTER, which was incorporated October 5, 1891. When Cox College (q.v.) was moved here from LaGrange, it was decided to change the name of the town to College Park, which was approved December 16, 1895.

COLLEGE TEMPLE, Newnan. Started as a college for women in 1853. It was chartered in 1854 by Moses and Harriett Kellogg from Vermont. The school closed in 1888, but the remaining building yet stands at 73 College Street.

COLLIER (STATION), Monroe County. Also called COLLIERS. This former community was located five miles west of Forsyth on the Central of Georgia Railroad. Was named for Cuthbert Collier, who came here from Virginia in the eighteenth century.

COLLINS, Tattnall County. Named for Perry Collins, a prominent citizen, this town was incorporated April 9, 1894.

COLLINSVILLE, DeKalb County. A community located one mile east of Lithonia. Incorporated as a town October 24, 1887. Derivation is unknown.

COLOMOKEE CREEK, Clay County. This is the alternate spelling of KOLOMOKI CREEK (q.v.).

COLOMOKEE (Militia) DISTRICT, Early County. The name is a variant of Kolomoki (q.v.).

COLONEL'S ISLAND, Liberty County. This island was previously known as HERON, and also BERMUDA before given its present name. It is located near the mouth of the Midway River, and believed named for Colonel Heron who received a grant of land here in 1748. There are others who claim it was named for both Colonel James Maxwell and a Colonel Law.

COLOPARCHEE CREEK, Monroe and Bibb counties. A variation in spelling of COLAPARCHEE CREEK (q.v.).

COLQUITT, CS Miller County. Established as the county seat in 1856. Incorporated as a town December 19, 1860 and as a city in 1905. Was named in honor of Senator Walter Colquitt. *See* Colquitt County.

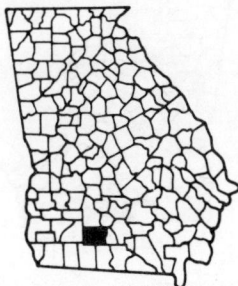

COLQUITT COUNTY. Created February 25, 1856 with 563 square miles taken from Lowndes and Thomas counties. Named for Virginia-born, Walter Terry Colquitt (1799-1855), a Methodist preacher, attorney, judge, and then U. S. Senator from Georgia. The county seat is Moultrie (q.v.). The court house was destroyed by fire in 1881.

COLUMBIA COUNTY. Created December 10, 1790 with 290 square miles taken from Richmond County. Named for the great navigator and discoverer of the Western Hemisphere, Christopher Columbus (c. 1446-1506). The county seat was first at Cobbham (q.v.) and is now Appling (q.v.).

COLUMBIA THEOLOGICAL SEMINARY, Decatur. Established by the Presbyterian Church in Lexington, Georgia in 1828. Moved to Columbia, South Carolina in 1830, move from which it derived its name. In 1924, it was decided to bring the school back to Georgia, this time to the Atlanta metropolitan area.

COLUMBUS, CS Muscogee County. "The South's Oldest Industrial City," also called "The Fountain City." Incorporated December 24, 1828. The city and county were consolidated January 1, 1971. Was built on a plain at the head of navigation on the Chat- tahoochee River, two miles from Coweta Town (q.v.). The city was laid out July 10, 1828, by Methodist minister and surveyor, Edward Lloyd Thomas, who also planned the town of Oxford in Newton County. On December 24, 1827 it was officially determined that the proposed town here was to be named Columbus in honor of the immortal navigator. At Broadway and Fourth is the Oglethorpe Marker, a boulder to commemorate General Oglethorpe's visit to Coweta Town in the summer of 1739. *See also* Koockogey. COLUMBUS COLLEGE in Columbus is a part of the University System of Georgia, and was established in 1958.

COMER, Madison County. Incorporated as a town December 13, 1893. Named for the settler family of A. J. Comer.

COMMERCE, Jackson County. Incorporated in 1884. The post office opened in 1825 when the community was called HARMONY GROVE. The name used before that was GROANING ROCK (q.v.). When cotton production thrived in the state, this became a center for buying cotton and was an active trade center. The name was changed to Commerce August 6, 1904 to suggest its commercial dominance.

COMMISSIONER, Jones County. Formerly the railroad name of McINTYRE (q.v.).

COMMISSIONER CREEK. Rises in Jones County and flows through Wilkinson County to the Oconee River. Named in honor of the commissioner who arranged for the acquisition of the lands here from the Indians.

CONASAUGA LAKE, Murray County. Located 15 miles northwest of Ellijay, this 25-acre lake at 3,200 feet elevation is the highest body of water in Georgia. CONASAUGA RIVER is pronounced locally "Conny-Sawgee." Has also been spelled CONNASAUGA. It rises in northwest Fannin County to enter Tennessee before flowing south to form the border between Murray and Whitfield counties, then enters Gordon County before flowing into the Coosawattee River northeast of Calhoun. The Cherokee word *Conasauga* was used as the name of several ancient settlements in Tennessee and Georgia. The derivation of the name is from the Cherokee, *kahnasagah,* "grass." *See also* Gansagi and Connesauga.

CONCORD, Pike County. Incorporated as a town October 24, 1887. Named after the Concord Primitive Baptist Church, which was deeded in 1833, and built here about 1842. The community center shifted to here from the nearby hamlet of Hard Head, and grew up around Isaac Strickland's store.

CONEY, Crisp County. Incorporated as a town November 7, 1889, at which time the name was changed from the former, GUM CREEK. The community is located five miles west of Cordele. It was either named for Ordinary, Judge S. W. Coney, or less likely was named from the Choctaw Indian word, *konih,* "skunk."

CONNESAUGA, Gilmer County. A former post office located nine miles northwest of Ellijay (1901). A map of 1887 shows a post office of CONNESAUGA located 12 miles north of Spring Place in Murray County. The name is a variant of Conasauga (*see* Conasauga River for derivation.)

CONNESENA CREEK, Bartow County. Flows southerly into the Etowah River just west of Kingston. The Cherokee name is from *Cunsena,* the name of a family that lived in the area, and the word means "dragging canoe."

CONSTITUTIONAL COUNTIES. This term refers to the eight counties which were created in the State's first formal constitution in 1777: Burke, Camden, Chatham, Effingham, Glynn, Liberty, Richmond, and Wilkes.

CONYERS, CS Rockdale County. Incorporated as a town February 16, 1854. In 1843-44, the Georgia Railroad was laying track through this community which was then known as ROCKDALE, and was unable to acquire the property of the blacksmith, Mr. Holcombe, for the station. A banker from Covington, a Dr. Conyers then bought the necessary site for the railroad station and the right of way, whereupon the railroad named the stop CONYERS STATION in his honor.

COOGLE'S MILL, Macon County. A former community which was located eight miles west of Oglethorpe on Buck Creek where Joseph M. Coogle was a millwright.

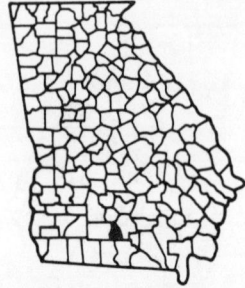

COOK COUNTY. Created July 30, 1918 with 226 square miles taken from Berrien County. Named in honor of General Philip Cook (1817-1894), a native Georgian who was a lawyer, soldier, state senator and secretary of state. The county seat is Adel (q.v.).

COOKSVILLE, Heard County. A community located seven miles southwest of Franklin. In 1881 the postmaster was J. D. Cook.

COOLIDGE, Thomas County. Incorporated December 10, 1901. Established in 1900 as a rail stop on the old Tifton, Thomasville and Gulf Railroad, and was named for its president.

COOLEEWAHEE CREEK, Baker County. Unites with the Flint River at Newton. The probable meaning of the Muskogean name is, "White-oak-acorns are scattered."

COOPER, Jackson County. A former post office of which Thomas Cooper was the postmaster from July 26, 1882 to April 24, 1883. The name of the post office was changed to the present NICHOLSON (q.v.) February 2, 1882.

COOPER'S CREEK, Fannin County. Flows southerly into the Toccoa River near the Union County line. Named for early (1698) traders, William and Joseph Cooper.

COOPERVILLE, Screven County. A former community which was located 12 miles southwest of Sylvania. Established about 1790 by William Cooper. Holingsworth said it was named for the early settlers, the first of which was George Cooper, father of congressman Wilson Cooper. Brinkley said it was named for George Washington Cooper, inventor of the Cooper plow.

COOSA, Floyd County. First known as MISSIONARY STATION, after a Baptist mission established here in 1821 by Rev. and Mrs. Elijah Butler. Later he was imprisoned by authorities and then run out of the state. The present name is for the river on which this community is situated.

COOSA CREEK, Union County. A former community located 4½ miles southwest of Blairsville, which was named for the stream which flows north from here into Nottely Lake. For derivation, *see* Coosa River.

COOSA OLD TOWN, Floyd County. This was an Indian village on the Coosa River near the present Rome. It was destroyed on or about October 17, 1793 by General John Sevier, an early governor of Tennessee, who was called Nollichucky Jack by the Cherokee Indians.

COOSA RIVER. The major portion of this waterway of which is in Alabama, begins at Rome in Georgia, where the Oostanaula and Etowah Rivers join. It has also been spelled KOOSA RIVER in the past. The name may be derived from the Abikha or Coosa (Kusa) Indian tribe of the Creek Confederation, or from the town by this name on the river. It has also been asserted that the name is a Muskogean Indian word meaning "cane" or "canebrake."

COOSAWATTEE, Murray County. This was an early community, named from its location on the Coosawattee River (q.v.). The place is now called CARTERS (q.v.).

COOSAWATTEE (Militia) DISTRICT, Gordon County. Located in the northeast corner of the county, and named after the Coosawattee River.

COOSAWATTEE OLD TOWN, Murray County. This was once a busy Indian settlement located on the Coosawattee River. It has been suggested that the Cherokee Indian name *Coosawattee* (or *Kusawetiyi*) means "Old Creek Place."

COOSAWATTEE RIVER. Has also been spelled COOSEWATTEE, its probable meaning is "River of the Coosas." The lower portion was once labeled ELLIJAY RIVER. The Coosawattee River rises at Ellijay in Gilmer County, flows southwestward into southeast Murray County, forms part of the border on northern Gordon County and winds its way southwesterly to be joined by the Conasauga River northeast of Calhoun to form the Oostanaula River.

CORDELE, CS Crisp County. Pronounced "Cor deal'." Called "The Hub City" and also the "Watermelon Capital of the World." Founded in 1888 by J.E.D. Shipp from Americus, and was incorporated December

22, 1888. Named after Miss Cordelia Hawkins, eldest daughter of Colonel Samuel H. Hawkins, who was president of the Savannah, Americus and Montgomery Railroad.

CORDRAY, Calhoun County. A former community located seven miles north of Leary on Ichawaynochaway Creek. Named for the general store and post office of J. A. Cordray.

CORINTH, Heard County. Incorporated as a town December 21, 1839. This community is located ten miles southeast of Franklin. This meeting of the highways was named for the famous cross-roads city of Corinth, Greece.

CORK, Butts County. This community is located eight miles southeast of Jackson. It was named for the city of this name in Ireland.

CORNELIA, Habersham County. "Home of the Big Red Apple" Incorporated October 22, 1887. The community of BLAINE was first settled here when the Charlotte Air-Line Railroad was graded through this section about 1872. After this the stop was called RABUN GAP JUNCTION in 1882. A few years later, an attorney for the railroad, Judge Pope Barrow secured a depot for the town, which was then named in honor of his wife Cornelia. This is the state's largest apple growing center.

CORNISH CREEK, Gwinnett County. This is a tributary of the Alcovy River. Goff said it was possibly named for an early squatter or "trespasser" who once lived here.

CORNUCOPIA, Jones County. The name is from the Latin, meaning "Horn of Plenty." This former community, previously called GRAB ALL, was located at the extreme northwest corner of the county.

CORSICA, Tattnall County. A former post office, probably named for the Corsica pine tree *(pinus laricio)*. The place is now called COBBTOWN (q.v.).

COTTON, Mitchell County. Established in 1899, this community was incorporated as a town August 11, 1913. Was first called MAPLETON after Gid Maples who had an estate here, but that name was already in use in Georgia. It was then decided to call it Cotton, because it was believed that the soil was adaptable for production of this crop.

COTTON RIVER, Henry County. Derivation is possibly from a previous Indian name of PANALAHATCHEE, meaning

"Cotton River." This is in reality a large creek, and presently called BIG COTTON INDIAN CREEK. It rises in the northern section of the county and flows southeasterly until reaching the South River, which forms the boundary between Henry and Newton counties. A former community of COTTON RIVER was located 6½ miles north of McDonough.

COUNCIL, Clinch County. A community located six miles southeast of Fargo. Established in the early 1900's with the large saw mill, called American Mfg. Co., owned by John M. and C. C. Council of Americus.

COUPER'S POINT, St. Simons Island. Located across the Hampton River from Butler Point (q.v.). The ruin of a tabby slave cabin here, which was built by a Mr. Couper or James Hamilton, has been alleged to be a Spanish ruin.

COURTESY, Floyd County. The early name of SIX MILE (q.v.).

COVENANT COLLEGE, Lookout Mountain. This Presbyterian coeducational institution was established in 1955 in what was an inn called Castle in the Clouds, previously Lookout Mountain Hotel. The word *covenant* means "a solemn vow to defend and support the faith and doctrine of the church."

COVINGTON, CS Newton County. "City of Beautiful Homes" Incorporated as a town December 6, 1822, and as a city in 1854. The original community was called NEWTONSBORO(UGH) (q.v.) and then given its present name in honor of General Leonard Covington (1768-1813), distinguished at Fort Recovery in 1794, and was a U. S. congressman from Maryland. The Covington post office was established in 1828.

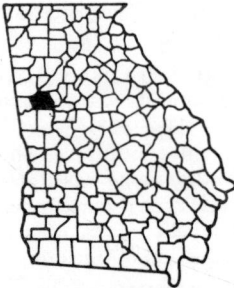

COWETA COUNTY. Pronounced "Coweeta" or "Kie-eeta." Created June 9, 1825 and December 11, 1826 with 443 square miles acquired by Creek cessions of January 24, 1826 and March 31, 1826. Named Coweta to perpetuate the fame of the head chief of the Coweta Indians, General William McIntosh, half-blood Creek Indian (*see* McIntosh Old Place). *Coweta* may mean "falls" or "where there are falls," from the falls on the Chattahoochee River at present-day Columbus, Georgia. The county seat is Newnan (q.v.).

COWETA TOWN, Muscogee County. Called "The Red War Town." This was the name of the old Muskogee Indian village at the site of the present COLUMBUS (q.v.). French maps of 1733 showed the name as CAOUITA and COUITA. Maps dated 1818 had it written COWETAU or KAWITA. A map of 1825 spelled the name COWETAW.

COW HELL, Laurens County. This name was applied to a dense swamp in the upper section of the county along the east side of the Oconee River at the mouth of Buckeye Creek. Named for the treacherous bogs encountered by cattle that ventured into this bovine Hades.

COWHOUSE ISLAND, Ware County. Located at the northeast corner of Okefenokee Swamp. It was said to have been given this name during the War Between the States, because the neighboring stockmen drove their cattle here when the Union forces were foraging on the land. Another source claims the island was named by the early settlers who drove their cattle here for the winter months.

COWPEN (or MUSGROVES COWPEN), Chatham County. This was the descriptive designation applied to the later WHITEHALL PLANTATION when Mary Musgrove kept cattle here (her Indian name was Coosaponakee). This plantation was later called GRANGE (q.v.).

COWPEN CREEK, Washington County. Located in the northern section of the county, and originally called JONES COWPEN CREEK. John Goff found this to be one of the oldest English place-names west of the Ogeechee River. Presumably it was named for a squatter or Indian countryman named Jones who set up a cowpen on it in the mid-Eighteenth Century.

COWPENS, Walton County. Also known as EASLEY'S COWPENS, this was temporarily the county seat when Walton County was first formed in 1818. It was located three miles south of Monroe. Named after "Colonel" Roderick Easley who kept cattle pens here. In 1912, the name was changed to PANNELL (q.v.).

COX COLLEGE. Founded in LaGrange in 1843, and first called LA GRANGE FEMALE SEMINARY. The campus was moved near Atlanta in 1895 where it was first known as SOUTHERN FEMALE COLLEGE. It was later named COX FEMALE COLLEGE in honor of its president, I.F. Cox. After continuing at its College Park (q.v.) location until 1923, it closed to reopen again in 1932. The city hall, library, and auditorium are on the site of the old campus.

COX (Militia) DISTRICT, Monroe County. Located just southwest of Forsyth. Named for the family of Frances R. Cox (1821-1911), wife of wheelwright Henry Rumble (1815-1889).

COXES (Militia) DISTRICT, Cobb County. Located just northeast of Austell. Was created in 1836 with elections being held at the house of Robert R. Cox.

COX'S CROSSROAD, Atlanta. This was the early name of the intersection of Moore's Mill and Howell Mill roads. Named for Carr Cox, who was postmaster in 1881 of HOWELL'S MILL post office here.

CRABAPPLE. Fulton County. "Garden Spot of North Fulton." This community above Roswell was established in 1874 when a log cabin school house was built beside a knarled crabapple tree.

CRACKERS NECK, Greene County. This post office in the lower part of the county in the 1830's was thought to have referred to "Crackers" who had a hard time making a living here.

"CRACKER STATE." A long time nickname of Georgia. The word "Cracker" is a corruption of a common term used anciently in Scotland to designate a certain yeomanry class of independents who were obnoxious to the aristocracy. There are also authorities who regard it as a shortened form of corncracker, which refers to the fact that cracked corn was long the chief article of food among the poor whites and hill dwellers of the South.

CRANE-EATER, Gordon County. This was the early name of the present community of RED BUD (q.v.), and was given the original

name after CRANE-EATER CREEK nearby. The stream is believed to be named from a Cherokee Indian that lived in the vicinity.

CRANE'S HILL, Lumpkin County. Located in east Dahlonega, it was named for Stephen D. Crane, who was a prominent lawyer here.

CRAVEN'S ISLAND, Charlton County. Also called OLD ISLAND, it is located about five miles north of Stephen Foster State Park in the Okefenokee Swamp. Was discovered by John Craven, a famous hunter and trapper of the swamp, who lived at nearby Hickory Hammock. Also named for him is nearby CRAVEN'S HAMMOCK.

CRAWFISH CREEK, Walker County. Arises three miles above LaFayette and flows northerly to enter Chickamauga Creek. Also spelled CRAYFISH, the name is derived from the Cherokee word, *Tsistuna'yi* meaning "crayfish place."

CRAWFORD, Oglethorpe County. Incorporated February 28, 1876. This town was previously named LEXINGTON DEPOT, later changed to honor William H. Crawford (*see* Crawford County).

CRAWFORD COUNTY. Created December 9, 1822 with 313 square miles taken from Houston County. Named for Virginia-born William Harris Crawford (1772-1834), who became president of the U. S. Senate, Minister to Paris, Secretary of the Treasury, and candidate for the President in 1824. The county seat is Knoxville (q.v.). The courthouse was destroyed by fire in 1829. There is a CRAWFORD MEMORIAL of granite in the town of Crawford (q.v.), and also CRAWFORD SQUARE in Savannah was named in honor of Senator Crawford. *See also* WILLIAM H. CRAWFORD HIGHWAY.

CRAWFORDVILLE, CS Taliaferro County. Was named in honor of William H.

Crawford (see Crawford County). Located here is Liberty Hall which was the home of Alexander Stephens, vice president of the Confederacy (see Alexander H. Stephens State Park).

CRESCENT, McIntosh County. A community located 11 miles north of Darien on Georgia 99. Named for the crescent or bend made by the inlet of the Atlantic Ocean.

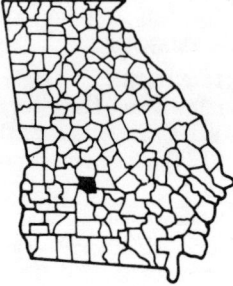

CRISP COUNTY. "Empire County of the Empire State of the South" Created August 17, 1905 with 296 square miles taken from part of Dooly County. Named in honor of Charles Frederick Crisp (1845-1896), who was born in Sheffield England of American parents. He was a soldier, judge, actor, producer of plays, state senator, and was elected to the U. S. Congress where he became Speaker of the House. The county seat is Cordele (q.v.).

CROMER'S, Franklin County. This community is located six miles south of Carnesville on Georgia 106. In 1881, J. D. Cromer had gin, grist, and saw mills here.

CROOKED RIVER, Camden County. Descriptively named in reference to its winding course. CROOKED RIVER STATE PARK, Kingsland. This 500-acre park is named from the river on which it is located. Other streams descriptively named CROOKED CREEK are found in eastern Putnam County and in Jackson-Banks counties.

CROSS KEYS, DeKalb County. A post office of this name was established in 1832 at the site of the present CHAMBLEE. The name "Cross Keys" originated on the sign of an inn. The name CROSS KEYS was also given to a northeast Bibb County suburban town, which is now a part of Macon.

CROSS PLAINS, Whitfield County. Incorporated as a town in 1839. The name was

changed to DALTON (q.v.) in 1847 when this was made the county seat.

CROSSROADS, Bryan County. This descriptively named community is now called RICHMOND HILL (q.v.). The county seat was moved here from Hardwick (q.v.) in 1797. CROSSROADS was also an early name of LITHONIA (q.v.) in DeKalb County. It was also called GEORGE'S STORE.

CRYSTAL MOUNTAIN, DeKalb County. An early name of STONE MOUNTAIN (q.v.).

CUBA, Early County. This community located six miles southeast of Blakely was named for the Caribbean island by this name. It is in the CUBA (Militia) DISTRICT. Of the same derivation was CUBANA CITY near Thomasville in Thomas County, which was incorporated December 20, 1893.

CUFITACHIQUI. An alternate spelling of COFITACHIQUI (q.v.).

CULLODEN, Monroe County. The town was first settled about 1739 when this was a junction of Indian trails from Columbus to Indian Springs and Alabama to Augusta. Was named in honor of William Culloden, a Scotch Highlander who opened a store here in 1780. The Methodist Church here, built in 1893, is the denomination's oldest ·brick church in Georgia.

CULPEPPER CREEK, Crawford County. Formerly called INTACHCOOCHEE CREEK (q.v.).

CULVERTON, Hancock County. A community located five miles northeast of Sparta on the Georgia Railway. Originally called MOUNT CARMEL, it was later changed to honor pioneer settler Hardy Culver who came here about 1835.

CUMBERLAND, Camden County. This community was located twenty miles northeast of St. Marys on Cumberland Island (q.v.) for which it was named.

CUMBERLAND ISLAND, Camden County. About 24,000 acres in size, it is the southernmost and largest of the Golden Isles. The Indians called the island MISSOE, WISSOO, or WISO (pronounced "why-so"), meaning "sassafras." It was named SAN PEDRO (St. Peter) by the Spaniards. General Oglethorpe changed the name to Cumberland at the request of Toonahawi, the nephew of Tomochichi, who wished to honor the young Duke of Cumberland, a brother of King

George II, who had presented the little Indian boy a gold watch during his visit to England. Other early names were HIGHLANDS, ISLE OF WHALES, and ST. ANDREW. On October 23, 1972 President Nixon signed a bill to make the semitropical island a national seashore. *See also* Little Cumberland Island, Dungeness, and Fort William.

CUMBERLAND PLATEAU. Also called LOOKOUT PLATEAU, it generally includes the area of Dade County. Named after the Cumberland Mountains of Tennessee.

CUMBERLAND RIVER, Camden County. This waterway lies inland from the north section of Cumberland Island.

CUMBERLAND SOUND, Camden County. This waterway lies inland from the south section of Cumberland Island.

CUMMING CS Forsyth County. Incorporated December 22, 1834 at which time it was designated the county seat. The post office was established here January 13, 1834. Was named for Colonel William Cumming of Augusta, a distinguished lawyer and editor, who fought a duel with the celebrated George McDuffie of South Carolina. CUMMING was also the previous name of the community of BARNETT in northwest Warren County.

CUNNINGHAM STORE, Jackson County. This post office, established from 1828 to 1845, was named for the first postmaster, Joseph T. Cunningham.

CURRAHEE MOUNTAIN, Stephens County. Located four miles southwest of Toccoa, with an elevation of 1,740 feet. The derivation is from the Cherokee Indian name *gurahiyi,* which means "water cress place" or may mean "standing alone." There was at one time an Indian settlement in eastern Habersham County called CURRAHEE.

CURRY'S CREEK, Jackson County. Rises in Jefferson, flows southeasterly, then easterly to enter the Oconee River. This stream was formerly called TOBSKESOFESKEE or TOBESOFOSKEE *(see* Tobesofkee Creek).

CURRYVILLE, Gordon County. This community is located on Georgia 156 near the Floyd County line. Originally named LITTLE ROW, after the little row of houses first built here, or possibly LITTLE ROE, for an Indian chief. It was then named after David W. Curry, a wholesale druggist of Rome, who suggested his own name to the postmaster.

CURTWRIGHT FACTORY, Greene County. Also known as LONG SHOALS FACTORY, this cotton mill town was established in the 1840's, 13 miles south of Greensboro on the Oconee River. The Curtwright Factory post office was opened in 1860, but the community declined soon afterward.

CUSSETA, CS Chattahoochee County. Was made the county seat and laid out, April 10, 1854 and incorporated as a town December 22, 1855. Named at the suggestion of William G. Wooldridge, and is derived from the Muskogean *Kashihta,* meaning a "Trading Place." CUSSETA TOWN was the name of the "White Peace Town" which was located on the Chattahoochee River, at the site of Fort Benning's Lawson Field, and was the largest trading town of the Muskogee Indians. The naturalist William Bartram called it USSETA.

CUTHBERT, CS Randolph County. Was incorporated and made county seat December 26, 1831. Named in honor of Colonel John Alfred Cuthbert (1788-1881) of Baldwin County, editor, jurist, and elected to the U. S. House of Representatives. He was a soldier in the War of 1812.

(THE) CUT OFF, Macon County. This section of farm land was originally part of Sumter County, with Camp Creek as the dividing line. The inhabitants in 1851 petitioned the state legislature to "cut off" that corner to be added to Macon County, so they would be closer to the county seat when on jury duty. This locality was first settled in the 1830's by Mr. and Mrs. Jim M. Wicker from South Carolina. There was also a post office in old Milton County named CUT OFF.

CUTTINGBONE CREEK, Rabun County. Located about four miles southeast of Clayton. The name is possibly from the Cherokee Indian word for "scratcher" referring to a ceremonial scratching device made of bone. Brinkley said the name refers to an Indian rite in which warriors cut the calves of their legs with a sharp bone. But more likely it is a corruption of the possible early names used of Crittingtons or Crittentons Creek. George R. Stewart points out that Crittington was the name of a Cherokee-English family.

CYCLONETA, Tift County. Originally this site was known as IRBY. The Southern Railway adopted this railroad station name of Cycloneta after a cyclone struck the lumber yards here during the late 1800's. The com-

munity has since changed to its present
commendatory name of SUNSWEET (q.v.).
There was also a place called CYCLONE in
northern Screven County.

CYCLORAMA, Grant Park, Atlanta. This
name is a Greek word which means "Circle
View." It here refers to a painting, completed
in 1886 by a group of German artists, portray-
ing the Battle of Atlanta during the Civil War.
This is one of the world's largest paintings,
being 400 feet in circumference, 50 feet in
height, and weighs over 18,000 pounds. It was
brought to Atlanta in 1892, and cost at that
time $40,000.

CYPRESS POND, Lowndes County.
Located on the edge of the town of Twin
Lakes, and was named after the cypress trees
here.

CYRENE, Decatur County. This is a stop on
the Atlantic Coast Line Railroad, six miles
northwest of Bainbridge. It takes the name of
the ancient Greek port of the kingdom of
Cyrenaica, which was active in the 7th century B. C. In Greek mythology, Cyrene was a
nymph beloved by Opollo.

D

DACULA, Gwinnett County. Incorporated as a town August 7, 1905. Was first called FREEMANTOWN. The first postmaster John W. Freeman coined the present name using three letters each from Atlanta and Decatur.

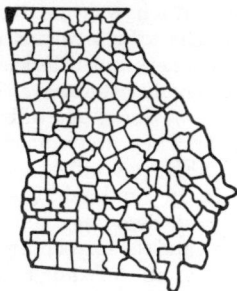

DADE COUNTY. Called "The Free State of Dade" or "The Independent State of Dade," because the only way to reach this county was through either Alabama or Tennessee, until Georgia highway 143 was completed in 1942. Created December 25, 1837 with 168 square miles taken from part of Walker County. It was named for Major Francis Langhorne Dade (1793-1835) of Virginia, who was killed while fighting the Seminoles. The county seat is Trenton (q.v.). The court house was destroyed by fires in 1865 and 1895.

DAHLONEGA, CS Lumpkin County. Pronounced "Dah-lahn-e-ga." Incorporated as TALONEGA December 21, 1833 when it was designated the county seat, after previously being at Auraria (q.v.). Was incorporated as a town December 11, 1858. This is the center of the historic gold mining region, and was the site of one of the nation's first gold rushes, in the 1820's. Other previous names of the town have been MEXICO, NEW MEXICO, and LICK LOG. The old mining camp here was known as HEAD QUARTERS. The early name of Licklog came about because salt was placed in a log for cattle, on what is now the public square. The present name is translated from the Cherokee, *Tau-la-ne-ca*, or *atela-dalanigei*, meaning "golden color" or "yellow money." A branch of the U. S. Mint was established here from 1838 to 1861. In 1958, a caravan of wagons from Dahlonega carried 43 ounces of gold leaf which was donated by citizens of Lumpkin County, and applied to gild the state capitol dome in 1959.

A dahlia and a daylilly have been named Dahlonega because of their golden color.

DAISY, Evans County. Incorporated June 13, 1923. The original name of this town was CONLEY, in honor of the early Methodist minister here, Rev. W. F. M. Conley. The post office was given the name Daisy to honor Daisy Leola Edwards, daughter of one of the first settlers, T. J. Edwards, and sister of state legislator, C. B. Edwards.

DALE'S MILL, Wayne County. This 19th century community was located near Satilla Creek, just north of the present town of Screven. The postmaster in 1881 was F. W. Dale who ran a saw mill here.

DALLAS, CS Paulding County. Created as county seat in 1851 and incorporated February 8, 1854. Named for George Miflin Dallas (1792-1864) of Pennsylvania, who was a U. S. senator, foreign minister, and vice president under Polk's administration.

DALTON, CS Whitfield County. Called "Tufted Textile Center of the World" or "Carpet Center of the World." The original name of this place was CROSS PLAINS. It was incorporated as a town and given its present name on December 29, 1847, in honor of Captain Edward White's mother, whose maiden name was Mary Dalton, and who was the daughter of U. S. Senator Tristram Dalton of Boston. Captain White was an early settler who came here from Massachusetts. The English place-name Dalton means "village in a valley." Dalton became the county seat when Whitfield County was formed in 1851. DALTON JUNIOR COLLEGE is part of the University System of Georgia, and was established here in 1966.

DAMASCUS, Early County. This old community in the eastern part of the county was named for the capital of Syria. Damascus, Syria was the highway terminus of three caravan routes. When the Georgia Pine Railroad was built through this site, the community was then called KESTLER (q.v.), but the depot was given the name Damascus from what was then the larger community nearby, which is now called Old Damascus (q.v.). The post office of the original Damascus closed, and Mrs. Adna McNair who was the postmaster, moved over to Kestler to become the postmaster there. Most of the other residents moved also, and the town changed its name to Damascus August 11, 1914. The original Damascus is now referred to as OLD TOWN.

DAMES FERRY, Monroe County. This rural community is located twelve miles east of Forsyth. George and John Dame made a ferry in 1810 which crossed the Ocmulgee River here for over a century. Their house here was built as a fort for protection against Indian attacks. The post office here was once known as EBENEZER (1887). *See also* S. A. Hodge, Senior, Bridge.

DANIEL FIELD, Augusta. This municipal airport was named by the Augusta city council in honor of Mayor R. H. Daniel, who promoted the local aviation program.

DANIELL'S MILL(S), Douglas County. A former community on Dog River, 12 miles southwest of Douglasville. Named for the J. B. and G. M. Daniell Flour and Grist Mill.

DANIEL SPRINGS, Greene County. This community is located six miles east of Union Point on Georgia highway 44. Named for the family of James K. Daniel, who owned 117 slaves in Greene County.

DANIELSVILLE, CS Madison County. Was made county seat in 1812 and incorporated November 27, 1817. Named for General Allen Daniel, an officer of the militia here, who had been a captain in the Revolution. General Daniel donated lands for the first public buildings.

D'ANTIGNAC SWAMP, Burke County. Located on the Savannah River near Hancock's Landing. This was formerly part of the William D'Antignac plantation.

DANVILLE, Elbert County. This former village was on the Broad River, although the exact location is not certain. It was laid out about 1798 by Clairborne Webb (1760-1830), but failed to survive. Derivation of the name is unknown. There was also a place called DANVILLE in Sumter County, located on the Flint River, ten miles east of Americus.

DANVILLE, Twiggs County. Established as a railroad town about 1891, and was first called HUGHES. The post office was established April 1, 1892, and named for Daniel Greenwood Hughes, father of Congressman Dudley M. Hughes (*see* Dudley, Laurens County). The town was incorporated August 22, 1905.

DARIEN, CS McIntosh County. Incorporated as a town December 12, 1816 and established as a port of entry December 19, 1816. Was made county seat and incorporated as a city December 18, 1818. Was once called "Queen of the Delta" and also known as DARIEN CITY. This was a prominent community in early colonial times, and was established at the site of the former Fort King George (q.v.), which was garrisoned from 1721 to 1727. The town was first settled by Scottish Highlanders under the leadership of John McIntosh Mohr, who arrived in 1736 on the ship *Prince of Wales,* piloted by Captain George Dunbar. They first named the place NEW INVERNESS (q.v.) after their county of Inverness-shire in Scotland. They then established a post here they named FORT DARIEN (q.v.), and the surrounding area was then called Darien. An Indian settlement called HUSPAW TOWN was located here previously. During the Civil War, Reverend Mansfield French, who was called the "White Jesus," formed a Gospel Army of black hymn-singing crusaders who burned Darien July 11, 1863, sparing only five buildings.

DARK CORNER, Douglas County. A former post office located 4½ miles west of Douglasville. Named for the Cherokee leader known as The Dark, who developed the first toll road into Cherokee lands.

(THE) DARK ENTRY, Camden County. A descriptive name for a remote, isolated, and lonesome route which extends ten miles northwest from St. Marys. It passes several miles to the north of today's Georgia highway 40.

DARLINGTON SCHOOL, Rome. A college preparatory school for boys. Founded in 1905 by John Paul and Alice Algood Cooper. Named in honor of Joseph James Darlington, teacher and later an attorney.

DARTMOUTH, Elbert County. Was located two miles above Fort James on the peninsula between the Savannah and Broad rivers. Settled in 1776 by some Virginians who took the name from the town of Dartmouth in Virginia. Was also said to have been named after the Earl of Dartmouth, after he had influenced the King to grant special privileges to the colonies. This was the third town to be established in Georgia, but it soon expired and gave place to Petersburg (q.v.) which was then established nearby. *See also* Bobby Brown State Park.

DART RIVER. This river runs along the south border of Elbert County. It was named about 1772 by provincial governor James Wright, in honor of the Earl of Dartmouth. This is now known as the BROAD RIVER. *See also* Dartmouth and New Purchase.

DASHBOARD, Carroll County. This community is located just below Bowdon. According to J. T. Phillips, president of Brewton-Parker College, the name originated after Slick Chambers' mule kicked the dashboard of Cecil Spruell's new buggy here.

DASHER, Lowndes County. Incorporated March 14, 1967. This town located six miles south of Valdosta was established about 1912, and named for the first settler of this area, Mr. O. P. Dasher.

DAVENPORT MOUNTAIN, Union County. Located just southwest of Nottely Lake, and named for John Davenport who came to this section to settle in 1838.

DAVISBORO, Washington County. Incorporated in 1894. This town was believed named about 1827 for the grandfather of T. J. Davis, who settled here from North Carolina. In 1842 when the Central of Georgia Railroad passed through here, the station was named NUMBER 12.

DAVIS HILL, Atlanta. Located near Bankhead Highway and Chappell Road. Named for Union general, Jeff C. Davis, who occupied the site July 22, 1864.

DAWSON, CS Terrell County. "World's Largest Spanish Peanut Market" Incorporated as a town December 22, 1857 when it was named for William C. Dawson (*see* Dawson County).

lawyer, soldier, who was elected to the U.S. Senate (1849-1855). The county seat is Dawsonville (q.v.).

DAWSONVILLE, CS Dawson County. Incorporated as a town December 10, 1859, and named for William C. Dawson (*see* Dawson County).

DAWSONVILLE, Gordon County. A previous name of CALHOUN (q.v.) and was called this to compliment a Mr. Dawson who owned a general store here.

DEAD MAN'S BRANCH, Walton County. The forces of Elijah Clarke defeated the Indians in a battle here September 21, 1787, after which the "Americans" buried their dead among the canes of this stream, in the eastern section of the county.

DEAN, Evans County. Named for Mrs. W. H. (Dean G.) Hodges. This former post office was established about 1906 at the site of the present DEANS CROSSING, four miles south of Claxton. There was a place called DEAN in McDuffie County at the turn of the century, and this was also an early name of WACO, Haralson County. And DEAN is the first name by which AURARIA (q.v.), Lumpkin County was called.

DEARING, McDuffie County. Incorporated as a town August 13, 1910. The post office of LOMBARDY was established here February 3, 1823. The name was changed April 1, 1893 to honor Mr. William Dearing, on the board of directors of the Georgia Railroad.

DECATUR, CS DeKalb County. Incorporated as a town and also designated as the county seat on December 10, 1823. This is the oldest town in the county and was named for Commodore Decatur (*see* Decatur County).

DAWSON COUNTY. Created December 3, 1857 with 209 square miles taken from Gilmer and Lumpkin counties. Named for William Crosby Dawson (1798-1857), Georgia-born

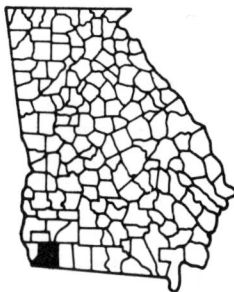

DECATUR COUNTY. Created December 8, 1823 with 586 square miles taken from part of

Early County. Named for Stephen Decatur (1779-1820) of Maryland, an illustrious U. S. Navy commodore, who was killed in a duel by Commodore James Barron. The county seat is Bainbridge. (q.v.).

DEEPSTEP, Washington County. First incorporated as a town December 15, 1900. A local legend explains that an Indian accidently put his foot down in a large hole here and exclaimed, "Ugh. Deep step!" Actually the first postmaster, Gus Avant, submitted the name taken from the nearby Deepstep Creek (q.v.), which flows along the town's southeastern border.

DEEPSTEP CREEK, Washington County. A tributary of Buffalo Creek, this stream was formerly called DEEP CREEK because the banks near the present town of DEEPSTEP (q.v.) were steep and had to be crossed downstream where it was less steep.

DE FOORS FERRY ROAD, Atlanta. Named for Martin DeFoor, pioneer settler who purchased (in 1853) and operated the old Montgomery Ferry across the Chattahoochee River.

DE KALB COLLEGE, Clarkston. A junior college established by the DeKalb County School District, which opened on a 100-acre site in the fall of 1964.

DEKALB COUNTY. Pronounced "Dee Kab'." Created December 9, 1822 with 269 square miles taken from Fayette, Gwinnett and Henry counties. Named in honor of the German-born hero of the Revolution, "Baron" Johann DeKalb (1721-1780), who accompanied LaFayette to America. He was not a real baron at all, but the son of a Bohemian peasant. He was one of a number of Europeans who came to help the colonists in the Revolutionary War. DeKalb was inspector general of the army, and was with

Washington at Valley Forge. The county seat is Decatur (q.v.).

DELANO, LAKE, Franklin D. Roosevelt State Park. This 15-acre lake was named in honor of the late president's mother, Sara Delano Roosevelt.

DELEGAL'S FORT, St. Simons Island. Was built at Sea Point in 1736, but there is now no trace of the structure. Named for and was under the command of Lieutenant Philip Delegal. The larger Fort Saint Simons (q.v.) was built nearby two years later.

DELHI, Wilkes County. A rural community located about twelve miles northwest of Washington, named from the city in India.

DEMOREST, Habersham County. Incorporated November 13, 1889. Laid out by J. A. Reynolds in 1890 at the site of a sawmill camp which was operated by Mr. Henry Rossingnal. A group of people from the North had come here to establish a prohibition town. With them was a Mr. W. Jennings Demorest for whom they named the place. He was a leading prohibition speaker and leader, who died in New York in 1895. DEMOREST LAKE is located here.

DENMARK, Bullock County. This community in the southern section of the county was named from the country in Europe. In earlier years there existed another community of DENMARK, located in Crawford County, four miles west of Knoxville.

DENNIS, Murray County. This community was located eleven miles southeast of Spring Place, where Dennis Johnson operated a general store.

DENSON'S MILL, Twiggs County. Located near Bullard, this post office opened June 15, 1869, with the first postmaster being Elias J. Denson.

DENTON, Jeff Davis County. Incorporated August 21, 1911. This town is thought to have been named for Samuel Denton (1806-1846) from South Carolina, who moved to Georgia about 1815-20.

DE SOTO, Sumter County. Incorporated November 7, 1889. This town was named for the famed Spanish explorer, Hernando DeSoto (1500?-1542), who reportedly crossed through Georgia during his unsuccessful search for a rich empire. On March 29, 1540 DeSoto crossed Chokee Creek and camped here. Also named for this Spanish cavalier was DE SOTO, Floyd County. Incorporated as a town January 22, 1852, it was a suburb of Rome, and is now a part of that city's Fourth Ward. There is today a LAKE DE SOTO, in Rome's Mobley Park. And this explorer's name has also been applied to the 400-foot high DE SOTO FALLS, located one mile south of Neels Gap in Lumpkin County.

DEVEREAUX, Hancock County. A community located seven miles southwest of Sparta. The station of the Georgia Railroad was named for Mrs. Samuel M. (Annie Lloyd) Devereaux, after her husband provided the land needed.

DEVIL'S BRANCH, Rabun County. This fork of little Persimmon Creek in the western section of the county is named to reflect its rugged character. Another DEVIL'S BRANCH rises near the Screven-Effingham line. It was so designated because of the dense swamp that fringes its banks. Other streams by this name are found in northwest Clinch County, and in Wilkinson County, east of Allentown. DEVIL'S COVE in Walker County was the name given to a narrow and rough little valley a mile or so southwest of the former community of Estelle. In Georgia there are at least three river bends that have been called DEVIL'S ELBO. These are found on the Savannah, Oconee, and St. Marys rivers, and are applied to sharp curves which are difficult to navigate. DEVIL'S HALF ACRE, located ten miles southwest of Eatonton in Putnam County, originated about 1806, and was given this name after a vice ridden dram shop was established at this crossroad. It was later known as THE HALF ACRE and finally adopted the present name of the community, STANFORDVILLE.

DEWITT, Mitchell County. A community located 13 miles north of Camilla on Georgia highway 3. Named for its founder, Dewitt C. Bacon.

DEWY ROSE, Elbert County. This community is located seven miles northwest of Elberton. John Goff said it was named about 1900 by postmaster Uncle Jack Christian for a dew-covered rose his small daughter brought in while he was considering a name for the new post office.

DEXTER, Laurens County. Incorporated August 22, 1891. This town was settled in 1889 by Reverend John W. Green. Derivation of the name is not known.

DIAMOND, Gilmer County. This community is located 16 miles northeast of Ellijay. Located here were the Diamond Gold Mine and Diamond Silver Mine.

DICKERSON'S STORE, Seminole County. *See* STEAM MILL.

DICK'S RIDGE, Floyd County. Named for an old Indian chief, Dick, who lived near this ridge, which is located in East Armuchee Militia District.

DILLARD, Rabun County. Incorporated as a town August 21, 1906. Named for John and James Dillard, early settlers and Revolutionary War veterans.

DIP, Hall County. This was the former name of the town of CLERMONT (q.v.). In 1913, the first postmaster, Harvey Keith, decided on this short name as he had no cancellation stamp, and wished a short name to write by hand. Brinkley said that "Dip" referred to the location between the mountains and ridges.

DIRTSELLER MOUNTAIN, Chattooga. Located about eight miles southwest of Summerville. This 1,293-foot peak was given its name which was translated from that used by the Cherokee Indians, KARTE KUNTEESKY.

DISMAL COVE, DISMAL GAP, and DISMAL KNOB. Located on the Blue Ridge at the Towns-Rabun line. These descriptive terms are applied to unpromising areas which are not suitable for farming. DISMAL MOUNTAIN is located about five miles southeast of Hiawasse, in Towns County.

THE DIVIDINGS, Rabun County. This was the descriptive name given to an old Indian trail intersection at the site of the present CLAYTON.

DIXIE, Brooks County. Incorporated as a town August 17, 1908. Was established in 1861 when the railroad came through, first being called NUMBER 17 or GROOVER'S STATION (*see* Grooverville). When the post office was transferred here, it was given its present name. "Dixie" is a term by which the Southern States of the U. S. are often called, but the origin is not certain. However, there are three theories: 1. From the slang for the French *dix* (ten) dollar bills once used in Louisiana. 2. A name originating with Negro slaves, referring to a kindhearted slaveholder from New York named Dixie. 3. Derived in reference to the Mason and Dixon Line that divided the free from the slave states. There is also a community of DIXIE in Newton County, located five miles southeast of Covington on Georgia highway 142. And there is a community named Dixie Heights near Albany in Dougherty County.

DOCTORS CREEK, Long County. Rises about six miles north of Ludowici, and flows southward into the Altamaha River. Was probably named for Indian chief, Captain Alleck (*see* Alecks Creek).

DOCTORTOWN, Wayne County. Has also been written DOCTOR'S TOWN. This community was established in 1827 upon the site of an old Indian settlement on the Altamaha River, which was the abode of Indian chief, Captain Alleck. For derivation, *see* Alecks Creek. The first white establishment here was FORT DEFENSE (q.v.). However, over the years the original Indian designation prevailed. John Goff points out that this is one of few Creek Indian town sites which retains its original name.

DOCTORTOWN SWAMP, Wayne County. Located on the upper end of large Penholloway Swamp. For derivation, *see* Alecks Creek.

DODGE COUNTY. Created October 26, 1870 with 499 square miles taken from Montgomery, Pulaski, and Telfair counties. Named in honor of William E. Dodge (1805-1883), an industrialist and temperance leader of New York. He had purchased an estate comprising most of the present Dodge, Laurens, Pulaski, Telfair, and Montgomery counties. The county seat is Eastman (q.v.).

DOERUN, Colquitt County. Incorporated as a town December 20, 1899. The name came about in the early days when there was a deer run or trail between the head of a stream on the north side of town and one on the south side.

DOGWOOD VALLEY, Catoosa County. Located at the southeast corner of the county. Said to have been named for an Indian chief, Dogwood, or for an early Cherokee town.

DONALSONVILLE, CS Seminole county. Was incorporated December 8, 1897. This started as a sawmill town, and was named after John E. Donalson who owned the sawmill.

DOOLING, Dooly County. A community located 14 miles northwest of Vienna. Founded by John A. Jenkins of North Carolina, and named for his second wife, Miss Ellen Dooling.

DOOLY COUNTY. Created May 15, 1821 with 394 square miles acquired by Creek cession of January 8, 1821. This was an original county, named for Colonel John Dooly (1740-1780) who was murdered by Tories in the Revolution (*see also* Tory Road). He had commanded a regiment at Kettle Creek (q.v.). The County seat is Vienna (q.v.). The court house was destroyed by fire in 1847.

DORAVILLE, DeKalb County. Incorporated December 15, 1871. The post office here was first named CROSS KEYS. The town was named for Dora Jack, whose father was an official of the Atlanta and Charlotte Air Line Railway.

DORCHESTER, Liberty County. Located on Georgia 38, six miles east of Midway. Settled in 1843 and named for the Dorchester family of England, Massachusetts and South Carolina.

DOUBLE BRANCHES, Lincoln County. This old community was named in reference to its location between two tributaries of the Little River, ten miles southeast of Lincolnton.

DOUBLE RUN, Wilcox County. Located midway between Fitzgerald and Cordele, about nine miles southwest of Rochelle. The community was given this name because of its being at the junction of two railroads. DOUBLE RUN CREEK flows southward from Double Run and into Turner County where it goes into the Alapaha River.

DOUBLE KNOB MOUNTAIN, Gilmer County. Located eight miles north of Ellijay. Named for its twin peaks of about equal height.

DOUGHERTY, Dawson County. This crossroad in the southeastern section of the county was called SAVANNAH (q.v.) until about 1890. Some say it was named for an Irishman, Cornelius Dougherty, who was a trader that lived at Quanasee (q.v.), said to have died in 1690 at the age of 120. Goff believed that the most probable derivation was for a prominent Cherokee, who long resided here, named James Dougherty, Sr.

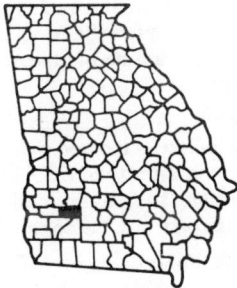

DOUGHERTY COUNTY. Pronounced "Dority." Created December 15, 1853 with 326 square miles taken from Baker County. Named for Charles Dougherty (? - 1853 or 1854), a prominent lawyer and jurist of Athens. The county seat is Albany (q.v.). This county contains more pecan trees than any other county in the nation.

DOUGLAS, CS Coffee County. Established and made the county seat in 1858. Incorporated as a town December 10, 1895. Named in honor of Stephen A. Douglas (*see* Douglas County).

DOUGLAS COUNTY. Created October 17, 1870 with 201 square miles taken from Campbell and Carroll counties. The county was first settled prior to 1848 by the Vansant brothers from South Carolina, Abe, Reuben and Young. Young settled at Flat Rock, two miles west of the present court house. He deeded 40 acres for the first county seat at

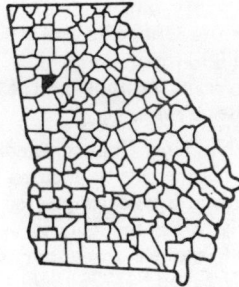

Skint Chestnut (q.v.), January 9, 1871. Douglas County was named in honor of U. S. Congressman Stephen Arnold Douglas (1813-1861) who was born in Vermont and lived in Illinois. He was the South's candidate for the President, and was defeated by Lincoln in 1860. The county seat is Douglasville (q.v.).

DOUGLASVILLE, CS Douglas County. "The Dynamic City" Incorporated as a town February 25, 1875. Named for Douglas County (q.v.). The original settlement here was known as SKIN(T) CHESTNUT (q.v.). The court house was destroyed by fires of 1896 and 1956.

DOVER, Screven County. This post office and community is located ten miles south of Sylvania by the Bulloch County line. It is believed this name was chosen in connection with the Dover Association Report of the Baptist Church (1832).

DOVER BLUFF, Camden County. Located between the Satilla and Little Satilla rivers near their mouths. The name is believed transferred from that of the Cliffs of Dover in England. DOVER CREEK, Camden County. This is a channel near the mouth of the Satilla River, near Dover Bluff.

DOVE'S CREEK, Elbert County. This former community was located seven miles southwest of Elberton near Dove's Creek, which flows southward into the Broad River.

DOWDELL'S KNOB (or THE KNOB), Harris County. This knob is 1,395 feet elevation and projects into Pine Mountain Valley near Franklin D. Roosevelt State Park. This was one of President Roosevelt's favorite picnic spots. Was named for pioneer settlers Lewis and James Dowdell who came here from Virginia in 1828.

DOWNING (FERRY) ROAD. Was also known as the ROME ROAD or ALABAMA ROAD. It extended from eastern Dawson County through northwest Forsyth County,

Cherokee County, and westward to Alabama. Named for the man who ran a ferry where Field's Bridge was later built across the Etowah River, at the upper end of the present Alatoona Reservoir.

DRAYTON, Dooly County. Incorporated in 1869. This community is located nine miles west of Vienna. It was designated the county seat shortly after the county was formed (1821), and named in honor of Colonel William Drayton (1776-1846) of South Carolina. The county seat was moved from Drayton to Berrien (q.v.) in 1839.

DREW, Forsyth County. A rural community about four miles west of Cumming. Drew E. Bennett was the first postmaster when the post office was established August 23, 1889. It was discontinued November 21, 1904.

DREWRYVILLE, Spalding County. This former community was previously known as ABNER, and was located on the Flint River southwest of Griffin. In 1881 the postmaster J. A. Drewry operated a general store and handled real estate.

DRIED INDIAN CREEK, Newton County. This is a tributary of the Yellow River which flows southward through Covington. Indian lore relates that it was so named after finding the dried remains of an old Indian chief near the banks of the stream.

DROWNDING BEAR CREEK, Whitfield County. Flows southeasterly from Dalton to the Conasauga River. Named for a Cherokee Indian who lived in this area.

DRUID HILLS, Atlanta. This section of northeast Atlanta was once a suburban community. The name was selected in 1908 when it was incorporated by a group of investors headed by Asa G. Candler, at a site selected and planned by Joel Hurt. In ancient times, druids were priests and medicine men of Celtic people, reported to have been magicians.

DRY BRANCH, Twiggs County. A community settled in 1808 with its post office established January 17, 1879. Many theories are told as to the derivation, but it is not related to the stream called DRY BRANCH. John Goff determined that the place was so named because of the removal of moonshine stills from the local streams prior to establishing the post office.

DRY CREEK. There are many wet weather streams of this name found in the state, such

as in Bartow-Paulding counties, Early County, Wayne County, etc.

DRY POND, Stephens County. The early name of TOCCOA (q.v.).

DUBIGNONS CREEK, Glynn County. Located in the northwest section of Jekyll Island. Named for Le Sieur Christophe Anne Poulain du Bignon (1739-1825), a French naval captain who purchased Jekyll Island about 1793. DUBIGNON HAMMOCK is located in the northwest section of Glynn County.

DUBLIN, CS Laurens County. "The City That's 'Doublin' Daily'." The first post office was established July 1, 1811, and the town was incorporated December 9, 1812. An Irishman, Jonathan Sawyer, agreed to donate a site for the public buildings for the town, provided that it be named for Erin's capital. It was said he did this to please his wife who was from Dublin originally. The county seat was then moved here from its original site of Sumpterville (q.v.). DUBLIN was also the early name of Resaca (q.v.) in Gordon County.

DUCK CREEK, Walker County. An early community which was located in the vicinity of the present community of CENTER POST (q.v.). It was near the stream called DUCK CREEK, a tributary of Chatooga Creek.

DUCKTOWN, Forsyth County. This post office existed from October 5, 1899 to October 17, 1903. Located near the western border of the county, it may have been named from the town of Ducktown in Tennessee.

DUDLEY, Laurens County. This town originated with a railroad station which opened in 1891. Originally called ELSIE, for the wife of Joshua Walker who owned the land here. Because of another station and post office by that name in Georgia, it had to be changed. It was then named for U. S. Senator Dudley Mays Hughes (1848-1927) of Twiggs County. He was president of the Macon, Dublin and Savannah Railroad. Senator Hughes was co-author with Senator Hoke Smith, also of Georgia, of the National Vocational Education Act of 1917. Also named for him was the DUDLEY M. HUGHES HIGH SCHOOL of Macon.

DUE WEST, Cobb County. This community was apparently named for its location five miles due west of Marietta.

DUFFIE, Wilcox County. This former community was located ten miles west of Abbeville, and was settled by the McDuffie family.

DUG GAP, Whitfield County. Was so named because a pioneer road, cut out of a hillside, passed through a cleft in Rocky Face Ridge at this point. Located just south of Dalton.

DUKES CREEK, White County. This was an old Cherokee Indian name which was applied to the present NACOOCHEE RIVER (q.v.).

DULUTH, Gwinnett County. Incorporated February 28, 1876. Named in 1875 by a Mr. Howell, grandson of Evan Howell, who came from North Carolina in 1821 to settle here. The name of the original community was HOWELL'S CROSSROAD. The present name of this town was chosen in commemoration of a speech made by U. S. Congressman J. Proctor Knott (D.Ky.) ridiculing a suggestion to appropriate financial help for the insignificant town of Duluth, Minnesota. He asked, "Where in the world is Duluth?" The northern city is named for the 17th century French explorer, Daniel Graysolon DuLuth.

DUNAWAY GARDENS, Coweta County. Located at the Wayne P. Sewell Plantation six miles northwest of Newnan. Consists of 20 acres overlooking Cedar Creek, which was opened to the public around 1940 and closed up about 1963. Established by and named for Mrs. Hettie Jane Dunaway Sewell.

DUNBAR ROAD, Houston County. Located northwest of Warner Robins. Named from a former post office of DUNBAR, located 3½ miles east of Byron. Named for the plantation home of Captain George Dunbar (*see also* Darien).

DUNGENESS, Cumberland Island. This was originally a hunting lodge, and then a post office near the southern end of the island. It was erected and named by General Oglethorpe after an English county seat of which he was the owner, in the county of Kent. Buried here was Henry "Light-Horse Harry" Lee (1756-1818), gallant cavalry officer of the Revolution, and father of Robert E. Lee. The Thomas Carnegie family came here in 1811 and Tom's widow, Lucy Coleman Carnegie, built the third Dungeness on this site, which burned in 1959.

DUNWOODY, DeKalb County. Named in honor of Major Charles Dunwoody, a prominent citizen of Roswell, who developed this unincorporated community.

DUPONT, Clinch County. A community located nine miles southwest of Homerville. This was known as STATION NUMBER 12 when the railroad first came through here. Its earliest name when settled in 1858 was SUWANNOOCHEE, after the nearby stream by this name. The name was later changed to LAWTON until May 3, 1874, at which time the town was incorporated as DuPont. It was named in honor of the first settler here, Captain J.P.A. DuPont, who moved his family here from Darien about 1858.

DURAND, Meriwether County. Previously named STINSON, after early settler, Dr. James Winslow Stinson. The name was changed to Durand when the Central of Georgia Railroad came through this community in the early 1900's.

DURDAN, Emanuel County. Also called KEA'S MILL, this former community was located in the vicinity of today's town of Stillmore. William Durdan operated a general store here in 1881.

DURDIN (Militia) DISTRICT, Morgan County. Located in the southwest section of the county. It was named for the Durden family, descendents of John Durden, an early state representative of the county.

DUTCH ISLAND, Chatham County. Lies north of Skidaway Island. This was formerly named LIBERTY ISLAND, and may have been called HERB ISLAND.

DUTCHTOWN, Henry County. This former community was located about six miles west of McDonough. The derivation has nothing to do with the Dutch, but only with the Palatines and Switzers, who were then called Dutch (Deutsch). It has also been said that the first settlers were Germans who had immigrated to America by way of Holland, which is why they were called "Dutch."

DYKESBORO, Bleckley County. The early community was named for Burrell B. Dykes, a public spirited settler who gave land for various purposes here. The name has since been changed to COCHRAN (q.v.).

DYKES CREEK, Floyd County. This stream flows south into the Etowah River about five miles east of Rome. It was named after Dr. G. J. Dykes, who settled in Rome in 1836.

E

EAGLE CLIFF, Walker County. This community in the northwest section of the county is located about one mile east of EAGLE CLIFFS where eagles once established their aeries.

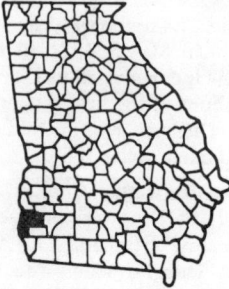

EARLY COUNTY. Created December 15, 1818 with 526 square miles acquired by Creek cession of August 9, 1814. This was an original county, named for judge, congressman, and the tenth governor of Georgia, Peter Early (1773-1817), a native of Virginia. The county seat is Blakely (q.v.). *See also* Fort Early.

EASLEY'S COWPENS, Walton County. *See* COWPENS.

EASTAHATCHEE CREEK, Decatur County. Has also been spelled EASTERHATCHE and ESTAHATCHEE. The name is of Muskogee origin, from *itsi,* "people," plus *hachi,* "stream," perhaps because of an early Indian settlement along its banks. It is now known as SANBORN CREEK (q.v.).

EASTANOL(L)EE, Stephens County. Located about four miles northwest of Avalon, this community was named for the stream which flows by it.

EASTANOLLEE CREEK. Flows eastward through Stephens and Franklin counties, emptying into Hartwell Reservoir. The name is believed to be a Cherokee word meaning "shoally" (*see* Oostanaula), although some have claimed it to be derived from the Müskogean *Isti nol-li,* their term for "White Man." Some old spellings have been ESTANOLA, EASTANOLA, EASTANOLEE, and EASTINAULEE.

EASTERTOY, Rabun County. This was an old Cherokee Indian town, thought to have been located in the vicinity of the present Dillard. The meaning of this Cherokee name is unknown, and has been written variously at other places as ESTATOWTH, ESTOTOWEE, ESTATOE, etc.

EAST JULIETTE, Jones County. Incorporated as a town August 11, 1924. This was originally a railroad settlement on the opposite side of the Ocmulgee River from Juliette (q.v.). East Juliette was at one time known as GLOVERS after Dr. W. P. Glover who inherited the property here.

EAST LAKE, DeKalb County. Incorporated August 14, 1908. This community was named from the lake on the property of the Atlanta Athletic Club, which is so called due to the fact that it lies east of Atlanta.

EASTMAN, CS Dodge County. "Candy Capital of Georgia" Incorporated as a city August 22, 1905. Settled in 1840 and originally known as STATION NO. 13. Named for William Pitt Eastman, an early settler who arrived here in 1870 from New Hampshire.

EAST POINT, Fulton County. Called "The City of Homes and Industry" and "Georgia's 7th Largest City." Incorporated August 10, 1887. Was given this name when it was the eastern terminus of the Atlanta and West Point Railroad.

EATONTON, CS Putnam County. Was made county seat in 1808 and incorporated as a town December 12, 1809. Named for diplomat and general, William Eaton (1768-1811) of Connecticut. This is the birthplace of writer, Joel Chandler Harris (*see also* Uncle Remus Route).

EBENEZAR, Schley County. This community lies five miles southwest of Ellaville. The name is a variation of Ebenezer (q.v.).

EBENEZER, Effingham County. This old settlement, later referred to as OLD EBENEZER, was established by the Lutheran Salzburgers from Germany in 1734. It was located about four miles below the present town of Springfield, near EBENEZER CREEK, which was named for this early community. The Salzburgers chose the site and here set up a stone they called Ebenezer, which means in German, "Stone of Help." It was named this in commemoration of their final deliverance from their enemies, and primarily the bigotry of the Archbishop of Salzburg. NEW EBENEZER was established nearby after the original location had proven unsatisfactory. This site was 34 miles from Savannah, on a ridge called Red Bluff (from the peculiar color of the soil). This was once the county seat of Effingham County, and served briefly as the capital of Georgia when the legislature met here in February 1796. The original settlement was converted into a cowpen in 1738, and by the year 1855, there were but two residences remaining of the original Ebenezer, one being vacant. The Jerusalem Church which was built here in 1767 houses a museum, and is the only structure still standing. The community of OKI (q.v.) later replaced the dead town. Communities named EBENEZER have been established in Dooly County (was also known as COUNTRY STORE), Harris County (five miles east of Hamilton, and named for the Ebenezer Baptist Church established here in 1873), Monroe County (later known as DAMES FERRY q.v. post office), and Morgan County (located ten miles northwest of Madison River, and which was also called REESE).

EBO LANDING, St. Simons Island. Named for the less favored Ebo Negroes of Africa, who were among the many slaves bootlegged into this secluded spot on Dunbar Creek, two miles south of Fort Frederica.

ECHACONNA, Bibb County. This community had one of the earliest post offices in the county. The name is a variation of Echeconnee (see Echeconnee Creek).

ECHECONNEE, Houston County Pronounced "Eechyconny." This old community is located at the junction of Bibb, Peach and Houston counties. Was named from the nearby stream.

ECHECONNEE CREEK. Called "Itchy Creek" by local youths. Rises in upper Crawford County, forms the border of Bibb County with Crawford and Houston counties before it enters the Ocmulgee River north of Warner Robins. The name is a Creek Indian word meaning "Deer Trap Creek." It was so named because deer that came here to drink from the stream were attacked by Indians before they could escape up the steep banks. Old variations of spelling have included IT-CHEECONO, ICHO-CONNO, ECHE-CONNEE, ITCHOCUNNO, and ICHO-CON-NAUGH. It has also been called LITTLE TOBESOFKE CREEK. This stream

was the site of mass "skinny dipping" during the 1970 Atlanta Pop Festival (see Byron). LITTLE ECHECONNEE CREEK in northeast Crawford County is a tributary of Echeconnee Creek.

ECHETE, Baldwin County. This was thought to have been an old Hitchiti Indian town in the vicinity of today's Milledgeville.

ECHOLS COUNTY. Created December 13, 1858 with 425 square miles taken from Clinch and Lowndes counties. This is the state's least populous county, having fewer than 2,000 inhabitants. Named after General Robert M. Echols (? - c. 1846), who was president of the Georgia Senate and died in Mexico during the War with Mexico. The county seat is Statenville (q.v.). The court house was destroyed by fire in 1897.

ECIMNA CHATE. The Indian name for the RED HILLS Region (q.v.).

ECTOR, Meriwether County. This was an early community located a few miles northwest of Greenville, near old Ector Mill. The Ectors were among the settlers of this region.

ECUN HUT COO CHEE, Chattahoochee County. This is an area along the south side of Upatoi Creek within the present Fort Benning Reservation, and its Creek Indian name means "Little White Ground."

ECUNHUTKENENE PATH. The Creek Indian word means "White Ground Path." This was an Indian trail which extended to the Chattahoochee River, in what is now Fort Benning Military Reservation.

EDEN, Bryan County. Named from the Biblical Garden of Eden. The only post office in the county in 1849, it was located approximately midway between Pembroke and Richmond Hill. Was the site of the first county seat, and was also called BRYAN (q.v.). There is today a community of EDEN near the southernmost tip of Effingham County.

EDGEHILL, Glascock County. A post office existed here from February 25, 1902 to September 14, 1903. This descriptively named community is located six miles south of Gibson. It was formerly called JULE WILCHER QUARTERS, and was then named by school teacher, Mrs. J.C.A. Wilcher, after a small village in her native state of Virginia.

EDGEWOOD, Fulton County. Located in original DeKalb County, it was incorporated as a town December 9, 1898, and became part of Atlanta January 1, 1909. It was so named because of its location on the edge of Atlanta. EDGEWOOD AVENUE of Atlanta was named from this early community.

EDISON, Calhoun County. Incorporated as a town December 6, 1902. Originally called NUBBINTOWN, it was afterwards named for Thomas Alva Edison (1847-1931) the inventor. *See also* Menlo.

EDWARDS LAKE, Bibb County. Located just east of Herbert Smart Airport, at or near the estate of distinguished Southern author, Harry Stillwell Edwards (1855-1938). This lake is formed by a dam on Swift Creek.

EDWARDSVILLE, DeKalb County. This community was located seven miles northeast of Atlanta on the Airline (Southern) Railroad. Was made a post office December 26, 1876 which was discontinued in October 1892. The first postmaster was Hiram Edwards.

EELBECK, Chattahoochee County. Was located nine miles northeast of Cusetta. Previously called MILLVILLE, it was a post office in the Henry J. Eelbeck home.

EFFINGHAM, Effingham County. This was designated the county seat February 7, 1799 after previously having been at Elberton (q.v.). It was later moved to Springfield (q.v.).

quired by Creek cession of May 20, 1733. This was an original county, previously organized in 1758 as the parishes of St. Mathew and St. Philip. Named for Thomas Howard (1746-1791), the third Earl of Effingham. He was an Englishman who was a friend of the colonies, and resigned his commission as an officer rather than take up arms against them. The county seat is Springfield (q.v.).

EGG ISLAND, McIntosh County. Located in the delta of the Altamaha River. Was so named as this is a favorite hatching place or incubator for thousands of sea birds who lay their eggs here.

EGYPT, Effingham County. This community is located in the northwest section of the county. It was named for the country in northern Africa because of the fertile soil also found here to produce abundant corn. There was formerly a community of EGYPT in northeastern Oglethorpe County.

EIGHT MILE CREEK, Burke County. This name refers to the length of the stream. It flows under Georgia highway 56 just before entering Buckhead Creek.

ELBA ISLAND, Chatham County. Located in the Savannah River just below Savannah. Was believed to have been given this name in the Napoleonic era, after Elba Island which lies off of Tuscany in the Tyrrhenian Sea, where Napoleon was exiled (1814-15).

ELBERTA, Houston County. Incorporated as a city March 21, 1958, and is located north of Warner Robins. The charter was repealed March 24, 1970, and this is now part of Warner Robins. Named for the Elberta peach crop which was successfully produced here in 1875 by Samuel Rumph (*see also* Marshallville).

EFFINGHAM COUNTY. Created February 5, 1777 with 480 square miles ac-

ELBERT COUNTY. Created December 10, 1790 with 359 square miles taken from Wilkes County. Named for General Samuel Elbert

(1740-1788), a native of South Carolina who fought in the Revolutionary War. He became governor of Georgia in 1785. The county seat is Elberton (q.v.).

ELBERTON, Effingham County. Was located on the north side of the Ogeechee River near Indian Bluff. This was the county seat from 1787 to 1796, after originally being at Tuskasee-King. *See also* Effingham.

ELBERTON, CS Elbert County. "The Granite City" Incorporated as a town December 10, 1803. Was made county seat in 1790, and was first called ELBERTVILLE and later ELBERT COURT HOUSE. Was named for Samuel Elbert (*see* Elbert County). This vicinity produces from its 26 quarries more granite monuments than any other city in the world.

ELDORADO, Tift County, Pronounced "El' duh-ray'-duh." This station on the Georgia Southern and Florida Railway is about six miles south of Tifton. Originally called FENDER (q.v.). it was renamed by the railroad in 1888 to signify the rich growth of pines in the area. The Spanish term *El Dorado* means "The Golden One." (The post office here is still called Fender.)

ELIJAH CLARK STATE PARK, Lincoln County. Located six miles northeast of Lincolnton. This 447-acre park contains the grave and memorial of General Elijah Clarke, the great Revolutionary hero for which the park was named. *See also* Clarke County.

ELIZABETH, Cobb County. Located on the north border of Marietta. Was incorporated October 5, 1885, but a mayor or city council were never elected. Believed named for Elizabeth Brown, the daughter of Georgia's Governor Joseph E. Brown. This "non-town" is located in ELIZABETH DISTRICT No. 1897, one of the last militia districts to be created.

ELLAVILLE, CS Schley County. Laid out in 1858 and incorporated November 23, 1859. The town was named for Ella, the oldest daughter of a leading citizen of this section, Robert Burton, who sold 150 acres for the establishment of the county seat. This was the site of the settlement POND TOWN which had sprung up in 1812, and was the first community in the county.

ELLERSLIE, Harris County. This post office was established in 1828, and is about eighteen miles from Columbus on the old Wire Road (q.v.). Believed to have been named for Captain Ellerslie from one of Scott's novels.

ELLICOTT'S ROCK SCENIC AREA, Rabun County. The large boulder here, called ELLICOTT'S ROCK, was used to designate the northeast corner of the state. It is located on the Chattooga River at the North Carolina line, and was in 1811 established as the natural marker to indicate the 35th degree of North Latitude. Named after Major Andrew Ellicott of Lancaster, Pennsylvania, who was a famous surveyor assigned by Georgia's Governor David B. Mitchell to determine the true boundary between the two states after years of dispute. March 26, 1811, Major Ellicott established the mark to designate where the 35 degree parallel crossed. The rock is marked with an "N" and a "G" to indicate North Carolina and Georgia. It is now determined to be about 500 feet too far north. The establishment of the new boundary line brought about the extinction of Georgia's first Walton County (q.v.) which found itself in North Carolina. Also named for him is ELICOTT'S MOUND just above Moniac in Charlton County, so designated when Major Elicott surveyed Georgia's southern boundary in 1796-1800. *See also* Camac's Rock.

ELLIJAY, CS Gilmer County. Incorporated December 20, 1834, at the time it was also designated the county seat. The town retained the name it had as a community in Indian days. Some people suggest that this was the name of a Cherokee Indian chief, while others would have it mean "Place of Green Things," "Many Waters," or "New Ground." Some former spellings of the place have been ALLE-JOY, ALLJAY, ALLJOY, ELIJA, ELLIJA, and ELECHAYE. The naturalist William Bartram labeled it ALLAGAE (1773-78). This name was also applied to the lower Coosawattee River. *See also* Sanderstown.

ELMODEL, Baker County. A community on the Chickasawhatchee River, nine miles north west of Newton. The name is a coined word, either from the Spanish "the model" or from "Elmo-dell."

EMANUEL COUNTY. Created December 10, 1812 with 686 square miles taken from Bulloch and Montgomery counties. Named for Colonel David Emanuel (1744-1808), who was born in Pennsylvania, and became governor of Georgia in 1801. The county seat

is Swainsboro (q.v.). The court house was destroyed by fires in 1841, 1855, 1857, 1919 and 1938.

EMANUEL COLLEGE, Franklin Springs. First opened in 1919 under the name FRANKLIN SPRINGS INSTITUTE. The name was later changed to Emanuel, from the Hebrew, which means "God With Us."

EMERSON, Bartow County. Incorporated as a city November 11, 1889, at which time the name was changed from STEGALL'S STATION to honor Georgia's governor during the Civil War, Joseph Emerson Brown (1821-1894). *See also* Fort Brown.

EMERY HIGHWAY, Macon. Named for the first commander of Camp Wheeler (q.v.) during World War II, General Ambrose R. Emery.

EMORY COLLEGE, Oxford. Also called EMORY AT OXFORD, or OXFORD COLLEGE (q.v.). Chartered in Newton County December 19, 1836 under the name Emory College, in honor of Dr. John Emory, bishop of the Methodist Episcopal Church. Emory moved to its Atlanta campus in 1919, and became Emory University (q.v.), with Oxford College remaining as an active campus at its original site.

EMORY UNIVERSITY, Atlanta. Was first established as EMORY COLLEGE (q.v.) at Oxford, Newton County, which became the liberal arts division of this university in 1919. The momentous impetus for the move was an outright gift of $1 million from Asa G. Candler Sr. toward the endowment of this new university. The first two dormitories were DOBBS HALL and WINSHIP HALL, named for their donors, Samuel Candler Dobbs and George Winship. Similar gifts determined the names of the JOHN P. SCOTT LABORATORY OF ANATOMY and T. T. FISHBURNE LABORATORY OF PHYSIOLOGY, built in 1917. The old CANDLER LIBRARY was named for the

university's major benefactor, while the CANDLER SCHOOL OF THEOLOGY was named for Bishop W. A. Candler. GLENN MEMORIAL CHURCH was dedicated in 1931, and presented to the college by Thomas K. Glenn and Mrs. Howard Candler in memory of their father, Wilbur Fisk Glenn.

EMPIRE, Bleckley County. Incorporated August 12, 1911, with the boundaries of the town to be in both Dodge and Pulaski counties. The community came within the border of Bleckley County when it was created the following year. Was named by John Anderson and John W. Hightower in 1886, when they had high hopes of booming success after they bought a sawmill which had been built here the previous year by Mr. Jim Few.

ENCHANTED MOUNTAIN, Union County. Located near the Towns County line. Brinkley said that, "In folklore, unusual occurences were associated with the Indian markings found in the nearby soapstone deposits.

ENECKS, Screven County. This town was located on the Savannah River about 12 miles east of Sylvania. T. J. Enecks was postmaster and wharf manager, who also had a grist mill here.

ENIGMA, Berrien County. Incorporated as a town August 21, 1906. Bernice McCullar explains that the derivation is an enigma, as nobody knows where the name came from or why.

ENTERPRISE, Morgan County. A former community located nine miles southeast of Madison. First known as ADAM, it was renamed for the Enterprise Compress Company of Augusta, producers of cotton seed oil.

EPHESUS, Heard County. Incorporated as a city March 3, 1964. Is located 13 miles northwest of Franklin. The name is that of an ancient Ionian city on the west coast of Asia Minor. There was formerly another community called EPHESUS in western Douglas County, located six miles southwest of Douglasville.

EPWORTH, Fannin County. Incorporated as a town August 18, 1906. This community was originally named ATALLA. The Methodists built a seminary here called Epworth, after which the post office changed its name to Epworth. John Wesley, the founder of Methodism, was born at Epworth in England. The Methodist Church was organized here by Rev. Alexander Haren in 1865. There was at that time no other Methodist Church in Georgia.

ESTATOAH CREEK, Rabun County. This stream enters the right side of the Little Tennessee River on the northeast side of Dillard. It is also called ESTATOAH FALLS CREEK or MUD CREEK. The name is a variation of the old Cherokee town name, Eastertoy (q.v.).

ETNA, Polk County. The name of this community is a Greek place-name describing "where Vulcan had his smithy." Just northwest of here is the 1,247-foot high ETNA MOUNTAIN. Etna (or Aetna) is a volcanic mountain in Italy.

ETON, Murray County. The name of this community is thought to have been taken from the noted school of England, perhaps because of the early establishment here of the largest school in the county.

ETOWAH INDIAN MOUNDS, Bartow County. Located three miles south of Cartersville. This was a large active Indian settlement about 1,000 to 1,500 A.D., and was named after the Etowah Indian tribe. The derivation is from the Cherokee, *Itawa,* the name of several Cherokee Indian settlements. The origin is obscure, possibly from the Cherokee, *etawaha,* "deadwood," or loaned from the Creek, *italwa,* "town." The name has often been corrupted to "Hightower" (q.v.). ETOWA(H), incorporated December 24, 1833 was the early name of CANTON (q.v.), Cherokee County.

ETOWAH RIVER. Rises in the mountains of Lumpkin County, and flows through Dawson, Cherokee and Bartow counties, then into Floyd County. At Rome it joins the Oostanaula River to form the Coosa River. The Etowah River and the ETOWAH VALLEY through which it flows were both named for the Etowah tribe of Indians.

EUDORA, Jasper County. A community located nine miles northwest of Monticello. Named for the Greek term, *eudora,* meaning "generous (or good) gifts."

EUFALA, LAKE. Named after the town of Eufala, Alabama which got its name from the old Abeika Indian town of Eufales in Alabama. Georgians prefer to call this LAKE GEORGE or WALTER F. GEORGE RESERVOIR (q.v.).

EUGENE TALMADGE MEMORIAL BRIDGE, Savannah. Carries U. S. Highway Alternate 17 across the Savannah River to Hutchinson Island. Named to honor former governor of Georgia, Eugene Talmadge (1884-1946). Also named for him is the state-owned EUGENE TALMADGE MEMORIAL HOSPITAL in Augusta, which was dedicated in 1956. *See also* Rock Eagle 4H Center.

EUHARLEE, Bartow County. Incorporated as a town September 16, 1870. Originally called BURGE'S MILL, this community is located eight miles west of Cartersville. Was previously incorporated January 12, 1852 as the town of EUHARLEYVILLE. *Euharlee* is a Cherokee Indian word which means, "She laughs as she runs," or may be corrupted from the Creek Indian name, *Eufala* (q.v.).

EUHARLEE CREEK. Flows northeasterly from southern Polk County into the southeast corner of Bartow County to enter the Etowah River at Euharlee (q.v.). This stream was formerly called LIMESTONE CREEK.

EUREKA, Dooly County. This former community was located twelve miles northeast of Vienna. The name is derived from the Greek, *Heureka,* meaning "I have found (it)." EUREKA SPRINGS was the name given to a water source in Screven County when the discoverer learned of the curative powers of the water.

EVA, Peach County. An early community in what is now Peach County. *See* Houser Mill.

EVANS COUNTY. Created August 11, 1914 with 186 square miles taken from Bulloch and Tattnall counties. Named for General Clement Anselm Evans (1832-1911), who commanded Gordon's famous division, was a Methodist minister, candidate for governor of Georgia, and was commander in chief of the United Confederate Veterans. The county seat is Claxton (q.v.).

EVERETT SPRINGS, Chattooga County. A community located 18 miles north of Rome on EVERETT SPRINGS ROAD and Johns Creek. Named for an early settler, Elkanan Everett.

EXCELSIOR, Candler County. A community located southeast of Metter. First known as LITTLE CREEK, and was also known as RED BRANCH. Renamed at the suggestion of Miss Ida Middleton who felt that the name of the school here was to symbolize, "to rise (or to excel)."

EXILE CAMP, Terrell County. Was located on Main Street at the north edge of Dawson. So named when Governor Joseph E. Brown sent about 300 refugees here after the fall of Atlanta in 1864. The camp existed during Reconstruction until it was closed April 30, 1868.

EXPERIMENT, Spalding County. A community located on the northern outskirts of Griffin, and also a station on the Central of Georgia Railway. The Georgia Agricultural Experiment Station was moved to this 2,000-acre site in 1889, one year after having been first established at the University of Georgia in Athens.

F

FACTORY CREEK, Early County. Flows northwesterly into the Chattahoochee River. A factory was built on this stream in 1855 to make thread and cloth, with the creek furnishing power for the machinery.

FACTORY SHOALS, Douglas County. The name of this site was derived from the Sweetwater Manufacturing Company, which was established here in 1852 to process cotton and wool. It was located on Sweetwater Creek (q.v.) in the northeast section of the county. The workers lived in Sweetwater Town which had a population of about 350. It was four miles north of the factory, within the city limits of today's Austell.

FAIRBURN, Fulton County. This town was incorporated February 17, 1854, and named after an English township in the county of York. It was made county seat of old Campbell County October 17, 1870, when the seat was moved from Campbellton. Settled in the 1830's, the place was earlier called CARTERSVILLE and BERRYSVILLE.

FAIRCHILD(S), Seminole County. The most southwesterly community in the state. Is thought to have been named for an early settler, a Mr. Fairchild. The 255-acre FAIRCHILD STATE PARK is located here.

FAIRCLOTH, Mitchell County. Named for John G. Faircloth, who was a physician and druggist here. The community is now called BRANCHVILLE (q.v.).

FAIRFAX, Ware County. Incorporated as a town for 20 years beginning August 12, 1907. Was a former post office and station on the Brunswick and Western Railroad, 17 miles west of Waycross.

FAIRMOUNT, Gordon County. Located 19 miles southeast of Calhoun. Incorporated as a town August 6, 1908. So named by the settlers for their old home, Fairmont, West Virginia. It was the county's only town on the old Tennessee (stagecoach) Road.

FAIRVIEW, Chattooga County. A former village located five miles northwest of Summerville. Named this for the excellent view of the mountains here.

FAIRYLAND (Militia) DISTRICT, Walker County. Located in the northwest corner of the county. Named for the principal theme of the Rock City Gardens (q.v.) and Mother Goose Storyland.

FALL LINE (sometimes called OLD FALL LINE). A geologists' term that refers to what was once the shoreline of an ancient ocean about 100 million years ago. It is called this as it marks the place where streams of the Piedmont Plateau drop to the Coastal Plain in falls or rapids. This Fall Line in Georgia extends from Columbus through Macon to Augusta. Along this belt is found 80% of the kaolin in the United States.

FALLING CREEK, Elbert County. Rises at Elberton and flows southerly to the Broad River. Named for John Falling, a brother-in-law of James Vann, forefather of the Cherokee Vann clan. *See also* Vann, Murray County.

FANNIN COUNTY. Created January 12, 1854 with 396 square miles taken from Gilmer and Union counties. Named in honor of a native Georgian, Colonel James W. Fannin (1809-1836). He perished in what was known as "Fannin's Massacre" at Fort Goliad in southern Texas, in the War of Texas Independence. The county seat is Blue Ridge (q.v.).

FARGO, Clinch County. The abandoned post office at nearby Dayton was transferred here and renamed Fargo. Ben Leviton served as postmaster at both places, and his grandson owns a modern store here now. Today's postmaster, S. H. Croft, explains that Fargo is a coined word, and was so named when the G. S. Baxter Lumber Co. built a railroad from Valdosta, and this was just as FAR as it would GO.

FARMINGTON, Oconee County. Incorporated as a city August 18, 1919. Located six miles south of Watkinsville, and so named because of its being in an agricultural region.

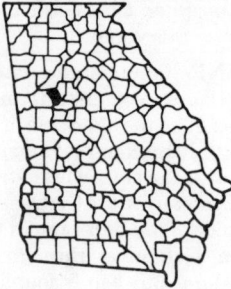

FAYETTE COUNTY. Created May 15, 1821 with 199 square miles acquired by Creek cession of January 8, 1821. An original county, it was named in honor of the Marquis de Lafayette (1757-1834) of France, who fought against England in the American Revolution (*see also* LaFayette). The county seat is Fayetteville (q.v.).

FAYETTEVILLE, CS Fayette County. Incorporated and made county seat on December 20, 1823. For derivation, *see* Fayette County. The court house which was built in 1825 is the oldest in the state.

FDR, Seminole County. This school site in the middle of the county is so designated from the initials of the three consolidated schools: Fairchild, Desser and Reynoldsville.

FEAGIN ROAD, Houston County. *See* Wellborn's Mills.

FEDERAL CROSSING, Hall County. Located about one mile north of the town of Flowery Branch. This is a byway that is a remnant of the Old Federal Road (q.v.) which crossed Flowery Branch (stream) here.

FEDERAL FORT, Bartow County. Located on the hill east of U. S. highway 41 at the Etowah River. General Sherman built this fort in 1864 to protect the river bridge.

FEDERAL ROAD. *See* OLD FEDERAL ROAD, and *see also* Macon.

FEDERAL TOWN, Baldwin County. An old tobacco village which was established about 1792 on the east bank of the Oconee River. It was the first settlement in the county, but perished with the coming of cotton. The name was changed to FORT FIDIUS (q.v.) when that post was erected at the site.

FEDERAL WIRE ROAD (Marker at Knoxville Court House). This name is in reference to the telegraph line which paralleled this road, the first such line to be erected in Georgia (1848). The road ran from Washington D. C. through Richmond to Augusta, Sparta, Milledgeville, Macon, and Knoxville to Coweta Town (Columbus), and then on westward to New Orleans. It was also known as FEDERAL ROAD, having previously been called MAIL ROAD.

FENDER, Tift County. A post office and community named for the Frank Fender turpentine works. The railroad name for the place is ELDORADO (q.v.).

FICKLINGS MILL, Taylor County. Named for a Dr. Fickling who lived here, and was a surgeon in the Confederate Army. The dam on Patsiliga Creek (where now crossed by Georgia 137) was originally built here before the Civil War. Fickling was an ancestor of Macon realtor, Bill Fickling.

FIFTEEN MILE CREEK, Candler County. Flows southerly to enter the Canoochee River below Metter. Named for the distance at the big bend, being 15 miles from Ten Mile Creek.

FIGHTINGTOWN CREEK, Fannin County. Flows northeasterly to enter Tennessee at McCaysville. The name is a translation of the Cherokee term, *Unulsti yi,* "fighting place," a meeting place of war chiefs.

FILLMORE, Whitfield County. A former community and post office which was five miles northeast of Dalton. Named for Millard Fillmore, president of the United States, 1850 to 1853.

FINDLAY, Dooly County. A community located four miles north of Vienna. Founded by a Mr. Findlay who set up a sawmill here in the early 1900's.

FINHALUI. A Lower Creek Indian town. *See* Penholoway Creek.

FINNEY (Militia) DISTRICT, Jones County. The Benjamin Finney family were early residents of Jones County. Mr. Finney fought in the American Revolution, and died in Jones County in November 1824.

FISH, Polk County. Located about six miles east of Cedartown on the Seaboard Coastline Railroad. This was an early trading station, with the railroad name of FISH CREEK STATION, named from nearby FISH CREEK.

FISHING CREEK. Arises in eastern Jones County and flows easterly to enter the Oconee

River at Milledgeville in Baldwin County. The name is a translation from the original Indian name of THLATHLOASA (or THLOCK-LAUSO).

FITZGERALD, CS Ben Hill County. "The Colony City of Georgia" Named for Philander H. Fitzgerald, a newspaper publisher from Indianapolis, who settled the town in 1895 with families of Union veterans who became tired of northern winters. Was first incorporated as a city December 2, 1896. The little village of SWAN (q.v.), also called "Shack Town," was here originally. The president of the Confederacy, Jefferson Davis, was arrested five miles from here in Irwin County on May 10, 1865.

FITZPATRICK, Twiggs County. A community located seven miles northwest of Jeffersonville. Earlier known as ELMWOOD, it was renamed to honor the prominent family of Benjamin S. Fitzpatrick.

FIVE FORKS, Madison County. Incorporated as a town December 8, 1899 at a place where the roads forked off into five directions. The town became COLBERT (q.v.) in 1909.

FIVE MILE BRANCH. Also called FIVE MILE CREEK. Arises in lower Sumter County, and flows southwesterly into Lee County where it joins Muckalee Creek. The name refers to its length. It was formerly called SUOXOMAHA, a Creek Indian word meaning "Hog Potato Creek."

FIVE MILE CREEK. Arises in Appling County, then separates that county and Wayne County before it empties into the Altamaha River. This name was applied to the stream because it ends five miles above Fort James Bluff.

FIVE MILE CREEK. Coffee County. This stream was given its name by General Blackshear (see Blackshear), although it is not known why.

FIVE NOTCH ROAD, Heard County. This was a trail blazed through the woods by early settlers on the west side of the Chattahoochee River. Five axe-marks in the trees at about 100-yard intervals identified the trail. See also Three Chop Road.

FIVE POINTS, Atlanta. This constitutes Atlanta's hub, from which principal thoroughfares radiate in five directions to all parts of the metropolitan area. This wedge-shaped area is at the intersection of Peachtree, Decatur, and Marietta streets and Edgewood Avenue. This intersection is called, "The Wall Street of the South," as it is the state's financial center. Originally the town well was at this spot, and for a long time a flag pole stood here. FIVE POINTS is a descriptive name for a place at which five roads or trails converge, and is also found in the following counties: Dougherty (part of Albany), Lowndes, Macon, Randolph, Taylor, and Thomas.

FIVE SPRING TRAIL, Walker County. A former Cherokee Indian trail running the entire length of Broomtown Valley (q.v.). Named after five cold, clear springs of pure water located along this trail.

FLAT CREEK, Fayette County. A community located eight miles southwest of Fayetteville, within the city limits of the present Peachtree City. The nearby stream, FLAT CREEK, from which it derived its name, arises near Tyrone and flows southerly into Line Creek. FLAT CREEK as a stream name indicates a creek with little gradient, therefore having quiet or "flat" water, and not considered desirable for a mill. In the following counties are found streams with this name: Berrien (2), Clay, Dawson, Emanuel, Fannin, Fayette, Gilmer, Hall, Houston, Meriwether-Troup, Miller, Montgomery, Rabun, Spalding, Twiggs, Walton and White.

FLAT SHOALS, Butts County. This was the name of a hamlet on the bank of the South River. Union General, J. W. Geary, reported it as "Float Rock" during Civil War action here October 11, 1864.

FLAT SHOALS, Pike County. Once a busy river town in the early days of the county, it was located on the Flint River about five miles west of the present community of Concord.

FLAT SHOALS CREEK, Harris County. Flows southerly into the Chattahoochee River in the northwest corner of the county. So named due to the sandbar created where the stream joins the Chattahoochee.

FLAT SHOALS CREEK, Hart County. Rises about three miles east of Bowersville and enters Hartwell Reservoir above Hartwell. Was descriptively named.

FLAT TOP MOUNTAIN, Gilmer County. With an elevation of 3,800 feet, it is located near the Fannin County line. Named for the flat appearance of the summit.

FLAT WOODS, Elbert County. A former community and post office about ten miles southeast of Elberton. Named for an unusual level and rich stand of hardwoods.

FLEMINGTON, Liberty County. Located two miles northeast of Hinesville, this community was settled before 1814. Originally called GRAVEL HILL, it was then named after its first settler, William Fleming.

FLETCHERVILLE, Thomas County. Incorporated March 5, 1856. This former town was named from FLETCHER INSTITUTE, a Methodist school which was incorporated in 1854, and located just outside of Thomasville.

FLINT, Mitchell County. A station on the Seaboard Coastline Railroad located six miles north of Camilla, it was originally named COCHRAN'S MILL (q.v.), and later given its present name after the nearby Flint River.

FLINT HILL, Talbot County. This rural community as well as FLINT HILL (Militia) DISTRICT are located in the northwest corner of the county, west of the Flint River.

FLINT RIVER. This 350-mile river, rises from a stream in College Park, flowing southward until it joins the Chattahoochee River at the southwest corner of the state. The name is reportedly from the Indian name for the waterway, THRONATEESKA (q.v.), which name refers to a source of flint stone. John Goff said that the Muskogee Indian name for the Flint River was HLONOTIS-KAHACHI. It was named RIO DE CAPACHEQUI by Hernando DeSoto when he discovered these inland waters near Bainbridge, Friday March 5, 1540. The Spanish later called it the RIO PERDERNALES (*see* Pedernales).

FLINTSIDE, Sumter County. This community name describes its location on the west bank of the Flint River (now Lake Blackshear).

FLINTSTONE, Walker County. A community located four miles southwest of Rossville. Named for a nearby source of the flint stone, used by the Cherokee Indians.

FLIPPEN, Henry County. This community was established with the Southern Railroad when it was built through here, and it was named for a Mr. Flippin, one of its officials. The post office was established in 1886 when it was moved from Guess (q.v.) by A. G. Harris who founded Flippen.

FLORENCE, Stewart County. Was incorporated for ten years beginning December 14, 1837. This shipping point on the Chattahoochee River was built to replace Roanoke (q.v.), three miles downstream, which was burned by Indians in 1836. Adiel Sherwood listed the name as LIVERPOOL in his *Gazateer* published in 1837. An earlier settlement, three fourths of a mile from the present Florence, was called MILLEN, and later referred to as OLD FLORENCE. *See also* APALACHEE.

FLORIDA (or LA FLORIDA). In the Spanish era, this name was applied to the region which included present day Georgia. The name which was chosen by Ponce de Leon means "flowered (or flowery)."

FLORIDA PASSAGE. A portion of the Atlantic Intracoastal Waterway (q.v.) between Bryan County and Ossabaw Sound on the route to Florida.

FLOVILLA, Butts County. This town was incorporated October 6, 1885, at the same time it changed its name from that of INDIAN SPRINGS (q.v.).

FLOWERY BRANCH, Hall County. Incorporated as a town August 17, 1903. The first house was built here in 1875, one mile from the stream from which the name of the town was derived. FLOWERY BRANCH had been called NATTAGASSKA by the Cherokee Indians, and it means "blossom creek," in reference to the floral beauty along its banks.

FLOYD COUNTY. Created December 3, 1832 with 514 square miles taken from part of the original Cherokee County. Named for General John Floyd (1769-1839) of South Carolina, an Indian fighter and U. S. congressman. The county seat is Rome (q.v.).

FLOYD JUNIOR COLLEGE of Rome opened in the Fall of 1970 and is part of the University System of Georgia.

FLOYD(S) ISLAND, Charlton County. Located six miles northeast of Stephen C. Foster State Park in the Okefenokee Swamp. Named by General Charles Floyd for his father, General John Floyd (*see* Floyd County), a famous soldier who drove the Seminoles out of the swamp in 1838.

FLOYD SPRINGS, Floyd County. Located four miles north of Armuchee on Floyd Springs Road. Named for General John Floyd (*see* Floyd County).

FODDER CREEK, Towns County. Rises on the southern slope of Brasstown Bald, and flows northeasterly until it enters the Hiawassee River. Near this stream is a site that was called FODDER CREEK after the Cherokee Indian Chief Fodder, who lived here with his tribe. His Indian name was Saluwaugah. The place is now called BALD MOUNTAIN PARK.

FOLKSTON, CS Charlton County. Incorporated as a city August 19, 1911. The county seat was moved here from Traders Hill (q.v.) in 1901. Named in honor of a prominent family of Charlton County, related to Dr. A. P. Folks of Waycross.

FORD, Bartow County. A former village and post office located four miles southwest of Kingston. Named for Joseph Ford, an early settler.

FORD ISLAND, Bryan County. Located in the Ogeechee River, just below Richmond Hill (q.v.) where Henry Ford (1863-1947) owned several plantations.

FORK DISTRICT, Hall County. This militia district was given this name because of its location at the fork of the Chestatee and Chattahoochee rivers.

FORK FERRY, Gordon County. The early name of CALHOUN. *See* New Echota.

FOREST PARK, Clayton County. Incorporated as the town of FORREST PARK August 14, 1908. So named for the many park areas here. The early rail stop here was called QUICK STATION.

FORESTVILLE, Floyd County. A former village located eight miles northwest of Rome. Named for General Nathan Bedford Forest (1821-1877) of Tennessee, a noted hero of the Confederacy.

FORSYTH, CS Monroe County. Incorporated December 10, 1823 when this was also designated the county seat. To lay out the city, 202½ acres were purchased for $700 from John T. Booth, February 18, 1823. Named in honor of John Forsyth (*see* Forsyth County). Railroading in Georgia got its actual start December 8, 1838 when two passenger cars on the Macon and Monroe Railroad left Macon for a 63-minute run to Forsyth. The first county seat of Monroe County was Johnstonville (q.v.).

FORSYTH COUNTY. Created December 3, 1832 with 223 square miles taken from Cherokee County. Named for John Forsyth (1780-1841), a native of Virginia and famed Georgia diplomat and statesman. He served as governor of Georgia 1827-29, and was secretary of state under President Van Buren. His home still stands in Augusta at Milledge and Cumming roads. The county seat is Cumming (q.v.). The court house was destroyed by fire in 1972 and 1973.

FORSYTH PARK, Savannah. Laid out in 1851 and named for John Forsyth (*see* Forsyth County).

FORT ADVANCE, Baldwin County. An early Indian fort, built by Elijah Clarke in 1794 on the Oconee River, on the opposite shore from Fort Fidius (q.v.). The site is about two miles below Milledgeville on Georgia highway 112. It was believed named because of its forward position. *See also* Trans-Oconee Republic.

FORT ALERT, Charlton County. This community was also known as TRADERS HILL (q.v.).

FORT ARGYLE, Bryan County. Built in 1733 by General Oglethorpe and Captain James McPherson, and named for John Campbell, Duke of Argyle. Was located about forty miles from Savannah on the west bank of the Ogeechee River, about one mile above the mouth of the Canoochee River. The site is now within Fort Stewart reservation.

FORT AUGUSTA, Richmond County. The first white settlers here were fur hunters Kennedy O'Brien and Roger deLacy. They established a trading post here to be closer to the Indians than Savannah Town. For their protection the trustees ordered the erection of Fort Augusta in 1736. During the American Revolution, it was called FORT CORNWALLIS (q.v.). *See also* Augusta.

FORT BARRINGTON, McIntosh County. Built in 1760 by Lieutenant Robert Baillie who garrisoned the fort with 25 rangers. It was established at a strategic crossing of the Altamaha River, twelve miles northwest of Darien, and was intended as a first line of defense against the Indians. After several years it was abandoned until the coming of the Revolution, at which time it played a vital part under the name FORT HOWE (q.v.). It was also garrisoned by the Confederate forces during the Civil War. Named in honor of Lt. Col. Josiah Barrington, a friend and kinsman of General Oglethorpe. In 1773, John Bartram the famous colonial botanist noted the remnants of an ancient Indian village at this site, which is now known as OLD FORT BARRINGTON.

FORT BARTOW, Chatham County. Located on a sandy bluff above St. Augustine Creek, four miles southeast of Savannah at a site known as Causton's Bluff (q.v.). Known as CAUSTON'S BLUFF BATTERY before 1863, the name was changed to honor General Francis S. Bartow (*see* Bartow County).

FORT, BEARDS BLUFF, Long County. *See* FORT TELFAIR.

FORT BENNING, Chattahoochee County. "The West Point of the South" This is the world's largest infantry camp, covering 284 square miles, just south of Columbus. It was established at the beginning of World War I, by order of General Pershing in 1917. Originally called CAMP BENNING, it was changed to Fort Benning in 1922, having been named in honor of General Henry Lewis Benning (1814-1875), "Old Rock" of Confederate fame. He was one of the most widely known and highly esteemed men in Georgia, considered great as a lawyer, judge, soldier, and patriot. LAWSON FIELD at Fort Benning was named in honor of Captain Walter B. Lawson, who was awarded the D.S.C. for heroism during World War I.

FORT BROWN, Chatham County. Was located at Savannah's Roman Catholic cemetery. Built at the beginning of the Civil War for defense of the city. Believed named for Georgia's governor during that war, Joseph Emerson Brown (1821-94). *See also* Emerson, Bartow County.

FORT BUFFINGTON, Cherokee County. Located six miles northwest of Canton, near Waleska. Was also called BUFFINGTON (q.v.).

FORT CEDARTOWN, Polk County. Was erected in the 1830's as a stockade or fort for rounding up Cherokees for removal to the West in 1838. Named from the town of Cedartown (q.v.).

FORT CHASTAIN, Towns County. Was established for the handling of Indians as at Fort Cedartown (q.v.). Derivation of the name is not known.

FORT COCKSPUR, Chatham County. *See* COCKSPUR FORT.

FORT CORNWALLIS, Augusta. Named after General Charles Cornwallis, 1st Marquis (1738-1805). Erected by the British at the site of the previous FORT AUGUSTA (q.v.). It was captured in 1780 by Colonel Elijah Clarke (*see* Clarke County) and Colonel James McCall.

FORT CUMMINGS, Walker County. This was an old Indian stockade, built by the United States government in 1836 on a hill above Big Spring at the northwest edge of LaFayette. Is thought to have been named for Rev. David B. Cummings, who was a well known Methodist preacher and missionary to the Indians.

FORT DAHLONEGA, Lumpkin County. Was an Indian removal stockade (*see* Fort Cedartown) named for the town of Dahlonega (q.v.).

FORT DANIEL, Gwinnett County. This fort was built as an outpost against the Indians, and was completed December 14, 1813. It was erected on a high hill near Hog Mountain, and presumably named in honor of General Allen Daniel (*see* Danielsville).

FORT DARIEN, McIntosh County. This was the first military post of the Scotch Highlanders at New Inverness (q.v.). Named by their leader Captain George Dunbar who brought them here in 1736, in memory of a former Scottish Colony (about 1696) in

Panama called Darien; it was claimed to be Balboa's mispronounciation of a native, Tarena. The Isthmus of Panama was formerly called the Isthmus of Darien, and today Darien is the name of the eastern part of Panama. *See also* Darien.

FORT DEARBORN, Clinch County. Was located at the confluence of the Suwanee River and Suwanoochee Creek. Commanded by Major G. Dearborn during the Indian troubles of the 1830's.

FORT DEFENSE, Wayne County. This stockade was established in post-Revolutionary years at the site of Doctortown (q.v.), and was so named as it was built to be used for the defense of the white settlers from Indian attacks.

FORT DEFIANCE, Baldwin County. Was established and commanded by General Elijah Clarke. The fort was burned September 28, 1794 after Clarke and his men were forced out in the action brought about to eliminate the Trans-Oconee Republic (q.v.) under command of Jared Irwin.

FORT DEPOSIT, Dawson County. Built on Thompson Creek in 1818 by Andrew Jackson. So named as it was used for the storage of food and supplies.

FORT EARLY, Crisp County. Was constructed in 1812 as an outpost against the Indians, on the banks of the Flint River at the western end of Blackshear Road (q.v.). It was given this name to honor the then current governor of the state, Peter Early (*see* Early County).

FORT EBENEZER, Effingham County. Erected at Ebenezer (q.v.) in 1757 by John Gerar William DeBrahm, His Majesty's Surveyor-General for the Southern District of North America. It was built for protection of the early settlers from Indian attacks.

FORT EDWARDS, Oconee County. In 1789, the Eagle Hotel building in Watkinsville, opposite the courthouse, was used as a blockhouse for protection against the Indians. It was called Fort Edwards, with derivation unknown.

FORT ERWIN, Washington County. Was located eight miles south of Tennille. A stockade erected by Governor Jared Erwin (1751-1818) and his three brothers for the protection of the settlers from Indian attacks.

FORT FIDIUS, Baldwin County. Es-

tablished in 1793 at a site two miles below the mouth of Fishing Creek, on the east side of the Oconee River. The derivation of the name is not known. In 1797, it was replaced by Fort Wilkinson (q.v.). *See also* FEDERAL TOWN.

FORT FLOYD. Was located near the northeast corner of Okefenokee Swamp. It was occupied November 15, 1838 to September 25, 1839, and named for the famed Indian fighter, General Charles Floyd.

FORT FREDERICA, Glynn County. An earthwork fortification established on St. Simons Island February 18, 1736 by General James Oglethorpe, and was the headquarters for his military operations against the Spanish in Florida during the Anglo-Spanish struggle of 1739-43. Oglethorpe's forces turned back the Spanish invaders in the Battle of Bloody Marsh a few miles south of the fort in 1742. *See also* Frederica.

FORT FROGTOWN, White County. Was located about 20 miles northwest of Cleveland. This was an army outpost and stockade for prisoners, used by U. S. troops during the Cherokee Indian removal of 1838. For derivation, *see* Frogtown Creek.

FORT GAINES, CS Clay County. "Queen City of the Chattahoochee". Incorporated as a town December 14, 1830. Was known to the Indians as A-CON-HOLLO-WA TAL-LOFA, "Highland Town." Named for the military fort which was erected in April 1814 on the crest of a bluff on the left bank of the Chattahoochee River to check Seminole and Creek incursions into South Georgia. The fortification was named for General Edmund Pendleton Gaines (*see* Gainesville), who proposed that this fort be established. The last garrison abandoned the post in 1865.

FORT GALPHIN. Located on Silver Bluff below Augusta on the South Carolina side of the Savannah River. The British called the fort, DREADNAUGHT (meaning "Fearless"), but the Americans named it for the wealthy Indian trader, George Galphin, who was active in Georgia, but whose residence was here.

FORT GEORGE, Chatham County. Was constructed on Cockspur Island (q.v.) in 1761 by John G. W. DeBrahm to guard the mouth of the Savannah River. It served at least up to 1775, and was dismantled in 1776. Believed to have been named for King George III of England. This name, FORT GEORGE, was soon after given to Fort Morris (q.v.) by the British.

FORT GILLEM, Forest Park. Activated June 30, 1974 and named in honor of Lt. Gen. Alvan C. Gillem, Jr. (1888-1973) of the U. S. Third Army. Was established on the site of the former Atlanta General Depot.

FORT GILMER, Clinch County. A place by this name was located about two miles southwest of Fargo on the Suwannee River. Derivation of the name is unknown.

FORT GILMER, Fulton County. Was located at the site of Atlanta's water works at Bolton. Also known as GILMER'S FORT, it was named for its builder, Lieutenant George Gilmer (see Gilmer County). The post was also called FORT PEACHTREE (q.v.), so named from the Indian town, Standing Peachtree, at the site.

FORT GILMER, Gilmer County. Was located one mile below the mouth of Cypress Creek, and named for Governor George R. Gilmer It was established in 1836, and occupied from July 30, 1838 to March 24, 1842.

FORT GORDON, Richmond County. The original name was CAMP GORDON (q.v.).

FORT GREENE, Pulaski County. Was located 6½ miles below Hartford at the site of the present Fort Pond. It was named for Nathanael Greene (see Greene County), famed Revolutionary general. This was one of four early forts built in the county for the defense of the settlers "from the savagery of the Creek and Seminole Indians." The others were Forts Pike, Lawrence, and Mitchell. It is believed that FORT GREENE in Chatham County was also named for General Greene. This fort on Cockspur Island was destroyed by a battering hurricane in 1804.

FORT GRIERSON, Augusta. Was located at or near the intersection of the present Reynolds and Eleventh streets. Named after the British officer, Lieutenant Colonel James Grierson, who commanded the fort, and was then shot by a Georgian. This was a temporary stronghold during the British occupation of Augusta, 1780-81. Was captured in May 1781 by an American force under General Andrew Pickens, aided by Colonel "Lighthorse Harry" Lee and Colonel Elijah Clarke.

FORT HALIFAX, Chatham County. Erected in 1759 on the bluff within the Savan-

nah city limits. Named for George M. Dunk, Earl of Halifax (1716-1771), who was called the "Father of the Colonies."

FORT HAWKINS, Bibb County. This was the first white settlement of Macon, and was constructed in 1806 on the site of OLD OCMULGEE FIELDS (q.v.). It was named for Benjamin Hawkins (1754-1816), who selected the site and had recommended its establishment, to be used as a trading post. The garrison was brought here from Fort Wilkinson (q.v.). This fort was in operation from 1807 to 1821. A replica of Fort Hawkins was erected in 1929 on Macon's Emery Highway, at the instigation of the Nathaniel Macon Chapter of the D.A.R. See also Old Agency and Hawkinsville.

FORT HEARD, Wilkes County. Was ordered built in 1774. and was constructed near the headwaters of Fishing Creek on the site of present Washington (q.v.). Named for Stephen Heard who settled here about 1773; it was also called HEARD'S FORT (q.v.).

FORT HEITZEL, Gilmer County. Was located on the present site of East Ellijay. Used for herding Indians during the removal of the Cherokees in 1838. It stood until about 1868. Derivation of the name is not known, and it was sometimes erroneously called Fort Gilmer (q.v.).

FORT HOWE, McIntosh County. Built on the Altamaha River in 1777 near the junction of McIntosh, Glynn and Wayne counties. Originally called FORT BARRINGTON (q.v.), it was then named for North Carolinian, Brigadier General Robert Howe (1732-1796), who fought in the Continental Army here during the Revolutionary War.

FORT HUGHES, Decatur County. Was located near the present Bainbridge. This was an eighteenth century trading post, but the derivation of the name is not known. The earthwork fort was used by the troops of General Andrew Jackson during the Indian War of 1817-21.

FORT JACKSON, Chatham County. Was established at the site of the former MUD FORT on Salters Island (q.v.), which was built in 1778. Fort Jackson was built in 1808 and used as a signal station in the War of 1812. Named in honor of General James Jackson (see Jackson County), it was called FORT OGLETHORPE from 1867 to 1907. It now houses the maritime museum of the Georgia Historical Commission.

FORT JAMES, Elbert County. Was built at the fork of the Broad and Savannah rivers in about 1776, to protect the settlers of the Dartmouth (q.v.) area. It was named in honor of Georgia's last colonial governor, James Wright (1714-1785). Twenty years later, another FORT JAMES was built in what is now Wayne County. It was located on the Altamaha River about four miles above the community of Madray Springs, on what is now called FORT JAMES BLUFF. It is on the opposite shore from, and about a mile above Beard's Bluff (q.v.), and two miles above the mouth of Beard's Creek. Derivation of the name is not known. During the Civil War, there was a Confederate fortification called FORT JAMES on the Ogeechee River.

FORT JONES, Stewart County. This was a fortification which was built about 1837 near Florence (q.v.), for protection from the Creek Indians who burned Roanoke (q.v.). The derivation of the name is not known.

FORT KING GEORGE, McIntosh County. This was the first fort to be established by the English to defy the Spanish and the French. It was constructed in 1721 near the mouth of the Altamaha River on the bluff at Darien. Colonel John Barnwell, a planter from South Carolina was in charge of establishing the fort. The fort was named for King George I of England, and was shortly afterward abandoned in 1727 by Carolina. The site was bought by the State of Georgia in 1938 to be preserved as a historical monument. Another FORT KING GEORGE was built at the junction of the Oconee and Ocmulgee rivers about 1720 by order of General Nicholson, then governor of South Carolina. This fort was destroyed by fire and not rebuilt.

FORT LAWRENCE, Taylor County. Established by Colonel Benjamin Hawkins at Old Agency (q.v.).

FORT LAWTON, Jenkins County. This 42-acre stockade was located within what is now Magnolia Springs State Park. It was the largest camp for receiving prisoners-of-war in the entire Confederacy, built to handle a capacity of 40,000 prisoners. Completed in October 1864, it later burned. Believed to have been named from the former town here of Lawtonville.

FORT McALLISTER, Bryan County. Designed by Captain John M. McCrady and built in 1861-62 at Genesis Point on the south bank of the Great Ogeechee River. Was the southern "anchor" in a chain of Confederate defenses to prevent attack by sea. Federal naval attacks against the fort during the years 1862-64 were unsuccessful, and it was finally captured by General Sherman's land forces December 13, 1864. This earthwork fort, which was recently restored, got its name from the nearby McAllister plantation.

FORT McINTOSH, Camden County. Erected on the northeast side of the Satilla River in 1777, fifteen miles south of Atkinson, it became an important post on the Southern frontier. This is the only Georgia fort to ever surrender to the enemy and to allow its men to be captured. Named for General Lachlan McIntosh (1725-1806), commander of the Georgia Battalion, and was built by his brother, Colonel William McIntosh. It was General McIntosh who killed Button Gwinnett in a duel (*see* Gwinnett County).

FORT McPHERSON, Fulton County. Called "The Pentagon of the South." Established in the southwest sector of Atlanta in 1867, and originally called McPHERSON BARRACKS. Named for Ohio-born Union general, James Birdseye McPherson (born 1828), who was killed by Confederate sharpshooters in the Battle of Atlanta, July 22, 1864. A monument stands at the spot where he lost his life, at Monument and McPherson avenues southeast. During the 1880's, the original post was sold and the present site was selected in 1885, with occupation taking place in 1889.

FORT McCREARY, Stewart County. The site is one mile north of Omaha. Built for the defense of Georgia's frontier along the Chattahoochee River. It was garrisoned during the Creek Indian War of 1836.

FORT MASSACHUSETTS, Baldwin County. Was located at the Rock Landing (q.v.) on the Oconee River, as recorded in 1791. The Commonwealth of Massachusetts in New England was so named in 1780, this being an Algonquian Indian name meaning "big hills at."

FORT MATHEWS, Clarke County. Built in 1793 for protection of the frontiersmen from the Indians. Was located on the Oconee River opposite Watkinsville (?). Named for Georgia governor, George Mathews (1739-1812).

FORT MITCHELL, Russell County, Alabama. Was located near the Creek Indian town, Coweta, on the Chattahoochee River, and within the area of the present city of Mitchell. It was completed in 1813 (when this was still part of Georgia) as a frontier post, and named for Georgia governor, David B. Mitchell (1766-1837).

FORT MONTPELIER, Baldwin County. Built in 1794 just east of Milledgeville during the Creek Indian troubles. The nearby Montpelier Church on Georgia highway 24 was named from this fort.

FORT MORRIS, Liberty County. Located on the Midway River, just below Sunbury, the town it was designed to protect during the Revolution. Built in 1776 and named in honor of the captain who led the Continental artillery company here. It was first garrisoned in 1778. The British Colonel Prevost captured the fort in January 1779, whereupon he changed the name to FORT GEORGE in honor of King George III.

FORT MOUNTAIN, Murray County. This community took its name from the nearby 2,835-foot mountain. FORT MOUNTAIN is located in the Cohutta· Mountains, and it derives its name from an ancient fortification of unknown origin, the ruins of which still stand on the high point of the mountain. These are possibly the oldest fortifications of North America, believed to have been built by Indians about 1530 as protection against DeSoto's conquering legions. It has also been thought to have been built in 1560 by the Spanish party of Tristan DeLuna. Is located in the northern section of FORT MOUNTAIN STATE PARK. This 1,897-acre park was presented to the State of Georgia in 1934 for development as a state park by Ivan Allen Sr. of Atlanta.

FORT NEIL, Greene County. The early name of WHITE PLAINS (q.v.).

FORT OGLETHORPE, Catoosa County. Built in 1902-04 as a U. S. military reservation, and named for General James Edward Oglethorpe (*See* Oglethorpe County). It was used as a training post during World Wars I and II. The fort was closed in 1947, and then the town of FORT OGLETHORPE was established here, incorporated February 17, 1949. *See also* FORT JACKSON, and Macon, Bibb County (Fort Oglethorpe).

FORT PEACHTREE, Fulton County. First called FORT GILMER (q.v.), it was established from 1814 to about 1821 as part of a chain of communications and supply. It was located in what is now Atlanta, on a knoll on the north side of Peachtree Creek where it flows into the Chattahoochee River at Atlanta's Water Works. For derivation, *see* Peachtree Creek.

FORT PERRY, Marion County. Completed in 1813 at the direction of General John Floyd. (*see* Floyd County). Was located on the Old Federal Road, 12 miles north of Buena Vista. Named in honor of Commandant O. H. Perry (*see* Perry).

FORT PICKERING, Charlton County. Located at Coleraine (q.v.), it was one of the earliest government forts built for the protection of white settlers. A marker on the west side of St. Marys states that Fort Pickering was built there in the War of 1812, but this location (near the marker) appears unlikely.

FORT POND, Pulaski County. Located six and one-half miles below Hartford. This small lake was named in reference to Fort Greene (q.v.), which had been established here.

FORT PRINCE WILLIAM, Camden County. See FORT WILLIAM.

FORT PULASKI, Chatham County. Situated on Long Island at a site selected by Major Babcock about 1829. Captain J. F. K. Mansfield of the U. S. Engineer Corps was given charge of the erection which took almost sixteen years, and costing at that time nearly $1 million. Named in honor of Count Casimir Pulaski (*see* Pulaski County). This is one of the best preserved fortresses constructed for coast defense during the first half of the nineteenth century. Was greatly strengthened prior to the Civil War by R. E. Lee of U. S. Army Engineers. The fort was abandoned after the Spanish-American War, until the 537-acre FORT PULASKI NATIONAL MONUMENT was established here by presidential proclamation of October 13, 1924. The National Park Service then undertook to restore the fort so as to be preserved as it was at the time of its surrender in 1862.

FORT RECOVERY, Decatur County. See RECOVERY.

FORT ROMULOS, Monroe County. The proposed site for this fortification was near the Ocmulgee River opposite Tom's Ford (q.v.), but the post was never constructed. The location and name were designated by General John Twiggs (see Twiggs County). The name may be a variant of Romulus, who was the legendary founder and first king of Rome.

FORT ST. ANDREW, Camden County. Established in early 1736 by Captain Hugh Mackay on the northeast end of Cumberland Island. Saint Andrew was the patron saint of Scotland.

FORT ST. SIMON'S, Glynn County. Completed in 1736 on the south end of St. Simons Island where the lighthouse now stands. It was first called SOLDIER'S FORT and later referred to as THE FORT AT ST. SIMONS. Oglethorpe had ordered extensive fortification to be erected here. Records show that it was commanded by Lieutenant Delegal (see Delegal's Fort) in 1738.

FORT SCOTT, Decatur County. Built by Lt. Col. D. L. Clinch in 1816 on the west bank of the Flint River. Probably named for General Winfield Scott (1786-1860), who fought in the Seminole War. March 9, 1818, Andrew Jackson arrived and launched an unauthorized campaign against the Seminoles from this fort. It was first called CAMP CRAWFORD, named for Secretary of War, William H. Crawford. The post was abandoned in September 1821.

FORT SCREVEN, Chatham County. First acquired from John Screven and J. C. Rowland, by the United States, December 22, 1808, and was built on Tybee Island in 1875. The post office here was established in March 1898. It was manned during the Spanish-American War, World War I and II. First known as Fort Graham, it was then named in honor of General James Screven (see Screven County).

FORTSONIA, Elbert County. A community located eight miles southeast of Elberton. Named for George Hailey Fortson, a native son who was killed in the Philippines during the Spanish-American War.

FORT STEWART. First established as CAMP STEWART (q.v.).

FORT SUNBURY, Liberty County. Was built in the middle of the eighteenth century for protection against the Indians at Sunbury (q.v.). It was more commonly known as FORT MORRIS (q.v.).

FORT SWAMP, McIntosh County. This descriptively named fortification was es-

tablished in the middle of the eighteenth century on the south side of the Sapalo River at its mouth, 14 miles north of Darien.

FORT TATTNALL, Clinch County. Believed named for Governor Tattnall (see Tattnall County). It was built by General Charles Floyd during an expedition against the Indians of the swamp in 1838. Was located about ten miles northeast of today's Fargo, on the penninsula called The Pocket.

FORT TELFAIR, Long County. Also known as BEARDS BLUFF FORT as it was established at Beards Bluff (q.v.) on the Altamaha River for the protection against the Indians. Garrisoned on and off from 1776 to 1814. and named in 1790 for Governor Edward Telfair (see TELFAIR COUNTY and TELFAIRVILLE).

FORT TONYN. Built during the Revolutionary War at Scrubby Bluff on the St. Marys River. Named after the royal governor of Florida, Patrick Tonyn (1725-1792). A marker on the western edge of St. Marys indicates that this fort was located there, but Hemperley located a map showing its site on the Florida side of St. Marys River, opposite Coleraine (q.v.).

FORT TWIGGS, Hancock County. This frontier fort was named for General John Twiggs (see Twiggs County), and was erected in 1793 at the mouth of Shoulderbone Creek on the Oconee River.

FORT TWIGGS, Twiggs County. Was established during the War of 1812 near the present community of Tarversville. Erected and commanded by Colonel Ezekial Wimberly.

FORT TYBEE, Chatham County. Built about 1779 by Colonel Campbell at the north end of Tybee Island, not far from Fort Screven (q.v.).

FORT TYLER, Troup County. Was strategically located on top of a high hill on the northeast edge of West Point, for the defense of that town from Union attack, and to guard the two important railroad bridges across the Chattahoochee River. This was the last Confederate fort to fall. Named for Brigadier General Robert C. Tyler, who was killed at this small fort by General James H. Wilson's "Raiders," on Easter Sunday, April 16, 1865. The Union troops outnumbered this little garrison ten to one.

FORT UCHEE, Screven County. This was

an Indian trading post located 30 miles above Ebenezer on the Savannah River, commanded by Captain Thomas Wiggins who died in 1742. For derivation *see* Uchee Creek.

FORT VALLEY, Peach County. Called "The Peach Center" and "The Best Pecan Producing Area in the South." Incorporated March 3, 1856. Founded in 1820 by James A. Everett who established an Indian trading post here. The locality was first known as FOX VALLEY, because so many people from the Macon area would fox hunt in a small valley near Mossy Creek, a short distance from town. In 1825 the name was misread as "Fort Valley" when being submitted as an application for a post office. The congressman for the district who applied on behalf of the community scrawled the word "Fox" which was read as "Fort" in Washington. At that time, illegible writing was considered indicitive of intellectual profundity. There was actually never known to be a fort here. FORT VALLEY STATE COLLEGE is located here. The STATE TEACHERS AND AGRICULTURAL COLLEGE founded in 1902 at Forsyth, and the FORT VALLEY HIGH AND INDUSTRIAL SCHOOL, founded here in 1895, were combined in 1939 by the State to form Fort Valley State College, a part of the University System of Georgia.

FORTVILLE, Jones County. Was also known as OLD FORT or THE FORTIFICATION. This was the site of an early Indian trading post or fort, located about five miles east of today's Gray on Georgia highway 22.

FORT WALKER, Fulton County. The site is in Atlanta at the crown of the hill near the Atlanta Avenue and Boulevard entrance to Grant Park. Was erected with slave labor during the summer and fall of 1863, and was part of 10.5 miles of breastworks designed and supervised by Colonel L. P. Grant for the defense of Atlanta. Now standing is a restoration of the fort that stood to defend the southeast section of the city in the summer of 1864. Named in honor of General William Henry Talbot Walker (b. 1816) who was killed in the Battle of Atlanta, July 1864. *See also* Grant Park and Walker Monument. Another FORT WALKER was located on the west end of Chepucky Island (q.v.). General Floyd gave it this name, also in honor of General W.H.T. Walker.

FORT WASHINGTON, Wilkes County.

This was more commonly known as HEARD'S FORT (q.v.). The present county seat town of Washington (q.v.) is located on this site.

FORT WAYNE, Chatham County. Constructed in 1759 on Broad Street near the River in Savannah. Was used in the Revolutionary War and also in the War of 1812. In 1786, it was declared inadequate for compelling vessels to comply with the laws. Originally called FORT SAVANNAH, it was later renamed to honor Anthony Wayne (*see* Wayne County).

FORT WAYNE, McIntosh County. Built by the U. S. Government, and occupied October 21, 1821 to June 1823. Was named in honor of Anthony Wayne (*see* Wayne County).

FORT WILKINSON, Baldwin County. Established in 1797 on the Oconee River, three miles below Milledgeville. This was an early trading house for the Creek Indians, named in honor of General James Wilkinson (1757-1825) of Maryland, a scoundrel who was noted for his military activities during the Revolution. *See also* Fort Hawkins.

FORT WILLIAM (or WILLIAM'S FORT), Camden County. Built by General Oglethorpe about April 1740 at the lower end of Cumberland Island near Dungeness (q.v.). The garrison was sent here from Fort St. Andrew in June 1742. Nothing remains here now. Named for Prince William Augustus, Duke of Cumberland, for whom this island is named.

FORT WIMBERLEY, Chatham County. Built in 1741 to guard the narrows of the Skidaway River near Wormsloe (q.v.), the home of Noble Wimberly Jones.

FORT WINSTON, Baldwin County. An early fort built in 1794 which stood at the site of the present city of Milledgeville. This was a fortification of Elijah Clarke's Trans Oconee Republic (q.v.). Derivation of the name is not known.

FORT WORMSLOE, Chatham County. Built in 1735, this was one of Georgia's original fortifications against the Spanish. *See also* Wormsloe.

FORT YARGO, Barrow County. This old log fort or block house was built sometime in the 1790's by the Humphries brothers for protection against the Indians. *See* Fort Yargo State Park.

FORT YARGO STATE PARK, Barrow County. Located two miles south of Winder, this 1,680-acre park was named from the old fort (*see* Fort Yargo) here. *See also* WILL-A-WAY RECREATION AREA.

FOSTER, Brooks County. This former post office was established April 4, 1890 and transferred to Barney (q.v.) in 1897.

FOSTER'S STORE, Chattooga County. Located eight miles southwest of Summerville on the Chattooga River. Named for Captain Kinchen R. Foster who had a gin, general store, and grist mill here when he established the community. Later, in 1889, he was appointed superintendent of the newly established prison farm at Milledgeville.

FOSTERVILLE, Henry County. This was a post office in 1837, located near the Clayton County line. The settlement was made up of several Foster families.

FOUCHE, Floyd County. Located in the northwest section of the county on Lavender Creek. In 1881, the postmaster C. M. Fouche was in a partnership in operating grist, saw, and shingle mills. Brinkley says the community was named for Colonel Simpson Fouche, an early settler.

FOUR KILLER CREEK, Fulton County. This was translated from the Cherokee Indian name, *Nunggihtehe.* Chief Four Killer lived at the head of this stream, which is located between Roswell and Alpaharetta.

FOUR LANE HIGHWAY, Cobb County. The descriptive name of U. S. highway 41 through Marietta. This appellation has been used universally throughout the country for years, but a highway is rarely officially so labeled as it is here.

FOUR MILE CREEK, Forsyth County. *See* Two Mile Creek.

FOWL'S ROOST ISLAND, Okefenokee Swamp. This was so named as it was famous as a roosting place for water fowls of the swamp.

FOWL(S) TOWN, Decatur County. An old community located eight miles south of Bainbridge. The Indian name of the place was TOTALOSI TALOFA, but it was called Fowlstown by the whites. Elias Kemp was postmaster of the first post office here January 5, 1833; first named KEMP, the name was changed to Fowlstown July 15, 1833. Fifty years later, a post office named

AVIRETT was opened here March 12, 1883, with its name changed to Fowlstown by postmaster Abner Avirett, March 24, 1883. *See also* PERRYMAN.

FOX CREEK, Lee County. This is a tributary of Muckalee Creek. It was either translated from the Indian word for "fox" or the name was chosen because the first surveyor saw or killed a fox by the stream.

FOX VALLEY, Peach County. *See* FORT VALLEY.

FRANCISVILLE, Crawford County. Located six miles southwest of Roberta on State highway 128, near the site of Old Agency (q.v.). Was founded in 1825 by and named for Francis Bacon of Massachusetts, who was married to Benjamin Hawkins' daughter Jeffersonia. The community thrived until the 1850's, when the railroad was built between Macon and Columbus, but bypassing this section.

FRANKLIN, CS Heard County. Was a village as early as 1770, but not incorporated until December 26, 1831, at which time it was designated the county seat. They apparently "stole" the name from West Point (q.v.) in Troup County, thirty miles south, which was originally called FRANKLIN.

FRANKLIN COLLEGE, Clarke County. This was the name given to the first building of the University of Georgia (q.v.), to honor Benjamin Franklin who personified learning and wisdom. The University itself was referred to by this name in its early days.

FRANKLIN COUNTY. Created February 25, 1784 with 269 square miles acquired by Cherokee cession of May 31, 1783 and Creek cession of November 1, 1783. This was an original county, and was named in honor of Benjamin Franklin (1706-1790), the U. S. statesman, printer, scientist, and writer from

Philadelphia, who went to Paris in 1781 to sign the Treaty of Peace with England at the conclusion of the Revolution. The county seat is Carnesville (q.v.). This is one of 24 Franklin counties in the U. S., not counting Franklin Parish, Louisiana that were named for this great American. Also named in honor of Benjamin Franklin is FRANKLIN SPRINGS, Franklin County (Incorporated July 22, 1924), FRANKLIN SQUARE, Savannah, and FRANKLINVILLE, Lowndes County (see Lowndes Courthouse).

FRANKLIN D. ROOSEVELT STATE PARK, Harris County. This 4,980-acre park is located five miles southeast of Pine Mountain, and includes Lake Delano (q.v.) and LAKE FRANKLIN. Was created by President Roosevelt's C.C.C. (Civilian Conservation Corps) and named for the president, as he particularly liked and often visited this region during his term of office. The local residents still call it by its old name, PINE MOUNTAIN STATE PARK. Also named for this president is FRANKLIN D. ROOSEVELT HIGHWAY which runs from South Carolina through Cornelia, Newnan, Warm Springs, Columbus, and Albany, then on southward to the Florida Line.

FRANKLIN SPRINGS, Franklin County. Incorporated July 22, 1924. A community located 13 miles south of Lavonia.

FRANKLINVILLE, Lowndes County. This now dead village was located on the Withlacoochee River about nine miles northeast of Troupville (q.v.), and was the site of the county's first court house, which was built of logs in 1828. The post office was moved here from the original county seat of Lowndes Court-House (q.v.) July 7, 1828, at which time the name of the post office was changed to Franklinville. In 1833 it was decided to move the county seat here and change the name to Lowndesville (q.v.).

FRANKS, Jones County. This early community existed in the 1880's, and was located northeast of the Central of Georgia railroad station of Bradley. Named for Wiley Franks, a large landowner here, and his grandfather John W. Bradley (see Bradley, Jones County).

FRAZIER, Bleckley County. Incorporated as a town December 18, 1884 at which time it was in Pulaski County. It was located just above Empire. In 1881, the postmaster J. J. Frazier operated a general store here.

FREDERICA, Glynn County. Later called OLD TOWN, this old fort and settlement on St. Simons Island was named by General Oglethorpe after Frederick Louis (1707-1751), prince of Wales, eldest son of the King, and father of George III. It was established in 1736 for protection from the Spanish to the south. After determining the site, Oglethorpe returned to England to select the settlers, consisting of 40 families who would build the town and fort. This was a typical English village which was planned in England. Near this town was Orange Hall, which was the only home Oglethorpe ever occupied in the colony. By the year 1839 only two dwellings remained, and efforts to revivify the town proved utterly futile. In 1945 the 250-acre FORT FREDERICA (q.v.) site was established as a National Monument, a part of the National Park System.

FREDERICA COUNTY. On April 15, 1741 Georgia was divided into two so-called counties. Savannah County (q.v.) was the first established, and as the new settlements of Darien, Frederica, Barrimacke, etc. developed, it was decided to establish the new county with the county seat at Frederica. A president was never designated, so Frederica County never did become an actuality.

FREDERICA RIVER, Glynn County. Frederica (q.v.) is located on this channel between St. Simons Island and the mainland.

FREDONIA. Dr. John Goff explains that this is a coined name which was originally thought up in the early 1800's as a proposed national name for Americans and America. Believed to be a name built on the word "freedom," or meaning "Land of Freedom." Communities of this name have been found at various places in Georgia including: northwest Heard County near the Alabama line (1939), in Monroe County east of Forsyth on State highway 18, in Meriwether County, northeast of Thomasville in Thomas County, and a post office in Macon County (1851). And there is a Fredonia Church in Lamar County, southeast of Barnesville.

FREEDMEN'S GROVE, Liberty County. Located about three miles above Midway on U. S. highway 17. This is the descriptive name given to a Negro settlement on land deeded by the owner to his former slaves at the conclusion of the Civil War. The community is today designated as FREEDMAN.

FREEMAN, Gwinnett County. Early name of DACULA (q.v.).

FRIENDSHIP, Dooly County. This community took its early name from the Friendship Methodist Church here. The name has since been changed to BYROMVILLE (q.v.). Another community of FRIENDSHIP is located at the northwest corner of Sumter County.

FROGTOWN CREEK, Lumpkin County. This name (Frogtown) originally applied to a mountain peak northeast of the creek, and the name FROGTOWN (or WALASI-YI) also applied to an Indian settlement on the stream. For derivation, *see* Frogtown Pass.

FROGTOWN PASS, Union County. This was the name the Cherokee Indians gave to the present NEEL'S GAP (q.v.), a dent in the line of the Blue Ridge where U. S. highway 19-129 passes through. The ancient name was *Walasi-yi* "the place (or home) of Walasi, the Great Frog." *See* Walasiyi Inn.

FRONT RIVER, Chatham County. Descriptively named, it is that portion of the Savannah River which flows "in front of" Hutchinson Island (q.v.) at Savannah. *See also* Back River.

FULEMMY'S TOWN, Worth County. *See* PHILEMA.

FULLINGTON, Dooly County. Settled in the 1860's by John and G. W. "Doc" Fullington. The Southern Railroad built through here and changed the name to PINEHURST (q.v.).

FULSAMS CREEK, Hancock County. Has also been known as FOLSOMS CREEK. Named for Captain Benjamin Fulsam (or Folsom) who came to Georgia from North Carolina in 1773. He was attacked by Indians who killed him and burned his building in 1777. Shown as FULSOME CREEK on today's maps, it flows easterly into the Ogeechee River in the northeast section of the county.

FULTON, Fulton County. Now a section of Atlanta called BOLTON (q.v.), this early community was formerly called Fulton after the county name.

FULTON COUNTY. Created December 20, 1853 with 523 square miles taken from part of DeKalb County. The name of "Fulton" was accepted for the name of the new county after being proposed by Senator John Collier of

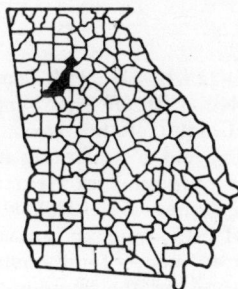

DeKalb County on December 7, 1853. It has been assumed by most historians that it was intended to be in honor of Robert Fulton (1765-1815) of Pennsylvania, who had gained notoriety with his steamboat *Clermont* in 1807. Franklin Garrett adds that "the weight of the evidence is that Dr. Needom L. Angier who came from New Hampshire had Robert Fulton in mind when he chose the name for this county." There have also been those who believe Georgia had no reason to honor Robert Fulton, in view of the fact that inventor William Longstreet of Augusta operated a steam powered vessel on the Savannah River in November 1808. It was then contended that the county was actually named after Hamilton Fulton, a noted English civil engineer, who was born and educated in Scotland, and who proposed and surveyed a railroad through what is now Fulton County. He was at that time the chief engineer of the state. The county seat is Atlanta (q.v.).

FUNKHOUSER, Bartow County. This community was named after the Funkhouser Co. which first owned the present Flex-a-tile Company here.

FURNACE, Dade County. A former community located two miles southeast of Rising Fawn. Named for the ore furnaces which were located near here by industrialist, Noah Edmondson. In Walker County is a stream named FURNACE CREEK which flows westerly into Armuchee Creek, two miles south of Villanow.

FUSHACHEE CREEK. Now known as PRUITT CREEK, it rises in southeast Randolph County and flows southward into Calhoun County where it joins Merrett Creek before emptying into Ichawaynochaway Creek. Variations of this name have included FUSIHATCHI and FOOSAHATCHEE. The word is of Muskogean origin, meaning "Bird-Stream" or "Clay Creek." An early English name of this stream was CLAYBANK CREEK.

G

GAINESVILLE, CS Hall County. Called "The Queen City of the Mountains" or "Poultry Capital of the World." Made the county seat and incorporated as a village named for Virginia-born General Edmund Pendleton Gaines (1777-1849), who served in the War of 1812, although it may have been named for a pioneer family named Gaines. In the early days, the community here was called MULE CAMP SPRINGS. The post office was opened in 1823. Gainesville is the Nation's leading center of broiler production in the chicken industry. GAINESVILLE JUNIOR COLLEGE is a part of the University System of Georgia, and was chartered here in 1965.

GALLOWS HALLOW, Lumpkin County. This is the name given to a deep ravine in back of the Dahlonega cemetery, so designated after Hamilton Sneed and a man named Jones were hanged here.

GALPHINTON, Jefferson County. This was an early trading post on the Ogeechee River, established by Indian trader, George Galphin prior to the founding of Georgia. This was later called OGEECHEE TOWN, and finally referred to as OLD TOWN. *See* Fort Galphin.

GAMMON THEOLOGICAL SEMINARY, Atlanta. Founded in 1883 for the education of Negro ministers. The name was chosen to honor Rev. Elijah H. Gammon, who gave generous financial aid to establish this school.

GANNET LAKE, Ware County. This 15-acre lake is in Grand Prairie (q.v.) in the southeast section of Okefenokee Swamp. So named because "black-end-wing gannet" water birds are here in large numbers.

GANSAGI, Gordon County. This was an active Cherokee Indian settlement near the present city of Calhoun. The earlier name of CONASAUGA (q.v.) was corrupted to the later "Gansagi." It is believed that DeSoto tarried a short time here in his 1540 expedition into this region. *See also* NEW ECHOTA.

GARDEN CITY, Chatham County. Incorporated February 8, 1939 as the town of INDUSTRIAL CITY GARDENS. The name was changed to the present one March 24, 1941, at which time it was reincorporated.

GARDI, Wayne County. Pronounced "Gardye." This community was named after the dense GARDI SWAMP nearby, where people had to guard their eyes when pushing through the thickets.

GARFIELD, Emanuel County. Incorporated as a town August 23, 1905. May have been named in honor of U. S. President James Garfield, who was assassinated in 1881.

GASCOIGNE'S BLUFF, Glynn County. Pronounced "Gas'-co-neeze." Located at the right of the St. Simons Causeway where it approaches St. Simons Island. Named for Captain James Gascoigne, commander of the man-of-war *Hawk,* which conveyed the two ships bringing settlers to Georgia in 1736. Among those arriving then were John and Charles Wesley and many German Salzburgers and Moravians. This section of the island yielded the live oak timbers for the U. S. Frigate *Constitution* or "Old Ironsides."

GATE CITY (Atlanta). This nickname for Georgia's capital city was first suggested in a toast at a banquet in Charleston in 1857, in reference to Atlanta's famous hospitality to travelers passing through the southwest.

GAY, Meriwether County. First settled by William Sasser who came here in a covered wagon in 1829. Incorporated as a town August 22, 1907 at which time W. F. Gay was appointed the first mayor.

GEECHEE, Jefferson County. This former community was located twelve miles from Louisville near Grange. Was so named because the place was settled with Negroes from the coast who spoke the Geechee dialect.

GENERAL COFFEE STATE PARK, Coffee County. This 1,495-acre park is located five miles east of Douglas. Named for General John E. Coffee (*see* Coffee County).

GENERAL'S CUT, McIntosh County. This name refers to a canal cut through the marshlands of General's Island (q.v.) between Frederica and Darien in 1808.

GENERAL'S ISLAND, McIntosh County. Located across the Darien River from Darien, it was named in honor of General Lachlan McIntosh (*see* McIntosh County) who established his home here in 1758.

GENEVA, Talbot County. Incorporated October 18, 1870. The name was taken from the city in Switzerland. First settled before 1840. In the 1850's the early community was called KOOCKOGEY (q.v.).

GENOLA, Carroll County. This was a suburban town, one mile west of Carrollton, and the site of the present West Georgia College. May have been named from the village of Genola in Italy.

GEORGE, LAKE. Borders Clay, Quitman and Stewart counties. Also called WALTER F. GEORGE RESERVOIR (q.v.).

GEORGETOWN, Bryan County. The original name of HARDWICK (q.v.), presumably named for King George II.

GEORGETOWN, CS Quitman County. Incorporated and designated the county seat December 9, 1859, and named for Georgetown, D. C. The name was changed from TABANANA (q.v.) September 21, 1836.

GEORGE WASHINGTON CARVER STATE PARK, Bartow County. This 307-acre park was developed for Negroes in the 1930's. Named in honor of Carver (1864-1943), who was born in Missouri of slave parents, graduated from Iowa State College, and taught at Tuskegee Institute in Alabama. He developed 300 products from the peanut plant.

GEORGE WASHINGTON HIGHWAY. The state highway from Savannah to Augusta was named after the Nation's first president.

GEORGIA. Charter was granted June 9, 1732 by the English sovereign, George II. The colony was named in his honor, taking the Latinized form for a place-name. Perhaps the earliest names given to the region which is now Georgia, were BIMINI (q.v.) and an early name the Indians gave to Georgia, E-CUN-NAU-NUX-ULGEE, which means "People greedily grasping after the lands of the red men." The Greek word *georgia* means "agriculture." In the 16th Century the Spaniards called the islands and coastal region GUALE (q.v.), and the inland territory they called TAMA (q.v.). As the colonies were being established further north in the 17th century, the present Georgia region was included in the land referred to as FLORIDA (q.v.). It is believed that the first map which showed this region with the name "Georgia" was one drawn in 1715 by Herman Moll (this was during the reign of George I who died in 1727). In the year 1717, Robert Montgomery proposed the establishment of a colony here to

be called MARGRAVATE OF AZILIA (q.v.). Five years later in 1722, the Swiss promoter Jean Pierre Purry interested the Board of Trade in a scheme to project the English settlement westward along the parallel of 33 degrees to be given the name of "Georgia" (in honor of King George I). The first public written mention of the name "Georgia" (honoring George II) was in *London Magazine,* June 3, 1732. The trustees surrendered their charter and Georgia became a royal province on June 23, 1752. On January 19, 1861, Georgia seceded from the Union; in 1871 representatives were readmitted to U. S. Congress. Georgia has no official sobriquet, but has sometimes been called "The Empire State of the South," "Peach State," "Goober State," "Cracker State" (q.v.), and "Yankee-Land of the South." The original charter to establish the Colony of Georgia assigned to the trustees the region between the Savannah and the Altamaha rivers, from the headwaters thereof, and westward to the Pacific. Today Georgia is the largest state east of the Mississippi River, with an area of 58,876 square miles, with a length of 315 miles, and a breadth of 250 miles. In the 1970 census, Georgia had a population of 4,627,309, ranking fifteenth in the United States. The capital city is Atlanta (q.v.), after previously being located at Savannah, Augusta, Louisville, and Milledgeville.

GEORGIA COLLEGE AT MILLEDGEVILLE. Established and chartered as GEORGIA NORMAL INDUSTRIAL COLLEGE in 1889, it became WOMAN'S COLLEGE OF GEORGIA in 1961. The present name was adopted in 1967 when the college became coeducational. It is a part of the University System of Georgia.

GEORGIA INSTITUTE OF TECHNOLOGY, Atlanta. Popularly referred to as "Georgia Tech," it is part of the University System of Georgia. In 1882, Representative (later governor) Nathaniel Edwin Harris of Bibb County, introduced a bill which provided for the establishment of a state technical school, at the suggestion of Macon industrialist, Major John Fletcher Hanson. It was chartered in 1885 and opened in 1888. The first two buildings were completed in 1888, the present ADMINISTRATION BUILDING and the OLD SHOP BUILDING. The early textile department was housed in the A. FRENCH BUILDING, named in 1899 for

Pennsylvania donor Aaron French. SWANN DORMITORY, finished in 1901, was named for Janie Austell Swann, wife of contributor James Swann. LYMAN HALL CHEMICAL LABORATORY was named for Lyman Hall (1860-1905), the second president of the University, responsible for its early growth and development. BRITTAIN HALL was named for the fourth president of the University, Dr. Marion L. Brittain. GRANT FIELD was named in memory of Hugh Inman Grant, the son of trustee of the University, John W. Grant.

GEORGIA MILITARY COLLEGE, Milledgeville. Established in 1879 in the old State Capitol Building, the building and grounds being a gift of the State. Originally called MIDDLE GEORGIA MILITARY AND AGRICULTURAL COLLEGE, the present name of this municipally operated high school was adopted in 1900.

GEORGIA STATE FAIR, Macon. Held annually in October at Macon's Central City Park. The first state fair was organized by the Southern Central Agricultural Society and held at Stone Mountain beginning in 1846. The fair was moved to Atlanta in 1850 and came to Macon in 1851.

GEORGIA STATE UNIVERSITY, Atlanta. Founded in 1913 as GEORGIA TECH EVENING SCHOOL OF COMMERCE. In 1947 it became the ATLANTA DIVISION OF THE UNIVERSITY OF GEORGIA, then GEORGIA STATE COLLEGE OF BUSINESS ADMINISTRATION in 1955, which was shortened to GEORGIA STATE COLLEGE in 1961. The present name was adopted in 1969.

GEORGIA SOUTHERN COLLEGE, Statesboro. Part of the University System of Georgia, it was founded in 1906. Opened in 1908 as FIRST DISTRICT AGRICULTURAL AND MECHANICAL HIGH SCHOOL. In 1924 it became GEORGIA NORMAL SCHOOL, then became SOUTHERN GEORGIA TEACHERS COLLEGE in 1929, and GEORGIA TEACHERS COLLEGE in 1939. The present name was adopted in 1959.

GEORGIA SOUTHWESTERN COLLEGE, Americus. Part of the University System of Georgia. Established in 1907 as a two-year college called THIRD DISTRICT AGRICULTURAL AND MECHANICAL

HIGH SCHOOL. The present name was adopted in 1933.

GEORGIA, UNIVERSITY OF, Athens. *See* UNIVERSITY OF GEORGIA.

GEORGIA VETERANS MEMORIAL STATE PARK, Crisp County. Deeded to the State by the Commissioners of Crisp County in 1946. This 1,307-acre park includes a military museum, and was named in honor of the State's men and women who served in World Wars I and II. It is located seven miles west of Cordele on the shore of Lake Blackshear, near the site of Fort Early (q.v.).

GERBER, Walker County. This former community was located in the northwest section of the county, where postmaster G. F. Gerber was a chemist and winemaker (1881).

GERMAINES ISLAND, Columbia County. *See* UCHEE ISLAND.

GERMAN(Y) CREEK, McDuffie County. Rises east of Thomson and flows northward into Clark Hill Reservoir. McCommons and Stovall said it was named for an early white settler who lived near this stream, while Brinkley writes that it was named for a group of German Quakers who settled here.

GERMAN VILLAGE, Glynn County. This was the name which referred to a former community two miles east of Frederica on St. Simons Island, where some of the German Salzburgers settled.

GHOST HOLE FORD, Charlton County. Located just over a mile above Moniac on the St. Marys River. It is said to be a name derived from a frontier killing involving a hold-up and shooting of a stage coach driver.

GIBSON, CS Glascock County. Incorporated August 20, 1913. Named in honor of Judge William Gibson (1822-1893) who donated $500 for Glascock County's first public buildings. As a colonel in the Confederate army, he was wounded at the Second Battle of Manassas and again at Gettysburg. The post office was established here March 31, 1858.

GILLSVILLE, Hall and Banks counties. Incorporated December 16, 1901. Named for a settler family of Gills. The original community here was called STONETHROW (in 1796) by railroad crews since it was such a short distance from Maysville.

GILMER COUNTY. Created December 3, 1832 with 439 square miles taken from part of Cherokee County. Named for George Rockingham Gilmer (1780-1859) in recognition

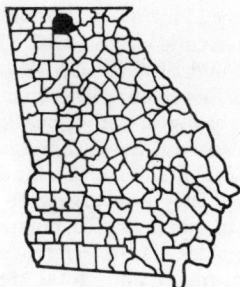

of his insistence that the Cherokee Indians be removed from this region. He served as U. S. Congressman (1824) and was the sixteenth governor of Georgia. *See also* Fort Gilmer. Governor Gilmer's home stands in Lexington, Oglethorpe County. The county seat is Ellijay (q.v.).

(THE) GLADE, Oglethorpe County. This was the early name of POINT PETER (q.v.). The word glade means "an opening among trees."

GLADE CREEK, Habersham County. Flows westerly to enter the Soquee River above Clarkesville through GLADE CREEK (Militia) DISTRICT. Named for the Glade Mining Company which operated in the area during the 1830's.

GLADE (Militia) DISTRICT, Hall County. Named after GLADE SHOALS which are in the North Oconee River east of Gainesville.

GLADESVILLE, Jasper County. A former community located 12 miles southwest of Monticello, sometimes called THE GLADES. Named for its location on a glade or grassy open plain. Nearby is GLADESVILLE CREEK which flows southerly to become Falling Creek near the Jones County line.

ta, who served in the War of 1812, also Seminole troubles of 1817, and was an officer of the state militia. He was elected to the U. S. House of Representatives in 1835. The county seat is Gibson (q.v.).

GLASGOW, Thomas County. A former community named for the city in Scotland by several Scotch families who settled here in 1826. Remaining is only the Glasgow Church, about ten miles southeast of Thomasville.

GLENDALE, Fulton County. Candler and Evans describe this as a hamlet in old Milton County, located five miles east of Roswell. The early residents probably gave this name for commendatory purposes.

GLENLOCH, Heard County. A former post office was established here in 1886, about three miles northeast of the community of Centralhatchee. The name is of Scotch origin, meaning "Glen lake" or "Lake-in-a-glen."

GLENVILLE, Tattnall County. "The Accommodating City" Incorporated as a city August 24, 1905. Named for the noted minister and educator, Glenn Thompson.

GLENWOOD, Montgomery County. Incorporated as a town August 11, 1908. This is believed to be a commendatory name.

GLOSTER, Gwinnett County. Pronounced "Gloss'tuh." A community located six miles southwest of Lawrenceville on the Yellow River. Named for a railroad official.

GLYNCO, Glynn County. Located just north of Brunswick, this U. S. Naval Air Station was established from 1942 to 1973. The name is a coined word made by dropping an "n" from Glynn Co.

GLASCOCK COUNTY. Created December 19, 1857 with 142 square miles taken from part of Warren County. Named for General Thomas Glascock (1780-1841), born in Augus-

GLYNN COUNTY. Created February 5, 1777 with 423 square miles acquired by Creek cessions of November 10, 1763 and November 12, 1785. This was an original county previously organized in 1765 as the parishes of St. David and St. Patrick. Named for John Glynn (1722-1779), noted member of Parliament, a friend of the colonies, and who was once Sergeant of London (that city's legal advisor). The county seat is Brunswick (q.v.). The court house was destroyed by storm in 1896.

GOAT ROCK DAM, Harris County. Completed in 1912 on the Chattahoochee River to create GOAT ROCK LAKE. Both were named from a large boulder on the river's edge which was called GOAT ROCK by Cullen and Abb Terry, who as boys liked to watch from here the goats of a Mr. Smith on the Alabama side of the river.

GOAT TOWN, Washington County. This name of a store and road intersection on the west side of Deepstep, was so named by a wag in reference to a large flock of goats kept by the early store owner.

GODFREY, Morgan County. This town was incorporated July 25, 1906, and named for early resident, Dr. Ervine Godfrey, who came here from Savannah.

GOGGINS, Lamar County. This community is located three miles east of Barnesville on the Central of Georgia Railway. Has also been called GOGGANSVILLE and GOGGANS STATION. Named for John F. Goggins, father of William J. Goggins who donated the site for the station.

GOLDEN GHETTO, Fulton County. A sobriquet of Sandy Springs (q.v.).

GOLDEN GROVE, Liberty County. In 1748, William Hester of North Carolina used this name for the first time in Georgia. This was a plantation site on the south side of the Midway River. Goldengrove was the name of Congressman James Gillespie's plantation at what is now Kenansville, N.C.

GOLDEN GROVE, Toombs County. This name applies to a bend and bar on the Altamaha River, about one mile below the bridge of U. S. highway 1. The name is thought to have been transplanted from a place in Wales or Great Britain. Or it may have been named by early rivermen in the fall of the year when the leaves are turning to a golden color.

GOLDEN ISLES. The name first applied to Georgia's coastal islands in 1717 by Sir Robert Montgomery. He wrote that this colony could become a golden opportunity to all comers (*see* Margravate of Azilia). These have also been called THE GOLDEN ISLES OF GUALE and SEA ISLANDS (although generally the Sea Islands are considered the islands lying below St. Catherines Sound). Included are Ossabaw, St. Catherines, Sapelo, St. Simons, Jekyl, and Cumberland islands. Historians say they were given the name by adventurers in search of gold, but more likely the name golden is in reference to less tangible treasures. With a total area of 600 square miles, these islands were separated from the mainland about 1,000 years ago.

GOLDEN TRIANGLE (GEORGIA'S). This commendatory name is a recent appellation which refers to the area delineated by a triangle formed by the cities of Brunswick, Folkston and Waycross.

GOLD NUGGET HIGHWAY. This name was given to State route 60 which extends from Dahlonega to Gainesville. The derivation is in reference to the old gold mining area around Dahlonega (q.v.).

GOOD HOPE, Walton County. Incorporated as a town August 11, 1905. Was named to indicate the early settlers' optimism for the future of their community.

GOPHER TOWN, Seminole County. Sometimes called "Go' Town." This name applied to a crossroads on Georgia highway 39 below Donalsonville. The name is said to be derived from the fact that an enormous gopher (or burrowing land turtle) was once killed nearby.

GORDON, Wilkinson County. Incorporated as a town October 7, 1885. This city was first established as a stop on the Central of Georgia Railroad, and named for its first president, W. W. Gordon (*see* Gordon County).

GORDON COUNTY. Created February 13, 1850 with 358 square miles taken from Bartow (then called Cass) and Floyd counties. Named for William Washington Gordon (1796-1842), attorney and graduate of West Point who was elected the first president of the Central of Georgia Railroad. The county seat is Calhoun (q.v.). The courthouse was destroyed by storm in 1888. A statue of W. W. Gordon is located at Wright Square, Savannah.

GORDON JUNIOR COLLEGE, Barnesville. Chartered first as MASONIC FEMALE SEMINARY in 1852. Then GORDON INSTITUTE was established here in 1872 by Charles E. Lambdin, its first president, who named it in honor of his good friend General John Brown Gordon (1832-1904). In 1927, the name was changed to GORDON MILITARY COLLEGE, and July 5, 1972, when it came under the University System of Georgia it became Gordon Junior College. RUSSELL HALL (library), was named for Senator Richard Russell, class of 1915 here. GORDON MONUMENT, Atlanta. A bronze equestrian statue of General John B. Gordon was placed on the capitol ground, which was unveiled May 25, 1907.

GORDONIA ALTAMAHA STATE PARK, Tattnall County. This 209-acre park is located within the city of Reidsville, and was originally called REIDSVILLE STATE PARK. The name was changed by act of the General Assembly, March 3, 1962, to memorialize the rare species named *Franklinia* or *Gordonia altamaha*. This is a small tree discovered in 1765 by naturalists John and William Bartram. It is known as the "Lost Camelia," belongs to the Theaceae family and is found naturally nowhere but Georgia.

GORMAN'S FERRY, Fulton County. The original name of AUSTELL'S FERRY (q.v.).

GOSHEN, Chatham County. This was an old Moravian settlement near old Knoxborough (q.v.), and was about two miles west of Abercorn and ten miles southwest of Ebenezer. The derivation is from the part of Egypt called the "Land of Goshen" in which the Israelites were settled by Joseph, and the meaning indicates fruitfulness and fertility. There is today a community called GOSHEN in upper Lincoln County.

GOUGH, Burke County. This community is located on Georgia highway 305 about twelve miles west of Waynesboro. Laid out in 1905, the first post office was on the plantation of J. P. Gough. *See also* Torbit.

GRAB ALL, Jones County. An alternate name of CORNUCOPIA (q.v.).

GRACEWOOD, Richmond County. Incorporated as a town December 24, 1884; located on the site of RICHMOND CAMP GROUND. The root word *grace* probably was used for its meaning of "divine mercy or forgiveness."

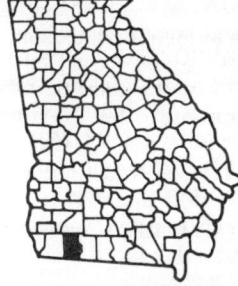

GRADY COUNTY. Created August 17, 1905 with 467 square miles taken from Decatur and Thomas counties. Named for Henry Woodfin Grady (1850-1889), who was the directing genius of *The Atlanta Constitution* as its managing editor, and was an orator who gained a national reputation as a spokesman for the New South. The county seat is Cairo (q.v.). The HENRY W. GRADY MONUMENT was placed at Marietta and Forsyth streets in Atlanta shortly after his death, and was dedicated October 21, 1891. In that same year construction was begun on the GRADY MEMORIAL HOSPITAL in his honor, which was dedicated May 25, 1891. Today it occupies twenty buildings in a two-block area. Also named in his honor are the HENRY GRADY HIGH SCHOOL of Atlanta, the former HENRY GRADY HOTEL there, and also HENRY W. GRADY MEMORIAL HIGHWAY which runs from Dalton via Gainesville to Athens, where his home still stands.

GRAHAM, Appling County. A community located ten miles northwest of Baxley. Named for a prominent citizen, J. H. Graham.

GRANBERY, Twiggs County. This post office existed from May 7, 1830 to June 20, 1837, and was named for its first postmaster, James M. Granbery. It was later changed to SONICERA, which appears to be a coined name.

GRAND BAY CREEK, Lowndes-Lanier counties. Also known as LITTLE RIVER (q.v.).

GRAND PRAIRIE, Charlton County. This is the largest of several such "prairies" in the Okefenokee Swamp, and covers 50 square miles. These are actually marshes of the swamp, and are so named as they resemble the prairies of the West.

GRANGE, Jefferson County. This community is located 12 miles northwest of Louisville. The name means "farm lands" and is believed to have come about here from The Grange, a farmers' organization which began in the 19th century. In Chatham County, GRANGE was the name that was given to a plantation on the Savannah River, previously known as COWPENS (q.v.), as it was used by John and Mary Musgrove for keeping cattle.

GRANITEVILLE, Coweta County. *See* GRANTVILLE.

GRANT PARK, Atlanta. Was first called L. P. GRANT PARK, named for its donor, Colonel Lemuel P. Grant (1817-1893), who was chief engineer of the Atlanta and West Point Railroad, and who became wealthy in real estate. He gave 100 acres of woodland in 1882 to create the park; 40 acres were added later. Included in the park are the CYCLORAMA (q.v.) and the CANDLER ZOO which was named in honor of Asa Griggs Candler, Sr. who became sole owner of Coca Cola in 1891 for $2,300. *See also* Grantville, Coweta County.

GRANTVILLE, Coweta County. Incorporated as GRANITEVILLE February 13, 1854. This was the early home of, and named for Colonel L. P. Grant (*see* Grant Park). The original community here was called CAL(L)ICO CORNER(S) until the railroad came through and it was changed to the present name June 1, 1852.

GRANTVILLE, Greene County. This former community was incorporated as a town October 10, 1868, and named for early settler Daniel Grant. It was located three miles north of Union Point.

GRAPEVINE, Barrow County. Located ten miles southeast of the present town of Flowery Branch. This was a 19th century community, so named because it was in a vineyard region.

GRATIS, Walton County. Incorporated August 17, 1908. Was said by Mrs. Sams to have been given this apt name when residents found that no money was required to open the

post office in 1893. Bob Harrell writes that the community was originally called FREE, but the officials in Washington felt Gratis was a better post office name.

GRAVES, Terrell County. A community located four miles west of Dawson. Established as GRAVES STATION on the Central of Georgia Railroad. Named for Iverson Graves.

GRAY, CS Jones County. Incorporated August 22, 1911. This town began as a settlement on the property of U. S. Congressman James Henderson Blount (1837-1903), and the names Dollytown and Blountston were suggested for the name of the place. It was first called JAMES, from Mr. Blount's given name, but afterwards changed to its present name in honor of its outstanding citizen, James Madison Gray, one of the larger financiers of the Confederacy. The county seat was moved here from Clinton (q.v.) in 1905. *See also* Blountsville.

GRAY COAT BRANCH, Jefferson County. This stream is also called GREAT COAT BRANCH (q.v.).

GRAYSON, Gwinnett County. Originally called TRIP(P) until December 16, 1901 when the town was incorporated under the name BERKELEY. This name was changed to Grayson with reincorporation December 17, 1902. Derivations of these names are unknown.

GRAYSON'S LANDING, Heard County. This old place was located on the Chattahoochee River. Named after a Scotchman by the name of Grayson, who was a great Indian trader who married an Indian wife. It was afterwards called PHILPOT'S FERRY.

GRAYSVILLE, Catoosa County. Located five miles north of Ringgold. Incorporated August 23, 1872, with John D. Gray as one of the five commissioners of the new town, which was founded in 1849 by Gray, a native of England. He was chief contractor for the Western and Atlantic Railroad, who laid the first tracks across the Appalachian barrier, built from 1838 to 1850. Skirmishes occurred here September 10, 1863, prior to the battle of Chickamauga.

GREAT COAT BRANCH, Jefferson County. This stream in the lower section of the county was given a toponym derived from the old name for an overcoat. It is frequently called GRAY COAT BRANCH by nearby residents. Today's maps label this creek, COAT CREEK; perhaps the cartographer copied only part of the name from a previous map.

GREAT OGEECHEE RIVER. *See* OGEECHEE RIVER.

GREEN, Evans County. An early community of Bulloch County located 7½ miles north of Claxton. Named for the postmaster and local merchant, M. J. Green.

GREENBUSH BRANCH, Walker County. Located in the southwest section of the county, it flows into West Armuchee Creek near the former community of GREENBUSH. The name of this place had been VICKSBURG until it was changed by Mr. S. Bomar, the postmaster, who had a beautiful green bush in his yard.

J. S. GREEN COLLEGIATE INSTITUTE, Demorest. This was the early name of PIEDMONT COLLEGE (q.v.).

GREENE COUNTY. Created February 3, 1786 with 403 square miles taken from Washington County. Named in honor of Major General Nathanael Greene (1742-1786) of Rhode Island, for his outstanding service in the Revolution. He heroically defeated the British in South Carolina September 8, 1781, and afterwards retired at Mulberry Grove Plantation (q.v.) near Savannah, which was given him by the State of Georgia. Also named in his honor is GREENE SQUARE in Savannah, and the GREENE MONUMENT, of which the cornerstone was laid by LaFayette in 1825 at Johnson Square in Savannah. The county seat is Greensboro (q.v.).

GREENSBORO, CS Greene County. First chartered in 1786, designated county seat December 1, 1802 and incorporated December 10, 1803 when the town's name was spelled

GREENSBOROUGH. Settled in the 1770's and named in honor of Nathanael Greene (*see* Greene County).

GREEN(')S CUT, Burke County. This community is located six miles north of Waynesborough on the Central of Georgia Railway, and was named for the railroad cut running through the plantation of Moses P. Green.

GREENVILLE, CS Meriwether County. Incorporated December 20, 1828, and originally spelled GREENEVILLE, but the middle "e" was later dropped. Laid out in 1828 on land owned by General Hugh W. Ector. The town was first settled by Adam B. Ragan who built a log cabin store on what is now the courthouse square. It was named for Nathanael Greene (*see* Greene County).

GREENWOOD, Mitchell County. This community located nine miles west of Camilla was established about 1880. Named for a beautiful grove of evergreen live oak trees found growing here.

GRESHAMVILLE, Greene County. This community is located ten miles northwest of Greensboro. Probably named for Volney Gresham, or his father. Brinkley says it was named for an old fort built near the Davis Gresham settlement in 1786.

GRESSTON, Dodge County. This community is located seven miles northwest of Eastman. Named for G. V. Gress, who in 1883 built one of the largest sawmills in the South, at this place.

GREY'S SWAMP, Liberty County. In 1784 it was recorded that George Grey had adjoining lands to this swamp.

GRIFFIN, CS Spalding County. "Pimiento Center of the World" Incorporated December 24, 1843 when this was within Pike County. The post office was first established here as PLEASANT GROVE, April 14, 1826, with the name being changed to Griffin, February 2, 1841. The town was laid out in 1840 when Colonel Lewis Lawrence Griffin purchased 800 acres here, and so the place was named for him. Later becoming a general, Griffin was president of the Macon and Western Railroad, also a banker, planter, and Indian fighter.

GRISWOLD(VILLE), Jones County. (Unincorporated) This dead town was located about ten miles southeast of Gray. The Griswold post office served until August 1, 1928. Named for himself by Samuel Griswold (1790-1867)

who came from Clinton (q.v.) in 1849 to establish the town. This became a flourishing manufacturing and agricultural center where Griswold produced the nation's best cotton gin, selling up to 1,200 gins per year. In March 1862, he converted from cotton gin machinery to making .36 calibre brass frame Confederate revolvers, and produced about 3,500. His factories as well as his mansion were burned by Brigadier General J. L. Kilpatrick's 3rd Cavalry Division, November 20, 1864.

GROANING ROCK, Jackson County. This was the first permanent settlement in the county, and was established January 20, 1784 when a land grant deed was acquired by a William Dunson, of German descent. The name of the place was probably derived from a rock by nearby Sandy Creek. Its been said it was because of the sound made by the wind blowing in the hollow of the rock formation there. The name was later changed to HARMONY GROVE (q.v.) and finally to COMMERCE (q.v.).

GROOVERVILLE, Brooks County. Incorporated as a town December 18, 1859. An early post office was established here July 16, 1833, at which time the site was within Thomas County. The first postmaster was Joshua Groover, and the village was named from several Groover families who lived in the vicinity. When the Atlantic & Gulf railroad came through in 1860-61, it missed Grooverville by a few miles, so a station was established on the line nearby called NUMBER 17 or GROOVER'S STATION. The post office was transferred to this new location February 28, 1879, when it adopted the name of DIXIE (q.v.).

GROVANIA, Houston County: A community among peach and pecan groves, located eight miles southeast of Perry. Incorporated as a town August 16, 1909.

GROVE CREEK, Banks County. This stream apparently derived its name from an adjoining area formerly known as THE GROVE.

GROVE CREEK, Oglethorpe County. Rises north of Crawford and flows northward into the South Fork of the Broad River. The name of this stream was altered in about 1800 from its earlier designation, GOLDEN GROVE CREEK (q.v.).

GROVE LEVEL, Banks County. This former community was located near GROVE CREEK. Still standing today is Grove Level Church, five miles south of Homer.

GROVETOWN, Columbia County. Incorporated as GROVETON September 29, 1881.

GUALDAQUINI, Glynn County. An early name of JEKYLL ISLAND (q.v.).

GUALE. Pronounced "Wallie." The Spanish established their first settlement in what is now Georgia on St. Catherines Island (q.v.) in 1566. They named the place "Guale" after the chief Indian of the tribe found on this island. Some historians have interpreted the name as having been derived from the Indian word *Wahali,* "The South." The Georgia coast constituted the district of Guale and the inland area was called Tama (q.v.). It was all part of what was named (La) Florida (q.v.) during the Spanish era. Even before that, the Spanish called the region Bimini.

GUALEQUINI, Glynn County. An early Spanish name of JEKYLL ISLAND (q.v.).

GUALQUINI, Glynn County. Pronounced "Wal-queen-ie." This was the old Indian name of ST. SIMONS SOUND, and means "Waters of Guale." *See* Guale.

GUAXULE, White County. Was a Cherokee Indian town (*see* Nacoochee).

GUESS, Henry County. This was an early post office located five miles northwest of McDonough. Named for the Cherokee Indian, Sequoyah, whose English name was George Guess (*see* Sequoyah Caverns). The post office was moved to Flippen (q.v.) in 1886.

GULLETTSVILLE, Monroe County. Was apparently named for George W. Gullett who was a large landowner here. The name of the community was changed to CABANISS (q.v.) in the late 1800's in honor of Judge E. G. Cabaniss of Forsyth.

GUM POND, Mitchell County. This former community was located east of Baconton. The residents selected this name as an alternative since none could spell their first choice, Cypress Pond.

GUNPOWDER SPRINGS, Butts County. The early name of INDIAN SPRINGS (q.v.), and of POWDER SPRINGS (q.v.), Cobb County.

GWINNETT COUNTY. Created by acts of December 15 and 19, 1818, with 436 square miles acquired by Cherokee cession of July 18, 1817 and Creek cession of January 22, 1818. This was an original county which bears the illustrious name of Button Gwinnett (1735-1777) who was a delegate from Georgia at the Continental Congress, and was a signer of the Declaration of Independence. The autograph of Button Gwinnett is considered the most expensive in the world, worth about $250,000 today. He purchased St. Catherines Island from Thomas Bosomworth about 1766. Gwinnett served Georgia a short while as governor until he died May 19, 1777 from injuries suffered in a duel with General Lachlan McIntosh. It is not known for sure where Gwinnett is buried, but it is believed to be in Savannah at Colonial Park Cemetery. In 1865, the first Negro to be lynched in the State of Georgia, suffered this fate in Gwinnett County. The county seat is Lawrenceville (q.v.). The court house was destroyed by fire in 1871. Also named in honor of Button Gwinnett is GWINNETT STREET in Savannah, and another street of the same name in Augusta.

H

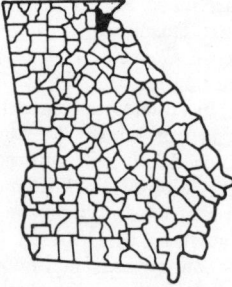

HABERSHAM COUNTY. This is an original county which now comprises 283 square miles, and was created December 15 and 19, 1818 with Cherokee cessions of July 8, 1817 and February 27, 1819. Named in honor of Major Joseph Habersham (1724-1790) of Savannah, who was a patriot of the Revolution, served as Postmaster General in the Cabinet of George Washington, and was speaker of the General Assembly of Georgia in 1785. The county seat is Clarkesville (q.v.). The court house was destroyed by fire in 1856 and blown up in 1898. There is also a town of HABERSHAM, about three miles southwest of Clarkesville, and also a LAKE HABERSHAM near here at the head of the Soquee River. In Chatham County is found HABERSHAM CREEK, which forms the west boundary of Wassaw Island (q.v.), and also HABERSHAM STREET in Savannah was named for Major Habersham.

HACHASOFKEE CREEK, Talbot County. Flows northeasterly into the Flint River. Variations of spellings have included HATCHASAUFKA, HATCHESAUFKA, and HACHASOFKA. A contemporary county map labels the stream HOCKOSOFKEE CREEK. The name undoubtedly means "Deep Creek" in Muskogee, with *soofka* or *sufki,* meaning "deep." On older maps it was called AUPIOGEE (1797) and AHAPIOKA.

HACK, Decatur County. This was an early name of ATTAPULGUS (q.v.).

HADDOCK, Jones County. Incorporated as a town August 23, 1905 to 1925. Joseph Caswell Haddock (1812-1883) was overseer of the wealthy Barnes family plantation here, and he married the Barnes' daughter Mildred. She gave the land for the depot and right of way for the railroad, so the stop was then called HADDOCK'S STATION.

HAGAN, Evans County. Incorporated as a city August 21, 1906. Named for Susan Hagan, wife of Marshall A. Smith who owned some of the land on which the town was established.

HAHIRA, Lowndes County. Pronounced "Hey high'-ra." Incorporated October 2, 1891. This town was founded in 1888, and reportedly named by Mr. Berry J. Folsom, and said to be from the name of a river in Liberia. The compiler was unable to find this river on any maps of that country. It has also been said to mean "good water." Another possible derivation is from the Biblical place, Hahiroth where the Israelites encamped during the initial stages of the Exodus. A legend was created which attributes the name to a locomotive engineer called Hira, who was hailed by friends with, "Hey, Hira!"

HAISTENTOWN, Fayette County. *See* BROOKS.

HALCYONDALE, Screven County. A community located fifteen miles south of Sylvania. Its post office was established May 20, 1842. Was first called STATION NO. 5 when the Central of Georgia first came through. It was changed later to the present name proposed by youthful local poet, Cuyler Young, and the meaning is "Peaceful Valley."

HALF ACRE (Militia) DISTRICT, Putnam County. Name is derived from the former community here of (THE) HALF ACRE. For derivation, *see* Devil's Half Acre.

HALL COUNTY. Created December 15 and 19, 1818 with 392 square miles acquired by Cherokee cessions of July 8, 1817 and February 27, 1819. This was an original county, and was named in honor of Dr. Lyman Hall (1724-1790), who was born in Connecticut, was a patriot of the Revolution, a delegate from Georgia at the Continental Congress, and was one of the three Georgians who signed the Declaration of Indepencence. Hall was elected governor of Georgia in 1783. The county seat is Gainesville (q.v.). The courthouse was destroyed by fires of 1851 and 1882, and by a tornado in 1936.

HALLOCA CREEK, Chattahoochee County. A tributary of Ochillee Creek, located about three miles north of Cusseta. Variations in spelling have included HALLOKA, HALLOKEE, HALLOCKEE and HALLOOKEE. This is a Chickasaw Indian word which possibly means "beloved" or "beloved bear ground."

HALLS, Bartow County. A community located five miles south of Adairsville. Also known as HALL'S MILL, it was a rail station named for L. H. Hall, an agent for the Western and Atlantic Railroad here.

HAMBURG, Macon County. A former community which was near the present community of Fountainville. Named after the city of Hamburg, Germany, by German brothers John H. Jones and William B. Jones, who were the first settlers here about 1830.

HAMBURG STATE PARK, Washington County. This 1,405-acre park is located 16 miles north of Sandersville on Georgia highway 248. It includes HAMBURG MILL POND, at the head of navigation of the Little Ogeechee River.

HAMILTON, CS Harris County. Incorporated as a town and made county seat December 20, 1828. Believed named for South Carolina's governor, James Hamilton, Jr. (1786-1857), who was chiefly responsible for the passing of the Nullification Ordinance of 1832, and who led armed forces to defend states' rights. This town now prefers to be called "Hamilton on the Square," after April 1969, when it opened the town square as a museum of the 1870-1920 era. It was rebuilt by Allen M. Woodall, Jr. of Columbus.

HAMILTON PLANTATION, St. Simons Island. Named after James Hamilton, a native of Scotland who acquired the tract of land in 1804 that was previously known as GASCOIGNE'S BLUFF (q.v.).

HAMPTON, Henry County. Incorporated as a town December 20, 1872, when the name was changed from the previous, BEAR CREEK (see BEAR CREEK STATION).

Named to honor the noted Confederate hero, General Wade Hampton (1818-1902) of South Carolina, who raised and commanded "Hampton's Legion." His grandfather was General Wade Hampton, hero of the Revolution. General Sherman's forces passed through here November 16, 1864. This town was the site of the first Atlanta Pop Festival, July Fourth weekend, 1969 (see also Byron).

HAMPTON, St. Simons Island. Was also known as BUTLER(S) POINT. It was originally named NEWHAMPTON by some of General Oglethorpe's soldiers who settled here, but they soon shortened it to Hampton. It is located at the northwestern point of the island. HAMPTON RIVER, separates St. Simons Island from Little St. Simons Island.

HAMPSTEAD, Chatham County. This was an early settlement, laid out in 1733 about one mile east of High Gate (q.v.), but did not survive, being entirely abandoned by 1740. It is believed the name was transferred from England.

HANNA, Dade County. An early post office established on the Hanna Plantation, near the site of present RISING FAWN (q.v.). The name was later changed to STAUNTON (q.v.) before the post office was named Rising Fawn.

HANNAHATCHEE CREEK, Stewart County. Rises near Richland and flows westerly to enter the Chattahoochee River near Omaha. The name is derived from the Muskogean word *achina,* "cedar," and *hachi,* "creek". Near this stream was the early settlement of HANNAHATCHEE which was sometimes called ANTIOCH (q.v.), and is now the community of LOUVALE (q.v.).

HANCOCK COUNTY. Created December 17, 1793 with 478 square miles taken from Greene and Washington counties. Named for John Hancock (1737-1793), Revolutionary patriot, president of the Continental Congress, and the first signer of the Declaration of Independence. The county seat is Sparta (q.v.).

HANOVER PARK, Brunswick. Named in honor of the King of England, George III of the House of Hanover.

HAPEVILLE, Fulton County. Incorporated as a city September 16, 1891. The first post office was approved April 23, 1875. Named for Dr. Samuel Hape, an Atlanta dentist who came from Maryland, and served as an officer in the Confederate Army. He purchased the land in 1871 to establish this town, later becoming the first postmaster and the first mayor.

HAPPY HOLLOW, McDuffie County. A commendatory name for a crossroads in the southwest section of the county, at the junction of Brier and Sweetwater creeks.

HARALSON, Coweta County. Incorporated as a town August 22, 1907. This former community was located in the southeast section of the county. Settled in the late 1820's, and believed named for an army officer, Hugh A. Haralson (see Haralson County).

HARALSON COUNTY. Created January 26, 1856 with 285 square miles taken from Carroll and Polk counties. Named for General Hugh Anderson Haralson (1805-1854), officer of the state militia, who served in the U. S. Congress. The county seat is Buchanan (q.v.).

HARDEE CREEK, DeKalb County. Located in East Atlanta, this is a small stream that flows into Sugar Creek where State highway 260 crosses U. S. Interstate 20. Believed named for General William J. Hardee (see Hardee Hall).

HARDEE HALL, Atlanta Army Depot. Named for Lieutenant General William Joseph Hardee (1815-1873) CSA, who was the

able leader in the Army of Tennessee and a corps commander during the Atlanta campaign.

HARD FORTUNE CREEK, McDuffie County. This stream rises south of Dearing and flows westerly into Headstall Creek near the boundary of Fort Gordon. This name is descriptive of pioneer way of thinking.

HARDING, Tift County. A community located in the northeast section of the county. The name is taken from the town of Harding, located on the railroad where Captain H. H. Tift (see Tift County) lived in Massachusetts.

HARDING, LAKE, Harris County. Located above Columbus, this 6,000-acre lake was formed by Bartlett's Ferry Dam (q.v.) in the Chattahoochee River, which was completed in 1926. This lake is named for Mr. R. M. Harding, who was general manager of the Columbus Electric and Power Company.

HARD LABOR CREEK, Morgan County. This stream flows easterly across the county to enter the Apalachee River. It was given its name by slaves who found the river-bottom fields difficult to till because of their swampy and marsh-like nature.

HARD LABOR CREEK STATE PARK, Morgan County. This 5,804-acre park is located just north of Rutledge on the stream for which it was named. See Hard Labor Creek. It is the largest state park in Georgia, and contains two lakes, BRANTLEY and RUTLEDGE, which were named for early settlers on this land.

HARDSCRABBLE, Fulton County. This name was applied to a section in the upper part of the county. It is a pessimistic appellation that was used here as it was difficult to make a living in the area.

HARDWICK, Baldwin County. An unincorporated town adjacent to Central State Hospital and Women's Rehabilitation Center. May have been named for Thomas W. Hardwick (1872-1944), U. S. Senator and governor of Georgia (1921-23). Is also called MIDWAY-HARDWICK.

HARDWICK(E), Bryan County. A settlement first called GEORGETOWN (q.v.) was established here in 1754 on a bluff at the "elbow" of the Ogeechee River's south side, about fourteen miles from its mouth. In February 1755, Governor John Reynolds visited the place and proposed that Georgia's colonial capital be moved here, and that the name be changed to Hardwick in honor of his relative, Philip Yorke (1690-1764), Earl of Hardwicke, and Lord High Chancellor of England. After 21,000 acres of land were granted here, lack of funds prevented its being developed as proposed, so the place finally died. This was designated as the Bryan county seat, but it was soon afterwards moved to Crossroads (q.v.) in 1797. An attempt was made to re-establish the town with incorporation March 21, 1866. HARDWICK COVE is the present name of a residential development here.

HARGETT, Harris County. This 19th century community was located 13 miles southwest of Hamilton. Postmaster H. V. Hargett operated gin and grist mills here.

HARLEM, Columbia County. Incorporated as a village October 24, 1870. The name originated directly or indirectly from the town of Haerlem in Holland. Harlem in New York was established in 1658 by Peter Styvesant, and remained farmland for nearly 200 years.

HARMONY GROVE, Jackson County. Incorporated as a town December 24, 1884 when the name was changed from that of GROANING ROCK (q.v.). The commendatory name of Harmony Grove prevailed until August 6, 1904 when the town was incorporated under the name of COMMERCE (q.v.).

HARNAGEVILLE, Pickens County. The early name of the present town of TATE (q.v.). Was named after Ambrose Harnage, who built and operated the first tavern here, which was located on the site of the later Tate family home.

HARPERS LAKE, McIntosh County. Located near Fort Barrington and named after Francis Harper. It was previously known as LEWIS LAGOON, after early settler here, Samuel Lewis, Sr.

HARREL MILL CREEK, Webster County. This is the present name of the stream known to the Indians as ARCHIBOOKTA CREEK (q.v.).

HARRELL'S) STATION, Grady County. The post office was established here May 26, 1868, and changed to WHIGHAM (q.v.) April 7, 1880. Named for John and W. W. Harrell who deeded ten acres of land for the depot. This is the same family for which the com-

munity of HARRELL'S STILL, north of here was named.

HARRIS COUNTY. Created December 14, 1827 with 465 square miles taken from Muscogee and Troup counties. Named for English-born Charles Harris (1772-1827), distinguished Savannah lawyer. The county seat is Hamilton (q.v.). The court house was set afire by Federal troops in 1865 but then quickly extinguished. There is also a community by the name of HARRIS, which is in Meriwether County about four miles south of Greenville.

HARRIS NECK, McIntosh County. Named for the Harris Plantation which was located on the narrow isthmus or neck along the Intracoastal Waterway.

HARRISON, Washington County. Incorporated December 21, 1886. Was named in 1883 for Green B. Harrison, a wealthy farmer who was the postmaster, the local railroad and express agent, a director of the road, and the town's first mayor.

HARRISONVILLE, Troup County. A community located ten miles north of LaGrange on Georgia highway 54. Was formerly called ASBURY (q.v.).

HART COUNTY. Created December 7, 1853 with 257 square miles taken from Elbert and Franklin counties. Named for Nancy Hart, heroine of the Revolutionary War, who served as a spy and also had captured a group of Tories who had come to her house demanding food. She was called "War Woman" by the Indians (see also War Woman Creek). The county seat is Hartwell (q.v.). The court house was destroyed by fires in 1900 and 1967. Also named HART was a former post office in Bibb County, ten miles west of Macon, which was established in 1883. Another community called HART was located in upper Gordon County. Derivations of these two places are not known.

HARTFORD, Pulaski County. Designated as the county seat December 13, 1809 and incorporated as a town December 14, 1815. Named in honor of Nancy Hart (see Hart County). Was established on the opposite bank of the Ocmulgee from Hawkinsville, and in 1804 came within one vote of becoming the capital of Georgia. The county seat was moved to Hawkinsville in 1837, and the place was abandoned by mid century "on account of its unhealthiness." There was also a place on record in 1909 called HARTFORD in Cherokee County, located nine miles southeast of Canton.

HARTFORD ROAD (or OLD HARTFORD ROAD). Extended from Milledgeville, when it was the capital of the state, through Baldwin, Wilkinson, Twiggs, and Pulaski counties, to the frontier at Hartford (q.v.). It was built about 1811, and found useful for movement of troops and supplies during the War of 1812.

HART(S) CREEK, McDuffie County. Rises in eastern Warren County and flows easterly into Clark Hill Reservoir. Named after an early settler of the county.

HARTSFIELD, Colquitt County. A community located 11 miles west of Moultrie on Georgia highway 37. Named for the John L. Hartsfield lumber mill.

HARTSFIELD INTERNATIONAL AIRPORT, Fulton and Clayton counties. Serving the metropolitan Atlanta area. Established in 1929 as the ATLANTA SPEEDWAY, a dirt auto race track, with Jack Gray Sr. its first manager. Its first name as an airport was CANDLER FIELD and soon afterwards called ATLANTA AIRPORT. Named WILLIAM B. HARTSFIELD ATLANTA AIRPORT in 1970 in honor of William Berry Hartsfield, who as mayor of Atlanta (1937-1961) had the vision to make this a major aviation center. It became "international" June 29, 1971 with the first direct flight to Mexico (by Eastern Airlines).

HART STATE PARK, Hart County. This 147-acre park is located three miles north of Hartwell on Hartwell Reservoir (q.v.). Named for Nancy Hart (see Hart County).

HARTWELL, CS Hart County. Incorporated as a town February 26, 1856, and named in honor of Nancy Hart (see Hart County). The main street was named HOWELL in honor of Howell Cobb (1815-1868), who served as the attorney to aid in the establishment of this as the county seat.

HARTWELL DAM, Hart County. Located on the Savannah River seven miles east of the city of Hartwell, for which it was named. The concrete section is 1,900 feet long, while it is 17,900 feet long overall, including earth embankments. It was constructed by the U. S. Corps of Engineers 1955-63 at a cost of about $88 million, and created the 61,900-acre HARTWELL RESERVOIR, also called LAKE HARTWELL, with a 960-mile shoreline. This recreation area attracts over 4 million visitors annually.

HARVEY ISLAND, Chatham County. Located between the Ogeechee and Little Ogeechee rivers, at their mouths. Believed named from that of early occupants.

HARWELLS (Militia) DISTRICT, Morgan County. Located in the southern section of the county, it was named for a Dr. Harwell, who bought lands here in 1839.

HASSLER'S MILL, Murray County. Established in 1879 on Holly Creek. Named for William Hassler.

HATCHETHLUCCO CREEK, Muscogee and Chattahoochee counties. An old Indian name meaning "Big Creek," which was formerly applied to UPATOI CREEK (q.v.).

HAT CREEK. Rises just north of Sycamore in Turner County and flows southeasterly through a corner of Tift County and into the Alapaha River in northwestern Irwin County. Received its name after Jesse Hobby lost his hat here during a hasty retreat from an Indian attack.

HATLEY, Crisp County. This community in the eastern section of the county was given this name by the Seaboard Coast Line Railroad when it established the station here. The first post office was called MALONE, the postmaster's name being W. H. Malone. This community is located within HATLEY (Militia) DISTRICT.

HAWKINS ISLAND, Glynn County. Lies two miles south of Frederica. Named in honor of Dr. Thomas Hawkins, an early doctor of Frederica.

HAWKINSVILLE, CS Pulaski County. "City of Thirteen Highways" Incorporated December 2, 1830, and the county seat was moved here from Hartford (q.v.) in 1837. Named in honor of Colonel Benjamin Hawkins (1754-1816), Revolutionary soldier and U. S. senator from North Carolina (1798-95). He had been a member of the Continental Congress and in 1796 was appointed by President Washington to be superintendent of all Indians south of the Ohio River. Hawkins kept detailed records which preserved many old Indian place-names in Georgia. He lived among the Creek Indians during his last twenty years, and he showed sympathy for and understanding of their problems. The BEN HAWKINS MONUMENT at Roberta is located in the center of town, having been placed there by the U. S. Government to honor the services of the noted Indian agent. He spent his later years and was buried at Old Agency (q.v.), six miles southwest of the monument, near where the COLONEL HAWKINS BRIDGE spans the Flint River. HAWKINS BRANCH is a tiny stream that flows into the Flint River in northeast Lee County. HAWKINS CROSSROADS is located southwest of Woodland in Talbot County. HAWKINS LINE is presently the boundary between Habersham and Banks counties. Was also called the FOUR MILE PURCHASE LINE. It was the boundary between Georgia and the Cherokee Nation from 1804 to 1818.

HAW POND, Crisp County. The name of this little lake is derived from the haw bushes growing along its banks.

HAYES CROSSING, Stephens County. Located southwest of Toccoa on Georgia Highway 184. Named for the family of William Hayes who settled here.

HAYNES CREEK, Gwinnett and Rockdale counties. A tributary of the Yellow River which rises west of Grayson in Gwinnett County. Named by Thomas Haynes after himself, when he built a gin, which was probably located on LITTLE HAYNES CREEK, a tributary.

HAYNEVILLE, Houston County. Located nine miles southeast of Perry on U. S. 341. Is one of the oldest communities in the county. The derivation of the name is unknown, but Grice wrote that it was said to "have been from an unimpeachable name."

HAYSTON, Newton County. A station on the Central of Georgia Railroad, two miles west of Mansfield. Alexander S. Hays and then his son A. S. Hays Jr. were postmasters for the entire 64 years of the post office service here (1893-1957). This is believed to be a record in post office history.

HAZELHURST, CS Jeff Davis County. Incorporated as a town August 22, 1891. Named for Colonel George H. Hazelhurst, civil engineer, who surveyed the Macon and Brunswick Railroad.

HEADSTALL, McDuffie County. This community in the southeast section of the county is located three miles from Avondale, on Headstall Creek, from which it derived its name.

HEARD COUNTY. Created December 22, 1830 with 301 square miles taken from Carroll, Coweta and Troup counties. Named for Stephen Heard (1740-1815), Revolutionary War hero who came to Georgia from Virginia, and later became president of the Executive Council of Georgia. The county seat is Franklin (q.v.). HEARD'S FORT, Wilkes County. Also called FORT HEARD (q.v.), it was named for Stephen Heard, who planted a colony here in 1773. Construction of the fort was begun January 1, 1774. This was the seat of government for Georgia for a short time during the Revolution, after which the British captured Savannah and Augusta. In 1780, the name of the town was changed to WASHINGTON (q.v.). There is also a place called HEARD in Butts County, five miles southeast of Jackson, which has also been known as INDIAN SPRINGS DEPOT.

HEARD community of Houston County was a region of almost 36 square miles surrounding Heard's Store as its voting precinct. The Heard post office was located seven miles northeast of Perry. HEARDMONT in Elbert County is a community located about 3½ miles east of Middleton. This was a little hamlet where Stephen Heard settled after the close of the Revolutionary War. HEARDS ISLAND, Elbert County. Is now called McCALLA'S ISLAND. Was given the original name for Stephen Heard, who was given a land grant, which included this island in the Savannah River.

HEBARDVILLE, Ware County. This former community in the Okefenokee Swamp was the site of the Hebard Cypress Company.

HEIFERHORN CREEK, Muscogee and Harris counties. The reason for this name is not known, but John Goff said that it may be in the category of rustic names like "Buck Head," "Possum Snout" and "Hog Jaw." The present name of the stream is STANDING BOY CREEK (q.v.).

HELEN, White County. Incorporated as a town August 18, 1913. Called the "Star of the North." The town was laid out by John E. Mitchell of St. Louis in 1912-13. When a name was being sought for the place, a lumber official suggested the name of his daughter, and inasmuch as most citizens worked for the lumber company, there was little opposition to the name offered. This is a Blue Ridge mountain village, which has recently been given an Alpine look as a tourist attraction, an idea suggested by John Kollock, an Atlanta artist.

HELENA, Telfair County. Incorporated as a city December 27, 1890. Derivation of the name is uncertain.

HELL GAP, Troup County. Is located on the Chattahoochee River below the mouth of Wehadkee Creek. So named as this is a shoaly stretch. HELL GATE in Camden County on the Great Satilla River, and HELL GATE SHOALS in Baker County (located on the Flint River, one mile below the mouth of Ichawaynochaway Creek) are so named as they are spots characterized by tortuous boat channels. HELL HOLE BRANCH in Rabun County is an appropriately named rugged fork of Wildcat Creek, which is a tributary of Tallulah (Terrible) River. Also in Rabun County is HELL HOLE MOUNTAIN with an elevation of 3,220 feet. HELL'S GATE is the name given to a strip of choppy water at the

mouth of the Ogeechee River. HELL KNOB of Towns County is an elevation located west of Dismal Mountain, eight miles southeast of Hiawassee. It is 3,455 feet high. HELL'S HALF ACRE in Burke County is a dense thicket and wooded area east of Magruder, and is so thick it is said a dog can not pass through it. It is far larger than a half acre.

HEMP, Fannin County. A community located four miles east of Morgantown. A post office here earlier was called HEMPTOWN. Named for a Cherokee chief, Tal-danigi-ski, translated by the whites as "Hemp-carrier (or toter)" since he traded in fabrics. Nearby HEMPTOWN CREEK flows northwesterly to enter the Toccoa River at Mineral Bluff.

HENCART ROAD. This was an early route from Macon to Savannah via Hawkinsville. The name is generally thought to have arisen because farmers carried chickens in carts to Savannah markets using this road. There is also evidence that suggests it may be a corruption of an earlier name, HAND CART ROAD.

HENDERSON, Houston County. This community in the southwest corner of the county was named after an early Indian trader, Solomon H. Henderson.

HENRY COUNTY. Created May 15, 1821 with 331 square miles acquired by Creek cession of January 8, 1821. Called "The Mother of Counties" because parts of Newton, Walton and Fayette counties were taken from Henry County in the first year of its formation. Named for Virginia patriot and orator, Patrick Henry (1736-1799). The county seat is McDonough (q.v.). The court house was destroyed by fire in 1824, and some records were destroyed by General Sherman's men December 16, 1864. HENRY (COUNTY) ACADEMY of McDonough was incorporated December 9, 1824 for college preparatory schooling, and opened January 15, 1827. It declined in the early 1850's and is said that the buildings burned during the Reconstruction period.

HENTOWN, Early County. Located ten miles southeast of Blakely. The name of this community came about when a Mr. J. D. Kilpatrick raised thousands of chickens here.

HEPHZIBAH, Richmond County. Incorporated October 24, 1870. Originally called BROTHERSVILLE (q.v.), this was one of Georgia's earliest settlements. The area was previously inhabited by the Uchee Indians. The present name of the town was taken from the Hephzibah Baptist Association which established a denominational high school here in 1860. The word *Hephzibah* is from the Bible, meaning "My delight is in Her," and is also a symbol for Zion.

HERBERT SMART AIRPORT, Bibb County. Now called MACON DOWNTOWN AIRPORT. Located east of Macon, it was named for Herbert Smart, who was mayor of Macon from 1934 to 1938 during which time the airport was built.

HERNDON, Jenkins County. This community is located on the Central of Georgia Railroad, ten miles west of Millen. Formerly called BIRDSVILLE (q.v.), it was then named in honor of Captain William Lewis Herndon, commander of the S. S. Central America. He saved all women and children when the vessel sank September 12, 1856, but went down with the ship along with the other men.

HEROD, Terrell County. Incorporated November 15, 1901. This community was established one mile east of INDIAN HEROD TOWN, which was one of the largest and most important Creek Indian villages. The chief's name was Herod.

HERON ISLAND, Liberty County. Was an early name of COLONEL'S ISLAND (q.v.). The heron is a large wading bird.

HIAWASSEE, CS Towns County. Incorporated May 17, 1956 (was incorporated as the town of HIWASSEE, October 24, 1870). The name is derived from the Cherokee Indian word *a-yu-wa-si,* meaning "meadow," "savanna" or "pretty fawn." *See* also Hiwassee River.

HICHITEE CREEK, Chattahoochee and Stewart counties. A variant of *Hichiti* (q.v.), the stream was formerly called HITCHITI CREEK (q.v.).

HICHITI, Chattahoochee County. Also spelled HITCHITI (q.v.). This was the name of an old Cusseta Indian village on the right bank of Thlucco Creek, about five miles southeast of Cusseta. The name is derived from the Creek, *achitchita,* "to look up (the stream)."

HICKORY. Several places in the state have taken the name from hickory trees found in their vicinities. HICKORY FLAT is a rural community in Cherokee County, located six miles southeast of Canton on Georgia highway 14. The name is a translation from the Cherokee Indian name of the place. HICKORY GROVE was a community in Crawford County, ten miles west of Knoxville. HICKORY HILL was the name of the plantation owned by James Butler on the south side of the Ogeechee River, in what was then Liberty County (before Bryan County was formed). An engagement of the Revolutionary War took place here in June 1779. HICKORY HILL is also the name that was given to Tom Watson's home in Thomson (*see* Thomas E. Watson Highway). HICKORY LEVEL is a rural community eight miles northeast of Carrollton in Carroll County. Settled in 1828, it was named for the almost level land with many hickory trees growing thereupon. HICKORY LEVEL was also the early name of Thomson (q.v.) in McDuffie County. HICKORY LOG is the name of a rural community three miles north of Canton in Cherokee County. It is translated from WANI I the Indian name of their village which was located here. Near here also is HICKORY LOG CREEK.

HICKS (Militia) DISTRICT, Macon County. Named for an early family who settled here from Crawford County in 1836. Jones Hicks established a saw mill and grist mill six miles south of Reynolds on Horse Creek.

HIGGSTON, Montgomery County. Incorporated August 17, 1903. Postmaster James Higgs ran gin and grist mills here.

HIGGSVILLE, Twiggs County. Thought to have been named for a Mr. A. Higgs, the first postmaster when the office was opened July 19, 1833. All that remains is Higgensville Church, located midway between Danville and Jeffersonville.

HIGH, Walker County. This descriptively named mountain community is now called LOOKOUT, and is located two miles south of Cloudland Canyon State Park.

HIGH BLUFF. Was given this name as it is the highest point on the Ocmulgee River between Hawkinsville and Macon. This was thought to have been an Indian sentinel point.

HIGH FALLS, Monroe County. Previous names of this former community have been HIGH SHOALS, TOWALIGA SHOALS and UNIONVILLE. The name is taken from the falls here on the Towaliga River. During the Civil War, the grist mill here was burned by retreating Confederate soldiers; rebuilt in 1866, and operated until 1960. The town died after the railroad was built through Jackson in the late 1880's.

HIGH FALLS STATE PARK, Monroe County. This 970-acre park was established July 1, 1966. Located eight miles southwest of Jackson, it includes the falls from which it was named, and also the 600-acre HIGH FALLS LAKE. *See also* High Falls.

HIGH GATE, Chatham County. This was one of Georgia's earliest communities, which was settled by French Huguenots about four miles southwest of Savannah. It was laid out in 1733, but did not survive for long.

HIGHLAND (or GEORGIA HIGHLAND). This is the descriptive name applied to the southern end of the older Appalachian mountain province in the north-central to northeastern part of the State, and comprises about 1,850 square miles.

HIGH POINT, Dade County. This is the designation applied to the highest elevation of Lookout Mountain, at 2,393 feet.

HIGH POINT, Walker County. This community is located on Chattanooga Creek, twelve miles northwest of LaFayette. Was given this name as it is near a high point on Lookout Mountain.

HIGH SHOALS, Walton County. Incorporated as a town March 2, 1872 at which time it was also included in corners of Clarke and Morgan counties. It was named from HIGH SHOALS, a rapid in the Apalachee River with sixty-foot falls, located twelve miles southwest of Athens. The community here is now called SHOALS, although the post office is still named High Shoals.

HIGH TOP, Gilmer County. A 2,700-foot peak located nine miles west of Ellijay. So named as it is the high point on the Cohutta Mountain Range.

HIGHTOWER. This name is a corruption of the Cherokee Indian word *itawa,* or as it is more often spelled, *Etowah* (*see* Etowah Indian Mounds). There is presently a community named HIGHTOWER in Forsyth County, located eight miles northwest of Cumming on HIGHTOWER CREEK. It was a center of government and commercial activities during Cherokee Indian days, and has also been known as SCUDDER'S (q.v.). In this section of Forsyth County is HIGHTOWER (Militia) DISTRICT. There was formerly a community of HIGHTOWER in Fannin County near Chestnut Gap, and another in Towns County near the former community of Visage. A HIGHTOWER CREEK in Laurens County flows south into Brewton Creek, northeast of Dublin. In Polk County, about nine miles southeast of Cedartown is found HIGHTOWER FALLS, HIGHTOWER LAKE and HIGHTOWER ROAD. The former community of HIGHTOWER MILL was previously located here. Another HIGHTOWER ROAD forms part of the boundary between DeKalb and Gwinnett counties.

HILLABAHATCHEE CREEK, Heard County. Rises in eastern Alabama and flows southeasterly to enter the Chattahoochee River near Franklin. The name means "Hillabee Creek," and it is derived from the fact that its headwaters were in the vicinity of the Hillabee Indian villages in Alabama.

HILL CITY, Gordon County. Located in the northwest corner of the county. Shortly after the Civil War, this town was given the name of MILLER after one of its pioneer families, while the post office was BLUE SPRINGS (BLUE SPRINGS CREEK here is a tributary of Camp Creek). Miller was often confused with Millen, Georgia so the local railroad agent J. T. Parsons suggested the name be changed to Hill City, descriptive of the region.

HILLMAN, Taliaferro County. Incorporated October 22, 1887. Mr. A. K. Hillman was one of the founders of this town which was established on a branch of the Georgia Railroad. Is now a rural community on Georgia highway 47, about ten miles south of Washington.

HILLSBORO, Floyd County. Incorporated February 25, 1856 to 1874, when this became SOUTH ROME (q.v.).

HILLSBORO, Jasper County. A community located ten miles south of Monticello. Named for the pioneer family from North Carolina, John and Isaac Hill. This was the birthplace of Senator B. H. Hill (*see* Ben Hill County).

HILOKA CREEK, Lee County. Rises on the western edge of Smithville and flows southward into Kinchafoonee Creek. This is a Muskogean Indian name from their word *hilukwa,* that is thought to mean "sweet gum tree."

HILTON, Early County. A community on the Chattahoochee River, southwest of Blakely. Named for Elisha Hilton who put up the first store here when the town was established about 1880. The post office was moved here from Sowhatchee, and Hilton was the first postmaster. He was also appointed the first mayor when the town was incorporated October 25, 1889.

HILTONIA, Screven County. Community and rural branch post office of Sylvania. Believed named for Lee H. Hilton (1865-?) of Sylvania who built a large mercantile business.

HINESVILLE, CS Liberty County. Incorporated July 24, 1916. Named in honor of Charlton Hines. A sharp skirmish occurred here December 16, 1864 as Sherman was drawing his lines about Savannah.

HIRAM, Paulding County. Incorporated October 6, 1891. This town was named for Hiram Baggett, its first postmaster.

HITCHITI CREEK. Spelled HICHITEE CREEK on current maps. Rises below Cusseta in Chattahoochee County and flows southerly into Stewart County before turning east to enter the Chattahoochee River. Hitchiti is the name of a tribe of Indians that separated from the Creeks long before Columbus made his westward voyage to the New World. *See also* HICHITI.

HITCHITI EXPERIMENTAL FOREST, Jones County. Located near Round Oak about eight miles northwest of Gray. For derivation, *see* Hitchiti Creek.

HITCHITUDSHI. The name means "Little Hitchiti." Located on Chattahoochee Creek. This was an Indian settlement which was a branch of the town, Hitchiti (*see* Hitchiti).

HIWASSEE, Towns County. The early spelling of HIAWASSEE (q.v.).

HIWASSEE RIVER (or CREEK), Towns County. Pronounced "High-wah-see." Flows past the town of Hiawassee (q.v.), and then

northward into North Carolina. The name is derived from the Cherokee Indian word *ayuhwasi,* signifying "Savannah." Previous names were EUFASEE and EUFORSEE.

HIX, Madison County. In 1882, A. H. Hix was the postmaster and thresher who operated a cotton gin. The community is gone, but the Hix Cemetery located four miles west of Ila, remains.

HIXTOWN, Carroll County. This was the early name of the present VILLA RICA (q.v.). Named for William Hix, who operated a tavern and general store here before 1830.

HLONOTISKAHACHI RIVER. This was the old Muskogee name for the Flint River, and translated, the name means "Flint River."

HOBOKEN, Brantley County. Incorporated as a city August 16, 1920. This town in the western part of the county has a name from the Algonquian word *hopocan,* meaning "tobacco pipe" or "pipe country." It may have been named from the city in New Jersey.

HOCKOSOFKEE CREEK, Talbot County. *See* HACHASOFKEE CREEK.

HODCHODKEE CREEK, Stewart and Quitman counties. A tributary of Pataula Creek. Means either "Small Potato Creek" or "Little Creek," from the Muskogee word *Hoti,* "Home," and *Chutki,* "Little."

HODO'S GAP, Talbot County. Located several miles northeast of Flint Hill (q.v.) community where a Mr. Hodo carried on a small trading business. It was said that Mr. and Mrs. Hodo were buried in a tomb where people could look upon their faces in the vault.

HOGANSVILLE, Troup County. Incorporated as a town October 12, 1870. When the Atlantic and West Point Railroad came through here in the 1860's, it adopted the station name, derived from William Hogan who was the original owner of the property upon which the town was built. HOGANSVILLE (Militia) DISTRICT here has the same derivation.

HOG CRAWL CREEK. Flows between Dooly and Macon counties, an affluent of Sweetwater Creek, rising in eastern Macon County. Was formerly called BEAVER CREEK. The name refers to a kind of pen or enclosure to hold hogs. It derives from the colonial Dutch word, *kraal* that is seemingly derived from the Spanish or Portugese, *corral.*

HOG HEAVEN BRANCH, Worth County. This stream, east of Sylvester, was so named as it was thought to be ideally suited for pigs.

HOG POTATO BRANCH, Sumter and Lee Counties. *See* FIVE MILE BRANCH.

HOG MOUNTAIN ROAD, Barrow and Oconee counties. Is coincident with present Georgia highway 53, running from Winder to Watkinsville. A native in the area relates that this was the route used for driving large numbers of hogs down the mountains to the markets. The more likely source of the name is that it was derived from its extending further to the elevation and community of HOG MOUNTAIN near Buford in Gwinnett County which was also known as CAINS (q.v.). The Cherokee name for the mountain was SIKWA. *See* Okoloco Trail.

HOLANNA CREEK. A tributary of Pataula Creek in the southwestern section of the state. William Read stated that it probably means "yellow potato," from the Creek *aha,* "potatoes," and *lani,* "yellow." It may also be from the Hitchiti, *olani,* which signifies "reed."

HOLLEY, Murray County. This community located seven miles south of Spring Place has also been called HOLLY CREEK (q.v.), named for the stream on which it is located.

HOLLY CREEK, Murray County. This is a tributary of the Conasauga River, and the name is translated from the Cherokee, *Oosetuste,* and called that because of the profusion of holly growing along its banks. Brinkley said it was named for one of the seven Cherokee clans.

HOLLY SPRINGS, Cherokee County. Incorporated as a town August 14, 1906. It was said to have been given this name from the presence of several holly trees beside a large spring in the western end of town. There is also a community named HOLLY SPRINGS in upper Jackson County.

HOLLYWOOD, Habersham County. A community located five miles northeast of Clarkesville. Originally an Indian settlement headed by a principal chief of the Holly clan.

HOLMESVILLE, Appling County. Designated the county seat December 8, 1828 and incorporated as a town February 7, 1854. It was built on land owned by Solomon Kennedy. The seat moved to Baxley in 1874, after which the town died. The derivation of the name is not known.

HOLTON, Bibb County. This community was established on the Ocmulgee River, ten miles northwest of Macon. Now known as ARKWRIGHT (q.v.), it was first named after Dr. Lee Holt, a physician and farmer.

HOMELAND, Charlton County. Established in 1906 as a new opportunity colony by Union veterans of the Civil War.

HOMER, CS Banks County. Incorporated as a town December 19, 1859. Named after Homer Jackson, a prominent early settler.

HOMERVILLE, CS Clinch County. Incorporated February 15, 1869. This place was originally called STATION NUMBER ELEVEN by the railroad. In February 1853, Dr. John Homer Mattox (1827-1859) established his home here and called the place Homerville after his own name, not thinking that later on a town would be built up on the same lot of land and retain the name. The Atlantic and Gulf Railroad was built through here in 1859, and the county seat was moved here from Magnolia (q.v.) in 1860.

HOMINY CREEK, Carroll County. An east bank tributary of the Little Tallapoosa River, which rises southwest of Villa Rica and then flows southwesterly. Is thought to be a translation from a possible Indian name, SOFKEEHATCHEE. *See* Sofkee Creek.

HONEY (BEE) ISLAND, Ware County. Located in the Okefenokee Swamp, about twelve miles north of the Florida line. Wild bees use this island as a home, as there are many wild "bee gums" found here.

HOOD, Harris County. This former community was established in 1877. Also known as OLD HOOD, it was named for Dr. E. C. Hood. After Hood declined, the community of Chipley (q.v.) was established one mile north of this site about 1879. There was also a community called HOOD, four miles southeast of Blairsville, in Union County.

HOOKER, Dade County. Named for Union general, Joseph Hooker, who advanced through the mountain pass here in the Civil War.

HOOPER, Haralson County. This rural community is located two miles west of Tallapoosa on U. S. 78. In 1882 the postmaster J. M. Hooper operated a cotton gin and wool carder as well as flour and grist mills.

HOOTENVILLE, Taylor County. This former community was located on the Flint River where it is crossed by the present U. S. 80. It was originally called HOOTEN'S FERRY, and this ferry was later taken over by Louis Cantelow. The old Indian trail, Toms Path (q.v.), passed through here. This section of the county is named HOOTENVILLE (Militia) DISTRICT.

HOPEFUL, Mitchell County. Located west of Camilla. The name of this community was selected by the first settlers who desired an optimistic name to call it. There was also a community named HOPEFUL in upper Forsyth County. The first settler was believed to be Herod Thornton Sr., who moved here from North Carolina in 1819.

HOPEULIKIT, Bulloch County. The original settlers invented the whimsical name for this community in the upper section of the county. Brinkley said this name was submitted in desperation after the U. S. postal authorities rejected all previous names proposed.

HOPEWELL, Fulton County. This old community about five miles north of Alpharetta was given its name by early settlers to denote optimism. Another community called HOPEWELL is located in Cherokee County near Canton.

HOPOETHYELOHOLO CREEK, Butts County. The Muskogee Indian name for SANDY CREEK, which flows easterly into Chief MacIntosh Lake at Indian Springs State Park.

HORNET'S NEST, Elbert County. This was the name given to that section of old Wilkes County, where there lived a number of Whigs "who were both enthusiastic and vindictive in their hatred of the Tories." Nancy Hart (*see* Hart County) lived in this region. This section of Wilkes County was taken in 1790 to create Elbert County.

HORNSBY'S, Fulton County. This was the name given to an old post office which was in operation from 1840 to 1844. Named for postmaster Joseph Hornsby. It was located a short distance west of the present East Point.

HORRY, Taylor County. Settled about 1828 when it was the first county seat of Marion County. It was located 7½ miles northeast of Tazewell. The derivation of the name is not known.

HORSELEG MOUNTAIN, Floyd County. Located just southwest of Rome, it is 1,526 feet high. Descriptively named because of its apparent resemblance to the hock and shank of a horse. *See also* Shinbone Ridge.

HOSCHTON, Jackson County. Pronounced "Hush'-ton." Incorporated September 19, 1891. The first post office established here August 21, 1878 was named HOSCH'S STORE, after postmaster Russell A. Hosch, who ran a general store here.

HOT HOUSE, Fannin County. This early settlement was located six miles north of Blue Ridge on HOT HOUSE CREEK. This stream rises at the North Carolina line and flows southwesterly to enter the Toccoa River three miles below McCaysville. Named for a sweat house, a small structure covered with earth, which was used by the Cherokees in extremely cold weather.

HOUSE CREEK, Harris County. Flows into the Chattahoochee River. Formerly called OLD HOUSE CREEK, it was named for a former house, hut or place of refuge located nearby.

(BIG) HOUSE CREEK, Wilcox County. Was known to the Indians as AL-KA-SAC-KI-LI-KI, signifying "a kettle boiling in a creek." It rises between Rochelle and Abbeville, and flows southeasterly to enter the Ocmulgee River at the southeast corner of the county. An affluent of House Creek is LITTLE HOUSE CREEK in Ben Hill County. It rises about ten miles northwest of Fitzgerald to enter (Big) House Creek three miles before it flows into the Ocmulgee River. There is also a similarly named stream, BIG HORSE CREEK in Telfair County, which enters the Ocmulgee River midway between Jacksonville and Lumber City.

HOUSER MILL ROAD, Peach County. Runs southward from Byron to Mossy Creek. Named from a former mill which was located seven miles east of Fort Valley on Mossy Creek. HOUSER MILL was named after Andrew Houser, who purchased Clark's grist mill in 1865. The community here was originally called EVA. The place was washed away in a flood in 1928.

HOUSTON, Heard County. Incorporated as a village December 23, 1840. Also known as LIBERTY HILL, it was located near the Troup County line. Named for the Rev. H. W. Houston, a Baptist preacher.

HOUSTON COUNTY. Pronounced "How'-stun." Calls itself "Georgia's Most Progressive County." Created May 15, 1821 with 379 square miles acquired by Creek cession of January 8, 1821. This was an original county, named for John Houstoun (1744-1796), son of Sir Patrick Houstoun, who was one of the companions of General Oglethorpe. John Houstoun was born in Waynesboro, Burke County, was a member of the Continental Congress and became governor of Georgia in 1778. The county seat is Perry (q.v.). Note: "Houstoun" was the 19th century spelling of today's "Houston." There is also a community of HOUSTON LAKE near Perry in Houston County, a HOUSTON AVENUE in Macon and a HOUSTON HEIGHTS district in Bibb County.

HOUSTON VALLEY, Catoosa County. Located just east of Taylor Ridge. The name is derived from either Robert Houston or Samuel E. Houston, both of whom resided in Catoosa County.

HOWARD'S MILL, Early County. Built about 1839 by John Howard (1812-1857) on Kirkland Creek five miles north of Jakin.

HOWELL, Echols County. Incorporated as a town August 2, 1905. This community is located about 14 miles east of Valdosta. Derivation of the name is unknown.

HOWELL MILL ROAD, Atlanta. Named for Clark Howell's (1811-1882) grist and planing mill on Peachtree Creek, which was established in 1852. HOWELL'S MILLS post office was established here from February 29, 1876 to 1891. *See also* COX'S CROSSROAD.

HOWELL'S CROSSROADS, Gwinnett County. This was the early name of DULUTH (q.v.).

HOWELL'S FERRY ROAD, Fulton County. Was called LICK SKILLET ROAD during the Civil War and prior to that time. This early name was taken from a village of LICK SKILLET at the site of the later ADAMSVILLE, which was located six miles west of the center of Atlanta. The later name was for Isaac Howell who operated a ferry on the Chattahoochee River in the late 1820's.

HUBER, Twiggs County. Originally known as PHILIP (STATION), it was changed to ADAMS PARK in 1916. The present name of this community is after J. M. Huber of the J. M. Huber Company here. The post office was given the name of Huber in 1939.

HUB JUNCTION, Newton County. Named after a gas station, which became what was claimed to be the busiest rural bus station in the world, called "The Hub." It was established by Robert Stanton in 1935 at the junction of Georgia highways 11 and 12, and became a bus station in 1937. Up to as many as 40 buses stopped daily during World War II.

HUCHING, Oglethorpe County. This small village three miles south of Crawford was first called RICE for George L. Rice, local farmer and business man. The name was later changed to honor Captain Huchins, who was conductor on the Georgia Railroad, which passes through here. The name was labeled as HUCHINS on a Thomas B. Moss map of 1894, and given this spelling in Mrs. Florrie Smith's, *History of Oglethorpe County.*

HUDSON RIVER. Rises in Banks County, flows southeasterly to form the boundary between Franklin and Madison counties, and Madison and Echols counties, before entering the Broad River six miles southwest of Elberton. Named after the Hudson River of New York, which was named for Henry Hudson (d. 1611?), English navigator.

HUFFER, Coffee County. A community originally called SHEPHERD (q.v.).

HUGUENOT, Elbert County. Was an old community located on the Broad River, five miles from its mouth. It is believed to have been named after the French Huguenots, or Calvinist Protestants, from which ancestry the early settlers were no doubt derived.

HULL, Madison County. Incorporated August 24, 1905. Believed named for Rev. Hope Hull (1763-1818), founder of the Methodist Church in Georgia (at Washington, Wilkes County). His grandson,

A. L. Hull, was secretary and treasurer of the University of Georgia.

HUMBUG SQUARE, Atlanta. This was an early designation for the block bounded by Whitehall, Alabama and Pryor streets and the Western and Atlantic Railroad. It was so named before the Civil War due to its use for circuses, medicine shows, fakirs, auctioneers, etc.

HUNGER AND HARDSHIP CREEK, Laurens County. Enters the Oconee River at Dublin. John Goff said it may have been given this name by a weary and hungry surveying party when first laying out the area in 1804-05.

HUNGRY HILL, Bryan County. Located in the eastern section of the county on Georgia highway 63; it is not a hill but is as flat as can be. This is a po' mouthin name, as is HUNGRY CREEK in southwestern Carroll County, and also HUNGRY VALLEY located west of Dalton in Whitfield County.

HUNTER FIELD, Savannah. This U. S. Air Force base was named for Major General Frank O'Driscoll Hunter, a native of Savannah who was a leading air ace in both World Wars. He received the highest decorations from his own country as well as from France and England.

HURRICANE CREEK. Streams by this name are fairly well distributed in Georgia, mostly in an east-west band across the state, through an area most frequented by hurricanes. One is located in Jeff Davis-Bacon-Pierce counties, and in the same vicinity is a stream called LITTLE HURRICANE CREEK. The HURRICANE CREEK in Jackson County was formerly called NUMSACOTA CREEK. Near the Tennessee Line in Catoosa County is found HURRICANE BRANCH, which is an affluent of South Chickamauga Creek.

HURRICANE SHOALS, Jackson County. This former community was settled about 1790, about three miles south of the present Maysville. A post office existed here from April 30, 1819 to January 6, 1844. It was located on the North Oconee River, taking its name from the shoals here.

HURRICANE TOWN, Dougherty County. This was an early Indian settlement located on the west bank of the Flint River, five miles below Albany. The name was translated from the original Indian name, HOTALI-HUYANA. This was derived from the Muskogee, *Hotali,* "Wind," and *Huyana,* "Passing."

HUSH-YOUR-MOUTH ISLAND, Camden County. Burnette Vanstory notes that this is a tiny island near Cumberland, which was descriptively named when the small islands here were used as hideouts for smugglers.

HUTCHINSON'S ISLAND, Chatham County. This large island is located in the Savannah River opposite downtown Savannah. Named by General Oglethorpe for a close friend and supporter, Archibald Hutchinson.

I

ICE, Pierce County. Believed named from the fact that so much ice was put off here by the railroad. The community, four miles northeast of Blackshear, is now called OWEN.

ICEBERG, Monroe County. Also spelled ICEBURG, this was the original name of JULIETTE (q.v.).

ICHABUCKLER CREEK, Stewart County. Enters the Chattahoochee River about 2½ miles north of the Quitman County line. Pronounced by local people, "Itcheebuckluh." The Muskogean name means "Tobacco Pipe Creek."

ICHAWAYNOCHAWAY CREEK (or RIVER). Forms the boundary between Randolph and Terrell counties, and flows southerly through Baker County and into the Flint River. This is a Muskogee Indian word that may be pertaining to beavers or possibly the male deer. Some authorities believe it means "Buck Sleeping (place) Creek," or "The Place Where the Deer Sleep."

ICHOCONNAUGH CREEK. An early spelling of ECHECONNEE CREEK (q.v.).

IDA CASON CALLAWAY GARDENS. This is the original name given to the present CALLAWAY GARDENS (q.v.), otherwise known as IDA CASON GARDENS.

IDEAL, Macon County. Incorporated as a town August 22, 1907. Before the railway came through, this place was called JOETOWN (q.v.). Later when two railroad executives were looking for a likely place for a stop, they arrived here, and one of them said that this site was "ideal." The other man proclaimed, "And you have just named it!" The post office named Ideal was opened in 1906.

IFCONJO CREEK, Monroe County. This is a tributary of the Ocmulgee River shown on an 1823 Tanner map. An 1818 map had it spelled IF-CON-JO-HATCHEE. The name is derived from the Creek, *ifkancho,* "tick" — probably referring to the cattle tick.

ILA, Madison County. Incorporated as a town July 28, 1910. This name is derived from the Choctaw word, *illa,* meaning "dead."

ILLA CREEK, Wayne County. Derivation is from the name Saint Illa, which is also the origin of the Satilla River (q.v.).

INDIAN. Some of the place-names in Georgia include the word "Indian" in reference to its former inhabitants, who were forcibly removed from this early homeland in 1838. INDIAN BRANCH in eastern Laurens County is an affluent of Pughes Creek. An old community of INDIAN CREEK in Jackson County was named for the stream on which it was located. Its post office was established from 1851 to 1858. Other streams called INDIAN CREEK are found in Carroll, Clayton, Dooly, Oglethorpe and Worth counties. The stream by this name in Dooly county is a tributary of the Flint River, and was called LONOTO CREEK by the Indians, a word meaning "flint." INDIAN LAKE in Colquitt County is located on LITTLE INDIAN CREEK, three miles south of Moultrie. INDIAN MOUNTAIN in Harris County was named for a legendary Indian fort atop this peak of the Pine Mountain range. INDIAN GRAVE GAP in Towns County was named for the isolated stone cairn here which supposedly marks an Indian's grave. INDIANOLA is a community in Lowndes County named "Indian" with a Latin-like ending. In this county is an INDIAN POND which contains peat, and is located three miles southwest of Lake Park. INDIAN SPRINGS in Butts County was incorporated as a "place" December 25, 1837. This was at one time the most fashionable watering place in the state. It was given its name because of the famous mineral spring water here that is rich in sulphur. This spring was first discovered by white men when Douglas Watson, an Indian scout, came upon the place in 1792 (*see* Watson Springs). The place was first called GUNPOWDER SPRINGS, because of the taste of the water. The official name was adopted in 1825 when the treaty with the Creek Indians was ratified, in which agreement the Indians were to give up all their lands in Georgia. The name of the town of Indian Spring (*sic*) was changed to FLOVILLA (q.v.) October 6, 1885 because of confusion caused by the adjoining town of McIntosh which had a post office called Indian Spring. To add to the confusion, the post office at Indian Spring was then called HEARD. INDIAN SPRINGS STATE PARK with 510 acres was established here in 1927, and is believed by some authorities to be the oldest state park in the U. S. Within the park is CHIEF McINTOSH LAKE (q.v.). The Creek Indian Chief William McIntosh built a hotel in the vicinity of the springs in 1819 (see McIntosh Old Place). INDIAN TOWN in Ware County is located on the western end of Mitchells Island, ten miles southwest of Camp Cornelia. This was the last Indian town in Georgia, where Seminole Indians remained until about 1850, in this most secluded area of the Okefenokee Swamp.

INDUSTRIAL CITY GARDENS, Chatham County. See GARDEN CITY.

INGLESIDE, DeKalb County. This name was bestowed by the Dabney's and a Mr. Almond of Conyers, who liked the sound of the name for this suburban community located just east of Decatur. Its post office opened February 20, 1892. This became AVONDALE ESTATES (q.v.) in 1925. A section of Macon has also been named INGLESIDE.

INMAN, Fayette County. This former town was incorporated August 21, 1911. It is now a rural community five miles southeast of Fayetteville.

INMAN PARK, Atlanta. Located less than two miles east of Five Points. Planned in the 1880's as the city's first suburban community by Joel Hurt who named it for his friend and business associate, Samuel M. Inman (? - 1915), an organizer of the Southern Railway Co.

INTACHCOOCHEE (stream), Crawford County. This was the previous Creek Indian name for the present CULPEPPER CREEK, and means "Little Beaver Dams (or Ponds)."

INTACHKCULGUA, Marion County. This was the name given to an old Uchee Indian town, and translates as "Beaver Ponds." It was located near the present community of Tazewell, on what was then called upper Opilthlucco Creek (q.v.).

INTRACOASTAL (INLAND) WATERWAY. See ATLANTIC INTRACOASTAL WATERWAY.

INTRENCHMENT CREEK, DeKalb County. Flows in a southerly direction to enter the South River at the town of Constitution. Goff believed it may have been named in reference to a stockade or trench of uncertain date. The former LITTLE IN-

TRENCHMENT CREEK in Hall County was inundated with the formation of Lake Lanier.

INVERNESS, McIntosh County. This was the name given to a former village on Sapelo Island, located twelve miles northeast of Darien. This place was so named by the Scotch settlers for the county of Invernessshire in Scotland. See New Inverness.

IRBYVILLE, DeKalb County. Was located at the corner of present West Paces Ferry and Roswell roads. This community was named for the pioneer settler of Buckhead (q.v.), Henry Irby, who came to Georgia from South Carolina. The post office here was open intermittently from 1841-1842, 1855-1861, and 1867-1879. There was formerly a village named IRBY in Tift County, located seven miles north of Tifton. The Georgia Southern and Florida Railroad named their stop here CYCLONETTA STATION (q.v.), which is now called SUNSWEET.

IRENE MOUND, Chatham County. Located on the banks of Pipemakers Creek in the northwest section of the county. It is believed to be the site of a schoolhouse established in 1735 by John Wesley, Benjamin Ingham, and the Moravians.

IRIC CREEK, Bulloch County. A tributary of Black Creek that begins above Arcola on U.S. 80 and joins upper Black Creek south of Stilson. Was named for Adam Eirick who applied for and received a grant of 500 acres on the stream in 1768. There was at one time a village named IRIC on this stream, located five miles southwest of Stilson.

IRISH SETTLEMENT, Jefferson County. See QUEENSBORO.

IRON CITY, Seminole County. Incorporated as a town December 20, 1900. Established as a rail town which was named to commemorate Georgia's venture as an iron-producing state. The ore from Cass (Bartow) County passed through here.

IRONVILLE, Bartow County. A former community located six miles northwest of Cartersville on Pettis Creek. Was so named as there was active iron mining in the vicinity. Another former community of IRONVILLE was the first county seat of Irwin County when it was formed in 1818. The seat was moved to Irwinville (q.v.) in 1831.

IRVINE, Cobb County. The early name of AUSTELL (q.v.).

IRWIN COUNTY. Created December 15, 1818 with 372 square miles acquired by Creek cessions of August 9, 1814 and January 22, 1818. This was an original county, named after Georgia governor, Jared Irwin (1751-1818), a native of North Carolina, who was of Irish descent. He was famous for his opposition to the Yazoo fraud, and when he was governor he rescinded the Yazoo law in 1796. The county seat is Ocilla (q.v.). A monument to Governor Irwin in Sandersville was the first monument to an individual erected by the State of Georgia. *See also* Irwinton.

IRWINS, Washington County. A community located ten miles southwest of Sandersville. Shortened from the earlier name of IRWIN'S CROSSROADS, named for the Irwin family who were early settlers here.

IRWINTON, CS Wilkinson County. First known as BETHEL, then later as HIGH HILL FRACTION, due to the lack of interest in the first railroad here. Established as the county seat in 1811 and incorporated as a town December 4, 1816. Named in honor of Jared Irwin (*see* Irwin County). The site of the courthouse is said to be the location of an early Indian trading post.

IRWINVILLE, Irwin County. Incorporated as a town December 22, 1857. This community is located ten miles northwest of Ocilla, and was the county seat from 1831 to 1906, when it was moved to Ocilla (*see also* Ironville). Jefferson Davis was captured two miles north of here, May 16, 1865 (*see* Jeff Davis County).

ISABELLA, Worth County. Incorporated as a city August 17, 1903. This community is located about three miles northwest of Sylvester, and was the county seat after it was moved from nearby San Barnard (q.v.). When the railroad came through, ISABELLA

STATION was established southeast of here, and later became the county seat, July 1, 1904, which was then named SYLVESTER (q.v.).

ISLAND FORD, Gwinnett County. Located about one mile below Buford Dam, above the mouth of Big Creek. This name is descriptive, as this was a place where people forded the Chattahoochee River, and in crossing traversed Bowmans Island, half a mile wide. Also in this vicinity is found ISLAND FORD ROAD and ISLAND FORD CHURCH.

ISLANDS FORD, Crawford-Taylor counties. This was used as a crossing place on the Flint River about seven miles due north of today's Reynolds. It is now called REEVES ISLAND and REEVES SHOALS, named for a family in the area. The Creek Indian designation of this ford was OTAULGAUNENE (q.v.).

ISLAND SHOALS, Henry-Newton counties. Located in the South Branch of the Ocmulgee River at the northern point of Butts County. The name is derived from a three-acre island in the river here. Joseph M. Bosworth attempted to establish a milltown on the Henry side of the river in 1880, but failed.

ISLE OF HOPE, Chatham County. Located a short distance directly south of Savannah. This is actually a peninsula, and was an early summer resort which was in 1840 called PARKERSBURG. The present name was adopted in colonial days. Noble Jones' plantation Wormsloe (q.v.) is adjacent to this place.

ISONDEGA (or ISUNDIGA). An early name of the SAVANNAH RIVER (q.v.).

ITATCHEE USCAW, Muscogee County. This was the name of an old Indian village in the northwest section of the county, located on Standing Boy Creek. The name means "Head of a Creek." It was later called HATCHE UXAU, meaning "End Creek," from the Muskogean, *hachiuksa,* meaning "At the Head (or End) of a Stream."

IVANHOE, Bulloch County. This old community is located in the southeast section of the county, ten miles west of Eden. The name is derived from novel *Ivanhoe* of 1820 by Sir Walter Scott, who was very popular in the early days.

IVEY, Wilkinson County. Incorporated as a town February 13, 1950. Is located three miles northeast of Gordon. Named for the James Ivey family of Baldwin County.

IVY STREET, Atlanta. Named after Hardy Ivy (c. 1780-1842), the first permanent white settler of Atlanta (q.v.). Other downtown streets there were named for Ivy's sons-in-law: ELLIS for James M. Ellis, CAIN for John J. Cain, and BAKER for Thomas Baker.

J

JACK'S CREEK, Walton County. Rises just north of Monroe and flows easterly, crosses the upper tip of Morgan County and empties into the Apalachee River. This stream was named for Lieutenant John "Jack" Clark (*sic*), son of Elijah Clarke. The younger Clark was wounded in the Battle of Jack's Creek against the Indians here September 21, 1787. He later became governor of Georgia (*see also* Clarkesville). A stream called JACKS RIVER rises in northern Gilmer County and flows northwesterly through Fannin County into Tennessee.

JACK'S ISLAND, Ware County. Named in honor of Jack Lee, one of the natives of the Okefenokee Swamp.

JACKSON, CS Butts County. Incorporated and designated the county seat, December 26, 1826. Named in honor of Andrew Jackson who stopped near here for two weeks in 1818 when en route to Florida to fight the Seminoles. He drew acclaim from Georgians with his campaign against these fierce Indians in the lower part of this state, which he defeated at Horseshoe Bend in Alabama. His stopover near Jackson was at JACKSON SPRINGS, Jasper County, designated by a marker on Georgia 11 south of Monticello.

JACKSONBORO(UGH), Screven County. Established as the county seat February 1, 1797 and incorporated as a town February 16, 1799. This former town was established by legislator Clement Lanier (*see* Lanier, Macon County). It was located at the center of the county on Beaver Dam Creek, six miles north of the present county seat, Sylvania (q.v.). Was founded in 1794 as a coach stop halfway between Augusta and Savannah. Named for Georgia's Governor, General James Jackson (1757-1806). The town declined after itinerant minister Lorenzo Dow put a curse on the residents in 1830. It was decided May 11, 1847 to move the county seat to Sylvania, as Jacksonborough was considered a town of bad character.

JACKSON COUNTY. Created February 11, 1796 with 337 square miles acquired from part of Franklin County. Named in honor of General James Jackson (1757-1806) of Revolutionary fame, who was the hero of the Yazoo affair when he left the United States Senate to come home and fight the Yazooists.

The first settlement in the county was at Yamacutah (q.v.). The county seat is Jefferson (q.v.).

JACKSON LAKE. This 4,750-acre lake is located at the juncture of Butts, Jasper, and Newton counties. It was developed as a state reservoir in 1910 by the construction of Lloyd Shoal Dam on the upper Ocmulgee River, and was named for General Andrew Jackson (*see* Jackson, Butts County).

JACKSON MONUMENT, Terrell County. Located five miles south of Dawson. Was erected to the honor of Andrew Jackson, who was the seventh president of the United States (*see* Jackson, Butts County).

JACKSON'S FOLLY, Charlton County. A canal which is one of the three entrances to Okefenokee Swamp. Named after Captain Henry Jackson (1845-1895), who attempted to get wealthy by draining the swamp in order to cut the valuable timber here. Now called SUWANNEE CANAL, it was dug in 1891 between the St. Marys River to the edge of the swamp. See Camp Cornelia.

JACKSON SPRINGS, Jasper County. *See* Jackson, Butts County.

JACKSON'S TRAIL. Also called the SEMINOLE WAR PATH, it was made by Colonel Arthur P. Hayne of Tennessee in 1818, under orders of General Andrew Jackson. It ran from Marion County through Chattahoochee, Stewart, and Randolph counties.

JACKSONVILLE, Telfair County. Settled in 1807 and incorporated December 14, 1815. Was the county seat until it was moved to McRae in 1871. Named for "Old Hickory" Andrew Jackson, who defeated the British at New Orleans in 1815, the same year this town was chartered. Another JACKSONVILLE is a community in Towns County, just south of Young Harris. It is not known which Jackson it was named for.

JAKIN, Early County. Incorporated as a town December 16, 1895. First settled in 1817, the post office was opened in 1891. Named by a former major in the Confederate Army, J. Morris Bivings; it is derived from the Biblical word *Joachin.*

JAMAICA, Glynn County. This former community was located sixteen miles northwest of Brunswick, and was named after Jamaica, New York, the home of an investor in the Atlantic Coastline Railroad.

JAMES, Jones County. Located about five miles southeast of Gray, this was originally a Creek Indian settlement. It was named by officials of the Georgia Railroad for Lemuel Photo James, Sr., a bridge builder for the railroad who settled here. JAMES was also the original name of GRAY (q.v.).

JAMESTOWN, Chattahoochee County. This former community was located seven miles southwest of Cusseta. It was named for John A. James who was overseer of construction of the road to Cusseta. Corporal John A. James, CSA of this family died in the battle of Chickamauga.

JASPER, CS Pickens County. Incorporated as a town December 22, 1857. Named in honor of Sergeant Jasper (*see* Jasper County).

JASPER COUNTY. Created December 10, 1807 with 373 square miles taken from part of Baldwin County. When first formed, the county was named RANDOLPH COUNTY after U. S. Congressman John Randolph (1773-1833) of Virginia, the state from which the early settlers here had come. Because of Randolph's opposition to the War of 1812, the county changed its name in 1812 to honor Sergeant William Jasper (1750-1779) of South Carolina, who fell mortally wounded at the siege of Savannah in the Revolution. The county seat is Monticello (q.v.). A statue to the honor of William Jasper stands at Madison Square, Savannah. *See also* Jasper Spring.

JASPER SPRING, Chatham County. This spring is on the edge of Savannah near Augusta Road, where sergeants Jasper and Newton rescued some American prisoners during the Revolution. *See also* Jasper County and Newton County.

JEFF DAVIS COUNTY. Created August 18, 1905 with 331 square miles formed from parts of Appling and Coffee counties. Named for Jefferson Davis (1808-1889), president of the Confederacy. The county seat is Hazelhurst (q.v.). JEFFERSON DAVIS MEMORIAL STATE PARK, Irwin County. Located two miles north of Irwinville, with Davis' bust located at the spot where he was captured May 16, 1865.

JEFFERSON CS, Jackson County. Incorporated as a town and designated the county seat November 24, 1806. This town was established in 1805 at the site of a previous Indian settlement called THOMOCOGGAN. The first post office was called JACKSON COURT HOUSE January 1, 1805 and the place was called JEFFERSONVILLE. The Community name was changed to JEFFERSONTON October 1, 1810, and finally to Jefferson June 30, 1824. Was named for Thomas Jefferson (*see* Jefferson County). The first use of ether for surgery occurred here March 30, 1842 (*see* Long County).

JEFFERSON COUNTY. Created February 20, 1796 with 532 square miles taken from Burke and Warren counties. Named for Thomas Jefferson (1743-1826) of Virginia,

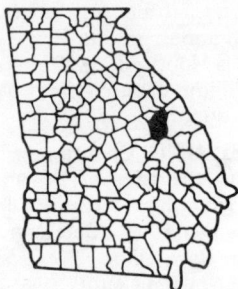

author of the Declaration of Independence, apostle of agrarian democracy, and the third president of the United States. The county seat is Louisville (q.v.).

JEFFERSON HALL, Greene County. Was located nine miles east of Greensboro, and named for Thomas Jefferson (*see* Jefferson County). Established by Lemuel Greene, who built a Greek Revival house here about 1830, after which this became a thriving community when it was made a railroad terminus about 1838. When the road was later extended to Augusta, it spelled the decline of the village, until finally only the Greene house remained.

JEFFERSONTON, Camden County. Laid out in 1800 on a high bluff on the south side of the Satilla River. The county seat was moved here from St. Marys in 1801. After many years the seat was returned to St. Marys, because the inhabitants suffered chills and fevers, as this place was found to be unhealthy. Still existent is the JEFFERSON CHURCH, located about 3½ miles west of Woodbine.

JEFFERSONVILLE, CS Twiggs County. Incorporated as a town November 29, 1901. The early community here was known as RAIN'S STORE, with a post office approved September 1828. The name of the town was changed in 1849 to honor the Jefferson family, leaders during the early development of the county. This became the county seat when it was moved here from Marion (q.v.) in 1868.

JEKYLL ISLAND, Glynn County. Pronounced "Jeck'-el," or as called by coastal folk, "Jack'-el." This island was originally called OSPO by the Indians, while the Spanish called it GUALDAQUINI, GUALE-QUINI and OBALDAQUINI. The French

named it ISLE DE LA SOMME (and the Satilla River they called the Somme). Some of the early English names of this island were JECKEL, JEEKEL, JEKIL and JEKYL. It's been speculated that the name originated from a Frenchman named Jocques who had dealings with the pirates on the island; supposedly the name was corrupted from JACQUES' ISLAND to JAKE'S ISLE and then to JAKYL. The island was in reality named in January of 1734 by General James E. Oglethorpe in honor of Sir Joseph Jekyll, (1663-1738), a lawyer and statesman who helped finance the colonial venture with a gift of £500. The Spanish first came about 1556 and maintained a Jesuit mission here until about 1742. In 1791 four Frenchmen bought the island and it was owned by the du Bignon family until 1886 (*see also* Dubignons Creek). Major William Horton was the first Englishman to settle here. He raised hops and established a brewery to supply the community of Frederica (q.v.) on nearby St. Simons Island. Jekyll was a millionaires' playground and retreat from 1888 to 1942, with names like Astor, Morgan, Pulitzer, Rockefeller, and Vanderbilt maintaining cottages here. It was purchased by the State of Georgia in 1947 for $675,000 for the creation of JEKYLL ISLAND STATE PARK, which includes 11,000 acres of tropical beauty, with ten miles of white sandy beach. JEKYLL POINT is the lower end of Jekyll Island which extends into St. Andrew Sound. JEKYLL RIVER (or CREEK) is the name of the channel separating the island from the mainland, and is part of the Atlantic Intracoastal Waterway (q.v.). JEKYLL SOUND is at the mouth of the Little Satilla River.

JENKINSBURG, Butts County. Incorporated as a town October 24, 1889. Derivation of the name is not known. This former community was located five miles northwest of Jackson on the Southern Railway.

JENKINS COUNTY. Created August 17, 1905 with 351 square miles taken from Bulloch, Burke, Emanuel and Screven counties. Named for Georgia's governor, Charles Jones Jenkins (1805-1883), a native of South Carolina, who was author of the famous Georgia Platform (1850). The name originally proposed for this county was "Dixie" (q.v.). Representative Joe Hill Hall from Bibb

County was the one who suggested the name for the county. The county seat is Millen (q.v.).

JENKINSVILLE, Pike County. This former community was located at or near the present town of Molena, and was named for the pioneer settlers here. In 1882 the postmaster was Mrs. M. A. Jenkins, and N. S. Jenkins ran the general store.

JEROME, Heard County. James Bonner believed that this former community was probably named after postmaster Jerome Ridley.

JERSEY, Walton County. Incorporated as a town August 24, 1905. The original name of the place was CENTERVILLE, because it was seven miles from Monroe, from Covington and from Social Circle. The present name of this community was adopted after a local planter proudly imported a Jersey bull.

JESUP, CS Wayne County. Pronounced "Jess'up." Incorporated as a town October 24, 1870. Named for General Thomas Sidney Jesup (1788-1860) of the U. S. Army, who rendered valuable service during the Creek War of 1836. The county seat was moved here from Waynesville (q.v.).

JEWELL(S), Hancock County. Located on the Ogeechee River, 13 miles east of Sparta on Georgia highway 16. It was first known as ROCK FACTORY and then called SHIVERS (on 1718 map), named after William Shivers who built a cotton mill on the river. Ultimately it was named for Daniel A. Jewell, who came from New Hampshire in 1856 and purchased the mill which he operated until 1883.

JEWTOWN, Glynn County. Located east of Gascoigne Bluff on the southwest end of St. Simons Island. Named after a Jewish merchant, a Mr. Levinson, who once owned a store here. He wished to call the community LEVINSONTON, but the Negroes of the vicinity insisted on calling it "Jewtown."

JOBLEY(S) CREEK, Burke County. A tiny stream which flows northerly into the Savannah River near Girard. It was first called TOBLER CREEK (q.v.), then TOBLAR and JOBBLER before finally evolving to the present name.

JOEL, Carroll County. An old community and post office located 14 miles southwest of Carrollton. In 1882 the postmaster was Joel F. Yates. An earlier name of the community was SPENCER.

JOETOWN, Macon County. This was the original settlement at the site of the present IDEAL (q.v.). Violet Moore says it was named for a solid old citizen here, Mr. J. C. "Joe" Tarrer.

JOHN MARSHALL UNIVERSITY, Atlanta. Includes colleges of Liberal Arts and Law. Named after John Marshall (1755-1835), American jurist and statesman, fourth chief justice of the United States, who was credited with establishing the power and prestige of the Supreme Court. *See also* Marshallville.

JOHN'S NEGRO ISLAND, Ware County. Located in the Okefenokee Swamp above the northeast tip of Blackjack Island. A thief stole a Negro slave from J. J. Johns of Charlton County and hid him on this island in slavery times.

JOHNSON COUNTY. Created December 11, 1858 with 313 square miles taken from Emanuel, Laurens and Washington counties. Named for Georgia's governor, Herschel Vespasian Johnson (1812-1880), who was a U. S. senator, and was candidate for vice president on the ticket with Stephen A. Douglas in 1860. The county seat is Wrightsville (q.v.).

JOHNSON ISLANDS, Harris County. Located eight miles below West Point on the Chattahoochee River. Named for Benjamin Johnson (1807-1882), who purchased the islands from William A. Callaway in 1851.

JOHNSTON STATION, Long County. The early name of LUDOWICI (q.v.), and was so called as Allen Johnston owned all the land where the present town is located. In the 1880's when Johnston Station had about 200 inhabitants, a Mr. T. F. Johnston operated a general store here.

JOHNSTONVILLE, Lamar County. Located four miles northeast of Barnesville. Established in 1821, this community was the first county seat of Monroe County. Mrs. Lambdin said it was named for the Thomas Johnston family, thought to be the first settlers here, while Winters reports that the first settler was John Johnston.

JOHNTOWN, Dawson County. A former community located 13 miles northwest of Dawsonville on Georgia 52. The postmaster in the 1880's was John S. Holden.

JOHNTOWN, Jackson County. The Negro section of Harmony Grove was so named after lots were sold by John Pittman, John A. Williford and Johnson Sanders.

JOHN W. TANNER STATE PARK, Carroll County. Located six miles west of Carrollton. This 128-acre park was acquired by the state in 1971 and includes a 1,000-foot white sand beach on a 27-acre lake. It was formerly a private resort called TANNER'S BEACH RECREATION AREA, which was founded by John Tanner.

JOLLY, Pike County. A stop on the Southern Railway 3½ miles northwest of Zebulon. The original community was called TRAVELERS' REST, as it was a rest stop for early wagon train drivers. When the railroad came through a laborer suggested the new name because of the good humor of the inhabitants.

JONES, McIntosh County. A community in the northern section of the county. Was originally called JONESVILLE, after its first settler, Samuel Jones.

JONESBORO, CS Clayton County. Settled about 1843, and incorporated as a town December 13, 1859. Called LEAKSVILLE (q.v.) until the railroad came through; it was then named JONESBOROUGH for Captain Samuel G. Jones (father of Alabama's governor, Thomas G. Jones), a civil engineer who surveyed for the Central of Georgia Railroad here. In the Civil War, Atlanta fell after the last rail line to the city was cut off with the capture of Jonesboro by Union forces September 1, 1864.

JONES COUNTY. Created December 10, 1807 with 402 square miles taken from part of Baldwin County. Named for James Jones (?-1801) of Savannah who became a legislator at the age of 23, was a U. S. Congressman, and served Georgia well before his early death at 32. The county seat is Gray (q.v.).

JONES CROSSING, Lowndes County. Settled by Mr. Francis Jones in the early 1800's. The name of the community was later changed to KINDERLOU (q.v.).

JONES CROSS ROADS, Harris County. Formerly called PAULINA post office, the community is located nine miles east of West Point. Named after early landowners, Christopher Columbus Jones and his son Monroe Jones.

JORDON, Pike County. Was located nine miles southeast of Zebulon. Named for the post office and general store of Henry G. Jordon.

JOSEPH B. MERCER BRIDGE, Glynn County. A bridge crossing the Turtle River on Georgia highway 303 northwest of Brunswick. Named March 31, 1965 in honor of Dr. Mercer (1925-c.1965) who was a physician and mayor of Brunswick.

JOSEPH'S TOWN, Chatham County. This dead town was located four miles below the mouth of Abercorn Creek on the Savannah River at Black Swamp. Settled about 1733 by two Scotchmen and thirty servants. They soon left after some of their numbers died of malaria. The British attacked General Moultrie here in 1799.

JOT 'EM DOWN STORE, Pierce County. A community located three miles northeast of Blackshear, and has a whimsical name invented by an early store owner. There was a store called SMITH'S JOT 'EM DOWN STORE in Doctortown, Wayne County, and also a JOT 'EM DOWN ROAD, which is a three-mile stretch of road that runs south of Chestatee in Forsyth County.

JOSEPH VANN HIGHWAY, Gordon and Murray Counties. State Route 225 through Spring Place was named November 3, 1955 to honor Chief Vann (*see* Vann).

JUG TAVERN, Barrow County. Incorporated as a town December 24, 1884. This was the earlier name of WINDER (q.v.), under which name it was reincorporated December 20, 1893. It was claimed that a tract of land here was cleared by settler Alanzo Draper in the shape of a jug, which gave it this name. Other versions of how the early community was named relate that it was after a tavern here which sold whiskey by the jugfull, or because this was a place where jugs were manufactured near a tavern.

JUGTOWN, Pike County. This former community, located eight miles south of Zebulon, was named for a family of potters who made jugs and pots here for over a century from native clay.

JULIETTE, Monroe County. This town was originally called ICEBERG or BROWNSVILLE. It was named for Juliette McCracken, whose father was the engineer who supervised the grading and laying of the tracks through here in 1882. On the opposite side of the Ocmulgee River is the larger town of East Juliette (q.v.).

JUNCTION CITY, Talbot County. Incorporated as a town August 21, 1906. The reason for this name is because it was established at the junction of the Central of Georgia and Talbotton railroads, as well as the junction of the Atlantic Coast Line and Central of Georgia tracks.

JUNIPER, on the border of Marion and Talbot Counties. The name of this community is derived from the stream on which it is located, JUNIPER CREEK, which has also been called UPATOY CREEK.

JUNO, Dawson County. This post office is in the home of postmaster, Miss Ruth Harben, eight miles south of Dawsonville. She was appointed April 8, 1940, replacing her mother who had served twenty years. Her grandfather, Z. C. Payne was postmaster in 1887. She has heard it said that the name is from Juno of Roman mythology, who was the consort of Jupiter.

K

KANSAS, Carroll County. This community is located five miles north of Bowdon. It is believed to have been named after the Kansas Territory, when this name was much in the news because of the slavery question in the 1850's. The earlier derivation is from the Indian tribe called *Kansa* by the 17th century French explorers.

KEA'S OLD MILL POND, Emanuel County. Located on Mulepen Creek just northwest of Norristown. Nearby is KEA'S CHURCH at the site of the former community of KEA'S MILL, which was also called DURDAN (q.v.). Postmaster Burrell C. Kea had a general store here in 1881. The town here is now called STILLMORE (q.v.).

KEDRON, Coweta County. A former community located northeast of Newnan on Line Creek. Named from the stream called Kidron near Jerusalem in the Holy Land.

KEG CREEK STATE PARK, Columbia County. Established February 26, 1953 to serve the Negro people of the area. This 867-acre park is located ten miles north of Appling on Clark Hill Reservoir. KEG CREEK, after which it was named, is a tiny stream that flows into the reservoir here. Named from a brewery or still in the vicinity, where the product was stored in kegs.

KEITH, Catoosa County. This community is located six miles east of Ringgold in the KEITH VALLEY. Both were named for the Keith family who lived near and established the Keith Baptist Church here.

KELLEYTOWN, Henry County. This community is located about nine miles east of Stockbridge. Named after Reuben Kelley (1800-1875), a first settler of this section.

KELLOG'S STORE, Jackson County. This former post office was established from 1826 to 1848, and named for the postmaster, Truman Kellog.

KEMP(S) CREEK, Wilkes County. Flows southward into Clark Hill Reservoir, nine miles east of Washington. Named for John Kemp, who settled on 300 acres near this stream.

KENNADY, Bulloch County. This was a small community in old Bryan County where W. Kenneday had a gin and a grist mill in 1881.

KENNARD'S TRAIL. This early route started at Jack Kennard's Place on Kinchafoonee Creek and extended eastward via Traders Hill to St. Marys. *See also* Canoy.

KENNESAW, Cobb County. This town was for many years known as BIG SHANTY (q.v.). It was incorporated September 21, 1887 under the name Kennesaw to preserve its war association after the famous Civil War battle fought at nearby KENNESAW MOUNTAIN, June 27, 1864. The mountain was named by the Indians, and is possibly a variation of Conasauga, the name of an Indian town that was located nearby. Reverend George White believed the place was named for an old Indian chief by the name of Kennesaw who signed the Treaty of Holston in 1791. He was also known as "Cabin." South of the town is the KENNESAW NATIONAL BATTLEFIELD PARK, covering an area of over 3,000 acres. KENNESAW JUNIOR COLLEGE in Marietta opened in 1966, and is part of the Georgia University System. It was named in 1965 for Kennesaw Mountain which can be viewed from the campus.

KENSINGTON, Walker County. Named by resort developers in 1895. The name of this community was transferred from Kensington, Pennsylvania, the origin of some of the first settlers here. Before that the name had come from the village in England, now a part of London.

KESTLER, Early County. Incorporated as a town December 6, 1900. Was first established about 1897 when a big sawmill operation was set up here near the Damascus railroad station. Its been said that it was named for an early family of German origin here by the name of Kestler, or possibly named after the favorite bird dog of the sawmill doctor, L. C. Ward. The name of the town was changed to DAMASCUS (q.v.) August 11, 1914.

KETTLE CREEK, Ware County. A tributary of the Satilla River. Captain David J. Miller of Ware County, who served in the Indian wars, relates that the name was chosen by a squad of soldiers who found an old iron kettle in the sands near the creek where they were camped, three miles west of Waycross. Another KETTLE CREEK rises in Oglethorpe County and flows through southwest Wilkes County into Little River. A famous Revolutionary battle was fought by this stream at War Hill (q.v.) eight miles west of Washington, on February 14, 1779. This engagement was a crushing defeat for the British.

KEYS FERRY ROAD. Extends from eastern Henry County through northern Butts County to Jackson Lake. Named from KEY'S FERRY which was located on the Ocmulgee River at the site of the present Jackson Lake. Tandy W. Key was authorized by the state on December 10, 1823 to establish this ferry.

KEYSVILLE, Burke County. Incorporated as a town December 29, 1890. Probably named for the Rev. Joshua Key (1786-1862), or his son Joshua Scott Key (1817-1876).

KIBBEE, Montgomery County. This community is located eight miles northeast of Mt. Vernon on the Seaboard Airline Railroad. Believed to have been named for Charles C. Kibbee.

KILLARNEY, Early County. This community in the southern section of the county was named for the famous lakes district of Ireland.

KINCHAFOONEE CREEK. With its source in Chattahoochee and Marion counties, it flows southeasterly until it empties into the Flint River at Albany. Hawkins recorded its name as KIT-CHO-FOON-E. This Indian name means "Bone Mortar," or "Mortar Nutshells," apparently a device for cracking nuts, from the Creek *Kicho,* meaning "Mortar," and *Funi,* "Nutshells." Named from the stream was KINCHAFOONEE COUNTY, the original name of WEBSTER COUNTY (q.v.). The name was also applied to KINCHAFOONEE LAKE of Marion, Webster and Stewart counties. This is a 4,400-acre recreational lake with an 85-mile shoreline, and was formed by a 4,000-foot long dam on Kinchafoonee Creek, about three miles northwest of Preston in Webster County.

KINDERLOU, Lowndes County. Located four miles west of Valdosta, this community was first known as JONES CROSSING (q.v.). It was then named KINDER-LOU for the sister of civil engineer, Captain George R. McKee, who had large farming interests here.

KINGS, Newton County. This post office was established in 1890, eight miles southwest of Covington. S. D. King was postmaster in 1902 when it was discontinued.

KINGS BAY, Camden County. Formerly called WESTERN SHORE RIVER, this is a channel which extends inland from Cumberland Sound. Was named after Thomas King (a brother of Roswell King, *see* Roswell) who settled on a tract here.

KINGS BAY ARMY TERMINAL, Camden County. This is a U. S. Army installation and shipping point located two miles north of St. Marys on Kings Bay (q.v.).

KING'S BENCH, Hart County. This was a post office which was established from 1832 to 1849. Named for postmaster and justice of peace, William King, and also after a sort of work bench where he would display liquor for sale.

KING'S GAP, Harris County. Located a few miles above Hamilton in what is now Franklin D. Roosevelt State Park. When established, this was a stop on the stagecoach route from Columbus to Newnan, and was abandoned after the coming of the railroad. The post office was established here from May 16, 1829 to October 7, 1856, and was named for KING'S GAP, village and mountain pass, which were named for an old white trader named King who lived here.

KINGSLAND, Camden County. Incorporated as a city August 6, 1908 at which time Mr. W. H. King was appointed the first mayor. This was established in 1894 as a flag station on the Seaboard Airline Railway.

KING'S ROAD. This old route was previously called EL COMINO REAL by the Spanish, meaning literally "The Royal Road," being named for the king of Spain. It extended from Jacksonville, Florida to Savannah.

KINGSTON, Bartow County. Established around 1832 and incorporated November 19, 1869. This town was named in honor of Judge John Pendleton King (1799-1888) of Augusta, once president of the Georgia Railroad and was elected to the United States Senate.

KING'S TRAIL(S). An early route running from West Point easterly to the Flint River. Named after the King's highways in Great Britain.

KING'S TOWN, Marion County. This was an ancient Indian village located near the present Buena Vista, and was the home of the Uchee Indian chiefs.

KINGWOOD, Colquitt County. Incorporated as a town August 13, 1903. Efforts were unsuccessful in establishing a town here.

KIOKEE, Columbia County. This early community was located eight miles northeast of Appling on Kiokee Creek (q.v.) from which it took its name. In 1772 was established here, not only the first regularly constituted Baptist church in Georgia, but the oldest one in continuous existence. The KIOKEE BAPTIST CHURCH was organized under the leadership of Reverend Daniel Marshall (1706-1784) from Connecticut, and was incorporated December 23, 1789.

KIOKEE CREEK. Rises in eastern McDuffie County and flows southeasterly into Columbia County, then flows northeasterly to enter the Savannah River four miles south of Clark Hill Dam. Was originally called OKIOKEE which means "Falls Creek," or its derivation may be from the Creek Indian, *ki,* "mulberry," and *oki,* "water," or possibly derived from *kowiki,* "quail." It has also been referred to as the KIOKAS RIVER. There is also a stream in Columbia County called LITTLE KIOKEE CREEK. Another KIOKEE CREEK rises in southeast Terrell County and flows southward into Dougherty County to enter Chickasawhatchee Creek at the southwest corner of that county.

KIOKEE (Militia) DISTRICT, Columbia County. Located in the central section of the county, it is believed named from the early community of Kiokee (q.v.).

KIOKEE LAKE. This 180-acre lake was created by a dam built in the 1970's on Kiokee Creek near the Columbia-McDuffie county line.

KIRKLAND, Atkinson County. This was a community in old Coffee County when first established. Believed to have been named for Timothy Kirkland (1799-1864), early plantation owner here, or for the William Kirkland general store.

KIRKWOOD, DeKalb County. Incorporated as a community in 1899. Named in honor of Irish-born James Hutchinson Kirkpatrick (1778-1853), one of the early settlers of the county, who came here from Morgan County in 1827. The town became incorporated into Atlanta in 1922.

KITCHOFOONE CREEK. An early spelling of KINCHAFOONEE CREEK (q.v.).

KITE, Johnson County. Incorporated September 11, 1891. The post office was established February 28, 1887. William N. Kight had a general store here and was the first postmaster. The land for the town was given by Shaderick Kight, and he chose the simplified spelling for the town's name, reportedly to facilitate mail service.

KLONDIKE, DeKalb County. This community is located on KLONDIKE ROAD, four miles south of Lithonia, and was served by the Klondike Post Office from January 4, 1898 to April, 1902. The name was inspired by the great gold rush to the Klondike in Yukon Territory during the late 1890's. It is an Athabascan Indian name. There is also a community called KLONDIKE in Hall County, about five miles below Gainesville, named for a trademark label of the Adams Canning Company, and another KLONDIKE in Houston County above Hawkinsville.

KNOXBOROUGH, Effingham County. This was one of the earliest white settlements in this part of the state, and was said to be sixteen miles from Savannah and sixteen miles from Ebenezer. Derivation is not certain, and may be named from one of three: Mr. Knox, undersecretary of state in London; William Knox (1732-1810) who was provost marshall of Georgia, or Revolutionary general, Henry Knox (1750-1806).

KNOX'S BRIDGE, Hart County. This was an old covered bridge which spanned the Tugaloo River for a road between Pendleton, South Carolina and Carnesville, Georgia. Built in 1854 by Colonel Samuel Knox of Franklin County.

KNOXVILLE, CS Crawford County. Designated the county seat in 1823, and was incorporated as a town December 24, 1825. Established back in the days of the stage coach, it was on the Federal Wire Road (q.v.). The town was named for General Henry Knox (1750-1805) of Boston, the first U. S. secretary of war. In 1835, sixteen-year-old Joanna E. Troutman of Knoxville made Texas' first flag, with a blue lone star on a banner of white silk (the colors were later reversed). Most of the inhabitants here moved a mile away to Roberta after the railroad was routed through that town.

KOINONIA (FARMS), Sumter County. Pronounced "Coy-noe-nee'-a." Located seven miles southwest of Americus on Georgia highway 49. This 1,400-acre interracial commune was founded in 1942 by Clarence Leonard Jordon (1912-1970). The name is found in the original Greek version of the New Testament, and means "fellowship" or "communion."

KOLOMI. A former Creek Indian town which was located on the Chattahoochee River, probably in what is now Clay County. Has also been spelled KULOMI and KULUMI. The Muskogean word *kolomi* may mean "where there are white oaks" plus a final element meaning "water." *See also* Kolomoki.

KOLOMOKI, Early County. This community is located five miles north of Blakely, and the name is derived from the Creek Indian word *kolomi* (q.v.). It is situated on LAKE KOLOMOKI, and both are included in the 1,293-acre KOLOMOKI MOUNDS STATE PARK. Named after the mounds of the Kolomoki Indians who occupied this area from about 1000 A.D. until sometime in the 13th century.

KOLOMOKI CREEK (also written COLOMOKEE CREEK). Rises in upper Early County and flows northwesterly into the Chattahoochee River, five miles south of Fort Gaines in Clay County. For derivation, *see* Kolomoki.

KOOCKOGEY, Talbot County. This was the name by which the present town of GENEVA (q.v.) was once known. Has also been written COCOGEE. It was named for Samuel Koockogey who built a hotel near the railroad tracks here about 1852. Koockogey, a Quaker from Pennsylvania, was the first settler in Columbus before moving here.

KOSALU. This was an early name of the SAVANNAH RIVER (q.v.). *See also* Casuppy Creek.

KULOMI. This is a variation in spelling of the Creek Indian town KOLOMI (q.v.).

KULSE' TSI, Fannin County. A former Indian village (*see* Sugar Creek).

L

LADDS, Bartow County. Located about two miles southwest of Cartersville on Georgia 16. This community was established as a shipping station for the Ladd Lime and Stone Company.

LaFAYETTE, CS Walker County. Pronounced "Luh-fay'-et." Called "Queen City of the Highlands." Incorporated September 30, 1885. The original settlement here was called CHATTOOGA (q.v.) and later changed to BENTON. In 1836 the town was given its name in honor of the French nobleman, the marquis Marie Joseph Yves Gilbert Du Motier LaFayette (1757-1834), who helped America in the Revolution, and was later imprisoned in France during the French Revolution. Also named in honor of this French general is LAFAYETTE (Militia) DISTRICT in Walker County, LaFAYETTE SQUARE in Savannah, Fayette County, and Fayetteville.

LaGRANGE, CS Troup County. "The Crossroads City" Incorporated as a town and also designated the county seat December 16, 1828. Incorporated as a city March 3, 1856. The post office was established here January 26, 1832. The name was proposed by Julius C. Alford, which is in honor of LaFayette's estate in France. LaGRANGE COLLEGE here was founded in 1831 as LaGRANGE FEMALE ACADEMY, and is Georgia's oldest independent college. In 1836, the school's name was changed to LaGRANGE FEMALE INSTITUTE. The Methodists purchased it in 1856 and gave it its present name. It became coeducational in 1953.

LAINGKAT, Decatur County. Pronounced "Lan' cat." Was spelled LAND CAT on a 1927 map. This community is located two miles south of Attapulgus. The name originated about 1900 when a New Yorker named Upson started a tobacco farm here he called "Deli Laing-Kat," after the port of Deli and the province of Langkat on the northeast coast of Sumatra. This was because Upson was raising Sumatran tobacco.

LAIRDSBOROUGH, Carroll County. A former community located ten miles southwest of Carrollton. First known as LAUREL HILL, it was renamed to honor merchant, Andrew J. Laird.

LAKES. In this compilation, lakes are generally listed alphabetically by their designated names.

LAKE BURTON, Rabun County. The community of this name was taken from the lake on which it was established. The lake was created by a dam on the Tallulah River, and was named after the former community of Burton which was located on the site of the lake.

LAKE CITY, Clayton County. Incorporated as a city February 12, 1951. It was descriptively named in reference to a lake which has since been filled in for a shopping center.

LAKELAND, CS Lanier County. The post office was established in 1832 and named MILL TOWN because of the various mills here then. Incorporated as a city August 11, 1925 and renamed Lakeland because of its being located near Grand Bay Lake, Lake Erma and Banks Lake. The original community was called ALAPAHA (STATION), named for the Alapaha River nearby.

LAKEMONT, Rabun County. This community was originally called MATHIS, and later descriptively named in reference to its location near the mountains and Lake Burton.

LAKE PARK, Lowndes County. This town was incorporated December 29, 1890. Founded in 1859 by Lawrence A. Wisenbaker, the name was suggested by Mr. John Young of Savannah, in reference to a nearby lake called Ocean Pond. LAKE PARK (Militia) DISTRICT is located in the southeast corner of the county.

LAKE TARA, Clayton County. Incorporated as a city February 17, 1950 to December 7, 1953. *See also* Tara.

LAKEVIEW, Catoosa County. This unincorporated town was established in 1925, and given a name describing its relationship to Lake Winnepesaukah (q.v.). There is another small community called LAKEVIEW in Peach County, east of Fort Valley. Also a town of LAKE VIEW in DeKalb County was incorporated from August 15, 1910 to August 16, 1913.

LAKEVIEW ACADEMY, Gainesville. Dedicated August 1970. This college preparatory school is located on 35 acres overlooking Lake Lanier.

LAKEVIEW VILLAGE, Hancock County. Named from a series of lakes or fish ponds which were dug to farm catfish. Located about half-a-mile north of the center of Mayfield, it was built in 1972 when 150 public housing units were constructed here at a cost of $2,388,500.

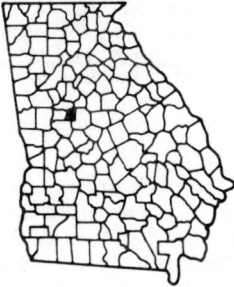

LAMAR COUNTY. Created August 17, 1920 with 181 square miles taken from Monroe and Pike counties. Named in honor of Eatonton attorney, Lucius Quintus Cincinnatus Lamar (1825-1893), who was a U. S. senator, secretary of the interior, and finally justice on the U. S. Supreme Court. The county seat is Barnesville (q.v.). There have been two small communities in Georgia named LAMAR, one in Sumter County, five miles north of Leslie, and another in Baker County, which was incorporated as a town March 4, 1856.

LAMAR'S MILL, Upson County. This community was located on the Flint River, eighteen miles southeast of Thomaston. H. J. Lamar had a flour mill and general store here in 1881.

LANCE MOUNTAIN, Union County. This 3,075-foot mountain near the North Carolina line was named for Thomas Lance, who settled at the foot of this peak.

LANE POND, Lowndes County. Located two miles west of Benevolence Baptist Church. Named for the owner, Mills B. Lane III, former banker of Atlanta.

LANES MILL CREEK, Lowndes County. Rises about two miles south of Lanes Pond (q.v.) and flows southward into Clyatt Mill Creek.

LANG, Carroll County. A former post office located east of Carrollton. Established in 1887 by postmaster Benjamin F. Lang.

LANIER, Macon County. The "Lost Town of Lanier" was the first county seat of Macon County, and was so designated December 29, 1838 when it was also incorporated as a town. It was then on the main stage line between Tazewell and Columbus, on the right bank of the Flint River, about six miles north of the present Oglethorpe. When the Central of Georgia Railroad extended its tracks to Oglethorpe, the residents moved out and the county seat was moved there in 1854. By 1870, not a stick or stone was left to mark the business center of Lanier. It was named for Clement A. Lanier, possibly a relative of Robert Lanier, father of Sidney Lanier (*see* Lanier County). LANIER was also the name of a small community in upper Bryan County, and is a station on the Seaboard Airline Railway.

LANIER COUNTY. Created August 7, 1920 with 167 square miles taken from Barrien, Clinch, and Lowndes counties. Named in honor of noted poet Sidney Clapton Lanier, who was also a linguist, mathematician, lawyer, and musician. He was born in Macon in 1842 and died in Baltimore, Maryland in 1881. The county seat is Lakeland (q.v.). Also named for Sidney Lanier is SIDNEY LANIER BRIDGE (q.v.) at Brunswick, which crosses the Marshes of Glynn, and the former LANIER HIGH SCHOOL in Macon. LANIER ISLAND, Glynn County. Lies southwest of St. Simons Island, in the vicinity of the Marshes of Glynn (q.v.). In Macon is found the SIDNEY LANIER COTTAGE where the poet was born, as well as LANIER PLAZA HOTEL, built in 1853, which was owned and operated by Sterling Lanier, grandfather of the poet. *See also* LANIER, LAKE.

LANIER, LAKE, Forsyth and Hall counties. "Houseboat Capitol of the World." Formed behind the Buford Dam (q.v.) which was constructed in 1957 to create the 35,000-

acre lake with a 760-mile shoreline. It draws over 11 million visitors a year, which makes it the most popular man-made lake in America. Named LAKE SIDNEY LANIER January 29, 1952 in honor of Georgia's famed poet (*see* Lanier County), who wrote the famous poem "Song of the Chattahoochee" about the river which feeds the lake.

(LAKE)LANIER ISLANDS. This is a $40 million state owned island resort completed in 1974 on islands of Lake Lanier (q.v.), with its business area called Village Harbor.

LANNAHASSEE, Webster County. This was the first white settlement (1836) in the county after the Creek Indians were forced out. Named after nearby Lannahassee Creek (q.v.). About 1851, the town moved a mile or two away and was called McINTOSH. The name of the settlement was changed to PRESTON (q.v.) in 1853 when Kinchafoonee County was created.

LANNAHASSEE CREEK. Rises in lower Marion County and flows southerly through Webster County until it enters Kinchafoonee Creek southeast of Preston. The name is believed to mean "Old Yellow Water, from *wi*, "water," *lani*, "yellow," and *hassi*, "old."

LAST CHANCE, Lumpkin County. Formerly a suburb of south Dahlonega. The name came about from an early sign over the road reading "First Chance" when coming into town, and "Last Chance" on the reverse side.

LATHAMTOWN, Cherokee County. This community is located ten miles east of Canton on Georgia highway 20. Named after a former merchant here, William A. Latham.

LATIMER'S STORE, DeKalb County. Was also called LATIMER'S CROSSROAD, and subsequently named BELMONT. Established in 1832 by William M. Latimer from Maryland, who was the first postmaster. The second postmaster was his brother, Charles Latimer, who owned and operated a tavern and store here. The latter was the father of Rebecca Latimer Felton (1835-1930), the first female to sit in the U. S. Senate. In 1845 the post office was moved three miles down the road to Lithonia.

LAURA S. WALKER STATE PARK, Ware County. Located ten miles southeast of Waycross. This 306-acre park is built around LAKE WALKER, and was named after Laura

Singleton Walker. She was a philanthropist who worked tirelessly for the well-being of her fellow man, and also for the conservation and preservation of the forests in this area.

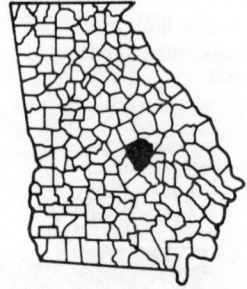

LAURENS COUNTY. Created December 10, 1807 with 811 square miles taken from part of Wilkinson County. Named for Lieutenant Colonel John Laurens (1754-1782) from South Carolina, who gained fame in the Revolutionary War, when he served as aide to General George Washington. The county seat is Dublin (q.v.).

LAURENS HILL, Laurens County. This post office was established 16 miles west of Dublin, August 20, 1835. Named for the estate of this name built by David Harvard between the years of 1833 and 1843.

LAVENDER, Floyd County. This community is located on the Central of Georgia Railway, ten miles northwest of Rome. It is located near LAVENDER CREEK which flows northeasterly into Armuchee Creek north of Rome. Also nearby is LAVENDER MOUNTAIN, a range about eight miles long, with an elevation of 1,701 feet. All three of these were named for George Michael Lavender, who settled near here and ran a trading post.

LaVISTA, DeKalb County. This is a small community located north of Atlanta with a Spanish name meaning "The View."

LAVONIA, Franklin County. Incorporated as a town December 23, 1896. Named in honor of Lavonia Hammond Jones (1827-1909), wife of Major John Henry Jones, who was president of the Elberton Air Line Railway.

LAWRENCEVILLE, CS Gwinnett County. "Garden Spot of Metro Atlanta" Incorporated and designated the county seat December 15, 1821. The name was suggested by the first postmaster here, William Maltbie from

Connecticut. It was named to honor Captain James Lawrence (1781-1813), a gallant naval officer of the *Chesapeake*. When mortally wounded, he commanded, "Don't give up the ship!" which became a popular naval battle cry.

LAWSON GENERAL HOSPITAL, Fulton County. Opened in 1941 at the site of the former CAMP GORDON (q.v.), it was named for a native Virginian, Brigadier General Thomas Lawson (c. 1789-1861), who was surgeon general in 1836.

LAWTON, Clinch County. The former name of DUPONT (q.v.).

LAZARETTO CREEK, Chatham County. Extends from Tybee River to the mouth of the Savannah River, at which point was located the LAZERATTO or quarantine station for newly imported slaves. The name is apparently derived from an Italian word meaning "pest house."

LAZER CREEK, Talbot County. Rises just south of Manchester and flows below Woodland, then northwesterly into the Flint River. Now commonly known as LIZA CREEK and sometimes called LIZER CREEK (q.v.). The original maps of 1826-27 showed the spelling as Lazer.

LEAKSVILLE, Clayton County. This was probably the second oldest town in old Fayette County, and named in 1823 for Garlington Leak, a prominent citizen in the early history of that county. The town was incorporated under the name JONESBORO (q.v.) in 1859, a year after Clayton County was formed.

LEDBETTER, Baker County. Located six miles northwest of Newton. The postmaster in 1881 was H. A. Ledbetter, who had a general store in this early community.

LEBANON, Cherokee County. Located seven miles south of Canton. The original name of this community was TOONIGH (q.v.), which is the present railroad name for the stop. The later name is for the country in the Near East, which became an autonomous district in 1864, and an independent republic in 1941.

LEDBETTER, Baker County. This community was located six miles northwest of Newton where H. A. Ledbetter was postmaster and had a store in 1881.

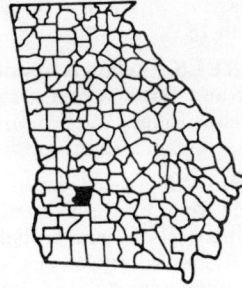

LEE COUNTY. Created June 9, 1825 and December 11, 1826 with 355 square miles, acquired by Creek cessions of January, 1826 and March 31, 1826. This was an original county which was named for General Richard Henry "Lighthorse Harry" Lee (1732-1794) of Virginia, who in 1776 stood up in Congress and proposed "that the colonies declare themselves free and independent." The county seat is Leesburg (q.v.).

LEESBURG, CS Lee County. Incorporated as WOOTEN (q.v.) in 1872; the new courthouse burned that same year. Incorporated as the town of Leesburg December 21, 1898. Derivation of the name is the same as Lee County (q.v.). The earlier county seat was at Starkville (q.v.), where the courthouse was destroyed by fire in 1856.

LeHARDY SPRINGS, Floyd County. Another name for CARLIER SPRINGS (q.v.).

LENA, Tift County. The early name of TIFTON (q.v.).

LENS, Colquitt County. This was the temporary name by which BERLIN (q.v.) was called during World War I. Lens is the name of an industrial city of northern France which was invaded by the Germans in April 1917.

LEONARD, Bryan County. A community which was located on Little Creek about 11 miles east of the present Pembroke. The postmaster in 1881 was Leonard F. Cox.

LESTER'S (Militia) DISTRICT, Burke County. Probably named after Ezekiel Lester, the grandfather of U. S. Congressman Rufus E. Lester of Savannah. A post office named LESTER'S DISTRICT was established here in the 1880's, later changed to MUNNERLYN (q.v.).

LESTERS (Militia) DISTRICT, Jones County. The Lester family came to Jones County from South Carolina, having originated from Virginia. The first of the family to arrive was John Lester, Sr. who came here in 1806.

LEVEL CREEK, Gwinnett County. Rises at Sugar Hill and flows westerly to enter the Chattahoochee River. The descriptive name suggests the stream's slight gradient.

LEWIS ISLAND, Glynn County. Located in the Altmaha River five miles from its mouth. This 6,000-acre island was probably named from an early owner, is mostly cypress forests and is an alligator sanctuary. It is now owned by the Georgia-Pacific Corporation.

LEXINGTON, CS Oglethorpe County. Incorporated and designated the county seat November 24, 1806. Named after the little town in Massachusetts where the first blood was shed in the American Revolution. *See also* Meson Academy and Shoals, Warren County.

LIBERTY COUNTY. Created February 5, 1777 with 510 square miles acquired by Creek cession of May 20, 1733. This was an original county, previously organized in 1758 as the parishes of St. John, St. Andrew and St. James. Named "Liberty" in recognition of the marked patriotism of the Midway (q.v.) community during the Revolutionary War, and in honor of American Independence, which was gained in the same year that this new county was created. At that time "Liberty" was the watchword of the radical Whigs. The county seat is Hinesville (q.v.). There is a community of LIBERTY CITY in Chatham County, near Savannah, and also a place called LIBERTY in the extreme southeast corner of Mitchell County. LIBERTY CITY was also an early name of LUDOWICI (q.v.). There is also a LIBERTY ISLAND in Chatham County, and Alexander Stephens' home LIBERTY HALL and a LAKE LIBERTY in Taliaferro County (*see* Alexander H. Stephens State Park).

LIBERTY HILL, Lamar County. This former post office was first established March 11, 1837 with the name VAN BUREN, after the eighth president of the U. S., Martin Van Buren, until he proved to be an Abolitionist. On June 1, 1841 the name was changed to DAVISVILLE, after John H. Davis, the first postmaster. The final change to Liberty Hill was approved April 17, 1844. *See also* HOUSTON, Heard County.

LICKLOG, Lumpkin County. An early name of DAHLONEGA (q.v.).

LICKLOG CREEK, Rabun County. A small stream that enters the Chattooga River east of Clayton. The name refers to the former use of a hollowed out log in which to place salt for cattle. LICKLOG MOUNTAIN in Fannin County is located nine miles southeast of Morganton, and is 3,472 feet high.

LICKSKILLET, Harris County. The name for this former community was adopted after a man so enjoyed his meal at a fish fry held here after the Civil War, that he offered to lick the skillet the fish was fried in. John Goff describes this as a poor mouthing name which was previously applied to ADAMSVILLE (q.v.) in Fulton County. Howell's Ferry Road (q.v.) was originally called LICKSKILLET ROAD. A LICKSKILLET (Militia) DISTRICT is found in Cherokee County, and another by this name in Schley County.

LICLOG, Gilmer County. This former community was located about ten miles southeast of Ellijay. The name is a variant of Licklog (*see* Licklog Creek).

LIFSEY, Pike County. The name of this community was shortened from the original LIFSEY SPRINGS, which was named for its developer, James Lifsey. Previous to that it was called LIFSEY'S STORE.

LIGHTSEY, Pierce County. *See* BRISTOL.

LIGON, Bartow County. This was a small community located on the old Chulio Road to Rome. It was named after James Oliver "Red" Ligon who lived here.

LILBURN, Gwinnett County. Incorporated as a town July 27, 1910. Established with the coming of the railroad in 1892. The origin of the name is unknown, but thought to be after an early railroad official. The community settled here in 1823 was called BRYAN, and after that it was named McDaniel, for John C. McDaniel, a cotton gin tycoon.

LILLY, Dooly County. Incorporated August 13, 1907 with J. A. Lilly one of the original commissioners. It was founded by brothers John, Frank and Robert Lilly, who settled here in 1902. The early community was first named MIDWAY because of its being equidistant from Cordele and Montezuma. When it was found Georgia already had a Midway, the present name was adopted.

LILY POND, Gordon County. This community was located five miles south of Calhoun. The early post office was named after a pond of lillies that once grew in a nearby marsh. It was an early trade center and shipping point.

LIME-KILN BLUFF, Burke County. So named as this was at one time the site of an old lime-kiln. It is 140 feet high, the second highest bluff on the Savannah River after Shell Bluff (q.v.).

LIMERICK, Liberty County. This station on the Seaboard Airline Railroad is about three miles northeast of Midway, and was an early community named by Irish settlers from the town of Limerick in Ireland.

LIME SPRING POND CREEK, Webster County. Formerly called TALLULGA CREEK (q.v.).

LIMESTONE CREEK, Polk County. This was an early name of EUHARLEE CREEK (q.v.).

LIMESTONE SPRINGS, Hall County. Descriptively named, this early community later became NEW HOLLAND (q.v.).

LINCOLN COUNTY. Created February 20, 1796 with 207 square miles taken from part of Wilkes County. Named in honor of General Benjamin Lincoln (1733-1810), distinguished officer who assisted Georgia during the Revolution, and surrendered at Charleston in 1780. In 1781 Lincoln became secretary of war, and in 1786 was the commander who put down Shay's rebellion. The county seat is Lincolnton (q.v.). Also named in honor of General Lincoln are LINCOLN STATE PARK, with 53 acres near Millen, and LINCOLN STREET of Savannah. *See also* Lisbon.

LINCOLNTON, CS Lincoln County. Incorporated as a town December 19, 1817, and named for Massachusetts-born General Lincoln (*see* Lincoln County).

LINE BRIDGE, Banks County. Carries Georgia highway 184 across the Middle Fork of the Broad River. So named as it was on the survey line of the "Last Four Mile Purchase Tract" bought from the Cherokee Indians.

LINE CREEK. A tributary of the Flint River, so named as it forms the boundary line between Coweta and Fayette counties.

LINTON, Hancock County. Was called "City of the Future." Located about ten miles south of Sparta, it was founded about 1833. Named for Judge Linton Stephens, brother of Alexander Stephens, vice president of the Confederacy. It declined after being bypassed by the railroad. Established here was Washington Institute which burned to the ground by the turn of the century.

LISBON, Lincoln County. Laid out in 1786 on the south side of the Broad River, when it was called TOWN OF LINCON. The name was later changed to the present Lisbon for the city in Portugal. The post office of Petersburg (q.v.) was changed to Lisbon July 2, 1844. There were Petersburg, Lisbon, and Vienna at that intersection at the same time!

LITCH, Greene County. This was the post office name of CAREY (q.v.), where a Mr. Litchfield had a store and no doubt was also the postmaster.

LITHIA SPRINGS, Douglas County. Incorporated as a town August 19, 1918 when the name was changed from SALT SPRINGS (q.v.). It is located on a spring-fed stream, rich in mineral salts.

LITHONIA, DeKalb County. Pronounced "Lie-thoe'-nya." Incorporated as a town March 5, 1856. Was settled about 1830, when it was first called CROSSROADS or GEORGE'S STORE. After this it was named LYTHONIA, from the Greek, *lithos,* "stone," and *onia,* "place," as it was built over underlying granite beds.

LITTLE ATTAPULGUS CREEK, Decatur County. Arises near Fowlstown and flows southeasterly to enter Big Attapulgus Creek (q.v.) just below the Georgia-Florida line.

LITTLE AUCHEHATCHEE. This was the early name of the LITTLE OCMULGEE RIVER (q.v.), as recorded in 1883. *See also* Au Che Ha Chee.

LITTLE BALD MOUNTAIN, Murray County. This 3,700-foot peak is located below Bald Mountain (q.v.), northeast of Chatsworth.

LITTLE BETTYS CREEK, Rabun County. Now called BETTY CREEK (q.v.).

LITTLE CREEK, Haralson County. This was once a thriving community located nine miles north of Tallapoosa on present Georgia highway 100. Named from the nearby stream, LITTLE CREEK, a tributary of Big Creek. All that remains of the former community is the LITTLE CREEK CEMETERY.

LITTLE CUMBERLAND ISLAND, Camden County. This 2,297-acre island is the northern section of Cumberland Island (q.v.), separated by Brockington and Christmas creeks.

LITTLE FORT MOUNTAIN, Union County. This 2,660-foot peak is located just north of Vogel State Park. Derivation is unknown. *See also* Fort Mountain, Murray County.

LITTLE GRAND CANYON, Stewart County. Located west of Lumpkin, this canyon was caused by grand scale erosion over the years. It is more commonly called PROVIDENCE CANYON (q.v.).

LITTLE HELL POINT, Burke County. Located in the southeast part of the county on the Savannah River, about a mile below Devil's Elbow. It was named after Little Hell Landing on the opposite South Carolina shore, which was a difficult stopping place.

LITTLE HOUSE CREEK, Ben Hill County. A tributary of House Creek (q.v.).

LITTLE-HUDSON CAMPGROUND, Hancock County. Located ten miles northwest of Sparta on the Oconee River. Named after the Little family and the Hudson family, former owners of the property here.

LITTLE NEW YORK, Carroll County. *See* New York.

LITTLE OCMULGEE RIVER. Rises in Twiggs County and flows southeasterly to empty into the Ocmulgee River near Lumber City in Telfair County. The Indians called this river AU CHE HA CHEE (q.v.). A dam in the river above McRae has created a 300-acre lake which is included in the 1,397-acre LITTLE OCMULGEE STATE PARK in Telfair County.

LITTLE OGEECHEE RIVER, Effingham and Chatham counties. A small stream which enters Ossabaw Sound just above the Ogeechee River (q.v.).

LITTLE RIVER, Lanier and Lowndes counties. The name is translated from the Creek Indian name WITHLACOOCHEE, which name also applies to Little Alapaha River (q.v.). Little River is also called GRAND BAY CREEK. The community of LITTLE RIVER in Wilkes County is located five miles south of Washington on Georgia highway 47, and is named for the nearby river. There is another stream called LITTLE RIVER in Cherokee County.

LITTLE ROE (or LITTLE ROW), Gordon County. *See* CURRYVILLE.

LITTLE SATILLA RIVER. Rises in Brantley County and then forms the border between Camden and Glynn counties before it empties into St. Andrews Sound above the mouth of the Satilla River (q.v.).

LITTLE ST. SIMONS ISLAND, Glynn County. Lies north and northeast of St. Simons Island (q.v.), and is separated from the larger island by the Hampton River.

LITTLE TENNESSEE RIVER, Rabun County. Rises three miles north of Clayton and flows into North Carolina. "Tennessee" was the name given by the Cherokee Indians to several of their settlements. They spelled it *Tanasi,* but the meaning is obscure. There is a possibility that the name is derived from the Creek word *Talasee,* meaning "Old Town," also seen in the name of Tallahassee in Florida. Tennessee was written by the Spanish in 1567 as *Tanasqui,* and the English in 1707 as *Tinnase.*

LIVERPOOL, Forsyth County. This community is located six miles southwest of Cumming. The name was taken from that of the English seaport, suggestive of a thriving city.

LIVINGSTON, Floyd County. Once the county seat, this community is located on the Coosa River, seven miles north of Cave

Spring. Derivation is not certain, but may have been named for Leonidas F. Livingston (1832-1912) from Newton County, who served in the Confederate Army as a private and was later elected to U. S. Congress.

LIZELLA, Bibb County. Pronounced "Lye'zell'-a." This unincorporated community was first called WARRIOR. The pioneer settler here was James A. Eubanks, who was also the first postmaster. To select a name for the new post office, he had to change from Warrior, as there already was a Warrior in Georgia. He felt it would be too conceited to use "Eubanks," and he didn't want to name it after one daughter in preference over the other. So he coined the name after both Lizzy and Ella Eubanks.

LIZER CREEK, Talbot County. Hawkins originally recorded this stream as LAZER CREEK (q.v.), and it was probably named for an early settler. The Indians had called it AUTHLUCCO, meaning "Big Potato Creek."

LLOYD SHOALS DAM, Butts and Jasper counties. Was completed by the Georgia Power Company in 1914 to create Jackson Lake (q.v.). Named after the shoals in the Ocmulgee River here, eight miles east of Jackson.

LOCHOCHEE CREEK, Terrell County. An affluent of Kinchafoonee Creek. This name means "Little Turtle," from the Creek, *locha, "turtle,"* and the diminutive suffix *-ochi.* An earlier name of the stream was BEAR CREEK, translated from the Creek, *Nokosi Hachi.*

LOCKACHAUTALOFAU, Carroll County. This was the site of Chief William McIntosh's large plantation. Also written LOCKCHAU TALOFAU, this Creek Indian name means "Acorn Bluff." The post office of McINTOSH OLD PLACE was later established here. Near here was established the present village of Whitesburg (q.v.). *See also* ROTHERWOOD.

LOCO, Lincoln County. This community is located three miles southeast of Lincolnton. It is believed to be a Chickasaw village name.

LOCUST GROVE, Henry County. Incorporated as a town December 20, 1893. It is said to have been named after a beautiful grove of flowering locust trees around the old home of William Carroll. LOCUST GROVE INSTITUTE here opened November 1, 1894 by B. J. Graham, pastor of the Locust Grove

Baptist Church. This was a noted coeducational school which existed until 1929. Another community named LOCUST GROVE is located near Sharon in Talieferro County. This was the site of Georgia's first Catholic Church, which opened under the leadership of Father J. M. O'Brian.

LODI, Coweta County. This community in the northwest section of the county was named from a city of northern Italy. It was also known as WILLCOXON'S and later called SARGENT('S).

LOFTIN, Heard County. This post office was located at or near the present town of Ephesus. The postmaster in 1889 was J. C. Loftin.

LOGANVILLE, Walton County. Incorporated as a town September 20, 1887. The first post office was named BUNCOMBE, probably from residents who had come from Buncombe County, North Carolina. The name was changed to Loganville in 1851, after James Harvie Logan, a shoemaker who settled here from Tennessee in 1842.

LOMBARDY, McDuffie County. The former name of DEARING (q.v.). This may have been named for the region of Lombardy in northern Italy near Switzerland.

LONE OAK, Meriwether County. This descriptively named community is in the northwest section of the county, and was incorporated as a town November 15, 1901. *See* Oak.

LONG COUNTY. Created August 14, 1920 with 403 square miles taken from part of Liberty County. Named for Dr. Crawford Williamson Long (1815-1878), who attended Franklin College in Athens where he studied medicine. Dr. Long was the first man in history to use sulphuric ether as an anesthesia for surgery, on March 30, 1842. The county seat is Ludowici (q.v.). Also named for him is the CRAWFORD LONG HOSPITAL of Atlanta. The CRAWFORD W. LONG MONUMENT stands in the public square in Danielsville. It was erected here in 1936, not far from Dr. Long's birthplace. DR. LONG'S OFFICE where the celebrated operation was performed, has been preserved as a museum in Jefferson, Jackson County.

LONG CANE, Troup County. This early community was located eight miles southwest of LaGrange on LONG CANE CREEK, from which it took its name.

LONG ISLAND, Chatham County. Also known as COCKSPUR ISLAND (q.v.), this island at the mouth of the Savannah River was descriptively named. On it was built Fort Pulaski (q.v.). Another descriptively named LONG ISLAND is located in the Chattahoochee River at the northwest corner of Atlanta city limits. LONG ISLAND CREEK of Fulton County, flows southwesterly and empties into the Chattahoochee River opposite Long Island, from which it was named.

LONG SHOALS, Greene and Oconee counties. Were located in the Oconee River before the formation of Wallace Lake. *See also* Curtwright Factory.

LONGSTREET, Pulaski County. This former community was located four miles northwest of Cochran, and also called COLEY STATION. The name was taken from LONGSTREET ROAD, which extends from the aforesaid community northeasterly to the Twiggs-Bleckley line. The term "Longstreet" was used here to apply to a rural stretch of highway that was relatively built up (like a city street).

LONG SWAMP CREEK. Rises in Pickens County and flows into Cherokee County where it empties into the Etowah River. The name is translated from the Indian NEUCONOHETA or GATIGUNAHITA. It was recorded as LOOCCUNNA HEAT by Hawkins in 1796. A former Indian settlement called LONG SWAMP was located at the intersection of this stream and the Etowah River, southeast of Ball Ground in Cherokee County.

LONG VIEW, Dodge County. This old community was located at or near Milan on the

Telfair County line. It was named to suggest the scenic beauty here.

LOO-CHAU PO-GAU, Heard County. This Muskogean Indian name means "The resort of terrapins." It was also spelled LOACHAPOKA or LUCHAW POGAU, and is seemingly today's BRUSH CREEK. The old Indian town was located near the former Chattahoochee Town (or Chat-to-ho-che). The stream rises six miles southwest of Franklin and winds its way easterly to the Chattahoochee River.

LOOKOUT MOUNTAIN, Dade County. This is in reality a range of about 2,000 feet elevation, and 83 miles long. It extends southwesterly from below Chattanooga, Tennessee, through Dade County, Georgia to near Gadsden, Alabama. Tradition relates that the name of the mountain was originated by some of General Andrew Jackson's forces who were here in 1812. At that time General Coffee used as a countersign for the night, "Lookout." Another legend tells of travelers who had been constantly warned to "look out" for dangers of Indians and river rapids in the area. The name was more likely taken from a translation of the Cherokee name, TALI-DANDA-GANU or O-TULLEE-TANNA-TA-KUNNA-EE, "Two Mountains Looking at Each Other." The mountain was also called CHATTANOOGA by the Indians, meaning "Rock-Rising-to-a-Point," and was spelled CHATANUGA by early explorers. The name was applied to LOOKOUT MOUNTAIN (Militia) DISTRICT in Walker County, and to LOOKOUT CREEK in Dade County. LOOKOUT PLATEAU in Dade County is also called CUMBERLAND PLATEAU (q.v.). A community of LOOKOUT or LOOKOUT MOUNTAIN is located on the Georgia-Tennessee line, near Lookout Creek. It is also known as HOOK. LOOKOUT MOUNTAIN EDUCATIONAL INSTITUTIONS of Dade County, founded by Christopher R. Roberts in 1866, existed for only six years.

LORANE, Bibb County. A small community located in the northwest section of the county was called LORRAINE, but the name was corrupted by the railroad spelling of the station. Previously it was named MIM'S CROSSING, after the Mim family who lived here.

C. T. LORD HIGHWAY, Wilkinson County. State highway 112 between Toomsboro and

Milledgeville was so named for County Commissioner Lord, who was killed on this road in 1929.

LORDAMERCY COVE, Union-White county line. John Goff told of this whimsical name for this deep, steep sloped little valley.

LORING'S HILL, Atlanta. Located within the forks of Tanyard Branch near the Atlanta Waterworks. Named for Major General William Wing Loring, CSA (1818-1886), who occupied this high hill July 20, 1864.

LOST ARCADIA, Richmond County. The name by which HEPHZIBAH (q.v.) is sometimes called. Arcadia was the district of ancient Greece which poetically envisioned a land of rural simplicity and loveliness.

LOST MOUNTAIN, Cobb County. A community located six miles west of Marietta on Georgia highway 120. Named after the nearby 1,520-foot high LOST MOUNTAIN.

LOST TOWN CREEK, Cherokee County. Flows southward into Shoal Creek about six miles northwest of Canton. It was named in Indian days, probably derived from the Cherokee *Tsuda ye lun yi,* and is apparently in reference to its detached location.

LOT POND, Lowndes County. Located four miles southwest of Lake Park. Derivation is from the old name, HORSELOT POND, and was formerly a clay pit. Charles W. Fortson, Jr. describes it as being a good source of quality peat.

LOTT'S MILL, Jenkins County. This former community was named after settler John Lott, Sr., who came here in 1764.

LOUISVILLE, CS Jefferson County. Pronounced "Lewis-ville." Georgia's third capital, and its first permanent one, it was established here from 1796 to 1806. The state purchased a 1,000-acre tract here for this purpose, and the town was laid out and incorporated in 1786. It was patterned after the early U. S. capital city of Philadelphia. It was named in honor of Louis XVI of France, in appreciation of French help in the Revolution. The old slave market which was built here in 1758, still stands after being yet preserved after General Sherman burned other city buildings. The famous burning of the Yazoo papers took place in front of the courthouse here February 15, 1796. Named after this city

was LOUISVILLE ROAD (*see* Ogeechee Road).

LOUVALE, Stewart County. Pronounced "Lou'-vul." Incorporated December 4, 1893. Previously called HANNAHATCHEE (q.v.), this community is located nine miles north of Lumpkin.

LOVEJOY, Clayton County. Incorporated as a town September 26, 1891. This name was modified from the original LOVEJOY'S, and is now U. S. Senator Herman Talmadge's home.

LOVERS LEAP, Harris County. This is a high and ragged cliff that projects boldly into the Chattahoochee River about twenty miles north of Columbus. The name is derived from an old Indian legend involving a tragic ending to a clandestine love affair. This is a story similar to others which have been created in regard to high places throughout the United States.

LOVES, Pickens County. This early settlement was named for a white man named Love who kept an inn here many years before the county was established. It stood where TALKING ROCK (q.v.) is now located.

LOVETT, Laurens County. Established as a railroad station in 1884, ten miles northeast of Dublin. Was incorporated as a town August 23, 1889, when E. A. Lovett was appointed one of the original councilmen. It was said to have been named in honor of Warren P. Lovett of Sandersville, at the suggestion of store owner J. M. "Sug" Hutchinson, who was the first railroad agent here.

LOWE, Schley County. This was a community located near the Macon County line, and was named for Rev. T. J. Lowe, Methodist preacher.

LOWER TALLONEY, Gilmer County. See Talona.

LOWES (Militia) DISTRICT, Henry County. Named for John H. Lowe (1815-1870), who was a large land and slave owner here.

LOWNDES COUNTY. Created December 23, 1825 with 506 square miles taken from part of Irwin County. Named in honor of William Jones Lowndes (1782-1822), a leader in the af-

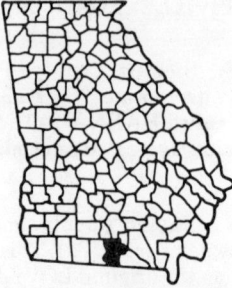

fairs of South Carolina during and after the Revolutionary War. The county seat is Valdosta (q.v.). *See also* Lowndes Court-House.

LOWNDES COURT-HOUSE, Lowndes County. This was the first county seat, and was established as such March 31, 1827. It was also the first post office of the county. The post office was moved July 7, 1827 to a new site which was given the name FRANKLINVILLE (q.v.). The county seat was also moved to the same place December 24, 1833, when its name was changed to Lowndesville (q.v.). Valdosta became the county seat December 7, 1860.

LOWNDESVILLE, Lowndes County. Named for William J. Lowndes (*see* Lowndes County), and designated the county seat December 24, 1833. The name of this town was changed to TROUPVILLE (q.v.) March 9, 1837.

LOYDS CREEK, Wilkes County. This stream was named after a settler of this region who came in the later 1750's.

LUCY POND, Gordon County. Located in the vicinity of Sugar Valley (q.v.). A legend relates how an Indian maiden called Lucy leaped to her death in this supposedly "bottomless" pond.

LUDOWICI, CS Long County. Pronounced "Loo'duh wee'-cee." Incorporated as a town August 23, 1905. The early settlement here was named JOHNSTON STATION (q.v.), also called LIBERTY CITY. The name was changed to honor a German immigrant, William Ludowici, who established a roofing tile business here in 1903, which he operated for ten years. He made a substantial contribution toward the building of the town's former Liberty High School in 1905 (when this was in Liberty County).

LUELLA, Henry County. Incorporated as a town August 19, 1912. Established as a

railroad stop in 1886. Named after the daughter of the president of the Georgia, Midland and Gulf Railroad. The post office here served many years until it closed in 1956.

LULA, Hall County. Formerly spelled LULAH, it was established in 1876 and incorporated as a town August 23, 1905. Reportedly named either for the daughter of railroad builder R. L. Moss of Athens, or for the daughter of Ferninand Phininzy of Athens.

LULAH FALLS, Dade County. The falls and LULA(H) LAKE are located in the upper section of the county. The name was shortened from Talulah (*see* Talulah Falls). Legend says that an Indian princess named Talulah jumped to her death here, after her father, the chief denied her hand to the lad she wished to marry. These places were descriptively called SECLUSION FALLS and LAKE SECLUSION in early days.

LUMBER CITY, Telfair County. Incorporated as a town September 3, 1889. Received its name due to the establishment here of the largest sawmill in the south, over one-hundred years ago. This place was first known as ARTESIAN CITY for the wells here.

LUMPKIN, CS Stewart County. Established March 30, 1829. It was incorporated and designated the county seat December 30, 1830. The first court house was built here in 1831 of hewn logs. Named in honor of Wilson Lumpkin (*see* Lumpkin County).

LUMPKIN CAMPGROUND, Dawson County. Organized in 1830 by Elius Bruce and Luke Hendrix. At this time it was within Lumpkin County, from which it took its name.

LUMPKIN COUNTY. Created December 3, 1832 with 291 square miles taken from

Cherokee, Habersham and Hall counties. Named for Governor Wilson Lumpkin (1783-1870), a Virginian by birth, who had been a U. S. congressman and U. S. senator from Georgia. Lumpkin was commissioned by President Monroe to mark the border between Georgia and Florida. The county seat is Dahlonega (q.v.).

LUMPKIN STATION, Burke County. This was the early name of MUNNERLYN (q.v.).

LUTHERSVILLE, Meriwether County. Incorporated as a town in 1872. It is located near the headwaters of Red Oak Creek. Derivation is unknown.

LUXOMNI, Gwinnett County. Pronounced "Lucks-ahm'-nee." The name may be from the Latin, to mean "All Light," or from the Muskogee, meaning "Terrapin."

LYERLY, Chattooga County. Incorporated as a town September 29, 1891. Named after Charles A. Lyerly of Chattanooga, Tennessee.

LYONS, CS Toombs County. "The Tobacco Center." Incorporated December 9, 1897, and was designated the county seat August 18, 1905. Named for a Mr. Lyons, the man who promoted the building of the Seaboard Railroad through the town.

LYTLE, Walker County. A community located three miles north of Chickamauga. Incorporated as a city August 18, 1917. Was earlier known as BATTLEFIELD STATION. Reportedly named for General William H. Lytle (1826-1863) of Ohio, a Union soldier who fell in battle here, in the Battle of Chickamauga.

M

MABLETON, Cobb County. Incorporated as a town, August 19, 1912 to August 17, 1916. The post office was established June 28, 1882 with the closing of Bryantville post office, about two miles southeast of here. The Southern Railway opened its station here in December 1881. On September 11, 1843, Robert Mable purchased about 300 acres of land in the vicinity. His plantation home still stands, on Floyd Road, just north of Clay Road in Mableton.

McARTHUR, Wheeler County. This was once an active community in the southern part of what is now Wheeler County, between the Oconee and Little Ocmulgee rivers. The postmaster in 1881 was A. G. McArthur.

McBEAN, Richmond County. This community was originally called McBEAN DEPOT, and is located on the Burke County line near McBEAN CREEK (q.v.). Early grants of land in Georgia, 1741-54, include a grant to a Mr. McBean. It is believed that the community and the stream were named after this early settler. McBean Creek rises east of Blythe and forms the border between Burke and Richmond counties, emptying into the Savannah River.

McDADE, Richmond County. This was an active community, located on Spirit Creek, ten miles southwest of Augusta. In 1881, the postmaster was J. T. McDade, who ran a general store.

McDANIEL, Gwinnett County. An early name of LILBURN (q.v.).

McDANIELS, Gordon County. This community located three miles south of Calhoun was originally called McDANIEL STATION. It was named for P. E. McDaniel who owned a 1,200-acre plantation which he had purchased here in 1860. A post office was established in 1888 which was called McHENRY, with the first postmaster being C. E. McDaniel.

McDONALD, Atkinson County. This was the original community that later became AXSON (q.v.). It was originally called McDONALD'S MILL. In 1881, at which time this was in Coffee County, James McDonald had a sawmill here.

McDONALD, Brooks and Thomas counties. Established in 1872, this town was originally named for James McDonald, its first postmaster. The name was changed to PAVO (q.v.) in 1895.

McDONALD SHOALS, Hart County. Located in the Savannah River, and named for James McDonald from Virginia who owned some land here.

McDONOUGH, CS Henry County. First settled in 1822, it was incorporated as a village and designated the county seat December 17, 1823. Named for Commodore Thomas McDonough (1783-1825), a naval officer in the War of 1812, and hero of Lake Champlain. HENRY ACADEMY (q.v.) was located here before the Civil War. McDONOUGH INSTITUTE was organized here in November 1886. It was in an octagon-shaped building, and existed until 1904.

McDUFFIE COUNTY. Created October 18, 1870 with 257 square miles taken from Columbia and Warren counties. Named for George McDuffie (1790-1851), great orator and statesman of South Carolina. The county seat is Thomson (q.v.).

MACEDONIA, Cherokee County. Located fourteen miles east of Canton, near the county line. This community took its name from the church that was first established here. Macedonia was an ancient country which is referred to in the New Testament. There is another community called MACEDONIA in Miller County, seven miles northeast of Colquitt.

McELVEENVILLE, Mitchell County. This was a former community, which was named for the first settler here, Dr. Robert McElveen.

McINTOSH, Butts County. Incorporated as a town from 1866 to 1900. This was once a village of nearly 400 inhabitants, located in the vicinity of Indian Springs (q.v.). Named for Chief William McIntosh (*see* McIntosh Old Place). The present town here is called FLOVILLA.

McINTOSH, Liberty County. This former community, located five miles southeast of Hinesville, once had a population of over 150. It was established as a station on the Atlantic Coast Line Railroad.

McINTOSH, McIntosh County (q.v.). This "village" was referred to in the State laws of 1834. The location of this place is unknown.

McINTOSH, Webster County. *See* LANNAHASSEE.

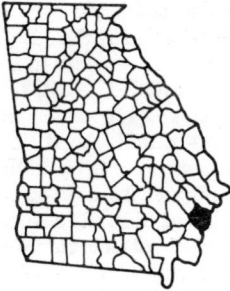

McINTOSH COUNTY. Created December 19, 1793 with 431 square miles taken from part of Liberty County. Named for the distinguished McIntosh family of Georgia. Captain John Mohr McIntosh was the leader of the Scots who in 1736, settled at Darien (q.v.), the county seat. His son, General Lachlan McIntosh (1727-1806), was a hero of the Revolution (*see* Fort McIntosh). The court house at Darien was destroyed by fire in 1864, 1872 and 1931.

McINTOSH FIELD, Camden County. Burnette Vanstory tells of this field on Cumberland which was named for Lachlan McIntosh, who owned some land here. *See also* Fort McIntosh.

McINTOSH OLD PLACE, Carroll County. Located on the west side of the Chattahoochee River about four miles southwest of Whitesburg. The place was also called LOCKACHAUTALOFAU (q.v.), and was the home of Chief William McIntosh (1775-1825), born in the vicinity of Wetumpka, Georgia (now Alabama). He was one of the chiefs of the Cowetas, one of the leading subtribal groups within the Creek Nation, and was called by the Creek Indians, Tustunugee

Hutkee, "White Warrior." McIntosh achieved the rank of Brigadier General in the U. S. Army, and fought in the War of 1812. The CHIEF McINTOSH MONUMENT is located here where he lived, died, and was buried. Another McINTOSH MONUMENT stands at the entrance of West Georgia College at Carrollton. *See also* Chief McIntosh Lake and McIntosh Reserve.

McINTOSH RESERVE, Carroll County. Refers to a one mile square at McIntosh Old Place (q.v.) which was devastated by the Lower Creeks in 1825, when they murdered Chief McIntosh.

McINTYRE, Wilkinson County. Incorporated as a town August 15, 1910. Originally called COMMISSIONER and then STATION NO. 16. Named for Mrs. Thomas (Sarah) McIntyre, a widow who was the first agent of the depot when it was established here. Her Irish-born husband was killed during the construction of a railroad bridge over the Oconee River.

McKASKY CREEK, Bartow County. Flows southerly into Allatoona Lake, four miles east of Cartersville. Formerly known as NOSES CREEK (q.v.).

MACKAY RIVER, Glynn County. Lies west of Saint Simons Sound. Probably named for Captain James Mackay who fought the Indians in General Oglethorpe's regiment.

McLELLAN'S MILLS, Worth County. Was located at the mouth of Mill Creek on the Flint River, 17 miles northwest of Sylvester. In 1881, D. G. McLellan was a millwright here.

McLEMORE'S COVE, Walker County. This is a valley between Pigeon and Lookout mountains which was named for a Cherokee Indian chief, John McLemore, who lived in this section. A skirmish of the Civil War occurred here September 11, 1863.

MACON, CS Bibb County. Called "Heart of Georgia" or "Flag City U. S. A." The early town was laid out and named December 23, 1822, and was incorporated December 8, 1823. It has today transformed its downtown Poplar Street into an "Avenue of Flags" with flags of all U. S. states and territories. Was established in the vicinity of Fort Hawkins (q.v.), which had been erected by order of President Jefferson in 1806, at the site of OCMULGEE OLD FIELDS (q.v.). The settlement around the fort was first called FORT HAWKINS, and in 1821 it became known as

NEWTOWN. Another small community located here by the Ocmulgee River called itself TROY. On the opposite shore of the river was established another settlement, referred to as TIGER TOWN (q.v.). Then in 1822, the early settlers who were mostly from North Carolina, chose to name this place "Macon" after Senator Nathaniel Macon (1757-1837), the patriot and statesman from their home state (see Macon County). The first Christian baptism in the U. S. is said to have taken place in the Ocmulgee River here in 1540. Thomas Tatum built a cabin opposite the fort in 1822 and lots were sold the following year. The streets were laid out in 1823 by surveyor, James Webb, with the assistance of Simri Rose and others. The plan of the ancient city of Babylon was followed, with wide streets and downtown parks. The downtown streets were named for trees, beginning with WALNUT, then MULBERRY, CHERRY, POPLAR, PLUM, PINE and HEMLOCK. ROSE HILL CEMETERY was established in 1840, laid out by and named for the botanist and journalist, Simri Rose, one of Macon's first settlers, who came to Ft. Hawkins in 1818. RIVERSIDE DRIVE was so named because it runs along the Ocmulgee River. It was originally called WHARF STREET or RIVER ROAD when cotton was loaded on river boats here, and much later changed to OCMULGEE STREET. COLLEGE STREET was given this name when it was running in front of Wesleyan Female College (q.v.) which formerly stood on the site of the present U. S. Post Office building here. COTTON AVENUE was given its name in the 1830's when it was on the route of the early cotton merchants, and was once part of the old FEDERAL ROAD that ran towards Milledgeville to the north, and out what is now COLUMBUS ROAD in the opposite direction toward Columbus. NAPIER AVENUE was named for the Napier family of Macon. Colonel Leroy Napier, Sr. made the largest individual investment in the Confederate Loan Fund (in 1861). His son Captain Leroy Napier, Jr. commanded the Macon Light Artillery (or Napier Artillery) in the Confederate service. On WASHINGTON AVENUE, across from WASHINGTON PARK, stands WASHINGTON MEMORIAL LIBRARY, which was endowed and presented to the city in 1919 by Mrs. Ellen Washington Bellamy in honor of her brother, Hugh Vernon Washington. TATTNALL SQUARE PARK comprises four city blocks adjacent to Mercer University, and was said to have been named for Governor Josiah B. Tattnall (see Tattnall County). This park area was offered as a site for the state capitol in 1911 and again in 1919, but local efforts to have the state offices moved here from Atlanta failed. DUNLAP PARK (on Third Street) was named in honor of civic leader, Samuel S. Dunlap, who led the Bibb County Cavalry during the War Between the States. DAISY PARK as well as PRICE LIBRARY, which was established in 1900, were named for S. B. "Daisy" Price, who was the mayor of Macon in the 1890's. The first bridge to be constructed in Macon was built across the Ocmulgee River by the State in 1826, and called OCMULGEE BRIDGE. The Spring rains of March 1933 washed it partly away, after which it was replaced by the FIFTH STREET BRIDGE. This was replaced in 1974 by OTIS REDDING MEMORIAL BRIDGE, named to honor the noted soul singer from Macon. STRIBLING MEMORIAL BRIDGE (Spring Street) was dedicated in 1935 and named for Macon prizefighter, W. L. "Young" Stribling. The city hall was built in 1837 and served as temporary capitol of Georgia from November 18, 1864 to March 11, 1865. The city's Municipal Auditorium has the world's largest copper dome. HERBERT SMART AIRPORT here was named for Mr. Smart who was Macon's mayor from 1934 to 1940. It has recently been renamed MACON DOWNTOWN AIRPORT. LEWIS B. WILSON AIRPORT was established on a part of the area formerly occupied by COCHRAN FIELD (q.v.), and was named in honor of Lewis Burgess Wilson (1901-1967), Georgia legislator, mayor of Macon (1947-1953), and airport manager (1956-1967.)

MACON COUNTY. Created December 14, 1837 with 399 square miles taken from Houston and Marion counties. Named in honor of

General Nathaniel Macon (*see also* Macon, Bibb County), a North Carolina statesman who served in the U. S. Congress for thirty-seven straight years. He became the speaker of the House of Representatives, and was also elected to the U. S. Senate. In 1874 he received twenty-four electoral votes for the vice presidency. The county seat is Oglethorpe (q.v.). The court house was destroyed by fire in 1857.

MACON COUNTY FERRY. *See* UNDERWOOD'S FERRY.

McPHERSON BARRACKS, Atlanta. This was the early name of FORT McPHERSON (q.v.).

McQUEENS ISLAND, Chatham County. Located between the South Channel of the Savannah River and Tybee River. This is the site of Fort Pulaski National Monument (q.v.). The name of the island is derived from the John McQueen family who once owned it. Records show that the only McQueen to arrive prior to 1741 was James Macqueen, who came to Savannah, January 10, 1736.

McRAE, CS Telfair County. Established as the county seat in 1870, and incorporated as a town March 3, 1874. The first settlers came here in the mid 1800's, and were Scottish Presbyterians from the Carolinas. The railroad station was built in 1870 and named in honor of the McRae clan or family. It was built on the plantation of Daniel M. McRae, who with William McRae was among the first of the town's commissioners. The county seat was moved here from Jacksonville in 1871. *See also* Alamo.

McTYEIRE INSTITUTE, Towns County. Now YOUNG HARRIS COLLEGE (q.v.), originally named for Holland N. McTyeire (1824-1889), Methodist bishop and principle founder of Vanderbilt University.

MADDOCKS CREEK, McDuffie County. Rises west of Thomson and flows northeasterly into Clark Hill Reservoir. Named for Joseph Maddox, Quaker leader who settled here from North Carolina (*see* Wrightsborough). The stream is spelled MAT-TOX CREEK on today's maps.

MADISON, CS Morgan County. Was established in 1809 and incorporated March 12, 1866. Named in honor of President Madison (*see* Madison County). It was Lancelot Johnson of Madison who first developed the

process of pressing oil from cotton seed. MADISON COLLEGIATE INSTITUTE of Madison was chartered by the Baptist Church, January 17, 1849, with its name changed to GEORGIA FEMALE COLLEGE in 1851. METHODIST FEMALE COLLEGE was chartered here January 26, 1849. These were among the first women's colleges in the U. S. and were both closed after being destroyed by fire.

MADISON COUNTY. Created December 5, 1811 with 281 square miles taken from Clarke, Elbert, Franklin, Jackson and Oglethorpe counties. Named for the fourth president of the U. S., James Madison (1751-1836), who was the chief drafter of the U. S. Constitution. The county seat is Danielsville (q.v.). There are nineteen Madison Counties in the U. S. plus Madison Parish in Louisiana. Also named after President Madison is MADISON SQUARE of Savannah, which was laid out in 1839, on which now stands a monument to Sergeant William Jasper (*see* Jasper County). MADISON SPRINGS of Madison County was reportedly discovered about 1800 by John Vinyard, who lived on a bluff above the springs and on the nearby Broad River. The community was first named ALEXANDERVILLE after James Alexander who purchased land here to develop a public resort. This was the principal watering place in Georgia before 1825, when it was called "Saratoga of the South." A post office was established here in 1825 at which time it was named Madison Springs, after the county. The resort community ended when its hotel burned January 30, 1871. The site is six miles northeast of Danielsville. *See also* Madison, Morgan County.

MADRAS, Coweta County. Incorporated in 1893. Originally called POWEL(L)VILLE (q.v.) or POWELL STATION, when it was named after city father, George Powell. It was settled in 1851 or before. The name was changed to Madras in 1902, a name chosen by Mrs. L. H. McGee, widow of George Powell. This community may have been named from the city in India, or possibly have been given this name, which is used to refer to the large bright colored kerchiefs worn as a headdress by Negroes.

MAGIC HILL, Talbot County. Located at the foot of Pine Mountain about five miles north of Woodland. It is so named because of the illusion that an automobile with its brakes released appears to roll uphill on the road here.

MAGNOLIA, Clinch County. Incorporated February 20, 1854. This former town was first called POLK in memory of President James K. Polk, and changed January 15, 1852 to Magnolia for the trees that abound here. At this time it was made the county seat. The court house burned in 1856, after which the county seat was moved to Number Eleven (q.v.) in 1860. Magnolia no longer exists today, except as MAGNOLIA (Militia) DISTRICT of southwestern Clinch County. There was also at one time a community of MAGNOLIA in Thomas County, above Newport on the St. Marks River. It too was apparently named this because of the magnolia trees in the vicinity. And there was also another MAGNOLIA post office in Mitchell County, which was located eight miles east of Camilla. MAGNOLIA SPRINGS STATE PARK in Jenkins County is located five miles north of Millen. The name for this 948-acre park refers to its crystal clear spring that flows an estimated nine million gallons of 64 degree cold water each day. This was the site of Fort Lawton (q.v.). MAGNOLIA SPRINGS (or MAGNOLIA VILLAGE) was an early name of PLAINS (q.v.) in Sumter County.

MALLORYSVILLE, Wilkes County. Was located fourteen miles north of Washington on S 902. Incorporated as a village December 9, 1819. William Mallory was one of the original commissioners.

MALVERN, Emanuel County. The name of this former community was derived from a watering place in England.

MANASSAS, Bartow County. This was the name selected to call CASSVILLE when the county name was changed December 6, 1861 (*see* Cass County). It was changed after General Cass had "...shown himself inimical to the South" and said "the South must be

subjugated, and the Union be preserved." The townspeople then decided to name their town in honor of Colonel Francis S. Bartow, who died in a battle at Manassas, Virginia, in which the Confederates were victorious. The Confederate postal authorities approved the change, but Washington would not. Another community in northeast Tattnall County subsequently gave itself the name MANASSAS, named for Manassas Foy, son of George Foy, who named his son after the Civil War battle of Manassas, Virginia.

MANCHESTER, Meriwether County. Called "The Magic City." Incorporated August 16, 1909. Named for the manufacturing town in England. This was also the early name of COLLEGE PARK (q.v.).

MANILA, Monroe County. A former community located eight miles south of Forsyth. Named to commemorate the 1898 Battle of Manila Bay.

MANSFIELD, Newton County. Incoroprated as a town July 22, 1903. The post office was established about 1898. Previously known as CARMEL and BOB LEE. According to legend, the early community named after one of the organizers of the town who remained sober at the celebration for its settlement.

MAPLETON, Mitchell County. Located nine miles southeast of Camilla. Incorporated as MAPLES August 13, 1904 and as Mapleton from 1905 to 1910.

MARBLEHILL, Pickens County. This community was named from its location at the northeast end of the marble quarry area. In 1900 there was recorded a community named MARBLE, six miles northwest of Moultrie in Colquitt County.

MARBLE WORKS, Pickens County. This was the name of an early post office at the present TATE (q.v.).

MARBURY CREEK, Barrow County. Rises west of Winder and flows southeasterly to the Apalachee River. It bears the name of two worthy early citizens of Georgia — Colonel Leonard Marbury of Columbia County and/or his son Captain Horatio Marbury. The General Highway Map of the county labels it MARBURG. Other variations in spelling include: MARBURY'S, MARBERRY'S and MARBRIES.

MARGRAVATE OF AZILIA. Or simply

called AZILIA, this was a fanciful name used by Sir Robert Montgomery when promoting a colony he wished to establish between the Savannah and Altamaha rivers. He received a grant in 1717 from the Lord Proprietors of South Carolina for this project, but he failed to secure settlers.

MARIETTA, CS Cobb County. "Gem City of the South" Was incorporated as a village and made county seat December 19, 1834. It is generally believed that this city was named after the wife of Judge Thomas W. Cobb, for whom the county was named. Another story would have this place named for two legendary, charming young ladies, whose Christian names were Mary and Etta. It has also been said to have been named for the famous pioneer town of Marietta in the Ohio Valley, settled in 1788 by General Putnam. This is the site of Lockheed Aircraft, the world's largest aircraft factory under one roof, and is the largest industrial plant in Georgia. MARIETTA NATIONAL CEMETERY, northwest from the city, contains the graves of 10,000 Union soldiers who died during General Sherman's march to the sea.

MARION, Twiggs County. Was known as "Legal Mecca of Georgia." Located six miles west of Jeffersonville on the Bullard Road, one half mile before it crosses U. S. highway I-16. Incorporated as a town December 12, 1816 and repealed December 10, 1834. Named for General Francis Marion (*see* Marion County). This was established as the county seat in December 1810, and its post office was approved October 26, 1812. It was in service until May 15, 1868 when the seat was moved to Jeffersonville, and the courthouse was literally "rolled" to its new location. The heyday for Marion was the 1830's when this city attained a population of 3,500. The place declined after refusing intrusion of the railroad, and it no longer exists as a town. The U. S. Geodetic survey in 1948 established the exact center of the state at a point about one mile south of Marion. There is also a community of MARION located 13 miles southeast of Ellijay in Gilmer County. OLD MARION ROAD in Twiggs County extends from US 23-129 in eastern Bibb County southeasterly to the site of Marion. *See also* ASHBURN.

MARION COUNTY. Created December 14, 1827 with 365 square miles taken from Lee and Muscogee counties. Named in honor of

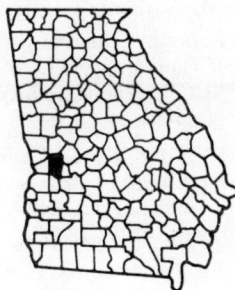

General Francis Marion (1732-1795) of South Carolina, a hero of the Revolution. He was dubbed the "Old Fox" by the British cavalry leader, Banastre Tarleton, and this sobriquet was changed by Marion's troops to "Swamp Fox." The county seat is Buena Vista (q.v.).

MARROW, Clayton County. This city was created and incorporated March 2, 1943, with its spelling corrected to MORROW (q.v.) February 23, 1945.

MARSHALLVILLE, Macon County. This is the oldest town in the county, and was settled by South Carolinians in the 1820's, but not incorporated as a town until February 20, 1854. In the official Act of the State Assembly to incorporate, the name was misspelled as MARTIALVILLE. It is said to have been named in honor of a much beloved Methodist preacher here, Reverend John Marshall, or was possibly named for the chief justice of the U. S. Supreme Court, John Marshall (*see* John Marshall University). Marshallville was the home of Samuel B. Rumph, originator of the Elberta peach, which he named for his wife. This was also the home of Georgia author, John Donald Wade.

MARSHES OF GLYNN, Glynn County. Immortalized by the poem of this name written by Sidney Lanier (*see* Lanier County). Consists of a five-mile network of tidal rivers and creeks — Terry Creek, Back River, Little River, Mackay River and the Frederica River, a part of the Intracoastal or Inland Waterway, and generally applies to the inland portion of St. Simons and Jekyll islands.

MARS HILL. The following minor locations in the state were named from local church sites, which name came from the Bible, Mars Hill being where the apostle Paul spoke to the idolatrous Athenians. MARS HILL road fork, Cobb County. Located two miles south of Acworth. MARS HILL CROSSROADS, Dooly County. Located north of Vienna on

Georgia 27. Another MARS HILL CROSS-ROADS, Forsyth County, four miles southwest of Cumming on U. S. 19. MARS HILL DISTRICT, Oconee County, five miles west of Watkinsville.

MARTHASVILLE, Fulton County. Named after Martha Lumpkin, this was the first name under which ATLANTA (q.v.) was chartered, December 23, 1843.

MARTIN, Stephens County. Incorporated as a town September 7, 1891. Named for John Martin (1730-1796) from Rhode Island, who was governor of Georgia (1782-83).

MARYSVILLE, Johnson County. A post office in the 1880's, located five miles southeast of Wrightsville. The postmaster was Mary P. Hutcheson.

MATT, Forsyth County. A community located six miles north of Cumming on Georgia highway 41. A post office was established here from May 5, 1896 to February 28, 1911. Derivation of the name is not certain, but is possibly for Matt J. Williams, one of the first Inferior Court justices of the county.

MATTOX CREEK, McDuffie County. Originally named MADDOX CREEK (q.v.).

MAUK, Taylor County. Incorporated as a town August 18, 1913 to February 28, 1939. The derivation of the name of this community is not known.

MAULDIN'S MILLS, Hall County. Located twelve miles south of Gainesville on the Mulberry River. In 1881, A. A. Mauldin operated a general store and a grist mill here, when the population was about 100.

MAXEYS, Oglethorpe County. Incorporated as a town August 22, 1907. First called SHANTY, it was named SALMONVILLE in 1834. Later it was changed to Maxeys for the Maxeys family, who were among the pioneer families of this section.

MAYFIELD, Hancock County. A community located ten miles northeast of Sparta, at the site of the former LATIMORES MILLS. Named for the plantation home of Judge William Smith.

MAYNARD'S MILL ROAD, Monroe County. Crosses Georgia highway 42, five miles south of Forsyth, and crosses Tobesofkee Creek over MAYNARD'S MILL BRIDGE where W. T. Maynard operated a flour and grist mill. The post office here was called MAYNARD'S MILL.

MAYSVILLE, Monroe County. Incorporated as a town September 30, 1879. First known as MIDWAY, it was later renamed for early settler John Mays. The post office was established from July 22, 1847 to August 21, 1897.

MEANSVILLE, Pike County. Incorporated August 6, 1913. This community located four miles south of Zebulon was said to have been named for pioneer settler John Means, who came here from South Carolina. It may also have been named for Dr. Alexander Means or early landowner B. A. Means.

MECHANICSVILLE, Lumpkin County. A city subdivision of east Dahlonega. Laid out and named by Dahlonega's first mayor, Colonel W. P. Price, in commemoration of the battle of Mechanicsville in Virginia, June 26, 1862. MECHANICSVILLE was also the name of a community and post office in Jasper County, ten miles northwest of Monticello.

MEDWAY, Liberty County. An early variation of MIDWAY (q.v.) as applied to the river and the town. The community was also referred to as MEDWAY CHURCH.

MEEKS, Johnson County. This community is located 13 miles southeast of Wrightsville, and was settled about 1888. Named for Elder Henry Meeks, a large landowner and prominent Primitive Baptist preacher.

MEIGS, Thomas County. This town was incorporated October 29, 1889. Named in honor of Josiah Meigs (1757-1822) from Connecticut, the first president of the University of Georgia. Also named in his honor is MEIGS STREET in Athens, Clarke County.

MELDRIM, Effingham County. A railroad junction established eighteen miles from Savannah. Believed named for Peter W. Meldrim of Savannah, attorney and state legislator, or for his ancestors.

MENLO, Chattooga County. Incorporated as a town August 11, 1903. Founded in 1883 in the heart of Broomtown Valley (q.v.) by Captain A. J. (Jack) Lawrence. Named in honor of Thomas A. Edison, whose workshop was in Menlo Park, New Jersey. George Stewart says that the name apparently was originally derived from Menlo (Park), California. Brinkley states that the name is of Creek Indian derivation.

MERCER UNIVERSITY, Macon. Named in honor of Jesse Mercer (1769-1841), an eminent Georgian, a distinguished Baptist clergyman, and principal organizer of the Georgia Baptist Convention. It first opened as MERCER INSTITUTE in Penfield, Greene County, January 14, 1833. The University was moved to Macon in 1871, and the Law School was started here two years later. The Medical School plans to open in 1976. The oldest dormitory on the campus, SHERWOOD HALL, was named for Baptist leader Adiel Sherwood (1791-1879), originally from New York, a teacher and Baptist preacher who wrote a *Gazateer of the State of Georgia,* 1826, 1829, 1837, 1839 and 1860. Another men's dormitory, SHORTER HALL, was named for benefactor, Edward Shorter, who made a substantial gift in 1948 for the erection of this building. PORTER GYMNASIUM was named for James Hyde Porter (1873-1949), a major benefactor of the University, and grandson of former Mercer trustee James M. Porter. ROBERTS HALL was dedicated in 1939, and named for Columbus Roberts, a leading benefactor and friend of Mercer. The HARDMAN BUILDING was named in honor of the mother of former Georgia governor, Lamartine Griffin Hardman. It was erected in 1907, rebuilt in 1937, and enlarged in 1953. It was formerly the Library and is now the Fine Arts Building. WILLINGHAM CHAPEL was named in honor of Broadus E. Willingham of Macon, who provided generous sums for improvements of the chapel as well as for a new organ. The WALTER F. GEORGE SCHOOL OF LAW was named for its distinguished graduate, Senator George (*see* Walter F. George Reservoir). The RYALS LAW BUILDING was named for Colonel Thomas Edward Ryals, Mercer alumnus, attorney, a university trustee, and major benefactor to build the Law Building. The GEORGE BOYCE CONNELL STUDENT CENTER, built in 1957, was named for Dr. Connell who served as Mercer's president from 1953 to 1959. KNIGHT HALL (humanities) was named to honor Professor Otis Dewey Knight (1898-1964). STETSON LIBRARY was given to the University as a memorial to Eugene William Stetson (1881-1959) by his wife and children. Stetson graduated from Mercer in 1901 and became an eminent New York banker. WARE HALL was named for Kathryn Cathings Ware, wife of Henry H. "Trot" Ware, who provided funds for its renovation for use as a music building in 1968. The WILLET SCIENCE CENTER was

opened in 1968, and named for Hugh M. Willet, class of 1886, a long time chairman of the Board of Trustees, and generous benefactor. Mercer University also has two campuses in Atlanta: Southern School of Pharmacy (q.v.) and Mercer University in Atlanta (q.v.).

MERCER UNIVERSITY IN ATLANTA, DeKalb County. This 500-acre campus is located five and one-half miles northeast of Atlanta. Chartered in 1964 as ATLANTA BAPTIST COLLEGE, it was acquired by MERCER UNIVERSITY (q.v.), Macon in December 1972.

MERIWETHER COUNTY. Created December 14, 1827 with 499 square miles taken from part of Troup County. Named for General David Meriwether (1755-1822) of Virginia, who served under George Washington in the Revolution. The county seat is Greenville (q.v.). The court house was destroyed by cyclone March 3, 1893. There was also a community of MERIWETHER, located eight miles northwest of Milledgeville in Baldwin County.

MERRILL, Heard County. In 1882 it was recorded that a Robert Merrill had a grist mill here on Hillabahatchee Creek, seven miles northwest of Franklin.

MERSHON, Pierce County. Named by Jack Dixon for Judge Martin L. Mershon of Brunswick.

MESENA, Warren County. A community located six miles northeast of Warrenton. The name was suggested by Dr. J. F. Hamilton, using the first letter of the first name of each of his six daughters.

MESON ACADEMY, Lexington. Opened in 1808, and was established with funds provided by Francis Meson, noted merchant and philanthropist. The name of the school was changed to OGLETHORPE COUNTY HIGH SCHOOL in 1920.

MESSIER MOUND, Early County. Located on the summit of a hill overlooking the valley of Little Colomokee Creek, about 12 miles east of the Chattahoochee River. Named for a Mr. Messier who owned a plantation here.

METASVILLE, Wilkes County. A community located eight miles east of Washington. May have been named for the Wampanoag Indian leader, Metacomet.

METTER, CS Candler County. Incorporated as a town August 17, 1903 at which time it was in Bulloch County. It was established as a stop on the Georgia Railroad, and said to have been named by a railroad official for his wife since he *met her* here.

MEXICO, Lumpkin County. This was an early name of DAHLONEGA (q.v.). The militia district at the southwest corner of Carroll County is named NEW MEXICO. These places may have been so named in the early 19th century because of sympathy with the Mexican struggle for independence.

MIAMI VALLEY, Peach County. A community located five miles east of Fort Valley. This is probably a Muskogean Indian name, and may mean "very large." Miami is also the name of a noted Indian tribe.

MICA, Cherokee County. A community located six miles east of Ball Ground. The name is descriptive as there are gold and mica mines in the vicinity.

MIDDLE GEORGIA COLLEGE, Cochran. Established in 1884 as the COLLEGE OF THE NEW EBENEZER ASSOCIATION, a Baptist denominational institution. Opened January 10, 1887, it was later chartered as a state school August 12, 1917. It became MIDDLE GEORGIA JUNIOR COLLEGE in 1928, and the present name was adopted in 1929. This is a unit of the University System of Georgia. The ROBERTS MEMORIAL LIBRARY here was named for Lucien Emerson Roberts, the third president of Middle Georgia College.

MIDDLE RIVER, Franklin County. Also known as MIDDLE FORK BROAD RIVER due to its position between two other streams, the Broad River and Hudson River. There was formerly a community of MIDDLE RIVER, ten miles west of Carnesville.

MIDVILLE, Burke County. Incorporated February 20, 1877. It was first established as a Central of Georgia railway center about halfway between Macon and Savannah. It is also approximately the mid point between Waynesboro and Swainsboro (Emanuel County). There was also a community of MIDVILLE in western Jenkins County.

MIDWAY, Liberty County. Incorporated as a town August 3, 1925. Originally settled about 1750 by road commissioner Audley Maxwell, who gave it the name LIMERICK after the county in south Ireland. Another early name was ARCADIA (q.v.). The settlement was called DORCHESTER by a group of Puritans who arrived here on May 16, 1752 from Dorchester, South Carolina. Their ancestors had originated from Dorchester, England in 1630. The district was already named MIDWAY when they arrived, having taken its name from the nearby Midway River. The river and the early community were written Midway and Medway almost interchangeably in early records. The tidal stream MIDWAY RIVER was believed to have been given its name from its supposed equal distance from the Ogeechee and Altamaha rivers. Some feel the river may have been named from the Medway River in England. There is also another MIDWAY in Baldwin County on the southern edge of Milledgeville, which was the original site of Oglethorpe University (q.v.). It is thought to have been given its name because of its location halfway between Milledgeville and Scottsboro. The present name is HARDWICK (q.v.) or MIDWAY-HARDWICK. There is another community named MIDWAY in Clinch County, located five miles southeast of Homerville. A former hamlet called MIDWAY was located seven miles north of Greenville in Meriwether County, and another community of MIDWAY is in Tattnall County. *See also* MAYSVILLE.

MILAN, Dodge-Telfair counties. Incorporated as a town October 21, 1891. It was named after the large city of Northern Italy.

MILFORD, Baker County. This community was given a coined name in reference to a grist *mill* and also a *ford* located on Itchawaynochaway Creek here.

MILKSICK COVE, Towns County. The name relates to a disease caused by drinking milk from cows that have eaten a certain plant. One such cove is located on the north side of the Blue Ridge, at the head of Cynth Creek. Another is on the Georgia-North Carolina line, to the northward of Sassafras Knob. In Rabun County, there is a

MILKSICK COVE on the east slope of the Blue Ridge, 2½ miles east of Mountain City.

MILL CREEK. The stream by this name in Dawson County came about apparently because of a grist or other mill here in early days. It is an affluent of the Etowah River, and has also been known as TENSAWATTE CREEK (q.v.). In Sumter County, MILL CREEK is an east bank affluent of Muckalee Creek, and was formerly called TULULGAH (q.v.) in Indian days before it was given its descriptive name, after a mill was placed on the stream. Other streams called MILL CREEK are located in Bulloch, Early, Walker and Worth counties. Whitfield County has a stream as well as a community called MILL CREEK. Also in Whitfield County is MILL CREEK GAP, otherwise known as BUZZARD ROOST. This is a natural gateway through Rocky Face Ridge.

MILLEDGEVILLE, CS Baldwin County. Designated the state capital December 12, 1804 and incorporated as a town December 8, 1806. Was laid out in 1803 as the site for the state capital, and the state offices were established here from 1807 to 1867. It is the only city in the United States that was established for the purpose of being a state's capital. Was named to honor Georgia's distinguished governor, John Milledge (1757-1818), who donated 633 acres in Athens for the establishment of the University of Georgia (q.v.). The city was established at the site of Fort Winston (q.v.) The State Sanitarium was established here after authorization by an act of December 26, 1837 (although it is actually outside the city limits). Now called the Central State Hospital, it has the world's largest kitchen, where up to 30,000 meals a day are prepared.

MILLEN, CS Jenkins County. Incorporated September 30, 1881 at which time the town was in Burke and Screven counties. Settled in 1835 by Robert Hendricks Gray, it was first called SEVENTY NINE or OLD 79, because of its distance from Savannah. When the Central of Georgia came through, it was called MILLEN JUNCTION or MILLEN STATION, apparently after McPherson B. Millen, superintendent of the railroad at Savannah. It has also been claimed to have been named for Captain John Millen (c. 1804-1843), a civil engineer of the railroad, or for Savannah attorney, John Millen. *See also* Florence.

MILLEN NATIONAL FISH HAT-

CHERY, Jenkins County. Located six miles north of Millen. Established in 1950 by the U. S. Department of the Interior, it has 25 ponds on 23.4 acres.

MILLER, Gordon County. This was an early name of HILL CITY (q.v.).

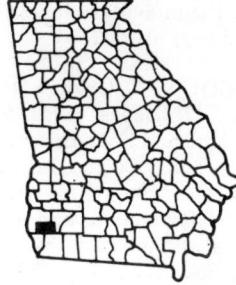

MILLER COUNTY. Created February 26, 1856 with 287 square miles taken from Baker and Early counties. Named for attorney, Andrew Miller (1806-1856), who was an outstanding state senator of Georgia, and was also president of the Medical College of Georgia. The county seat is Colquitt (q.v.). The court house was destroyed by fire in 1873.

MILLER'S BRANCH, Laurens County. This was the early name of the main tributary of Stitchihatchie Creek. Was seemingly named for James Miller, a chain carrier for surveyor Thomas Cooper, who surveyed here when this was in Wilkinson County. The stream is now called WHITLEY BRANCH (q.v.).

MILLHAVEN, Screven County. This community is located twelve miles north of Sylvania. The first post office in the county was established here March 27, 1908. The name is in reference to Paris' Mill, built here on Brier Creek before the middle of the 19th century.

MILLS POND, Screven County. Located six miles southeast of Hiltonia, on property owned by J. A. Mills of Sylvania.

MILLTOWN, Lanier County. Incorporated December 17, 1901 at which time it was in Berrien County. The early descriptive name came about in reference to the rice, grist and saw mills powered by the Alapaha River here. The name of the city was changed to LAKELAND (q.v.) August 11, 1925.

MILLWOOD, Ware County. Located nineteen miles west of Waycross on U. S. 82. Incorporated from August 24, 1905 to August

14, 1909. This descriptively named town no longer exists.

MILNER, Lamar County. Incorporated August 13, 1912 at which time it was in Pike County. This town was named for early settler, Willis R. Milner, who came from North Carolina to Blountsville in Jones County, and then moved here about 1855.

MILTON COUNTY. Created December 18, 1857 with 147 square miles taken from Cherokee, Cobb and Forsyth counties. It was merged into Fulton County January 1, 1932. Named for John Milton (1740-1824) who was active in the Revolution, and saved the official colonial records from the British at the capture of Savannah. In 1789 he became secretary of state for Georgia. Some authorities had claimed the county was named for Homer V. Milton, an officer of the War of 1812, and a descendant of John Milton. The county seat was Alpharetta (q.v.).

MINCIE MOUNTAIN, Lumpkin County. Located six miles east of Dahlonega, with an elevation of 1,860 feet. The name comes from the misspelling of an early settler family named Mincey.

MINEOLA, Lowndes County. This community is located about ten miles north of Valdosta. The name is from the old Indian word meaning "Much Water."

MINERAL BLUFF, Fannin County. This descriptively named town was incorporated September 26, 1889.

MINERAL SPRINGS, Whitfield County. This was an early settlement of undetermined location which was named for the mountain springs here which were said to be healthful. Another hamlet called MINERAL SPRINGS was recorded as having been in Pickens County, seven miles west of Tate.

MIONA SPRINGS, Macon County. Originally called MACON COUNTY SPRINGS, it was a popular resort before the days of the automobile. The name is from that of an Indian princess called Miona in a romantic story written by a Confederate soldier, Augustus Robinson.

MISSIONARY RIDGE, Walker County (and extends northward into Tennessee). Named for the missionaries who established the mission at Brainerd (*see* Brainerd Road). The soldiers during the Civil War called it MISSION RIDGE. There is also a community near the Tennessee line called MISSIONARY RIDGE. MISSIONARY STATION was the original name of COOSA (q.v.) in Floyd County.

MISSOE, Camden County. This was the commonly used name that the Indians gave to the present CUMBERLAND ISLAND (q.v.).

MISTLETOE, STATE PARK, Columbia County. This 1,920-acre park was opened in 1970. It is situated on the shores of Clark Hill Reservoir (q.v.) near Winfield, on the site of and named after the old community of MISTLETOE or MISTLETOE CORNERS. Its post office was discontinued in the early 1920's.

MITCHELL, Glascock County. Incorporated December 17, 1896. Established as a railroad town about 1886 and named for R.M. Mitchell, president of the Augusta Southern Railroad, who was responsible for putting the road through this spot. The post office was moved here from Scruggsville (q.v.) February 18, 1887.

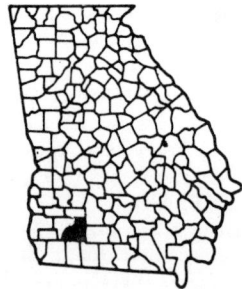

MITCHELL COUNTY. Created December 21, 1857 with 511 square miles taken from part of Baker County. Georgia laws say the county was named in honor of General Henry Mitchell (1760-1839), Revolutionary War hero, officer of the state militia, and president of the Georgia Senate. Some historians have claimed the county was named for Georgia governor, David Brydie Mitchell (1766-1837), who was born in Scotland and was general of the state militia. *See also* Fort Mitchell. The county seat is Camilla (q.v.). The court house was destroyed by fire in 1869.

MIZE, Stephens County. This community is located nine miles south of Toccoa on Georgia highway 106. Henry Mize settled here in 1808.

MOCCASIN CREEK STATE PARK, Rabun County. This 181-acre park is located 25 miles north of Clarkesville, on the upper end of Lake Burton where tiny Moccasin Creek enters the lake.

MOCCASIN GAP, Stewart County. This was the name given to an old trading post located north of Lumpkin. It was supposedly called this from the great number of water moccasins in the swamp here along Hannahatchee Creek.

MODESTO, Cherokee County. This was an early hamlet, located five miles southeast of Toonigh. This is a Spanish name meaning "modest" or "Modest Man."

MODOC, Emananuel County. A community located four miles north of Swainsboro on Georgia 56. Named from a northwestern Indian tribe which became nationally known due to an uprising in the 1870's over land disputes.

MOLENA, Pike County. Incorporated in 1888. This town was first called SNIDERSVILLE after store owner A. A. Snider, then JENKINSVILLE after Newt Jenkins who bought the business. It was changed to Molena and incorporated August 23, 1905 when the railroad came through. Derivation is not certain, but may be from the Spanish word *molina,* meaning "mill."

MONIAC, Charlton County. This community is said to have been named for old Fort Moniac which was located about one mile north on the Florida side of the St. Marys River. The log fortification was built during the Florida Indian wars.

MONROE, CS Walton County, Pronounced "Mun-roe." Was originally called WALTON COURT HOUSE, but was incorporated as a town November 30, 1821 when it was designated the county seat and named for President Monroe (*see* Monroe County).

MONROE COUNTY. Pronounced "Munroe" County. Created May 15, 1821 with 399 square miles acquired by Creek cession of January 8, 1821. This was an original county, named for the fifth United States president, James Monroe (1758-1831), author of the Monroe Doctrine of 1823. The county seat is Forsyth (q.v.).

MONROE FEMALE COLLEGE, Forsyth. Early name of TIFT COLLEGE (q.v.).

MONTEVIDEO, Hart County. Pronounced "Mount'vid-yo" or "Mont'vid'yo." This community on the Elbert County line was named for the city by the same name in Urguay, South America, because of the marvelous view of the surrounding countryside. It means, "A mountain saw I," and was named by Magellan in 1520. MONTEVIDEO was earlier the name of the Charles Colcock Jones plantation in Liberty County.

MONTEZUMA, Macon County. Incorporated as a town February 8, 1854. It began to develop in 1851 when the Central of Georgia Railway was built through here. Named for the emperor of the Aztecs by returning soldiers in the Mexican War. This is the largest and busiest of thirteen Montezumas in the United States. It was also claimed to have been named by the Indians in honor of their hero in Mexico, the last king of the Aztecs.

MONTGOMERY, Chatham County. This settlement on the Vernon River was an early Savannah area resort, and was named for General Montgomery (*see* Montgomery County).

MONTGOMERY COUNTY. Created December 19, 1793 with 235 square miles taken from part of Washington County. Named for Irish-born, Major General Richard Montgomery (1736-1775), soldier of the

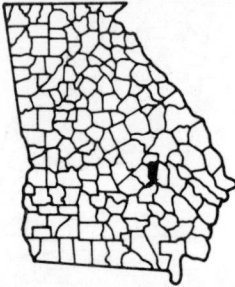

Revolution who was killed at the seige of Quebec, December 13, 1775. The county seat is Mount Vernon (q.v.).

MONTGOMERY CREEK, Lumpkin County. Rises in the northwest section of the county and flows into the Etowah River. Named after the Montgomery family who settled in this region.

MONTGOMERY FERRY ROAD, Atlanta. Named from a former ferry which crossed the Chattahoochee at present day Bolton. James McConnell Montgomery (1770-1842) settled here in 1821 and was given a state franchise for the ferry December 25, 1837. In 1853 the property and ferry were sold to Martin DeFoor (*see* DeFoor's Ferry). Montgomery was probably the first white man to settle permanently in what is now Fulton County.

MONTGOMERY ISLAND, Chatham County. This was the name by which the English called OSSABAW ISLAND (q.v.), this • being named after Sir Robert Montgomery.

MONTICELLO, CS Jasper County. Was laid out and made county seat December 10, 1808. Incorporated as a town December 15, 1810. Most of the original settlers here were native Virginians, which is the probable reason the town was named for the home of Thomas Jefferson near Charlottesville, Virginia.

MONTOUR VILLAGE, Hancock County. Incorporated December 22, 1857. A mill village within the corporate limits of Sparta. It is now called the OLD FACTORY.

MONTPELIER, Monroe County. Also known as MONTPERLIER STATION, it was located fifteen miles west of Macon. The name is from the city in France. MONTPELIER SPRINGS was once a noted health resort here, named in reference to the 14 springs in the area. The 800-acre site later became MONTPERLIER INSTITUTE which was

under the charge of Episcopal bishop, Stephen Elliott from South Carolina. It was the second oldest female school in Georgia, founded in 1842 and closed in 1876. MONTPERLIER AVENUE in Macon was probably an old "Montpelier Road" running west to the early settlement in Monroe County. In 1801 a town of MONT-PELIER was projected for Baldwin County.

MONTREAL, DeKalb County. A former post office established July 29, 1892, six miles north of Decatur on the Seaboard Railroad. The derivation is French, meaning "Royal Mountain" or "King's Mountain."

MONTROSE, Laurens County. Incorporated as a town August 21, 1929. This community was named for Mr. Dudley Montrose Hughes, a former landowner of Laurens and Twiggs counties, or possibly from Scott's *Legend of Montrose.*

MOODY AIR FORCE BASE, Lowndes-Lanier counties. Named after George Putnam Moody who was born in the Philippine Islands in 1908, graduated from West Point Academy, and died in an air crash in 1941.

MOORE'S MILL, Cherokee County. This former community was about seven miles northwest of Canton. In the early 1880's, a Mr. J. K. Moore had a grist mill on Shoal Creek here.

MOORE'S MILL ROAD, Atlanta. Named for Thomas Moore (1828-1914) who operated a sash-sawmill and a grist mill on Peachtree Creek above the confluence of Nancy Creek. He also served as postmaster of Boltonville (q.v.).

MOREHOUSE COLLEGE, Atlanta. Organized as AUGUSTA INSTITUTE in 1867 in Augusta, Richmond County. Moved to Atlanta in 1879 when it was renamed ATLANTA BAPTIST SEMINARY. In 1912 the present name was adopted to honor Reverend Henry L. Morehouse, corresponding secretary of the American Baptist Home Mission Society.

MORELAND, Coweta County. Incorporated as a town December 28, 1888. The original settlement began with the Mt. Zion Methodist Church, after which it was called MT. ZION. The name was changed to WRIGHT'S CROSSING about 1850 and to PUCKETT STATION in 1852. On September 1, 1888 it was changed to the present name to honor Dr.

John F. Moreland, the first doctor for the Atlanta and West Point Railroad.

MORGAN, CS Calhoun County. Incorporated as a city May 5, 1856, at which time Mr. Hiram Morgan was one of the original commissioners. The city was believed named after the Hiram Morgan family. The county seat was moved here from Arlington, August 6, 1929.

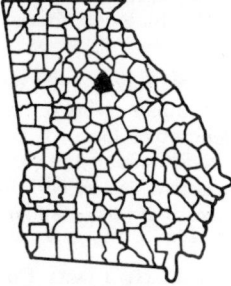

MORGAN COUNTY. Created December 10, 1807 with 357 square miles taken from part of Baldwin County. Named for hero of the Revolution, and later a U. S. congressman, Major General Daniel Morgan (1736-1802) who defeated the British at Cowpens, South Carolina in 1781. The county seat is Madison (q.v.).

MORGAN FALLS, Fulton County. Located twelve miles north of Atlanta on the Chattahoochee River, and is the site of the present MORGAN FALLS DAM. This was once called BULL SLUICE (q.v.). The present name is for Mrs. S. Morgan Smith, the mother of C. Elmer Smith. Mr. Smith helped establish the Atlanta Water and Electric Power Company, a predecessor of the Georgia Power Company.

MORGAN'S CREEK, Jackson County. This was called YOTOCOMPSA by the Indians. The derivation of the name and its location are not certain.

MORGANTON, Fannin County. Incorporated as a town March 5, 1856. Named by James H. Morris who came from Morganton, North Carolina in the 1840's, and that city was named for General Morgan (*see* Morgan County). The county seat was here originally until transferred to Blue Ridge on August 13, 1895.

MORGANVILLE, Dade County. Located on Lookout Mountain, six miles north of Tren-

ton. In 1881 the railroad and express agent was Mr. R. C. Morgan.

MORRIS BROWN UNIVERSITY, Atlanta. Established in 1881 as a coeducational institution for Negroes. Named in honor of Bishop Morris Brown of the African Methodist Church.

MORRISON'S STATION, Dade County. This was the original name of the present community of NEW ENGLAND (q.v.), which name was derived from an early landowner here, a Mr. W. G. Morrison.

MORROW, Clayton County. Incorporated as a city in 1943 with the name incorrectly recorded as MARROW. This was corrected February 23, 1945. The original settlement grew around the Philadelphia Presbyterian Church which was established here in 1825. The early community was called BIG SHANTY, and when the Macon and Western Railroad came through, this stop was named MORROW('S) STATION after the Radford E. Morrow family which owned most of the land, and had a store here. The depot was established in 1846 with Mr. Morrow as the agent. The post office at Morrow opened in 1871.

MORVEN, Brooks County. Incorporated as a town November 28, 1900. This is the oldest community in the county, having been settled in 1823. The first temporary county seat of Lowndes County was at the Sion Hall home, one and one-half mile north of Morven. The derivation is from a mountain in Scotland, and was changed from its former name of SHARPE'S STORE, July 21, 1853.

MOSSY CREEK, White County. This community is located six miles southeast of Cleveland, and is about one mile east of the stream of MOSSY CREEK after which it was named.

MOULTRIE, CS Colquitt County. "South Georgia's Market Place" Incorporated as a town December 13, 1859. The original name of the place was OCKLOCKNEY (q.v.) as it is located on the Ocklockney River. The post office with this original name was established in 1851. Its name was changed in 1857 to honor General William Moultrie (1731-1805) who served in the Revolution and was twice elected governor of South Carolina. SPENCE FIELD of Moultrie was named for Lieutenant Thomas Louis Spence, Jr. (1896-1919) from

Thomasville, who attended Georgia Tech and was killed in an airplane crash in France.

MOUNTAIN CITY, Rabun County. Incorporated as a town August 22, 1907. This was originally a village called PASSOVER (q.v.). It was given its present descriptive name as it is in Rabun Gap at the highest point of the old Tallulah Falls Railway. The Eastern Divide runs through the town with the waters draining off to the Atlantic Ocean on the east side, and with the west side flowing toward the Gulf of Mexico.

MOUNTAIN CREEK, Harris County. This stream originates in Franklin D. Roosevelt State Park, near the town of Pine Mountain and flows westward to the Chattahoochee. This descriptive name was applied by the original surveyor in 1827. A post office called MOUNTAIN CREEK was established in Harris County in 1830, and transferred nearby to the present Whitesville (q.v.) in 1835.

MOUNTAIN HILL, Harris County. The original name of this community was TALLEYTOWN, from a family here named Talley. When the post office was established in 1837, the postmaster Amos Smith from Maryland selected the new name because of his love for mountains and hills.

MOUNTAIN SCENE, Towns County. This former community was located seven miles southwest of Hiawassee on Hiwassee Creek. The name was adopted because of the delightful view afforded here.

MOUNTAINTOWN CREEK, Gilmer County. This stream took its name from an old Indian settlement of MOUNTAINTOWN, which was located 6½ miles northwest of Ellijay. The MOUNTAINTOWN (Militia) DISTRICT in the northwest section of Gilmer County was also named from an early Indian town.

MOUNTAIN VIEW, Clay County "Gateway to Clayton County" Incorporated as a city August 22, 1949. This was originally a community called ROUGH AND READY (q.v.) when it was in DeKalb County, and before it was given its present descriptive name.

MOUNT AIRY, Habersham County. Incorporated as a town March 3, 1874. Founded by Mr. M. C. Wilcox from Knoxville, Tennessee, who later built a hotel here in the early 1880's. In 1877 a Swiss colony, 1,700 feet above sea level, was established here under the leadership of a Mr. J. Staub. This town has a commendatory name which is descriptive of the climate of the locale with its abundant fresh air. It may have been named from the town of Mount Airy in North Carolina which was settled about 1850.

MOUNT BERRY, Floyd County. Incorporated from 1935 to 1973. Located on the north edge of Rome, the town was named for the family of Martha Berry, founder of Berry College (q.v.).

MOUNT ENON, Richmond County. This was an early summer resort settlement. The name is a simplified form of Aenon, mentioned in the New Testament as being a place where there was much water. MOUNT ENON ACADEMY (college) was established here in 1807.

MOUNT ENOTAH, Towns County. The peak of this mountain is called SUMMIT OF MOUNT ENOTAH, or more recently BRASSTOWN BALD (q.v.) which is the highest point in Georgia, with an elevation of 4,784 feet. The derivation of the Cherokee Indian name *Enotah* is not known.

MOUNT PISGAH, Catoosa County. Lies in a valley called "The Ridges" and is named from a mountain slope in the Holy Land.

MOUNT PLEASANT, Effingham County. Descriptively named, the site here is now referred to as OLD MOUNT PLEASANT. This was a former Uchee Indian town and English trading post on a bluff near the Savannah River about five miles up river from Clyo. The Georgia Colony maintained a fort and small garrison here under command of Captain Thomas Wiggin, an Indian trader.

MOUNT PLEASANT, Evans County. This community located three miles northeast of Claxton, was named from the early church here.

MOUNT PLEASANT, Wayne County. Located in the eastern section of the county community was probably meant as a joke, as there is not as much as a small hill in this region.

MOUNT VERNON, CS Montgomery County. Established as the county seat in 1813 and incorporated as a town August 26, 1872. Assumed to have been named for George Washington's home on the Potomac, which was named in honor of Admiral Edward Vernon of the British Navy, and was given this name by Lewis Washington, who willed the Virginia estate to his brother George. The Montgomery county seat may also have been named from an 18th century settlement about 25 miles south of Mount Vernon, as described by James E. Callaway, who explained how Oglethorpe sent Mary Musgrove in 1739:

> ... with her husband and twenty rangers 60 miles up the Altamaha where they placed a trading post known as Mount Vernon as an outguard against the Lower Creeks. The colony had been founded as the southern outpost of English civilization... As a military colony it was a success. But as a settlement for ambitious and worldly settlers there were definite drawbacks.

It was located near the junction of the Ohoopee River. There are some small places in Georgia called MOUNT VERNON, with one in Walton County, located four miles northeast of Monroe on U. S. 78. Another is in Whitfield County, located near Rocky Face, four miles west of Dalton on Georgia 201. It was settled in 1830 in what was then southeast Catoosa County. This community was also known as MOUNT VERNON VALLEY, with the name originating from the Mount Vernon Baptist Church here.

MOUNTVILLE, Troup County. This was the first settlement in the county and was located at the intersection of Oakfuskee and McIntosh trails. The post office was established here September 5, 1835, and was incorporated as a town November 29, 1897. This community was believed named by the first postmaster, Daniel Davis, because of the upland lay of the lands here.

MOUNT YONAH, White County. Also known as YONAH MOUNTAIN (q.v.).

MOUNT ZION, Carroll County. This community was first settled in 1811. The Methodist Episcopal Church made of logs was built here in 1867, and named Mount Zion at the suggestion of Dr. ·Hicks Martin. The name later spread to the community. Mount Zion in the Holy Land is a hill in the southwest section of Jerusalem. The MOUNT ZION SEMINARY was founded here in 1880, and it continued until 1937.

MOUNT ZION, Coweta County. This was the earliest name of MORELAND (q.v.), and was named after Mt. Zion Methodist Church

which was founded in 1843, but is now known as Moreland Methodist Church.

MOXLEY, Jefferson County. This small community was established five miles south of Louisville. In 1881 the postmaster was B. J. Moxley, who had a grist mill and general store here.

MUCKAFOONEE CREEK, Lee County. This is a white man's coined name which was applied to the combined Muckalee and Kinchafoonee creeks before they enter the Flint River.

MUCKALEE, Sumter County. This was an old Chehaw (Chiaha) Indian Village and its name is said to be derived from the Creek *am,* "me" and *ohkalita,* "pour on." Other scholars say Muckalee is from the Choctaw tribal name, Mukalasha, derived from the Muskogean, *Imuklash,* signifying "opposite people." MUCKALEE CREEK heads in Marion and Schley counties, drains through Sumter and Lee counties to Kinchafoonee Creek above Albany in Dougherty County. Many variations of the name have included, AMUCULLE, MUCALEE and MUCKLEE. The creek was named after the village, and Goff said it means "My People," "My Town" or perhaps, "My Home." Benjamin Hawkins called it AU-MUC-CU-LE, saying it meant "Pour on me."

MUCKALOOCHEE CREEK. A tributary of Muckalee Creek that arises in Marion County and enters the main stream in Lee County. It means "Little Muckalee," and has been written MUCKATOOCHEE on some later maps. Its upper fork is called LITTLE MUCKALOOCHEE, but it was originally called HENDRICKS CREEK, named for a member of the early survey party.

MUD CREEK. The stream in Bartow County called Mud Creek was descriptively named to differentiate from Clear Creek, immediately to the west. MUD CREEK in Cobb County unites with Nose's Creek to form Sweetwater Creek at Austell. A Civil War engagement occurred by this stream June 18, 1864. MUD CREEK in Lowndes County rises below Valdosta and flows southeasterly into Grand Bay Creek. MUD CREEK in Rabun County is also known as ESTATOAH CREEK (q.v.).

MUD FORT, Chatham County. *See* Fort Jackson.

MULBERRY. When the Georgia Colony

was first established, efforts were made by the Trustees to encourage the establishment of a thriving silk industry. And a great many mulberry trees were planted, besides those that already existed natively in the region. Consequently "Mulberry" has been found in various place-names in the state. The community of MULBERRY in Barrow County is located about one mile north of Winder, and about three miles south of MULBERRY CREEK. The first post office established here in 1825 was called BAINBRIDGE. The name of the post office was changed to PENTECOST MILL in 1829 after a mill owned by J.H. Pentecost, and in 1838 its name was changed to Mulberry. Another MUL-BERRY CREEK rises on the east border of Harris County and flows southeasterly into the Chattahoochee River. Its name was translated from the Muskogee, *Ketali*. This Indian word means, *ke*, "mulberry," and *tali*, "dead." Benjamin Hawkins had spelled it KETALEE in 1797. It had also been written, CATAULEE and CATAULA (q.v.). A crossroads near this stream in Harris County, about five miles north of Fortson has picked up the name, as it is called MULBERRY GROVE. Its post office by this name was established in 1831. It has also been suggested that mulberry trees were once common here. MULBERRY GROVE was also the name of a famous plantation in Chatham County, which was given to General Nathanael Greene (see Greene County) by the State of Georgia after his victories in the Revolution. It was here that Eli Whitney invented the cotton gin in 1793. General Sherman's army destroyed the plantation in 1864. The MULBERRY RIVER rises in southern Hall County, flows southerly and then easterly to form the boundary between Barrow and Jackson counties before emptying into the Middle Oconee River. The name is translated from the early Creek Indian name of TISHMAUGU (TISH-NA-GU or TISHMAGU). There is also a MULBERRY RIVER in Gwinnett County that rises east of Lawrenceville.

MULE CAMP SPRINGS, Hall County. The early name of GAINESVILLE (q.v.), named for the large number of mules kept here to move heavy mining equipment into the nearby gold mining region.

MULE PEN CREEK, Emanuel County. Flows southerly to enter the Ohoopee River at Norristown. Named for a nearby pen where early teamsters could obtain fresh mule teams.

MULLIS, Laurens County. A former town, incorporated August 1, 1906 with W. H. Mullis and D. E. Mullis appointed as two of the three commissioners.

MUNDY'S MILL, Clayton County. Located on a tiny stream and pond near Jonesboro, and is used for grinding corn. The mill was built in 1890 by E. T. Mundy and R. W. Mundy.

MUNNERLYN, Burke County. Located ten miles south of Waynesboro on the Georgia Railway. Was earlier called THOMAS (STATION), and was also known as LESTER'S DISTRICT and LUMPKIN'S STATION. The community was probably named to honor Colonel John D. Munnerlyn, attorney at law of Waynesboro. It could possible have been named for Charles James Munnerlyn (1822-1898), a Confederate congressman, who was a graduate of Emory College at Oxford, and who served as lieutenant colonel during the Civil War. MUNNERLYN (Militia) DISTRICT of Burke County is located southeast of Waynesboro.

MURDER CREEK, Baldwin County. This name is a translation from the Muskogean, CHATTOCHUCCOHATCHEE.

MURRAY COUNTY. Created December 3, 1832 with 342 square miles taken from part of Cherokee County. Named for attorney Thomas Walton Murray (1790-1832) who was a state legislator. The county seat is Chatsworth (q.v.).

MURRAYVILLE, Hall County. Settled in the 1830's. This community is located ten miles northwest of Gainesville, and was named for Patrick J. Murray who had a store and a boarding school here.

MURREL'S ROW, Atlanta. This was a disreputable section of the early city, on the north side of Decatur Street, between Peachtree and Pryor streets. Was named for the notorious Tennessee murderer, John A. Mur(r)el, who was active in Hall County and the surrounding area from about 1830 to 1853-56 or later. He posed as a preacher, but was said to have been the bloodiest villian of all time.

MUSGROVES COWPEN, Chatham County. More frequently called simply COWPEN (q.v.).

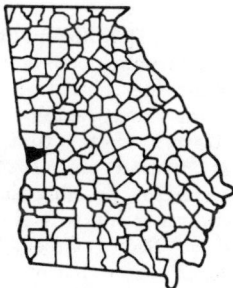

MUSCOGEE COUNTY. Created June 9, 1825 and December 11, 1826, with 220 square miles acquired by Creek cessions of January 24, 1826 and March 31, 1826. This name was given the county to perpetuate the name of the Muscogee (or Muskogee) Indians, the family of Indians to which the Creeks and Seminoles belong. The meaning is uncertain, but possibly signifies, "swampy," "pond," "open marshy land," or "dwellers in the swamps." The county seat is Columbus (q.v.). The court house was destroyed by fire in 1838.

MUSHMELLON CREEK, Tattnall County. This stream rises at Glennville and flows southward to the Altamaha River. The name is a corrupted form of muskmellon, so named because of the melons growing in the region. WATERMELON CREEK flows southerly a short distance to the west.

MYRICK'S MILL, Twiggs County. A former community, also called BIG SANDY (q.v.), which was visited by Marquis de Lafayette in 1825. General Stiph Parham Myrick, CSA (b. 1815), owned 3,700 acres here in 1863.

MYSTIC, Irwin County. Incorporated as a town August 18, 1903. The name was probably transferred from the city by this name in Connecticut, the original home of Nelson Tift (*see* Tift County). It is an Algonquian Indian word meaning, "big-(tidal)-river."

N

NACOOCHEE. The NACOOCHEE RIVER of White County flows through the beautiful NACOOCHEE VALLEY. The stream was formerly called DUKE'S CREEK; the present name was taken from the old Indian village of NACOOCHEE, located eight miles northeast of Cleveland. Signs indicate that DeSoto stopped in May 1540 at Nacoochee "Old Town" which was called CAUCHI by the Spaniards. Gold was discovered in this area about 1828, and was mined commercially until 1940. The name "Nacoochee" is from the Cherokee, *nagu 'tsi*, connected with *nak-wisi*, to signify, "evening star." Nacoochee was said to have been the name of an Indian princess in an old legend, who jumped to her death because of a thwarted love affair. It may also be from the Choctaw, *nakushi*, which signifies "little arrow." The site of the NACOOCHEE INDIAN MOUNDS is said to mark the center of an ancient Cherokee town called GUAXULE. LAKE NACOOCHEE (also called SEED LAKE) is located two miles southeast of Lake Burton in Rabun County, and at this site there previously existed a post office called Seed.

NAHUNTA, CS Brantley County. Incorporated as a city July 28, 1925. This was originally a freight station called VICTORIA. The Iroquoian (Tuscarora) Indian word *nahunta* is thought to mean "tall trees." This city is believed to have been named by a turpentine producer who came from Nahunta, North Carolina. It has also been said to have been derived from an Indian named N. A. Hunter. Another story relates that so much freight was consigned to a timber operator named N. A. Hunter that the railroad men called the town N. A. Hunter's siding, and finally Nahunta, shortly before 1900. A final theory states that Indians came here from the Okefenokee Swamp who spoke English poorly, and would grunt, "No-hunter."

NAIL'S CREEK, Banks County. This stream rises about three miles north of Homer, flows northeasterly into Franklin County, thence southeasterly until it enters the Hudson River. In the 19th century a community of NAIL'S CREEK was located seven miles northeast of Homer. All that exists here today is the NAILS CREEK CHURCH.

NAKED CREEK, Walton County. John Goff points this stream out as having a poor mouthing name.

NAMELESS, Laurens County. This post office was established 15 miles southwest of Dublin, from February 12, 1886 to December 31, 1901, after which the mail was sent to Dexter. It was so named from the fact that in a list of several hundred names submitted to the post office authorities, not one was found satisfactory, so it became "Nameless."

NANCY CREEK, DeKalb and Fulton counties. This stream commences above Doraville and flows southwesterly into Peachtree Creek just before the latter enters the Chattahoochee. Garrett claims that the name "Nancy" was first used here in 1824 as a name for the church nearby, possibly named by Mr. John L. Evins after his wife Nancy, when they settled on Nancy Creek. The name "Nancy" was first recorded in what is now Fulton County by the State's surveyor in 1821; thought to be named for an Indian woman who lived in that area. Another NANCY CREEK is located in Bartow County. It is a tributary of the Etowah River, and is located west of Cartersville. Goff believed it was named for the same Indian woman as the stream in Fulton County.

NANCY HART STATE PARK, Elbert County. Located about nine miles below Elberton on Georgia highway 17. This historical site consists of four acres of the original four hundred granted to Nancy's husband, Benjamin Hart. The reconstructed cabin of Nancy Hart is featured here. *See also* Hart County.

NANKIN, Brooks County. This community in the southeast corner of the county was named from the large city in China on the Yangtze River.

NANKIPOOH, Muscogee County. This community is located just northeast of Columbus. The name is from the Gilbert and Sullivan opera *The Mikado,* in which Nanki-Poo was the son of the Mikado.

NANTAHALA MOUNTAIN RANGE, Towns County. Formerly called AYOREE (or JORE) MOUNTAIN. A 50-mile range in North Carolina that extends southward into northeast Georgia to Tallulah Falls. The name is from the Cherokee word, *Nan-toh-ee-yah-heh-lih*, "Sun in the Middle," meaning "noonday." *See also* Sitting Bull Mountain.

NAOMI, Walker County. The name of this community (four miles east of LaFayette) is from the Bible. Naomi was Ruth's mother-in-law.

NASHVILLE, CS Berrien County. Incorporated as a town December 20, 1892. Like the capital city of Tennessee, this county seat was named in honor of General Francis Nash (1742-1777), a distinguished soldier of the Revolution.

NAYLOR, Lowndes County. Incorporated as a town August 21, 1906. It was named for railroad man, Captain Naylor. Also in northeastern Lowndes County is NAYLOR (Militia) DISTRICT.

NEAL, Pike County. This community was first called WILLIAMSVILLE, after a Dr. Williams who came here from Meriwether County about 1855. The name was changed to Neal when the railroad came through, to honor the H. B. Neal family who owned much of the land here.

NEAL DOW, Cobb County. This was the former name of SMYRNA (q.v.).

NEEDMORE, Echols County. It is believed the name of this community came about when critical customers of a general store here complained that they "need more" merchandise to buy.

NEEL(S) GAP, Union County. Named in honor of W. R. Neel, who was the surveyor of the American Scenic Highway through the gap about 1920. It was previously known as FROGTOWN GAP (q.v.). The elevation here is 3,108 feet.

NELLIEVILLE, Richmond County. Incorporated as a village from November 25, 1893 to 1961. The derivation of the name of this former community is unknown.

NELSON, Cherokee and Pickens counties. Incorporated as a town September 10, 1891. Named for John Nelson, a farmer and gunsmith, who was the original landowner here.

NEW BERLIN, Newton County. This old community was located eight miles from Covington on Hines Creek. The post office was established from 1883 to 1887, and was named from the capital city of GERMANY.

NEWBORN, Newton County. Incorporated as a town December 15, 1894. Originally known as CROSSROADS or SANDTOWN. It was settled by Rufus Broome of North Carolina, who became postmaster when he established the first post office in the county (then Jasper County) in 1824. The name of the community was adopted after the stirring sermons of Methodist evangelist Sam P. Jones, and the inhabitants then wished their town to be "born anew."

NEW BRIDGE, Lumpkin County. This early community was about ten miles southeast of Dahlonega, where a bridge was newly erected across the Chestatee River. There is also a NEW BRIDGE (Militia) DISTRICT in eastern Forsyth County.

NEW EBENEZER, Effingham County. This was the second community of the Salzburgers who had first settled at EBENEZER (q.v.). The Jerusalem Church here is the oldest church building in Georgia. It was erected 1767-1769, and has walls 20 inches thick of native bricks. The cemetery has been used since 1736.

NEW ECHOTA, Gordon County. Located at the junction of the Coosawattee and Conasauga rivers, near the present Calhoun (q.v.). It was founded in 1819, and the derivation of the name is from the Cherokee Indian word, *echota,* meaning, "town." It was known by various other names at different times, including NEW TOWN, FORK FERRY and GANSAGI (q.v.). On November 12, 1825 the Cherokee council assembled here and resolved to build a permanent capital at this site. A school and court house were then built, and in 1828 the first Indian newspaper in the United States, *The Cherokee Phoenix,* was published here. Ten years later, General Winfield Scott set up his headquarters here, where he commanded 8,000 troops who ruthlessly removed 13,000 Cherokee Indians to the West. On March 13, 1957, the state assembly authorized the reconstruction of New Echota, the last capital of the Cherokee Nation.

NEW ENGLAND, Dade County. Incorporated as a town September 27, 1891. Originally called MORRISON'S STATION (q.v.). It was christened New England City as it was intended that this be the future industrial capital of the New South by its Yankee promoters in 1889, who came from the New England states.

NEW GIBRALTER, DeKalb County. Incorporated as a town December 21, 1839. This was the second town (after Decatur) to be incorporated in the county. Was named after the famous Rock of Gibralter of southwest Europe. The name was changed to STONE MOUNTAIN (q.v.), December 24, 1847.

NEW GOETTINGEN, Burke County. This former community was located about 15 miles above the conjunction of Brier Creek and the Savannah River. Believed to have been established in the 1750's by the Germans of Ebenezer (q.v.) and their countrymen.

NEW HANOVER, Camden County. Established in 1755 on the Satilla River, thirty miles from its mouth, in the vicinity of the present Woodbine. Named in honor of King George III of England, of the House of Hanover. The place was settled by Edmund Gray, a "pretending Quaker" who lived here with 300 followers who were mostly outlaws and fugitives (*see* Wrightsboro). They were later driven out, and by 1761 the town was reestablished on Cumberland Island near the mouth of the Satilla River.

NEW HOLLAND, Hall County. This community was established about 1900 by the Pacolet Manufacturing Co., and planned as a neat attractive "flower garden city." A settlement called LIMESTONE SPRINGS was here in the early 1800's, later called NEW HOLLAND SPRINGS, a transplanted name from Europe.

NEW HOPE, Pike County. The name of the community was previously NEW HOPE CHURCH, after the early church established here in 1882. The area was originally called WILDERNESS OF MONROE when this region was included in Monroe County, but this settlement is now gone. There are today at least two small communities in the state called NEW HOPE, one in Lincoln County and the other is four miles northeast of Dallas in Paulding County. The three-day Civil War Battle of New Hope Church was fought in May 1864 near Dallas, Paulding County.

NEW INVERNESS, McIntosh County. This was the first Scotch colony in Georgia. Lieutenant Hugh Mackay sailed from Inverness October 18, 1735 with a band of 180 Scotch Highlanders, arriving in Georgia the following January. The name of their settlement was named from their former home county of Inverness-shire. It was later renamed DARIEN (q.v.).

NEW MEXICO (Militia) DISTRICT, Carroll County. Settled in 1838 by Isaiah Beck. *See also* Mexico.

NEWNAN, CS Coweta County. "City of Homes and Friendly People" The post office was established here in 1827. Incorporated as a town and designated the county seat December 20, 1828. The city began in 1827 with a small settlement two and one-half miles northeast of its present site, which was called BULLSBORO (q.v.). Named for General Daniel Newnan (c. 1780-1851) of North Carolina, who served in the Indian wars, the War of 1812 and later became a Georgia state assemblyman.

NEWNAN, Pike County. Incorporated and made county seat December 26, 1823. This former town was located one mile west of the present community of Meansville, and was named for General Newnan (*see* Newnan, Coweta County). When first established, it was the only town in the county. The county seat was moved to Zebulon in 1825, after which the town of Newnan died. The site later became known as RILEY'S CROSSROADS.

NEW PURCHASE. This name referred to a tract of land lying between the Broad and Savannah rivers, which became the original Wilkes County in 1777.

NEW SALEM, Dade County. An old community located five miles southeast of Trenton. Derivation is believed to be from the earlier Salem (q.v.), Trenton's original name.

NEW SAVANNAH BLUFF, Richmond County. Located on the Savannah River, 14 miles below Augusta. This was once an important shipping point for tobacco, at the lower end of Tobacco Road (q.v.). A $2 million SAVANNAH LOCK and DAM was built on the Savannah River at this site.

NEW SWITZERLAND, Habersham County. This is a small community located two miles northeast of Mount Airy. It was given this name by the Swiss who first settled this place in the 1800's.

NEWTON, CS Baker County. Designated the county seat in 1831 and incorporated January 20, 1872. The county seat had previously been at Bryan (q.v.), which site is now in Dougherty County. This city was named to honor Sergeant Newton (*see* Newton County).

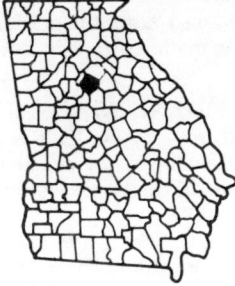

NEWTON COUNTY. Created December 24, 1821 with 273 square miles taken from Henry, Jasper and Walton counties. Named for Sergeant John Newton (1755-1780) of South Carolina, a Revolutionary celebrity who was taken prisoner with the surrender of Charleston, and died soon after of small pox. The county seat is Covington (q.v.).

NEWTON FACTORY BRIDGE ROAD, Newton County. Located about ten miles south of Covington, it crosses the Alcovy River just above Factory Shoals. The name originated from the former settlement of NEWTON FACTORY here.

NEWTON(S) BORO(UGH), Newton County. This was the original name of Covington (q.v.) when first laid out in 1822; it was renamed after a few months. The first county site was at Brick Store (q.v.).

NEWTOWN, Bibb County. The early name of MACON (q.v.). Also NEW TOWN is a community in Wilkes County, six miles northwest of Washington on S1444.

NEW YAMACRAW, Chatham County. Was located on the Savannah River at Pipemakers Creek. It was an old Indian town built in 1735 by Tomochichi, mico (chief) of the Yamacraws.

NEW YAUCAU, Heard County. Was also spelled NIUYAKA. This was an old Indian settlement on the east bank of the Chattahoochee River, in the upper section of the county. After the Creek Indian chiefs visited New York City in 1790 to negotiate a treaty with the United States, they returned and gave this name to their town.

NEW YORK, Macon County. This crossroads is located three miles northwest of Oglethorpe, and is named for New York City. There was another community of NEW YORK in Polk County (now part of Aragon), and at one time there was a small community and store in Carroll County called LITTLE NEW YORK. The settlement of NEW YORK in Oglethorpe County was located 5½ miles northeast of Lexington on S2164.

NEYAMI, Lee County. Located on the Central of Georgia Railroad, eight miles north of Leesburg. The site was called ADAMS STATION until the late 1920's. The newer name was coined from the first two letters of the names of three owners of a plantation here, at Mr. Newton, a Mr. Yancy and a Mr. Milner.

NICHOLASVILLE, Walton County. Located about five miles northwest of Monroe. Anita Sams wrote that it was called NICKELVILLE (on a liquor license granted here in 1887) because it contained the only store in the county selling a drink of whiskey for five cents. There is also a community of NICHOLASVILLE in Early County located about fifteen miles east of Blakely on Georgia highway 216.

NICHOLLS, Coffee County. Incorporated as the town of NICHOLS August 15, 1903. Established in 1895, it was named for Captain John Calhoun Nicholls (1834-1893), CSA, who was state senator and then a representative from Georgia in the U. S. Congress.

NICHOLSON, Jackson County. Incorporated as a town August 22, 1907. The post office here named COOPER (q.v.) was authorized February 2, 1882. The name was changed to Nicholson, February 2, 1882. Derivation of the name is unknown.

NICHOLSVILLE, Gordon County. Located nine miles northeast of Calhoun on Georgia highway 225. Also spelled NICKELVILLE, it is sometimes called LITTLE FIVE POINTS, because roads radiate in five directions from here.

NICKAJACK. There was formerly a community called NICKAJACK in Dade County, located on NICKAJACK MOUNTAIN, thirteen miles west of Lookout Mountain, with a nearby stream called NICKAJACK CREEK. It is now called COLE CITY CREEK, as it flows through Cole City (q.v.) and then northward into the Tennessee River after leaving Georgia. Also, there is an EAST NICKAJACK GAP through Missionary Ridge and a WEST NICKAJACK GAP through Lookout Mountain. Another NICKAJACK CREEK is located in Cobb County, below Marietta, which flows into the Chattahoochee. There is a nearby community also named NICKAJACK. The derivation of the Dade County places was related to a former Indian town of NICKAJACK which was located on the Tennessee River north of the present day Georgia - Alabama - Tennessee corner. The original laws stated that the Alabama - Georgia line was to run to Nickajack Town. According to legend, the derivation of Nickajack was said to be from an old Negro named Jack which the Indians referred to as "Nicko" instead of Negro. The stream in Cobb County was said to have been named for a Cherokee Indian of this name who lived on its banks. Bill Winn reports that *Nickajack* means "Old Creek Place."

NICKELVILLE. *See* NICHOLSASVILLE and NICHOLSVILLE.

NINE MILE CREEK, Coffee County. General David Blackshear (*see* Blackshear) named this stream about 1812-15, probably because of its distance from some particular place.

NIUYAKA, Heard County. An alternative spelling of NEW YAUCAU (q.v.).

NOAH, Jefferson County. This rural community is located about six miles east of Wrens. Named for the Biblical hero of the deluge. There was also a community of NOAH in Dawson County in the last century.

NO BUSINESS CREEK, Gwinnett and DeKalb counties. Rises at Snellville in Gwinnett County and flows southerly into Norris Lake on the Yellow River. John Goff describes this as a very old poor mouthing name.

NODOROC, Barrow County. This name refers to a mud volcano located 3½ miles east of Winder. It is similar to some found in Burma, and around which have been told many legends. The volcano erupted shortly after the area was settled, and was given its Indian name meaning "Hell," as it was thought that the devil dwelt here.

NOKETCHEE CREEK, Clarke County. A tributary of Sandy Creek, located northeast of Athens, on which William J. Barrett operated a grist mill and cotton gin. It is thought to be a pseudo-Indian name suggesting poor fishing. A bridge was built at Barrett's Mill to permit Nowhere Road (q.v.) to cross the stream.

NOKOMIS, Crawford County. This community is located six miles west of Fort Valley. George Stewart explains that Nakomis is named "...for the grandmother of Hiawatha, as made known by Longfellow's poem."

NO MAN'S FRIEND POND, Cook County. Located southwest of Adel. This is actually a dense woody swamp or bay, which is so thick that a person can easily get lost in it.

NOONDAY CREEK, Cherokee and Cobb counties. Flows northward from Marietta into Cherokee County where it enters Allatoona Lake. This name is the product of folk etymology. The Cherokee call both the sun and moon, *nunda,* according to William Read. There is also a community in Cobb County named NOONDAY, which is located about six miles north of Marietta.

NOONTOOTLA CREEK, Fannin County. Rises in the southern tip of the county and flows northerly into the Toccoa River. The name is Cherokee and means "The Land of the Shining Water," or may be a corruption of *Nantahala,* meaning "middle sun."

NORMAN PARK, Colquitt County. Incorporated as a town December 6, 1902. It was formerly called OBE before NORMAN COLLEGE was established here in 1901. Both the college and the town were named for Mr. J. B. Norman, who was the leader among the group who founded the college. This Baptist institution closed its doors in June 1971.

NORRISTOWN, Emanuel County. Incorporated as a town from August 16, 1907 to 1947. This community is located at the Truetlen County line. Derivation of the name is not known.

NORTH GEORGIA COLLEGE, Dahlonega. Founded in 1873 by the State of Georgia "... for the benefit of agriculture and mechanic arts." This is also a military college, requiring R.O.T.C. for all physically qualified male on-campus students. It was the first institution not located at Athens to be recognized as part of the University of Georgia. The name refers to its location in the northern section of the state.

NORTH HIGH SHOALS, Oconee County. Incorporated as a town March 24, 1933. Located on the Appalachee River at High Shoals Bridge. Its name is in reference to nearby High Shoals (q.v.).

NORTH PARK, Coweta County. Short for HARVEY H. NORTH PARK AND PLAYGROUND which is located just over one mile southwest of Newnan. Named for the former chairman of the Newnan Water and Light Commission.

NORWOOD, Warren County. Incorporated as a town October 7, 1885. This is probably a family name, or else meant to give the idea of "northwood."

NOSES CREEK, Bartow County. The former name of McKASKY CREEK (q.v.).

NOSES CREEK, Cobb County. Unites with Mud Creek to form Sweetwater Creek at Austell. John Goff explained that it was named for a Cherokee who lived on the stream.

NOTCHEFALOTEE CREEK, Stewart County. The obsolete name for today's TURNER CREEK. Rises at Providence Canyons and flows westerly to the Chattahoochee River. Exact meaning is unknown, but may have meant something like "dead asleep creek," from *noch,* "sleep," and *ili,* "dead." This name more than likely was meant to be "Camp Creek" (where someone camped or was asleep).

NOTCHWAY, Randolph County. The original settlement at the site of SHELLMAN. *See also* WARD.

NOTTELY RIVER, Union County. A tributary of the Hiawasee River, which was included in the vast TVA project, wherein the 2,300-foot long NOTTELY DAM was built, being completed in 1942. This created a 4,200-acre reservoir, NOTTELY LAKE, which is 20 miles long with a 106-mile shoreline. Further on down, near Vogel State Park is found NOTTELY FALLS, where the small stream descends 105 feet. William Read explained that the name is derived from an old Cherokee village called NADUHLI, said to mean "daring horseman."

NOWHERE ROAD, Clarke County. Located north of Athens, this old road crosses over Noketchee Creek (q.v.) at the site of Barrett's Mill. It was given this name since it extended northward from Barberville (of northeast Athens) on to nowhere.

NUCKOLLSVILLE, Lumpkin County. This was an early name of AURARIA (q.v.)

NUMBER ELEVEN (or STATION NUMBER ELEVEN), Clinch County. This was the early designation of HOMERVILLE (q.v.)

NUMBER ONE ISLAND and NUMBER TWO ISLAND, Ware County. These two islands in the Okefenokee Swamp were so named to differentiate between them, since they were of similar shape and size, as well as being near each other.

NUNEZ, Emanuel County. Incorporated August 6, 1903, this community is located nine miles south of Swainsboro. Named for Dr. Samuel Nunez, a Jewish doctor who arrived in Savannah in July 1733. He came at a time of urgent need, and was able to put a stop to a contagious epidemic that then raged in the new colony.

O

OAK. Within the borders of Georgia are found at least 23 species of the oak tree or shrub, genus *Quercus*. It is therefore not surprising to find a great many place-names which include "Oak" in their designation. There was once a community of OAK in south Barrien County, and also an OAK BOWER in Hart County, 4½ miles east of Hartwell. A post office in Fulton County named OAK-DALE was established from 1887 to 1899, when the name was changed to CHAT-TAHOOCHEE (q.v.). OAKFIELD is in northwest Worth County, and another OAK-FIELD in Crisp County, being incorporated December 6, 1900. Places with the name OAK GROVE have been found in Cherokee, DeKalb, Fulton and Macon counties. In Gilmer County, located below Ellijay, is an OAK HILL; there was also a community near Covington in Newton County called OAK HILL, and another located five miles northwest of Greensboro in Greene County. The town of OAKHURST in DeKalb County was incorporated August 13, 1910 and was incorporated into the town of Decatur, August 14, 1916. There was another OAKHURST in Cobb County, about six miles from Marietta. The town of OAKLAND CITY in Fulton County was incorporated December 12, 1894, and was located in what is now Atlanta, between West End and Fort McPherson. There have been communities named OAKLAND in four other counties: Glynn, Gwinnett, Lee and Meriwether. OAKLAWN is located in western Brooks County at the Thomas County line. The town of OAKMAN in Gordon County was incorporated March 24, 1939. It was so named from a local dealer in oak logs who was called "the oak man." OAK RIDGE was the name given to a community in Meriwether County, seven miles northwest of Greenville. In the northwest corner of Meriwether County is LONE OAK, and the county also has a RED OAK CREEK. OAK PARK, Muscogee County, was incorporated August 18, 1906, and is now a part of Columbus. The village of OAKWOOD in Hall County was incorporated August 12, 1903. In 1884, a Colonel Fort purchased 4,500 acres at OAK LAWN in eastern Houston County. *See also* ROUND OAK, Jones County and WHITE OAK, Camden County.

OAK CANE BRANCH, Jenkins County. Located on the north side of the Ogeechee River, two miles southeast of Millen. Goff found that this stream was originally called OCAIN'S BRANCH after Daniel O'Cain, who was given a grant of 300 acres in the vicinity in 1762.

OAKFUSKEE CREEK, Pike County. Empties into the Flint River west of Concord. The Muskogean name means "Down in a point of land," and was originally applied to the old trail, OAKFUSKEE PATH. It ran through the Upper Creek town of Oakfuskee in Dade County, Alabama and extended eastward through Greenville, Griffin, and Warrenton to Augusta.

OAKFUSKOOCHEE TALLAUHASSEE, Troup County. This was once a flourishing ancient Muskogee Indian town at a site three miles north of the present West Point. English traders from Charles Town visited here about 1685. The town existed until about 1790 when its inhabitants moved westward to settle on the Tallapoosa River.

OBALDAQUINI, Glynn County. An early Spanish name for the present JEKYLL ISLAND (q.v.).

OCEAN CITY, Chatham County. This island town on the Atlantic Ocean was incorporated October 15, 1887. The name was changed to TYBEE (q.v.) December 26, 1888, and is now called SAVANNAH BEACH (q.v.).

OCHEE FINNAU, Baldwin County. A Creek Indian name meaning "hickory bridge (or footlog)," from *ochi*, "hickory," and *fina*, "a crossing facility over a stream." This was what the Lower Creeks called the site of TOMS FORD (q.v.) on the Ocmulgee.

OCHILLEE CREEK, Chattahoochee and Marion counties. Now called PINK KNOT CREEK, it rises about six miles northwest of Buena Vista and flows westerly to Upatoi Creek. Originally the name was NOCHILLEHATCHEE or NOCHILLEE, with its meaning interpreted as "Camping Creek" or "Sleeping Creek." It has also been thought to signify "Dead Hickory," from the Creek, *ochi*, "hickory," and *ili*, "dead." A railroad station in Marion County was given the name OCHILLEE, and also a former village in upper Chattahoochee County, which is now a part of Fort Benning military reservation.

OCHISE (or OCHEESE) CREEK. This was the early name given to the OCMULGEE RIVER, presumably after the Yuchi Indians of the Creek coalition, who lived on its banks. The English called these early inhabitants the "Ocheese Creek Indians" and later shortened it to "Creek Indians," which is believed to be how the Creek Indians were so named. The Muskogee Indian word *ocheese* signifies "bubbling up of water from a spring."

OCHLOCKONEE RIVER. Called "Oaklocknee" by old timers in this region. Rises in Worth County and flows through Colquitt, Thomas and Grady counties and on into Florida. It was named GUACUCA by De Soto when he discovered this waterway in 1540. Some variations of spellings have included OKLOKNEE, OCHLOCHNEE, OCHLOCKNEE and OCKLOCKONY. OCKLOCKNEY was the early name of the present city of MOULTRIE (q.v.), and there is today a town in northwest Thomas County called OCKLOCKNEE, both named from the river. The Indian word means "Yellow Water," from the Hitchiti, *oki*, "water," and *lakni*, "yellow," as reported by William Read. It was also said to possibly mean "North River."

OCHWALKEE CREEK, Laurens and Wheeler counties. Often called OKEEWALKEE CREEK (q.v.), this is a tributary of the Oconee River. Means "dirty water," from the Creek, *oki*, "water," and *holwaki*, "dirty." This name of OCHWALKEE is given to a community in Wheeler County which is located near the Montgomery County line.

OCILLA, CS Irwin County. Pronounced "O-sill'-uh." Incorporated as a town November 24, 1897, it became the county seat in 1906 when the seat was moved from Irwinville. This is an old Indian name, a variation of Aucilla (*see* Aucilla River). Some sources have suggested it is derived from *Oswitchee*, an Indian town, or from the name of an Indian chief Ocilla who lived in Wiregrass, Coffee County. J. B. Clements claims to have traced the name back, first to ASSILE, and then AGLIE, AXILLA, AGULIL, OCHILE, and finally OCILLA.

OCKLAU CREEK, Pulaski County. William Read reports of this stream from an 1823 Tanner Map. He said that the derivation is probably from the Creek word, *aklowahi*, meaning "muddy."

OCMULGEE RIVER. Pronounced "Oak-mul'-gee," with a hard "g." Originates at Lake Jackson (q.v.) which is fed by the South River, Yellow River and Alcovy River. It flows southeasterly through the middle of the state until it is joined by the Little Ocmulgee and Oconee rivers above Hazlehurst to form the Altamaha. The early English settlers called it OCHISE CREEK (q.v.). The Indian name of this waterway is from the Hitchiti, *oki*, "water," and *mulgis*, "it is boiling (or bubbling)," The first element of the word has also been said to be from the Indian word *och*, meaning "in" or "down in." Some variations of spelling have included OAKMULGEE and OKMULGI. Today's maps no longer show some of the early communities with names taken from this river, such as OCMULGEE in eastern Monroe County, and OCMULGEE in the extreme northeast corner of Coffee County. There were two places called OCMULGEE WHARF, one in northern Jeff Davis County and another in eastern Wilcox County. An old post office of OCMULGEEVILLE was located nine miles west of Hazlehurst in what is now Jeff Davis County.

OCMULGEE MOUNDS, Bibb County. This 683-acre reserve was established as the OCMULGEE NATIONAL MONUMENT on December 23, 1936, following a request by U.S. congressman from Georgia, Carl Vinson. This is the site of the former OCMULGEE OLD TOWN (or OLD OCMULGEE FIELDS) which was the original Indian settlement at the site of the present MACON. From about 8000 B. C. to 1717 A.D., six different cultures are known to have inhabited the area: the Wandering Hunters, the Shellfish Eaters, the Early Farmers, the Master Farmers, the Reconquerors, and finally the Creek Indians.

OCONEE, Washington County. This community is located 12 miles southwest of Sandersville, near the Oconee River; incorporated as a town February 28, 1876. It was first settled when the Central of Georgia Railroad was built about 1842, when it was first called STATION NUMBER 14.

OCONEE COUNTY. Created February 25, 1875 with 186 square miles taken from part of Clarke County. Named for the Oconee River which forms its east boundary. The county seat is Watkinsville (q.v.).

OCONEE HEIGHTS, Clarke County. This community is located on the northwest edge of Athens, and is now a part of that city. Named from the Oconee River, it was formerly called BOHURON.

OCONEE OLD TOWN (or OLD OCONEE TOWN), Baldwin County. This former Indian town was located just below Rock Landing about four miles south of Milledgeville. The main body of the Oconee Indians lived here until the white men came in the 18th century. The Indians then established a town northwest on the Chattahoochee River about 1716 which they called LITTLE OCONEE, and then soon thereafter went to live in Florida. It was said that the Apalachee or Hitchiti town of OCONI was "missionized" as early as 1655. The mission list of 1680 referred to it as SAN FRANCISCO DE OCONI. *See also* COFAQUI.

OCONEE RIVER. This 250-mile waterway rises near Lula in Hall County and flows southward to join the Ocmulgee River above Hazelhurst to form the Altamaha. The name is derived from an early Creek Indian settlement in northeast Baldwin County called Oconee Old Town (q.v.). Variations of spellings have included OCONE, OCONI, OCONY, EKWONI, UKWU'NU and UKWU' NI. It was also known as ETOHO in the upper part. The MIDDLE OCONEE RIVER was formerly called ITHLOBEE by the Indians.

OCONEE WHITE SULPHUR SPRINGS, Hall County. Was also called WHITE SULPHUR SPRINGS (q.v.).

OCTAVIA, Cobb County. An early community which was located on Mud Creek, about 6½ miles southwest of Marietta. The name is believed derived from the sister of the Roman emperor Augustus, and wife of Marc Anthony.

ODESSADALE, Meriwether County. Now only a community, which was incorporated as a town August 23, 1905. Originally named XERXES (q.v.), it was later called ODESSA after Miss Odessa Jane Thompson, daughter of early settler from South Carolina, James W. Thompson. The post office was established here June 30, 1891.

ODINGSELL RIVER, Chatham County. Separates Wassaw Island from Little Wassaw Island. Lilla Hawes said it was probably named for the Charles A. Odingsell family.

ODUM, Wayne County. Incorporated as a town August 22, 1907. Mr. J. A. Odum was one of the original councilmen.

OGEECHEE RIVER. Also called the GREAT OGEECHEE RIVER, it is one of the 26 untamed rivers in the United States. This 233-mile long river begins near Union Point in Greene County, and flows southeasterly in the eastern part of the state, and enters the Atlantic Ocean on the south border of Chatham County. The Muskogean name is *Okeechee,* Which means "River of the Uchees" (or Yuchi Indians, *see* Uchee Creek). The English called the stream HOGEECHEE. A tributary in Screven County is called OGEECHEE CREEK. There was formerly a community in Jefferson County called OGEECHEE TOWN (*see* Galphinton). A community on the river in southwest Screven County is named OGEECHEE. It was originally known by its railroad name, STATION NO. 6½.

OGEECHEE ROAD. Followed the course of the Ogeechee River between Savannah and Louisville. It was an old post road established by the U.S. Post Office Department before 1800, and was later called LOUISVILLE ROAD. The present Georgia Highway 17 follows the same route.

OGLETHORPE, CS Macon County. Settled about 1840, incorporated as a town December 14, 1849, as a city January 22, 1852, and became the county seat in 1854, when it was moved here from Lanier (q.v.). At the site of the railroad depot, Timothy Barnard had established the first trading post in the area about 1770. Ulrich B. Phillips said that the town was established by E. G. Cabaniss in 1850 as the Central of Georgia Company was about to make this site the head of the railroad (*see also* Cabaniss, Monroe County). Named in honor of General Oglethorpe, founder of Georgia (*see* Oglethorpe County).

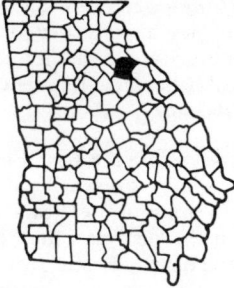

OGLETHORPE COUNTY. Called "Moth of Statesmen." Created December 19, 1793 with 432 square miles taken from part of Wilkes County. Named for General James Edward Oglethorpe (1696-1785), the founder of Georgia. The county seat is Lexington (q.v.). OGLETHORPE BENCH on Factors Walk in Savannah (q.v.) commemorates the spot where General Oglethorpe landed February 12, 1733. Also in Savannah is OGLETHORPE PARK, and the OGLETHORPE STATUE on Chippawa Square. Another statue honoring Georgia's founder was placed atop MOUNT OGLETHORPE. This 3,290-foot peak in northeast Pickens County was formerly called GRASSY KNOB. Also a monument to General Oglethorpe, dedicated in 1930, stands in Queens Square, Brunswick. South Broad Street in Savannah has changed its name to OGLETHORPE AVENUE. OGLETHORPE BARRACKS in Savannah was established from 1828 to 1884. OGLETHORPE BLUFF on the Altamaha River in Wayne County is located about six miles below the site of Fort James. Local legend tells that the name came about after General Oglethorpe once rode over the bluff into the river while being pursued by Indians. FORT OGLETHORPE in Macon was a Civil War encampment site, after which OGLETHORPE STREET here was named. *See also* FORT OGLETHORPE, Catoosa County.

OGLETHORPE TRAIL. Laid out along the Savannah River from Savannah to Augusta in 1736-37 at the direction of General

Oglethorpe (*see* Oglethorpe County). It was also called RIVER ROAD and sometimes PINE LOG TRAIL.

OGLETHORPE UNIVERSITY, Atlanta. Established as OGLETHORPE COLLEGE by the Trustees of Midway Seminary in 1835, with the dissolution of the Midway Seminary and the Gwinnett Institute, at Midway, Baldwin County. It was named after General Oglethorpe (*see* Oglethorpe County). First opened in January 1838, it was governed and controlled by the Presbyterian Church. Due to the hardships of the Civil War, it ceased operating from 1863 to 1866, and finally forced to close completely at Christmas 1872. Through the efforts of Dr. Thornwell Jacobs of Atlanta, the university was refounded in that city, and it reopened in the Fall of 1916 after being closed for almost 44 years. The present name was adopted in 1965.

OHOOPEE, Toombs County. Incorporated as a town August 19, 1907. This community in the eastern part of the county was named for the OHOOPEE RIVER which flows one mile east of this site. The stream is a tributary of the Altamaha River, and arises in southeast Washington County. George R. Stewart states that this Indian name is of uncertain language and meaning. Brinkley says it is an Anglicized form of the name of Creek-Seminole chief, Hopoy Hapo.

OKAPILCO CREEK, Brooks County. A tributary of the Withlacoochee River. William Read said the probable meaning is "Big Swamp Water" or possibly "Nighthawk Creek." A post office named OKAPILCO was established ten miles northwest of Quitman from 1846 to 1867.

OKAUHUTKEE CREEK, Talbot-Taylor-Macon counties. Now called WHITEWATER CREEK (q.v.).

OKEEWALKEE CREEK. Rises 12 miles below Dublin in Laurens County, and flows southeast through upper Wheeler County to the Oconee River. May have meant "Cow Creek," from Hitchitee, *Oke,* "water," and *waca,* "cow," or possibly "Place with water springs," from *u-ikai-walki.* Is also called OCHWALKEE CREEK (q.v.).

OKEFENOKEE SWAMP. Correct pronunciation is "Oakee-fen-oakee," but it is popularly called "O'kee fee no'kee." It is encompassed within the OKEFENOKEE NATIONAL WILDLIFE REFUGE which was purchased by the U. S. Government in 1937. This consists of a 681 square mile expanse of wilderness, the largest preserved fresh-water swampland in the United States. The name comes from the Seminole Indian word, *E-cun-fi-no-can,* which means "Trembling (or Quivering) Earth." and is so called because of the floating islands of the swamp. These are peat bogs that appear to be solid dry land; the peat is sometimes as much as 20 feet thick with the cypress trees rooted into its upper crust. There have been recorded over 77 different spellings of the name. Old maps of Georgia have labeled the swamp as EKANIFINAKA (1790), AKENFONOGA (1796), ECKENFINOOKA (1810), OKE-FINOKA (1813), OKE-FIN-A-CAN and OQUAFANAOKA (1818). Reverend George White wrote the name E-FI-NO-CAU. There was at one time a community called OKEEFENOKEE in Clinch County, located 30 miles southeast of Homerville, which was destroyed in the Civil War. OKEFENOKEE TRAIL was the designation of an early highway from Augusta to Florida.

OKEFENOKEE SWAMP PARK, Ware County. Located at the north entrance of Okefenokee Swamp (q.v.), at a site about eight miles south of Waycross. It is managed by the Okefenokee Association, Inc. which here provides tours and guides for visitors to the swamp.

OKI, Effingham County. This was a small settlement near Old Ebenezer (q.v.). The name is derived from the Hitchiti Indian word *oki,* meaning "water."

OKOLOCO TRAIL, Jackson County. This old Indian highway was the original boundary line between Gwinnett and Jackson counties. *Okoloco* is a Creek Indian word meaning "Hog Mountain" (*see* Hog Mountain Road).

OKTAHASASI (or OKTAHATAFLOFA), Fulton County. *See* SANDTOWN.

OKWHUSKE(E), Haralson County. The early name given to the TALLAPOOSA RIVER (q.v.).

OLA, Henry County. An early post office, named after the daughter of a Mr. Patten who lived here. Was located at the crossroads of Key's Ferry Road and Old Macon Road.

OLD AGENCY, Crawford and Taylor Counties. Was also called THE AGENCY or OLD CREEK AGENCY. The site is located six

miles southwest of Roberta on the banks of the Flint River. Indian agent Colonel Benjamin Hawkins (*see* Hawkinsville) in 1804 established the locality for transaction of his duties. It also included a plantation, mills, work shops, store houses, etc. After Hawkins died, the community declined, and was replaced by nearby Francisville (q.v.) which survived a little longer. Hawkin's grave is in a cow pasture on a beautiful knoll overlooking the river at the site of his home at Old Agency. He had established Fort Lawrence on the opposite (west) bank.

OLD DAMASCUS, Early County. This rural community, known locally as OLD TOWN, was originally called DAMASCUS (q.v.). When the Georgia Pine Railroad was built through nearby Kestler, the depot there was called Damascus, and eventually that community adopted this name. Old Damascus is about one mile northwest of Damascus.

OLD DOC SLOUGH, Long County. This is a creek or drain coming out of the river swamp about four miles above Doctortown. Goff said it was probably named for Indian chief, Captain Alleck (*see* Alecks Creek).

OLD EBENEZER, Effingham County. The original settlement of the Salzburgers. *See* Ebenezer.

OLD FALL LINE. *See* FALL LINE.

OLD FEDERAL ROAD. This thoroughfare became the earliest vehicular way of northwest Georgia, and the first postal route of this section. Beginning at Federal Crossing (q.v.), it crossed at Vann's Ferry (q.v.) and followed Georgia 141 to Coal Mountain, Forsyth County, and ran northwesterly through Cherokee and Pickens counties. It was so named because the Federal government secured right of passageway (by an agreement of 1803-04) from the Cherokees across their lands, to facilitate communication and travel between Tennessee and the lower Southeast.

OLD FLORENCE, Stewart County. *See* FLORENCE.

OLD HELL BIGHT, Wayne County. This is a big bend in the Altamaha River below the mouth of Penholoway Creek. The name was derived from the adjacent great swamp.

OLD ISLAND, Charlton County. One of the first islands in the Okefenokee Swamp to be discovered by the whites. It is now called CRAVEN'S ISLAND (q.v.).

OLD MOUNT PLEASANT, Effingham County. *See* MOUNT PLEASANT.

OLD NINE (or NUMBER NINE), Ware County. This was the early name of WAYCROSS (q.v.).

OLD OCMULGEE FIELDS (or OC-MULGEE OLD FIELDS), Bibb County. Was located on the site of OCMULGEE NATIONAL MONUMENT (q.v.). This was thought to be the location of the capital town of the so called Creek Confederacy.

OLD OCONEE TOWN, Baldwin County. *See* OCONEE OLD TOWN.

OLD POST ROAD. Georgia highway 77 between Elberton and Lexington. Officially given its original name March 10, 1964, as this old route had been in use for over 150 years, at first by post riders. It had recently been known as MATTOX BRIDGE ROAD.

OLD QUAKER ROAD. One of Georgia's earliest vehicular thoroughfares which was opened about 1769 to link Savannah with the Quaker settlement of Wrightsboro (q.v.). Georgia highway 24 follows this road quite closely.

OLD RIVER ROAD. Ran parallel to the Savannah River from Savannah to Augusta. John Goff said this was Georgia's first long, white man's thoroughfare, and was marked out in 1736-37 on orders of General Oglethorpe.

OLD RIVER ROAD. Was an important vehicular route which opened about 1777 along an Indian trail from Savannah to Rock Landing (q.v.). So named as it ran along the west side of the Ogeechee River to Bartow (Jefferson County).

OLD SCREAMER MOUNTAIN, Rabun County. A common name that was used to refer to SCREAMER MOUNTAIN (q.v.), now called BLECKLEY MOUNTAIN (q.v.).

OLD TOWN, Glynn County. This was the name given to FREDERICA (q.v.) on St. Simons Island in its declining years, as reported by Aaron Burr in 1804.

OLD TOWN, Jefferson County. This early community on the Ogeechee River was supposedly established by settlers from South Carolina before Oglethorpe established

Savannah. The settlement was originally called GALPHINTON (q.v.).

OLD WIRE ROAD. *See* WIRE ROAD.

OLICO CREEK, Lamar and Upson counties. *See* POTATO CREEK.

OLIVER DAM, Muscogee County (and Alabama). The dam was built on the Chattahoochee River to form LAKE OLIVER. This was the site of the famous old historic Clapp's Factory (textile mill), which was burned in 1865 by General Wilson's Raiders. The dam and lake were named for J. M. Oliver, who was general manager of the Georgia Power Company. There is also a community called OLIVER in Screven County, near the Effingham County line. Derivation of this name is unknown.

OLMSTEAD LAKE, Augusta. Located on the Augusta Country Club grounds. Possibly named for Colonel Charles H. Olmstead, CSA who was commander of Fort Pulaski (q.v.) when it was captured by Federal forces on April 11, 1861.

OLYMPIA, Lowndes County. This was an early trading center in the southern part of the county. Was named from the idea of the home of the Greek gods.

OMAHA, Stewart County. Incorporated as a town October 5, 1891. Was established on the Chattahoochee River, 15 miles northwest of Lumpkin, with the coming of the Seaboard Airline Railway, which was extended through here to Montgomery, Alabama. Derivation is from an old Indian tribal name which means "Upstream People" or "Against the Wind."

OMECRON, Wilkinson County. This was an early community which was located about eight miles northeast of Allentown, and is now the community of LINDSEY. The name is a variation of Omicron, the fifteenth letter of the Greek alphabet.

OMEGA, Tift County. Pronounced "O-mee'ga." Incorporated as a town August 22, 1905. Was established as a railroad town about 1889 when it was first called SURREY, located nine miles south of Tifton. *Omega* is the last letter of the Greek alphabet and signifies "the end," maybe of the railroad (there is no railroad here now).

ONIDA, Liberty County. This former community was located 15 miles northwest of

Hinesville. This is a simplified spelling of *Oneida,* an Indian tribal name.

OOSTANAULA INDIAN TOWN, Gordon County. This village was founded about the end of the American Revolution, after which it was replaced by New Echota (q.v.).

OOSTANAULA RIVER, Floyd and Gordon counties. The Conesauga and Coosawattee rivers join about five miles northeast of Calhoun to form the Oostanaula River which flows southwesterly to Rome. This is a swift river which is 45 miles long. The Cherokee Indian name means either "Shoally River," "The Rock that Bars Your Way," "A Rock Ledge Across a Stream" or "High Tower." Among the variations of spellings have been, OUSTANALE, OUSTANALEE, ESTANOLE, and USTANALI. There is also a community called OOSTANAULA in western Gordon County.

OOTHCALOOGA (or OOYOKILOKE), Gordon County. Was the early Cherokee Indian name for the present city of CALHOUN (q.v.). An early Indian village of OOTHCALOOGA in Bartow County was located five miles north of Adairsville.

OOTHKALOOGA CREEK, Bartow and Gordon counties. Rises just below Adairsville in Bartow County and flows northerly into Gordon County to enter the Oostanaula River west of Calhoun. The name is from a Cherokee word *tsutygilagi,* meaning "Beaver" or "Where there are Beaver Dams."

OPHELIA, Wilkes County. This was an early hamlet, located twelve miles northwest of Washington. "Ophelia" was the young, beautiful daughter of Polonius in Shakespeare's *Hamlet.*

ORANGE, Cherokee County. This community is located nine miles east of Canton on Georgia highway 20. May have been named for William III (1650-1702) of the house of Orange or from settlers coming from Orange County, North Carolina.

ORCHARD HILL, Spalding County. This descriptively named community, located five miles southeast of Griffin, was incorporated as a town August 19, 1912.

OREDELL, Polk County. Goff recorded that this is "A coined name for an iron-ore shipping point on the Southern Railway." There is no Oredell on the current county map, but is instead a stop called OREMONT, about six miles west of Cedartown on the Southern Railway.

ORLAND, Montgomery County. This former town was incorporated from August 11, 1908 until 1915, when its charter was repealed. It was located six miles northwest of Soperton on Georgia highway 29.

OSCEOLA, Oconee County. Was located at or near the present community of Bogart. Derivation is probably from the mixed-blood Creek-Seminole Indian chief of this name, which name refers to a medicine used by the tribe in certain ceremonies. It also may mean "Black Drink Singer," or "Black Drink Hollerer," referring to a call repeated while chiefs sipped the black drink made from asi leaves. Winn reports that it means "leaves," specifically leaves of the black yaupon, used for preparing the "Black Drink."

OSCEWICHEE SPRING, Wilcox County. This water source was reported to be located ten miles southeast of Abbeville. The name is probably a variant of Oswitchee (q.v.).

OSIERFIELD, Irwin County. This community located eight miles northeast of Ocilla was incorporated as a city August 19, 1912. Derivation is unknown.

OSKETOCHEE CREEK, Dougherty County. Early name of TALLAHASSEE CREEK (q.v.).

OSSABAW ISLAND, Chatham County. This is the northernmost of the Golden Isles, and bears what Goff says is one of the oldest place-names in Georgia, one given it by the Indians centuries before the white men settled here. *Ossabaw* is a Guale Indian word which means "Yaupon holly bushes place," from *asiape* or *asiaba.* The many variations of spelling have included, OSSEBAH, OBISPA, USSUYBAW, HUSSABA, HUSSAPAR, ASOPO, AUSABAW and OGECHE. The English in 1720 called the island MONTGOMERY, after Sir Robert Montgomery, who attempted to promote the Margravate of Azilia (q.v.). In 1970 this 40,000-acre island was reserved as a cooperative center for ecology. OSSABAW SOUND is the name which refers to the waters between Ossabaw and Wassau islands.

OSSAHATCHIE, Harris County. This former village near Ellerslie was known as

LOWES in pioneer days. For derivation, *see* Ossahatchie Creek.

OSSAHATCHIE CREEK, Harris County. Also spelled OSAHATCHEE, this is a tributary of Mulberry Creek. The name means "Pokeweed Creek," from the Muskogee, *osa,* "pokeweed," plus *hatchie,* meaning "creek," or possibly "Raccoon Creek" from Hitchitee *sawi,* "raccoon," and *hachi,* "creek." Some early spellings have been, OSAUHATCHEE, OSSOHATCHEE and OSOUHATCHEE.

OSWITCHEE, Chattahoochee County. This Indian town was located about nine miles south of Columbus, and existed until 1827. It was named for the Oscoochees, an Indian tribe of the Creek Confederation. The name was sometimes spelled OSWICHEE, and in much earlier days called OSCAYOOCHEE. The Muskogee Indian word means "switchers."

OTAULGAUNENE, Crawford-Taylor counties. Located on the Flint River in the vicinity of Old Agency (q.v.). This is the Creek Indian name for ISLANDS FORD (q.v.), from *oti,* "island," plus *algi* (or *ulga*), a plural suffix, plus *nini* (or *nene*), "trail (or path)."

OTISCA, Decatur County. A community located two miles southwest of Climax. Was named by railroad officials after Otisco Lake, New York. From an Iroquoian word meaning "water-dried," perhaps with the idea that the lake had shrunk.

OTTER CREEK, Coffee County. Rises about seven miles east of Broxton and flows southward into Seventeen Mile Creek east of Douglas. Probably named because of an otter slide here.

OUSLEY, Lowndes County. A community located eight miles west of Valdosta. Named after the two brothers, Joseph and William H. Ousley, who settled here in 1859.

OWENSBYVILLE, Heard County. This former community was located on the west side of the Chattahoochee River, ten miles west of Hogansville. John M. Owensby was an early postmaster here. The present OWENSBYVILLE ROAD in Troup County, about nine miles northwest of LaGrange, leads easterly into Heard County toward the river.

OWLTOWN, Gilmer County. The name of this early community was a translation of an old Cherokee Indian name. The village was an Indian meeting and council place. There is today a small community in Walker County named OWL HOLLOW, which probably has a similar derivation. It is four miles northwest of LaFayette.

OXFORD, Newton County. This town was incorporated December 23, 1839. Named in honor of the English university town where John and Charles Wesley were educated. It was laid out by Methodist minister, Edward Lloyd Thomas, who had also planned Columbus, Georgia.

OXFORD COLLEGE, Oxford. A branch of Emory University (q.v.), referred to as EMORY AT OXFORD. It was first named EMORY COLLEGE, in honor of Methodist bishop, John Emory (1789-1835). FEW HALL here was built in 1852, and named in honor of Dr. Ignatius Alphonso Few (c. 1789-1845), the first president of the college. PIERCE HALL here was named after George Franklin Pierce (1811-1884), the third president of Oxford College, and the first president of Georgia Female (Wesleyan) College. Also named after Bishop Pierce were PIERCE STREET in Oxford and PIERCE AVENUE, Macon. HAYGOOD AVENUE in Oxford was named in honor of Bishop George Franklin Haygood, graduate of Oxford College, and its eighth president. The administration building, SENEY HALL, was built with a grant received from New York banker and philanthropist, George I. Seney, in 1880. Its silver bell is reportedly from a ship of the Spanish Armada, and was given to the college by Queen Victoria. The institution is now used for an initial two-year program of Emory University.

P

PABST, Houston County. A stop on the Georgia Southern and Florida Railway, six miles east of Perry. This is the 700-acre site of the southeastern plant of Pabst Brewing Company, which started production in the Fall of 1970.

PACES FERRY ROAD, Atlanta. The Georgia governor's mansion is located at 391 West Paces Ferry Road Northwest. The original road here was named after Hardy Pace (1785-1864), who ran a ferry across the Chattahoochee River in the 1830's on the route to what is now Vinings (q.v.), Cobb County. Pace was a pioneer from North Carolina who came in the 1820's and built a house on what is now West Paces Ferry Road. A post office of PACE'S FERRY was established in the middle 1830's and continued until April 16, 1839 when Hardy Pace moved to the site of the present Vinings, changing the name of this post office to Cross Roads. Shortly after the present Vinings Mountain was given the name PACE'S MOUNTAIN, after Pace built a house at the foot of it.

PACHITLA CREEK, Randolph and Calhoun counties. This stream rises above Cuthbert and flows southward into Calhoun County to enter Ichawaynochaway Creek three miles west of Leary. The name PACHITLA is also applied to a rural community located about five miles east of Cuthbert, in Randolph County. This is believed to be the site of a former Indian town which was called Pachitla. This name is thought to be a Muskogee Indian word meaning "Dead Pigeon" or "Pigeon Town," or it may be from a Choctaw word that means "Opossum." Some variations in spellings have included, PACHITA, PACHUTA and PACHITTA.

PADSHILAIKA CREEK, Macon County. Gatschet wrote of a Yuchi Indian town at the junction of this stream and the Flint River called PADSHILAIKA or PAD-JEELEEGAU. He said it means "pigeon roost," from *padshi,* "pigeon," and *laikas,* "I sit down (am sitting)." Benjamin Harrison and his associates murdered sixteen warriors from this village.

PAINE COLLEGE, Augusta. Established in 1882 for Negroes by the Methodist Church, and was named in honor of Bishop Robert Paine. The WARREN A. CANDLER MEMORIAL LIBRARY here was named to honor Bishop Candler, who was a younger brother of Asa G. Candler, founder of the Coca Cola Company. The name of the museum, HAYGOOD HALL, honors the Methodist bishop, Dr. Atticus Green Haygood, a former president of Emory College.

PALATKEE, Evans County. This used to be an old Indian town, located near the crossings on Bull Creek and the Canoochee River. The name is from the Indian, *pilat-kee,* which signifies "a fording (or crossing) place."

PALMERS CREEK, Dawson County. This stream flows into the Etowah River above Dougherty. The name was corrupted from that of Silas Palmour, an Indian countryman who was an early settler on the stream.

PALMETTO, Fulton County. Founded by Willis T. Menneffee. Incorporated as a town February 18, 1854, at which time it was in old Campbell County. Named by a member of the Palmetto Guards, a South Carolina regiment that stopped in the area in 1847 when en route to the Mexican War.

PALMETTO, Oglethorpe County. This community is located about 12 miles east of Lexington, and was named by Daisy Rowe for the wild palmettos that were growing on Long Creek nearby.

PALMYRA, Lee County. Incorporated December 23, 1840; this is now a "ghost town." It was located on Kinchafoonee Creek, five miles north of Albany. Palmyra was the name of an ancient city of central Syria, founded by Solomon.

PANHANDLE. This descriptive term is used to denote a narrow strip of land extending out from a larger area. There are three such areas in Georgia given this name: 1. The strip of land in southeast Warren County. There was once a hamlet called PANHAN here, which was located seven miles southeast of Warrenton. 2. The extreme southwest tip of Clayton County. 3. The northeast section of Taylor County, because of the shape of militia district No. 768 here.

PANNELL, Walton County. This community was previously known as COWPENS (q.v.), and then changed in 1912 to honor resident here, Wiley Hill Pannell.

PANOLA MOUNTAIN CONSERVATION STATE PARK, Rockdale County. A

Rockdale County. A 537-acre park located on Georgia highway 155 west of Conyers, which was acquired by the state in 1971, and opened in Spring 1974. Named after PANOLA MOUNTAIN here, a million-year-old granite monadnock. One of the early communities of the county was named PANOLA. It was located on the South River, 12 miles south of Decatur. The name has also been given to PANOLA SHOALS in the South River where it is crossed by Georgia highway 155. *Panola* is a Choctaw Indian word which means "cotton."

PANTHER(S)VILLE, DeKalb County. This community is south of Decatur on Georgia highway 155. Franklin Garrett says that the name probably dates from the early or middle 1830's. He reports that tradition explains the derivation in a story in which a Mr. and Mrs. Johnson with their infant child were chased by a wild panther about 1830. However, Brinkley says the place was named for a Cherokee Indian clan. The Panthersville post office was established 1837-1856 and 1879-1901. Also given this name in DeKalb County is the PANTHERVILLE (Militia) DISTRICT, which was originally called GORDON'S DISTRICT until 1828 when it became PERRY'S DISTRICT.

PAOLI, Madison County. A community located eight miles southeast of Danielsville. Named for the town of Paoli in southeastern Pennsylvania.

PARAMORE (HILL), Jenkins County. This is a station on the Central of Georgia Railroad, and was named after an early resident here. John Goff said that PARAMORE'S BLUFF on the Ogeechee River in Jenkins County was called "Perrymore" Bluff by local residents. (See also SCULL'S BLUFF.) Estill and Weatherbe (1883) report a lumber station and post office here named PARRAMORE.

PARIS, Emmanuel County. The county seat was established here February 18, 1854 at which time the name of the town was changed from SWAINSBORO (q.v.) to Paris. An early post office called PARIS was located five miles south of Sharpsburg in Coweta County, and was named for the French capital.

PARKERTOWN, Hart County. Founded in 1832 in what was then Franklin County, and named for the Joseph A. Parker family who settled in Georgia from Virginia. It was located five miles northeast of Lavonia, and first called PARKER'S STORE.

PARKS, White County. A former post office which was located four miles north of Cleveland. Named for Benjamin Parks who found gold here in 1828.

PARK'S MILL, Greene County. This former community was named after early residents here, James B. Park and his uncle "Dickie" Park. The place was sometimes called RIVERSIDE, as it was located on the Oconee River, six miles southwest of Greensboro.

PARROTT, Terrell County. Incorporated as a town September 26, 1889. Named for settlers, James and John L. Parrott, who founded the community in the 1860's. John L. Parrott was the first mayor of the town.

PASSOVER, Rabun County. This community was located where one "passed over" the Blue Ridge divide. The name was changed to MOUNTAIN CITY (q.v.) when it was incorporated as a town in 1907.

PATAULA CREEK. Rises below Richland in Stewart County and flows southwesterly through Randolph and Quitman counties, then enters Lake Walter F. George in Clay County. *Pataula* is a Muskogean word which probably means "flat." The name is also applied to PATAULA (Militia) DISTRICT in southeast Stewart County.

PATAULA CREEK STATE PARK, Clay County. A 289-acre park developed by the U.S. Corps of Engineers about 1972. Located ten miles northwest of Fort Gaines where Pataula Creek (q.v.) enter Walter F. George Reservoir.

PATEVILLE, Crisp County. A former community which was located eight miles south of Cordele in what was then Dooly County. Named after J. S. Pate who first settled here in 1876.

PATSILIGA CREEK, Taylor County. Sometimes spelled PATSALIGA. Flows easterly across the northern section of the county to enter the Flint River northeast of Reynolds. George R. Stewart describes this as a Muskogean word meaning "pigeon-(roosting)-place."

PATTEN, Thomas County. A community located ten miles northeast of Thomasville on Georgia highway 122. This former town was incorporated from August 13, 1907 to 1912. Derivation is not known.

PATTERSON, Pierce County. This town was founded about 1873 and incorporated

December 1, 1893. Named for William Patterson from New York who operated a sawmill here in the early days. The original Atlantic and Gulf Railroad stop here was called NUMBER 7½.

PAUL A. GREEN BRIDGE, Rabun County. Located where U. S. highway 441 crosses Tiger Creek. Named March 28, 1961 for Mr. Green who was a state representative from Rabun County, 1947-1958.

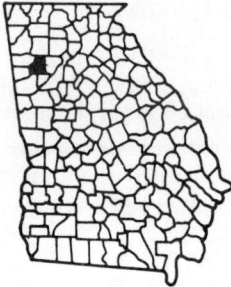

PAULDING COUNTY. Created December 3, 1832 with 318 square miles taken from part of Cherokee County. Named for a New Yorker, John Paulding (1759-1818), one of the captors of the British spy Andre, for which deed he was presented with a medal by George Washington. The county seat is Dallas (q.v.). *See also* Van Wert.

PAVO, Thomas and Brooks counties. Pronounced "Pay'-vo." Incorporated as a town December 22, 1898. Originally called McDONALD (q.v.), but had to be renamed because of the existant name of McDonald Mill, Georgia. *Pavo* is the Latinized form of "Peacock," named after Duncan D. Peacock, the first postmaster. Mr. Peacock came to McDonald in 1879, and was a store-owner, teacher, and community leader.

PAYNE CITY, Bibb County. A municipality completely surrounded by Macon, and located in the northwest section of that city. Calder Payne started Payne Mill here around 1899 which was sold to Bibb Manufacturing Company in early 1900. They incorporated the 70 acres of land as a mill town in 1913 so they could run it themselves. The homes here were originally owned by the company, but most of the people have bought them back.

PEACH COUNTY. Created July 18, 1924 with 151 square miles taken from parts of

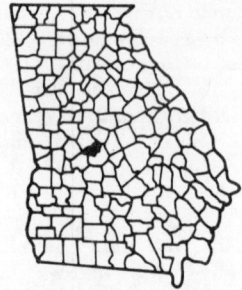

Houston and Macon counties. Georgia's youngest county was so named because of its location in one of the richest peach-growing regions of Georgia, and of the nation. The county seat is Fort Valley (q.v.).

PEACHTREE CITY, Fayette County. Incorporated March 9, 1959. The town was developed by the Phipps Land Company as an Atlanta suburban community at the site of the former town of ABERDEEN (q.v.). For derivation, *see* Peachtree Creek.

PEACHTREE CREEK, DeKalb and Fulton counties. Rises just east of Doraville and flows southwesterly to the Chattahoochee River. Named from an early Cherokee Indian village called PAKANAHUILI, meaning "Standing Peachtree." It has been natural to assume that the name was derived from there having been one or more Georgia peachtrees in the vicinity, although in fact they were not known in this area in the early days. Some historians attribute the name from an old pitch tree which was on a mound in the vicinity of the early village. The stream name has been applied to 15 PEACHTREE streets in Atlanta. The downtown PEACHTREE STREET is a divide, with the waters flowing from the east to the Atlantic Ocean and west to the Gulf of Mexico. *See also* Fort Peachtree.

PEACHTREE ROAD, Gwinnett County. The first road built in the county, at a cost of $150, to connect Fort Daniel on Hog Mountain with Fort Standing Peachtree.

PEACHTREE TRAIL, An early Indian road from the heart of the Cherokee Nation to the Creek Indian Village of Standing Peachtree (*see* Peachtree Creek). Later called DIXIE HIGHWAY, it is now U. S. highway 41.

PEA RIDGE, Marion County. Named from

the abundance of wild peavines in the area. This was the former name of BUENA VISTA (q.v.), and is the ridge on which this town stands.

PEARL, Elbert County. Community is located about two miles east of Middleton. Formerly called PEARL MILLS, and before that, BEVERLY (q.v.), the name under which it was incorporated.

PEARS (or PERRY) CREEK, Murray County. Tributary of the Conasauga River, in the upper section of the county. Goff reports that the name is derived from a man called "Sol Perry" or "Perry Spaniard," who lived by this stream on into Tennessee. It may have been Anglicized from his more probable Spanish name of Perez.

PEARSON, CS Atkinson County. Incorporated December 27, 1890, in what was then Coffee County. Laid out as a townsite when the railroad was built through here in 1870-71. It became the county seat in 1918, the year after Atkinson County was formed. Named in honor of Benjah Pearson (1811-1885), a wealthy and influential citizen of Coffee County, who served in the Indian War of 1838. S. J. Henderson built the first residence in Pearson in 1873, which house is now the Minnie F. Corbitt Memorial Museum.

PEAVINE CREEK, Walker and Catoosa counties. A tributary of the Chickamauga River, named because of the wild peavines found in the area. Named for the same reason is the nearby PEAVINE RIDGE, the site of Civil War skirmishes in September 1863. PEAVINE was also the early name of BOYNTON (q.v.) in Catoosa County.

PECAN CITY, Dougherty County. The name of this community was adopted because of its location in the center of the world's leading paper shell pecan region. There was also an early community called PECAN in Clay County, located eight miles northeast of Fort Gaines.

PECK'S MILL CREEK, Lumpkin County. A recent cartographer apparently applied this name to what had been known as BALL PLAY CREEK (q.v.), because of a mill on this stream.

PEDENVILLE, Pike County. A community located near the Flint River about four miles northwest of Concord. Named for the

Reverend A. G. Peden who came here from South Carolina.

PEDERNALES RIVER (or RIO PEDERNALES). This was an early Spanish name which was applied to the FLINT RIVER (q.v.). Derivation is from the Spanish word, *pedernal,* which means "flint."

PEEKSVILLE, Henry County. Now extinct, this community was located six miles east of Locust Grove on PEEKSVILLE ROAD. Named for W. H. Peek, a state representative of Henry County.

PEEPER ISLAND, Chatham County. This was the early name of LONG ISLAND (q.v.) in the Savannah River. John Wesley gave it this original name by which it was known during the Colonial period.

PELHAM, Mitchell County. Incorporated as a town September 14, 1881. The site for the town was selected as it was found to be the highest point of the South Georgia and Florida Railway. Named in 1868 by the chief engineer of the railroad, Major J. A. Maxwell to honor his comrade, Major John Pelham of Alabama, the "boy artillerist," mortally wounded in the battle of Kelly's Ford, Virginia, March 17, 1863.

PEMBROKE, CS Bryan County. Incorporated as a town August 23, 1905. The previous county seat was at Clyde (q.v.), but was forced to move to enable the subsequent occupancy of that area by Fort Stewart. The present seat is named for Pembroke Williams.

PENDERGRASS, Jackson County. This community was incorporated as a town December 30, 1890. Named for Dr. J. B. Pendergrass, a prominent physician of the county.

PENDLETON, Ware County. An early name of WAYCROSS (q.v.), Major Philip C. Pendleton settled in that portion of Waycross known as "Old Nine" in 1857. James Screven named the station "Pendleton," afterwards Major Pendleton caused the name to be changed to TEBEAUVILLE, after his father-in-law.

PENFIELD, Greene County. This little community has been referred to as the "Cradle of Mercer University." On December 28, 1838 the Trustees of Mercer University (q.v.) were given powers to run the government of the village. Named in honor of Josiah Penfield (c. 1785-1828) of Savannah, who gave the original bequest to establish Mercer Institute here in 1833, which became Mercer University in 1837. On the present Mercer University campus in Macon, the building housing the girls gymnasium is named PEN-FIELD HALL in his honor.

PENHOLOWAY CREEK. Rises in southern Wayne County, and flows northerly and then easterly into the Altamaha River. This Indian name was often misinterpreted to mean "Turkey Creek," but actually it is from the Creek, *fin' halui,* which means "high footlog," referring to a passage over a stream. Some sources say the name was first derived from a Lower Creek town of Finhalui. Old spellings have included, PENHOLLOWAY, PHENHOLLOWAY, FIN(N) HALLOWAY, PHINHOTOWAY, and PINHOLLOWAY (q.v.).

PENIA, Crisp County. The former community was located five miles east of Cordele on the Seaboard Airline Railroad. Was originally called PINIA, or PINA, relating to the many pine trees here. It was settled by a large number of Russian immigrants.

PENITENTIARY COVE, Lumpkin County. Located on Montgomery Creek (q.v.) in an inaccessible region, said to be as difficult to get out of as to escape the confines of a penitentiary. The name was also applied to the present Springer Mountain (q.v.), which was once known as PENITITIARY MOUN-TAIN. In northwest Fannin County, a stream called PENITENTIARY BRANCH flows into Jacks Creek.

PENNAHATCHEE CREEK, Dooly County. Rises about five miles west of Vienna, flows westerly into Turkey Creek which then enters the Flint River. Translated this name means, "Turkey Creek," from the Creek word, *pinwa,* "turkey," plus *hatchi,* "stream." *See also* Turkey Creek.

PENNINGTON, Morgan County. This community in the southern section of the county was named for the family who first settled here. In 1883 it was reported that J. C. Pennington was the postmaster here.

PEPPERTON, Butts County. Incorporated from November 1897 to 1966. Was site of Pepperton Cotton Mills.

PERCALE, Monroe County. Located 23 miles northwest of Macon on Georgia highway 87. Founded about 1966, it is the site of Bibb Manufacturing Company's Plant

Camilia, which makes cotton "percale" sheets and pillow cases.

(THE) PERIMETER, Fulton, Cobb, DeKalb and Clayton counties. The descriptive name given to U. S. highway I-285 which encircles metropolitan Atlanta. It opened in 1970, and has also been called THE LOOP.

PERRY, CS Houston County. "The Motel City" Incorporated as a town November 25, 1824. Settled in 1823 when it was first called WATTSVILLE. The following year it was changed to the present name to honor Oliver Hazard Perry (1785-1819), naval officer who defeated the British at Lake Erie, remembered best for his boast, "We have met the enemy and they are ours." The city is also called the "Crossroads of Georgia," after the suggestion of the prominent Methodist minister of Atlanta, the late Dr. Pierce Harris.

PERRY CREEK, Murray County. Variation of PEARS CREEK (q.v.).

PERRY HOUSE ROAD, Ben Hill County. Formerly called OLD OCILLA HIGHWAY, it runs south of Fitzgerald. Renamed in 1973 for M. P. House, general manager of the local Delco-Remy Company.

PERRYMAN, Decatur County. Now extinct, it was also called PERRYMAN TOWN. Named after either George Perryman who was onetime caretaker of Fort Scott (q.v.) or possibly after old 18th century trader here, Theophilus Perryman. This community had also been known as FOWL TOWN (q.v.) or OLD FOWL TOWN. Sherwood wrote that this was an old Indian town on the Chattahoochee River, southwest of Bainbridge.

PERSIMMON, Rabun County. Formerly a farmers' post office, now a court house located eight miles northwest of Clayton on PER-SIMMON CREEK, a stream which flows southwesterly into the Tallulah River. Settled in the 1820's, the community was named after trees, also called lotus trees, which grow wild in the area. Located here also is PERSIM-MON (Militia) DISTRICT.

PETERSBURG, Elbert County. In-corporated as a town December 1, 1802. In 1786 Dionysius Oliver erected a warehouse at Fort James (q.v.) about two miles below the earlier settlement of Dartmouth (q.v.). This was located at a fork between the Broad and Savannah rivers, and he named the place after Petersburg, Virginia where he was born. The post office was established here January

1, 1795, then moved to Lisbon (q.v.) July 2, 1844 and discontinued June 22, 1855. Petersburg turned into a tobacco farming center and tobacco inspection point, which became a thriving city, the third largest in the state. Among its residents was U. S. Senator Bibb (*see* Bibb County). The town died when cotton replaced tobacco as the major crop of the region. The site now lies beneath the waters of Clark Hill Reservoir.

PETERSBURG, Gordon County. Named for a German settler whose given name was Peter.

PETIT CHOU ISLAND, Chatham County. On the southern tip of Little Tybee Island. This name is a French term of endearment, meaning "little cabbage." Cabbage Island is two miles west of here.

PHILEMA, Lee County. Locally pronounced "Flimmee" or "Film' mee." The name of this community was first used to designate the railroad station here, and was taken from the nearby PHILEMA CREEK. Also called PHILEMA BRANCH, it is a tiny stream that rises in Sumter County and flows into the Flint River near Philema. This stream was originally called BEAVERDAM CREEK in the first surveys, and was then named after the Chehaw chief, Fullemy (or Philema).

PHILLIPS'S MILL, Coffee County. This former community was located ten miles west of Douglas. In 1883 it was reported that J. D. and J. J. Phillips had cotton and grist mills here, and also raised livestock.

PHILOMATH, Oglethorpe County. Pronounced "Fye-low-math." It was originally decided to call this community WOODSTOCK (q.v.), but the name was rejected, as a post office of this name was already in use, so Alexander H. Stephens (*see* Stephens County) was asked to suggest a name. He offered Philomath, meaning "Love of Knowledge." This was the site of the "Great Buffalo Lick" in earlier days, described by the Philadelphia naturalist William Bartram as a rock with a salty taste. The Bartram Trail Society Library is now located here.

PHINHOLLOWAY RIVER and PHINHOLLOWAY SWAMP, Wayne County. A variation in spelling of the name PENHOLOWAY (q.v.).

PHOENIX, Putnam County. Community located about six miles northeast of Eatonton. This name is derived from that of the

mythological bird that rose from its ashes, probably adopted to express the idea of a hopeful future for the place, as it was rebuilt after Indians had burned the early settlement.

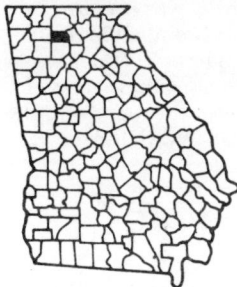

PICKENS COUNTY. Created December 5, 1853 with 225 square miles taken from Cherokee and Gilmer counties. Named for General Andrew Pickens (1739-1817) of South Carolina, Revolutionary hero who defeated the British at Kettle Creek, and took part in the victory at Cowpens. He was known as the "Fighting Elder" because of his stern Presbyterianism. The Cherokee Indians called him the "Wizard Owl." The county seat is Jasper (q.v.). The court house was destroyed by fire in 1947.

PICKETTS MILL STATE PARK, Paulding County. This 468-acre park is located on the site of the ten-day battle of Pickett's Mill which began in late May, 1864. It is between New Hope and Kennesaw Mountain. The property was purchased by the state for $935,510 in 1973 for use as a park.

PIEDMONT (Region). Name is applied to the broken and hilly land lying between the Appalachian Mountains of North Georgia and the Atlantic Coastal Plains. *Piedmont* is a French term which originated from the Italian word *piemonte,* meaning "foot hills" or "foot of the mountain." PIEDMONT is the name of a community incorporated as a town October 14, 1891, which is in PIEDMONT (Militia) DISTRICT in the southwest corner of Lamar County. PIEDMONT COLLEGE in Demorest, first called J. S. GREEN COLLEGIATE INSTITUTE, was founded in 1897 by a Methodist ciruit rider. It is now under the auspices of the Congregational church, and adopted its present name in 1903. PIEDMONT INSTITUTE of Rockmart was established in 1880 by the North Georgia Methodist Conference. This school existed until 1912. PIEDMONT NATIONAL WILDLIFE REFUGE contains 31,192 acres in Jones and Jasper counties, which are included in the lower Piedmont Belt. Acquisition of the land in the refuge by the U. S. Government began in 1934. Atlanta's PIEDMONT PARK was acquired by the city when it was purchased July 1, 1887 from prior owner Benjamin F. "Doc" Walker for the site of the Piedmont Exposition of 1887. Atlanta then changed the name of Calhoun Street to PIEDMONT AVENUE.

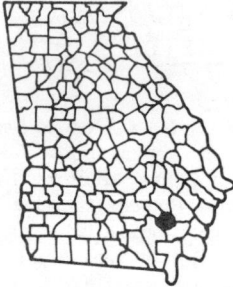

Territory, and discoverer of Pike's Peak in Colorado. The county seat is Zebulon (q.v.).

PIKES PEAK (Station),Twiggs County. This is a descriptive name for a high point on the Seaboard Coastline Railroad, located about nine miles northwest of Jeffersonville. *See also* Pike County.

PINAHACHI CREEK, Laurens County. An early Creek Indian name of the present TURKEY CREEK (q.v.).

PIERCE COUNTY. Created December 18, 1857 with 342 square miles taken from Appling and Ware counties. Named for the fourteenth president, Franklin Pierce (1804-1869) from New Hampshire, who gained the Democratic presidential nomination in 1852 as a candidate unobjectionable to the South. The county seat is Blackshear (q.v.). The court house was destroyed by fire in 1857. There is also a small community of PIERCEVILLE in Fannin County, located ten miles northwest of Blue Ridge.

PINDER TOWN, Worth County. This former community located 17 miles northwest of Sylvester was also spelled PINDAR TOWN. It is an old Indian name, possibly identical to FULEMMY'S TOWN (*see* PHILEMA). The post office was established here in 1825, and was one of the first in this section of the state.

PIGEON MOUNTAIN, Walker County. Located west of LaFayette, with an elevation of 2,329 feet. Sartain said the name was adopted when the white settlers first came and found millions of pigeons roosting on the mountain, feeding on chestnuts and acorns in early winter. Brinkley attributes the name to the mountain's shape or appearance of a pigeon breast.

PINE. At least 12 species of pine trees are found in the state, and these trees are undoubtedly the most prominent and valuable of those found here. It is therefore not surprising to find the large number of place-names in Georgia related to this tree. The term PINE BARRENS or GREAT PINE BARRENS is the designation that has been applied to the lower southeast half of the state, which was natively covered with forests of eight or ten varieties of pine trees on indifferent soil with scant underbrush. This southern region has also been referred to as the PINEY WOODS section. PINE BON ROAD of Chatham County was an old road that ran along the east side of the Ogeechee River. The name is undoubtedly a corruption of "Pine Barren." PINEBORO was a community in Quitman

PIKE COUNTY. Created December 9, 1822 comprising 230 square miles taken from part of Monroe County. Named for General Zebulon Montgomery Pike (1779-1813), a hero of the War of 1812, explorer of the Louisiana

County. PINE GROVE is a community in Newton County, which was formerly called SHOAL CREEK (q.v.). PINE HARBOR is a community in McIntosh County. A section of Columbus is called PINE HILL. The town of PINEHURST in Dooly County was incorporated December 16, 1895. Settled in the early 1860's when the early village was called FULLINGTON (q.v.). PINE ISLAND in Chatham County lies southeast of Little Wassaw Island. PINE KNOT CREEK in Chattahoochee and Marion counties was formerly called OCHILLEE CREEK (q.v.). The city of PINE LAKE in DeKalb County was incorporated December 29, 1937. PINELAND is a community in eastern Echols County. The community of PINE LOG in northeast Bartow County is named from PINE LOG MOUNTAIN (2,300 feet elevation), which extends eastward from Beasley Gap on State route 14 in west Cherokee County southwestward into neighboring Bartow County. LITTLE PINE LOG MOUNTAIN extends eastward of U. S. highway 411. PINE LOG CREEK arises at the northeast edge of Pine Log Mountain and flows northwesterly to join Salacoa Creek. A tributary is called LITTLE PINE LOG CREEK. PINE LOG TOWN was a Cherokee settlement on Pine Log Creek, three miles east of Pine Log in Bartow County. The Cherokee name of the town was NOTETSENSCHANSIL which signifies "Pine Footlog Place." Another PINE LOG CREEK is above Ballard Mountain in northeast Union County. PINE MOUNTAIN in Cobb County is an elevation located northwest of Marietta, which has also been called PINE HILL or PINE KNOB. It was the scene of skirmishes in June 1864 when General Leonidas Polk was killed here. The PINE MOUNTAIN range of northern Harris and southern Meriwether counties was given this name in the 1820's or before. The park here was formerly called PINE MOUNTAIN STATE PARK, and was then changed to the present FRANKLIN D. ROOSEVELT STATE PARK (q.v.). The town formerly called CHIPLEY (q.v.) in Harris County adopted the name PINE MOUNTAIN February 14, 1958. There is another community called PINE MOUNTAIN in northeast Rabun County. In Bartow County the 1,552-foot PINE MOUNTAIN is located two miles east of Cartersville. PINE MOUNTAIN in western Upson County has an elevation of 1,257 feet. A community of PINE MOUNTAIN VALLEY in Harris County was

established in 1935 by Roosevelt's New Deal agencies as an experiment to demonstrate a new method of absorbing surplus labor. It was earlier called VALLEY OF HOPE or VALLEY PLAINS. PINE PARK in Grady County was incorporated as a town August 15, 1910 at which time the community was in Thomas County. It was established as a station on the Atlantic Coast Line Railway. In Twiggs County, the post office named PINE RIDGE was established May 15, 1879. The community of PINE VALLEY is located about five miles below Covington in Newton County. The town of PINEVIEW in Wilcox County was incorporated December 10, 1902. PINEVILLE in Sumter County was located twelve miles east of Americus on the Flint River, and was the first post office in the county. Another PINEVILLE was in Marion County, eight miles west of Buena Vista. *See also* Penia.

PINHOLLOWAY, Wayne County. A former community which was located near Doctortown, and named from nearby PIN HOLLOWAY CREEK. Adiel Sherwood wrote that the stream was so named because an Indian shot a turkey high on a tree near the creek bank, thus *halloway*, "high up," and *pinaway*, "turkey." For actual derivation, *see* PENHOLOWAY CREEK.

PINK CREEK, Heard County. Originally known as PUNK CREEK. Goff said derivation is probably from the old Indian village of Punk Knot or *Tukpafka*, or possibly from the Indian translation of *Tukpafkahachi*, or "Punk Creek." The stream rises on the north border of Heard County above the town of Centralhatchee, and flows southeasterly into the Chattahoochee River.

PINK KNOT CREEK, Chattahoochee-Marion counties. *See* PINK CREEK and OCHILLEE CREEK.

PIONEER VILLAGE, Ware County. A model settlement established on PIONEER ISLAND by Okefenokee Swamp Park to demonstrate the lifestyle of the swampers in the pioneer days.

PIO NONO AVENUE, Macon. Pronounced "Pie-a Noe-na." The name originated from PIO NONO COLLEGE, founded in May 1874, with its name changed to Saint Stanislaus College in 1889. It was operated by Jesuits until it was destroyed by fire about 1922. The location of the school was in the vicinity of the present Stanislaus Circle near Vineville

Avenue. The original name of the college was from the Italian *Pio Nono* for Pope Pius IX.

PIPE MAKER(S) CREEK (or CANAL), Chatham County. Named for a meeting place where colonial officials would meet with the Indians "to make peace" or to "pipe talk."

PISCOLA CREEK, Brooks County. A tributary of the Withlacoochee River. Read wrote that it is probably derived from the Creeks, *pisi*, "milk," and, *kala*, "white oak acorns," from a place where oil was pressed from acorns. There was a settlement of PISCOLA by this stream, seven miles southwest of Quitman.

PISGAH, Gilmer County. This was an early village located eight miles east of Whitepath. From a Hebrew word meaning "peak" and is the name of a mountain in Palestine.

PISTOL, Wilkes County. Also called PISTOL CREEK, this was a village and early post office, 15 miles northeast of Washington. The name was taken from that of a nearby stream that flows into the Savannah River.

PITTMAN'S CREEK, Jackson County. Located in the vicinity of Commerce, and named for P. C. "Dick" Pittman who had a corn mill on this stream. There is also a community named PITTMAN, located four miles southwest of Duluth in Gwinnett County.

PITTS, Wilcox County. This town was incorporated August 23, 1905. Derivation of the name is from an early settler family of H. H. Pitts.

PITTSBURG, Henry County. A community located eight miles northwest of McDonough. Believed named from the city in Pennsylvania.

PLAINFIELD, Dodge County. This tiny community located seven miles northeast of Eastman was incorporated as a town August 7, 1912. Believed descriptively named.

PLAINS, Sumter County. Sometimes referred to locally as THE PLAINS. The home town of Georgia's present (1974) governor, Jimmy Carter. The post office was established August 17, 1839 and the town was incorporated December 17, 1896. The name is derived from an older location about one mile to the north, which was called PLAINS OF DURA. The Biblical Plain of Dura near Babylon was where Nebuchadnezzar erected a golden idol. The earlier settlement in Sumter County was founded in the mid 1830's, and

was also called MAGNOLIA SPRINGS or MAGNOLIA VILLAGE.

PLAINVILLE, Gordon County. Incorporated July 30, 1903. Captain E. G. Barney, president of the Selma, Rome and Dalton Railroad (1870) that was built through here, named the place for his home town, Plainville, Connecticut.

PLANTER, Madison County. This early community was in the western section of the county, and it was named to suggest the grain and cotton planted in the vicinity.

PLEASANT. Stewart reports that this descriptive adjective is used in at least 1,000 place-names in the U. S. for quasi-descriptive and commendatory reasons, usually coupled with names to indicate physical features. The community of PLEASANT GROVE in Johnson County, which is four miles from Wrightsville, was named after the Pleasant Grove Missionary Baptist Church which was established in 1881. A small settlement called PLEASANT GROVE in Catoosa County, was also named from a church here by this name. PLEASANT GROVE was the early name of GRIFFIN (q.v.). Other communities called PLEASANT GROVE are located in northeast Forsyth County and in southwest White County. PLEASANT HILL is the name given to a small place in upper Talbot County. PLEASANT HILL (Militia) DISTRICT above Lexington in Oglethorpe County was named from the former Pleasant Hill School which was a polling place. *See also* WOODLAND. PLEASANT RETREAT was a former community in White County, four miles southwest of Cleveland. PLEASANT VALLEY in Catoosa County was given this name because of the productive and beautiful land here. It lies north of Ringgold, and is a continuation of Woodstation Valley. There is also a community called PLEASANT VALLEY, which is located near Vienna in Dooly County, and another in western Upson County.

PLUM NELLY, Dade County. Not actually a town, but a sort of farm name. The place was given this name due to the fact that it is "Plum" out of Tennessee and "Nelly" out of Georgia. It is a two-acre crafts center in the New Salem community, located on a spur of Lookout Mountain. It is owned by artist, Miss Fannie Mennen, who was noted for her annual "clothes line" art show, which she conducted for 26 years through 1974.

PLUM ORCHARD, Camden County. A site

on Cumberland Island at which George Carnegie built a mansion by this name in 1898. There is also a community of PLUMORCHARD on the east slope of the Blue Ridge in extreme west Rabun County, as recorded at the State Surveyor General's Office.

POBIDDY CROSSROAD, Talbot County. Located three miles east of Talbotton on U. S. highway 80, at the junction with POBIDDY ROAD which extends northward to Thomaston. A legend relates how a mother hen here had a brood of little "biddies" and one of them ran out in the road and got killed by a horse, which prompted the exclamation, "That's the end of that po' biddy!" Dr. Goff concluded that the name originated when a dinner was being served near here, and one guest took the last piece of chicken, which prompted another to remark, "There goes the last of the po' biddy!"

POCATALIGO, Madison County. Pronounced locally, "Pokey tally go." Incorporated as a town July 21, 1920. The census spelling of the name of this community is POCOTALAGO. This same spelling is also found in the name of the POCOTALAGO (Militia) DISTRICT here. This is apparently a Yamasee Indian word borrowed from an old Indian town by this name in South Carolina. Several possible meanings have been suggested, such as "Big Gathering Place Town," "Big Ball (or Ball Play) Town," "Border Town," or "Gathering Place." A local legend regarding the name says that, to make a balky mule (or in another version, a pulled-in turtle) to go, was to "poke'e tail'e go." POCATALIGO was the Indian name of SANDY CREEK (q.v.), which flows through Madison County. (In West Virginia there is a Pocatalico River as well as a community called Pocatalico, both located north of Charleston.)

POETRY, Chattooga County. *See* TULIP.

POINSET, Murray County. This was the early name of SPRING PLACE (q.v.), and is believed to have been named by early settlers from South Carolina after that state's representative in Congress, Joel Roberts Poinsett (1779-1851), who also became Secretary of War.

POINT LOOKOUT, Elbert County. This elevation overlooking the Savannah River, was the highest point in the territory, where watchmen used to signal the approach of supply boats coming from Augusta.

POINT PETER, Camden County. Located just east of St. Marys on the St. Marys River, where (POINT) PETER CREEK enters the river. The name was probably derived from veterans of the French and Indian War who received grants from the English Crown in this area. These men had fought in Nova Scotia and probably brought this name south with them (Peter Point is in Queens County, Nova Scotia). Candler and Evans, in describing the War of 1812, wrote: "On January 15, 1815, a force of some 1,500 British was sent against Point Petre from Cumberland Island, but the movement was defeated by the militia under Captains Tattnall and Messias."

POINT PETER, Oglethorpe County. Community located ten miles northeast of Lexington. A local farmer named Peter sold whiskey by the pint, so it was suggested that the post office be named "Pint Peter," but instead the name "Point Peter" was used. The community was first called THE GLADE (q.v.).

POLK, Clinch County. Designated to be the county seat February 14, 1850 at which time it was named in memory of President Polk (*see* Polk County). On January 15, 1852, the name of the town was changed to the more euphonious, MAGNOLIA (q.v.). The court house was built in 1852, and was destroyed by fire in 1856. The county seat was then moved to Homerville in 1860.

POLK COUNTY. Created December 20, 1851 with 312 square miles taken from Floyd and Paulding counties. Named for the 11th U.S. president, James K. Polk (1795-1849) of North Carolina, who was previously a congressman and then governor of Tennessee. The county seat is Cedartown (q.v.).

PONCE DE LEON AVENUE, Atlanta. Pronounced "Ponst-de-Lee-on." Named after

PONCE DE LEON SPRINGS, which were located at the site of the present Sears-Roebuck store on Ponce de Leon Avenue. The spring were discovered in 1868 in a shady beech grove owned by John M. Armistead. They were named in 1870 by Dr. Henry L. Wilson, after it was found the water had surprising medicinal and curative value. The Spanish explorer, Ponce de Leon (1460?-1521), was looking for the "fountain of youth" when he discovered Florida. PONCE DE LEON PARK (no longer in existence) was the baseball park of the "Atlanta Crackers."

POOLER, Chatham County. Incorporated as a town October 25, 1907. Located northwest of Savannah, and believed named for Quentin Pooler.

POOLE'S CREEK. Rises at Forest Park in Clayton County and flows northerly to the South River. Garrett says it was named for Adam Pool who operated a grist mill on the stream. See also Poolesville.

POOLESVILLE, DeKalb County. A post office established 1831-37 and 1840-47. This was a settlement of Adam Poole at the site of today's apartment development, BLAIR VILLAGE. The post office moved to Rough and Ready (q.v.) in 1847. See also Poole's Creek.

POOR JOE BRANCH, Sumter County. This is a tributary of Lime Creek in the eastern section of the county. Goff said it may be a po' mouthing name or might have been applied to recognize a former resident near the stream.

POOR ROBIN SPRINGS, Wilcox County. Located just north of Abbeville on the Ocmulgee River. Possibly named after an Indian chief Robin, who was said to have been healed by bathing in the waters of the spring. There is a POOR ROBIN BLUFF on the Ocmulgee River, as well as on the Oconee River in Lauren County, and on the Savannah River in Screven County. In Screven County are also found, POOR ROBIN LAKE (slough), POOR ROBIN LANDING, POOR ROBIN LOWER POINT and POOR ROBIN UPPER POINT.

POPES FERRY, Monroe County. In 1819, a ferry operated by Cullen Pope was begun on the Ocmulgee River, about 12 miles upriver from the present Macon. Later a depot and post office were opened to serve the community.

POPLAR SPRINGS, Catoosa County. This was an early community which was so named from a spring nearby, above which grew a large poplar tree. Still standing is Poplar Springs Church, on the southwest edge of Ringgold. Another place called POPLAR SPRINGS was located on the Tallapoosa River in Haralson County.

PORTAL, Bulloch County. Incorporated as a town July 29, 1914. Derivation is unknown.

PORTERDALE, Newton County. This once prominent mill town was established about 1880 at the site of the former STEADMAN (q.v.). Believed to have been named for Oliver S. Porter, who purchased the thread factory here from Enoch Steadman, who had built the plant about 1868. The mill was in 1898 merged with Bibb Manufacturing Company of Macon.

PORTER MILLS, Habersham County. Incorporated as a town November 13, 1889. On February 19, 1951 a State act was passed ". . . to repeal the charter and laws incorporating the town of Porter Mills and to completely abolish the same." Was named from the Porter Manufacturing Company located here.

PORT WENTWORTH, Chatham County. Incorporated as a city February 6, 1957. This seaport town was named about 1917-18 for a prominent resident who lived here. When established as a shopbuilding town during World War I, there were two sections here, named BIG VILLAGE across the viaduct, for white citizens, and LITTLE VILLAGE for colored on the south side. This information was supplied by Port Wentworth mayor, P. B. Edwards.

POSS CREEK, Clarke County. Located west of Athens, and flowing into the Oconee River. Named after early resident William Poss, who ran a store nearby.

POSSOM SNOUT, Haralson County. This was an early name of TALLAPOOSA (q.v.).

POSSOMTROT BRANCH, Walker County. This stream is a tributary of Duck Creek, located northwest of LaFayette. John Goff said this is an old derisive term for designating nondescript localities.

POSTELL, Fannin County. This former settlement was located in the southern section of the county near the Toccoa River, and believed named for the early postmaster

J. McD. Postell who had a general store here in the 1880's.

POTATO CREEK, Lamar and Upson counties. Rises on the west edge of Barnesville and flows southwesterly to the Flint River. Earlier known as OLICO CREEK, the name is thought to have been translated from the Creek *aha* (or *auha*).

POULAN, Worth County. Incorporated as a town December 21, 1889. Mrs. Grubbs said the name was adopted to honor Judge W. A. Poulan.

POVERTY CREEK, which rises is southwest Lumpkin County, and POVERTY HILL in lower Jones County (six miles from Macon), are what Goff calls "po' mouthing" names.

POWDER MILL BRANCH, Hart County. This creek is a tributary of Big Cedar Creek, and was named for a mill here that made gunpowder for use in the War of 1812.

POWDER SPRINGS, Cobb County. The place was originally called GUNPOWDER SPRINGS, and was incorporated as the town of SPRINGFIELD AT POWDER SPRINGS December 29, 1838. The name originated from the smell of sulphur in the water here, which is also rich in magnesia. *See also* Swift's Lithia Spring.

POWELTON, Hancock County. Incorporated as a town December 13, 1816 to 1901. The Georgia Baptist Convention was organized here on June 27, 1822. The Baptist church here was organized July 1, 1786. Named after an early resident.

POWEL(L)VILLE, Coweta County. This was the name by which MADRAS (q.v.) was first known, and the name came from that of the early postmaster, George Powell, who had a general store here.

POWERS' CROSSROADS, Coweta County. Located on Georgia highway 34, midway between Newnan and Franklin. Named for the Powers family of which the present Tom Powers is the sixth generation to live here. The Powers' Crossroads Country Fair & Art Festival held annually here is the world's largest, with over 1,500 exhibitors.

POWERS FERRY ROAD, Cobb and Fulton counties. Named after the early ferry across the Chattahoochee River, established in 1835 by James Power (1790-1870). Garret relates how Powers Ferry was used by units of Sherman's army during July of 1864. It was replaced by a bridge built about 1903.

POWERSVILLE, Peach County. Located four miles below Byron. This community was established as a stop on the Macon and Southwestern Railroad, and named for Colonel Virgil Powers, the civil engineer for the railroad company.

THE PRAIRIES, Charlton County. Are also called GRAND (q.v.) and CHASE prairies. They are more like marshes, and were probably so named from their appearance from a distance, similar to the prairies of the Midwest.

PRATT(S)VILLE, Monroe County. This post office was established August 8, 1844, and was named for Daniel Pratt, an architect from New Hampshire who moved here from Clinton, Georgia. It has been said that the present city of Prattville, Alabama was named for the same family. The post office existed here to September 10, 1850, when it was transferred to nearby Bolingbroke (q.v.).

PRESTON, CS Webster County. Incorporated as a town December 22, 1857. Originally called LANNAHASSEE (q.v.), the derivation of this name is not certain, but is thought to be in honor of Senator William C. Preston (1794-1860), a leader in the Confederacy from South Carolina. *See also* TURIN.

PRETORIA, Dougherty County. Incorporated as a town August 22, 1907. Named from the large city of South Africa, which in turn was named for Boer leader Andries Pretorius.

PRIESTS LANDING (or PRIEST LAND), Skidaway Island. A monastery was built by the Benedictine Order on property acquired here in 1859 by the Bishop of Savannah. The monastery ruins are about one mile inland on the east side of the island.

PRIMROSE, Meriwether County. This tiny community about seven miles north of Greenville was incorporated as a town August 17, 1908. Probably named from the flower.

PRINCE EDWARD, Gilmer County. This was an old post office near the present Cartecay. Thought to have been named after the county in Virginia.

PRINCETON, Rockdale County. This small community is located seven miles northeast of Conyers, and believed to have been named after an early Prince family who lived here.

PRINGLE, Washington County. A community located 16 miles southeast of Sandersville, named for the C. R. Pringle family.

PROCTOR(S) CREEK, Dawson County. This stream in the southeast section of the county flows southerly into the Etowah River. Named for John Proctor, a part Cherokee, who lived in the vicinity and owned a mill on the creek.

PROVIDENCE, Fulton County. This early community in the upper section of the county was believed to have been given this name to denote optimism, or possibly named after Providence, Rhode Island. PROVIDENCE ROAD and PROVIDENCE CHURCH are today located northwest of Alpharetta. There was also a community called PROVIDENCE at the southwest border of Sumter County, on Kinchafoonee Creek. It was named for a church settlement, Providence Methodist Church of the early 1800's. The Union soldiers confined in Andersonville Prison (q.v.) at northeast Sumter County named a water source there PROVIDENCE SPRING.

PROVIDENCE CANYON STATE PARK, Stewart County. This 1,061-acre park was opened in July 1971, and is located about six miles' west of Lumpkin. Named from the PROVIDENCE CANYONS here, which in turn were named after the Providence Methodist Church here. Other names of the canyons have included, PROVIDENCE CAVERNS, GRAND CANYON OF GEORGIA, LITTLE GRAND CANYON(S) (q.v.), ROYAL GORGE OF THE CHATTAHOOCHEE, and sometimes known locally as the "BIG GULLY." The largest canyon is GRANDFATHER CANYON which is one-half mile long, 300 feet wide and 150 feet deep. The destructive erosion to create these canyons covers 3,000 acres, but started only about 150 years ago.

PRIUTT CREEK, Randolph and Calhoun counties. Rises about four miles south of Shellman in southeast Randolph County and flows southerly into Calhoun County where it enters Merrett Creek, an affluent of Ichawaynotchaway Creek. Earlier names of this stream have been FUSHATCHEE CREEK(q.v.) and CLAYBANK CREEK.

PUBLIC SQUARE, Greene County. *See* TEMPERANCE, Greene County.

PUDDLEVILLE, Cook County. The former name of Adel (q.v.).

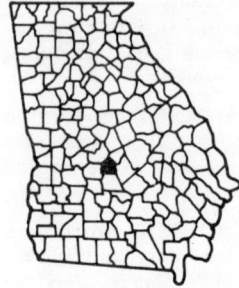

PULASKI COUNTY. Created December 13, 1808 with 254 square miles taken from part of Laurens County. Named for Count Kazimierz (Casimir) Pulaski (1748-1779), exiled Polish general, and hero of the Revolutionary War, who was killed while defending Savannah against the British. The county seat is Hawkinsville (q.v.). A statue to his honor, PULASKI MONUMENT, was placed in Monterrey Square in Savannah, October 12, 1855. FORT PULASKI (q.v.) and FORT PULASKI NATIONAL MONUMENT (q.v.) were also named for the Polish count. The town of PULASKI in Candler County was incorporated August 24, 1905, at which time it was in Bulloch County.

PULLTIGHT, Decatur-Grady counties. Goff described this community on the county line, east of the Big Slough, which he said was given a "whimsical poor mouthing name." This was a farmers' post office of Decatur County in the 1880's. There is also a PULLTIGHT HOLLOW in Tennessee which drains into the upper edge of Georgia's Dade County.

PUMPKIN (TOWN), Paulding County. This early community was named after PUMPKINTOWN FERRY on PUMPKINTOWN CREEK, located four miles west of Dallas. PUMPKINVINE CREEK rises about nine miles west of Dallas, and flows northeasterly into Bartow County to enter the Etowah River. May have been named for a Cherokee Indian, Pumpkin Vine. PUMPKINVINE CHURCH is about three miles southwest of Dallas.

PUNK CREEK, Heard County. This is a variation in spelling of PINK CREEK (q.v.).

At the request of George Washington he
selected the site for West Point Military
Academy on the Hudson River in New York
State. The county seat is Eatonton (q.v.).
There is also a community named PUTNAM
in Marion County, located near the Schley
County line.

PUTNEY, Dougherty County. A community
located eight miles south of Albany. Named
for Francis F. Putney, born in England in
1837, who had large plantation interests in
Dougherty and adjoining counties.

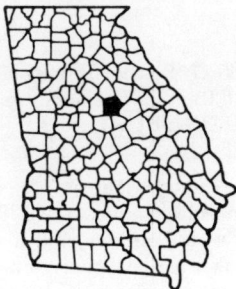

PUTNAM COUNTY. Created December 10,
1807 with 341 square miles taken from part of
Baldwin County. Named for General Israel
Putnam (1718-1790), a Revolutionary War
hero, who was born in Salem, Massachusetts.

PYE, Wayne County. This early community
was located on Goose Creek, fifteen miles
northwest of Jesup. The postmaster in 1882
was Solomon Pye.

Q

QUAKER RESERVE, McDuffie County. Early name of WRIGHTSBORO (q.v.) when the site was first settled by Quakers.

QUAKER ROAD. *See* OLD QUAKER ROAD.

QUAKER SPRING(S), Richmond County. Located on Washington Road, seven miles from the center of Augusta. Settled by Quakers in 1750, who departed after becoming alarmed at the murders committed by the Cherokees in the vicinity. The site was also known as SHERILL'S FORT (q.v.).

QUANASEE, Towns County. John Goff relates that this was an old Indian town, which was thought to have been located on the left bank of the Hiawassee River. The meaning of the name is not known. Variations in spelling have included QUANASSEE and QUANASSIE.

QUARTZ, Rabun County. A former post office located eight miles northwest of Clayton. Named for a deposit of silicon dioxide (quartz) found in the area.

QUEBEC, Union County. This was an early village located 14 miles south of Blairsville on Coopers Creek near the base of Blood Mountain. Some authorities say it is from a Cherokee word meaning, "being shut," "Narrow" or "fearful rocky cliff." Others believe it may have come from the province by this name in Canada, which is from the French term, *quel bec!,* "what a beak!"

QUEENSBORO(UGH), Jefferson County. Established in 1769 as a trading post, eight miles northwest of Galphinton (q.v.). Now extinct, it was located on the Ogeechee River at the fork of Lambert's Creek. The settlers were Scotch-Irish, and named the place for Queen Anne (1665-1714), the first queen of Great Britain and Ireland. The community was also called QUEENSBURY and IRISH SETTLEMENT.

QUILL, Gilmer County. A community located ten miles southeast of Ellijay on Tickanetley Creek. Brinkley said it was named for a Cherokee scribe who lived near here. He was among those who rushed to teach the Sequoian alphabet, in hopes that through a written language the Cherokee Nation could be saved.

QUITMAN, CS Brooks County. Incorporated as a town December 19, 1859. Named in honor of General John A. Quitman (*see* Quitman County).

QUITMAN COUNTY. Created December 10, 1858 with 170 square miles taken from Randolph and Stewart counties. Named for General John Anthony Quitman (1799-1858), who served under General Zachary Taylor in the war with Mexico. He was later governor of Mississippi and then elected to the U. S. Senate from that state. The county seat is Georgetown (q.v.).

R

RABBIT, Taylor County. This former community was located ten miles west of Butler. All names suggested for the post office were found to be in use, so this name was chosen in desperation when a rabbit ran in front of the postmaster.

RABBIT HILL, Bryan County. Community located about three miles southeast of Richmond Hill. The name is said to have been adopted because residents had to rely on rabbit meat as a food in order to "get by."

RABUN BALD, Rabun County. This is the second highest point in Georgia, with an elevation of 4,784 feet, and was named "Bald" because of its being bare of trees on the top.

RABUN COUNTY. Pronounced "Ray'-bin." Created December 21, 1819 with 369 square miles acquired by Cherokee cession of February 27, 1819. Named in honor of William Rabun (1771-1819), a native of North Carolina, who served as governor of Georgia (1817-1819). The county seat is Clayton (q.v.).

RABUN GAP, Rabun County. This small settlement is in a narrow pass at an altitude of 2,100 feet, and is three miles from the North Carolina line. It was sometimes called HEAD OF TENNESSEE as it is on the Little Tennessee River. This is the location of the RABUN GAP-NACOOCHEE SCHOOL, a five-year boarding high school for vocational and academic training, and recently gained fame with its publication of the *Foxfire Book.*

RABUN GAP JUNCTION, Habersham County. This was the former name of CORNELIA (q.v.).

RABUN, LAKE, Rabun County. Located on the White County line, it was created with the construction of Mathis Dam on the Tallulah River. In the upper end is RABUN BEACH RECREATION AREA, maintained by the U. S. Forest Service.

RACCOON. Several place-names in Georgia were given the longer and literary form for "coon." In some cases it is a translation from the Creek, as in *Sowhatchee* (q.v.), to signify RACCOON CREEK. There was formerly a town of RACCOON in Chattooga County, whose corporate limits were defined November 22, 1899. Located on Raccoon Creek in Chattooga County was a settlement of RACCOON MILLS, three miles southwest of Summerville. The Raccoon Manufacturing Company here manufactured cotton goods. There is also a RACCOON CREEK in Early County, and another in Paulding County. RACCOON ISLAND lies in Ossabaw Sound of Chatham County.

RACEPATH CREEK, Rabun County. An affluent of Persimmon Creek, thought to have been named from a mill race once constructed along the stream.

RACEPOND, Charlton County. Community located 13 miles northwest of Folkston on U. S. 1-23. Established as a station on the Seaboard Coast Line Railroad, and was named after RACE POND, a round cypress pond two miles distant.

RADIUM SPRINGS, Dougherty County. This resort is located four miles south of Albany, and its springs produce more water than any in the state. The main spring yields at the rate of 70,000 gallons a minute of clear 68 degree water. The Creek Indians had called the area SKYWATER and it was later referred to as SKYWATER PARK, and the springs were called BLUE SPRINGS. The name was changed to Radium Springs in 1925 when the present facilities were developed, because the water tested was found to contain 7.12 mache units of radium emanation "radron" per litre.

RALEIGH, Meriwether County. Incorporated as a city August 17, 1925. This small community was believed named after the English colonizer, Sir Walter Raleigh (1552?-1618).

RALSTON, LAKE, Stephens County. *See* YONAH, LAKE.

RAMHURST, Murray County. A small community located five miles south of Chatsworth. The place was formerly named RAMSEY. Estille and Weatherbe record that the postmaster A. K. Ramsey was a cattle raiser, and had a general store and grist mill here.

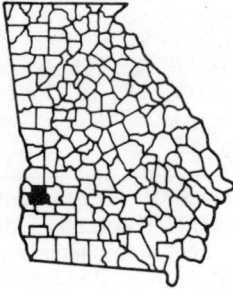

RANDOLPH COUNTY. Created December 20, 1828 with 436 square miles taken from part of Lee County. Named for John Randolph (1773-1833) of Virginia, Republican congressman, and descendant of Pocahontas. His name had previously been given to what is now Jasper County during the period 1807-1812, and had been changed because of his dovish attitude regarding the War of 1812. The county seat is Cuthbert (q.v.).

RANGER, Gordon County. Incorporated as a town August 15, 1910. Lulie Pitts wrote that the name was selected in 1895 by the new postmaster, Mr. J.W. Ashworth. It has also been reported that the name was chosen by the post office department from several names suggested by a Mrs. Horton when this was put on the Star Route from Calhoun. Her sister lived in Ranger, North Carolina.

RATHERWOOD, Carroll County. Later spelling of ROTHERWOOD (q.v.). *See also* RUTHERWOOD.

RAY CITY, Berrien County. Established about 1863 as RAYS POND, on the Lanier County line. Incorporated as a city, originally called RAY'S MILL, August 16, 1909. It was later moved to the railroad, and the present name was adopted August 6, 1915.

RAYMOND, Coweta County. Established in 1908 by Mr. and Mrs. R. F. Shedden. Mrs.

Shedden named the community in honor of her mother, Mrs. John (Mary) Ray. In 1901 a dam was built here to create the present 60-acre LAKE RAYMOND, five miles southeast of Newnan.

RAYSVILLE, Lincoln and McDuffie counties. This former settlement was located on both sides of Little River, and was named for Joseph Ray who settled here January 7, 1793. He built and operated mills here. A post office for the community was established in the 1830's.

RAYTOWN, Teliaferro County. Located eight miles east of Crawfordville. This is the oldest community in the county, and was originally called RAY'S PLACE, after a Ray family from 'New York who lived in Washington, Georgia.

REBECCA, Turner County. Incorporated as a town August 15, 1904 when this was in Wilcox County. Hal Brinkley says it was named for Rebecca Clark, daughter of Zach H. Clark, a prominent Turner County family.

RECOVERY, Decatur County. The southwesternmost community in the state, located on the east side of the Flint River, 21 miles southwest of Bainbridge. First established during the First Seminole Indian War as a hospital base for soldiers sent from Fort Scott to recover, and used during hostilities of 1817. Originally called FORT RECOVERY, it was also said to have been the site of a Confederate hospital during the Civil War.

REDAN, DeKalb County. Community located four miles northwest of Lithonia. A coined word, named after original residents, Mr. N. M. Reid and Mrs. Annie (John) Alford.

RED BLUFF, Effingham County. This was the ridge on which the Salzburgers established their second Ebenezer (q.v.) settlement. It was named from the peculiar color of the soil.

RED BLUFF CREEK, Clinch and Atkinson counties. Rises at the south border of Atkinson County and flows southeasterly to the Satilla River, and was descriptively named.

RED BONE, Talbot County. This early community was located at the site of the present YPSILANTI (q.v.). The name is taken from an old Indian chief Red Bone who was born here.

REDBUD, Gordon County. Originally called CRANE EATER (q.v.), this community is located on Pine Log Creek. The name was adopted because of the presence here of the redbud, genus *Cercis,* a small ornamental tree.

RED CLAY, Whitfield County. This descriptively named community was the site of a former Indian council ground, (1832-38), which the Cherokee called ELAWA'-DIYI which means "Red-earth place." Located 15 miles north of Dalton, it has also been called COUNCIL GROUND, COUNTY LINE and STATE LINE.

REDDISH, Wayne County. This former community was located near the Altamaha River, 12 miles northwest of Jesup. Also called REDDISHVILLE, it was believed named after early postmaster, G. R. Reddish.

RED HILLS REGION or SOUTHERN RED HILLS. This is an area that extends southwestward from Houston County, and downward into Alabama. The name was applied by the Indians, years before the white men came; they called the region ECIMNA CHATE, which signifies "Red Earth."

RED HOLLOW ROAD. An early trail from Savannah to Augusta and beyond, passing "Red Hollow House" which was located in what is now Martin, Stephens County. This inn was named from a red hollow stump close by.

RED HOUSE FORD, Catoosa County. This early crossing of the Old Federal Road on West Chickamauga Creek was descriptively named for the distillery that formerly operated on the west bank.

RED OAK, McDuffie County. An early post office established in 1833 when this was part of Columbia County. There is also a community in lower Fulton County called RED OAK. These names are for the common red oak tree found in the state.

RED OAK CREEK, Meriwether County. This stream in the northern section of the county flows into the Flint River. Named for the red oak trees here.

RED TOP MOUNTAIN STATE PARK, Bartow County. Located six miles southeast of Cartersville on the shore of Lake Allatoona (q.v.). This 1,246 - acre park was an old Indian meeting and play area, as well as the site of a Civil War battleground. It was named for REDTOP MOUNTAIN here, which was named from an Indian war town (red town).

REED BINGHAM STATE PARK, Colquitt County. Located about eight miles west of Adel. Designated a state park March 3, 1962, when it was named in honor of Mr. Reed Bingham who was the driving force responsible for the establishment of this 1,605-acre park. He also created the Colquitt County Rural Electric Cooperative, the second such cooperative to be established in the United States. A dam was constructed across Little River here to create BINGHAM LAKE. The dam broke in 1966 and was later rebuilt.

REED BLUFF CREEK, Clinch and Atkinson counties. Enters the Satilla River in eastern Atkinson County. The name came about because of the tall bamboo like grasses commonly found along the streams.

REED CREEK, Hart County. Located six miles north of Hartwell on Georgia 51. This community was named from the stream called REED CREEK, which flows into Hartwell Reservoir here. Another creek by this name is in Irwin County, and flows southeasterly to the Willacoochee River. REEDY CREEK rises in southeast Warren County and flows easterly through upper Jefferson County to enter Brier Creek at Keysville.

REEVES, Gordon County. Originally called REEVES STATION, it is a community located four miles southwest of Calhoun. Named for Osborne Reeves, local landowner who gave property for the railroad right-of-way.

REEVES CREEK, Henry County. A tributary of the Cotton River, named for an old settler who lived on the stream.

REGISTER, Bulloch County. An old community located eight miles southwest of Statesboro on Georgia highway 46. Derivation is probably from a family name.

REGISTERVILLE, Lanier County. Named after Samuel Register, Sr.; the community is now called STOCKTON (q.v.).

REHOBOTH, DeKalb County. A community located about three miles northeast of Decatur. Named from Rehovoth, a city of north central Israel. This is a Hebrew word which is thought to mean "wide places."

Another community named REHOBOTH is in Harris County, about seven miles northeast of Columbus. There was formerly a community of REHOBOTH in southeastern Oglethorpe County. REHOBOTH CEMETERY in Madison is 12 miles north of Madison in Morgan County, at the site of the early community of REHOBOTHVILLE.

REIDSVILLE, CS Tattnall County. Incorporated as a town December 31, 1838. When the post office was opened here at the county seat in 1832, it was named "Reidsville" in honor of Robert Raymond Reid (1789-1841) of Augusta, judge of the Superior Court, later territorial governor (1839-1841) of Florida. REIDSVILLE STATE PENITENTIARY (or GEORGIA STATE PRISON) is located seven miles south of town. It was completed in 1936 at a cost of $1½ million. REIDSVILLE STATE PARK, just west of town is now called GORDONIA ALTAMAHA STATE PARK (q.v.).

REINHARDT COLLEGE, Waleska. Founded in 1883 by Captain A. M. Reinhardt of Atlanta, and first named REINHARDT NORMAL SCHOOL in honor of pioneer settler Lewis Warlick Reinhardt. Chartered in 1891, and given its present name in 1909.

RELEE, Coffee County. A community located 18 miles northwest of Douglas on Georgia 107. Named for Robert E. Lee.

REMERTON, Lowndes County. Located northwest of Valdosta, and incorporated as a town February 19, 1951.

REMUS, Paulding County. A former post office located seven miles northwest of Dallas. Named from the Uncle Remus stories of Joel Candler Harris.

RENO, Grady County. Community located ten miles southwest of Cairo. Incorporated as a town April 18, 1913. Derivation believed to be from a personal name.

RENWICK, Lee County. Listed as a post office in 1859-60. The name was changed to SMITHVILLE (q.v.) April 18, 1863.

RENTZ, Laurens County. Incorporated as a town August 21, 1905. Named for E. P. Rentz of the Rentz Lumber Company here. Dr. C. E. Rentz was one of the five original aldermen.

REPOSE, Haralson County. This was the original settlement on the Little River of the present BREMEN (q.v.), and was named to suggest the peace and quiet of this locale.

REPPARD'S MILL, Clinch County. Former community located four miles northwest of Homerville. Named for Aaron Reppard, owner of a large steam mill, whose son was the distinguished Robert Blair Reppard of Savannah.

REPUBLICAN, McDuffie County. Also known as REPUBLICAN COURTHOUSE, this was a post office established August 17, 1839 when this was in Columbia County. It existed until 1868 when it was discontinued. Was not named for the Republican political party, which was not organized until 1854, but more likely for the philosophy of representative government.

RESACA, Gordon County. Pronounced "Ree-sac'a." Incorporated as the town of RESACCA February 15, 1854 and as the town of "Resaca" December 13, 1871. Originally called DUBLIN when first established in the 1840's. The soldiers returning from the Mexican War renamed it in honor of their great victory at Resaca de la Palma, which in Spanish means, "Dry River Bed of the Palm." An absurd legend has related how a young brave was to select an Indian maiden for his bride from several who were brought before him with sacks over their heads. After making a choice, her face was revealed to him, whereupon he commanded, "Resaca!" In the Civil War Battle of Resaca, May 14-15, 1864, General John B. Hood's corps attacked the Confederate forces in the first major battle of the Atlanta Campaign.

REX, Clayton County. Incorporated as a city August 16, 1912 to August 11, 1922. The name of this community is the Latin word meaning "King."

REYNOLDS, Taylor County. Incorporated as a town September 26, 1883. Founded in 1853 by a Dr. Coleman and was named for L.C. Reynolds, chief engineer of the Central of Georgia Railroad.

REYNOLDS SQUARE, Savannah. Laid out in 1733, and named in honor of John Reynolds (1700-1776 or 1781), sea captain and first provincial governor of Georgia (1754-56).

REYNOLDSVILLE STATE PARK, Seminole County. This 100-acre park is located on the shores of Jim Woodruff Reservoir, 16 miles west of Bainbridge on Georgia highway 253. Named for the nearby community of Reynoldsville.

RHINE, Dodge County. Town was incorporated September 1, 1891. Derivation of the name is not known.

RICEBORO, Liberty County. This town was originally settled about the beginning of the Revolutionary War. Was laid out February 1, 1797 and designated the county seat in 1798. Incorporated with the name of RICEBOROUGH December 21, 1819, and as the city of Riceboro August 20, 1927. The court house was moved to Zouck's Old Field in 1836. The name was derived from the fact that the early community was active in the rice trade.

RICHARD B. RUSSELL BRIDGE. Crosses Lake George from Georgetown, Quitman County to Eufala, Alabama. Named March 28, 1961 " . . . to perpetuate the stature of Senator Richard B. Russell, a great patriot, leader, public servant, and faithful son of the State of Georgia." Also named in honor of Senator Russell (1897-1971) is RICHARD B. RUSSELL SCENIC HIGHWAY, Union and White counties. A 15-mile stretch of winding mountain road (Georgia 348) east of Vogel State Park. RICHARD B. RUSSELL DAM was authorized in 1966 and named in 1973. It is scheduled for completion by June 1978, and will create the 25,000-acre LAKE RUSSELL, and is located on the Savannah River between Hartwell Dam and Lake, and Clark Hill Reservoir. *See also* Russell.

RICHLAND, Stewart County. The area was first settled in 1827 by Henry Audulf from Germany, who named the place CHISHOLM. Its post office was established May 6, 1839 and it was incorporated as a town September 28, 1889. The present name was derived from the Richland Baptist church here, which probably got its name from Richland District, South Carolina, where many of the settlers of Stewart County originated. The post office name was changed by postmaster John Audulf to Richland, December 16, 1899. In early times the settlement was nicknamed "Box Ankle" after a drunk broke his ankle when falling over a box.

RICHLAND CREEK, Greene County. Rises at the edge of Greensboro and flows southerly to the Oconee River. Was so named because of the rich land through which the creek runs.

RICHLAND CREEK, Twiggs County. Goff reports that this was first called SCUFFLE CREEK when the area was surveyed in 1806, but the residents apparently desired an antonym of its original poor mouthing name.

RICHMOND BATHS, Richmond County. The early name of the present community of BATH (q.v.).

RICHMOND COUNTY. Created February 5, 1777 with 325 square miles acquired by Creek cession of May 20, 1733. This was an original county previously organized in 1758 as the Parish of ST. PAUL. Named for Charles Lennox (1735-1806), the third Duke of Richmond, a military officer, ambassador, secretary of state, and a warm friend of American liberty. The county seat is Augusta (q.v.). RICHMOND ACADEMY (or ACADEMY OF RICHMOND COUNTY) in Augusta was the first public school in Georgia. Chartered in 1783, it opened April 12, 1785, in a building erected on Bay Street. *See also* Augusta College.

RICHMOND HILL, Bryan County. Incorporated as a city May 3, 1962. Previously here was the community named WAYS STATION (q.v.). Henry Ford (1863-1947) acquired property here in 1925 and built a winter house at the nearby Richmond Plantation. He developed a model community and gave the town its present name. RICHMOND HILL STATE PARK comprises 191 acres, and is located on the Ogeechee River about ten miles east of Richmond Hill, adjacent to Fort McAllister (q.v.).

RICHWOOD, Dooly County. Community on the Crisp County line, may have been named for the rich pine forests in this section. Believed established before 1900 when the Parrott Lumber Company moved into the area to cut the rich timber lands.

RIDDLEVILLE, Washington County. Incorporated as a town December 17, 1859. Located in the southeast section of the county and named for pioneer, Anderson Riddle, who came to Georgia in 1815 and gave land for the village.

RIDGE VALLEY, Floyd County. Valley is twelve miles long, extending northeasterly from Rome to Plainville. Named for Indian chief, Major Ridge, whose English name probably derived from his military rank in the Creek War of 1814.

RIDGEVILLE, McIntosh County. Community located three miles northeast of Darien on Georgia highway 99, earlier known as THE RIDGE. During the Civil War, the inhabitants from Darien fled to this settlement for refuge.

RIDGEWAY, Harris County. This former settlement was established about 1829 on the highest ridge, near the edge of the Harris and Talbot county line. The old Federal Wire Road (q.v.) passed through here.

RIDGEWAY (Militia) DISTRICT, Gilmer County. Located in the west section of the county, and named for an old Indian community here formerly.

RINCON, Effingham County. Pronounced "Rink'on." Incorporated August 3, 1927. This town was established in the early 1890's and has a Spanish name meaning "Corner" or "Nook."

RINGER'S CROSS ROAD, Carroll County. *See* TEMPLE.

RINGGOLD, CS Catoosa County. Incorporated December 23, 1847, and designated county seat March 16, 1854. The town bears the name of Major Samuel Ringgold, who died of wounds received in the Mexican War, when engaged in the battle of Palo Alto in 1846.

RINGGOLD, Spalding County. Was located five and one-half miles northeast of Griffin on Georgia 16. An early community, older than the county, settled around the Ringgold Masonic Lodge 90 which was established near here October 31, 1849.

RINGGOLD GAP, Catoosa County. Located east of the town of Ringgold, from which it was named. This was the site of a Civil War engagement on November 27, 1863.

RIO, Spalding County. Rural community located about six miles west of Griffin. *Rio* is the Spanish word for "river."

RIO DULCE. An early name of the SAVANNAH RIVER (q.v.).

RIO VISTA, Dougherty County. Community near Albany overlooking the Flint River. This is a Spanish term meaning "River View."

RIPLEY, Twiggs County. Former community which was located six miles north of Jeffersonville. Was originally named RIPLING June 11, 1892, by leading citizen John Walker Jones. The name was changed to Ripley August 6, 1892, and the post office continued to serve here until July 16, 1921.

RISING FAWN, Dade County. Incorporated as a town September 15, 1881. Romantic and fanciful accounts relate that the name is derived from a beautiful Indian princess called Rising Fawn, who supposedly lived in this area, but there is no substance to such legends. Dr. John Goff said that the name is actually derived from the Cherokee, *Kunnattetah, Kenotetah,* or *Agi-na-gi-li,* which translates literally, "Young He Is Rising." The real significance of the name is not known, but there were half a dozen male Cherokees who had that name. There was also an old Indian town of this name, named after one of these Indians who lived on upper Lookout Creek, near the present site of Rising Fawn. The name of this town was mentioned in Reverend George White's *Statistics of the State of Georgia* (1849) as "Rising Town," and Sherwood in 1860 listed it as "Rising Farm" post office. Here originally was the post office of HANNA (q.v.), later changed to STAUNTON (q.v.).

RISNER, TUGALOO H., MEMORIAL HIGHWAY and BRIDGE, Hart County. Named March 13, 1957 to honor Tugaloo Harvey Risner, who served the Georgia General Assembly and Senate, 1947-1954. The bridge is where Georgia 51 spans Lightwood Log Creek, and the highway so designated is that part of Georgia 51 between Hartwell to its end.

RIVER FERRY, Macon County. *See* UNDERWOOD'S FERRY.

RIVERDALE, Clayton County. Founded in 1886 as a railhead known as RAPE'S CROSSING on the Atlanta-to-Fort Valley Line. Incorporated as a town July 30, 1908, when it was named for Mr. and Mrs. W. Spratlin Rivers who gave land to the railroad here.

RIVER ROAD. One of the first pioneer roads to be established along the Ocmulgee River. It was made by widening the primitive Indian trail following the east bank of the stream from its headwaters down to the seacoast. *See also* Oglethorpe Trail.

RIVERSIDE, Colquitt County. Incorporated as a town August 22, 1907. The descriptive name came about because of its location beside the Ochlockonee River.

RIVERSIDE ACADEMY, Gainesville. Founded in 1907 as a military school, this 250-acre campus was named in reference to its location near the Chattahoochee River.

THE RIVER STYX, Charlton County. The headwaters of the St. Marys River in the lower section of the county was so called as it flows through a wild uninhabited tract. In Greek mythology, the Styx was the "River of Hate," that flowed nine times round the infernal regions.

RIVERTOWN, Fulton County. A former town located in old Campbell County when first settled. Also known as CROSS ANCHOR, it was about nine miles northwest of Palmetto, and given its name because of its site on the Chattahoochee River. The present RIVERTOWN ROAD (S698) extends about ten miles west of Fairburn.

RIVES, Dougherty County. Also called DUCKER'S STATION, this former community was located 13 miles southwest of Albany. In 1882 the postmaster was A. P. Rives, who was also the railroad and express agent.

RIVOLI, Bibb County. A suburban community near Macon in the vicinity of Wesleyan College. The name is taken from a town in Italy, near Turin.

ROANOKE, Stewart County. Incorporated as the town of ROAN-OAK' December 22, 1832. Established in 1831 on fifty acres purchased from Richard Mathias. It was located on the Chattahoochee River at the site of a former Indian village. The name may have been transferred from Roanoke Island of North Carolina where Sir Walter Raleigh's first colony was established in 1585, and then mysteriously disappeared. The derivation of that name is probably from the Algonquian, *Roanoak,* thought to mean "Place of White Shells," or "Indian Shell Money." On Friday May 13, 1836, this Georgia town was attacked by Creek Indians who burned the town and murdered most of the inhabitants. This act ignited a three-year war that eventually ended in Florida in 1842. The town was not rebuilt, but was replaced by Florence (q.v.)

about three miles upstream on the Chattahoochee River.

ROARING CREEK, Muscogee County. Enters Lake Oliver just above the dam. Named in 1826 by Willis P. Baker, surveyor. The earlier Indian name was CHISSEHULCUH (q.v.).

ROASTING EAR ISLAND, Ware County. Located in the Okefenokee Swamp near Soldier Camp Island. This name was adopted after it was discovered that a hill of corn was growing on the island.

ROBERTA, Crawford County. Incorporated as a town December 26, 1890. This town developed when the railroad came through, by-passing the county seat. Before long the settlement from Knoxville moved here. Roberta was named for the seven year old daughter of Hiram McCrary, who is now Mrs. Mattie Roberta McCrary Champion. He gave land for the early settlement, "He sold an acre and gave an acre." The BEN HAWKINS MONUMENT was placed here at the city square in 1930 by the U. S. Government to honor Colonel Hawkins, the first white settler in this area (*see also* Hawkinsville).

ROBERTS (Militia) DISTRICT, Jones County. The Reuben Roberts (1752-1845) family from Virginia came to Jones County in 1807. The community where he lived was called ROBERTS STATION. A post office named ROBERTS was located south of Clinton.

ROBERTSTOWN, White County. Incorporated from August 16, 1913 to August 12, 1921. Was located a few miles above Helen. Established in 1913 by a Mr. Pitner and named for Englishman, Charles Roberts, who had owned the property on which the town was built.

ROBINS AIR FORCE BASE, Houston County. This base covers 6,400 acres, and is located at Warner Robins (q.v.). It employs more people than any other establishment in the State of Georgia, and is the hub of the vast Warner Robins Air Material Area. Was built starting August 20, 1941, with original construction costs of $15 million. Named for General A. W. Robins.

ROCHELLE, Wilcox County. Town was incorporated December 15, 1888. The French name was suggested by the daughter of a railroad president who was touring the area

Rock 194 Georgia Place Names

with her father in the late 1800's, after a trip to Europe.

ROCK, THE. *See* THE ROCK.

ROCK BRANCH, Elbert County. Rural community located one mile east of ROCK BRANCH CREEK, an affluent of Coldwater Creek, about eight miles northeast of Elberton.

ROCK CITY (GARDENS), Dade County. Called the "Eighth Wonder of the World." Advertised as being *near* Chattanooga, Tennessee, but it actually is *in* Georgia. This 10-acre site was acquired in 1924 by Mr. and Mrs. Garnett Carter, who devleoped it into a tourist attraction. The area was named by early settlers because of its remarkable rock formations, which include LOVERS LEAP, 1,700 feet above the valley below.

ROCKDALE, Rockdale County. Established as a post office in 1834, 36 years before the county of Rockdale (q.v.) was created. In 1845, this post office was re-established as CONYERS (q.v.).

ROCKDALE COUNTY. Created October 18, 1870, it is Georgia's second smallest county (after Clarke County), with 128 square miles taken from Henry and Newton counties. Named for the Rockdale Church here, which was named after the subterranean bed of granite that underlies this region of the state. The first battle for prohibition was fought in Rockdale County. The county seat is Conyers (q.v.).

ROCK EAGLE 4H CAMP, Putnam County. Located six miles north of Eatonton, it is also called the STATE 4H CLUB CENTER. First opened in 1955, this is the world's largest 4H camp, and has facilities to host up to 50,000 persons. The 1,200-seat auditorium was named for Senator Herman E. Talmadge

of Georgia. The camp was named after a giant (120-foot) white quartz mound here in the form of a large bird, possibly an eagle. It has been described as being the most perfect effigy mound in North America, and is believed by archeologists to have been constructed by pre-Indian people at least 5,000 years ago. Here also is the 110-acre ROCK EAGLE LAKE, and on the opposite shore from the 4H camp is ROCK EAGLE PARK.

ROCK HILL, Early County. Community in the southwest section of the county, named for a large rock hill here. The Rock Hill court house was built here in 1886.

ROCKINGHAM, Bacon County. A community located three miles east of Alma. Named for the North Carolina town by settlers from that state.

ROCK LANDING, Baldwin County. Descriptively named, this site on the east side of the Oconee River is located four miles southeast of Milledgeville. Three Indian trails converged here, and also this was the official residence of James Seagrove, appointed the first U. S. Indian agent to the Creeks in September 1791. The Creek settlement, Oconee Old Town (q.v.) was located just below Rock Landing.

ROCKLEDGE, Laurens County. Incorporated as a town August 17, 1908. The post office was first established in 1889. The name of this community is derived from a ledge of rock which crops out along the Dublin and Mount Vernon highway.

ROCKMART, Polk County. Called "City on the Move." Incorporated as a town August 26, 1872. Derivation evolved from the original name of the place, ROCK MARKET. This was the offspring of Van Wert (q.v.). Slate deposits here were discovered in 1849, and are world renowned. *See also* Piedmont Institute.

ROCK MOUNTAIN, DeKalb County. This was one of the first names used by white men in referring to the present STONE MOUNTAIN (q.v.).

ROCKTOWN, Walker County. This name refers to an uninhabited rock formation resembling a town, located on top of Pigeon Mountain near Bronco. It is about 240 million years old.

ROCKVILLE, Putnam County. Located 12 miles east of Eatonton. Was an active community and post office in the 19th century.

ROCKY COMFORT CREEK. Rises in Warren County and flows down through Glascock and Jefferson counties to enter the Ogeechee River below Louisville. Its name is believed to have been translated from an original Indian name.

ROCKY CREEK. Rises in southeast Monroe County and flows easterly across Bibb County to the Ocmulgee River. William Bartram called it STONY CREEK. Benjamin Hawkins called it both STONEY CREEK and ROCKEY CREEK. It is probably an English translation of a Muskogee Indian word, *chattohachi*, from, *chatto*, "rock (or stone)" and *hachi*, "stream." In Greene County, ROCKY CREEK is an affluent of Richland Creek.

ROCKY FACE, Whitfield County. A community located five miles northwest of Dalton. Named for a nearby mountain on which a face-like rock formation can be seen on the brow. An earlier name for the community was AXOKA, which was a Cherokee Indian settlement.

ROCKY FORD, Screven County. This town was named in reference to a fording place on the Ogeechee River, south of here.

ROCKY MOUNT, Meriwether County. Incorporated as a town February 17, 1877. This community was descriptively named.

ROCKY TOP, Union County. A descriptively named mountain with an elevation of 3,075 feet. Located 3½ miles northeast of Ivy Log community.

ROLAND SPRINGS, Bartow County. Sometimes called ROWLAND'S MINERAL SPRINGS, it is shown five miles northeast of Cartersville on an 1882 map. Named for John S. Rowland who purchased the land in 1843 to develop a health resort. Today's county map indicates a Rowland Spring Church here now.

ROLLINS, Paulding County. A former community that was located six miles southwest of Dallas on Pumpkinvine Creek. The postmaster here in 1881 was W. L. Rollins.

ROME, CS Floyd County. "City of Seven Hills" Incorporated as a town December 20, 1834 and as a city December 29, 1847. Located in the ROME VALLEY where the Oostanaula and Etowah rivers join to form the Coosa River. The Cherokees originally had a post office here called HEAD OF COOSA. A small village called CHIHAHA (q.v.) then grew up on this site. Rome was founded in 1834 when five travelers met at a spring here, agreeing it

would be a fine place to start a city. They each tossed in a suggested name in a hat, and the one offered by Colonel Daniel R. Mitchell, a lawyer from Canton, was drawn. He had recalled the seven hills of ancient Rome on the Tiber, and therefore proposed this name. The county seat was transferred here from Livingston (q.v.) in 1834. BATTEY GENERAL HOSPITAL in Rome was named for Dr. Robert Halsey Battey (1828-1895) noted physician and surgeon, who was one time president of the A.M.A. The first bauxite (aluminum ore) to be found in the United States was discovered northeast of Rome in 1887.

ROOPVILLE, Carroll County. Incorporated as a town October 7, 1885. This community was built around a granite quarry, and was laid out by John K. Roop, farmer and business-man who lived here.

ROOSEVELT, Gilmer County. An early community located four miles southwest of Ellijay. Named for Theodore Roosevelt (1858-1919), 26th president of the U. S.

ROOSEVELT STATE PARK, Harris County. *See* FRANKLIN D. ROOSEVELT STATE PARK.

ROOSTERVILLE, Heard County. Located due east of Ephesus. Bob Harrell reported that, as the community was becoming established in 1905, an early resident Joe Spratlin suggested, "Let's call it Roosterville," because of the many nearby farms and roosters crowing most all of the time.

ROOTY CREEK, Putnam County. Rises above Eatonton and flows southeasterly into Lake Sinclair. Descriptively named in reference to the prevalence of roots in the stream banks.

ROSCOE, Coweta County. A rural settlement established in the early 1800's. The post office was established February 15, 1882. Believed named after U. S. Senator (1867-81) Roscoe Conkling (1829-88) from New York who was active in reconstruction plans for the Southern States.

ROSS LAKE. Turner County. Located near where Deep Creek flows into the Alapaha River. Named for early settler, W. D. Ross, who once owned the land on which the lake is located.

ROSSVILLE, Walker County. Incorporated as a city August 24, 1905. The first post office in northwest Georgia was established here April 5, 1817, with John Ross (1790-1866) the postmaster. Brinkley said it was first known as POPULAR SPRINGS. The town was named after Ross, around whose house the place grew. He was of mixed blood, being of Scottish and Indian ancestry, and was for forty years the head chief of the Cherokee Nation. This city is within ROSSVILLE (Militia) DISTRICT.

ROSWELL, Fulton County. Incorporated as a town February 16, 1854. Established at the site of a former Indian village on the Chattahoochee River. The city was first colonized in 1837 by Connecticut-born Roswell King (1765-1844), his family and a few friends. They established Roswell Manufacturing Co. here December 11, 1839. This is the location of "Bulloch Hall," the home of Theodore Roosevelt's mother. Union forces entered the town in July 1864. The earlier name of the original settlement here was ROSWELL JUNCTION, named for Roswell King who had been overseer for Pierce Butler's plantation on St. Simons Island. *See also* Chamblee.

ROTARY LAKE, Floyd County. Located southwest of Rome. So named after the Rotary Club of Rome donated a dam on Horseleg Creek to create the lake.

ROTHERWOOD, Carroll County. A post office was established here February 27, 1829 to 1868. It later reopened as RATHERWOOD until 1897. It was located at a site known to the Creek Indians as LOCKCHAU TALOFAU (q.v.), near the present town of Whitesburg. It was named Rotherwood after this was suggested by an English lady who noted that the countryside here resembled that described in Scott's novels. The Carroll County map shows a Rutherwood Church here now.

ROTTENWOOD CREEK, Cobb County. Rises at South Marietta and flows southeasterly to the Chattahoochee River. Goff explains that the stream was named for a Cherokee Indian who lived near its banks.

ROUGH AND READY, DeKalb County. This post office was established April 5, 1847 to June 24, 1869, in what was then Fayette County, having been moved here from Poolesville (q.v.). Its name was inspired by General Zachary Taylor's famous nickname (*see* Taylor County). An 1893 newspaper clipping

reported that the citizens here were "rough and always ready to fight." The town of MOUNTAIN VIEW (q.v.) later was established in this vicinity.

ROUGH CREEK, Murray County. This stream in the eastern part of the county, runs through what John Goff describes as rough territory, then into the Conasauga River.

ROUL, Habersham County. A station on the Southern Railway, about 1½ miles south of Alto. This is believed to have been the early name of the present ALTO (q.v.).

ROUND MOUNTAIN, Dade County. A hump on the back of Lookout Mountain, a few miles south of Lulah Lake. Descriptively named because of its almost circular elevation.

ROUND OAK, Jones County. Incorporated as a town August 17, 1914. Was reportedly first called SYLVANIA, and later given its present name for a huge ancient oak tree, under which the Indians held their powwows.

ROUND TOP, Gilmer County. A former post office located 11 miles southwest of Ellijay. Named for the nearby mountain which has a rounded appearance at its summit.

ROUSSEAU CREEK. Forms the border between Columbia and McDuffie counties before it enters Clark Hill Reservoir. Also in this vicinity was the resort of ROUSSEAU (POINT), located near ROUSSEAU SPRINGS. This latter is a mineral spring, rich in iron, located in the northern part of McDuffie County. It was named for William Rousseau, who purchased the land here from John McMurran (or McMurrin). The post office of Rousseau Springs was established here January 10, 1833 to April 6, 1839. McMurran came from South Carolina and acquired 350 acres here on Cane Creek. The five-acre tract including the springs was purchased in 1824 by General John Twiggs for $100 (*see* Twiggs County).

ROWLAND MINERAL SPRINGS, Bartow County. See ROLAND SPRINGS.

ROYAL LODGE, Harris County. Located on Georgia highway 190 near Warm Springs. Established and incorporated in 1973 by wealthy land developer John B. Amos of

Columbus. He named this community after the original hunting lodge on the site, and because of the proposed English village format.

ROYSTON, Franklin County. Incorporated December 29, 1890 at the junction with the Hart and Madison county lines. Believed to have been named for W. A. Royston, who had a general store here when the place was first settled.

RUBY FALLS, White County. Also called ANNA RUBY FALLS (q.v.), which are two separate falls, side-by-side. One on Curtis Creek drops 153 feet and on York Creek a drop of 50 feet. The falls were named for the only daughter of James H. "Captain" Nichols, who settled near here soon after the Civil War.

RUCKERSVILLE, Elbert County. Commissioners of the village were appointed December 9, 1822. Was settled in 1773 by Virginia aristocrats, John Rucker and John White, and named after their home of Ruckersville, Virginia. John Rucker's son Joseph "Squire" Rucker (1788-1865) was a businessman and banker who became Georgia's first millionaire.

RUM CREEK, Monroe County. Rises above Forsyth and flows southeasterly to enter the Ocmulgee River below Dames Ferry. Named for an early sugar cane mill, located at the present Todd-Ray place, which produced rum as a by-product.

RUNNING SPRING, Floyd County. A former community located six miles north of Rome. Translated from the Indian name for the spring located here, TANTATANARA.

RURAL VALE, Whitfield County. This was a tiny community which was located on Deep Creek, 11½ miles northeast of Dalton, and given a commendatory descriptive name.

RUSKIN, Ware County. Community located six miles southwest of Waycross. Founded in the 1890's by a group from Tennessee who established a communal type colony here, and its school had the first twelfth grade in Georgia. The early town was named for John

Ruskin (1819-1900), the English essayist and art critic.

RUSSELL, Barrow County. Incorporated as a city December 18, 1902. A station on the Seaboard Coast Line Railroad on the southeast edge of Winder. Believed named for the family of Georgia's Senator Richard Brevard Russell (1897-1971). *See also* Gordon Junior College and Russell Lake.

RUSSELL LAKE, Habersham County. Located two miles south of Cornelia. This 100-acre artificial lake was named for the late Senator Richard B. Russell of Georgia. RUSSELL WILDLIFE AREA is also located here. *See also* Richard B. Russell Bridge.

RUSSELLS CREEK, Dawson County. Flows southerly into the Etowah River below Dawsonville. This stream was named from a site of Russell's Mill, once located on the waterway. The earlier name of the stream was CHILD TOTERS CREEK (q.v.).

RUSSELLVILLE, Monroe County. A community located nine miles south of Forsyth on Georgia highway 42. Believed named for early resident, Alexander Russell. This section was previously (1821) called the 12th DISTRICT.

RUTH, Greene County. Was located near the Oconee River, 11 miles south of Greensboro. This early post office was believed named after early postmaster, Ruth Williams.

RUTHERWOOD, Carroll County. Rutherwood Church is located 2½ miles southwest of Whitesburg. *See also* ROTHERWOOD.

RUTLEDGE, Morgan County. Incorporated as a town December 13, 1871. It is said the town was named for a Rutledge family who settled here from South Carolina. LAKE RUTLEDGE is located north of the town within Hard Labor Creek State Park (q.v.).

RYONVILLE, Liberty County. This early post office was located 14 miles northwest of Hinesville, within the present Fort Stewart. It was believed to have been named for early postmaster and store owner, W. H. Ryon.

S

SABACOLA, Seminole County. An old Spanish settlement which was located where the Chattahoochee River is joined by the Flint River. The village here was burned by the English in 1685. The name, also known as SAVACOLA, comes from the Spanish mission, Santa Cruz de Sabacola el Menor, established here in 1680. There was also an Indian town in that same period, further north on the Chattahoochee, in the vicinity of Stewart County, called SABACOLA (or SAVACOLA) EL GRANDE.

SAFFOLD, Early County, A rural community located 19 miles south of Blakely on the Chattahoochee River, named from a plantation family who lived here.

S. A. HODGE, SENIOR, BRIDGE. On April 2, 1963 the Georgia State legislature passed an act proposing that ". . . the bridge over the Ocmulgee River which connects Jones and Monroe Counties on Georgia Highway 18 be named for the Honorable S. A. Hodge, Senior," who owned and operated Dames Ferry (q.v.), one of the last ferryboats in Georgia.

SAINT ANDREW'S PARISH. Created January 11, 1758 when the Georgia colony was divided into eight parishes. This parish comprised the district around Darien, and it was the intention of Govenor Ellis that the Church of England would establish a church here to be called Saint Andrew's, after the patron saint of Scotland. In 1777, Saint Andrew's merged with Saint John's and Saint James' parishes to form the original Liberty County.

SAINT ANDREWS SOUND, Camden County. Located at the mouth of the Satilla River, and named from Saint Andrew's Parish. (q.v.).

SAINT AUGUSTINE CREEK, Chatham County. A channel between Oatland Island and McQueens Island. Believed named by the early Spaniards in reference to Saint Augustine, the first white settlement on the continent. in today's Florida, which was named for St. Augustine of Hippo. *See also* Augustine Creek.

SAINT CATHERINE'S ISLAND, Liberty County. This was the home of the Indian chief, Guale (q.v.), and the site of the first white settlement of present-day Georgia. In April 1566, Pedro Menedez de Aviles made his first visit to the northern Georgia coast, and landed at what is now called St. Catherine's Island. He then established here what was the first of the island missions, and the head mission, which the Spanish named Santa Catalina de Guale. It burned in 1597 and was rebuilt in 1604 half a mile inland. The Spanish called the island SANTA CATALINA, and the English settlers later Anglicized it to the present name. It is believed that the first book written in America, a grammar by Brother Domingo, was written here in about 1568. The 25,000-acre island was owned by Mary Musgrove in 1759 and later sold to Button Gwinnett, who may be buried here. On Saint Catherine's Island was the headquarters of the Nation's first black Separatist Empire, which was established here by order of General William T. Sherman in 1865. SAINT CATHERINE'S SOUND lies between Saint Catherine's Island and Ossabaw Island.

ST. CHARLES, Coweta County. A small community located nine miles south of Newnan. Incorporated as a town from December 9, 1893 until March 22, 1935.

SAINT CLAIR, Burke County. Community located 12 miles northwest of Waynesboro on Georgia 80-305. Was originally called KILPATRICK ESTATE. Probably named for General Arthur St. Clair (1735-1818) of the Revolutionary War a friend of George Washington.

SAINT DAVID'S PARISH. Created October 7, 1763, and was merged with Saint Patrick's Parish in 1777 to form Glynn County. Probably named for David, king of the Hebrews (c. 1012-c. 972 B.C.).

SAINT GEORGE, Charlton County. Community located southeast of the Okefenokee Swamp. Originally called BATENVILLE, and later CUTLER STATION by the railroad. Was incorporated as a city from August 21, 1906 to August 6, 1924.

SAINT GEORGE'S PARISH. Created January 11, 1758, and consisted of the district of Halifax, which included all of the present Burke, and parts of Screven and Jefferson counties. Named for the patron saint of England since about 1348. A log cabin Church of England was built to serve this parish. It became the original Burke County in 1777.

SAINT JAMES' PARISH. Created January 11, 1758, and consisted of Frederica (q.v.) and all the sea islands south of the Altamaha River. Named either for the apostle, St. James the Great, brother of John and the patron saint of Spain, or for the palace of St. James in London. In 1777, St. James' Parish merged with St. John's and St. Andrew's parishes to form Liberty County. Telfair Square (q.v.) in Savannah was originally named SAINT JAMES SQUARE, after the palace of St. James in London.

SAINT JOHN'S PARISH. Created January 11, 1758, and comprised all of the present Liberty County, which included at that time the two settlements of Midway and Sunbury. Named after either the apostle Saint John, or Saint John the Evangelist. In 1777, St. John's Parish merged with St. James' and St. Andrew's parishes to form Liberty County.

ST. MARKS, Meriwether County. Community located nine miles northwest of Greenville. Incorporated as a town December 15, 1897. Named for Saint Mark, the patron of Venice, who wrote the second book of the New Testament.

SAINT MARYS, Camden County. Claims to be "America's Second Oldest City." Incorporated as the town of St. Mary *(sic)*, November 26, 1802, and as the city of St. Marys, December 13, 1858. This is the most southeasterly town in Georgia. Laid out in 1788 by James Findley on 1,672 acres of land, purchased for $38 from Jacob Weed. It was first named SAINT PATRICK (q.v.) and in 1792 changed to Saint Marys, named after the former Saint Mary's Mission in this vicinity, which the Spanish called *Santa Maria de Guadeloupe* (q.v.). The mission was founded in 1568 by Pedro Menendez de Avilles, founder of St. Augustine, Florida. It is believed that St. Marys was the site of an Indian village, TLATHLOTHLAGUPHTA, to which Captain Jean Ribault came in 1562.

SAINT MARY'S PARISH. Created October 7, 1763, after the English occupation, of what afterwards in 1776 became Camden County (q.v.), after being merged with St. Thomas Parish. Derivation is the same as St. Marys (q.v.).

SAINT MARYS RIVER. Rises in the lower Okefenokee Swamp and forms the border of Florida below Charlton and Camden counties. The Indian's name for this river was THLATHLOTHLAGUPHKA or PHLAPHLAGAPHGAW, which means "Rotten Fish," but the white men couldn't pronouce it. Ribault, upon finding it May 1, 1562, called it the SEINE. The present name originated from that of the early mission *(see* Saint Marys).

SAINT MATTHEW'S PARISH. Created January 11, 1758 when the colony was divided into eight parishes. This one included all of the present Effingham and much of Screven County, including the settlements of Abercorn and Ebenezer. Named for Saint Matthew, the disciple who wrote the first book of the New Testament.

SAINT PATRICK, Camden County. The first county seat of Camden County after it was formed in 1777. It is suspected that an Irishman was among one of the early settlers, to account for the name of the patron saint of Ireland. The name of the town was changed to SAINT MARYS (q.v.) December 5, 1792, and the county seat was moved to Woodbine in 1923.

SAINT PATRICK'S PARISH. Created March 25, 1765. Was merged with St. David's Parish in 1777 to form Glynn County. St. Patrick (c. 385-461) was a Christian missionary, called the Apostle of Ireland.

SAINT PAUL'S PARISH. Created January 11, 1758, it included all of the present Richmond, Columbia, McDuffie counties, and a part of Warren County. Named for the great apostle and missionary of Christianity, who was the author of the principal Epistles of the New Testament.

SAINT PHILIP'S PARISH. Created January 11, 1758, it included the south side of the Ogeechee River, west of Liberty County. Named for one of the twelve disciples of Jesus, and a missionary of the early church.

SAINT SIMONS ISLAND, Glynn County. The Indians' name for the island was ASAO, and the Spanish at first called it ISLA DE ASAO. Three Spanish missions were established here, with the central one being *San Buenaventure.* The others were the Mission Asao, plus a substation, *Ocotonico.* The Spanish changed the name of the island to the present one, undoubtedly after the one disciple who was a fisherman. The first English settlers arrived on Saint Simons Island February 22, 1736 (A comparative date: George Washington was born on February 22, 1732). SAINT SIMONS (village) is located on the southeast edge of the island, and is a resort community. There was also a former community of SAINT SIMONS MILLS on the west coast of the island.

SAINT SIMONS SOUND, Glynn County. Located south of Saint Simons Island (q.v.) from which it was named. It was previously called WALLEGONY BAY (1725), a corruption from its Spanish name, BARRA DE GUADALQUINI. Ribault had called it the LOIRE.

SAINTS ROW, White Sulphur Springs, Meriwether County. Old name for an unpaved road on the west side of present Georgia highway 18, because of the farm and plantation owners living along here who were "God-fearing" and church-going people.

SAINT THOMAS' PARISH. Created March 25, 1765. In 1777 it was merged with St. Marys Parish to create Camden County. St. Thomas was one of the twelve apostles who doubted the Ressurection until he saw Jesus and touched his side.

SALACOA CREEK. Pronounced "Sallacooee" or "Sallycooee" by old timers. A tributary of the Coosawattee River, which rises in southwest Pickens County, flows through corners of Cherokee and Bartow counties, and up through southeast Gordon County. The stream, as well as the SALACOA VALLEY, were probably named for an old Indian town of SAL(L)ACOA in northwest Cherokee County. Some families from Virginia settled here in 1850, and adopted the old Cherokee Indian name for the place, which is on Salacoa Creek. Hawkins recorded the name as SA LE QUO HEH, which he said meant, "Silke Grass." John Goff reported the name is of Cherokee origin, and signifies "Silk Grass Place" or "Bear Grass Place." He said the town was in Gordon County, on Pine Log Creek, eight miles east of Calhoun. Mooney wrote that the Indian word is from *Salikawa' yi* or "Bear Grass." Lloyd Marlin relates that the name is from the Indian word *Selu-egwa,* to signify "Big Corn," alluding to the fertility of the area.

SALE CITY, Mitchell County. Incorporated as a city August 12, 1910. Settled about 1901 and named for T. D. Sale, an active promoter.

SALEM, Dade County. Settled in 1830, it became the county seat in 1837, and was renamed TRENTON (q.v.) in 1840. "Salem" is a shortening of Jerusalem, which is taken to mean "peace."

SALEM, Oconee County. Incorporated November 24, 1818, in what was then Clarke County. A rural community which is located in the southern part of the county, and its name is a Hebrew word meaning "peace." SALEM (Militia) DISTRICT is located in the nothwest corner of Jackson County. SALEM VALLEY in Catoosa County was named from an old church that was established here in 1854.

SALIVAGE RIVER, Elbert County. An early name of the BROAD RIVER (q.v.).

SALTERS CREEK and SALTERS ISLAND, Chatham County. Located southeast of Savannah near Five Fathoms Hole. The island was previously known as DAWBUSS' ISLAND, and was in 1741 acquired by a brick mason, Thomas Salter, after which it and the stream were named. In 1772 the area was called Turckenham (q.v.) or Twickenham. Fort Jackson (q.v.) was established here in 1808.

SALT SPRINGS, Douglas County. Incorporated as a town December 12, 1882. Previously known as DEER LICK by the Cherokee Indians, as deer frequently licked the rocks here to benefit from the healthful healing salts from the springs. The place was also called BOWDEN, after Judge John C. Bowden, who discovered the great value of the water and made an analysis. The early community produced salt for the Confederacy during the Civil War. The name of the town was changed from Salt Springs to LITHIA SPRINGS August 19, 1918.

SAN BARNARD, Worth County. The first county seat when Worth County was established in 1853. It was Georgia's first summer resort, and was named for Saint Bernardine by General Brisbane, a Catholic who proposed building a monastery here. The name of this early resort was popularly given a "cracker" corruption to SANGUINARD. The succeeding county seat was Isabella (q.v.).

SANBORN CREEK, Decatur County. Located in the extreme lower part of the county, commencing near Faceville, and running into Jim Woodruff Reservoir at the Flint

River. The derivation of this name, which was bestowed by white men, is not known. The former Muskogee Indian name of the stream was EASTAHATCHEE (q.v.).

SANDERSTOWN, Gilmer County. Was located on the Old Federal Road, one mile northwest of Talking Rock. Was the site of CARMEL (q.v.) or TALONEY STATION (q.v.). The name is derived from the Cherokee chief, George Sanders, who once kept a house of entertainment here.

SANDERSVILLE, CS Washington County. Called "The Kaolin City" or "Kaolin Center of the World." Established as the county seat in 1796 and incorporated as a town November 27, 1812. The name is derived from SAUNDERS CROSS ROAD, its original name, which was named after a Mr. M. Saunders, who once owned land and a store here. In early times it was also called SAUNDERSVILLE.

SAND HILL, Carroll County. A former town, which was located eight miles north of Carrollton, and incorporated August 17, 1903.

SANDHILLS, Liberty County. Descriptively named, because of its location in sandhills adjoining the headstreams of the North Newport River. The name of the post office here was later changed to WALTHOURVILLE (q.v.).

SANDTOWN, Fulton County. This was an important early community, located along the east side of the Chattahoochee River below Utoy Creek. The name is a translation from the ancient Indian town here called, OKTAHASASI or OKTAHATALOFA. This place was first listed as BUZZARD ROOST (q.v.). SANDTOWN TRAIL began here, running through the middle of present Atlanta to Decatur. The name was later changed to SANDTOWN ROAD and then CASCADE ROAD. SANDTOWN is also the name of a community in northeast Wilkes County.

SANDY CREEK, Butts County. A descriptively named stream, which flows easterly into Chief McIntosh Lake. It was called HOPOETHYLELOHOLO by the Indians. Another SANDY CREEK rises in lower Madison County and flows westerly through lower Jackson County to the Oconee River. It was called POCATALIGO (q.v.) by the Indians, which is also the name of a community in Madison County. At least three other streams called SANDY CREEK are

found in Georgia, located in Coweta and Heard counties, Turner and Irwin counties, and in Jasper County. BIG SANDY CREEK is in Twiggs and Wilkinson County.

SANDY CROSS, Oglethorpe County. A community located 5½ miles northeast of Lexington. So named on account of the white sandy soil found here, and because several roads cross here, going in the four directions of the compass.

SANDY RIDGE (Militia) DISTRICT, Henry County. Located in the southeast section of the county. There was also a SANDY RIDGE post office here in the 1830's through the end of the century. It was believed named by early settlers after a natural sandy ridge in the red clay hills here.

SANDY SPRINGS, Fulton County. Called "Golden Ghetto" because it is an affluent community. A large suburban area lying north of Atlanta — a non-city with no local government or legal boundaries. Originally here was a spring bubbling through the sand used by Creek Indians and horse riders to Atlanta. A Methodist Church congregation later fathered the community. The original spring exists today in a yard on Sandy Springs Circle.

SANFORD, Stewart County. A community in the southwest section of the county. Thought to have been named for noted Indian fighter, General John W. A. Sanford (1798-1870).

SANGUINARD, Worth County. This name is the "cracker" corruption of SAN BARNARD (q.v.).

SANSAVILLA BLUFFS, Wayne County. Located on the Altamaha River at the mouth of Alex (Alecks) Creek. The name is derived from an early Indian town located on the bluffs, called SANTA SAVILLA (or SANCTA SAVILLA). The origin of the Indian town name is not certain, and there is no evidence of any former Spanish mission, fort, or settlement here. There was also a white settlement called SAINT SAVILLA on the Upper Sansavilla Bluff, later called WILLIAMSBURG (q.v.).

SANTA CLAUS, Toombs County. Incorporated as the City of SANTA CLAUSE, March 27, 1941. A community located below Lyons. The spelling of the name was changed to the present, March 13, 1970. Named for the patron saint of children, and is a corruption of the Dutch form of Saint Nicholas.

SANTA MARIA DE GUADELOUPE MISSION, Camden County. A mission built by the Spanish in 1568 in the vicinity of the present Saint Marys (q.v.).

SANTA MARIA STATE PARK, Camden County. Located two miles north of St. Marys. The 65-acre site includes ruins of a sugar mill built about 1825 by John Houstoun McIntosh (1773-1836). It had been widely circulated that this was the ruins of the Santa Maria de Guadeloupe Mission (q.v.), which accounts for the name.

SANTO DOMINGO BOYS ESTATE, McIntosh County. A self-governing boys' town, founded in 1946 on the Elizafield Plantation. Named after and located at the site of the former SANTO DOMINGO STATE PARK. The former 350-acre park was donated to the state by Cator Woolford. It is reputedly on the site of old Santo Domingo de Talaxe Mission, on the Altamaha River, one-half mile west of U. S. 17. *See* Talaje.

SAPELO ISLAND, McIntosh County. Pronounced "Sap'a-lo." Named for the Sixteenth Century mission of San Jose de Zapala, after which the island was called ZAPALA by the Spanish and the Indians. Zapala is the name of a province in Spain. Oglethorpe entered the picture, and Anglicized the name to Sapelo, which was sometimes spelled SAPELOE. Sapelo was called "Nigger Heaven" by envious planters because of Thomas Spalding's treatment of the slaves on his plantation here (*see also* Spalding County). SAPELO RIVER arises at Eulonia and flows southeasterly toward Sapelo Island. SAPELO SOUND lies between Sapelo and Saint Catherines islands.

SARDIS, Burke County. Incorporated as a town August 16, 1912. Believed named after the Sardis Baptist Church, established here in 1810. The church name is for the ruined city in Asia Minor, which was destroyed by Tamerlane. A community of SARDIS is located in northwest Talbot County. It was settled in the 1820's.

SARDI(N)S CREEK, Emanuel County. Other variations of spelling have included SARTINS and SERTAINS. Arises at the Johnson-Jefferson county line, and flows southeasterly across northwest Emanuel

County to the Ohoopee River. Was originally called SARTAINS CREEK, and was named for James Sartain who acquired property along the stream as early as 1794.

SARGENT, Coweta County. Previously a farming community called LODI (q.v.). In 1866 the name was changed to honor Captain H. J. Sargent and his brother George Sargent, founders of a cotton mill here that same year.

SASSER, Terrell County. Incorporated as a town December 29, 1890. Named in honor of a Mr. William Sasser.

SATILLA, Brantley County. A community located on the Satilla River (q.v.), 30 miles south of Jesup.

SATILLA, Wayne County. A community named from the Satilla River (q.v.), and was also called HASLAM. It was settled at the approximate site of the present town of ODUM, ten miles from the Little Satilla River, and ten miles northwest of Jesup.

SATILLA BLUFF, Camden County. This was an early community located three miles east of Woodbine, just east of highway I-95, where it crosses the Satilla River (q.v.). It was on the south bank, just above Burnt Fort.

SATILLA RIVER. Pronounced "Satilly" by old timers here, and is often called the GREAT SATILLA RIVER. Ribault had first called it the SOMME in 1562, and it was later given the name AI(S)NE by La Moyne. The present name is a corruption of SAINT ILLA, the name given the river by the Spanish invaders in honor of a captain in their King's army by that name. The name "Satilla River" was rendered in a decision by the U.S. Board of Geographic Names in 1892.

SATOLAH, Rabun County. Located Georgia highway 28, it is the most northeasterly community in the state. The name is derived from a Cherokee word meaning "six."

SAUNDERSVILLE, Washington County. Also called SAUNDERS CROSSROAD, this was the early name of the county seat, SANDERSVILLE (q.v.), and it was named for a Mr. Saunders.

SAUTEE, White County. Located three miles east of Helen at the junction of Chickamauga Creek and SAUTEE CREEK. The Cherokee town of ITSA TI near this site was called SANTA by Colonel Hawkins (1796). Bernice McCuller said that Sautee was named for a legendary Indian lad who was the lover of Nacoochee (q.v.). The post office name here is SAUTEE NACOOCHEE.

SAVACOLA, Seminole County. *See* SABACOLO.

SAVAGE CREEK, Twiggs County. Flows into the Ocmulgee River at the southwest corner of the county. The name was given this stream because white families living near here were massacred by savage Indians. A smaller stream named SAVAGE CREEK is in Bibb County. It flows through the northern residential section of Macon, and into the Ocmulgee River.

SAVANNAH, CS Chatham County. Established February 12, 1733, when General James Edward Oglethorpe landed at the Indian settlement on YAMACRAW BLUFF (q.v.), and founded Georgia. OGLETHORPE BENCH on Factors Walk marks the spot where Oglethorpe's landing was made (*see also* Oglethorpe County). The town was named by Oglethorpe after the Savannah River (q.v.), on the banks of which it is located. In the earlier days it was often referred to as SAVANNAH TOWN. TOMOCHICHI BOULDER on Wright Square was placed there in honor of the famous Yamacraw Indian chief, Tomochichi, (c. 1642-1739) who befriended Oglethorpe's colonists. Peter Gordon completed the plan of the town within the first year of their arrival. It became the first municipality in America to be built on the system of city squares. The streets that were then named KING, PRINCE and DUKE (as this was a royal colony), after the Revolution, in 1803 were changed to PRESIDENT, STATE and CONGRESS streets respectively. BULL STREET was named for Colonel William Bull (1683-1755), Surveyor - General of South Carolina, who helped Oglethorpe lay out the city of Savannah. JOHNSON SQUARE was laid out in 1733, and named in honor of Robert Johnson (c. 1676-1735), colonial governor of South Carolina, who aided Oglethorpe in the settlement of Georgia. ELLIS SQUARE was also laid out with the original city plan, and later named in honor of the second colonial governor of Georgia, Henry Ellis (1756-1759). JONES STREET was named in honor of Major John Jones, who was killed in the siege of Savannah in 1779. EMMET PARK was named for Irish patriot, Robert Emmet (1778-1803). CHIPPEWA SQUARE was laid out in 1813, and named to commemorate the July 5, 1814 Battle of Chippewa in Canada. Located here is a magnificent bronze statue of General James E. Oglethorpe. MONTERREY SQUARE was named in 1848 to commemorate the Battle of Monterrey, Mexico in 1846. FACTORS ROW consists of East Bay Street between Bull and Abercorn streets, and was named for the cotton factors (or agents) who made the nineteenth century a period of flourishing trade for Savannah. WRIGHT SQUARE was named for Sir James Wright (1714-1785), Georgia's last colonial governor (1760-1776). VICTORY DRIVE was named in reference to the victory of the Allies in World War I. Savannah was the place in 1733 of the first agricultural experimental station ever to be established (*see* Trustees' Garden). The Savannah post office was established in 1764, with Robert Bolton its first postmaster. The S. S. Savannah sailed here in 1819, which was the first steamboat to cross the Atlantic. Juliette Low founded the Girls Scouts of America in Savannah in 1912. Some of the city's nicknames have included, "Georgia's First City," "Cradle of Georgia," "Hostess City of the South," "Forest City of the South," and "Port City."

SAVANNAH BEACH, Chatham County. The easternmost town in Georgia. Located east of Savannah on Tybee Island, it was previously called TYBEE (q.v.) until the present descriptive name was adopted August 1, 1929.

SAVANNAH COUNTY. In the mid-1700's, Georgia divided into two so-called counties, Savannah and Frederica (q.v.), named from the two principle towns. Colonel William Stephens was made president of Savannah County April 15, 1741. With Frederica County, it was joined under one government in June 1743

SAVANNAH DISTRICT, Dawson County. Georgia Militia District No. 931, in the southern part of the county, was named for the old community of Big Savannah (q.v.).

SAVANNAH RIVER. This 314-mile river originates at Hartwell Dam (q.v.) and is the boundary between South Carolina and Georgia. Along with its tributaries, it drains more than 10,000 square miles. The Frenchman Jean Ribault called this river the

GRANDE in 1562, and then the Spanish called it RIO DULCE, meaning "Soft (or Sweet) River." Some attribute the name to the Spanish word *sabana,* meaning "flat lands" or "plains," and others believe it comes from the Indian, *shawano,* "the southerners." Then there are those who say it is a Creek corruption of the name of the Shawnee Indians, who formerly lived on the Savannah River. George Stewart relates that the name was probably derived from that of an Indian tribe, which may have been called this by the Spanish on account of the savannas found here, to mean "meadow," "open glade," or "treeless plain." The Indians' name for the river was ISONDEGA, or such variations as ISUNDIGA and ISONDIGA, which means "blue water" (although the water was never blue). The Mills Atlas of 1825 labels this the Isundiga River. The Indian name has also been said to be a corruption of *I' su nigu,* the name of an important Cherokee settlement in South Carolina that the whites called Seneca, meaning "muddy water." The Westoe Indians named the river WESTOBOU, or "River of the Westoes." In the upper part (in North Carolina) it is called the Whitewater River, and further down, Keowee River ("place of mulberries"), then Seneca River (these latter two in South Carolina), which flows into Hartwell Reservoir at the head of the Savannah River.

SAVANNAH STATE COLLEGE, Savannah. Established in 1890, it is now a part of the University System of Georgia.

SAVANNAH TOWN, Chatham County. An early name which referred to Savannah. There was also a noted trading post of the early 1700's called SAVANNAH TOWN, across the Savannah River in South Carolina, opposite the present city of Augusta.

SAW DUST, Columbia County. A community located in the southern corner of the county, one mile east of Harlem. The name was adopted because of the lumber produced from several saw mills here, which were powered from Big Kiokee Creek.

SAWHATCHEE CREEK, Early County. This stream name is now generally spelled SOWHATCHEE (q.v.).

SAWMILL, Chattooga County. This was a former community in the northwest corner of the county, located on Little River, which

provided the power for the mill referred to in the name.

SCANTVILLE, Carroll County. A former settlement in the western part of the county. Its name refers to the habit of local bootleggers of watering down the product so that the real liquor was scanty.

SCARBORO, Jenkins County. Incorporated as a town in "Scirven" (*sic*) County, December 19, 1859, according to the State Acts. One of the original five commissioners was Enos H. Scarborough, who was the first postmaster when the post office was established here about 1839. The original community was named for him and first called SCARBOROUGH. When the Central of Georgia Railroad was built through here, they named the stop, STATION NUMBER SEVEN.

SCARECORN CREEK, Pickens County. Flows northwesterly to enter Talking Creek. Brinkley relates how an Indian farmer was said to have merely "scared the corn" as he whooped through the field trying to scare away the birds.

SCHATULGA, Muscogee County. A rural community located nine miles east of Columbus. Goff explained that the name is a Creek Indian word meaning, "Crawfishes" or "Crawfish Place."

SCHLEY COUNTY. Pronounced "Sly." Created December 22, 1857 with 162 square miles taken from parts of Marion and Sumter counties. Named for William Schley (1786-1858), governor of Georgia (1835-37), legislator, and jurist of distinction. The county seat is Ellaville (q.v.).

SCOTLAND, Telfair and Wheeler counties. Incorporated as a town August 19, 1911. The original name of the town was McVILLE which was sometimes confused with McRae, so it was changed to the present name because of the predominance of Scotch settlers here.

SCOTT, Johnson County. Incorporated as a town August 6, 1904. The post office was established May 21, 1897, with James V. Carter the first postmaster. Derivation of the name is unknown.

SCOTTDALE, DeKalb County. This northeast suburb of Decatur was named for himself by Colonel George W. Scott (1829-1903), who built the Scottdale Cotton Mill here in 1900. He was originally from Florida, where he was elected governor in 1868. Scott was also an Atlanta broker, and benefactor of Agnes Scott College (q.v.).

SCOTT HIGHWAY, WILLIAM FRED, SR. Georgia highway 155-212, running southeast from Decatur. Named March 10, 1964 to honor this former state senator and U. S. congressman from Georgia.

SCOTTSBORO(UGH), Baldwin County. This early community was located four miles south of Milledgeville, and named for General John Scott of the state militia, whose modest house here was later enlarged by one of Georgia's richest planters, Farish Carter, and still stands (see Cartersville).

SCREAMER MOUNTAIN (or OLD SCREAMER MOUNTAIN), Rabun County. This 3,200-foot mountain was purchased in 1971 by Modern States Life Insraunce Co. One legend relates that the name was adopted because an Indian squaw once screamed all night at its top, and another tradition is that she leaped to her death rather than leave the mountains when the Indians were expelled from the state in 1838. The name of this mountain was changed March 24, 1839 to BLECKLEY MOUNTAIN (q.v.), in honor of Logan E. Bleckley (see Bleckley County).

SCREVEN COUNTY. In the original act creating the county, December 14, 1793, the name was spelled SCRIVEN, and it is not believed to have ever been changed to the correct spelling officially (see also Scarboro). Screven County comprises 651 square miles taken from parts of Burke and Effingham counties. It was named for General James Screven (1744-1778), public official and Revolutionary War hero, who lost his life fighting the British near Midway Church in Liberty County. The house of Benjamin Lanier was used for the first courthouse of the county until 1797 (see Jacksonboro). The county seat is now Sylvania (q.v.). The courthouse was destroyed by fires in the 1860's and in 1896. There is also a town by the name of SCREVEN, which is in Wayne County. It was incorporated August 19, 1907.

SCRUGGSVILLE, Glascock County. A post office established January 22, 1886. It was moved and changed to Mitchell (q.v.) February 18, 1887, when the railroad came through.

SCUDDERS, Forsyth County. Named for notable white settler, Jacob M. Scudder (1788-1870), who came here in 1815 from Wilkes County, Georgia, and was the first state senator from Cherokee County. Scudder established the first post office in the county here in 1833, and this was a center of government and commercial activities during Cherokee Indian days. The present community here is now called HIGHTOWER (q.v.).

SCULL SHOALS, Greene County. Located on the Oconee River, in the northwest part of the county. This post office was established in 1825, and the town here at one time had a population of about 600. Thought to have been named because of skulls and skeletons found in the nearby area of Indian mounds. Coulter said that this was the site of an early paper mill established in 1810 by Zachariah Sims, who also built and operated a toll bridge here. The factory ruins are preserved by the United States Park Service.

SCULL'S CREEK, Jenkins County. Located in the southern section of the county, it flows into the Ogeechee River. Goff presumed it was named for a colonial family by the name of Scull. SCULL'S BLUFF on the Ogeechee River in Jenkins County was previously known as INDIAN BLUFFS, and later was called PARAMORE'S BLUFF after a resident here (*see* Paramore Hill).

SEABROOK, Liberty County. A rural community located between the Midway and North Newport rivers. Was descriptively named in reference to a small stream flowing into the sea.

SEA ISLAND, Glynn County. This community on the island from which it was named, was laid out in 1828. The Cloister Hotel here is one of Georgia's oldest and most exclusive resort facilities. Sea Island has also been called LONG ISLAND in the past. The series of beautiful semitropical islands that extend along the Georgia coast from the Florida border to St. Catherine's Sound are called the Golden Isles (q.v.) and sometimes were referred to as the SEA ISLANDS. The name Sea Island has later been applied specifically to this privately owned resort island, which lies on the seaward side of Saint Simons Island.

S. EARNEST VANDIVER BRIDGE. The name designated for the bridge where highway I-85 crosses the Tugaloo River between Hart County, Georgia to South Carolina. Named March 28, 1961 in honor of S. E. Vandiver and his family. He was a member of the State Highway Board and his son S. E. Vandiver, Jr. was governor of Georgia (1959-63).

SEAY, Meriwether County. Was located three miles east of Mountville, at which time the site was in old Troup County. SEAY'S POST OFFICE was in service from March 18, 1830 to September 1835. The first postmaster was James Seay, well-to-do plantation-owner here.

SECLUSION FALLS and SECLUSION LAKE. *See* LULAH FALLS.

SEED LAKE, Rabun County. Also called NACOOCHEE LAKE (q.v.).

SEITUAH, Chatham County. A former settlement on Skidaway Island (q.v.) where General James Oglethorpe built a stockade in 1834 for protection against Indians. *Seituah* is believed to be a Yamacraw Indian name of unknown origin.

SEMINOLE COUNTY. Created July 8, 1920 with 254 square miles taken from Decatur and Early counties. The county is

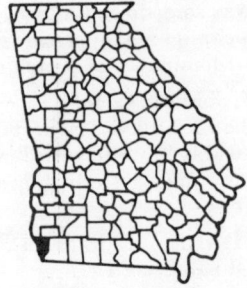

named for the Seminole Indians, an important Muskhogean tribe that lived primarily in what is now Florida and in the Okefenokee Swamp. They are a mixed people, combining aborigines of the area, migratory Creeks, and Negro slaves. The name is a Creek Indian word meaning, "separatists," "runaways," or "wanderers." The county seat is Donalsonville (q.v.). The Jim Woodruff Reservoir in the southwest corner of the county is also called LAKE SEMINOLE. It covers 37,500 acres, and has a 243-mile shoreline. On its shores is SEMINOLE STATE PARK which was established March 17, 1960. The 343-acre park is located 16 miles south of Donalsonville. There is also a smaller SEMINOLE LAKE in lower DeKalb County, which drains into Conley Creek. It is located almost four miles south of Panthersville.

SENOIA, Coweta County. "Home of Friendly People." First settled in 1860 by Rev. Francis Warren Baggerly, and incorporated December 12, 1866. John Williams suggested the name of the town, after an old Indian chief who had lived near the present community of Sargent. May also have been corrupted from "Shenoywa," a possible Indian title of Creek chief, William McIntosh.

SEQUOYAH. This was the Indian name of George Gist (usually corrupted to Guess) (1770-1843), a halfbreed Indian who by 1821 had invented the Cherokee syllabary (alphabet), which made literature of all kinds available to the Indians. Sequoyah became the accepted Indian name (*Sikwayi*) for the "Lonely Lame One," which is the same name they gave to the white man's pig, and also to the possum, as the Indians thought the opossum was an animal of mixed breed. It is for this Georgia Indian that the gigantic redwoods of California were named, and he was also the only Indian to merit being in the National Hall of Fame. The SEQUOYAH STATUE to his honor faces the memorial arch at the city limits of Calhoun. Named for him are the SEQUOYAH CAVERNS of Walker County, and LAKE SEQUOYAH, at 2,800 feet elevation in Pickens County, six miles northeast of Jasper.

SETTENDOWN, Forsyth County. *See* Settingdown Creek.

SETTINGDOWN CREEK. Rises in upper Forsyth County and flows westerly to enter the Etowah River just inside the Cherokee County line. Also spelled SITTINGDOWN, it was named for Cherokee Indian chief, Setten Down. He was called this because he allowed some of the white settlers to "set down" and live peaceably near his village. The village called SETTENDOWN was located on this stream, four miles northwest of Cumming.

SEVEN BRIDGES, Bibb County. This descriptive name designates a district in the vicinity of seven separate bridges located in a ¾ mile stretch of U.S. 41, beginning below the city limit of Macon.

SEVEN ISLAND ROAD, Jasper and Morgan counties. This was an old highway that connected civilization with the red man; an old Indian trail that crossed the Ocmulgee River at the SEVEN ISLANDS.

SEVENTEEN MILE CREEK, Coffee County. Warren Ward said it was given this name about 1812-15 by General David Blackshear, undoubtedly because of its length. Brinkley states that the name refers to the distance to another stream or military point.

SEVENTY NINE (or OLD 79) Jenkins County. The early name of MILLEN (q.v.).

SEVILLE, Wilcox County. Pronounced "Seeville." Incorporated as a town December 27, 1890. Named for the famous province and its capital in Spain, that is called *Sevilla* by the Spanish.

SEYMOUR, Jackson County. This former community was located near the bridge across the Mulberry River on Georgia 11, between Jefferson and Winder. It was named for Anderw J. Seymour, who was the postmaster here from 1893 to 1902.

SHADY DALE, Jasper County. Incorporated November 13, 1889. It is a commendatory descriptive name for this community which is located nine miles northeast of Monticello. Another community which is descriptively called SHADY GROVE is located in Carroll County on the Little Tallapoosa River, 5½ miles northeast of Carrollton. The same name has also been given to communities in Forsyth, Towns, and Twiggs counties.

SHAFTESBURY KNOLL, Chatham County. This is the name that was long ago given to the only high place on the old SHAFTESBURY PLANTATION on Argyle Island. The early owner James Deveaux named his plantation for the Earl of Shaftesbury, Anthony Ashley Cooper (1621-1683).

SHAKE RAG. This name was applied to various early railroad stops, referring to the waving of a signal flag. This was the early name of the present WADLEY (q.v.), and is still the name of two rural communities, one in upper Fulton County, six miles east of Alpharetta (*see* SHELTONVILLE) and another in Fayette County near Senoia. A stream called SHAKERAG BRANCH in Towns County is located southeast of Hiwasesee, and flows into lower Chatuge Lake.

SHAKING ROCK PARK, Lexington. This park was named in reference to a 20-ton boulder which can be rocked with one hand because of its pivotal balance.

SHANGRI-LA LAKE, Rabun County. This fishing pond is located just above Clayton. The name originated from the mythical land of eternal youth described by James Hilton in his 1933 novel, *Lost Horizon.*

SHARON, Taliaferro County. Incorporated December 24, 1884. The name of this town has a Biblical origin, and is from the Hebrew, meaning "A Plain."

SHARON GROVE, Fayette County. *See* BROOKS.

SHARP, Carroll County. This former settlement was named for old Uncle Hiram Sharp, probably the first settler in this part of the county, who lived to be 90. The place was later called FARMVILLE. Of the same derivation is SHARPE (or SHARPS) CREEK, which flows northerly into Spence Lake in Carroll County, near the Haralson County line.

SHARPE, Walker County. Located six miles southwest of LaFayette. This small community was named for Thomas A. Sharpe, early settler and delegate to the Secession Convention in 1860.

SHARPE'S STORE, Brooks County. Named for Hamilton W. Sharpe, who built a store out of logs here in 1826. This was the second post office in the original Lowndes County, having been approved April 2, 1853. The name of the place was changed to the present MORVEN (q.v.), July 21, 1853.

SHARPSBURG, Coweta County. Founded in 1825 by Anglo-Saxon descendants of Connecticut settlers. Incorporated as a town December 13, 1871. Named after Judge Elias Sharp (c. 1813-1884), who was one of the original town commissioners. The post office was built here in 1870 and still stands.

SHARPS CREEK, Carroll County. *See* Sharp.

SHARP TOP MOUNTAIN, Pickens County. Located four miles northwest of Jasper with an elevation of 2,600 feet. Usually thought to be a descriptive name, but Brinkley says the origin is probably from a Cherokee family of Sharp Fellow or Peggy Sharp who lived here.

SHAWNEE, Effingham County. A community located ten miles northwest of Springfield. Named after the Shawnee Indian tribe of the Algonquian linguistic family. Their chief was Tecumseh (1768?-1813).

SHEARER SPRINGS, Henry County. Incorporated December 13, 1871 by owner John Shearer.

SHELL BLUFF, Burke County. Was a thriving community and post office in early colonial days, and located about one mile from SHELL BLUFF LANDING, from which it was named. The bluff extends forty miles along the Savannah River below Augusta, and was so named after the common oyster fossil which is found in abundance here. This is the highest bluff on the river, and rises up to 150 feet elevation. SHELL BLUFF (Militia) DISTRICT is located at the northeast corner of Burke County.

SHELLMAN, Randolph County. Originally incorporated as WARD (q.v.), the town was incorporated as SCHELLMAN October 6, 1885, with the spelling corrected July 30, 1908. Named to honor W. F. Shellman who contributed generously for the academic institute.

SHELTONVILLE, Forsyth County. The post office was established here October 27, 1848, with the first postmaster being Vardy B. Shelton. The name of the community was later changed to SHAKERAG (q.v.).

SHENANDOAH, Coweta County. Established at a site east of Newnan in 1971. The idea for this planned city of 70,000 (by the year 1993) was conceived in 1969 by developer Scott Hudgens of Atlanta. Mrs. Douglas Wilson of Senoia submitted the name which was selected from over 1,000 entries. For this she was given $5,000 by Hudgens. *Shenandoah* is an Algonquian Indian word meaning "spruce-stream."

SHEPERDS (Militia) DISTRICT, Morgan County. Located in the lower section of the county, and named for early landowner here, Carter Shepherd (*sic*).

SHEPHERD, Coffee County. Located six miles northeast of Douglas. The name was adopted because of this being a center of sheep raising and wool carding. The community here is now known as HUFFER.

SHERRILL'S FORT, Richmond County. Established in 1751 by Quaker families who abandoned the settlement because of Indian attacks. The settlers returned in January 1774 under the leadership of Sherrill, and built a fort. While it was under construction, the Indians attacked, killing some of the settlers including Sherrill, and set the fort aflame.

SHILOH, Harris County. Incorporated as a city February 14, 1961. This name was taken from the Shiloh Baptist Church here. It is of Biblical origin, from the city of Shiloh in Ephraim, north of Bethel. There is also a SHILOH (Militia) DISTRICT, located in Lowndes County, below Salem District.

SHINBONE RIDGE, Chattooga County. Located in the northwest section of the county. The name is in reference to the anatomy of a horse, as associated with nearby Horseleg Mountain.

SHINGLER, Worth County. Incorporated as a town August 16, 1912 to July 9, 1924. Derivation of the name of this community is unknown. It is located five miles northeast of Sylvester.

SHOAL CREEK, Newton County. An early

community named from the nearby stream, and centered around Shoal Creek Baptist Church. It is now known as PINE GROVE community.

SHOALS, Walton County. Formerly called HIGH SHOALS (q.v.).

SHOALS, Warren County. A rural community in the southwest section of the county, which was first called LEXINGTON. An industrialist named Colonel William Bird from Virginia settled here in 1794, and established what is believed to have been the first woolen mill and iron foundry in Georgia. The community was also called VILLAGE SHOALS and SHOALS OF OGEECHEE.

SHOOTING CREEK BALD, Towns County. Located in the northeast section of the county, this peak has an elevation of 4,317 feet. Named after Shooting Creek in North Carolina, which is derived from a translation of the Cherokee, *du-stagalan'yi,* "where it made a great noise."

SHORTER COLLEGE, Rome. Founded August 2, 1873 as CHEROKEE BAPTIST FEMALE COLLEGE by Colonel Alfred Shorter, his wife Martha Baldwin Shorter, and Luther Rice Gwaltney. The school opened October 6, 1873 with Gwaltney the first president. In 1876 the present name was adopted to honor Mr. and Mrs. Shorter.

SHOULDER, Hancock County. A former community, which was located nine miles northwest of Sparta. It took the name from its location on Shoulderbone Creek (q.v.).

SHOULDERBONE CREEK. Rises in lower Greene County and upper Hancock County, and empties into the Oconee River. Named in 1784, although the derivation is not known. A famous treaty was signed with the Creek Indians near the mouth of this stream, November 3, 1786, wherein all lands east of the Oconee River were ceded to the white men.

SIDNEY LANIER BRIDGE, Glynn County. Opened July 18, 1956. A one-mile long span where U. S. highway 17 leaps the confluence of the Brunswick and Turtle rivers. Named for Georgia-born poet, Sidney Lanier (*see* Lanier County). Ten people were killed November 7, 1972 when the ship *African Neptune* struck the span of the bridge, causing it to collapse.

SIDSHA' LIDSHA, Chattahoochee County. This was the name of a branch town of the Cusseta Indians. The name signifies, "Under Blackjack Trees."

SILCO, Camden County. This community in the western section of the county is located on the headwaters of the Crooked River. It is probably a coined name, but it also may be from the Creek word, *silkosi,* meaning "narrows" or "narrow place."

SILK HOPE, Chatham County. This early community was about five miles west of Savannah. It was named when the Georgia colony was first formed, reflecting aspirations of establishing a flourishing silk industry here.

SILLYCOOK MOUNTAIN, Habersham County. Located 11 miles northeast of Mount Yonah near the Rabun County line. The name is the white man's corruption of the Cherokee, *Saligugi,* which signifies, "turtle," because of the shape of the formation.

SILOAM, Greene County. The community was originally settled as SMYRNA in the early 1840's. At the request of the post office department that a new name be adopted, it was decided to use the Biblical name from the Tunnel of Siloam, used by Hezekiah in the defense of Jerusalem.

SILVER BLUFF. Located on the east side of the Savannah River opposite a place called Spanish Cut. The Spanish thought there was silver under Silver Bluff.

SILVER CITY, Forsyth County. Originally called TATUM (q.v.). The post office of Silver City existed seven miles north of Cumming from April 7, 1886 to June 22, 1907. It is believed the name was taken from one of the western mining towns.

SILVER CREEK, Floyd County. This community is five miles south of Rome, located on the stream called SILVER CREEK. The name of this stream was adopted because of the mining of silver in the vicinity.

SILVERTOWN, Upham County. Incorporated July 27, 1929 to February 21, 1958. Established as a company town by the B. F. Goodrich Company, which built one of the world's largest plants here for the production of tire cord. The town was given the trade name of the company. It was located above Thomaston, and annexed to that city in 1958.

SIMSTON (Militia) DISTRICT, Oglethorpe County. Located east of Lexington. Originally called SIMSTOWN for resident John Maze Sims.

SIMS TOWN, Oconee County. An early community located on Hog Mountain Road (q.v.) near the Barrow County line. It was named for the earliest settlers here who were called Sims.

SIMSVILLE, Carroll County. A former community located on the Little Talapoosa River, twelve miles north of Carrollton on Georgia highway 113. The place was named for the local pastor, Rev. S. T. Sims.

SINCLAIR, LAKE. Located on the borders of Baldwin, Hancock and Putnam counties. This 15,330-acre reservoir with a 420-mile shoreline was created by the 3,000-foot long SINCLAIR DAM on the Oconee River. Both the lake and dam are named in honor of the late Benjamin W. Sinclair, who served the Georgia Power Company for many years as manager of production.

SITTING BULL MOUNTAIN, Towns County. This is the middle summit of the Nantahala Mountains (q.v.), and its elevation is 5,046 feet. Named for the noted Indian chief, Sitting Bull (c. 1837-1890), medicine man of the Sioux Nation.

SITTINGDOWN CREEK. Also spelled SETTINGDOWN CREEK (q.v.).

SITTON('S) GULCH, Dade County. A picturesque canyon located on the west side of Lookout Mountain near Trenton. Named for Jacob Sitton (1807-1892), who got land here by lottery and established a mill. The name of SITTON'S GULCH STATE PARK here was changed to CLOUDLAND CANYON STATE PARK, December 11, 1953.

SIXES CREEK, Cherokee County. Named after the once noted Sixes Gold Mine of the 1830's, which was owned by Allen Lawhorn, and located about six miles southwest of Canton. The mine had been named after a former Cherokee village, SIXES OLD TOWN, and Goff said it was probably translated from the Cherokee word, *sutali,* meaning "six." The site of the mine is now covered by the waters of the Alatoona Reservoir.

SIX FLAGS OVER GEORGIA, Cobb County. Located west of Atlanta, just past the Chattahoochee River on Interstate 20. This 276-acre amusement park presents the discovery, founding and development of the State of Georgia, and was named from the fact that in past history, the following flags have flown over the state: Spanish, French, English, Georgia, Confederate and United States. The park boasts the world's largest and fastest roller coaster.

SIX MILE, Floyd County. The name of this community refers to its distance south of Rome on the Southern Railway. It was first called COURTESY.

SIX MILE CREEK, Forsyth County. *See* Two Mile Creek.

SKIDAWAY ISLAND, Chatham County. Located just south of Savannah. Oglethorpe had a fort built here in 1734 on the northeast point of the island. He sent ten families to colonize the area, but the settlement was soon deserted. Various spellings have been: SKIDWAY (1735), SKIDAWAY (1737, 1883), SKEEDWAY (1737), SKEDOWAY (1738), SKEEDOWAY (1740), SKEEDAWAY (1745), SKIDDOWAY (1749), SHIDOWAY (1767), and SKIDOWAY (1878). Not enough is known of the Yamacraw language to hazard a guess as to the meaning of Skidaway, assuming that it is of Indian origin. Brinkley says it is an Anglicized form of Scenawki, the wife of Tomochichi, for whom Oglethorpe named the island. It was reached only by boat until June 1971, when a causeway and highway bridge were completed. A bridge built here prior to the Civil War was destroyed about 1864. The 480-acre SKIDAWAY STATE PARK is now being developed. Also located on the island is SKIDAWAY INSTITUTE OF OCEANOGRAPHY, a unit of the Georgia University System. The SKIDAWAY RIVER lies on the island's western shore. *See also* Priests Landing.

SKIN(T) CHESTNUT, Douglas County. Early name of DOUGLASVILLE (q.v.). Mr. Young Vansant was the original settler who built a store here. This was said to have been an old Indian ground, where it is believed they stripped bark from a chestnut tree which stood at the site of the present Kirkley's Store.

SKITT MOUNTAIN, White County. With an elevation of 2,076 feet; it is located on the Hall County line. Derived from "skit," a form of humorous story, because of the wild stories and hoaxes told by miners here.

SKYUKA SPRING, Dade County. Located two miles west of Rock City Gardens. This water source was named for an old Cherokee chief, Skyuka (or Wyuca).

SKYWATER PARK, Dougherty County. An early name of RADIUM SPRINGS (q.v.).

SLABTOWN, Atlanta. Jonothan Norcross put up a sawmill on the site of present Decatur Street opposite Pratt Street. The place here was so named when Norcross gave slabs of wood to poor people for use in building cabins in the locality.

SLAUGHTER GAP, Union County. The name of the pass between SLAUGHTER MOUNTAIN and Blood Mountain. Located about 1½ miles southwest of Vogel State Park. The name was applied because of a legendary savage Indian war fought on this mountain, when the Cherokees are said to have defeated the Creek, who were encroaching on their territory.

SMARR, Monroe County. Community and post office located five miles southeast of Forsyth. Named for the Andrew Smarr family, prominent in the area for many years.

SMITH CREEK, White County. Located above Anna Ruby Falls. Named for the former Nathan Smith settlement.

SMITHFIELD, Carroll County. Joe Cobb said this was a settlement on the western section of the county, near the Alabama line. Named for the large number of Smith families residing here.

SMITHSONIA, Bibb County. A 280-acre development for the juvenile detention home, located just south of Herbert Smart Airport. Named in 1926 for juvenile court judge, Bridges Smith.

SMITHSONIA, Oglethorpe County. Incorporated as a town August 23, 1905. Named for Colonel James M. Smith (1839-1915), one of the three original councilmen.

SMITHVILLE, Lee County. Incorporated as a town April 18, 1863. Has also been known as RENWICK. Derivation of the name is not known.

SMYRNA, Cobb County. "The Jonquil City" Incorporated as a town August 23, 1872. The first community here was called NEAL DOW, in honor of a friend of Stephen H. Young, Western and Atlantic Railroad engineer. It was also called VARNER'S STATION. The present name was taken from the Smyrna Campground here, which name was taken from Smyrna, the ancient seaport of Asia

Minor, the birthplace of Homer. *See also* SILOAM, Greene County.

SNAKE NATION, Atlanta. A tenderloin district or settlement, so named as it consisted of criminal and immoral elements. It was sprawled along the old Whitehall Road (later Peters Street). The section was cleaned out in the early 1850's.

SNAKE NATION, Fannin County. A community located three miles south of the city of Blue Ridge. The name is derived from the old Cherokee Nation which had leaders such as Going Snake Speaker and Speckled Snake Chief.

SNAPFINGER CREEK, DeKalb County. An undocumented story relates that when DeKalb County was being surveyed, one of the surveyors tripped at the edge of an unnamed creek and broke his finger. Because he "snapped" his finger, the creek became known as Snapfinger Creek. Brinkley declares the name of the stream was adopted because it is a "branch" or "finger" of Snapping Shoals Creek. Union general, George Stoneman was involved in a skirmish by this stream July 27, 1864. The stream name has also been applied to the community of SNAPFINGER and also to SNAPFINGER ROAD in the South Decatur area.

SNAPPING SHOALS. Located on the South River east of McDonough. Rainer said the name was adopted because of the rapid current of the stream. Brinkley wrote that it was "named for an old Indian fishery where the fish could be pitched out or 'snapped' as they passed over the shallow shoals." A post office of SNAPPING SHOALS was established on the Newton County side of the river from 1850 to 1902, and the community here had a reported population of 200.

SNELLVILLE, Gwinnett County. Incorporated as a town August 20, 1923. Settled in the 1870's by two Londoners, Thomas Snell and James Sawyer. The first post office was named SNELL and opened in 1885.

SNOW SPRINGS, Dooly County. A community located three miles west of Unadilla. The name was expanded from an earlier designation of SNOW, so derived because of bubbling springs that washed over white sand around which the settlement was established.

SOAP CREEK, Cherokee County. Its original name was SOPE CREEK after a flows through Lincoln County into Clark Hill Reservoir.

SOAPSTONE RIDGE, Clayton, Fulton and DeKalb counties. Covers an area of approximately 25 square miles in a triangular shape. At least 450 million years old, it is predominently of metapyroxenite — a rock type which has been locally (but inaccurately) called soapstone. Indians quarried stone here about the time the pyramids were being built in Egypt.

SOCIAL CIRCLE, Walton County. Incorporated as a village December 22, 1832. The post office was transferred here from Sunup (q.v.) in 1900. The derivation of this name is not certain, but it was most likely transferred from a former Social Circle in Bulloch County, as shown on an 1818 map of Georgia. Goff related that local tradition held that it was named in the 1820's when a group who first gathered here to start a settlement, passed around a jug of spirits; they looked upon themselves as a happy social circle, and thereupon decided on this name. Brinkley claims it was, "Named for a rest station of the early overland drives where 'crackers' would swap stories and socialize while passing the jug."

SOCOHACHEE CREEK, Randolph Creek. Believed to be a tributary of Ichawaynochaway Creek, located east of Shellman. William Read wrote that the name is of Creek Indian origin, from *sukha,* "hog," and *hachi,* "creek."

SOCRATES, Monroe County. Candler and Evans record this former community which was located in the northwest section of the county on a branch of the Towaliga River. Named for the ancient Greek philosopher of Athens.

SOFKEE, Bibb County. A small community, ten miles south of the center of Macon, which was begun as a railroad junction point. The present name was shortened from its previous, TOBESOFKEE, which undoubtedly was taken from nearby Tobesofkee Creek (q.v.). There was also a community named SOFKEY near Cairo in Grady County on Sofkee Creek (q.v.).

SOFKEE CREEK, Grady County. Flows easterly to enter Tired Creek four miles south of Cairo. In an early survey of this region, the stream was labeled "SOFKA CR." The meaning is not certain, but may mean "Hominy

Cherokee chief called Old Sope, who once lived on this stream. It was later corrupted to Soap Creek. There is another SOAP CREEK in Cobb County, and also a SOAP CREEK which rises in eastern Wilkes County and Creek," or it may derive from the Indian word *sufki* or *soofka,* signifying "deep."

SOLDIER CAMP ISLAND, Charlton and Ware counties. Located about ten miles south of Camp Cornelia. Was used as a camping place during the Civil War for deserters from the army, and soldiers hunting for deserters.

SOLDIERS BRANCH, Telfair County. Brinkley says this was a camping spot for General Blackshear's troops in the War of 1812. The name of the stream was adopted after one of his soldiers died and was buried here.

SOMME. This was the name (of a French river) given by Ribault to the present SATILLA RIVER (q.v.).

SOPERTON, CS Treutlen County. "The Million Pine City" Incorporated as a town December 17, 1902. It is said to have been named for a Mr. Soper, construction engineer with the Macon, Dublin and Savannah Railroad. On March 31, 1933, the *Soperton News* printed its newspaper on pine-pulp paper for the first time of any newspaper in the United States.

SOQUE(E) RIVER. Rises in Habersham County and flows southwesterly into Lake Sidney Lanier in Hall County. Its name was taken from a former Cherokee town of SOQUE or SAKWIYI, which was located eleven miles northwest of Clarkesville on the Soque River.

SOULE, A. CHARLES, BRIDGE, Gilmer County. Spans the Cartecay River at the city limits east of Ellijay. Named March 25, 1958 in honor of former Mayor Soule of Ellijay.

SOUTH END POINT, Chatham County. A descriptive designation that was given to the site on Wilmington Island (q.v.) where remnants of Confederate breastworks can still be seen.

SOUTHER FIELD, Americus (q.v.). Named in honor of Major Henry Souther, who was a noted aviation engineer during World War II.

SOUTHERN SCHOOL OF PHARMACY, Atlanta. Opened in 1903 as an independent college by Dr. R. C. Hood, Dr. Edward

Everhart and Dr. Hansell Crenshaw. A board of trustees assumed control of the school in 1938, then in July 1959 it was merged with Mercer University (q.v.).

SOUTHERN TECHNICAL INSTITUTE, Marietta. Established in 1948 at Chamblee as the TECHNICAL INSTITUTE. The name was changed to the present in 1949, and moved to its Marietta location in 1961. It is now a branch of Georgia Institute of Technology (q.v.).

SOUTH GEORGIA COLLEGE, Douglas. The first state-supported Junior College in Georgia. Established in 1906 as the ELEVENTH DISTRICT AGRICULTURAL AND MECHANICAL SCHOOL. In 1927 the present name was adopted. It came under the State University System in 1932. PETERSON HALL (1908) was named for Benjah Peterson of Douglas who gave the original 300 acres of land for the college. DAVIS HALL (1908) was named for Charles Wesley Davis, first principal of the school, and POWELL HALL (1908) for Josiah W. Powell, the second principal. FRASER HALL was named for Charles West Fraser, the third principal.

SOUTH NEWPORT, McIntosh County. A community located 19 miles north of Darien on the SOUTH NEWPORT RIVER. The name is believed to be derived from Newport, Rhode Island.

SOUTH RIVER. Flows out of underground springs in downtown Atlanta, and runs easterly to Jackson Lake. In early days it was known as SOUTH BRANCH, OCMULGEE RIVER before the name was shortened to "South River."

SOUTH ROME, Floyd County. Incorporated as a town February 20, 1874, and incorporated into Rome October 24, 1889.

SOWHATCHEE RIVER, Early County. Pronounced locally, "Sye hatchy." Flows southerly from below Blakely to the Chattahoochee River. Originally called SAWNOOK HATCHIE. Goff says that the name is of Muskogean origin, meaning "mad river." However Read claims it is from the Hitchiti, *sawi,* "raccoon," and *hatchi,* "creek." There was formerly a community with a post office called SOWHATCHEE, located two miles east of Hilton (q.v.).

SPALDING, Macon County. Incorporated

as a town from March 16, 1869 to March 21, 1958. This community is located just east of Montezuma.

SPALDING COUNTY. Created December 20, 1851 with 201 square miles taken from Fayette, Henry and Pike counties. Named for Thomas Spalding (1774-1851), who was born at Frederica, and purchased Sapelo Island (q.v.) where he was a prominent planter. Spalding was also an early political leader, and a member of the Constitutional Convention of 1798. The county seat is Griffin (q.v.). This county's first clerk of court was Major Henry B. Holliday, father of the notorious gunman of Texas, John Henry "Doc" Holliday.

SPANIARD MOUNTAIN, Towns County. With an altitude of 3,786 feet, it is located six miles south of Hiwasee. Brinkley attributes the name to the legendary explorations into north Georgia by Juan Pardo in 1566, as directed by Menendez.

SPANISH CREEK, Charlton County. Flows southerly to enter the St. Marys River below Folkston. Named for a Seminole Indian called Spanish John, who lived in this vicinity.

SPARKS, Cook County. Incorporated as a town December 26, 1888. The original community here was called AFTON. In the 1880's, when the Georgia Southern & Florida Railroad was built through here from Macon to Jacksonville, Florida, the people of Afton decided to re-name the place for a Mr. Sparks, who was the railroad division president. Brinkley said it was named for Sparks Hunter, an early settler of the 1820's. In later years at the nearby town of Adel, a saying came into being to the effect that "Adel is so close to Hell you can see Sparks."

SPARTA, CS Hancock County. Established in 1795, made the seat of justice in 1797, and incorporated as a town December 3, 1805. Was named by its founder, Major Charles Ambercrombie, Revolutionary soldier from North Carolina. The original old world Sparta was a famous classical Greek city state. This new world Sparta, along with Athens (q.v.), helped inspire Georgia's Greek revival.

SPELMAN COLLEGE, Atlanta. Founded in 1881 by Misses Sophia B. Packard and Harriet E. Giles of the Women's American Baptist Home Mission Society of Boston. It was originally called ATLANTA BAPTIST FEMALE SEMINARY, and was the first college ever established for black women students. The name was changed to SPELMAN SEMINARY in 1884 in honor of Mrs. Harvey Buel Spelman, mother of the school's benefactor, John D. Rockefeller of New York. This is now one of five colleges that make up the Atlanta University Center (q.v.). The education building was built in 1886 and named ROCKEFELLER HALL, as this was the first major gift of John D. Rockefeller to education. SISTERS CHAPEL was dedicated in 1935, and was named to honor Rockefeller's mother and aunt. The FLORENCE MATILDA READ HEALTH AND RECREATION BUILDING was dedicated in 1951, and named in honor of Miss Read, who served as president of the college from 1927 to 1953.

SPEWRELL BLUFF, Upson County. Overlooking the Flint River about eight miles west of Thomaston. Named for Jeptha Sprewell, an early settler of upper Talbot County. SPEWRELL BLUFF PARK was established nearby on Old Alabama Road. Efforts to establish a "Spewrell Bluff Dam" on the Flint River were defeated by the state assembly in February 1974. *See also* SPREWELL BLUFF.

SPIERS TURNOUT, Jefferson County. Has also been recorded as SPEAR'S TURN OUT. Established in the 1850's, this was the original name of the present town of BARTOW (q.v.). It was named for William Spier who had kept a commisary for railroad hands here.

SPIVEY, LAKE, Clayton and Henry counties. A 550-acre private lake located east of Jonesboro. Claims to have the world's largest man-made beach. Was formerly owned by Dr. Walter B. Spivey.

SPOIL CANE CREEK, White County. Goff explained that this name evolved from the original surveyor's naming this stream,

SPOIL'D CANE CREEK (1820), somehow related to the use of cane as a forage plant. From the edge of Georgia highway 75, just short of Unicoi Gap, one can look down on the very head of Spoil Cane Creek.

SPREAD, Jefferson County. Incorporated as a town August 15, 1903. The post office here was first known as SPREAD OAK, and later shortened to "Spread." The name of the town was changed to STAPLETON (q.v.) August 17, 1917.

SPREWELL BLUFF, Upson County. By executive order in early March 1974, Governor Jimmy Carter corrected the spelling from its former name, SPEWRELL BLUFF (q.v.).

SPRING BLUFF, Camden County. This bluff is located near U. S. highway 17 on the south side of the Little Satilla River. Goff said that it had this name for over 200 years, and it refers to the mineral spring three miles to the east.

SPRING CREEK. Rises in southeast Clay County and flows through Early and Miller counties, thence down near the western boundary of Decatur County into Lake Seminole. Named for the artesian springs at its source.

SPRINGER MOUNTAIN. Located at the juncture of Dawson, Fannin and Lumpkin counties. Its elevation is 3,782 feet, and it is the southern terminus of the Appalachian Trail (q.v.). The peak is about one mile north of the Dawson County line. It was previously known as PENENTIARY MOUNTAIN (q.v.). Derivation is not certain, but may be named for John Springer, the first Presbyterian minister to be ordained in Georgia, July 22, 1790. The name was officially approved in 1959 by the Georgia Appalachian Trail Club. If this was a later designation, it was most likely for William G. Springer, an early settler of Carroll County who was appointed (c. 1833) by Governor Lumpkin to implement legislation to improve conditions for the Indians.

SPRINGFIELD AT POWDER SPRINGS, Cobb County. An early name of the town of POWDER SPRINGS (q.v.).

SPRINGFIELD, CS Effingham County. Founded in 1799 and incorporated as a town December 31, 1838. Thought to have been named for the plantation of General David Blackshear (*see also* Blackshear). The original county seat was at Tuckasee-King (q.v.).

SPRING HILL, Chatham County. This section of Savannah was descriptively named as it was the site of some never failing springs of water.

SPRING PLACE, Murray County. Designated the county seat in 1834 and incorporated as a town October 9, 1885. The original settlement was called POINSET (q.v.), but it was later renamed for the former Spring Place Mission (q.v.), which was located southwest of the present town. The county seat was moved to Chatsworth in 1913. Nearby stands the home of the former Cherokee Indian chief, Joseph Vann, who was a wealthy plantation owner (*see also* Vann).

SPRING PLACE MISSION, Murray County. Located southwest of the town of Spring Place (q.v.). Founded in 1801 by Moravian Brethren from Salem, North Carolina, and was the first school among the Cherokees. It was named for a noted spring in the locality, which had made this a famous resort of the Indians.

SPRINGVALE, Randolph County. A commendatory name for a community located eight miles northwest of Cuthbert. Was incorporated as a village October 25, 1870.

STALKINGHEAD CREEK, Jasper and Jones counties. Rises about five miles south of Monticello and flows southward to enter Little Falling Creek in northwest Jones County. Derivation is the same as for Stocking Head Branch (q.v.).

STALLINGS ISLAND, Columbia County. Located eight miles northwest of Augusta in the Savannah River. Was also known as INDIAN ISLAND. Found here is one of the most important shell mound sites in the Southeast, with pottery from a period prior to 1700 B.C. The name is believed to be from that of an early owner of the island.

STAMP CREEK, Bartow County. Rises in western Cherokee County and flows southward into Allatoona Lake. Originally known as LICK CREEK in the state surveys of 1832. A lick or stamp was an area in which cattle were fed, and they stamped their feet while licking salt or feeding.

STANDING BOY CREEK. Rises in lower Harris County and flows into upper Muscogee County, entering the Chattahoochee above Columbus. The Indian spellings were CHUCETHLOCCO, CHUSSETHLUCCO and HATCHAUXA, which do not translate directly. Goff said, that properly spelled to mean "Standing Boy Creek," it should have been written, *Chiponusihuili.* The stream is now called HEIFERHORN CREEK (q.v.).

STANDING PEACHTREE, Fulton County. Was located on both sides of the Chattahoochee River at the mouth of Peachtree Creek. This name is an English translation of the Indian name for the Creek Indian village, PAKANAHUILI. James Montgomery was the postmaster of the early community here (*see* Montgomery Ferry Road). *See also* Peachtree Street.

STANFORDVILLE, Putnam County. *See* DEVIL'S HALF ACRE.

STANLEY CREEK, Fannin County. Flows into the Toccoa River about six miles southeast of Blue Ridge. Brinkley says it was named for the John Stanley rest station of 1818.

STAPLETON, Jefferson County. Was called SPREAD (q.v.) when it was incorporated August 15, 1903. The present name is in honor of a Colonel James Stapleton.

STARKVILLE, Lee County. Incorporated and designated the county seat December 26, 1852. Was located on the west side of Muckalee Creek, several miles to the eastward of present Leesburg (on the east side of the creek was a Chehaw Indian town). Named in honor of Major General John Stark (1728-1822) of Revolutionary War fame. The county seat was moved to Leesburg in 1872, after which this eventually became a dead town.

STARRSVILLE, Newton County. A community located six miles southeast of Covington, on Georgia highway 213. Settled in 1820-21 by the Starr and Epps families. Named for Silas H. Starr, Sr., popular state legislator.

STATE LINE, Heard County. An early community which was located at or near the present community of Waresville. It was descriptively named regarding its location on the Alabama state line. This same name has also been applied to the community of Red Clay (q.v.), Whitfield County.

STATENVILLE, CS Echols County. Incorporated as the town of STATESVILLE (q.v.) December 13, 1859. It was known as TROUBLESOME until 1858 when this tative in the Georgia legislature from Clinch County (from which Echols County was formed). It is located within the STATEN-VILLE (Militia) DISTRICT.

STATESBORO, CS Bulloch County. "The Tourist City." In 1803 it was decided that the county seat would be "Statesborough" but there was no record of a town by the name of Statesboro until 1805. Was incorporated as a town and designated the county seat December 20, 1866. This is the only Statesboro in the United States, and no doubt was named for the State of Georgia.

STATESVILLE, Echols County. The name by which STATENVILLE (q.v.) was formerly designated, and is the name by which it is now popularly known.

STATHAM, Barrow County. Pronounced "Stattum." Incorporated as a town from December 20, 1892 to December 6, 1902. In 1846 it was called BARBERS CREEK, after the nearby stream. The name was changed to DELAY in 1854, and the present name was adopted in 1892, in honor of Dr. Charles Statham, chancellor of the University of Georgia.

STAUNTON, Dade County. A former community located just south of Rising Fawn. The post office here was called HANNA. The station was named for a Mr. Staunton who built the Alabama Great Southern Railroad through here.

STEADMAN, Newton County. Incorporated as a town February 21, 1866, so that Enoch Steadman would be enabled to build a large manufacturing establishment on the falls of the Yellow River known as Henry Shoals. On this site is today's town of PORTERDALE (q.v.).

STEADMAN ISLAND, Chatham County. Located in the Little Ogeechee River south of Savannah. Believed to have been named for its early occupants.

STEAM MILL, Seminole County. Located near the Chattahoochee River, eight miles southwest of Donalsonville. This little community was given its name when there were steam-operated cotton gins and grist mills here. It was also known as DICKERSON'S STORE, with this name from storeowner S. H. Dickerson.

STEARNESVILLE, Pike County. Named for John T. Stearnes who operated a general

became the county seat. On April 1, 1965, the town of Statesville was re-incorporated as the town of Statenville. Named for Captain James W. Staten, who was the first representative store here. This was an early name of WILLIAMSON (q.v.)

STEKOA CREEK, Rabun County. Flows from Clayton northeasterly to the Chattooga River. The name is a misspelling of STICOA, an early Cherokee village.

STELLAVILLE, Jefferson County. Incorporated as a town September 11, 1891. This community was first established in 1817 as a Baptist church called DARCY'S MEETING HOUSE, and then later changed to WAYS CHURCH, for a Mr. William Way. It was called SISTERVILLE until 1871, when it adopted its present name after Stella Brinson, the daughter of John Brinson.

STEPHEN C. FOSTER STATE PARK, Charlton County. This 80-acre park is located on Jones Island in Okefenokee Swamp, and is on the Suwannee River, 18 miles northeast of Fargo. Named for Stephen Collins Foster (1826-1864) of Pittsburgh who wrote *Old Folks at Home* (1851), also known as *Swanee River*.

STEPHENS, Oglethorpe County. Community located eight miles southwest of Lexington. Originally called ANTIOCH or AN-TIOCH DEPOT, after the local Baptist church. Later named for Alexander H. Stephens (*see* Stephens County).

STEPHENS COUNTY. Created August 18, 1905 with 180 square miles taken from Franklin and Habersham counties. Named in honor of Alexander Hamilton "Little Alec" Stephens (1812-1883), who opposed secession, but was made vice president of the Confederacy. He was selected governor of Georgia shortly before he died. The county seat is Toccoa (q.v.).

STEPHENS MEMORIAL STATE PARK. *See* ALEXANDER H. STEPHENS STATE PARK.

STERLING CREEK, Bryan County. Enters the Ogeechee River two miles below Richmond Hill. Named for two Scotch brothers, William and Hugh Sterling, who in 1734 received a grant of 500 acres in this area from General Oglethorpe. They left after being refused permission to introduce slaves.

STEVENS POTTERY, Baldwin County. Community located nine miles southwest of Milledgeville, which was sometimes called WHITING. Established in 1858 by Henry Stevens (1813-1883) who came to America in 1831 from County Cornwall, England. He built and operated a clay manufacturing plant here which was burned to the ground by General Sherman's soldiers. A post office was later established here in 1870.

STEWART ARMY AIR FIELD. *See* Camp Stewart.

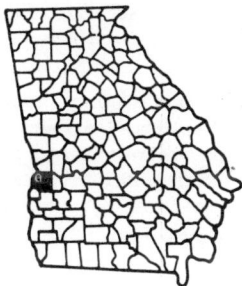

STEWART COUNTY. Created December 23, 1830 with 463 square miles taken from part of Randolph County. Named for General Daniel Stewart (1759-1829), scion of the famous Midway settlement, who served in the Revolutionary War and the War of 1812. The county seat is Lumpkin (q.v.). The court house was destroyed by fire in 1922.

STICOA, Rabun County. A former Cherokee town. *See* Stekoa Creek.

STILESBORO(UGH), Bartow County. Incorporated March 21, 1866. This community located eight miles southwest of Cartersville was named for William H. Stiles who settled here in 1838.

STILLMORE, Emanuel County. The community of KEA'S MILL (q.v.) was here originally. When the town was first established, the U. S. Post Office authorities sent a list of names to choose from, and also indicated that if none were acceptable they would send "still more." So this last suggestion was used for the name of the post office.

STINK CREEK, Union County. Rises near the White County line and flows northwesterly into Nottely Lake. This name is a literal translation of the Cherokee word *sunga,* which referred to a strong offensive odor, such as found with wild onions.

STINSON, Meriwether County. First named for early settler Dr. James Winslow Stinson, the community is now called DURAND (q.v.).

STITCHIHATCHIE CREEK, Laurens County. Rises west of Dexter and flows northeasterly into Rocky Creek. Read wrote that, "The first part of this name probably means *Indian,* from Creek isti *man* and chati *red.* The second part is from Creek hachi *creek.*" Goff on the other hand said it is a garbled form of the earlier name TICKEHACHEE, meaning "Crossing Creek" or "Fording Creek."

STOCKBRIDGE, Henry County. Incorporated as a town in 1895 and as a city August 6, 1920. First established in 1882 as a railroad stop. Vessie Rainer said it was named after a Professor Stockbridge who taught school here before the war at what is now known as OLD STOCKBRIDGE, which is on the north edge of the present town. Brinkley wrote that it was, "Settled in the 1820's and named for Thomas Stock, State Surveyor and later President of the Georgia Senate."

STOCKING (or STOCKIN') CREEK, Burke County. Arises a mile or so to the northeast of St. Clair and flows northerly to join Bushy Creek. The name is a shortened variation of the original name, STALKING HEAD BRANCH (*see* Stocking Head Branch).

STOCKING HEAD BRANCH, Candler County. Flows southerly to enter Fifteen Mile Creek on the northeast edge of Metter. Goff said that the name is in reference to a camouflage of a deer head worn by Indian hunters when stalking their prey. In Jasper and Jones counties there is a similarly named Stalking Head Creek (q.v.). *See also* Stocking Creek.

STOCKTON, Clinch County. Incorporated as a town February 28, 1876. This community changed its name from REGISTERVILLE (q.v.) to honor a Mr. Stockton, who was in charge of grading for the railroad through here.

STONE HOUSE SHOALS, Putnam County. Located on Murder Creek at Resseaus Crossroads. The name is a translation of the Creek Indian word *Chattochookohatchie,* which means "Stone House Creek."

STONE MOUNTAIN, DeKalb County. This descriptive name is given to the largest exposed granite rock in the world, which is 650 feet high and two miles long. It is located sixteen miles east of Atlanta. The Indians had called it LONE MOUNTAIN or CRYSTAL MOUNTAIN, and the white men later named it ROCK MOUNTAIN or ROCK FORT MOUNTAIN, and sometimes NEW GIBRALTER (q.v.). A town called STONE MOUNTAIN was established here, with a post office which opened July 18, 1834. It was incorporated as New Gibralter in 1839, with the name being changed to Stone Mountain, December 24, 1847. In 1885 there was some agitation to move the county seat of DeKalb County here from Decatur. This dispute came to a head in 1896 and 1897, which resulted in an election in which Stone Mountain won a majority vote, but not the required two-thirds. The 3,000-acre STONE MOUNTAIN PARK is located on the east edge of the town of Stone Mountain (and encompasses the mountain). It was dedicated to Confederate soldiers and sailors.

STONE PILE GAP, Lumpkin County. *See* TRAHLYTA'S CAIRN.

STONEWALL, Fulton County. Located five miles northeast of Fairburn. It was incorporated as a town August 18, 1911. Believed to have been named after the nickname of Confederate general, Thomas Jonothan "Stonewall" Jackson (1824-1863).

STORY, LUTHER, BRIDGE. Spans the Flint River on Georgia highway 27 between Americus and Vienna. Named March 10, 1959 in honor of Luther Story of Sumter County, who was posthumously awarded the Congressional Medal of Honor for heroism in the Korean conflict.

STRAIGHT GUT VALLEY, Walker County. A descriptive name for this beautiful valley; the word "gut" refers to a channel or stream.

STRIBLING LAKE, Jones County. A seven-acre lake located at the Macon YMCA Camp on Highway 18. Named in 1972 in honor of W. L. "Young" Stribling who died in October 1933. *See also* Macon, Stribling Memorial Bridge.

STROUD(S), Monroe County. Located five miles northeast of Culloden. This community was originally called STROUD CROSSROADS, named for the first settlers of the community, Levi Stroud Sr. and his wife Frances, who arrived here about 1830.

STUBBS, Mitchell County. A former community which was located in the southwest corner of the county. Named for the mill of John Stubbs.

STUCKEY, Wheeler County. A community located 7½ miles southwest of Mount Vernon. Believed named for early postmaster H. T. Stuckey who had a general store here, when this was part of Montgomery County.

STYX, RIVER. See RIVER STYX.

SUBLIGNA, Chattooga County. Incorporated October 28, 1870. A community located on Taylor Ridge (q.v.) named by a Dr. Underwood for himself. This is a Latinized form of his name, from *sub,* "under," and *ligna,* "wood."

SUCHES, Union County. Pronounced to rhyme with "touches." Located 18 miles north of Dahlonega, this community is over 75 years old, and may be derived from a family name.

SUGAR CREEK, Fannin County. Located two miles west of Blue Ridge. The name is derived from an earlier Cherokee Indian village called KULSE' TSI, meaning "sweet place," which was named from the honey locust.

SUGAR HILL, Gwinnett County. Incorporated as a town March 24, 1939. The origin of this name is not known. There is also a community of SUGAR HILL in Hall County, located near Gainesville.

SUGAR VALLEY, Gordon County. The post office was established here by Elias King in 1849, and the town was incorporated October 24, 1887. This community is located a few miles south of Resaca. Four different explanations have been offered as to the origin of the name: 1. It was said to have been covered with sugar maples when first settled to account for the name. 2. Pioneer John Bough named it in 1831, because it was the sweetest valley he had ever seen. 3. Brinkley reports that it was named for the Cherokee Indian called Su-A-Ga who settled in the area under the protection of the treaty of 1817. 4. Orrin Davis introduced sugar cane here and it became SWEET VALLEY then Sugar Valley.

SULENOJUHNENE FORD, Crawford-Taylor counties. Located about one-half mile above Islands Ford (q.v.). There was another Sulenojuhnene fording place upstream from the U. S. 80 bridge. This Creek Indian word means "Buzzard Roost Trail," although it was here used to designate a ford on the Flint River. It was used as a crossing of a branch trail of Toms Path (q.v.).

SULPHUR SPRINGS, Hall County. This was a descriptive name given to this once celebrated resort, located six miles northeast of Gainesville. It was also called OCONEE WHITE SULPHUR SPRINGS or WHITE SULPHUR SPRINGS (q.v.). There is also a rural community in Dade County called SULPHUR SPRINGS, located 13 miles south of Trenton on the Southern Railway.

SUMACH, Murray County. Community located ten miles north of Spring Place on SUMACH CREEK, which is a tributary of the Conasauga River. Sumach is a translation from the Cherokee, which they called *Qual-la-kia-ica-ie,* and this name was adopted by them because of the sumac trees or shrubs found in the area. Hawkins translated it on to maps as SHEWMAKE or SHOEMAK.

SUMMERTOWN, Emanuel County. Incorporated as a town August 21, 1906. Community located ten miles northeast of Swainsboro on Georgia 56. The name was adopted as residents established summer homes here to flee the mosquitos along the Ogeechee River.

SUMMERVILLE, CS Chattooga County. "City of Young Men" Incorporated as a town and designated the county seat December 21, 1839. The origin of the name is uncertain, but is thought to have been named because of its picturesque environment in a beautiful mountain valley.

SUMMERVILLE, Richmond County. Incorporated as a village December 16, 1861, and 50 years later was incorporated into the city of Augusta. It is now a suburban area of that city known as THE HILL. It was believed given the original name by its early residents who included many distinguished families, such as Hugh Nesbit and

John Milledge, because of its unusual advantages for summer residence.

SUMMIT, Emmanuel County. Incorporated as a town April 23, 1898. This descriptively named community was combined with Graymont in 1924 to create TWIN CITY.

SUMNER, Worth County. Incorporated August 9, 1883. This community was once also known as ALFORD. The first settlement here was on land belonging to John C. "Jack" Sumner, and the place was named for him. It was certainly *not* named for the ardent anti-slavery spokesman from Boston, Senator Charles Sumner!

SUMPTERVILLE, Laurens County. In 1807 this became the first county seat of Laurens County. It was located on the west side of the Oconee River on Turkey Creek, eight miles from the present county seat of Dublin. The derivation of this name is not known.

SUMTER COUNTY. Created December 26, 1831 with 485 square miles taken from part of Lee County. Named for Major General Thomas Sumter (1734-1832) of Revolutionary War distinction, who was born in Virginia and died in South Carolina. He was given the nickname "Fighting Gamecock" by the British. The county seat is Americus (q.v.). *See also* Andersonville. There is also a community named SUMTER in the lower section of the county.

SUNBURY, Liberty County. Incorporated December 8, 1791, the town government continued to function to about 1825. This dead town was one of the early settlements of Georgia. Located on the south side of the Midway River at the site of restored Fort Morris (q.v.). It was believed to have been named for Sunbury on the Thames River in

Middlesex County, England, or possibly for its sunny location on the banks of the Midway River. First settled in 1752 by the families of Benjamin and Samuel Baker of South Carolina, the community was established June 20, 1758. It became a point of entry in 1761, soon rivalling Savannah as a port. The post office served about half a century until discontinued December 8, 1841. This was the home of Governor Lyman Hall, a signer of the Declaration of Independence. Several factors caused the town's demise, but the coup de grace was delivered by one of Sherman's divisions in 1864. SUNBURY ACADEMY was authorized in February 1788 and established in 1793, after which it existed for over forty years. Located in King's Square in Sunbury, this was for many years the most famous school in South Georgia. SUNBURY CHANNEL is the designation of the harbor lying between the bluff at Sunbury and a small island. SUNBURRY CREEK, also in Liberty County, is a tidal stream located several miles downriver from the site of Sunbury. (OLD) SUNBURY ROAD was laid out about 1792, at which time it was the longest vehicular route of post-Revolutionary Georgia. It extended from Sunbury to Greensboro in Greene County, and was variously called, SUNDBURY, LUNSBURY, SUNBERRY, SUNSBURG and SUNS-BERRY Road.

SUNDALHATCHEE CREEK, Heard County. This stream is now called CENTRALHATCHEE CREEK (q.v.). William Read wrote, "Sundalhatchee may have been altered from Creek sandalakwa, *perch* (a fish) and hachi *creek.* Folk etymology must be responsoble for the change of Sundal to Central."

SUNHILL, Washington County. A commendatory name given this community when it became a station on the Central of Georgia Railroad, four miles east of Tennille. There was once an early community called SUNNY DALE, six miles west of Summerville in Chattooga County, where there is today a SUN-NYDALE ROAD. And another commendatorily named community of SUNNYSIDE in Spalding County is located on the Central of Georgia Railroad, near the Henry County line. It was incorporated December 20, 1897.

SUNSWEET, Tift County. Formerly known as CYCLONETA (q.v.), Brinkley said it was first known as LITTLE PENNSYLVANIA by the Pennsylvania investors who reclaimed the cotton lands here. A bountiful peach crop of 1894 led to the Sunsweet name which is still in use in the fruit industry.

SUNUP, Walton County. A post office which was established in 1887 and transferred to Social Circle in 1900.

SUOMI, Dodge County. Pronounced "Sue oh' mee." Community located in the eastern part of the county just east of Chauncey. This was the native and official name of Finland, and the name was first applied to the railroad siding or station, perhaps by early lumbermen for their homeland.

SURRENCY, CS Appling County. Incorporated as a town August 21, 1911. Named for Millard Surrency, an early settler of Hazelhurst, Jeff Davis County.

SURREY, Tift County. The early name of OMEGA, it was named from the county in England.

SUTALLE, Cherokee County. Community located eight miles west of Canton. Was also spelled SUTTALLEE. The name is a translation of *Sutali,* an Indian word referring to six or sixes, a Cherokee settlement.

SUTHERLANDS BLUFF, McIntosh County. Overlooks the Sapelo River about 1½ miles south of Shellman Bluff. Named for Lieutenant Patrick Sutherland, who was granted this property on the recommendation of General Oglethorpe, in recognition of Sutherland's service in the Battle of Bloody Marsh.

SUWANEE, Gwinnett County. Incorporated February 25, 1949. A community in the northwest section of the county. Established in 1871, when what is now the Southern Railroad was put through here. The name is taken from a former Cherokee Indian village of SUWANNEE OLD TOWN, a short distance to the west, which had earlier been called SUWANI. The Cherokees said the name was of Muskogean origin, possibly meaning "echo," or may have been named for the Shawnee Indians. *See also* Suwannee River.

SUWANEE CREEK. Rises in southwest Hall County and flows southwesterly through the town of Suwanee (q.v.) in Gwinnett County, and then enters the Chattahoochee River.

SUWANNEE RIVER. Commences in the Okefenokee Swamp (q.v.), flows through Clinch and Echols counties, and runs down through Florida to the Gulf of Mexico. When the Spaniards with DeSota first crossed this river, they called it RIO DE VENADO, or "River of the Deer," which has no connection with its present name. Its name is derived from a former Seminole village on its banks, which took its name from a Cherokee settlement of SUWANI, which was in what is now Gwinnett County (see Suwanee). The river had also been called LITTLE SAINT JOHN(S), LITTLE SAN JUAN or SAN JUANITO (pronounced "Wah-nee'toe"), which some have suggested was corrupted to Suwannee. Another theory is that the name is attributed to a noble chieftainess, Su-wan-nee, who ruled over the Seminoles in early times. See also Stephen C. Foster State Park.

SUWANOOCHE CREEK. A tributary of the Suwannee River, that rises in Clinch County, and flows southeasterly to join the mother river in Echols County.

SWAINSBORO, CS Emanuel County. "Pine Tree Country." Also called "Crossroads of the South," as U. S. highways 1 and 80 cross here. Established as the county seat February 18, 1854 when the name of the town was changed from Swainsboro to PARIS. Was incorporated again as the town of Swainsboro December 22, 1857. Named for Colonel Stephen Swain of the state legislature.

SWAMP CREEK, Decatur County. Rises along the west border of Grady County, flows southwesterly into Decatur County, thence into Florida to enter Attapulgus Creek. Descriptively named for the swampy region through which it flows.

SWAN (TOWN), Ben Hill County. Settled by the Drew brothers of North Carolina, who named the village after the steamship *Swan,* which had originally brought them up the Altamaha-Ocmulgee River from Darien. The land here was purchased in 1895 by the American Tribune Soldier Colony Co. which established the present city of FITZGERALD (q.v.).

SWEDEN, Pickens County. A former community which was located eight miles west of Talking Rock, at the northwest section of the county. Its name is from the Scandanavian country.

SWEET GUM, Fannin County. A rural community located near the North Carolina line. Named for the deciduous tree, Sweet Gum, which was found in abundance here.

SWEETWATER. This place-name is frequently used to identify a source of potable water, and may sometimes be a direct translation from the Spanish term, *agua dulce.* A former community named SWEETWATER in Gwinnett County was located seven miles northwest from Lawrenceville. In McDuffie County, SWEETWATER was the name of a post office which was established December 21, 1826. It was named from the nearby stream called SWEETWATER CREEK. SWEETWATER BRANCH in Camden County flows easterly along the northern edge of St. Marys' airport to the North River. SWEETWATER CREEK in northeast Crawford County, according to Goff, was one of the oldest recorded names of interior Georgia (1775). Another SWEETWATER CREEK rises in northeast Douglas County. It flows through Paulding and Cobb Counties, returning to Douglas County where it enters the Chattahoochee River. The 35-mile stream is named after a Cherokee Indian chief, AmaKanasta, or Chief Sweet Water. Named also for this chief was SWEETWATER TOWN on the aforementioned creek, in the vicinity of the present Austell in Cobb County (see Factory Shoals). And lastly, a SWEETWATER CREEK rises south of Andersonville, then forms the border between Macon and Sumter counties before entering the Flint River. Legend relates that the name is derived from an accident in which a barrel of homemade cane syrup tumbled into this stream, in the last days of the Civil War.

SWIFT'S LITHIA SPRING, Elbert County. Believed to have been located in the southern part of the county. Named for I. G. Swift who purchased the spring in 1806 from Mrs. Sallie L. Bell. An earlier name for this once noted watering place was POWDER SPRING.

SWORDS, Morgan County. A rural community located 3½ miles east of Buckhead. Incorporated as a town August 16, 1909. Previously called BLUE SPRING, it was named after John Buchanan Swords (?-1940) who settled here around 1889 to 1900, and was the greatest benefactor of the town.

SYCAMORE, Turner County. Incorporated as a town September 29, 1891 when this was in part of Irwin County. Named for the sycamore trees in the area.

SYLLSFORK, Oglethorpe County. This early community was located eleven miles southeast of Lexington, on SYLLSFORK CREEK from which it was named.

SYLVAN BOWER, Walker County. This name signifies a secluded (or wild) location. The post office department refused this name, so it was necessary to change the name of the place to BRONCO (q.v.). In Rabun County northwest of Clayton is found SYLVAN FALLS, at the north end of SYLVAN LAKE, which means "Wood Lake." SYLVAN GROVE was the name of an old community located in northwestern Jefferson County.

SYLVANIA, CS Screven County. "The Welcome Station City" Established as the county seat December 24, 1847. The post office was opened August 10, 1848, and the town was incorporated February 20, 1854. The name was suggested by Cuyler Young of Halcyondale (q.v.). *Sylvania* is a Latinized form for "Place in the Woods" or "Forest Land," suggestive of the Arcadian beauty of the woods here. The decision was made May 11, 1847 to transfer the county seat here from its previous location of Jacksonborough (q.v.). *See also* Round Oak.

SYLVESTER, CS Worth County. "Heart of Hunting Land" Laid out in 1893 and incorporated as a town December 21, 1898 to August 15, 1904. The original community here was called ISABELLA STATION (q.v.). The present name was adopted in 1894, with the derivation from the Latin words, *silva,* meaning "wood," and *vester,* meaning "your." Brinkley says the town was named for a pioneer family. *See also* WILLINGHAM.

T

TABANANA, Quitman County. The Tabanana Post Office was established January 10, 1833, named after TABANANA CREEK, now called TOBANNEE CREEK (q.v.). The name of the community was changed to GEORGETOWN (q.v.) September 21, 1836.

TAHOMA, Richmond County. Community located twelve miles south of downtown Augusta. The meaning is unknown, but the terminal element of the name is *homa,* Chickasaw-Choctaw for "red."

TAIL(S) CREEK, Gilmer County. Located in the eastern section of the county, it is a tributary of the Coosawattee River. The stream was named after some Indians called Tail who lived along its banks. Named for the stream was a former community of TAILS CREEK, located eight miles west of Ellijay.

TALAJE, Glynn County. The site of a 17th century mission established by the Spanish, SANTO DOMINGO DE TALAXE or SANTO DOMINGO AT TALAJE. E. Merton Coulter believes it was located on the western side of St. Simons Island. The region at the mouth of the Altamaha River (RIO DE TALAJE) was called TALAJE PROVINCE by the Spaniards. Domingo was the patron saint of the island, and *talaje* is a Spanish word meaning "pasturage" or "grazing."

TALAPAGEE CREEK, Stewart County. Flows southwesterly into Walter F. George Reservoir. A recent county map labels the stream, TALIPAHOGA RUM CREEK, and it is often called simply RUM CREEK. William Read wrote that the name means "Little Corncob Creek," from the Creek, *talapi,* "corncob." Goff said that it could also mean "grass water town" or "swamp water town," from the Muskogean, *taliwa pahi.*

TALASEE COLONY, Jackson County. Established in 1786, in what was then Franklin County, by a group of settlers from Effingham County, under the leadership of Richard Easley. The community was located on the north side of the Tishmaugu River (now Mulberry River) near Talasee Shoals (q.v.) from which it was named.

TALASEE SHOALS, Jackson County. Named for Talasee King who lived on the road from the shoals to Athens. *See also* Talasee Colony.

TALAXE, Glynn County. A variant of TALAJE (q.v.).

TALBOT COUNTY. Created December 14, 1827 with 390 square miles taken from part of Muscogee County. Named for Governor Mathew Talbot (1762-1827), who came to Georgia from an aristocratic family of Virginia, who had also served as president of the state senate. The county seat is Talbotton (q.v.). The court house was destroyed by fire in 1890.

TALBOTTON, CS Talbot County. Incorporated as a town and designated the county seat December 20, 1828. The first meeting of Georgia's supreme court was held January 26, 1846 in the dining room of the old Claiborne Hotel here. This city is where Bavarian refugee, Isadore Straus, started the merchandising career that led to his ultimate ownership of the R. H. Macy Company of New York City, which company now owns Davison's department stores in Georgia. *See also* Centerville, Talbot County.

TALIAFERRO COUNTY. Pronounced "Toliver" or "Tolaferro." Created December

24, 1825 with 195 square miles taken from parts of Greene, Hancock, Oglethorpe, Warren and Wilkes counties. Named for Colonel Benjamin Taliaferro (1750-1821), a Revolutionary War hero from Virginia, who in Georgia was trustee of Franklin College (q.v.), state senator, and a judge. The county seat is Crawfordsville (q.v.). TALIAFERRO CREEK in Chattooga County, enters the Chattooga River just below Lyerly. The station of TALIAFERRO on the Chattooga, Rome and Southern Railroad was located seven miles south of Summerville.

TALIPAHOGA RUM CREEK Stewart County. Originally called TALAPAGEE CREEK (q.v.).

TALKING ROCK, Pickens County. Incorporated as a town September 24, 1883. The early settlement was established on the site of the former community of LOVES (q.v.). Several explanations have been offered regarding the origin of the present name of this town: 1. It was supposedly so named when Irishmen building the railroad would leave money on a big rock, and Indians would pick up the cash and leave jugs of native whiskey. 2. Reportedly so named from a rocky cliff in the stream, which at one time produced peculiar echoes. 3. From a story about a rock with which some of the Indians played a trick on one another. 4. The most probably origin is that it is a translation of a Cherokee name, *Nuny-gunswani-ski*, which Brinkley says means, "the talker" or "place of the talkers."

TALLAHASSEE CREEK, Dougherty County. Commences in the northwest section of the county, near the Terrell County line, and joins the west side of Kiokee Creek about one mile below the crossing of Georgia highway 234. The name is from the Muskogean word, *Talwaahasihachi,* signifying "Old Town Creek," from *talwa,* "town," *ahasi,* "old," and *hachi,* "stream." It was formerly called OSKETOCHEE CREEK.

TALLAPOOSA, Haralson County. Incorporated as a town December 20, 1860. In the 1880's it was promoted as "A Yankee City Under the Southern Sun." Named after the nearby Tallapoosa River (q.v.); the early village was called POSSUM SNOUT, a nickname for an old Indian chief. Before this it was called OKWHUSKE or OKFUSKI.

TALLAPOOSA RIVER. This 268-mile waterway originates at the southwest corner

of Paulding County, flows through Haralson County into Alabama, and on southward to join the Coosa River near Selma. Its earlier name was OKWHUSKE or OKFUSKI. The meaning of the Creek name, *Talapoosa,* is uncertain. One explanation is that it means "Swift Current," while another authority says that it means "Newcomer" or "Stranger." A third source believes it signifies "Pulverized Rock," while a fourth says the meaning is "Golden River," because of its yellowish tinge. And lastly, that it is derived from the name of an early Creek town, the first part of the word from *talwa,* meaning "town."

TALLONEY, Gilmer County. See Talona.

TALLUGA CREEK, Webster County. See TALLULGA CREEK.

TALLULA, Habersham County. A post office established in 1858, four miles from Tallulah Falls (q.v.) from which it was named. The name was changed to TURNERVILLE in 1882.

TALLULAH FALLS, Rabun County. Incorporated as a town October 7, 1885. A resort hotel was built here in the 1770's, and the town began to grow in 1882 with the extention of the Tallulah Falls Railroad here. After the river was diverted in 1913 by a tunnel around the falls for hydroelectric power, the town declined, and was last chartered in 1943. It was named after the former cascade of TALLULAH FALLS, which was a spectacular 1,000-foot waterfall on the Tallulah (Falls) River (q.v.). The Cherokee Indians called the falls UGANYI or UGUNYL earlier, and later variations of the name have included TELULA, TELULEE, TARURI, TORURO and TURROR. In 1835 it was stated that the meaning of the name was "terrible," because of the wild roaring and plunging of the falls. Another theory is that the name is derived from the Choctaw, *talulu,* which means "bell." Again it has been suggested that the name was from *tululu,* for the cry of the frog, or possible to mean "frog place" from the Cherokee, *Tu-lu-lu-li,* "The Frogs Cry There." Still another has thought its origin was from *Atalulu,* meaning "Unfinished," or from the Cherokee, *nunyu,* "rock," and *tsiwanihu,* "I am talking." John Mooney, authority on the Cherokee language, has held that the name is from the Indian word *Talulu* or *Taruri,* which he said is not translatable. The late actress Tallulah Bankhead was named for her grandmother, who was named after Tallulah Falls. Despite vigorous opposition led by Mrs. Helen D. Longstreet of Gainesville, the Georgia Power Company constructed in 1912-13, the TALLULAH FALLS DAM at Indian Arrow Rapids, the point where U. S. Highway 23-441 crosses the river. From the dam the water is carried through a tunnel to a powerhouse nearly a mile and a half away, where generators produce 72,000 kilowatts.

TALLULAH FALLS DOME. Located in northeast Georgia. This is a natural geological feature in the earth's crust, which is a uniform circular unwrap, about 150 square miles in area which contains rocks over one billion years old.

TALLULAH GORGE, Rabun and Habersham counties. Was called "The Niagara of the South." Located below Tallulah Falls Dam, it is 600 feet deep and three miles long. The chasm was crossed on a 1,449-foot tightrope in 1886 by "Professor Leon" (J. A. St. John). This feat was repeated July 18, 1970 by "The Great" Karl Wallenda, who at the age of 65 walked a 1,000-foot cable stretched 700 feet above the rocky stream bed, for a $10,000 fee. A point of the west side of the gorge was afterwards named WALLENDA POINT.

TALLULAH (FALLS) RIVER. Commences in North Carolina, and enters Georgia at the northeast corner of Towns County, then flows southeasterly, emptying into Tugaloo Lake. The Cherokee name for the stream was TERRORA, and they had an ancient village on the river, some distance above the Falls, which they called TA-RU-RI. WITCHES HEAD is a rock formation protruding over the river, and was descriptively named from the configuration of the profile in the rock. *See also* Tallulah Falls and Tallulah Gorge.

TALLULGA(H) CREEK, Webster County. Enters the south side of Kinchafoonee Creek in southeast Webster County. It was also called TALLUGA CREEK, and means "abounding in palmettos." The present name is LIME SPRING POND CREEK.

TALLY MOUNTAIN, Haralson County. Located just southeast of Tallapoosa, it has an elevation of 1,520 feet. Was called by the Creeks, CHUN-NE-MIC-CO, which means "Kings Mountain" or "Pilot Mountain." Tally has been said to be a family surname, or possibly comes from the Cherokee word *tali*,

signifying "mountain." A third supposition is that it is a nickname for Tallapoosa. Brinkley says it is a shortened form of TALI WA, a battle site of the middle 1700's between the Cherokee and Creek Indians.

TALMADGE MEMORIAL BRIDGE, Savannah. *See* EUGENE TALMADGE MEMORIAL BRIDGE.

TALMO, Jackson County. Incorporated as a town August 9, 1920. Named from the Creek word *Talomeco*, "Home of the Chief Tallassee." In the late 1800's this became a station of the Gainesville, Jefferson and Southern Railroad.

TALONA, Gilmer County. A rural community located seven miles south of Ellijay. It was formerly called UPPER TALLONEY, and is derived from the Cherokee Indian name, *To-lo-ney*. The oldest post office in the county was at TALLONEY (or LOWER TALLONEY), which was later spelled TALONEY. This ancient village stood seven miles south of the present Talona, and was the location of CARMEL (q.v.), the second mission to the Indians in Georgia. In all, five separate places had been named Talloney. The present one was sometimes called SANDERSTOWN (q.v.).

TALONA MOUNTAIN, Gilmer County. With an elevation of 2,115 feet, it is located four miles south of Ellijay. Named from the Cherokee Indian town of Talona (q.v.).

TALONEGA, Lumpkin County. Incorporated December 21, 1833. *See* DAHLONEGA.

TAMA. This was the name given by the Spanish to the inland area of what is now Georgia (*see* Guale). The name was also given to a former Indian village at the point where the Oconee and Ocmulgee rivers flow together to form the Altamaha (q.v.). The meaning of the word Tama is not certain, but the Indians and the Spanish in Texas used the same term for someone who was a "pusher" or overseer who saw to it that things got done when they should be. There is also today a town of Tama (pronounced "Tay'-muh") in Iowa, which was named after a lower chief Taimah of the Fox tribe, who was known as "The Bear."

TAMA LAKE(S), Bibb County. A private resort lake in the southwest section of the county, which was formerly called BANKSTON LAKE after the previous owner, Mr. R. E. Bankston. The spring-fed 74-acre lake was given this old Indian place - name (*see* Tama) by its present owner Mrs. Hazel M. Harvey, so named as it was apparently in a formerly active Indian community where many primitive artifacts have been found, including arrowheads, trading beads, etc. Mrs. Harvey had seen the name mentioned in an Atlanta newspaper as being an old Indian place-name.

TANNER'S BEACH RECREATION AREA, Carroll County. Now known as JOHN W. TANNER STATE PARK (q.v.).

TANTATANARA, Floyd County. This is an old Indian name for a fresh-water spring located at the Chieftans (q.v.), three miles north of Rome. The Cherokee name means "Running Waters."

TANYARD BRANCH, Lumpkin County. This little stream runs from Dahlonega southwesterly into Yahoola Creek. It was named after a tan yard, which was operated by Dr. J. A Moody. In southwest Monroe County, TANYARD CREEK flows easterly into Echeconnee Creek. Derivation is unknown.

TARA. This is undoubtedly the most famous plantation in Georgia, and is known throughout the civilized world. It is an imaginary place created by Margaret Mitchell for her novel *Gone With The Wind* (1936), and does not represent any actual plantation. The name for the O'Hara place in the book is probably derived from the Hill of Tara in Ireland. TARA LAKE is a community near Jonesboro in Clayton County, in which vicinity some people have speculated that Mrs. Mitchell meant Tara to be.

TARKILN BRANCH, Hart County. This stream is thought to have been named because of tar that was run from kilns along its banks. John Baker said it entered the Tugaloo River near the Andersonville Ferry.

TARRYTOWN, Montgomery County. Located eight miles northwest of Vidalia. Incorporated as a town August 19, 1912. Derivation of this name is unknown, but may be from the family name of Tarry.

TARVERSVILLE, Twiggs County. Unincorporated. Named for Hartwell Hill Tarver (1791-1851), a wealthy planter in the community, who was one of the large slave owners in the South. His name was given to two post offices in the county. The first opened September 29, 1826 as TARVER'S STORE,

and the second on September 27, 1876. H. H. Tarver was the first postmaster at Tarver's Store. That name was changed to Tarversville, May 24, 1831. There is also a community of TARVER in southern Echols County, which was incorporated October 15, 1887, and there was an earlier TARVERSVILLE in northwest Burke County.

TATE, Pickens County. Established about 1818 as a tavern site on the old Federal Road, first called HARNAGEVILLE (q.v.). The post office was originally called MARBLE WORKS, after the discovery of high quality marble here in almost unlimited quantity. In the early 1880's the name of the community was changed to TATEVILLE or Tate, after Colonel Samuel C. Tate, who purchased the property in 1834. There is also a community, as well as a militia district, called TATE CITY, located in the northeast corner of Towns County. This derivation is not known.

TATTNALL COUNTY. Created December 5, 1801 with 493 square miles taken from Montgomery County. Named for Governor Josiah Tattnall (1764-1803), who was born near Savannah, and was a state senator, and a brigadier general in the state militia. The county seat is Reidsville (q.v.). Also named for this governor is TATTNALL SQUARE PARK in Macon (q.v.) and TATTNALL STREET in Savannah.

TATUM, Dade County. A former community, possibly named for the family of Colonel Robert H. "Uncle Bob" Tatum, who lived in Dade County in the 1840's, and later in 1860 became a member of the Georgia House of Representatives. A widespread legend has it that he proclaimed that Dade County was seceding from Georgia at the outset of the Civil War.

TATUM, Forsyth County. A post office established November 12, 1880. This is believed to have been named for a family of early settlers in this area, near and in Dawson County. The post office name was changed to SILVER CITY (q.v.) April 7, 1886.

TAURULABOOLE CREEK, Jackson County. This Creek Indian word means "Screaming Panther Creek," and was the previous name for the present BEECH CREEK (q.v.).

TAX, Talbot County. This was a well known community in the early 1900's, which was located in the northwest section of the county. A mercantile store here contained the post office, and it was so called because county tax officials stopped here to receive tax returns.

TAYLOR, Crawford County. An early community which was located eight miles north of Fort Valley. The postmaster in 1882 was a Mr. James Taylor.

TAYLOR COUNTY. Created January 15, 1852 with 400 square miles taken from Macon, Marion and Talbot counties. Named for the twelfth U. S. president, Zachary Taylor (1784-1850), who was a native of Virginia. He won his nickname "Old Rough and Ready" in the Indian Wars, and he also served in the War of 1812 and the war with Mexico. The county seat is Butler (q.v.). *See also* Rough and Ready, DeKalb County.

TAYLOR'S CREEK, Liberty County. A former community which was located about seven miles northwest of Hinesville on the present Georgia highway 27. It was named for nearby stream, TAYLOR'S CREEK, which flows easterly then northerly to Canoochee Creek.

TAYLOR(S) RIDGE, Chattooga and

Walker counties. From the Tennessee line near Graysville, it runs southwesterly through Chattooga County. Named for a prominent Cherokee chief by the name of Richard Taylor who lived near Ringgold, and had signed the treaty at Red Clay in 1835. A Civil War battle was fought on this ridge November 7, 1863.

TAYLOR SPRINGS, Pike County. Named after the developer of the springs as a resort, U. L. Taylor, Sr., who came from Upson County.

TAYLORSVILLE, Bartow County. Incorporated as a town August 19, 1916. Named for a Mr. Taylor who surveyed the town about 1870.

TAZEWELL, Marion County. A community located at the headwaters of Buck Creek. Incorporated as the town of TAZWELL (*sic*) February 20, 1854. Named for Henry Tazewell (1753-1799) of Virginia, who was a U. S. senator from 1794 to 1799. The county seat was moved here from Horry (q.v.) December 27, 1838. The court house burned November 3, 1845, and the county seat was then moved to Buena Vista.

TEARBRITCHES CREEK, Murray County. Goff said this was a waggish tab applied by old timers to this stream flowing through thick bushy areas. It rises on the north side of Little Bald Mountain, just inside of Murray County from the Fannin County line, and runs northerly to join the Conasauga River at the Murray-Fannin boundary.

TEBEAUVILLE, Ware County. An early name of WAYCROSS (q.v.). *See also* PENDLETON.

TELFAIR COUNTY. Created December 10, 1807 with 440 square miles taken from part of

Wilkinson County. Named for Scottish-born, Edward Telfair (1735-1807), patriot of the Revolutionary War, a U. S. congressman, and the second governor of Georgia after the United States was established. The county seat is McRae (q.v.). The court house was destroyed by fire in the early 1900's. TELFAIR's MILL, owned by Governor Telfair, was located on Beaverdam Creek in Burke County. There was also once a village of TELFAIRVILLE (or FORT TELFAIR, q.v.) in Burke County, located fifteen miles east of Waynesboro, on a ridge between Brier Creek and the Savannah River.

TELFAIR SQUARE, Savannah. Laid out in 1733, it was first named SAINT JAMES SQUARE in honor of the palace of Saint James in London. After the Revolution, it was renamed in honor of the Telfair family in recognition of their services to the city. TELFAIR ACADEMY OF ARTS AND SCIENCES is in the TELFAIR HOUSE which was built by William Jay, and herein are exhibited art treasures of the City of Savannah.

TELOGA CREEK, Chattooga County. This is a Muskogee name that signifies "Pea Creek," from *telogi,* "pea." Located in the northwest corner of the county, in the vicinity of the stream, is a rural community called TELOGA, and also nearby is TELOGA SPRINGS.

TEMPERANCE (BELL), Greene County. Located three miles north of Union Point, it was earlier called PUBLIC SQUARE. This former community was named after a great temperance revival here in 1826-27.

TEMPERANCE, Telfair County. A rural community in the extreme west corner of the county. This name was adopted by the Methodists who had a large camp ground here before the Civil War.

TEMPLE, Carroll County. Incorporated August 28, 1883. The earlier name of the town was RINGER'S CROSS ROAD, after original settler B. R. Ringer. The Georgia Pacific Railroad reached here in 1883, and the station was named for a Mr. Temple, the civil engineer of the railroad.

TEN MILE CREEK, Appling County. Flows easterly across the northern section of the county before entering the Altamaha River. Named because of its distance from Fort James Bluff (q.v.).

TENNESSEE ROCK, Rabun County.

Located in Black Rock Mountain State Park (q.v.), and was so named because it overlooks the Tennessee River (in North Carolina).

TENNGA. Murray County. Pronounced "Tenngee" by old timers here. Brinkley said it was first known as WHIP, for the Cherokee Indian called Whip-poor-will. The name was later changed to signify the location of the community on the Tennessee-Georgia line. There is also a TENNGA (Militia) DISTRICT here.

TENNILLE, Washington County. Pronounced "Tin'-il." Incorporated as the town of TENNELLE (*sic*) March 4, 1875, and as the town of Tennille October 24, 1887. This was originally a Central of Georgia railroad stop called NUMBER THIRTEEN C.R.R. about 1842, and then reportedly (by E. Mitchell) renamed for Benjamine Tennille, who owned much land here. It has also been said to have been named for Colonel Robert Tennille, a veteran of the Indian Wars, and finally for Mr. Francis Tennille, a public spirited citizen.

TENSAWATTEE, Dawson County. An old Cherokee village, which was probably the central meeting place of the Big Savannah (q.v.) community. The name means "Tennessee Old Town," and it was also called NEW TOWN. Variations of spellings have included, TINSWATTE, TENSAW WATEE, TENSAU WATER, and TENNESSE WATER. The name was probably transferred from another "Tensa" place, according to Goff.

TERMINUS (or THE TERMINUS), Fulton County. A name which was adopted after civil engineer Stephen H. Long (1784-1864) designated this site for the hub or terminal point of the Georgia Railroad (Long is the explorer for whom Long's Peak in Colorado was named). This railroad center had also been called THRASHERVILLE (q.v.), later named MARTHASVILLE, and finally ATLANTA (q.v.).

TERRELL COUNTY. Pronounced "Tare'-ul." Created February 16, 1856 with 329 square miles taken from Lee and Randolph counties. Named for Dr. William Terrell (1778-1885) of Sparta, who was a noted state and U.S. congressman. He established the chair of agriculture at the University of Georgia. The county seat is Dawson (q.v.). A community named TERRELL in Worth County is located eight miles northeast of Sylvester.

The TERRY, Augusta. This name is shortened from THE TERRITORY, which was the designation of the Negro section of Augusta.

TERRY'S MILL POND, DeKalb County. A pond created by the impounded waters of Sugar Creek (near Glenwood Avenue), where Tom Terry (1823-1861) operated a grist mill.

TESNATEE, White County. An early community which was located six miles west of present day Cleveland, where Town Creek runs into TESNATEE CREEK. TESNATEE GAP is a mountain pass at 3,138 feet elevation in White County. The Cherokee word *tesnatee* is thought to mean "turkey" or "wild turkey."

TEXAS, Heard County. A rural community located six miles southwest of Franklin. Was named during the 1844 presidential contest when the expansionist movement became popular in the South, over the annexation of Texas Territory. *Texas* is said to be an Indian word used as a token of friendship, or to mean "friends." It was the name of an Indian tribe in the West.

THAD, Chattahoochee County. An early post office located eight miles southeast of Columbus. In 1882 the postmaster here was E. T. "Thad" Hickey.

THE HILL, Richmond County. A descriptive name for an exclusive residential section of Augusta, which name has been adopted for the former SUMMERVILLE (q.v.).

THE ROCK, Upson County. Incorporated as a town February 22, 1877. This community was so named because it is located upon a rock, out-croppings of which appear over the site. In early times, it was said that mail was deposited in a secret hole in the rock, which was covered with a flat stone. Stage drivers were instructed to "Leave the mail at The Rock," after which the post office adopted this name.

THIGPEN TRAIL. This old road cut through North and South Carolina, Georgia and Florida, over 250 years ago, built by James Thigpen of North Carolina. It was the first military road cut through Georgia, which avoided all swamps and great rivers. It passed through Arabi, west of Isabella, west of Parkersville, and near Doerun. THIGPEN TRAIL MONUMENT in Colquitt County is located on the trail, three miles west of Sylvester on U. S. 82 in Worth County.

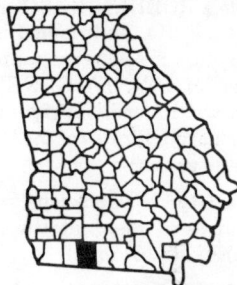

THOMAS COUNTY. Created December 23, 1825 with 540 square miles taken from Decatur and Irwin counties. Named after General Jett Thomas (1776-1817), veteran of the War of 1812, and the builder of the first university building in Athens, as well as of the state house in Milledgeville. The county seat is Thomasville (q.v.).

THOMAS E. WATSON HIGHWAY. Runs from the North Carolina line to Savannah Beach via U. S. routes 23 and 41, through Cornelia, Atlanta, Macon and Augusta. Named in honor of Thomas Edward Watson (1856-1922), "Sage of Hickory Hill" who was the state and national leader of the People's or Populist Party, was vice presidential candidate in 1896 and then candidate for the presidency in 1904. He was an agrarian rebel who published the *Weekly Jeffersonian,* and also introduced the first resolution in U. S. congress for rural free delivery. The THOMAS E. WATSON STATUE to his honor stands on the capitol grounds in Atlanta. *See also* Thomson.

THOMAS MILLS, Floyd County. An early community which was located on Cedar Creek, 13 miles southwest of Rome. In 1882, L. T. Thomas had a grist mill and saw mill on the stream.

THOMASTON, CS Upson County. Has been called "Tire Cord Capital of U. S." Incorporated as a town and designated the county seat June 11, 1825. Named in honor of General Jett Thomas (*see* Thomas County), or possibly for John Thomas, one of the first justices of the Inferior Court. *See also* Silvertown.

THOMASVILLE, CS Thomas County. Called "The City of Roses," being the home of an annual rose festival. Established and made county seat in 1826, it was incorporated as a town December 26, 1831, and named for General Jett Thomas (*see* Thomas County). Thomasville's RODDENBERRY PARK was established in 1914, and named in honor of S. A. Roddenberry, congressman from the Second District. FINNEY GENERAL HOSPITAL here was named for Brigadier General John Miller Turpin Finney of the U. S. Army's Medical Reserve Corps.

THOMOCOGGAN, Jackson County. An early Indian settlement at the site of the present JEFFERSON (q.v.).

THOMSON, CS McDuffie County. "Camelia City of the South." The whole town was once owned by plantation-owner John Langston. In earlier days it was called FROGPOND, HICKORY LEVEL and the SLASHES. Then named Thomson in 1853 for J. Edgar Thomson, the civil engineer who surveyed the right-of-way for the Georgia Railroad through here in 1833. Thomson was also the one who named Atlanta (q.v.). When this was part of Columbia County, Thomson was incorporated as a village February 15, 1854. Located here is HICKORY HILL, which was the home of Senator Tom Watson (*see* Thomas E. Watson Highway).

THOMSON'S MILLS, Jackson County. A post office was established here from 1878 to 1903, and the community now uses the Hoschton post office. It was believed named for J. M. Thomson who was a wool carder, had a general store here and a saw mill on Mulberry Creek.

THORNTON'S CROSS ROAD, Greene County. First settled in 1775 and named for early resident Redman Thornton, whose 1780 house was moved to Atlanta's McBurny Art Memorial in 1960. When the railroads came through, the town was given its present name of UNION POINT (q.v.).

THRASHERVILLE, Fulton County. An early Atlanta (q.v.) area settlement, located between White Hall and the Chattahoochee River. Named for John J. "Cousin John"

Thrasher, who arrived here from Newton County in 1839, when the county was entirely covered with forest. With a partner he established the first store in what is now Atlanta, called Johnson and Thrasher.

THREE CHOP ROAD. Laid out in 1803 across the Cherokee Nation, from Greensboro, Georgia to Walnut Hill on the Mississippi River. The route was marked by three chops made with an axe on one tree after another through the forests by General Winfield Scott's soldiers. The Indians were driven west from Georgia on this road. *See also* Five Notch Road.

THRONATEESKA RIVER. *Thronateeska* (also spelled THLONOTIASKE) is said to be the Indian name for the FLINT RIVER (q.v.), but it is not clear which Indian language this word is from. The Muskogee word for "flint" is *ronoto*, or according to Goff, the Flint River was called HLONOTISKAHACHI.

THUNDERBOLT, Chatham County. The first English settlers to occupy Georgia were given grants here, according to Lilla Hawes. Hetherington and others came here before 1732. This was the site of early fortifications and was later a Civil War garrison. The derivation of the name is described by Oglethorpe as being traced "to a rock which was here shattered by a thunderbolt, causing a spring to gush from the ground, which continued ever afterward to emit the odor of brimstone." By an act of the state assembly of March 3, 1856, the name of the town was changed to WARSAW (q.v.), under which name it was then incorporated. Custom refused to sanction the change, and so the original name remained. The name of the town was officially changed back to Thunderbolt July 22, 1921. This is today the center of Georgia's shrimp industry.

THUNDERING SPRINGS, Upson County. Located in the northwest section of the county, two miles from the Flint River. The name was adopted because of the rumbling noises like distant thunder that formerly arose from the depths of these springs.

TIAH RIVER. An early name of the CHATTAHOOCHEE RIVER (q.v.).

TICKANETLEY, Gilmer County. This was the name of an early Cherokee Indian community located thirteen miles east of Ellijay. Nearby TICKANETLEY CREEK was named after this town, as was TICKANETLEY (Militia) DISTRICT in the eastern section of

Gilmer County. Located eight miles northeast of Ellijay is TICKANETLEY BALD MOUNTAIN, with an elevation of 4,054 feet.

TICKE(E)HATCHEE CREEK, Dodge and Laurens counties. A Creek Indian word meaning "Crossing (or Fording) Place," or possibly "House Creek." This is an obsolete designation for the present STITCHIHATCHEE CREEK (q.v.).

TIFT COLLEGE, Forsyth. Established in 1847 as FORSYTH FEMALE COLLEGIATE INSTITUTE, with its name changed in 1867 to MONROE FEMALE COLLEGE. In 1898 the college became the property of the Georgia Baptist Convention, and in 1907 its name was changed to BESSIE TIFT COLLEGE in honor of its benefactress, Mrs. Bessie Willingham Tift. The present name was adopted in 1956.

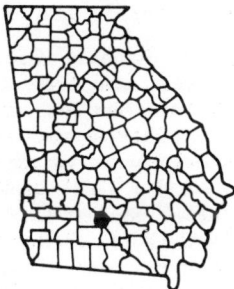

TIFT COUNTY. Created August 17, 1905 with 266 square miles taken from Berrien, Irwin and Worth counties. Named for Colonel Nelson Tift (1810-1891), state congressman and later U. S. representative from Georgia (1868-69). The county seat is Tifton (q.v.).

TIFTON, CS Tift County. Called "The Friendly City" and "The Tomato Plant Capital." Settled in 1872 and incorporated as a city December 29, 1890. Founded by Connecticut-born Henry Harding Tift, who first named the village LENA for his sweetheart. But a sawmill worker, George Badger, put up a sign with the word "Tifton" on a pine tree, after his boss, and the name stuck. H. H. Tift therefore allowed that the place be named for his uncle, Colonel Nelson Tift of Albany (q.v., *see also* Tift County). FULWOOD PARK of Tifton was named for Columbus Wesley Fulwood, close friend and legal adviser of Henry H.

Tift, who gave the land to the city from which the park was created.

TIGER, Rabun County. Incorporated as a town August 13, 1904. Named for the Cherokee chief, Tiger Tail. Located ¾ mile northwest of Tiger is TIGER MOUNTAIN, with an elevation of 2,856 feet. TIGER (Militia) DISTRICT of Rabun County is located south of Clayton.

TIGERTOWN, Bibb County. Settled in 1822-23 by immigrant "squatters." This was Macon's first suburban settlement, and was located on the opposite (west) side of the Ocmulgee River from the original community by Fort Hawkins. It was named after the ugly and ferocious leader of the settlement, Tiger Jenkins.

TIGHT SQUEEZE, Fulton County. This was the name of a low grade suburb of early Atlanta near the present Tenth and Peachtree streets, where it was commonly said that it took "a mighty tight squeeze to get through here with one's life." This district is today known as THE STRIP.

TIGNAL, Wilkes County. Incorporated as a town August 22, 1907. Derivation of this name is not known.

TIMPSON CREEK, Rabun County. Originally called TIMSON CREEK, Goff said it was named for a Cherokee family of John Timson, who reportedly lived along this stream. There was an early community of TIMSON on the creek, which was located five miles west of Clayton.

TINSLEY'S TRAIL. Dougherty County. A trail that ran from the northeast, and crossed the Flint River just north of Albany. Was named for a pioneer called Tinsley who settled here, and was murdered with his family by Indians.

TIPPETTVILLE, Dooly and Wilcox counties. A rural community located ten miles east of Vienna on S672. Founded in 1890 when brothers Abner and Ezekiel Tippett came here from Rochelle, Wilcox County, and established a store.

TIRED CREEK, Grady County. Flows southerly through the middle of the county to enter the Ochlocknee River about nine miles south of Cairo. Its name is believed to reflect the sluggishness of the stream's flow.

TIRED CREEK STATE PARK, Grady County. A 2,933-acre park located six miles northwest of Cairo, opened in 1974 and named after Tired Creek (q.v.).

TISHMAUGU RIVER, Hall, Barrow and Jackson counties. An old Indian name of the present MULBERRY RIVER (q.v.).

TLATHLOTHLAGUPHTA, Camden County. Believed to have been a former Indian village to which Captain Jean Ribault (c. 1520-1565) came in 1562. Its site was said to be at the location of today's St. Marys (q.v.).

TOBACCO ROAD. This old road was laid out about 1789 for rolling tobacco hogsheads to the warehouses at New Savannah Bluff (q.v.). It ran south from Augusta on the present Georgia route 56 (OLD SAVANNAH ROAD).

TOBANNEE CREEK, Quitman County. This stream reaches the Chattahoochee River just below Georgetown. The name was first listed as TO-BE-NA-NIE, and later as TOBE-NAHNEE. Stewart says that the Muskogean name probably means "tree-crooked," for a landmark tree, or as interpreted by Read, from *ito,* "tree," *api,* "trunk," and *yanahi,* "crooked." The name has also been thought to mean "Hurricane" Creek. *See also* TABANANA.

TOBESOFKEE CREEK. Rises in central Monroe County and flows southeasterly through Bibb County, emptying into the Ocmulgee River below Macon. The Purcell Map of about 1770 calls this creek, TOBASAUGHKEE. The naturalist William Bartram in 1776 mentions the stream as TOBOSOCHTE, and William DeBrahm a little later as TOBOSOPHSKEE. Benjamin Hawkins spelled it (c. 1790's) variously as TOBOSAUFKEE, TOBA SAUFEKE and TOBESAUKE. On H. S. Tanner's map of 1825, we find it called CHUPEE CREEK. Read interprets the meaning of *Tobesofkee* to be "Sofky Stirrer," - from the Creek *atapa,* "stirrer," probably a wooden ladle, and *safki,* "corn gruel." Sherwood presented a more colorful explanation in stating that the name came from the Indian word *sofskee,* an Indian dish prepared of meal or corn, and *tobe,* "I have lost," supposedly after an Indian had lost his provisions while crossing the stream. Stewart on the other hand translates *sofkee* as meaning "deep," but says the rest is uncertain.

TOBESOFKEE, LAKE, Bibb County. Comprises 1,750 acres, and was created by a $2 million dam on Tobesofkee Creek (q.v.), begun in late 1963. The lake is six miles long with a 35-mile shoreline, and is located immediately west of Macon. The TOBESOFKEE RECREATION AREA here is a park which is owned and operated by Bibb County, and was opened in 1969.

TOBLER CREEK. Pronounced "Tobe-ler" and sometimes locally "Tobe-ly." This name is applied to at least three separate streams. One in Lamar County is at times called SWIFT CREEK in the lower part. Another arises in northwest Baldwin County, and is also called TAYLORS CREEK. A stream called TOBLERS CREEK arises in southeast Monroe County. The origin of the name is said to be from a Creek Indian named Tobler who was a picturesque character and a grand rascal of the Georgia frontier. It has also been thought to be after a Swiss called William Tobler, who sold liquor to Indians against regulations, along Toms Path, through the area of these streams. *See also* Jobley Creek.

TOCCOA, CS Stephens County. "The Furniture, Thread and Steel City." The original settlement here was named DRY POND, because of a pond which stood by the crossroads here and was dry much of the time, especially in summer. This became a coaling station for the railroad between Atlanta and Charlotte, North Carolina. The town of Toccoa was laid out in lots in 1873, and was incorporated February 26, 1875. This became the county seat of Stephens County, August 18, 1905. The Georgia Baptist Assembly occupies the facilities bought from industrialist, Robert LeTourneau, who had established a company recreation center here. Also located here is the TOCCOA FALLS INSTITUTE which was founded in 1911 by Rev. R. A. Forrest. At that time he purchased the vacation hotel, Haddock Inn, as the original site for this independent Christian school. Within the school property are the TOCCOA FALLS on TOCCOA CREEK, which cascade like a veil of mist over a 186-foot precipice. The TOCCOA RIVER commences in lower Fannin County and flows northward into Tennessee. TOCCOA LAKE in Fannin County is sometimes called BLUE RIDGE LAKE. The name Toccoa is said to be derived from the Cherokee, *Tagwahi,* "Where the Catawbas Lived." It has also been said that the word toccoa means "beautiful." The Spanish spelled the name, TOCAX.

TOKOGALGI. An early Yuchi Indian set-tlement which was located on Kinchafoonee Creek, but the exact location is not known. The name means "Tadpole Place."

TOLEDO, Charlton County. A community located on the Saint Marys River, twelve miles south of Traders Hill. It was named for the province in Spain.

TOLOMATO MISSION, McIntosh County. A major Spanish mission that was founded by Pedro Ruiz in 1595. The full Spanish name of the mission was NUESTRA SENORA DE GUADELUPE DE TOLOMATO. There has been some uncertainty as to the site of this former mission. After research and study, Coulter concluded that "it is reasonable to as-sume that Tolomato was near Darien." Lan-ning places it five miles northeast of pre-sent Darien, on Pease Creek.

TOM BELL DISTRICT, Hall County. This militia district was thought to have been named for state congressman, Thomas M. Bell.

TOMS PATH. This was an old Indian trail through central Georgia, from the Flint River near Old Agency (q.v.) through Milledgeville to Old Town on the east side of the Ogeechee River, about nine miles southeast of Louis-ville in Jefferson County. Goff explains that it was either named for an old Indian chief called Tom, for a Cussetta Indian courrier named Tom, or possible for Samuel Tomes (or Thomas) of Washington County.

TOMS SHOALS, Baldwin County. Also called TOMS FORD, it is located just east of Milledgeville at the place on the Oconee which was crossed by Toms Path (q.v.). The Creeks called this fording place, OCHEE FINNAU, which signifies "Hickory Bridge (or Footlog)."

TOM WATSON BRIDGE. On which U. S. Highway 78 crosses Little River between McDuffie and Wilkes counties. Named in honor of Senator Watson (see Thomas E. Wat-son Highway).

TOOKABATCHIE, Haralson County. A former Indian town, thought to have been an old Creek capital. Was located one mile north of the present business section of Tallapoosa. The name means "Crossed Sticks."

TOOMBS COUNTY. Created August 18, 1905 with 369 square miles taken from Em-

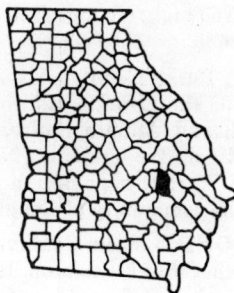

manuel, Montgomery and Tattnall counties. Named for Robert Toombs (1810-1885), U. S. congressman and senator from Georgia, who as a general had fought at the second battle of Bull Run and at Antietam, after having resigned his appointment as the Confederate secretary of state. At the conclusion of the Civil War, he escaped to New Orleans and then became a refugee in London. Toombs refused to ever again pledge allegiance to the United States. The county seat is Lyons (q.v.). The court house was destroyed by fire in 1919. The TOOMBS OAK stood for many years on the University of Georgia campus until near the end of the century, and the location was afterward marked with a marble sun-dial. This was the spot where the noted statesman had once made a famous speech when he was a student at the university.

TOOMSBORO, Wilkinson County. In-corporated as a town August 15, 1904. The early community began when the railroad stop was moved here from its previous location of Emmet, which was 1½ miles east of here. The town was named in honor of Robert Toombs (see Toombs County).

TOONIGH, Cherokee County. This com-munity is now called by its early post office name of LEBANON (q.v.), although its railroad name has remained Toonigh. Brink-ley explains that the probable derivation of the name is from *Tooantuh,* meaning "spring frog," and was the name of a Cherokee chief. A popular legend has it that the place was given its name because it was "too nigh" other places to become a full fledged town of itself, or more specifically that it was too nigh (near) to Woodstock to be part of Holly Springs and vice versa. Another story tells that when the train station was brought on a flat car and set beside the track, one man walked down the track to see that it was not too close. As the other moved it away, he kept calling, "Too nigh, too nigh," so that is what they called it.

TORBIT, Burke County. A station at the crossing of the Georgia Railroad and the Savannah and Atlanta Railroad, 12 miles northwest of Waynesboro. Named after Dr. A. M. Torbit, a physician who helped develop the community of Gough.

TORY POND, Lincoln County. Located six miles northeast of Lincolnton. It is said that the Tories who murdered Colonel John Dooly were hanged here (*see* Dooly County).

TOTO CREEK, Dawson County. This is a western tributary of the Chestatee River. According to Goff, the derivation is for a prominent, well-to-do Cherokee named Child Toter (meaning "Child Carrier"), who lived not far from the creek.

TOWALAGA, Spalding County. A railroad station located five miles northeast of Griffin. The name is a variation of Towaliga (*see* Towaliga River).

TOWALIGA RIVER. Pronounced "Tow-a-lee-ga" or "Tye lye' gee." Rises in southern Henry County near Hampton, and flows southeastward across Henry, Spalding, Butts and Monroe counties to enter the west side of the Ocmulgee River above the little town of Juliette. An earlier spelling was TOWELAGGEE. William Read said that the probable meaning is "Sumac Place," from the Creek *tawa,* "sumac," and *laigi,* "place." Goff believed its meaning may be "About (or Among) Trees," or possibly "an old place (or spot)." Sherwood and Stewart offer a doubtful supposition that the name was derived from the Muskogean word *Towelaggie,* to mean "Roasted Scalps" or "Scalp Place," being a spot where war parties halted to dry scalps. TOWALIGA was also the name of an early settlement on the Towaliga River, located seven miles west of Jackson. The falls on this river in Butts County were formerly called TOWALIGA FALLS, and this was also the earlier name of the later community there of HIGH FALLS (q.v.).

TOWN CREEK, Gilmer and Pickens counties. Flows southerly into Talking Rock Creek. Named for an old Indian town on its banks, due west of Talona. The early meeting and council place was referred to as TOWN CREEK.

TOWN OF LINCOLN, Lincoln County. Named for General Lincoln (*see* Lincoln County), this was the original name of the present LISBON (q.v.).

TOWNS, Telfair County. A community located on the Little Auchehatchee River in the eastern section of the county. Named for Johnson C. Towns, one of the first settlers here, and the first postmaster.

TOWNS COUNTY. Created March 6, 1856 with 166 square miles taken from Rabun and Union counties. Named in honor of Georgia governor, George Washington Towns (1802-1854). The county seat is Hiawassee (q.v.).

TRACK ROCK, Towns County. This was an earlier name of the settlement BRASSTOWN (q.v.). The name is translated from the Cherokee word *Datsu' nasgun' yi,* "Where there are tracks," or *Degayelun' ha,* "Printed (or Branded) Place," and refers to petrographs on soapstone rocks here.

TRACK ROCK GAP, Union County. A mountain pass located five miles east of Blairsville. For derivation, *see* Track Rock.

TRADERS HILL, Charlton County. A community on the Saint Marys River, which was earlier known as FORT ALERT. The name originated because it was established as a trading post, and was a thriving center of trade about 1755. Trader's Hill was designated the county seat in 1854, when Charlton County was formed. In 1901 the county seat was moved to Folkston.

TRAHLYTA, LAKE, Lumpkin County. Located nine miles above Dahlonega, near the grave of the Cherokee Indian princess, Trahlyta, for which it was named. The location of this grave is called TRAHLYTA'S CAIRN, and has also been referred to as STONE PILE GAP, because the Indians traditionally placed additional stones on the cairn each time they passed by. The nearby springs were earlier called TRAHLYTA SPRINGS, and were reputed to bring eternal youth. They later became known as PORTER SPRINGS.

TRAHLYTA, LAKE, Union County. Located within Vogel State Park. Said to have been named after the beautiful daughter of a Cherokee chieftan who lived on top of Cedar Mountain.

TRAIN ROAD (or OLD TRAIN ROAD). The name refers to the wagon trains that used this route, which terminated at Saint Marys. This was first an Indian trail, and was also once a Spanish bridle path. It now includes some parts of the Dixie Highway, and it passed through the present Waycross on what is now Gilmore Street.

TRANS, Walker County. A community located in the southeast corner of the county. This name means "across," and was named by Professor E. I. F. Cheney, who went across the mountain to teach here.

TRANS-OCONEE REPUBLIC. An independent republic established in 1794 when the Indian situation was most threatening. It was organized under the leadership of Elijah Clarke (*see* Clarke County) in the regions west of the Oconee River, with its headquarters near the present Milledgeville. He drew up a written constitution for a new government, and erected Fort Advance, Fort Defiance (q.v.), and Fort Winston in this section. This enterprise lasted only a few months, and ceased to exist after the U. S. government officials became panicky, and forced its dissolution. *See also* Clarke County.

TRAVELER'S REST, Stephens County. Located six miles east of Toccoa, just off U. S. highway 123. One of the oldest inns of Georgia, it was erected in 1785 by Major Jesse Walton, Revolutionary soldier and Indian fighter. The tavern was later called JARRETT MANOR after Devereaux Jarrett bought it from James Rutherford Wylie (or Wyly), August 21, 1838. TRAVELER'S REST was also the name of a stage coach stop in Macon County, located two miles below Oglethorpe. The community was settled in 1830 and incorporated as BRISTOL (q.v.) in 1838. Another TRAVELERS' REST was in Pike County, with the place later called JOLLY (q.v.).

TRAY MOUNTAIN, White County. Has an elevation of 4,430 feet, and is located on the Towns County line. The name was believed corrupted from the original TRAIL MOUNTAIN, so named because of various trails leading to the summit. Near its peak is TRAY GAP at the county line, with an elevation of 3,847 feet.

TREE, Towns County. A former post office at the site of present TATE CITY.

TRENTON, CS Dade County. The first settlers arrived here in 1830, and the early community was first known as SALEM (q.v.), presumably transferred from a Salem in the North. This was made the county seat in 1837, and the name was changed to Trenton in 1840. The town was incorporated February 18, 1854. It was named in honor of industrial developers from Trenton, New Jersey, who came here looking for iron and coal.

TREUTLEN COUNTY. Created August 21, 1917 with 194 square miles taken from Emanuel and Montgomery counties. Named for John Adam Treutlen (1726-1782), who was the first elected governor of the State of Georgia under the State Constitution of 1777. He was born in Austria, and a member of the Salzburger church at Ebenezer (q.v.). He defeated Button Gwinnett, his opposing candidate by a good margin, and served as governor from 1777 to 1778 during which time he resisted efforts by South Carolina officials to annex Georgia. There is no record of his death, but tradition relates that he was brutally murdered by Tories in Orangeburg, South Carolina. The county seat is Soperton (q.v.).

TRIBLE, Clarke County. This former community was located ten miles southeast of Athens. Early settler F. Trible was a farmer and notary in 1882.

TRICKUM, Walker County. A community in the southeast section of the county, originally called GRAYSVILLE after a store owner by the name of Gray, who allegedly tricked and swindled customers in his dealings. It was said he once swindled a drunk out of twenty dollars. There is also a TRICKUM in Whitfield County, six miles west of Dalton, and another in Carroll County, 8½ miles south of Carrollton. There is today a rural community in Gwinnett County called TRICUM, also known as LOWELL.

TRION, Chattooga County. Incorporated as a town December 9, 1862. Originally known as TRION FACTORY, and named after the Trion Mills, built here in 1846-47 by a "trio" of founders, Judge A. P. Allgood, Judge Spencer Marsh, and Colonel W. K. Byars (or Briers).

TRIP, Gwinnett County. First called Trip. Incorporated under the name BERKELY December 16, 1901, and reincorporated with the present name GRAYSON (q.v.) in 1902.

TROUBLE CREEK, Oglethorpe County. This name was shortened from its original, TROUBLESOME CREEK, which flows through what was considered a difficult area. Another TROUBLESOME CREEK was located in upper Spalding County, and is now a "forgotten" name.

TROUBLESOME, Echols County. An early name of the present STATENVILLE (q.v.).

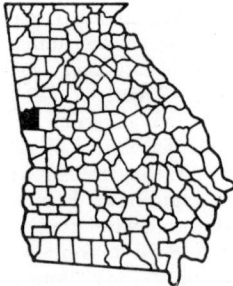

TROUP COUNTY. Created June 9, 1825 and December 11, 1826 with 447 square miles acquired by Creek cessions of January 24, 1826 and March 31, 1826. This was an original county, and was named for George Michael Troup (1780-1856). He was the governor of Georgia, and also was elected to the U. S. Senate, then later nominated to be president

of the United States. *See also* Troupsville. The county seat is LaGrange (q.v.). The court house was destroyed by a mysterious fire November 4, 1936. TROUP SQUARE in Savannah was also named for Governor Troup.

TROUP FACTORY, Troup County. An early community located ten miles southeast of LaGrange. Named for the Troup Cotton Factory which was operated by the Robertson, Leslie & Company, textile manufacturers. James M. C. Robertson and Thomas Leslie purchased Brooks Mill in 1846. The mill was built about 1841, and operated by power supplied by Flat Shoals Creek here. A post office was established for the community April 5, 1847 to June 5, 1867, and November 16, 1875 to May 15, 1902.

TROUPSVILLE, Carroll County. The original name of CARROLLTON (q.v.). Named in honor of Governor Troup (*see* Troup County), who had worked so aggressively to remove the Indians from Georgia, although he himself was a cousin of Creek chief William McIntosh (*see* McIntosh Old Place).

TROUPVILLE, Lowndes County. Incorporated December 14, 1837. Established on what was thought to have been the site of an old Spanish town, four miles northwest of the present Valdosta, or about one mile above the junction of the Little and Withlacoochee rivers. This place was made the county seat July 7, 1828. It was first called LOWNDESVILLE (q.v.), and then adopted its later name to honor Governor Troup (*see* Troup County), with the post office being moved here from Franklinville (q.v.) May 9, 1837. The post office remained in service until November 1, 1860 when it was moved to Valdosta (q.v.).

TRUETT McCONNELL COLLEGE, Cleveland. A Baptist school founded in 1946, it was named for George W. Truett and Fred C. McConnell, who had conducted a Christian academy at Hiawassee, which had been founded in 1887.

TRUSTEES' GARDEN, Savannah. America's first public agricultural experiment station. Established on a 10-acre tract in 1753 by General James Oglethorpe for the purpose of cultivating mulberry trees (for silk) and spices. Recently restored, it was in the northeast corner of colonial Savannah. The Herb House here is the oldest house in Georgia.

TUCKAHOE, Jefferson County. A former community which was located above Wrens. The Algonquian Indian word, *tuckahoe,* refers to a plant or tuber, the pioneers called "Indian bread." Another community named TUCKAHOE was located in Screven County, ten miles northeast of Sylvania.

TUCKASEE-KING, Effingham County. The first county seat of Effingham, established February 26, 1784. The site was near the present Clyo on the Screven County line. The seat was moved to Elberton (q.v.) in 1787.

TUCKASEEKING LAKE, Effingham County. William Read described this as, "A small lake tributary to the Savannah river" but is not found on today's maps. The name is believed derived from an ancient Cherokee town of TUCKASEEKING or TUCKASEGEE. It was also said to have been transferred by folk-etymology, possibly from the Creek word, *Tukaskina* (or *Tukashina*), meaning "Pepper Grass." Some old variations of spellings have been, TUCKASEE KINGS and TUCKASEE CREEK.

TUCKER, DeKalb County. A community named for Henry Holcomb Tucker (1819-1889), a leading Baptist in the South, one time president of Mercer University, and later chancellor of the University of Georgia.

TUCKER BRIDGE, HUGH C., Jasper County. A bridge over Gap Creek on State Route 83. Named for H. C. Tucker, businessman of Monticello and member of the Board of Tax Assessors for Jasper County for many years.

TUCKERSVILLE, Wayne County. The original county seat of Wayne County, located one mile from Waynesville. Derivation of the name is not known.

TUGALO, Stephens County. A rural community in the northeast section of the county, named from an Indian town of TUGALOO, which site is now under Lake Hartwell.

TUGALOO LAKE. Created by the Turnerville Dam on the Tugaloo River, on the border of Habersham and Rabun counties.

TUGALOO RIVER. Pronounced "Too' ga lo" or "Too'goo loo." This name is applied to an upper section of the Savannah River, where it borders between Stephens County and South Carolina. The naturalist William Bartram spelled the name TUGILO. The name Tugaloo (or Tugalo) is derived from an early Cherokee settlement called DUGILUYI, which was situated at the confluence of Toccoa Creek with the Tugoloo River. *Dugilu* may refer to a place at the forks of a stream. Or it is possibly from the Cherokee, *Ama-tu-gwa-luny,* which means "Water rolling over rocks there," or "Rough flowing water."

TUGALOO STATE PARK, Franklin County. A 393-acre park located on the shore of Hartwell Reservoir, six miles north of Lavonia. For derivation of the name, *see* Tugaloo River.

TUKPAFKA. This was an 18th century Creek Indian settlement on the upper Chattahoochee River, but its exact location is not known. It was recorded as TOAPAFKI in 1832, and was also called TOTE-PAUF-CAU. The Muskogean word means "punk knot," "punky wood," "rotten wood" or "tinder."

TULIP, Chattooga County. A station on the Central of Georgia Railroad, located near the Floyd County line. The name is derived from the tulip tree (yellow poplar). Re-established as the town of POETRY in 1973 by Anne C. Otwell who wanted to put "poetry" on the map, and create a colony of poets.

TULULGAH CREEK, Sumter County. Goff relates that this was an old Indian name of the present MILL CREEK (q.v.), and means "Where palmettoes abound."

TUMBLING SHOALS, Jackson County. A solid rock dam built by nature, located about one mile below Hurricane Shoals on the North Oconee River. The name is a translation from the Indian, *Yamucutah,* "To tumble."

TUNNEL HILL, Whitfield County. Incorporated as a town March 4, 1856. Named after the Western and Atlantic Railroad tunnel which penetrated the Chetoogeta Mountain on the southeast edge of Tunnel Hill (town), October 30, 1849.

TUNNO'S ISLAND, McIntosh County. Located in the Altamaha River near its mouth. Named after a Mr. Tunno who was an early proprietor of the island.

TUPIQUE, Liberty County. An early town at which the Spanish built a church in the 1570's. It was located in the vicinity of Sunbury, and was destroyed by young Chief Juan in 1597.

TURIN, Coweta County. Incorporated as a town December 27, 1890, at which time the post office was established. The present community is located in the southeast section of the county, and was also known as LOCATION. In 1830 an earlier community called PRESTON was settled about one mile south of present Turin. When the Savannah, Griffin and North Alabama Railroad came through in 1870, Preston moved to the present site near the railroad, and the name was then changed to Turin. It was named after the city in northwest Italy, which name means "City of the Bull."

TURKEY. The wild turkey, or *Meleagris gallopavo,* has been the source of several place-names in Georgia. Some had been translated from their former Indian names, such as TURKEY CREEK in Laurens County which was named by the Creeks, PINAHACHI or PENNOHATCHEE, the derivation being, *pinawa,* "turkey," and *hachi,* "stream." It rises in southwest Baldwin County, and crosses Wilkinson County southeasterly to the Oconee River. TURKEY CREEK in Carroll county was named for the numerous droves of wild turkey in the area. It rises at the southwest edge of Bremen and flows southwesterly to enter Big Indian Creek west of Bowdon. TURKEY CREEK in Dooly County rises at the Houston County line, and is an east bank tributary of the Flint River. It was previously known as BEAVERDAM CREEK. There was once a community in Dooly County of TURKEY CREEK near the present Lilly. The TURKEY CREEK (Militia) DISTRICT in Carroll County was named for the stream there. TURKEY MOUNTAIN in Floyd County was named for the stream there. TURKEY MOUNTAIN in Floyd County has an elevation of 1,280 feet, and is a recreation area about ten miles north of Rome. TURKEY MOUNTAIN LAKE is located 2½ miles south of this mountain.

TURNER AIR FORCE BASE (or TURNER FIELD), Albany. Named for Sullins Preston Turner, an Air Force officer born in Oxford, Georgia in 1914, and killed in an air crash at the beginning of World War II.

TURNER COUNTY. Created August 18, 1905 with 293 square miles taken from Dooly, Irwin, Wilcox and Worth counties. Named in honor of Captain Henry Gray Turner (1839-1904), who was wounded at Gettysburg and later became a U. S. congressman from Georgia, and also served as justice of the

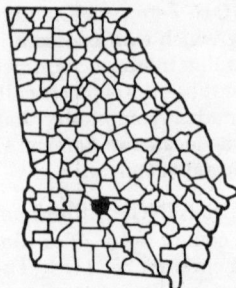

Georgia Supreme Court. The county seat is Ashburn (q.v.).

TURNER CREEK, Stewart County. Formerly called NOTCHEFALOTEE CREEK (q.v.).

TURNERVILLE, Habersham County. The post office was first established here in 1858 which was named TALLULA, after Tallulah Falls (q.v.) which were five miles north. The present name was adopted in 1882.

TURNIPTOWN CREEK, Gilmer County. An affluent of the Ellijay River, located northeast of Ellijay. The name is translated from the Cherokee name, ULUNYI, which means "Tuber place." TURNIPTOWN MOUNTAIN, with an elevation of 3,800 feet, is located seven miles east of Ellijay. There was an early Indian village named TURNIPTOWN, located four miles northeast of Ellijay.

TSILGIS' TCHO' KO, Chattahoochee County. This was a branch town of Cusseta, and the Muskogean name means, "clapboard."

TUSKIO-MICCO PATH. A former Indian trail that crossed the Ocmulgee River in lower Jones County and joined with Toms Path (q.v.). Assumed to have been named for Tussekiah Mico (Tasikaya Miko), the Warrior King of the Cussetta Indian tribe.

TUSSAHAW CREEK, Henry and Butts counties. Pronounced locally, "Tusseehaw." Rises in eastern Henry County and enters Branch Creek before it reaches Jackson Lake. Labeled TUSSY HAW on an 1821 map, the Muskogean Indian word means "Stream of Life," according to Rainer. However, Goff's research and study concludes it to mean, "To inflict pain on you" (as a wasp or bee sting), or "Warrior shooting at you."

TWEED, Laurens County. An early community which was located 12 miles southeast of Dublin, off of Georgia Highway 199. Believed to have been named after the river in Scotland.

TWENTY MILE CREEK, Coffee County. Rises about five miles northwest of Douglas and flows easterly to Seventeen Mile Creek. Was named about 1812-15 by General David Blackshear, probably because of its distance from another point.

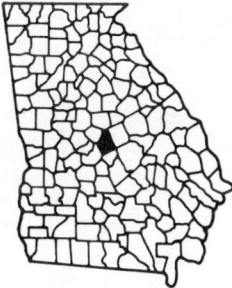

TWIGGS COUNTY. Created December 14, 1809 with 365 square miles taken from part of Wilkinson County. Named for Major General John Twiggs (1750-1816), a soldier of Georgia during the Revolutionary War. Within this county is the geographic center of the state, located near Marion (q.v.). The county seat is Jeffersonville (q.v.). The court house was destroyed by fire in 1901. *See also* Fort Romulos and Fort Twiggs.

TWIGGSVILLE, Twiggs County. A former post office which opened June 1, 1853 and was discontinued October 31, 1903. It was located eight miles south of Jeffersonville, and named for General Twiggs (*see* Twiggs County).

TWIN CITY, Emanuel County. This descriptive name was adopted when the towns of SUMMIT and GRAYMONT were incorporated into one, August 9, 1920.

TWIN LAKES, Lowndes County. Now a suburban community of Valdosta, it was established in 1825. Named for the two clear spring lakes upon which it is situated.

TWO MILE CREEK, Forsyth County. Flows parallel to Four Mile Creek and then Six Mile Creek, but they all join just before entering the Chattahoochee River. The names were designated as they measured the distance along the former Middle Cherokee Trading Path from Augusta.

TYBEE, Chatham County. Incorporated in 1887 as the town of OCEAN CITY, and in December of 1888 as the town of Tybee. August 1, 1929 the name was changed to SAVANNAH BEACH. For derivation, *see* Tybee Island.

TYBEE ISLAND, Chatham County. Sometimes spelled TIBY in the early days, the name means "salt" in the Uchee Indian language, or it may be derived from the name of the Choctaw chief, *Iti ubi*, which means "Wood killer." Located here is the famous lighthouse, TYBEE LIGHT. The first lighthouse here was built by Noble Jones of Wormsloe in 1736, on order of General James E. Oglethorpe. This is believed to be the third lighthouse in the United States. The present lighthouse was completed in October 1867, and soars 144 feet above sea level.

TYBEE ROADS, Chatham County. The bay at the entrance of the Savannah River, north of Tybee Island (q.v.). Margaret Godley said it was referred to by the Spanish as LOS BAJOS, "The Bay of Shoals."

TYRE, Douglas County. An early community which was located sixteen miles southwest of Douglasvile. Named after one of the great cities of the ancient world, in Phoenicia, which city today is called Sur, Lebanon.

TYRONE, Fayette County. Incorporated as a town August 18, 1911. Located nine miles west of Fayetteville, it was named from a county in Ireland.

TY TY, Tift County. Incorporated as a town August 28, 1883. Named after the nearby stream, Ty Ty Creek (q.v.). Mrs. Ida Belle Williams wrote that storekeeper and first postmaster "Daddy" Jelks suggested the name Ty Ty for the post office because of the many heart land railroad ties cut and sold at this community. It has been said that there was once a newspaper correspondent here in TyTy named Lulu Bobo.

TY TY CREEK. Rises in Worth County and flows through Tift and Colquitt counties, emptying into the Little River. The name is derived from the white titi (ironwood trees), or black titi (buckwheat trees) which grow along the stream, and which have white tassel-like flowers. Goff also adds that it may be from "Tight-Eye," an early coined name for a thick place that was difficult to see through. *See also* Ty Ty, Tift County. There is also a TY TY CREEK in Sumter County, which flows southerly below Plains to Kinchafoonee Creek.

TYUS, Carroll County. Located about ten miles southwest of Carrollton. It was said that two men were running for justice of the peace, with the agreement that the place would be named after the winner, who turned out to be H. M. Tyus. Actually the community was named for Jackson "Jack" Buchanan Tyus, who owned a farm and a general store here when the post office was established.

U

UCHEE CREEK, Columbia County. Pronounced locally, "Oochee." Indian scholars spelled it YUCHI and pronounced it "Yoochee." Rises in the lower section of the county and flows northeasterly into the Savannah River. Named after the Yuchi Indians (or Uchees), who were members of the Creek coalition. The Muskogean word *yuchi* means "seeing far away." When DeSoto passed through the Augusta area he found the Uchee Indians, which he called Appalachees, occupying both sides of the Savannah River. There are also several other streams in the state named UCHEE CREEK.

UCHEE ISLAND, Columbia County. Now called GERMAINES ISLAND, it is located in the Savannah River north of Augusta. The Uchee tribe of Indians resided in a town on the Georgia side of the river and cultivated fields on the island. *See also* Uchee Creek.

UCHEE PATH, Bleckley County. This route was opened around 1729 when the Uchee Indians began removing to the Uchee Town on the Chattahoochee River (on the Alabama side). Also called UCHEE TRAIL, it passed through the present Dublin, Cochran, Hawkinsville and Montezuma, thence to Uchee Town. *See also* Uchee Creek, and Upper Uchee Path.

UCHEE TOWN, Screven County. (Spelled YUCHI by Gatschett.) An early Indian town which was founded about 1729 on the banks of the Savannah River, 25 miles above the site of Ebenezer. For derivation *see* Uchee Creek. *See also* Fort Uchee.

UGLY CREEK, Twiggs County. An affluent of Big Sandy Creek in the northeast section of the county. Probably named by a surveyor in an attempt to be cute.

ULCOFAUHATCHIE RIVER. The early Indian name of the ALCOVY RIVER (q.v.).

ULCOHACHEE CREEK, Crawford County. A tributary of the Flint River. The Muskogean name means "Pawpaw Stream."

UNADILLA, Dooly County. Incorporated as a town December 24, 1891. First settled by Alexander Borum and John Edward Ransom. It was named by the Georgia Southern and Florida Railroad when laying the tracks through here in 1887-88. The name is an Iroquois Indian word that means "council place" or "place of meeting."

UNAWATTI CREEK. Rises in Franklin County and flows southwesterly into the North Fork of the Broad River. The name means "Old Bear Creek," possibly for a Cherokee by this name who once lived on its banks. Goff traced back to earlier names for the stream, such as YANUHWETI, YONA WATTOE and YONE WATER CREEK.

UNCLE REMUS ROUTE. This memorial highway runs from the North Carolina border, through Clayton, Cornelia, Athens, Madison, Milledgeville, Dublin, McRae, Douglas, Pearson, and Homerville to the Florida line. It was named in honor of Joel Chandler Harris (1848-1908) and his famous story book character, Uncle Remus. *See also* Eatonton and Wren's Nest.

UNDERGROUND ATLANTA. Reopened in 1969. This is a newly developed tourist attraction, and is located between the capitol building and Five Points, with its entrance on Central Avenue above Hunter Street. This subterranean district evolved with the construction of viaducts over the original rail yards to alleviate traffic snarls. It was completed in 1929, leaving assorted shops of the 1890 era, which were subsequently abandoned.

UNDERWOOD'S FERRY, Macon County. The last operating ferry in the state. Crosses the Flint River four miles southwest of Marshallville on Georgia Route 127. It is now run for the State Highway Department by brothers Lester and Homer Cromer. Originally named for Henry Underwood who owned the ferry and had a mill on the west bank of the river. It is now known as RIVER FERRY or MACON COUNTY FERRY.

UNICOI GAP, White County. A mountain pass in the northern section of the county, with an elevation of 2,963 feet. It was the first pass in the Georgia Blue Ridge through which a public road was constructed, and was named from this road, the Unicoi Turnpike (q.v.).

UNICOI NATIONAL OUTDOOR RECREATIONAL EXPERIMENT STATION, White County. Located north of Helen, this was established at the site of the former Unicoi State Park (q.v.). It is a state research facility governed by the North Georgia Mountains Authority which was created in 1968, with title to 1,013 acres of land for experimental use.

UNICOI STATE PARK, White County. Given this name December 12, 1953 as per the "desire of the citizens of White County." Established here in 1968 was the Unicoi National Recreational Experiment Station (q.v.).

UNICOI TURNPIKE, White County. An early toll road which was built about 1812-13. Some say it was built by a company of coastal traders, and it was also claimed to have been built as a public road by the Cherokees between their villages. The road started on the Tugaloo River, below the mouth of Toccoa Creek, went through the present Clarkesville, Nacoochee Valley, and left Georgia near Hiawassee. Stewart records that *Unicoi* is a Cherokee word meaning "White," while Bob Harrell said that it means "New Way." Earlier spellings of the name have included, UNICOY, UNAKA and UNEGA.

UNION CITY, Fulton County. "The Progressive City." Incorporated as a city August 17, 1908, when this was in Campbell County. So named when this became the meeting place of two railroads, the Atlanta and West Point and the Seaboard Coast Line.

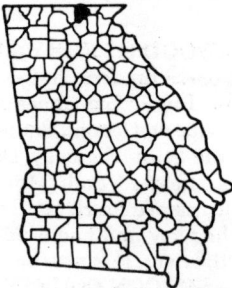

UNION COUNTY. Created December 3, 1832 with 319 square miles taken from part of Cherokee County. When the question as to the name of the new county was introduced in the state legislature, John Thomas, who was representing this region answered, "Union, for none but Union men reside in it." The tariff issue was a lively one at the time, creating a conflict between sectional interests and Union loyalty. The county seat is Blairsville (q.v.). The court house was destroyed by fire in 1859.

UNION POINT, Greene County. Incorporated as a town December 14, 1901. This name was adopted when the railroad junction was established in the 1830's for the two separate lines of the Georgia railroad. The original name of the settlement was THORNTON('S) CROSS ROAD (q.v.), and later it was called SCRUGGSVILLE, for local blacksmith, Mr. Scruggs.

UNION STREET, Brunswick. Named in honor of the union of England and Scotland as one kingdom (1707).

UNIONVILLE, Lamar County. *See* CHAPPELL.

UNIONVILLE, Tift County. Named in 1889 for the Union Lumber Company; it adjoins Tifton.

UNITY, Franklin County. A rural community near Carnesville. Named for an early church settlement. The name comes from Ephesians 4:3, "Endeavoring to keep the *unity* of the Spirit in the bond of peace."

UVALDA, Montgomery County. This town was incorporated July 22, 1910. Derivation of the name is unknown.

UNIVERSITY OF GEORGIA, Athens. This is claimed to be the nation's first state university, chartered January 27, 1785. The University of North Carolina disputes this claim, despite the fact that it was not chartered until 1789; it however opened its doors and began operating in 1795, which was six years before the University of Georgia opened. The university in Athens actually opened in 1801 on a 633-acre tract, which had been purchased from Mr. Daniel Easley by John Milledge, who donated the property to the trustees of the university. MILLEDGE HALL for men's residence was named in his honor (*see also* Milledgeville). The first building was completed in 1806, and called FRANKLIN COLLEGE in honor of Benjamin Franklin. This structure still stands and is now called OLD COLLEGE, and is used for administration offices. A second structure was built nearby in 1823, which is called NEW COLLEGE. The UNIVERSITY CHAPEL was erected that same year. DEMOSTHENIAN HALL was built in 1824 and named after the Greek, Demosthenes, the greatest orator of all time. Another early building, PHI KAPPA HALL, was named for an honorary fraternity, and built in 1834. MEIGS HALL (Psychology) honors Josiah

Meigs, the first president of the university (*see
also* Meigs, Thomas County). BALDWIN
HALL (Education) honors Abraham
Baldwin, one of the founders, and BARROW
HALL named for David C. Barrow, who was
chancellor of the university. HOKE SMITH
ANNEX (Agriculture · and Extension) for
Governor Smith who was elected governor of
Georgia in 1906. LUMPKIN LAW SCHOOL
was named for Joseph Henry Lumpkin, who
founded the law school in 1859, along with
William Hope Hull and Thomas R. R. Cobb.
Lumpkin was the first chief justice of
Georgia's Supreme Court. SANFORD
STADIUM was dedicated in 1929 and named
for Dr. S. V. Sanford, former president of the
university and long a leader in Southern
athletics. The Athens campus now comprises
3,500 acres. The entire University System of
Georgia includes 29 campuses throughout the
state (1974), with a total enrollment of over
85,000. *See also* Athens.

UPATOI, Muscogee County. A community
in the eastern section of the county on the
present U. S. 80, near Upatoi Creek (q.v.).
About 1790 this place was founded as a
satellite settlement of Cusseta Town (*see*
Cusseta).

UPATOI CREEK. Pronounced "You'-pa-
toy." Rises in lower Talbot County and flows
southwesterly, forming the border between
Chattahoochee and Muscogee counties before
entering the Chattahoochee River at Fort
Benning. The name may   signify "furthest
out" or "on the fringe," and it may also be
from the Muskogean, *apata-i,* "sheet-like
covering"   or   possibly   from   *apatana,*
"bullfrog." In Indian days the stream was
called HATCHEETHLUCCO or "Big Creek."
Many variations in spelling have included,
UPATOIE, UPATOY, UPTOIS, AU-PUT-
TAU-E, EUPHAUTAUS, OPATOHWAY,
OPATOY, EPITOY and APATI-I. This place-
name has also been applied to the UPATOIE
(Militia) DISTRICT in Muscogee County.

UPELIKEE CREEK, Terrell County. The
main headstream of Chickasawhatchee
Creek. Sometimes spelled UPELIKIE, the
Muskogean Indian word means "Big
Swamp."

UPPER (Militia) DISTRICT, Dade County. This might have been descriptively named
because of its being in the upper (northern)
part of the state, however it is in the extreme
lower (southernmost) section of the county.

UPPER UCHEE PATH. This early Indian
trail ran from Uchee Town on the west side of
the Chattahoochee River, at the mouth of
Uchee Creek below Columbus, to the present
Montezuma. From there it ran east across the
Ocmulgee, over past the Tarversville area,
turned north passing to the west of Jefferson-
ville, then by Rock Landing and on to Fort
Wilkinson. The trail was given this name in
1729 to differentiate from the Lower Uchee
Path which ran through Hawkinsville and
Cochran (*see* Uchee Path). In 1807, surveyor
William Dowsing Sr. labeled the Upper Uchee
Path, BLUFF TRAIL (q.v.).

UPSHAW, Cobb County. This early settlement was located on Wild Horse Creek,
about eight miles southwest of Marietta, in
the vicinity of the present community of
Macland. In 1882 the postmaster, Isaac D.
Upshaw, was a teacher and a blacksmith, and
also had a general store here.

UPSON COUNTY. Created December 15,
1824 with 333 square miles taken from
Crawford and Pike counties. Named in honor
of Stephen Upson (1786-1824), who was born
in Connecticut and educated at Yale. He was
forced to go south for his health, and became a
successful attorney in Oglethorpe, after
which he became a jurist of distinction, and
from 1820 to 1824 served in the state
legislature. The county seat is Thomaston
(q.v.).

UPTON CREEK, Henry County. Named for
a Mr. Upton, an early settler who lived on the
south side of Panther Creek near where Upton
Creek joins it, at which site he operated UP-
TON FORD FERRY. There is also a community named UPTON in Coffee County,
three miles northwest of Douglas, and a site
called UPTON MILL in Taylor County.

URENA, Banks County. A former community which was located about ten miles

northeast of Homer, and its name is from that of a particular herb or shrub.

USELESS BAY, Clinch County. A large swampy wooded area northwest of Homerville, which Goff said was so named because natives proclaim, "Hit's hard to get about in, and ain't fit fer nuthin'."

USSETTA, Chattahoochee County. *See* Cusseta.

USTANALI, Gordon County. A variant of OOSTANAULA (q.v.), and the early Indian name of CALHOUN (q.v.). Named from the nearby Oostanaula River.

UTOY, Fulton County. A former stagecoach stop and a post office from March 9, 1836 to July 7, 1866. Was located on Cascade Road near the south fork of Utoy Creek (q.v.).

UTOY CREEK, Fulton County. Located in the western section of the county. It was called by this name as early as 1823. Believed to have been named for the Utoy Indians, whose name signifies "final (or last) people." The name is also thought by some to be a garbled form of Upatoi (q.v.).

V

VADA, Mitchell County. Pronounced "Vay' da." Located five miles east of the Flint River on the Decatur County line. This community was first called PULL-TIGHT, after which it was known as HARRELL. It is presently named for Vada Wooten, daughter of a former justice of the peace.

VALDOSTA, CS Lowndes County. Called "The Azalea City," "Vale of Beauty," and "Naval Stores Capital of the World." Pronounced "Val dah' sta." Incorporated as a town December 7, 1860. The name of the city was suggested by Colonel Leonoreon de Leon, editor of the *South Georgia Watchman.* It is derived from *Val de Osta,* Italian for "Beautiful Valley." Valdosta was the name of Governor Troupe's country home in Laurens County. Lowndes County seat was moved to Valdosta from Troupville (q.v.) in 1860. The city supplies 80% of the world's supply of naval stores. FORCE STREET in Valdosta was named for Mr. Benjamin Force, who refugeed with his family from Rome, Georgia to Valdosta in 1863. MOODY FIELD of Valdosta was named for George Putnam Moody (1908-1941), who was born in the Philippine Islands, was a graduate of West Point, and died in an air crash in Kansas.

VALDOSTA STATE COLLEGE, Valdosta. Now part of the University System of Georgia, it was chartered in 1906 as SOUTH GEORGIA STATE NORMAL COLLEGE FOR WOMEN, and became coed and adopted its present name in 1950. The first building erected on campus was CONVERSE HALL, named in honor of W. L. Converse. The RICHARD HOLMES POWELL LIBRARY was named for the first president of the college. WEST HALL (classrooms and administration) was named in honor of the late Senator W. S. West, author of the first charter of the college, and first president of its board of trustees. NEVIN'S HALL (science) is named for Dr. Beatrice I. Nevins, professor of biology. The JEWEL WHITEHEAD CAMELIA TRAIL on the campus was a gift to the college from Mr. and Mrs. R. B. Whitehead of Valdosta, and in the south woods of the campus is DREXEL PARK, named after the city's landscape architect, R. J. Drexel.

VALONA, McIntosh County. A community located on Shellbluff River, nine miles northeast of Darien, off Georgia highway 99. Named after the seaport town of Valona in Albania.

VAN BUREN, Lamar County. *See* LIBERTY HILL.

VAN CREEK, Elbert County. Rises four miles northeast of Elberton and flows southeasterly to the Savannah River. Named after Van's Church, established in 1785 by Rev. Dozier Thornton. The church had been named for David Van, a benefactor friend of Reverend Thornton.

VANDIVER, S. ERNEST, BRIDGE. Spans the Tugaloo River on Interstate highway 85 between Hart County, Georgia and Oconee County, South Carolina. Named March 28, 1961 to honor Mr. Vandiver, who served as member of the State Highway Board, and who's son, Samuel Ernest Vandiver, Jr., was governor of Georgia (1959-63).

VANN, Murray County. An early trading station which was located north of Spring Place. It was sometimes called VANN'S (OLD) TOWN. This was the home of the notorious half breed chief, James Vann, a benevolent leader and constant trouble maker, son of the Scot, Clement Vann and a Cherokee mother named Wawli. His son Joseph was a wealthy slave-owning planter who built a substantial brick mansion in Spring Place about 1790, which is now one of the state's buildings of historic importance. *See also* Vann's Ferry.

VANNA, Hart County. Incorporated as a town August 19, 1912. This community is located four miles southeast of Royston, and established a post office here about 1893. Named by the railroad mail agent, Mr. Ezra Bowers, for his cousin, Miss Vanna Ballinger.

VANN'S CREEK, Floyd County. Located in VAN(N)'S VALLEY, which extends southwestward from Six Mile Station to Cave Spring. Named for Indian sub-chief David Vann who lived at Cave Spring. There was once a community and post office named VAN'S Valley in the late 1800's. VAN VALLEY CHURCH is located seven miles northeast of Cave Spring on U. S. 53-411.

VANN'S FERRY, Forsyth County. The first ferry on the Chattahoochee River, which was located 1½ miles southeast of Oscarville. This site is now beneath the waters of Lake Sidney Lanier. The ferry opened about 1805 by James Vann (*see* Vann), and the place was later known as VANN'S, and finally after transfer of ownership, WILLIAM'S FERRY.

VAN WERT, Polk County. Incorporated and designated the original county seat of Paulding County, December 27, 1838. This was the first town in the state to have a water system of its own, which was installed before 1887. Named for Isaac Van Wert, the companion of John Paulding, who assisted him in the capture of the British spy, Major John Andre (which thwarted Benedict Arnold's plot to betray West Point to the British). *See also* Paulding County.

VARNELL, Whitfield County. Incorporated as a city April 8, 1968. Originally called RED HILL, it was later known as VARNELL'S STATION, named for Mr. M. P. Varnell who was the early railroad agent here. General Wheeler defeated Union cavlary forces here which were led by Colonel LaGrange, May 9, 1864. VARNELL (Militia) DISTRICT is also located here.

VARNER'S STATION, Cobb County. An early name of SMYRNA (q.v.).

VASHTI SCHOOL FOR GIRLS, Thomasville. Pronounced "Vash-tie." Also known as VASHTI INDUSTRIAL SCHOOL. Originally established in a former Cubana cigar factory, it later expanded to twenty buildings. Methodist owned and operated, it was founded in 1908. Named in honor of Mrs. Vashti Blasingame, mother of the founder, Walter P. Blasingame.

VEAZEY, Greene County. A community in the southern section of the county, named for early postmaster Eli A. Veazey, who was a prosperous farmer who also had a general store here.

VEGA, Pike Community. A community located seven miles southeast of Zebulon. Vega is the name of a brilliant star of the first magnitude, and the word means "vulture."

VEREEN BELL HIGHWAY, Ware County. The access road, Georgia highway 177 which extends to Okefenokee Swamp Park (q.v.). Named for Lieutenant Vereen Bell, USNR, Georgia patriot and writer. His novel *Swamp Water* was made into two motion pictures by Fox Studios, in 1942 and 1952.

VERNONBURG(H), Chatham County. Also spelled VERNONBORG, it has sometimes been called WHITE BLUFF. Incorporated as the Town of Vernonburg, March 6, 1866. It was settled in 1742, making this one of Georgia's earliest settlements. Brinkley said it was "named by the early settlers of Salzburgers for one of their sponsors in America, James Vernon." It is located on the banks of the Vernon River.

VERNON RIVER, Chatham County. This stream enters Ossabaw Sound just above the Ogeechee River. There is uncertainty as to the origin of the name. Some say it bears the name of James Vernon, a member of the first Board of Trustees of the colony; others say it perpetuates the memory of Admiral Edward Vernon, who helped Oglethorpe drive the Spaniards from Georgia.

VESTA, Oglethorpe County. A community located 15 miles east of Lexington on Georgia highway 77. Named in honor of Miss Vesta Johnson, daughter of early resident, W.C. Johnson.

VICKERY CREEK (Militia) DISTRICT, Forsyth County. Located in the west-central part of the county. The post office was first established here as ALLENSVILLE (q.v.), became VICKERY'S CREEK January 13, 1846, and was changed to VICKERY on March 28, 1895. Named for the leading Cherokee Indian chieftan, Henry Vickery who died here in 1834 or for his wife Charlotte Vickery. The former community reportedly had a population of over 100 inhabitants.

VICTORIA, Brantley County. The early name of NAHUNTA (q.v.). There was also recorded that a community of VICTORIA existed in Etowah Valley of Cherokee County. Both places were probably named after Queen Victoria Alexandria (1819-1901) of England.

VICTORIA BRYANT STATE PARK, Franklin County. Located four miles west of Royston. This 380-acre park was established in 1954 on property given by Mr. Paul Bryant as a memorial to his mother, for whom it was named.

VICTORY (Militia) DISTRICT, Carroll County. Located east of Bowdon. Named from the early post office, VICTORY, on the Tallapoosa River, 12 miles southwest of Carrollton. The community was also known as McDANIELS MILLS, and the postmaster was Victoria Hines. *See also* LISBON, Lincoln County.

VIDALIA, Toombs County. Pronounced "Vye-dale'yuh." "A Modern Town for Modern Living." The town was named by the daughter of the man who built the old Savannah, Americus and Montgomery Railroad. It is a coined name from *via-dalia,* "by way of (the) dalias."

VIDETTE, Burke County. Incorporated as a town Augusta 17, 1908. A community located 13 miles west of Waynesboro on Georgia highway 24. Named after a Dr. Vidette.

VIENNA, CS Dooly County. Pronounced "Vy-enna." Incorporated as a city February 8, 1854. Formerly called BERRIEN (q.v.), the name was changed to CENTERVILLE in 1840. The present name was adopted February 8, 1841.

VIEW, Habersham County. A community located five miles west of Cornelia, named for the unusually good view from here of the distant mountains.

VILLAGE HARBOR. See (Lake) Lanier Islands.

VILLANOW, Walker County. A crossroads community located in the southeast section of the county. The name is believed to have been taken from that of a magnificent palace, "Villanow," described by Jane Porter in her novel *Thaddeus of Warsaw* (1803). Sartain however reported that Mrs. Constantine Wood, mother of Captain J. Y. Wood, proposed the name, saying, "It is no longer a hamlet, but is now a village, or village now, i.e. 'Villanow'."

VILLA RICA, Carroll County. Pronounced "Viller-ricka." Incorporated as a town December 24, 1842. The original settlement here was called HIXTOWN (q.v.), and started as a small colony of settlers who came from the North. This is said to be the oldest town in western Georgia. Gold had been discovered here in 1826, which led to its being named from the Spanish, *villa rica,* meaning "village of gold" or "rich town."

VILULAH, Randolph County. A former settlement that was located on present U. S. highway 27 about eight miles south of Cuthbert. Named after the Vilulah Baptist Church, which took its name from an old hymn, "Vilulia."

VINEGAR HILL (Militia) DISTRICT, Walton County. The name was said to have originated when an innkeeper, Jasper

Newton "Jack" Smith, watered down his liquor on one occasion to provide for a large number of guests who found it had turned to vinegar. It was also thought to have been named for the famous battle of Vinegar Hill between Irish rebels and the English in 1798. This was also known as LINDLEY'S DISTRICT.

VINEVILLE, Bibb County. An early residential community of 300 to 400 inhabitants, on the hill one mile from the original town of Macon. Named for the vineyards which were growing in the area. Incorporated into the city of Macon in 1903, with the present VINEVILLE AVENUE extending through this section.

VINEYARD ROAD, Spalding County. Runs east and north just above Griffin. So named as this is a noted fruit growing region where particularly fine grapes are produced. There was formerly a community and farmers post office three miles north of Griffin named VINEYARD.

VININGS, Cobb County. The early post office of VININGS STATION was established here in October 1868, named for one of the civil engineers who laid the tracks for the Western and Atlantic Railroad. The name was at one time VININGS BRIDGE, but the official name became simply "Vinings" in 1904. Much earlier than this, Hardy Pace moved his post office here from Paces Ferry (q.v.) in 1839 and called the place CROSSROADS. VININGS MOUNTAIN nearby had previously been called PACE'S MOUNTAIN after Pace had built a home at its base.

VINSON BRIDGE, Macon. This Second Street bridge over the Ocmulgee River was named in honor of Carl Vinson (1883-   ) of Milledgeville, who was U. S. representative from Georgia's Sixth District for over fifty years, a record unparalleled in House history. Also named for Congressman Vinson is VINSON VILLAGE of Macon, located in the southwest corner of the city. *See also* Ocmulgee National Monument.

VIOLA, Heard County. Community located three miles southwest of Franklin. Named for a Miss Viola Franklin.

VIOLA BEND, Dougherty County. Formerly called HORSESHOE BEND due to its shape. Located south of Albany's Oakwood Cemetery. Its present name was adopted after a boat called *Viola* smashed into the rocks on the side of the Flint River here and sank in 1846.

VIOLET, Meriwether County. A former post office from March 23, 1886 to March 23, 1903, which was located ten miles northwest of Greenville. The name was suggested by the first postmaster, James Cunningham Russell, who was fond of violets.

VISAGE, Towns County. A former community which was located seven miles southeast of Hiawassee. Its name is related to its view of the picturesque region.

VOGEL STATE PARK, Union County. This 221-acre park is located eleven miles south of Blairsville, and is at an elevation of 2,450 feet. It is Georgia's second oldest state park (after Indian Springs), and is located on Lake Trahlyta (q.v.). In 1928 August Vogel gave the land for the park which was named in his honor. There is also a community named VOGEL located in Clinch County.

VULCAN, Walker County. A former community named for an early iron works located here. In Greek mythology, Vulcan was the god of fire. As Lagondakis pointed out, "Etna was where Vulcan had his smithy."

W

WACO, Haralson County. Incorporated as a town September 23, 1885. Was also referred to as WACOVILLE, and previously called DEAN. *Waco* is a Muskogean Indian word meaning "heron."

WADLEY, Jefferson County. Incorporated as a town February 21, 1876, it was previously named SHAKE RAG (q.v.) and earlier yet known as BETHANY. Its present name, suggested by William Donovan, is for a native of New Hampshire, William Morrill Wadley (1813-1882). He began work as a blacksmith in Georgia, after which he eventually rose to be president of the Central of Georgia Railroad, as well as many other railroad and steamship companies. During the Civil War, Wadley was appointed by President Davis to serve as Superintendent of Transportation for the Confederacy. The magnificent bronze WADLEY STATUE, at the intersection of Third and Magnolia streets in Macon, was erected in 1886 by the employees of the railroad. *See also* Bolingbroke.

WAHACHEE CREEK, Elbert County. Rises five miles southeast of Elberton and flows southerly by Nancy Hart State Park and into the Broad River. Has also been spelled WAHATCHEE CREEK. William Read said it was probably named for a chief of the Lower Towns, Wauhatchie, derived from the Muskogean word *Waya-chi*, "Mighty Wolf."

WAHOO, Lumpkin County. A rural community which was located ten miles east of Dahlonega on Wahoo Creek. The WAHOO CHURCH is located on Georgia 52 at the Hall County line. WAHOO CREEK rises in southwest White County, flows through the southeast corner of Lumpkin County, then continues southward into Hall County to enter Lake Sidney Lanier. Various spellings of the name have included, WAWHOO, WARHOO, WAUGHOO, etc. Another WAHOO CREEK is located in Coweta County. It rises above Newnan, and flows westerly to the Chattahoochee River. WAHOO ISLAND of McIntosh County was originally named WAWHOO ISLAND. It is located east of U. S. highway 17, off the south bank of the South Newport River. WAHOO RIVER is a tidal stream that leads into the South Newport River. The derivation is believed to be from the Creek Indian word *uhawhu*, which means "cork" or "winged elm."

WAINWRIGHT, Charlton County. A former community which was located seven miles northeast of Traders Hill. The postmaster here in 1882 was F. D. Wainright who also had a general store. The place was later renamed UPTONVILLE.

WAKOFUDSKY CREEK, Clay County. A tributary to Cemocheckobee Creek. Read thought it to mean "Heron Point," from the Creek, *wako*, the "Little Blue Heron," and *fudsky* or *faski*, "sharp (or pointed)." A recent county map labels the stream WAUKEEFRISKEE CREEK.

WALASIYI INN, Vogel State Park. This lodge was named after the legendary great frog that the Cherokees called Walasiyi, which was described as being as big as a house and would hop across the valleys.

WALDEN, Bibb County. A small community located nine miles south of Macon on Echeconnee Creek. WALDENS CREEK is a tributary of the Ochlocknee River, and rises in Mitchell County, then flows into Thomas County. The name was possibly derived from Walden Pond, south of Concord in Massachusetts, publicized by Thoreau in his book *Walden* of 1854.

WALESKA, Cherokee County. Incorporated as the town of WALESCA (*sic*) November 13, 1889. First settled in 1835 by the Lewis W. Reinhardt family, the place was named after Warluskee, the daughter of an Indian chieftan who lived in this section. Brinkley says it was named from the Cherokee, *Walasi'yi* (*see* Walasiyi Inn).

WALKER COUNTY. Created December 18, 1833 with 445 square miles taken from part of Murray County. Named for Virginia-born

Major Freeman Walker (1780-1827) of Augusta, attorney who later served as U. S. senator from Georgia (1819-1821). The county seat is LaFayette (q.v.). The court house was destroyed by fire in 1883.

WALKER, LAKE, Ware County. Located in Laura S. Walker State Park (q.v.)

WALKER MONUMENT, Atlanta. This memorial features a cannon barrel aimed skyward. Located at the corner of Wilkinson Drive and Glenwood Avenue, the spot where General W. H. T. Walker, CSA (b. 1816) was killed July 22, 1864. *See also* Fort Walker.

WALKER MOUNTAIN, White County. With an elevation of 2,585 feet, it is located six miles southwest of Cleveland. Named for early settler, Richard Walker.

WALKER(S)VILLE, Pierce County. Was located nine miles north of Blackshear. Established about 1885 by Jackson Walker, a large landowner here. His son Lander Walker opened the post office in 1895, and was postmaster until it closed in 1910.

WALK-IKEY CREEK, Terrell County. Flows into Ichawaynochaway Creek southwest of Dawson. Goff said it is probably "Cow Creek," from *waca,* "cow."

WALLACE DAM, Putnam and Greene counties. Located 15 miles east of Eatonton. Construction of the 2,400-foot long dam on the Oconee River was begun in 1972. It was built by the Georgia Power Company to create LAKE WALLACE, a 35-mile long reservoir covering 18,000 acres.

WALLEGONY BAY, Glynn County. An early name of SAINT SIMONS SOUND (q.v.).

WALLENDA POINT, Habersham County. *See* Tallulah Gorge.

WALNUT. The existence of walnut trees, genus *Juglans* has been responsible for several place-names in Georgia. WALNUT was the name of a hamlet which was located ten miles north of Dahlonega in Lumpkin County. WALNUT CREEK rises in southeast Hall County and flows easterly into Jackson County until it reaches the Oconee River four miles west of Jefferson. It runs near the WALNUT CHURCH, three miles east of Braselton in Jackson County. This is the site of a former town of WALNUT, in which a post office was established from 1878 to 1890. Another WALNUT CREEK is found in Jones

County. It rises 4½ miles northwest of Gray, and flows southerly until it enters the Ocmulgee River at Macon in Bibb County. The early Indian name for the stream was OKENCHULGA, OCHUNCOOLGA, OKENCHULGEE, OKENCHULGO and OAKCHUNCOOLGAU. Goff explained that this would actually translate, "Stream where rock moss abounds," and would have been better called Moss Creek. A Civil War skirmish occurred by this stream in Bibb County, November 20, 1864. The town of WALNUT GROVE in western Walton County was incorporated August 23, 1905. It was named by early settler, Thomas Evans, because of an inviting group of walnut trees here. An early community of WALNUT HILL in Franklin County was located six miles southwest of Carnesville.

WALTER F. GEORGE RESERVOIR. Created by the construction of the WALTER F. GEORGE LOCK AND DAM on the Chattahoochee River at Fort Gaines, Clay County. Named for distinguished U. S. senator from Georgia, Walter Franklin George (1878-1957), who served in that office from 1922 to 1957. (*See also* Mercer University). The reservoir is also called LAKE GEORGE, LAKE CHATTAHOOCHEE, LAKE FORT GAINES, and particularly by Alabamans, LAKE EUFALA (q.v.). The lake has never been officially named by Congress, but the U. S. Corps of Engineers refers to it as Walter F. George Reservoir.

WALTHOURVILLE, Liberty County. Pronounced "Wall'ti ville." Incorporated as a town in 1974. Established as an early resort community and a stop on the Atlantic Coast Line Railroad. The post office was named for rich planter, Andrew Walthour. He donated property here for WALTHOURVILLE ACADEMY, which was incorporated November 21, 1823.

WALTON COUNTY. Created December 15

and 19, 1818 with 333 square miles acquired by Creek cession of January 22, 1818. This was an original county that was named for Virginia-born George Walton (1749-1804) of Augusta, in which city the street WALTON WAY was named in his honor. He was a delegate to the Continental Congress, and one of the three Georgians who signed the Declaration of Independence. Walton also served as U. S. representative from Georgia, and was the first governor of this state to serve after the Republic was established. He was made judge of the superior court in 1793 and elected to the U. S. senate in 1795. The county seat is Monroe (q.v.), earlier called WALTON COURT HOUSE (*see also* Cowpens).

WALTON COUNTY (extinct). Created by Act No. 106 of the Georgia General Assembly, April 24, 1802. It was located in what is now Transylvania and Jackson counties, North Carolina, due to a dispute as to the location of the state line. It was in the territory referred to as the "Orphan Strip." This county is shown on Wofford's map of c.1808 (Georgia Surveyor General Department). The state line was established at its true latitude in 1811, after which the county ceased to exist. *See also* Ellicott's Rock Scenic Area.

WARD, Randolph County. Settled in 1837 when it was known as NOTCHWAY. Established as WARDS STATION in 1858, named for rail agent John Ward. Incorporated as a town September 5, 1883. The name was changed to SCHELLMAN (now SHELLMAN, q.v.), October 6, 1885.

WARE COUNTY. Created December 15, 1824 with 912 square miles taken from part of Appling County. Ware is the largest in area of any county in the state, and was named for Nicholas Ware (1769-1824), Virginia-born Georgia legislator, who served as mayor of

Augusta and was elected to the U. S. senate, serving from 1821-24. The county seat is Waycross (q.v.). The home of Nicholas Ware in Augusta was called WARE'S FOLLY. WARESBORO(UGH) in Ware County was also named for Nicholas Ware. Settled in 1824, it was incorporated as a town December 11, 1858. In 1849 George White showed this to be the county seat and the only post office in the county. There is also a community of WARES CROSSROADS located near LaGrange in Troup County, and a community of WARESVILLE in Heard County.

WAR HILL, Wilkes County. A steep bluff located on the south side of Kettle Creek, eight miles west of Washington. It was so named because of the famous battle of Kettle Creek, resulting in a decisive victory for the American patriots here on February 14, 1779.

WARM SPRINGS, Meriwether County. First incorporated as BULLOCHVILLE (q.v.) in 1893 and as the city of Warm Springs August 6, 1924. The name is derived from the warm (87 degrees F.) spring mineral water of famous curative powers. The water is heated by the inner earth in a pocket of rocks 3,800 feet deep, and the springs produce 800 gallons per minute. Franklin D. Roosevelt first made use of the pools here as treatment for his polio in 1924, and this became a favorite second home for him after he became president and established his "Little White House" here. He died while at Warm Springs in 1945. The WARM SPRINGS FOUNDATION, a 900-acre facility was established here in 1927 to battle polio. It was purchased by the state of Georgia in 1973.

WARNER, LAKE, Hall County. Named for General A. J. Warner. This former Lake was created by Dunlap Dam on the Chattahoochee River, which was completed in 1908 and went out in 1936. This area was covered by Lake Lanier in 1957.

WARNER ROBINS, Houston County. "The International City" The original community here was for many years known as WELLSTON (q.v.). The municipality of Warner Robins was incorporated March 5, 1943, named for General Augustine Warner Robins (1882-1940), a pioneer officer of the U.S. Army Air Force, and designer of the USAF Materiel system. The Robins Air Force Base (q.v.) is located here.

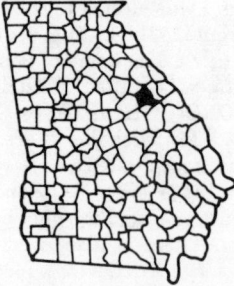

WARREN COUNTY. Created December 19, 1793 with 284 square miles taken from Columbus, Hancock, Richmond and Wilkes counties. Named in honor of Major General Joseph Warren (1741-1775) of Massachusetts, who fell in the battle of Bunker Hill. The county seat is Warrenton (q.v.). The court house was destroyed by fire in 1909.

WARRENTON, CS Warren County. Incorporated as a town December 8, 1810. Named for General Joseph Warren (*see* Warren County).

WARRIOR CREEK, Worth and Colquitt counties. It empties into the Little River. An upper tributary is called Indian Creek, and like Warrior is named in reference to the early inhabitants of the region. Brinkley said it was named for Long John or Warrior John, a Seminole Indian. WARRIOR was also the early name of LIZELLA (q.v.) in Bibb County.

WARSAW, Fulton County. This former community was located seven miles southeast of Alpharetta. It was the third post office to be established in Forsyth County, and was approved January 13, 1834. The WARSAW CAMP GROUND here was incorporated December 27, 1842. The community was later brought into Milton County when it was formed in 1857, and afterwards into Fulton County. The name is believed corrupted from the Indian word *wiso,* meaning "sassafras," and was also the derivation of Wassaw Island (q.v.) on the Georgia coast, and Wassau in Florida. Some have thought the name was transferred from the capital of Poland, during a time of revolutionary fervor. There is also a community of WARSAW located in northwest McIntosh County. The town of THUNDERBOLT (q.v.) was incorporated with the name of WARSAW March 5, 1856.

WARTHEN, Washington County. Pronounced "Wur'-then." Incorporated in 1812. This is the oldest community in the county, located eight miles north of Sandersville. Named for the George D. Warthen family, whose grandfather Robert Wicker from Maryland was given grant to the land here in 1787.

WARWICK, Worth County. Incorporated as a town August 22, 1905. The northernmost town of the county, which was moved from its original location after the coming of the railroad. Named after Warwick, Rhode Island, which was the birthplace of Nathanael Greene (*see* Greene County).

WAR WOMAN'S CREEK, Rabun County. Starts three miles east of Clayton and flows easterly to the Chattooga River. Reportedly given its name during the Revolution, as this was the stream near which Benjamin Hart lived, with his wife Nancy, who was known as the "War Woman" among the Indians of this section (*see* Hart County). Another source has explained that the name was adopted in reference to a female dignitary among the Cherokee, with the authority to decide the fate of prisoners of war. She was reportedly friendly with whites, and once saved some early settlers from a raid.

WASHINGTON, CS Wilkes County. "City of Ante-Bellum Homes" Is frequently referred to as WASHINGTON-WILKES, to differentiate from Washington D. C. Incorporated as a town in 1804. Washington is said to have more ante-bellum homes than any city in the state. This was previously the site of FORT WASHINGTON or HEARD'S FORT (q.v.), and the name of the place was changed to Washington in 1780 when the town was laid out. The Stephen Heard family was the first to settle here, having arrived December 31, 1773, and they named the place after George Washington who had been their neighbor in Virginia. This is said to be the first town in the nation to be incorporated in the name of George Washington, and is one of 36 Washington's in the United States. In this town was the first cotton mill in the South (1810), the first Southern woman newspaper editor (Sarah Hillhouse), and the first woman hanged in Georgia (1806). Located here is the Cooper-Sanders-Wickersham house, where Jefferson Davis dissolved the Confederate Government, May 5, 1865.

WASHINGTON COUNTY. Created February 25, 1784 with 674 square miles acquired by Creek cession of November 1, 1783.

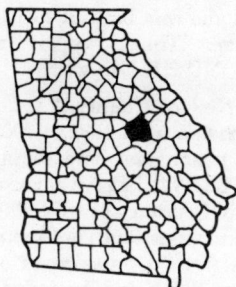

Named for General George Washington (1732-1799). The county seat is Sandersville (q.v.).

WASSAW ISLAND, Chatham County. The name is derived from the Creek word *wiso*, pronounced "wee' so," meaning "sassafras." Variations in spelling have included WESSO, WARSAW (q.v.), WASSA and WASSAU. GREAT WASSAW ISLAND is actually the eastern section of Skidaway Island. LITTLE WASSAW ISLAND lies southwest of the large Wassaw Island. WASSAW RIVER empties into WASSAW SOUND. The Spanish name for this sound on the early charts was BARRA DE AGUADULCE, meaning "Sweetwater Inlet (or Bar)," or BAHIA DE LA CRUZ, "Bay of the Cross."

WATERLOO, Irwin County. A rural community near the western boundary line of the county. Supposedly named by Joe Young who bought up property here, and afterwards his business deals went bad and he "met his Waterloo."

WATERMELON CREEK, Tattnall County. Flows southward into Bluff Lake which is located in swamplands along the Altamaha River. So named as this is in a melon growing region; nearby is Mushmellon Creek (q.v.).

WATKINSVILLE, CS Oconee County. Incorporated as a town December 14, 1815. Was made county seat of Clarke County in 1802, and became the county seat of Oconee County when it was formed in 1875. The town was named either after Colonel Robert Watkins, attorney of Augusta, or for Revolutionary soldier, Major John Watkins of Augusta.

WATSONBURGH, (Chatham County?). A place which was previously called YAMACRAW, mentioned in the 1758 will of Joseph Watson.

WATSON MILL STATE PARK, Oglethorpe County. This 140-acre park is located on a country road off of Georgia highway 22, eight miles north of Lexington. The longest covered bridge in Georgia, WATSON MILL BRIDGE, is on park property. The bridge spans Big Clouds Creek.

WATSON SPRINGS, Greene County. Located 11 miles northwest of Greensboro on Georgia highway 15. Named for Douglas Watson who purchased the spring in 1786 from Jesse Sanders. *See also* Indian Springs.

WAUHATCHIE BRANCH, Dade County. An affluent of Lookout Creek, located in the northeast corner of the county. Nearby is WAUHATCHIE SPRING. Both are named for Cherokee chief, Wauhatchie, who fought the Creeks in the War of 1812, serving under Major General Andrew Jackson's command. The name means "terrible wolf," from the Cherokee, *way achie*.

WAUKEEFRISKEE CREEK, Clay County. Ealier known as WAKAFUDSKY CREEK (q.v.).

WAVERLY, Camden County. A community located 16 miles southwest of Brunswick, which took its name from the old Waverly Plantation on which it was located. The plantation took its name from Sir Walter Scott's historical novels, which characterized its hero Captain Edward Waverly of Waverly Honor.

WAVERLY HALL, Harris County. The post office was established here February 2, 1829, and was given this name by the first postmaster, William Osborne, because of his appreciation of Scott's novels (*see* Waverly).

WAYCROSS, CS Ware County. Incorporated as the town of "Way Cross" March 3, 1874. Was first settled about 1820 after the land here was acquired from the Indians in 1814 and 1818. There was at one time a post office here called YANKEE TOWN (q.v.). This was for many years a small railroad stop called OLD NINE or NUMBER NINE, the railroad station number. It was afterwards called PENDELTON after an early settler, Philip C. Pendleton, and later in 1857 to TEBEAUVILLE in honor of Captain F. E. Tebeau (incorporated under this name in 1866). The present name of the city was chosen by three local leaders because of the many roads crossing here.

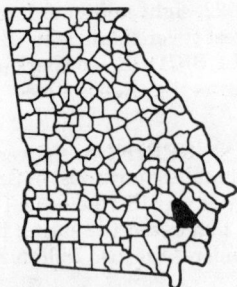

WAYNE COUNTY. Created May 11, 1803 with 646 square miles acquired by Creek cession of June 16, 1802. This was an original county and was named for General Anthony "Mad Anthony" Wayne (1745-1796) from Pennsylvania, who was a famous Revolutionary soldier, built Fort Wayne in Indiana, and settled in Georgia after the war, to the place where he had successfully defeated the British forces. He was subsequently made commander in chief of the western army to settle the Indian disputes in the plains states. The county seat is Jesup (q.v.), its originally having been at Waynesville (q.v.).

WAYNESBORO, CS Burke County. "Bird Dog Capital of the World" laid out in 1783 and incorporated as a town December 10, 1803. Named in honor of Anthony Wayne (see Wayne County).

WAYNESVILLE, Brantley County. A community located 35 miles east of Waycross on U. S. 84. This was the first county seat of Wayne County. The seat was moved to Jesup (q.v.) after Charlton County was cut off in 1854.

WAYSIDE, Jones County. A community located six miles northwest of Gray. Was first named LOUSY LEVEL and after that BLACK ANKLE. When the Central of Georgia Railroad came through in the 1880's, a more attractive name was desired, so the present one was adopted.

WAYS (STATION), Bryan County. The county seat was moved here from Hardwick (q.v.) in 1797 at which time this community was named CROSS ROADS. The later railroad stop was named for one of the Ways families, of which many inhabit this section. A model community was later developed by Henry Ford of Detroit. He began operations here with the purchase of several plantations in 1925, finally acquiring a total 70,000 acres in Bryan and Chatham counties. His own

winter home was built at nearby Richmond Plantation. The town is now named RICHMOND HILL (q.v.).

WEBB, Newton County. A former post office which existed from 1832 to 1902. Named for the first postmaster here, John Webb. Later called WEBBVILLE, it was incorporated as a villlage in February of 1854, and was located about nine miles south of Covington. Among the first five commissioners of the village were John Webb and Augustus J. Webb.

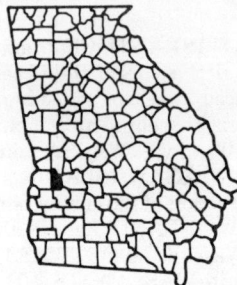

WEBSTER COUNTY. Created December 16, 1853 with 195 square miles taken from part of Stewart County. Residents had at first named their county KINCHAFOONEE (q.v.) which brought laughter across the state, so the name was changed in 1856 in honor of the U. S. representative from New Hampshire, Daniel Webster (1782-1852), who supported Clay's Compromise of 1850. The county seat is Preston (q.v.). The court house was destroyed by fire in 1914.

WE(E)LUSTEE CREEK, Bulloch and Bryan Counties. Early Indian name for BLACK CREEK (q.v.).

WEHADKEE CREEK. Flows southward from Randolph County in Alabama and joins the Chattahoochee River in Troup County, Georgia. The name means, "White Water Creek," from the Creek, wi, "water," and hatki, "white." It was labeled HOITHLE TIGUA by Benjamin Hawkins in 1798.

WELBORN (Militia) DISTRICT, Franklin County. The name is believed corrupted from Wilburn (q.v.).

WELCOME, Coweta County. A community located about one mile west of Newnan on the Franklin Road. Named by J. B. Hutchens after his friend Welcome Carter, a farmer who was one of the original settlers of this section. A resident here recently explained that the name came about because the Indians were friendly to the early settlers and made them feel welcome here. The post office was established in 1890.

WELLBORN'S MILLS, Houston County. Named for William Wellborn, who was a prominent resident of the county. The place was later known as FEAGIN SETTLEMENT, after an early postmaster G. T. Feagin. The present FEAGIN ROAD is located three miles south of Warner Robins.

WELLSTON, Houston County. Until 1943, this was the name of the community that became WARNER ROBINS (q.v.). It was named for a Mr. Wells (initials unknown), an engineer for the Georgia Southern & Florida Railway, who was a friend of R. H. Watson and Henry S. Feagin, Jr. Before the railroad name Wellston, the community had a post office named YORK, about one mile from Wellston station.

WERACOBA CREEK, Muscogee County. Flows southerly through Columbus to the Chattahoochee River. Goff said it could mean "big water," from *wewa,* "water," and *rakketa,* "very large."

WESLEY, Emanuel County. A community located nine miles south of Swainsboro. Incorporated as a town August 18, 1913, and believed named after John Wesley (*see* Wesleyan College).

WESLEYAN COLLEGE, Macon. Incorporated December 23, 1836 as GEORGIA FEMALE COLLEGE, which opened in Macon, January 7, 1839. It is the first chartered college in the world to grant degrees exclusively to women. The Methodist Church assumed supervision of the college December 19, 1839, and changed its name to WESLEYAN FEMALE COLLEGE in honor of John Wesley (1703-1791), the founder of Methodism. Wesley was brought to the Georgia Colony in 1735 by General Oglethorpe to minister to the colonies, although his personal interest was to Christianize the Indians. The present name of the college was adopted in 1919, and it was moved from its College Street location to its present 240-acre campus at suburban Rivolvi in September 1928. The CANDLER MEMORIAL LIBRARY here was built in 1928 as a gift of Atlanta judge, John Slaughter Candler, in honor of his father and mother. The former railroad station name of

Rivoli by the Wesleyan College campus was changed to WESLEYAN STATION. WESLEY('S) OAK on Saint Simons Island is a water oak under which John Wesley preached before Christ Church was built here. Emory University's WESLEY MEMORIAL HOSPITAL was named in honor of John Wesley, and opened in 1922. The magnificent bronze WESLEY STATUE, sculptured by Marshall Dougherty of Mercer University, is located in the center of Reynolds Square in Savannah.

WEST BROW (Militia) DISTRICT, Dade County. Descriptively named in reference to its location on Lookout Mountain.

WEST END, Fulton County. Incorporated as a town October 10, 1868. Now part of Atlanta, this early suburban community was named because of its relationship to downtown Atlanta. It was established at the site of WHITE HALL (q.v.), at the intersection of Newnan and Sandtown roads. The descriptive name WEST END is also applied to a part of the city of Rome, Floyd County.

WESTFIELD ROAD, Gilmer County. A 25-mile section of the present U. S. highway 76 from Chatsworth across the Cohutta Mountains to Ellijay. Named after the man who built the original road, David Westfield (1786-1865), an Irishman from South Carolina.

WEST GEORGIA COLLEGE, Carrollton. First organized in 1907 as the FOURTH CONGRESSIONAL DISTRICT AGRICULTURAL AND MECHANICAL SCHOOL, this college is now a part of the University System of Georgia. It became a junior college in 1933, and a senior college in 1957. The oldest building on campus is the THOMAS BONNER HOUSE (alumni office) which was erected in 1843. ADAMSON HALL (women's residence) was named for U.S. congressman, William C. Adamson, while AYCOCK HALL (men's residents) honors one of the founders of the college, Colonel J. A. Aycock. The MARTHA MONRO BUILDING (classrooms) was named for the wife of former college president, Dr. David S. Ingram, and the SANFORD BUILDING (administration) was named to honor the late chancellor, Steadman V. Sanford. The CASON CALLAWAY SCIENCE BUILDING was completed in 1962 and was named for Cason J. Callaway, one of the original members of the Board of Regents (*see* Callaway Gardens).

WEST GREEN, Coffee County. Incorporated as a town July 29, 1914. This community was first called THE TWENTY when it was established about 1900, being 20 miles south of Hazelhurst. Some years later the name was changed to GARRANT, and finally adopted its present name to honor a member of the Westbrook Company.

WESTLAKE, Twiggs County. Located in the southwest corner of the county, this old community was originally called BUZZARD ROOST (q.v.). The present name was adopted in 1885 because of its relationship to a lake to the west of the settlement.

WESTMINSTER, Fulton County. Incorporated as a town July 26, 1904. Believed named for a Presbyterian church of the former community here.

WESTOBOU. An early name of the SAVANNAH RIVER (q.v.).

WESTON, Webster County. Previously called HARD MONEY, the present name was adopted when it was incorporated March 6, 1856. It was either named to honor one of the original commissioners, Joseph L. Weston, or because of its location in the western part of the county as well as of the state.

WESTONIA, Atkinson County. An early settlement of old Coffee County, located six miles west of Pearson. Believed named after early postmaster, J. O. Weston, who was the local railroad and express agent, and also had a saw mill here.

WEST POINT, Troup County. "The Home of Textiles" The original settlement began here with the building of the first store about 1829. The place was called FRANKLIN at the suggestion of Dr. G. W. Hill. In 1831 the new county seat of Heard County was given the name Franklin (q.v.), so Franklin in Troup County changed its name to West Point, December 24, 1832. This present name was adopted because of the town being the westernmost community on the Chattahoochee River in Georgia. It later became the western terminal of the Atlanta and West Point Railroad which ran from East Point near Atlanta.

WEST POINT LAKE, Troup and Heard counties. A 26,900-acre reservoir completed in 1974, with a 525-mile shoreline and extending 34 miles up the Chattahoochee River. The 7,000-foot long WEST POINT DAM was built by the U. S. Corps of Engineers at a total project cost of $115 million. Its generators have a capacity of producing 193,000,000 kilowatt hours of electricity annually.

WESTVILLE, Stewart County. A newly developed "Living History Center," representing an 1850 Georgia town. It is located on 58 acres of land on the southeast edge of Lumpkin, which was donated by the Sam Singer family. Named for Colonel John Word West, history professor and former president of North Georgia College, whose extensive collection was purchased when this venture was begun. The idea for the town was conceived by director, Joseph B. Mahan. The first historic building was brought here in January 1968.

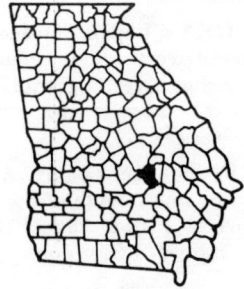

WHEELER COUNTY. Created August 14, 1912 with 306 square miles taken from part of Montgomery County. Named for General Joseph Wheeler (1836-1906), illustrious soldier of two wars. He was a Confederate cavalry leader, and later was commander of a cavalry division in the Spanish American War. The county seat is Alamo (q.v.). Its court house was destroyed by fire in 1916. *See also* Camp Wheeler.

WHELCHEL DISTRICT, Hall County. This militia district was claimed by some to have been named for early postmaster, William P. Whelchel, who was also a farmer, legislator and justice of the peace. Others have said it was named after John and David Whelchel, who settled on the Little River here.

WHIGHAM, Grady County. Originally called HARRELL'S STATION (q.v.), the name Whigham was adopted in 1880 for Robert Whigham, who had established a big mercantile store here. The town was incorporated December 23, 1896 when this was still part of Decatur County.

WHITE, Bartow County. Incorporated August 7, 1919. Named for James A. White who came from the vicinity of Pine Log (q.v.), and from North Carolina before that. He settled here about 1870 and established a store, a cotton gin, and was the first postmaster of the town.

WHITE BLUFF, Chatham County. *See* Vernonburgh.

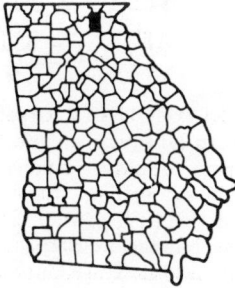

WHITE COUNTY. Created December 22, 1857 with 243 square miles taken from part of Habersham County. Derivation of the name is not certain, but it is believed to have been named by State Representative William H. Shelton in honor of David Thomas White (1812-1871), a native of Davidson, North Carolina, and representative from Newton County, who backed the bill to form White County. Lucian Lamar Knight, and Candler and Evans had earlier claimed that the county was named for Colonel John White of Chatham County, who was a hero of the Revolution. The original court house in Cleveland (q.v.) was built in 1857, constructed of handmade brick, laid by slave labor and paid for in Confederate currency.

WHITE HALL, Chatham County. A plantation, six miles south of Savannah on the Savannah River. Was the estate of attorney and statesman, Thomas Gibbons, which was previously known as COWPENS (q.v.).

WHITEHALL, Clarke County. Incorporated as a town October 15, 1891. Now a rural community, it is located south of Athens. At this site, John White from Ireland built in 1827 the first cotton mill south of the Potomac to take the raw product and manufacture it into clothing.

WHITE HALL, Fulton County. The post office existed here from 1835 to 1840, when Charner Humphries (1795-1855) was the postmaster. This was at the present intersection of Lee and Gordon streets, and was a suburban community of Atlanta at a section called WEST END (q.v.). White Hall was the first established name of present ATLANTA (q.v.) and was given this name because Humphries' place was the first structure to be painted white in this region. After the railroad was established, the community south of the tracks was sometimes referred to as BLACK HALL, as contrasted to White Hall on the opposite side of the tracks. The 530th militia district which included White Hall, became known as the BLACK HALL DISTRICT in the 1830's and 1840's.

WHITE HOUSE, Henry County. A community located six miles north of McDonough at the forks of Georgia 155 and the road to Kelleytown. The settlement was established around the Silas Moseley place and was named after the white house of his daughter, Martha Moseley, who married Rufus W. Love. A post office existed here in the 1850's.

WHITE OAK, Camden County. A community about four miles north of Woodbine on U. S. 17 and on WHITE OAK CREEK, a tributary of the Satilla River.

WHITEPATH, Gilmer County. An early post office, located about five miles northeast of Ellijay. Named after the noted Cherokee chief, White Path (c. 1768-1838) of the Turniptown region. Also named for this chief is nearby WHITEPATH SPRINGS.

WHITE PLAINS, Greene County. Incorporated as the town of "White-plains" March 3, 1856. This town adopted its name because of the sandy white soil here in the "white land section," originally occupied by small poor white owners. The place was previously called FORT NEIL.

WHITESBURG, Carroll County. Incorporated as a town March 2, 1874. The Coweta chief, William McIntosh (*see* McIntosh Old Place), had previously owned a vast plantation near here which was called LOCKCHAU TALOFAU (q.v.), "Acorn Bluff." McIntosh was killed and his estate here was destroyed May 1, 1825 with a reported property loss of $40,000. Mr. J. A. McMullen was the first white settler, who came in 1872 and built the first store and a house. The town was laid out about 1873-74 when the Savannah, Griffin and North Alabama Railroad came through, and was named for Mr. A. J. White, who was then president of the railroad.

WHITE SULPHUR SPRINGS, Hall County. Also known as OCONEE WHITE SULPHUR SPRINGS. This was once a noted health resort located six miles northeast of Gainesville near Lula. The waters were found to be rich in sulphur and magnesia. A railroad station of WHITE SULPHUR was located on the Southern Railroad, two miles northwest of the spring.

WHITE SULPHUR SPRINGS, Meriwether County. Incorporated as a town August 22, 1907. Located on Mountain Creek, five miles northeast of Pine Mountain. This was once a popular summer resort. It adopted its name because the mineral springs here were found to be strongly impregnated with sulphur.

WHITESVILLE, Harris County. Incorporated as a town from December 25, 1837 to December 27, 1842, and then again incorporated February 10, 1854. The post office was established here in 1835, after having been transferred from Mountain Creek (q.v.). Was named in honor of the wealthy and influential White family who once lived here. Wiley White was one of the town's commissioners when it was first incorporated.

WHITEWATER CREEK. Rises in the southwestern section of Heard County, and flows southeasterly into Troup County and then southward to the Chattahoochee River. Derivation is from an early name of the stream, WEHUTKEE, a Creek word meaning "white water," apparently because of the frothy appearance from the numerous shoals in the stream. It was labeled HATCHE SOOF, KEE by Benjamin Hawkins in 1798 (for derivation, see Hachasofkee Creek). Another WHITEWATER CREEK is found in Laurens County. It enters the Oconee River near the southeast corner of the county. There is also a WHITEWATER CREEK which rises in southeast Talbot County and flows through Taylor County and into Macon County where it enters the Flint River. A translation from the former name OKAUHUTKEE CREEK. Named for it is the new WHITEWATER CREEK STATE PARK in Macon County. This 426-acre park is located four miles north of Oglethorpe on Georgia highway 128. And lastly, a WHITEWATER

CREEK rises at Fairburn and Union City in Fulton County, flows southward, entering the northwest corner of Fayette County and continues southerly to enter Line Creek at the southwest corner of Fayette County.

WHITFIELD COUNTY. Created December 30, 1851 with 281 square miles taken from part of Murray County. Named after the celebrated evangelist, Reverend George Whitefield (1714-1770), who established the famous orphanage at Bethesda (q.v.) near Savannah in 1741. The county seat is Dalton (q.v.). An early community named WHITFIELD in Pulaski County was located eight miles southwest of Hawkinsville. Also named for Reverend Whitefield (sic) is WHITFIELD SQUARE in Savannah.

WHITLEY BRANCH, Laurens County. A tributary of Stitchihatchie Creek, located southeast of Dexter. It is not known when or why this name was given to this stream, which was formerly called MILLER'S BRANCH (q.v.). An early community of WHITLEY was located on the present Ben Hill-Irwin county line.

WHITNEY, Calhoun County. A community located four miles northwest of Morgan. Incorporated as a town December 14, 1871. Incorporated as DICKEY in 1900.

WHITTINGTON, Worth County. An early settlement in the southeast section of the county located on TyTy Creek, and believed named for the Whittington family. S. C. Whittington was an early postmaster and N. B. Whittington had a general store here.

WHOOPING CREEK, Carroll County. Rises below Carrollton and flows southward into the Chattahoochee River. Bonner wrote that the name of this stream was translated from the Creek Indian word *wetumcau,* meaning "rumbling water."

WICKED(S) CREEK, Hall County. A west-bank affluent of the Chattahoochee River, named for a Cherokee family of Wickeds. Variations in spelling have been WICKET or WICKETT.

WIGHT, ISLE OF, Liberty County. Located two miles east of Midway. Was undoubtedly named for the island off Hampshire in southern England.

WILBURN, Franklin County. Was established as a station on the Southern Railroad, located four miles northwest of Lavonia. Incorporated as a town from August 8, 1910 to August 4, 1914. It is within WELBORN (sic) MILITIA DISTRICT.

WILCOX COUNTY. Created December 22, 1857 with 383 square miles taken from Dooly, Irwin and Pulaski counties. Named for Major General Mark Wilcox (1800-1850) of Telfair County, who was a soldier, railroad pioneer and legislator. The county seat is Abbeville (q.v.).

WILKES COUNTY. Created February 5, 1777 with 470 square miles acquired by Cherokee cession and Creek cession, both of June 1, 1773. Named in honor of John Wilkes (1727-1797), a distinguished member of the British Parliament, who strenuously opposed those harsh and unjust measures towards the colonies which finally led to the Revolution. The county seat is Washington (q.v.). *See also* New Purchase.

WILKINSON COUNTY. Created May 11, 1803 and June 26, 1806 with 428 square miles acquired by Creek cessions of June 16, 1802 and November 14, 1805. This was an original county which was named for General James Marion Wilkinson (1757-1825), a soldier of the Revolution and the War of 1812, noted Valdosta attorney at law, and railroad president (*see also* Fort Wilkinson). The county seat is Irwinton (q.v.). The court house was destroyed by fires in 1829, 1854, 1864, and 1924.

WILLACOOCHEE RIVER, Irwin County. Sometimes called WILLACOOCHEE CREEK. The name is derived from the Creek word, *Wihlakuchi,* meaning "Little River." It has also been interpreted as being from the Creek word for wildcat. The town of WILLACOOCHEE in Atkinson County was incorporated November 12, 1889.

WILL-A-WAY RECREATION AREA, Bartow County. Also called CAMP WILL-A-WAY. This is a section of Fort Yargo State Park (q.v.) which was completed in 1970 and dedicated June 20, 1971. It was designed as a park area for disabled persons. The Department of State Parks conducted a contest for the naming of the recreation area. The winning suggestion was submitted by Mrs. Bascom S. Deaver of Macon, who condensed the phrase, "Where there's a will there's a way."

WILLIAM B. HARTSFIELD ATLANTA INTERNATIONAL AIRPORT. *See* HARTSFIELD INTERNATIONAL AIRPORT.

WILLIAM C. CRAWFORD HIGHWAY. A state route (now U.S. 78) between Atlanta and

Augusta, through Athens, named in honor of Senator Crawford (see Crawford County).

WILLIAM HOWARD TAFT HIGHWAY, Chattooga and Walker counties. Runs parallel and west of U. S. 27 between Summerville and LaFayette. Named in honor of President Taft (1857-1930), who was also Secretary of War and Chief Justice of the Supreme Court.

WILLIAMSBURG(H), Calhoun County. Incorporated as a town August 4, 1887. This is now a vanished Georgia town, which was once called "the sickliest place in Georgia" due to the prevalence of malaria here. Is located on the Central of Georgia Railroad, six miles south of Morgan.

WILLIAMSBURG, Clinch County. A former community which was located on the west side of the Suwanee River. Derivation of the name is unknown.

WILLIAMSBURG, Wayne County. Incorporated in 1792. This place was first called SAINT SAVILLA (q.v.) and then Williamsburg, after which it reverted to its original name before it disappeared to become a ghost town. It was believed named after the incorporators, which were William Williams, Farr Williams, John William Lambert, William Cook and the last commissioner, Roswell King on whose land the town was partially laid out.

WILLIAMSON, Pike County. Incorporated as a town August 17, 1908. The original name of this place was DRIVER, after innkeeper Giles Driver. It was then called STEARNSVILLE after John Stearns who bought the inn, and finally for Judge Isaac Wiliamson, slave owner, farmer, and money lender.

WILLIAMSTOWN, Jackson County. A settlement area of old Harmony Grove (now Commerce), named for early builder and contractor Harmon Williams.

WILLIAMSVILLE, Pike County. The early name of NEAL (q.v.)

WILLIE, Liberty County. A former community which was incorporated as a town August 4, 1915. Was located 12 miles northwest of Hinesville.

WILLINGHAM, Worth County. Believed to have been the original settlement of the present SYLVESTER (q.v.), named from the pioneer settlers here. This was the location of Hugh Willingham and Company, dealing in naval stores. An early postmaster here was W. B. Willingham.

WILLOWBROOK, Oglethorpe County. A residential area between Lexington and Crawford. Established in 1965 by Charles Clifford Brooks.

WILMINGTON, Chatham County. A community on Wilmington Island (q.v.).

WILMINGTON ISLAND, Chatham County. Located below Savannah, east of Skidaway Island and west of Tybee. Thought to have been named for Spencer Compton, Earl of Wilmington (1673-1743), who was prominent in English politics and had colonial interests.

WILMINGTON RIVER, Chatham County. The channel beside Wilmington Island (q.v.).

WILMOTS, Banks County. An early community, located five miles northeast of Homer. In 1882, the postmaster was H. E. Wilmots. It was also known as CHEAP.

WILSON AIRPORT, Bibb County. See Macon.

WINCHESTER, Macon County. A stop on the Georgia Railroad, located two miles southwest of Marshallville. Believed named for the city in England.

WINDER, CS Barrow County. "The Work Clothing Center of the World" Pronounced "Wine-der" or "Wine-duh." This was originally the site of an Indian settlement called SNODON, after which the white men came and called their first community JUG TAVERN (q.v.), which was located at what was then the junction of Jackson, Walton and Gwinnett counties. It was called BRANDON after this. When the Seaboard Air Line Railroad was built through here in 1893, the town was incorporated and its name was changed to honor the president of the railroad, John H. Winder of Raleigh, N.C. He is thought to have been related to General John Henry Winder CSA, who supervised Andersonville (q.v.) and other Confederate prisons during the Civil War.

WINDSOR, Walton County. An early settlement which was located four miles northeast of Loganville. All that remains today is Windsor Church and Cemetery. The name was believed transferred from England, from the name of a prominent town there as well as of the royal castle. A section of Savannah is called WINDSOR FOREST, and a part of Columbus is named WINDSOR PARK.

WINFIELD, Columbia County. A community located 17 miles northeast of Thomson. First settled on 700 acres granted Leonard Clairborne in 1767 by King George III. This is obviously an English name, but the derivation is unknown. The community is called COBBHAM by a few people, perhaps in relation to the former town in adjoining McDuffie County named Cobbham (q.v.).

WINFIELD SCOTT, LAKE, Lumpkin County. Located six miles south of Lake Trahlyta, near Dahlonega. Named for "Old Fuss and Feathers," General Scott (1786-1866), who fought in the War of 1812, the Seminole War, Mexican War, and was a United States presidential candidate in 1852.

WINNEPESAUKAU, LAKE, Catoosa County. Located within the city of Lakeview. Also spelled WINNEPESAUKAT, it was once known as GREEN'S LAKE. It was then purchased by Mr. and Mrs. Carl O. Dixon, who gave it the present Indian name, which is said to mean, "Beautiful Lake of the Highlands," or "Place of Abundant Waters."

WINSTON, Douglas County. Incorporated as a town August 20, 1906, it was disincorporated since 1950. The community is located four miles west of Douglasville. Named for early settler and preacher here, "Uncle Jackie" Winn, originally from South Carolina.

WINTERVILLE, Clarke County. Incorporated as a town August 15, 1904. The original railroad name was WINTERS in 1882 when John Winter was the railroad and express agent.

WIREGRASS REGION. This is a name that refers to roughly the southern third of the state of Georgia, where the grass *Aristida stricta* abounds. This wiregrass grows in bunches or tufts in the south Georgia piney woods section, and has long wire-like blades. There was once a community named WIREGRASS, 11 miles south of Homerville in Clinch County, which took its name from this region in which it was located.

WIRE ROAD. *See* FEDERAL WIRE ROAD.

WISDOM'S STORE, Harris County. An early community which was located eight miles northwest of Hamilton, and was the home of William C. Wisdom (1833-1898) from Virginia, who was judge of the county court and a state representative.

WISO, Camden County. Pronounced "Weeso." The Indian name for CUMBERLAND ISLAND (q.v.) and was their name for "sassafras."

WITHLACOOCHEE RIVER. The upper section in eastern Tift County is called Camp Creek. It flows southeasterly into Berrien County then southerly into Lowndes County and forms part of the boundary with Brooks County, and continues southward into Florida. William Read explains that the name means "Little River" (q.v.) and the derivation is from the Creek Indian word *Wihlakuchi*, from *wi*, "water," *lako*, "big," and *-uchi*, "little." He adds that it is a by-form of Willacoochee (q.v.).

WOLF CREEK, Bibb County. Rises northwest of Macon's Weslyan College, and flows southward about three miles into Rocky Creek. The surveyor who named this stream, probably killed or at least saw a wolf nearby.

WOLF FORK DISTRICT, Rabun County. Named from its location in the WOLF FORK VALLEY. WOLFFORK is also the name of a rural community in Rabun County, seven miles northwest of Clayton. WOLF CREEK ROAD is located three miles north of Clayton. WOLF FORK GAP is between Mountain City and Rabun Gap.

WOLFPEN. Pens were devices for catching wolves, which were commonly found in early settlement days of Georgia, but have now disappeared. The name "Wolfpen" has been applied to place-names in various sections of the state. A stream called WOLFPEN BRANCH is an upper affluent of Lotus Creek in western Bulloch County. The name of streams called WOLFPEN BRANCH are also found in Bryan, Habersham, and McIntosh counties. WOLFPEN GAP is in lower Union County, while WOLFPEN RIDGE is on the line between Union and Towns counties. WOLFPEN MOUNTAIN is located in Gilmer County. There is also a WOLF PIT (Militia) DISTRICT in Stephens County, which is from another name for a wolf trap.

WOLFSKIN (Militia) DISTRICT, Oglethorpe County. Located southwest of Crawford. Named when the last wolf of this region was killed in 1823, and its skin nailed to a door of the trading post.

WOLLEY FORD, Hall County. Located in the western section of the county, this crossing on the Chestatee River was named for Bazel Wolley, who came to this area in 1821.

WOODBINE, CS Camden County. Incorporated as a town August 13, 1908, and became the county seat in 1923. Woodbine is the common English name for the honeysuckle, *Lonicera*. A new Thiokol plant was recently established here to build the nation's largest solid-fuel rocket engines.

WOODBURY, Meriwether County. Incorporated as a town August 23, 1872. Probably named in reference to the wooded country here, but it may have been from a personal name or from the town in England.

WOODLAND, Talbot County. Incorporated as a town July 30, 1908. Named in honor of C.S. Woods of Virginia, who purchased the surrounding land and laid it off into town lots. The post office was opened March 5, 1907. The site was originally known as PLEASANT HILL.

WOODROW WILSON COLLEGE OF LAW, Atlanta. Named for the 28th president of the United States, Thomas Woodrow Wilson (1856-1924), who practiced law in Atlanta for a short period. He married Ellen Lou Axson of Rome, Georgia, in Savannah in 1885 (*see also* Axson). Wilson's boyhood home was located at Telfair and Seventh streets in Augusta.

WOODROW WILSON SPRING, Richmond County. Located adjacent to State Route 25 at McBean Creek. Named by a resolution of the General Assembly of Georgia, January 1960, to perpetuate the memory of President Wilson, who spent his boyhood in Augusta (*see* Woodrow Wilson College of Law).

WOOD(S) STATION, Catoosa County. A rural community located nine miles south of Ringgold. The first post office was in Johnny Wood's store, and was named WOODSTATION. Coincidentally this was a place that did a lively trade in lumber production. The locale is referred to as WOODSTATION VALLEY.

WOODSTOCK, Cherokee County. Incorporated as a town December 9, 1897. Named after a novel called *Woodstock* by Sir Walter Scott, which was published in 1826.

WOODSTOCK, Oglethorpe County. The name of this community was rejected as a post office as it was already in use (*see* Woodstock, Cherokee County), so Alexander H. Stephens was asked to suggest a name. He offered "Philomath" (q.v.).

WOODSTOWN, Henry County. Now a dead town, it was located ten miles east of McDonough. The post office was established in July 1893. Named for William Woods the original postmaster and the first settler here, who came directly from Ireland.

WOODVILLE, Greene County. Incorporated as a city August 21, 1911. An early settlement which was located five miles north of Union Point, and was first known as BEEMAN, named for a Mr. Beeman who owned a large store here. The later name is said to have been adopted because trains loaded up with wood here.

WOODY GAP, Lumpkin County. A mountain pass in the Blue Ridge at an elevation of 3,164 feet, located ten miles north of Dahlonega on U.S. highway 19. It was named for an early postmaster of Dahlonega, John Woody.

WOOLEY'S BRIDGE, Bartow County. Located one mile west of Kingston. In 1864 this covered bridge spanned the Etowah River on the plantation of Andrew F. Wooley.

WOOLSEY, Fayette County. Incorporated as a town December 15, 1893, this community is seven miles southeast of Fayetteville. Was formerly located on the Southern Railroad. Derivation is unknown.

WOOTEN, Lee County. Incorporated as a town August 23, 1872. The name was changed to LEESBURG (q.v.), February 28, 1874.

WOOTTEN'S MILL, Telfair County. An early community located on the Ocmulgee River, 15 miles south of McRae. The postmaster in 1882 was John Wootten who had a grist mill here.

WORMSLOE, Chatham County. A 750-acre tract on the Isle of Hope, below Savannah, which is the oldest estate in Georgia. Noble Jones gave it its name when he gained possession of the property in 1733. Wormsloe was retained by the Craig Barrow family, heirs of Noble Jones, until 1972 when the estate was donated to the state of Georgia. It has been explained that Jones set out mulberry trees here for the culture of silkworms — hence the name, "Wormsloe."

WORSE CREEK, Rabun County. Located in lower Rabun County where it flows into Tugalo Lake. Goff said the name is quite descriptive of the stream flowing in a rugged area, not far from Bad Creek.

WORTH, Turner County. A small community located about three miles above Auburn. Incorporated as a town from August 13, 1910 to February 16, 1943.

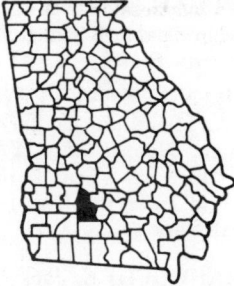

WORTH COUNTY. Created December 20, 1853 with 580 square miles taken from Dooly and Irwin counties. Named in honor of Major General William James Worth (1794-1849) of New York, a distinguished soldier of the Mexican War, and son-in-law of Zachary Taylor. The county seat is Sylvester (q.v.).

WRENS, Jefferson County. Incorporated as a town December 17, 1901. The first election was held at the store of Wren and Phillips. The community was established in 1884 when the Augusta Southern Railroad came through here, and was named after W. J. Wren who then built a home and a store.

WREN'S NEST, Atlanta. Located at 1050 Gordon Street, S. W., this former home of Joel Candler Harris (1848-1908) is a memorial to the creator of the Uncle Remus stories. It was given this name when a wren built her nest in

the mail box, and Harris built another mail box so as not to disturb her. *See also* Uncle Remus Route.

WRIGHTSBORO(UGH), McDuffie County. One of the oldest communities of upper Georgia, it was located on Little River, about five miles northwest of the present-day Thomson. Was said to have been settled not later than 1754 by pretending Quaker, Edmund Gray of Virginia. They called their community here, BRANDON (q.y.). In 1767, Sir James Wright made a grant of 12,000 acres to the Quakers (who were under the direction of Joseph Maddock), and the area was called the QUAKER RESERVE. Later it was titled WRIGHTSBOROUGH TOWNSHIP. The Quakers all left by 1806 because of their opposition to slavery. The town of Wrightsborough was founded in 1770 and incorporated in 1799, but declined after the coming of the railroad in the 1830's, as the residents refused to allow the road to come through here.

WRIGHT SQUARE, Savannah. Laid out in 1733. Originally named EGMONT SQUARE for John Percival, Earl of Egmont. The name was changed in 1763 to honor Sir James Wright (c. 1714-1785), Georgia's last colonial governor, who served during the period 1760-1776.

WRIGHTSVILLE, CS Johnson County. Laid out in 1859 on land donated by William P. Hicks. The post office was established March 10, 1860, and the town was incorporated February 23, 1866. James B. Wright was on the committee which selected the site for the town, and it was named for him. He later was elected to the state legislature.

WYNN'S MILL, Henry County. A former community which was located in the southeast corner of the county. In 1882, J. A. C. Wynn owned a grist mill and saw mill here.

X

XERXES, Meriwether County. Located at the site of the present community of ODES-SADALE (q.v.). The Xerxes post office was established here from August 3, 1887 to June 15, 1900. Named for the Xerxes Plantation (later called Cedar Hill Plantation), owned by Colonel Henry Richard Harris (1781-1858), who named the place after Xerxes the Great, who was king of Persia from 486 to 465 B. C. Colonel Harris was looking for a name that was not already in use.

Y

YAHOOLA, Lumpkin County. An early community which was located five miles north of Dahlonega, near Yahoola Creek (q.v.). Said to have been named YAHOLI I, or "Yahula Place" by the Cherokees, after the prosperous stock trader named Yahula who lived here prior to the Revolution.

YAHOOLA CREEK, Lumpkin County. A tributary of the Chestatee River, which arises in the upper section of the county. Said to be from the Creek Indian word *Yahulo,* a cry the Indians used at the start of their drinking ceremony. Another theory is that it is from the Cherokee, *yahula,* meaning "doodle bug." *See also* Yahoola.

YAMACUTAH, Jackson County. Originally an old Indian settlement on the old Etoho River, now the North Oconee River, and is the site of the first white settlement in the county. Jordan Clark and Jacob Bankston came here from Virginia and settled in 1784. The name is a Cherokee Indian word signifying "to tumble," in reference to the tumbling shoals in the river nearby.

YAMACRAW BLUFF, Chatham County. The original name given to the settlement where Savannah was established, and the site where Oglethorpe landed to establish Georgia's first town in 1733. It takes its name from the tribe of Yamacraw Indians who lived in this area at that time. They were outlaw Creeks, who had been banished from the Creek Nation several years before General Oglethorpe's arrival. John Musgrove of South Carolina had established a trading post here in 1732, a year before Oglethorpe landed to establish the Georgia colony. His half-breed bride, Mary Musgrove, acted as interpreter for Oglethorpe (*see also* Cowpen).

YAMACRAW VILLAGE, Chatham County. A name long used to designate the "black" section of Savannah, lying just west of the downtown business district. It has now been converted into public housing. For derivation *see* Yamacraw Bluff.

YAM GRANDY STATE PARK, Emanuel County. An 11-acre day use park located near Swainsboro. Named after YAMGRANDY CREEK, which arises near the park and flows southerly to enter the Ohoopee River just above Oak Park.

YAMTRAHOOCHEE, Jackson County. A former settlement on the west branch of the North Oconee River. The Indian name means "hurricane shoals."

YANKEE TOWN, Ware County. Was located at the site of the present WAYCROSS. This post office was so named because northern people operated the stage coaches here.

YATESVILLE, Upson County. Incorporated as a town December 17, 1896. Believed named after A. J. Yates, who was the postmaster here in 1882, and had a general store and cotton gin.

YELLOW CREEK, Dawson County. An early settlement in the southwest section of the county, named for the stream on which it was located. YELLOW CREEK enters the Etowah River at the western corner of the county. Also located here is YELLOW CREEK (Militia) DISTRICT.

YELLOW DIRT, Heard County. A community and former post office located 4½ miles northeast of Centralhatchee. Was named after nearby Yellow Dirt Creek (q.v.).

YELLOW DIRT CREEK, Heard County. Bonner said this was originally labeled YELLOW LAND CREEK. The name could be a translation of the Indian named Fokelani, which is Creek for "yellow dirt," or may be translated from the Muskogean Indian word, *Ikanlanihachi.*

YELLOW RIVER. A tributary of the Ocmulgee River, which arises in Gwinnett County and flows through a corner of DeKalb, as well as Rockdale and Newton counties, and then enters Jackson Lake. The name is a translation from the early Creek Indian name of the river, COC-LAU-PAU-CHEE or WELAUNEEHATCHEE. There was at one time a community called YELLOW RIVER, near the stream at the approximate site of today's Luxomni in Gwinnett County.

YONAH MOUNTAIN, White County. Also called MOUNT YONAH, with an elevation of 3,167 feet, it is located 3½ miles northeast of Cleveland. A dam on the Tugaloo River in upper Stephens County forms a reservoir called LAKE YONAH. It was previously called LAKE RALSTON, named for a family by the name of Ralston that owned land here. A rural community and post office named YONAH was located eight miles southwest of Cornelia in what is now Habersham County. The Cherokee word *yonah or yonu* means "bear" or "big black bear." The name has also been spelled YANUH.

YONNKER, Dodge County. Incorporated August 20, 1906. The present community spelled YONKERS is located 12 miles north of Eastman on Georgia highway 257. It is within the YOUNKER (Militia) DISTRICT. May have been named from Yonkers, New York, there derived from the Dutch word, *Jonkheer,* a courtesy title similar to "Squire."

YORK, Houston County. An early community and post office in the northeast corner of the county, where WARNER ROBINS (q.v.) is now located. There is also a rural community named YORK in Rabun County near Rabun Gap. The name is believed to be derived from the county in England.

YOUNGCANE, Union County. A rural community located eight miles southwest of Blairsville; takes its name from the nearby YOUNG CANE CREEK. The stream was named for the son of the Cherokee chief, Long Cane.

YOUNG DEER CREEK, Forsyth County. Arises in the eastern section of the county to the northeast of Cumming, and flows southerly to enter the Chattahoochee River. John Goff said this is probably a personal Cherokee Indian name borne by an individual who lived on the stream.

YOUNG HARRIS, Towns County. Incorporated as a town December 5, 1895. The original community here was called McTYEIRE. The circuit-riding Methodist minister, Reverend Artemus Lester founded McTYEIRE INSTITUTE (q.v.) here in 1885. It later was renamed YOUNG HARRIS COLLEGE to honor its first benefactor, Judge Young Loftin Gerdine Harris (1812-1894) of Athens. The town thereafter was called Young Harris. The oldest building on the 35-acre campus is the SUSAN B. HARRIS CHAPEL, which was named for the wife of Judge Harris, while the newest structure is the SHARP MEMORIAL UNITED METHODIST CHURCH, which is a memorial to Dr. J. A. Sharp. The PRUITT-BARRETT BUILDING was named in honor of benefactors, Mr. J. C. Pruitt and Mr. Guy Barrett.

YOUTH, Walton County. Anita Sams wrote that this "neat little town (was) said to have been named by Collie Shelnutt, and bears the wistful title of Youth."

YPSILANTI, Talbot County. Pronounced "Ipp'-see-lan'-tee" or "Yipsie" for short. The original settlement here was named RED BONE (q.v.). This present name was transplanted from the city in Michigan, which was named after Demetrios Ypsilanti, who in 1821 was the first to lead his fellow Greeks on the path of national freedom.

YUCHI TOWN, Screven County. *See* UCHEE TOWN.

YUKON, Gilmer County. A community located four miles east of Talona. The name is believed to have been transferred from the Yukon River and the Yukon Territory of Canada. When the gold strikes occurred, the excitement caused various places in this country to adopt the name, which is derived from the Apathascan word, *Yukon-na,* which means "big river."

Z

ZEBULON, CS Pike County. Incorporated as a town and designated county seat November 25, 1825. The original county seat had been at Newnan (q.v.). The first court house at Zebulon was of hewn logs. Mrs. D. S. Patterson, an early settler of the county, suggested the name for the town. She took the given name of Zebulon M. Pike, the man for whom Pike County (q.v.) was named.

ZELLNER, Monroe County. A former community located five miles west of Forsyth. Named for Andrew Zellner.

ZENITH, Crawford County. A rural community located seven miles south of Roberta. Its commendatory name means, "The culminating point of prosperity." Brinkley says it was "Named for the high point or summit of its location."

ZERO MILE POST, Atlanta. A stone post that marked the terminus of the Western and Atlantic Railway in the 1890's. It is the symbolic spot where Atlanta began, and is located on lower Wall Street, across the railroad tracks from Underground Atlanta (q.v.).

ZIRKLE, Pierce County. Originally (1904-05) known as DIXON SIDING, it was located six miles southeast of Patterson. A depot was erected about 1910, named Zirkle in honor of local lumberman, L. A. Zirkle. The town declined after the Davis-Zirkle Lumber Co. mill closed down in 1926.

ZOAR, Bulloch County. A former community located seven miles north of Statesboro. This is a Biblical name, the city of Zoar, to which Lot fled from Sodom.

ZOUCK'S OLD FIELD, Liberty County. Designated the county seat December 30, 1836 when it was moved here from Riceboro (q.v.). Derivation is undoubtedly from the name of a Liberty County family. It is recorded that Samuel H. Zoucks was the sheriff of Walthourville, Liberty County in 1882.

SELECTED BIBLIOGRAPHY
CITY AND COUNTY HISTORIES

Baker, John William. *History of Hart County.* Atlanta: Foote Davies Co., 1933.

Baldwin, Nell H. and Millhouse, A.M. *An Intelligent Student's Guide to Burke County (Ga.) History.* Waynesboro, Ga.: Published by the authors, 1956.

Barfield, Louise Calhoun. *History of Harris County Georgia.* Columbus: Columbus Office Supply Co., 1961.

Battey, George Magruder, Jr. *A History of Rome and Floyd County.* Atlanta: Webb and Vary Co., 1922.

Beeson, Leola Selman. *County History Stories of Milledgeville and Baldwin County.* Macon: J. W. Burke Company, 1943.

Bonner, James Calvin, *A Short History of Heard County.* Milledgeville, Georgia, 1958, 1962.

Bowen, Eliza A. *A Story of Wilkes County Georgia.* Marietta, Georgia: Continental Book Co., 1950.

Broome, Dean. *History of Pierce County Georgia, Volume 1.* Blackshear: Broome Printing & Office Supplies, 1973.

Butler, John C. *Historical Record of Macon and Central Georgia.* Macon: J. W. Burke Company, 1879.

Cain, Andrew W. *History of Lumpkin County for the First Hundred Years.* Atlanta: Stein Printing Co., 1932.

Church, Mary L. *The Hills of Habersham.* Atlanta: Foote & Davies, Inc., 1962.

Clark, William Henry Harrison. *History of Catoosa County.* 1972.

Clements, J. B. *History of Irwin County.* Atlanta: Foote & Davies Co., 1932.

Cobb, Joe. *Carroll County and Her People.* Published c. 1907.

Conyus, Lucy Josephine. *The History of Bartow County, Formerly Cass.* Cartersville, Ga.: Tribune Publishing Co., Inc., 1933.

Cook, Mrs. Anna Maria Green. *History of Baldwin County, Georgia.* Anderson, S. C.: Keys Hearn Printing Co., 1925.

Cooper, Walter G. *Official History of Fulton County.* Atlanta: History Commission — Ivan Allen, Sr., Chairman, 1934.

Covington, W. A. *History of Colquitt County.* Atlanta: Foote & Davies Co., 1937.

D.A.R., Fort Early Chapter. *History of Crisp County.* 1916.

D.A.R., General James Jackson Chapter. *History of Lowndes County, Georgia.* Valdosta, 1941.

D.A.R., Governor Treutlen Chapter, Fort Valley. *History of Peach County, Georgia.* Atlanta: Cherokee Publishing Co., 1972.

D.A.R., Hawkinsville Chapter. *History of Pulaski and Bleckley Counties, Georgia.* 2 volumes. 1957, 1958.

D.A.R., Sergeant Newton Chapter. *Newton County History.* Covington, Ga., 1937.

D.A.R., Thronateeska Chapter. *History and Reminscences of Dougherty County Georgia.* Albany, Ga.: Herald Publishing Co., 1924.

Davidson, Victor. *History of Wilkinson County.* Macon: J. W. Burke Co., 1930.

Dooly County Sesquicentennial Corporation. *History of Dooly County.* 1971.

Elrod, Frary, *Historical Notes on Jackson County, Georgia.* Jefferson, Ga., 1967.

Faulk, J. Lanette O'Neal and Jones, Billy Walker. *History of Twiggs County, Georgia.* Columbus: Columbus Office Supply Co., 1960.

Flanigan, James C. *History of Gwinnett County,* 2 volumes. Hapeville, Georgia: Tyler and Co., 1943.

Fleming, W. P. *Crisp County Georgia Historical Sketches,* Vol. 1. Cordele, Georgia: Ham Printing Co., 1932.

Garrett, Franklin M. *Atlanta and Environs, A Chronicle of its People and Events,* 2 volumes. Athens: University of Georgia Press, 1954.

Georgia Historical Records Survey, WPA. *Inventory of the County Archives of Georgia. No. 50 Echols County (Statenville).* Atlanta, 1940.

Gregory, G.A. *Savannah and its Surroundings.* Savannah: Press of the Morning News, 1890.

Grice, Warren, editor. *History of Houston County.* Typed manuscript, 1934.

Grubbs, Mrs. Lillie Martin. *History of Worth County Georgia.* Macon: J. W. Burke Co., 1934.

Harden, William. *History of Savannah and South Georgia,* volume 1. Chicago: Lewis Publishing Co., 1913.

Hardman, Thomas C. *History of Harmony Grove - Commerce Jackson County, Georgia.* Athens: McGregor Co., 1949.

Hart, Bertha Sheppard. *The Official History of Laurens County Georgia.* Athens: McGregor Co., 1941.

Hays, Louise Frederick. *History of Macon County, Georgia.* Atlanta: Stein Printing Co., 1933.

Hicky, Louise McHenry. *Rambles Through Morgan County.* Morgan County Historical Society, 1971.

Hines, Nelle Womack. *Teasure Album of Milledgeville and Baldwin County, Georgia.* Macon: J. W. Burke Co., 1936.

Hodges, Lucile. *A History of Our Locale Mainly Evans County Georgia.* Macon: Southern Press, Inc., 1965.

Hollingsworth, Clyde. *Pioneer Days, A History of the Early Years in Screven County.* Circa 1947.

Hull, Augustus Longstreet. *Annals of Athens, Georgia, 1801-1901.* Athens, 1906.

Huxford, Folks. *History of Brooks County Georgia.* Athens: McGregor Co., 1949.

——————————— *History of Clinch County Georgia.* Macon: J. W. Burke Co., 1916.

Jones, Frank S. *History of Decatur County.*

Jones, Mary G. and Reynolds, Lily. *Coweta County Chronicles for One Hundred Years.* Atlanta: Stein Printing Co., 1928.

Lambdin, Mrs. Augusta, editor. *History of Lamar County.* Barnesville, Georgia: Barnesville News - Gazette, 1932.

Lee, Fitzhugh. *Newton County's History.* Covington: By compiler, 1937.

Lee, F. D. and Agnew, J. L. *Historical Record of the City of Savannah.* Savannah: J. H. Estill, 1869.

Lunceford, Alvin Mell, Jr. *Early Records of Taliaferro County, Georgia.* Crawfordville, 1956.

McCommons, Mrs. W. C. and Stovall, Miss Clara. *History of McDuffie County Georgia.*

McDaniel, Susie Blaylock. *Official History of Catoosa County, Georgia.* Dalton: Gregory Printing & Office Supply, 1953.

McIntosh, John H. *The Official History of Elbert County.* Athens: McGregor Company, 1940.

MacIntyre, W. Irwin. *History of Thomas County.* volume 1. Thomasville, 1923.

McQueen, Alex S. *History of Charlton County.* Atlanta: Stein Printing Co., 1932.

Mann, Floris Perkins. *History of Telfair County.* Macon: J. W. Burke Co., 1949.

Marlin, Loyd G. *The History of Cherokee County.* Atlanta: Walter W. Brown Publishing Co., 1932.

Melton, Quimby, Jr. *History of Griffin.* Griffin: Griffin DailyNews, 1959.

Mitchell, Ella. *History of Washington County.* Atlanta: Byrd Printing Co., 1924.

Nottingham, Carolyn Walker and Hannah, Evelyn. *History of Upson County, Georgia.* Bacon: J. W. Burke Co., 1930.

Pate, John Ben. *History of Turner County.* Atlanta: Stein Printing Co., 1933.

Perry, Jowl W. *Some Pioneer History of Early County.* 1871.

Pitts, Lulie. *History of Gordon County.* Calhoun: The Calhoun Times, 1933.

Powell, N. J. *Brief History of Jasper County.*

Powell, Nettie. *History of Marion County Georgia.* Columbus: Historical Publishing Co., 1931.

Rainer, Vessie Thrasher. *Henry County, Georgia: the mother of counties.* McDonough (?), Georgia, 1971.

Raper, Arthur F. *Tenants of the Almighty* (Greene County). New York: The Macmillan Co., 1943.

Reeve, Jewell B. *Stories of Gordon County.* Calhoun (?), Georgia, 1962.

Rice, Thaddeus Brockett. *History of Greene County Georgia.* Edited by Mrs. Carolyn White Williams. Macon: J. W. Burke Co., 1961.

Ritchie, Andrew Jackson. *Sketches of Rabun County History.* Clayton, Georgia, 1948.

Rogers, N. K. *History of Chattahoochee County, Georgia.* Columbus: Columbus Office Supply Co., 1933.

Rogers, R. W., Rev. *History of Pike County from 1822-1922.* Zebulon, Georgia, 1922.

Rogers, William Warren. *Ante-Bellum Thomas County 1825-1861. Tallahassee: Florida State University, 1963.*

Rowe, H. J., Publisher. *History of Athens and Clarke County.* Athens: McGregor Co., Printers, 1923.

Sams, Anita B. *Wayfarers in Walton.* Doraville: Foote Davies Co., 1967.

Sartain, James Alfred. *History of Walker County Georgia.* Dalton: A. J. Showalter Company, 1932.

Shadburn, Don L. *Forsyth County's Historical Heritage.* Cumming: Forsyth County Historical & Geneological Society, 1972.

Shriner, Chas. H. *History of Murray County.* Dalton, Ga.: A. J. Showalter Co., 1911.

Smith, Clifford L. *History of Troup County.* Atlanta: Foote & Davies Co., 1933.

Smith, Elizabeth Wiley. *The History of Hancock County, Georgia volume 1.* Washington, Ga.: Wilkes Publishing Company, 1974.

Smith, Florrie C. *History of Oglethorpe County.* Washington, Georgia: Wilkes Publishing Co., 1970.

Tate, Luke E. *History of Pickens County.* Atlanta. Walter W. Brown Publishing Co., 1935.

Terrill, Helen Eliza and Dixon, Mary Marshall. *History of Stewart County, Georgia.* Columbus: Columbus Office Supply Co., 1958.

Thomas, Mrs. Z. F. *History of Jefferson County.* Macon: J. W. Burke Co., 1927.

Trogden, Kathryn Curtis. *History of Stephens County Georgia.* Toccoa: Toccoa Womens Club Inc., 1973.

Vochelle, James T. *History of Camden County, Georgia, 1914.* Kingland, Georgia: Southeast Georgian, 1967.

Walker, Laura Singleton. *History of Ware County.* Macon: J. W. Burke Co., 1934.

Ward, George Gordon. *The Annals of Upper Georgia Centered in Gilmer County.* Carrollton: Thomason Printing & Office Equipment Co., 1965.

Ward, Warren P. *Ward's History of Coffee County.* Atlanta: Foote & Davies Co., 1930.

Whitfield County History Commission. *Official History of Whitfield County, Georgia.* Dalton: A. J. Showalter Co., 1936.

Williams, Carolyn White. *History of Jones County Georgia.* Macon: J. W. Burke Co., 1957.

Williams, H. J., Mrs. *History of Schley County.* Ellaville (?), Circa 1932.

Williford, William B. *Americus Through the Years.* Atlanta, 1960.

Willingham, Robert Marion, Jr. *We Have This Heritage, The History of Wilkes County Beginnings to 1860.* Washington, Ga.: Wilkes Publishing Co., 1969.

Wilson, G. J. N. *The Early History of Jackson County Georgia.* Atlanta: Foote & Davies Co., 1914.

Winters, Larry M., Chairman Historical Book Committee. *Forsyth-Monroe County Georgia, Sesquicentennial 1923-1973.* Forsyth: The Monroe Advertiser, 1973.

Yates, B. C. *Historic Cobb County.* Marietta: Cobb County Federal Savings and Loan Association.

Young, Ida, Gholson, Julius and Hargrove, Clara Nell. *History of Macon, Georgia.* Macon: Lyon, Marshall & Brooks, 1950.

OTHER BOOKS CONSULTED

Anderson, Mrs. Kirby-Smith. *Taverns and Inns of Early Georgia.* Typewritten bound volume, 1939.

Bartram, William. *Travels.* Mark Van Doren, Editor. New York: Dover Publications, 1928 (First published in Philadelphia, 1791).

Bolton, Herbert E. and Ross, Mary. *The Debatable Land.* New York: Russell & Russell, 1968.

Brinkley, Hal E. *How Georgia Got Her Names.* Lakemont, Ga.: CSA Printing & Bindery, Inc., 1967.

Bullock, Henry Morton. *A History of Emory University.* Nashville: Parthenon Press, 1936.

Callaway, James E. *The Early Settlement of Georgia.* Athens: University of Georgia Press, 1948.

Candler, Allen D. and Evans, Clement A. *Cyclopedia of Georgia,* 3 volumes. Atlanta: State Historical Association, 1906.

Candler, Allen D. *The Colonial Records of the State of Georgia.* Atlanta: Charles P. Byrd, State Printer, 1911.

Cate, Margaret Davis. *Our Todays and Yesterdays.* Brunswick: Glover Bros., Inc., 1926.

Clark, Walter Augustus. *A Lost Arcadia, or the Story of My Old Community.* Augusta, Ga.: Chronicle Job Print, 1909.

Corbin, Harriet Turner (Poiter). *History and Geneology of Chief William McIntosh, Jr.* Long Beach, Calif.: Carl C. Burdic, Editor, 1967.

Coulter, E. Merton. *Auraria.* Athens: University of Georgia Press, 1965.

_____ *Georgia, A Short History.* Chapel Hill: University of North Carolina Press, 1947.

_____ *Old Petersburg and the Broad River Valley of Georgia.* Athens: University of Georgia Press, 1965.

English, Thomas H. *Emory University 1915-1965.* Atlanta: Higgins McArthur Co., 1966.

Estill, J. H. and Weatherbe, Ch. F., Publishers. *Georgia State Gazeteer, Business and Planters' Directory 1883-84.* Savannah: Morning News Printing House, 1883.

Evans, Lawton B. *A History of Georgia.* New York, Chicago, etc.: American Book Co., 1908.

Fish, Tallu. *Sidney Lanier.* Darien: Darien News, 1963.

Flags of Five Nations: Being a collection of historical sketches, legends and stories of the Golden Isles of Guale.

Fleming, Berry, Compiler. *Autobiography of a Colony.* Athens: University of Georgia Press, 1957.

Fries, Adelaide Lisetta. *Moravians in Georgia 1735-1740.* Raleigh, N. C.: Edwards & Broughton, 1905.

Gannett, Henry. *American Names: A Guide to the origin of place names in the United States.* Washington D. C.: Public Affairs Press, 1947.

Gatschet, Albert S. *Towns and Villages of the Creek Confederacy in the XVIII and XIX Centuries.* Montgomery, Ala.: Brown Printing Co., 1901.

Georgia Historical Commission. *Georgia Civil War Historical Markers.* Atlanta, 1964.

Gleazer, Edmund J., Jr., Editor. *American Junior Colleges,* 7th Edition. Washington D. C.; American Council on Education, 1967.

Glore, L. Harold. *History of Mableton, Cobb County, Georgia.*

Godley, Margaret W. *Georgia County Place Names.* Atlanta: The Author. (M.A. Thesis, Emory University), 1935.

_____ *Historic Tybee Island.* Savannah Beach: Savannah Beach Chamber of Commerce, 1958.

Grice, Warren; Edited by E. Merton Coulter. *Georgia Through Two Centuries,* 3 volumes. New York and West Palm Beach: Lewis Publishing Co., 1965.

Hatcher, George, editor. *Georgia Rivers.* Athens: University of Georgia Press, 1962.

Hopkins, John M. *Forty-Five Years with the Okefenokee Swamp, 1900-1945.* Atlanta(?): Georgia Society of Naturalists, 1946(?).

Jones, Charles C. *Dead Towns of Georgia.* Savannah: Morning News and Printing House, 1878.

Kaiser, Albert. *College Names, Their Origin and Significance.* New York: Bookman Associates, Inc., 1952.

King, Spencer Bidwell, Jr. *Georgia Voices, A Documentary History to 1872.* Athens: University of Georgia Press, 1966.

———————— Unpublished manuscript: *The Darien Story, The Death and Rebirth of A Southern Town* (tentative title), Circa 1969.

———————— *Ebb Tide As Seen Through the Diary of Josephine Clay Habersham 1863.* Athens: University of Georgia Press, 1958.

Knight, Lucian Lamar. Georgia's Landmarks, Memorials, and Legends, 2 volumes. Atlanta: Byrd Printing Company, 1913-14.

———————— *A Standard History of Georgians,* 6 volumes. Chicago: Lewis Publishing Co., 1917.

Lambert, Eloise and Pei, Mario. *The Book of Place Names.* New York: Lothrop, Lee and Shepard, Inc., 1959.

Lanning, John Tate. *The Spanish Missions of Georgia.* Chapel Hill: The University of North Carolina Press, 1935.

Lovell, Caroline C. *The Golden Isles of Georgia.* Boston: Little, Brown, and Company, 1933.

McCullar, Bernice. *This is your Georgia.* Northport, Ala.: Southern Publishing Company, 1966.

Malone, Henry T. *Cherokees of the Old South.* Athens: University of Georgia Press, 1956.

Mathews, Mitford McLeod. *Some Sources of Southernisms.* University, Ala.: University of Alabama Press, 1948.

Mooney, James. *Myths of the Cherokees.* Washington D. C.: Smithsonian Institution, Bureau of American Ethnology 19th Annual Report, part 1, 1897-1898.

Northen, William J. *Men of Mark in Georgia,* 6 volumes. Atlanta: A.B. Caldwell, 1907-12.

Perkerson, Medora Field. *White Columns in Georgia.* New York: Rinehart & Co., Inc., 1952.

Phillips, Ulrich Bonnell. *A History of Transportation in the Eastern Cotton Belt to 1860.* New York City: Columbia University Press, 1908.

Pope, G. D., Jr. *Ocmulgee National*

Monument, Georgia. Washington D. C.: Historical Handbook Series No. 24, 1956 (Reprint 1961).

Pound, Merritt B. *Benjamin Hawkins — Indian Agent.* Athens: University of Georgia Press, 1951.

Reed, Thomas Walter. *David Crenshaw Barrow.* Athens: McGregor Co., 1935.

Richards, William Carey, Editor. *Georgia Illustrated.* New York: Gould Newman and Saxton, 1841, 1842.

Russell, Franklin. *The Okefenokee Swamp, The American Wilderness.* New York: Time-Life Books, 1973.

Scruggs, Carroll Proctor, Compiler. *Georgia Historical Markers.* Valdosta: Bay Tree Grove, 1973.

Sherwood, Adiel. *A Gazateer of the State of Georgia.* Charleston: W. Riley, 1827. Philadelphia: J. W. Martin and W. K. Boden, 1829. Washington: P. Force, 1837. Atlanta: J. Richards, 1860.

Stewart, George R. *American Place Names.* New York: Oxford University Press, 1970.

Stoutenburgh, John L. *Dictionary of the American Indian.* New York: Philosophical Library, 1960.

Suddeth, Ruth Elgin, and Associates. *Empire Builders of Georgia.* Austin, Texas: The Steck Co., 1963.

Swanton, John R. *Early History of the Creek Indians and their Neighbors.* Washington: Government Printing Office, 1922.

Taylor, Francis Long. *Crawford W. Long & Discovery of Ether Anesthesia.* New York: Paul B. Hoeber, Inc., 1928.

Thomas, Ruby F. R. (Mrs. Eli A.). *Historic Spots and Places of Interest in Georgia.* Published by the author, 1935.

United States Department of Interior. *The National Register of Historic Places 1969.* Washington D. C.: National Park Service.

Vanstory, Burnette. *Georgia's Land of the Golden Isles.* Athens: University of Georgia Press, 1956.

White, George. *Historical Collections of Georgia.* New York: Pudney & Russell, 1855.

———————— *Statistics of the State of Georgia.* Savannah: W. Thorne Williams, 1849.

Wightman, Orrin Sage and Cate, Margaret Davis. *Early Days of Coastal Georgia.*

Winn, Bill. *The First Georgians.* Atlanta: Atlanta Journal, 1968.

Woodward, Grace Steele. *The Cherokees.* Norman: University of Oklahoma Press, 1963.

Worsley, E. B. *Columbus on the Chattahoochee.*

Writers' Program, Georgia. Revised by George G. Leckie. *Georgia, A Guide to its Towns and Countryside.* Atlanta: Tupper & Love, 1954.

PERIODICALS, INDIVIDUALS, AND OTHER SOURCES CONSULTED.

Allen, Mary Moore. *Origin of Names of Army and Air Corps Posts, Camps and Stations in World War II.* Unpublished paper.

Ashmore, Otis. "Wilkes County, Its Place in Georgia History." *Georgia Historical Quarterly.* Vol. I, No. 1, March 1917. pp. 59-69.

Bartow, Rev. T. B. "Memoirs of Frederica." *Georgia Historical Quarterly.* Vol. 1, No. 4, December 1917. pp. 347-49.

Cohen, Hennig. "Two Poems from English Magazines on the Naming of Georgia." *Georgia Historical Quarterly.* Vol. 35, No. 4, December 1951. pp. 319-22.

"On The Word Georgian." *Georgia Historical Quarterly.* Vol. 37, No. 4, December 1953. pp. 347-48.

Corbitt, D. C. "Some Papers Relating to Bourbon County, Georgia." *Georgia Historical Quarterly.* Vol. 19, No. 3, September 1935. pp. 251-263.

Goelchius, Henry R. "Columbus Georgia and General Henry L. Benning." *Georgia Historical Quarterly.* Vol. 3, No. 1, March 1919. pp. 3-10.

Goff, John H. "Short Studies of Georgia place names." *Georgia Mineral Newsletter,* vols. 7-16, 1954-1965.

Gray, Jim. "Satellite Cities." *Atlanta Constitution.* 45-part series, January 13, 1974 to February 26, 1974.

Harrell, Bob. "Date Line Georgia." A daily column appearing in the *Atlanta Constitution.* Information abstracted during period, 1969-1973.

Hawes, Mrs. Lilla M., Director, Georgia Historical Society. Information received, March, 1973.

Irvine, William S. "Terminus and Deanville, Local Names of Long Ago at the Site of Atlanta" *Atlanta Historical Bulletin,* Vol. III, No. 13, April 1938. pp. 101-119.

Lagondakis, Charles. "Greece In Georgia" *Georgia Historical Quarterly.* Vol. XLCII, June 1963. pp. 189-192.

McMurry, Richard. "Early History of DeKalb County" *Georgia Magazine,* Vol. V, No. 2, August-September 1961. pp. 19-22.

Mallard, John B. "Liberty County, Georgia" (an address). *Georgia Historical Quarterly,* Vol. II, No. 1, March 1918. pp. 1-21.

Mitchell, Eugene M. "Queer place names in old Atlanta" *Atlanta Historical Bulletin,* Vol. I, April 1931. pp. 22-31.

Moore, Violet. Montezuma, Georgia. Freelance writer. Information given to compiler.

Nottingham, Zera Pendleton. "Macon's Wesleyan" *Georgia Magazine.* Vol. VI, No. 2, August-September 1962. pp. 20-22.

Read, William A. "Indian Stream-Names In Georgia" *International Journal of American Linguistics,* Vol. 15, April 1949, pp. 128-132, Vol. 16, October 1950. pp. 203-207.

Sears, Joan N. "Town Planning in Georgia" *Georgia Historical Quarterly.* Vol. LIV, No. 1, Spring 1970. pp. 20-40.

State Parks, Georgia Department of. Descriptive leaflets and supplementary information provided.

Suddeth, Ruth Elgin. "Land of Mystery and Magic" *Georgia Magazine.* Vol. II, No. 2, Aug.-Sept. 1958. pp. 31-33.